# Justice
## BEHiND THE WALLS

# Justice
## BEHiND THE WALLS

## Human Rights
## in Canadian Prisons

## MICHAEL JACKSON

Douglas & McIntyre
VANCOUVER/TORONTO

Douglas & McIntyre
2323 Quebec Street, Suite 201
Vancouver, British Columbia
V5T 4S7

NATIONAL LIBRARY OF CANADA CATALOGUING IN PUBLICATION DATA

Jackson, Michael, 1943–
   Justice behind the walls

   Includes index.
   ISBN 1-55054-893-X

   1. Prisoners—Legal status, laws, etc.—Canada. 2. Human rights—
Canada. 3. Prisons—Canada. I. Title.
KE9416.J32 2002          344.71'03564          C2002-910047-X
KF9731.J32 2002

Editing by Barbara Pulling
Copy-editing by Robin Van Heck
Cover photograph by Shane Jackson: Segregation, Matsqui
Cover design by Val Speidel
Interior photographs by Shane Jackson: p. xi: Main corridor, Kent;
   p. 13: Segregation exercise yard, Matsqui; p. 75: Segregation cell, Matsqui;
   p. 185: Segregation unit, Kent;  p. 285: Interview room, segregation unit, Kent;
   p. 433: Open visiting area, Matsqui; p. 573: Screened visiting area, Kent;
   p. 605: The fence, Matsqui
Text design and typesetting by Julie Cochrane
Printed and bound in Canada by Friesens
Printed on acid-free paper

The publisher gratefully acknowledges the financial support of the Canada Council for
the Arts, the British Columbia Ministry of Tourism, Small Business and Culture, and the
Government of Canada through the Book Publishing Industry Development Program
(BPIDP) for our publishing activities.

*For Melissa and Shane*

# Contents

# Preface

*Justice behind the Walls* is available in both book and Internet versions. The latter was written and designed not only to complement the book but also to enhance its use for students and for legal and correctional practitioners. The Internet version contains two additional chapters—one on the Special Handling Units and one on visit review boards—and many of the chapters in the book appear on the website in expanded form, with additional case studies and a more extensive legal and policy commentary. The book avoids the conventional academic practice of extensive footnoting, but the Internet version is hyperlinked to a large body of relevant legislation, policy directives, jurisprudence, and research that is available online. The website also provides a window to many other sites that address the themes with which *Justice behind the Walls* is concerned. New developments in both law and policy will be posted on the website as they arise. In addition, readers will find online a photo gallery that provides visual references for individuals and places referred to in the book.

The Internet version can be found at www.justicebehindthewalls.net.

# INTRODUCTION

# Introduction

This book is both a personal and a public journey in search of justice. The journey begins and ends in a place—the federal penitentiary—where most people have never been, and where they hope neither they nor their loved ones will ever be sent. Yet while the penitentiary lies beyond the borders of most Canadians' personal experience, it is a looming presence in the public imagination. More so now than at any time since the birth of the penitentiary, the issues of crime and punishment are anchored in the stone and concrete of the prison. It is a rare day indeed that we are not confronted with a newspaper, radio, or television story in which justice is measured by the length of sentence a judge imposes or the appropriateness of a prisoner's release by a parole board.

The prison's powerful influence in shaping visions of justice is not solely a function of media fixation. Since the end of the eighteenth century, when imprisonment replaced the gallows and deportation as the primary penalty for serious crime, the intertwining of crime and punishment with the prison has been played out in literature, music, theatre, and film. The success of *Kiss of the Spider Woman*, as a novel, a film, and most recently a musical, is neither surprising nor accidental. It is a reflection of the huge space the prison occupies in the physical and moral architecture of punishment—bars cast deep shadows on the stage, as they do over the lives of prisoners. *Kiss of the Spider Woman* also illustrates a central theme of this book: that the personal, public, political, and cultural threads of life are interwoven in the search for justice and human dignity behind prison walls.

When I began my work in prisons thirty years ago, justice and respect for human rights were distinguished by their absence. In 1972, at the end of my first study of the prison disciplinary process, I concluded that the Canadian peni-tentiary was an outlaw of the criminal justice system. I suggested that the arbi-trariness of prison discipline could be attributed to the scant attention the legal system paid to the rights of prisoners and to the courts' attitude that the deci-sions of prison administrators were not reviewable. From a legal perspective, a great deal has changed since my indictment. The Supreme Court of Canada has brought the prison within the scope of judicial review, the Canadian *Charter of Rights and Freedoms* has entrenched in the Constitution fundamental human rights that apply to prisoners, and a new *Corrections and Conditional Release Act* has been passed by Parliament. Paralleling these developments, the Correctional Service of Canada (CSC) has developed a Mission Statement that incorporates respect for human rights and dignity. Volumes of correctional policy and case management manuals have been developed to guide prison officials and correc-tional officers in implementing both the new law and the Mission Statement.

Questions about the exercise of justice in prisons today must be placed in the context of these significant legal and policy developments. However, one of the lessons of prison research, in this country and in others, is that the law and policy carefully crafted by judges, legislators, and senior administrators are not neces-sarily translated into the daily practice of imprisonment. This book addresses that issue first by examining how imprisonment has changed, then by identify-ing pathways to achieving justice as *both* a matter of law and a matter of practice.

The changes over the last thirty years have not taken place only within prison walls. Perhaps the most significant change has been the hardening of public atti-tudes about crime and punishment. Disturbingly, just as the issue of prisoners' rights has emerged from the legal shadows onto a clearly defined landscape, it appears dangerously close to being eclipsed by rising concern for victims of crime and a growing fear about the erosion of public safety (a fear strangely imper-vious to the decrease in the rate of violent crime). The divide on the inside, between the keeper and the kept, now has a counterpoint on the outside, as the rights of victims and the public are increasingly asserted against the rights of prisoners.

My journey to better understand what we do in the name of justice when we sentence men and women to prison has taken me inside federal penitentiaries as a university researcher, an advocate and lawyer for prisoners, and a human rights activist and reformer. I have interviewed hundreds of prisoners, some considered to be among the most dangerous men and women in the country. I have also interviewed the men and women charged with guarding and "correcting" those sentenced to prison. I have been inside prisons in the midst of riots, hostage-takings, homicides, and stabbings, and I have borne witness to the explosive power of prisoners' rage and frustration. My journey has taken me into segrega-tion units—contemporary versions of Dante's Inferno—where prisoners scream abuse and hurl their bodily fluids and guards respond violently with fire hoses and nightsticks. I have sat with prisoners hopeless beyond tears as they contemplate suicide, and I have knelt at a segregation cell door, scanning through the narrow food slot the barren interior of a prisoner's world, begging a man not to use a razor blade to slash his eyeballs.

Not all of my journey has been so dark. I have witnessed the marriage of prisoners to partners who saw in them a capacity to love, something prisons do little to nourish; I have participated in Aboriginal powwows where uplifted voices carried a message resonant with joy, where uplifted hands were the natural accompaniment to the beat of a drum, where the glint came not from a plunging knife but from the reflected glow of an ancient and shared heritage. I have seen acts of courage by correctional officers who have put their jobs, and even their lives, on the line to protect another—even though the "other" was a prisoner.

In my previous accounts of imprisonment, my focus has been almost exclusively on the experiences of prisoners. This book also includes the reflections of correctional staff on the most significant milestones in the life of the Correctional Service of Canada. But although *Justice behind the Walls* endeavours to capture the stories of prisoners and prison staff alike, its ambition is a broader one. These stories are located within the larger framework of change and continuity in the practice of imprisonment and the role of the law in achieving justice.

## Locating *Justice behind the Walls* on the Correctional Map

Canada's prison system includes federal prisons and provincial and territorial institutions. For reasons rooted in nineteenth-century political history, prisoners sentenced to terms of two years or more are committed to the federal system, where they fall under the authority of the Correctional Service of Canada. The federal prison population in the year 2000 was approximately 22,000, with 13,000 offenders incarcerated and 9,000 on conditional release in the community. CSC has a budget in excess of $1.3 billion and employs more than 14,000 staff. The federal "carceral archipelago" spans the geography of Canada, with forty-seven federal penitentiaries for men, classified as maximum, medium, or minimum security, and seventeen community correctional centres for offenders on day parole, which are designated as minimum security institutions. There are five regional facilities for federally sentenced women and, until its closure in 2000, the federal Prison for Women.

Although I have interviewed prisoners and staff in many federal prisons, my research and advocacy has concentrated on prisons in the Pacific Region. In 1972, I conducted an intensive study at Matsqui Institution, then the principal medium security prison in the region. This study, the first of its kind in Canada, looked at how Wardens' Courts were conducted. Subsequently, with the help of students at the University of British Columbia's Faculty of Law, I began offering legal assistance clinics to prisoners at Matsqui and the B.C. Penitentiary, then the maximum security penitentiary for the Pacific Region. With the closure of the B.C. Pen in 1980, Kent Institution received its first prisoners, following an opening ceremony in which the Solicitor General described it as the "Cadillac of Canadian penitentiaries." In 1983 I conducted a study at Matsqui and Kent to see how much progress had been made in the administration of prison justice. My 1972 and 1983 studies form the backdrop for the third and most intensive of my prison studies, the results of which are featured in *Justice behind the Walls*. This third study began in 1993, during my sabbatical year from U.B.C.'s law school. That original year stretched into seven, my research continuing as I resumed my teaching duties.

My research for *Justice behind the Walls* followed a relatively straightforward trajectory. During 1993–94, first at Matsqui and then at Kent, I sat as an observer at disciplinary court hearings, segregation review and visit review hearings, case management meetings, meetings between staff and management, and meetings of management and inmate committees. I interviewed prisoners, correctional staff, and managers and, with the permission of the prisoners involved, reviewed official correctional files. Between 1994 and 2000 I continued to visit Matsqui and Kent, although on a less regular basis, to build an inventory of case studies that would provide a secure foundation for my assessment and recommendations. Except where otherwise indicated, the events described in this book are drawn from my research notes, personal interviews, and official documents.

The decision to concentrate my research on Matsqui and Kent was not based simply on geographical proximity. Indeed, their locations forty-five and ninety miles, respectively, from my home in Vancouver make them unattractive places to conduct intensive research, which often requires a daily presence in the institution. However, the issues with which this book is concerned are confronted more often at these prisons than at any other in the Pacific Region. Matsqui, one of four medium security institutions in the region, is in the minds of both correctional officials and prisoners the toughest of the mediums. This can be seen not only in the kinds of prisoners sent there but in the fact that Matsqui has the largest segregation unit and the longest disciplinary court docket. Its prisoners are also more likely to be transferred to maximum security. Given that the trilogy of discipline, segregation, and transfers is central to my study of prison justice, Matsqui Institution was the natural choice for my research at the medium security level. There was also another reason for selecting Matsqui. Through my earlier research, I had become familiar with the dynamics of the institution and so I was in a good position to assess change and continuity over three decades.

Matsqui, opened in 1966, was for the first few years of its operation a specialized institution for drug offenders. In 1968 it began accepting a full range of federal offenders, although a heavy emphasis on "treatment" pervaded the institutional philosophy well into the 1970s. In its early days, Matsqui was regarded as a relative haven from the harsh regime of the maximum security B.C. Penitentiary because of the freedom prisoners had to move about within the prison and the amount of time they could spend out of their cells. Fast-forward to 1981, and the scene is quite different. That summer, Matsqui went up in flames in a riot that left the main cellblocks badly damaged and resulted in the establishment of a tent city to temporarily house prisoners. Following the riot, there were many changes in the prison's physical and cultural architecture. Relationships between prisoners and staff tightened, as did the security regime; walkways that had once been open were enclosed with chain-link fences. The prison closed in on itself. During the years following the riot, Matsqui increasingly took on the character and atmosphere of the penitentiary from which it had once been a welcome relief.

By 1993, there were only a few staff members at Matsqui who remembered the riot, and even fewer prisoners who did. On the surface, the institution presented a less harsh face, thanks to the awnings covering the walkway from the front gate, some landscaping and the presence of a large teepee less than two hundred feet from the main cellblock. The extent to which these external changes were indicative of the interior dynamics of Matsqui is a story left for later in this book.

I selected Kent as the second site for *Justice behind the Walls* because it is the Pacific Region's only maximum security institution. Located at the eastern end of B.C.'s Fraser Valley, just a few miles from the resort town of Harrison Hot Springs, Kent looks out to a panorama of forested mountain slopes. However, prison vistas are deceiving; they look very different when viewed from inside a cell.

> A tarmac
> A fence
> Some glass
> Another double fence
>
> The trees
> And
> The side
> Of a mountain
>
> Some dusty shelf
> In a forgotten corner
> Of a vast
> Warehouse

Scarred
Inside their memory

("Lost Ones," one in a series of poems that originated as a creative writing exercise in the University Education Program at Kent Institution, reproduced in [1992] 9/10 *Prison Journal* at 157)

Opened in 1979, Kent had a troubled first few years involving a series of violent incidents, including a riot and hostage-takings. The intensely hostile relationship between prisoners and staff lightened somewhat as the 1980s turned into the 1990s, although an undercurrent of violence continues to erupt periodically. One principal change at Kent over the years has been the physical division of the institution into two populations, "General Population" (GP) and "Protective Custody" (PC). Initially, the number of prisoners officially designated as PC was quite small. They were largely men who had committed sex offences against children and brutal assaults on women, had given evidence for the Crown against fellow prisoners, or had been victims of sexual predation within the prison. PC prisoners typically were segregated from the general population. In the 1980s the number of prisoners claiming protective custody rose dramatically for a variety of reasons, including the greater number of sex offenders being prosecuted and convicted and the institutional drug trade's distinctive form of debt enforcement. This led the CSC to designate certain penitentiaries as PC institutions. Mountain Institution, situated on the penitentiary reserve adjacent to Kent, was one such medium security prison. At Kent, efforts to provide greater freedom and access to programs for PC prisoners led to the designation of several of the eight as living units for their use. In 1987, a decision was made to split the institution literally down the middle, with four units on one side of the central courtyard being designated GP and the four on the other side PC, coupled with the operational imperative that "never the twain shall meet." Kent has henceforth been run virtually as two institutions, with different times of access to the common dining room, recreation yards, and gymnasium, as well as two separate program regimes. The move between general population and protective custody is irreversibly one-way. A prisoner in GP can "check in"—become a PC prisoner and move to the other side of "the House"—but there is no going back. However, prisoners who can only glare from opposite sides of the courtyard at Kent sometimes find themselves side by side down the road, in one of a number of medium security institutions that practise "integration" of populations. In these prisons, GP and PC prisoners are expected to live together, if not in friendship, then at least without overt hostility. Mission and William Head are two such integrated mediums in the Pacific Region. Matsqui is too hardcore to accept integration, and thus only GP prisoners can move from Kent to Matsqui.

The split population at Kent had direct implications for the issues under inquiry in this book. During the period of my research, half of the segregation unit at Kent held PC prisoners who had sought refuge there after burning their bridges in the PC population. Protecting the rights of such prisoners not to be subject to lengthy segregation is one of the most intractable problems facing the Correctional Service of Canada.

There is another important institution in the Pacific Region that appears throughout the book. This institution, opened in 1974 as the Regional Psychiatric Centre, fulfills a number of functions within a maximum security perimeter. First, it is a psychiatric hospital to which prisoners who are mentally ill or otherwise disturbed can be sent. Some prisoners (for example, those diagnosed as schizophrenic) spend their whole sentences in this institution. Others are sent there temporarily, after a suicide attempt or a psychotic breakdown, and kept until they are deemed sufficiently recovered to be returned to a regular prison. The institution is also the site of a number of intensive treatment programs for violent offenders and sex offenders. During its history, the institution has been known as the Regional Psychiatric Centre (RPC), the Regional Medical Centre (RMC), and, most recently, the Regional Health Centre (RHC). Because of the different time frames of the events presented in *Justice behind the Walls,* the institution is referred to in the text by the name it had at the relevant time.

The Regional Psychiatric/Medical/Health Centre is not the only thing that has changed its name over the years of my research. Wardens became Directors and then reverted to Wardens; Case Management Officers (CMOs) have become Institutional Parole Officers (IPOs). While I have endeavoured to give people their appropriate titles, the change from CMO to IPO that officially took place in January 1998 has not yet permeated the everyday language of the penitentiary; hence, in their interviews with me many staff and prisoners continued to use the old titles.

In the summer of 1997, I entered the deep end of the two parts of Canada's system of justice that have occupied most of my professional life. On June 16 and 17, I was in the Supreme Court of Canada appearing as co-counsel in *Delgamuukw* v. *Attorney General of B.C.,* the final stage in the landmark Aboriginal title case brought by the Gitksan and Wet'suwet'en Hereditary Chiefs of northwest British Columbia. The case had begun in the courts of British Columbia a decade earlier, but as with the history of the penitentiary, it was grounded in the events, and challenged the attitudes, of earlier centuries. On June 18 and 19 I entered the gates of Quebec's Special Handling Unit (SHU) in Ste.-Anne-des-Plaines and spent two days interviewing prisoners regarded as the most dangerous in Canada. The contrast could hardly have been greater. In the Supreme Court building I sat amid the formality of the Court, surrounded by marble, polished hardwood, deep red leather, and the rustling of gowns, and listened to the barristerial tone of arguments on the nature and scope of Aboriginal rights. In the Special Handling Unit, my surroundings were made up of chainlink fences, razor wire, steel doors, guns, and the bang of electronic locks being thrown; what I listened to there were accounts of the precarious state of prisoners' rights in Canada's harshest prison.

Special Handling Units were opened in 1977 at Millhaven Institution in Ontario and the Correctional Development Centre in Quebec to contain those prisoners regarded as "particularly dangerous." Although conceived as an alternative to long-term administrative segregation, places where prisoners could participate in specially designed, phased programs to earn increasing privileges, the new units proved to be a cruel parody of reform. In my 1983 book *Prisoners of Isolation,* I described how at the Millhaven SHU the "library" was a cell furnished with an empty bookcase, the "music room" was a cell with a shelf on which a single guitar rested, and the "gym" was a double cell equipped with a punching bag and exerciser. CSC opened two new Special Handling Units in 1984, one in Prince Albert Penitentiary and the other in Ste.-Anne-des-Plaines. Although the new units had better physical amenities—larger cells and a modern well-equipped gym—the architects of the new SHUs had taken to heart the panoptical vision of English political reformer Jeremy Bentham in laying out the observation galleries: these permitted total surveillance of prisoner activity. Separation of prisoners from staff by glass and steel barriers was a central theme of these units, allowing total control over prisoner movement and intensifying the repressive nature of imprisonment. For a brief period in the late 1980s the units were called "High Maximum Security Institutions," a name change accompanied by little more than new policy that made it easier to transfer a prisoner there. A few years later, the units reverted to their former designation. In 1995, a decision was made to close the Prince Albert SHU, and since 1997 the Quebec Special Handling Unit has been Canada's only super-maximum penitentiary. In the Internet version of this book I devote a separate chapter to the development and operational reality of the Special Handling Units. In this printed edition, I have woven into several chapters the experiences of prisoners who have served time in both the first- and second-generation SHUs. Readers may draw their own conclusions about whether intensifying the pains of imprisonment contributes in the end to increased public safety.

## The Organization of *Justice behind the Walls*

*Justice behind the Walls* is divided into six parts, which I have called Sectors— prison terminology for the different areas of an institution. Sector 1 begins with an overview of the social and historical scholarship that has invigorated the study of imprisonment. I then review the contours of organizational change in the Correctional Service of Canada over the past twenty years, a change spearheaded by the aspirational Mission Statement, a new model for institutional management, and a research-based cognitive model for prison programs. I end Sector 1 by charting the principal developments in the interface between corrections, the courts, and the Constitution of Canada. Since this book is intended to reach not only lawyers, judges, prisoners, correctional staff, law students, and criminology students but also concerned members of the public, I endeavour to equip readers with a working knowledge of the evolution of contemporary corrections law, including the key concepts in administrative law, such as the duty to act fairly, the impact of the *Canadian Charter of Rights and Freedoms,* and the genesis of the 1992 *Corrections and Conditional Release Act.*

Sector 2 of the book moves to the reality of life inside Kent and Matsqui Institutions. The guiding voices here are not those of criminologists, the Commissioner of Corrections, and the Supreme Court of Canada but those of the correctional officers and prisoners whose lives intersect as the keepers and the kept. The warring elements of repression and rehabilitation are represented physically in the geographical proximity at Matsqui of the segregation unit and an Aboriginal sweatlodge. They are also expressed dynamically in two events that occurred during my first month of research there, one culminating in a powwow, the other in "Operation Big Scoop," a crackdown involving the segregation of thirteen prisoners. By tracking the manoeuvres of Operation Big Scoop, I open the first window on the relationship between operational reality and the law. Sector 2 also opens a window onto the world of maximum security. By chronicling a prison killing and the subsequent court proceedings, I expose the harsh lessons of survival in a maximum security institution, revealing how the same evidence that demonstrates justifiable self-defence in the eyes of the law can, in the eyes of correctional authority, be considered a justification for harsher punishment.

In Sector 3 of the book I return to the questions that took me to the gates of Matsqui Institution in 1972 to study the internal disciplinary system, a private criminal code to which only prisoners are subject. I trace a historical path from a time, not so long ago, when prisoners to be disciplined were marched into the Warden's office and required to stand on footprints painted on a concrete floor to the contemporary disciplinary system, presided over by independent judges, in which the footprints of justice are etched in the due process of law. Based on my observations of more than five hundred hearings, I present samples from the weekly docket of disciplinary court and offer my assessment that, although independent adjudication has resulted in greater fairness, faultlines remain. Because *Justice behind the Walls* seeks to provide more than just a history and ethnography of imprisonment, Sector 3 sets out what I see as the necessary legal and administrative reforms to the prison disciplinary process.

If the disciplinary process is the leading edge of prison justice, its hurting edge, the subject of Sector 4, is what is euphemistically referred to as "administrative segregation." Under very broad discretionary powers given to wardens, a prisoner may be placed in administrative segregation, there to be confined in a cell indefinitely for twenty-three hours a day without the necessity for either a formal disciplinary charge or a conviction in disciplinary court. Because the time spent in administrative segregation can extend to months, even years, it represents the most powerful form of carceral authority; historically, it has also been the most abused. In *Prisoners of Isolation,* I revealed how the regime of solitary confinement, conceived by the founders of the penitentiary as a humane response to the abuse of power, had become by the twentieth century the very epitome of that abuse. In 1974 I helped a group of prisoners who had spent years in the "Penthouse," the solitary confinement unit atop the B.C. Penitentiary, challenge the conditions of their confinement as cruel and unusual punishment in the case of *McCann* v. *The Queen.* Yet despite the apparent victory of a declaration by the Federal Court of Canada, the csc's mean-spirited interpretation of the Court's judgement resulted in only minimal changes.

In the face of csc's obvious inability to reform itself, *Prisoners of Isolation* set out a reform agenda in the shape of a Model Segregation Code, the centrepiece of which was independent adjudication. Sector 4 of *Justice behind the Walls* travels further along this path, tracking the legal developments to the segregation regime that culminated in the *Corrections and Conditional Release Act.* Based on my observations of the segregation review process at both Matsqui and Kent, my judgement on how far the csc has come in curbing the abuses of segregation is not favourable. Neither was that of Madam Justice Louise Arbour, whose inquiry into events at the Prison for Women in 1994 concluded that the csc had developed a culture with little respect for the Rule of Law and the rights of prisoners. That report also recommended that a system of independent adjudication be introduced to establish a fair and just segregation process.

The csc's response to the Arbour Report included establishing a national Task Force on Administrative Segregation. In Sector 4, I chronicle the work of this Task Force and its principal recommendations: first, that the Correctional Service of Canada enhance its own capacity to ensure full compliance with the law and, second, that the Service conduct an experiment in the use of independent adjudicators. The Commissioner of Corrections moved on the first recommendation but rejected the second. To test the Commissioner's confidence in the Service's capacity for internal reform, Sector 4 concludes with a review of events at Kent in the two years following the *Report of the Task Force on Administrative Segregation,* including the "Deadly July" of 1997 during which one prisoner was killed and another narrowly escaped death.

Many of the prisoners profiled in this book have experienced not only the formal disciplinary process and lengthy administrative segregation but also involuntary transfer from medium to maximum security or from maximum security to the Special Handling Unit. Involuntary transfers, the subject of Sector 5, are the site of intersecting and competing interests—those of the warden to maintain a safe and peaceful prison and those of prisoners not to be subject to greater pains of imprisonment without a fair hearing. These transfers have also consistently been the source of more complaints filed with Canada's Correctional Investigator than any other area of prison justice. A set of powerful images and metaphors has grown up around the involuntary transfer. What wardens refer to as "Greyhound therapy" is often used as an administrative alternative in cases where the evidence against a prisoner is insufficient to secure a disciplinary conviction. Prisoners who are objects of involuntary transfers have been characterized by judges as "barbarian princes." Critics have questioned the practice of basing this Greyhound therapy on secret information provided by "faceless informers." The first part of Sector 5 charts the existing boundaries of justice surrounding involuntary transfers and suggests some fairer landmarks.

Sector 5 also addresses how the Supreme Court of Canada jurisprudence on the *Charter* right to be free from unreasonable search and seizure operates in a prison context. To combat the flow of drugs and other contraband and to ensure security and safety within the prison, correctional administrators maintain that they must be given broad powers to search prisoners and their cells. Prisoners maintain with equal vigour that routine searching undermines their dignity and privacy—two of the most precious and scarce human resources in a prison. After tracking the *Charter* protection of privacy through to the *Corrections and Conditional Release Act,* I go on to examine how law was translated into operational reality at Kent when prison officials received information that there was a gun and ammunition in the possession of prisoners.

In a further examination of the conflicting interests of prison administrators and prisoners, the Internet version of Sector 5 addresses a key development in the operation of modern prisons: the liberalization of the regime governing visits between prisoners and their family and friends. From a correctional administrator's perspective, this liberalization has a dark underside: every step in opening up the inside to the outside results in potential holes in the security regime through which may flow a seemingly unending supply of drugs. In examining how prison administrators balance prisoners' visiting rights and security in the war against drugs, I conclude that one of the casualties is fairness.

One difficulty in writing about the Canadian prison experience is finding the appropriate language. Great novels like Aleksandr Solzhenitsyn's *The Gulag Archipelago* and Oriana Fallaci's *A Man* have deepened our understanding of the terror and privation of totalitarian prison systems. Books written by political prisoners themselves, such as Jacobo Timerman's *Prisoner without a Name, Cell without a Number* and Pramoedya Ananta Toer's *The Mute's Soliloquy,* have given expression to the horrifying nature of imprisonment without trial and the fate of the disappeared in the dictatorships of Argentina and Indonesia. Canadians reading these accounts can only stand in awe of the men and women who have survived these experiences with their spirit—if not their bodies—unbroken. In the face of these appalling abuses of human rights, how does a Canadian prisoner

without the lodestar of political or intellectual conviction explain what imprisonment means to the "common criminal"? Over the years, I have met a number
of prisoners with the verbal ability to take us beyond the physical plane of
imprisonment into an interior space from which the experience of justice and
injustice is articulated. The words of some of these prisoners are woven into the
book, and the last part of Sector 5 is devoted to the life and times of one such
prisoner, Gary Weaver.

Sector 6 of *Justice behind the Walls* takes a hard look at remedies, an issue at
the core of human rights protection. Prison litigation has a number of limitations: the expense of lawsuits, the limited availability of legal aid, and the high
threshold for judicial review, which accords prison administrators the right to be
wrong. For this reason, the effectiveness of two non-judicial remedies created in
the 1970s—the Correctional Service's internal grievance process and the Office
of the Correctional Investigator (CI), the federal prison ombudsman—assume
particular significance. Since the CSC has been largely unresponsive to the CI's
recommendations, the Correctional Investigator has recently recommended the
establishment of an administrative tribunal with jurisdiction to enforce the CSC's
compliance with legislation and to provide remedies where necessary. Madam
Justice Arbour also found fault with the CSC's internal grievance system and the
Service's lack of responsiveness to the Correctional Investigator. She recommended that the courts develop a new remedy to respond to those cases in which
there had been illegalities, gross mismanagement, or unfairness in the administration of a prisoner's sentence. To close Sector 6, I review these proposals in the
context of my own recommendations for the expansion of independent adjudication to the areas of administrative segregation and involuntary transfers.

In December 1998, at various places across Canada and around the world, quiet
celebrations marked the fiftieth anniversary of the Universal Declaration of
Human Rights. One of the celebration sites was the National Headquarters of
the Correctional Service of Canada. That week I was in Ottawa preparing for a
case before the Supreme Court, in which I would argue that B.C. prisoners have
a right, under the legal aid scheme, to be represented by a lawyer at disciplinary
hearings which could end in their solitary confinement. The events at CSC headquarters celebrated the passage into Canadian domestic law of international
human rights standards. The arguments soon to come before the Supreme Court
of Canada were about making those rights a reality. At the conclusion of *Justice
behind the Walls,* I offer my report card on how far we have come and how far we
have yet to go in living up to the ideals of the Universal Declaration.

# SECTOR 1

## CHAPTER 1

# Change and Continuity in the Canadian Prison: Lessons from Scholarship

Since its adoption in Europe and North America in the late eighteenth century as the principal form of punishment for serious crime, the prison has left indelible marks on our culture. These are recorded in great works of literature by writers such as Victor Hugo and Aleksandr Solzhenitsyn; they can be seen in the architecture of high-walled fortress penitentiaries and high-tech correctional institutions. Less visibly, they are etched on the lives of those who have endured the pain of imprisonment. Although these experiences sometimes see the light of day in accounts by former prisoners, more often than not they remain hidden in the graffiti of prison cells or explode into public consciousness in the form of violent riots.

Less evident and less accessible than great literature or imposing architecture, and less immediate than violent rebellion, is a library of scholarly work on the prison: its origins and historical evolution, its professed and covert purposes, its character as a social institution, its distinctive culture of the keeper and the kept, its successes and failures as a state institution, and its place in a system of social control that extends far beyond prison gates.

In this chapter I will reach into this body of work to place my study—which is largely confined to two institutions in Western Canada in the late twentieth century—in a larger historical, geographical, and conceptual space. My primary purpose in doing so will be to examine the myriad of questions raised by the prison as an institution and by the practice of imprisonment, specifically with reference to the role of the law, lawyers, and the courts. Studies by lawyers that are grounded in the reality of imprisonment are relatively absent from the literature. As I ask my students at the beginning of their first year of law school, is it not strange that lawyers and judges, as gatekeepers of the only process that can result in a sentence of imprisonment, know or care so little about what happens inside prisons? Lawyers and judges who participate in criminal trials well understand the rules of criminal procedure and the principles of substantive criminal law. It is in the acquittals or convictions that flow from the application of process to principle that we see the model of justice according to law. But what happens when justice results in a prison sentence, once all appeals have been exhausted, is rarely subject to scrutiny by the legal profession. The point at which the criminal justice system will have its greatest impact on the individual is the point at which for the legal profession the process has run its course. It is simply assumed that the prison sentence, whether by deterring, apportioning just deserts, rehabilitating, or simply incapacitating the prisoner for the duration of the sentence, serves the ends of justice. A significant part of this book will be directed to challenging the legal profession to take seriously its responsibility to those men and women who are sentenced to imprisonment, as well as to challenging the assumption that the prison sentence, as administered by prison administrators and staff, does indeed serve the ends of justice.

The broadened context of my inquiry is not solely for the benefit of the legal profession. A good deal of my time inside prisons has been spent talking with and observing the way prison administrators and staff make decisions affecting prisoners. Although they work in institutions with a deep intellectual and social history, most administrators and staff are unfamiliar with that history, or feel disconnected from it in their daily work. In the eyes of the law, correctional staff are important participants in serving the ends of justice, yet they receive little acknowledgement, and even less validation, of their difficult and at times dangerous responsibilities. While television is not a reliable guide to the realities of crime or the criminal justice system, the saturation of network prime time with programs about police officers and lawyers, and the exclusion of programs about prison life (the American series *Oz* being the only exception), speaks volumes about how the work of correctional staff is disconnected from the practice of justice. My interviews with correctional staff were, for many, the first time in their professional lives that someone from outside the correctional establishment had sought their views. In this respect, staff, like prisoners, are disenfranchised as participants in the justice system. By bringing together the library of prison scholarship with the actual experiences of correctional staff, I hope to expose some of the challenges and contradictions that these people encounter in their work.

My horizon in connecting scholarship to practice, however, lies beyond the borders of the legal and prison establishments. A sentence of imprisonment, more so than any other form of censure in our society, is a public judgement visited upon those who have committed public wrongs. A sentence is designed to send a message both to the person upon whom it is imposed and to the rest of us, in whose name, and at whose expense, it is invoked. Engaging the scholarship of imprisonment is thus also of critical importance at a time when the public seems to be demanding more, rather than less, use of imprisonment. In the face of declining crime rates, Canada's incarceration rate continues to rise, ranking among the highest in the world. Even the appearance that we in Canada may be "soft" on crime in comparison to the United States, the most punitive country in the world, disappears when it comes to rates of locking up young people. In this Canada eclipses even the U.S. Yet there is currently a public clamour for more young people to be tried in adult court and for sentences to be made longer, parole more difficult, and prison regimes more rigorous. Politicians seem unable to resist the political benefits perceived to flow from stepping up the war on crime, deploying imprisonment as the principal artillery.

What is rarely heard in the public debate is that the invocation of imprisonment and the practices that accompany its execution have been punctuated over the course of two centuries by a succession of crises. These crises have led to commissions of inquiry and reports cataloguing both the abuses of power taking place within prison walls and the prison's pervasive tendency to make prisoners more dangerous and more anti-social. The 1989 report of the Canadian Sentencing Commission introduced its discussion of sentencing reform with a review of the findings of earlier commissions, which spanned the 150 years since Canada's first penitentiary was opened in 1835 in Kingston, Ontario. Again and again, these reports lamented the demonstrated failure of imprisonment to improve those subjected to its toils. In 1849 the Brown Commission reflected:

> The vast number of human beings annually committed to prison in every civilized country, and the reflection that there they may receive fresh lessons in vice or be led into the path of virtue that, after a brief space, they are to be thrown back on their own habits, more deeply versed than before in the mysteries of crime, or return to society with new feelings, industrious habits, and good resolutions for the future —must ever render the management of penal institutions a study of deep importance for the Statesman as well as the Philanthropist.
>
> In Canada . . . [w]e have but one penal institution for which the aim is reformation and the little success which has as yet attended its operations, it has been our painful duty to disclose. (*Second Report of the Commissioners Appointed to Investigate into the Conduct, Discipline, and Management of the Provincial Penitentiary: Journal of the Legislative Assembly* [1849], cited in *Sentencing Reform: A Canadian Approach* [Report of the Canadian Sentencing Commission] [Ottawa: Minister of Supply and Services Canada, 1987] [Chairman: J. R. Omer Archambault] at 41)

In 1938 the Archambault Commission reported:

> The undeniable responsibility of the state to those held in its custody is to see that they are not returned to freedom worse than when they were taken in charge. This responsibility has been officially recognized in Canada for nearly a century but, although recognized, it has not been discharged. The evidence before this Commission convinced us that there are very few, if any, prisoners who enter our penitentiaries who do not leave them worse members of society than when they entered them. This is a severe, but in our opinion, just indictment of the prison and past administrations. (*Report of the Royal Commission to Investigate the Penal System of Canada* [Ottawa: King's Printer, 1938] [Commissioner: Joseph Archambault], cited in *Sentencing Reform* at 41)

In 1977 the House of Commons Sub-Committee on the Penitentiary System in Canada, set up in the wake of a series of riots in Canada's maximum security penitentiaries, added these words to the collective indictment by its predecessors:

> The persistent recidivist statistic can be related to the fact that so many in prison have been irreversibly damaged by the system by the time they reach the final storehouse of the Criminal Justice System— the penitentiary . . . It was compounded in schools, foster homes, group homes, orphanages, the juvenile justice system, the courts, the police stations, provincial jails, and finally in the "university" of the system, the penitentiary.
>
> Most of those in prison are not dangerous. However, cruel lock-ups, isolation, the injustices and harassment deliberately inflicted on prisoners unable to fight back, make non-violent inmates violent, and those already dangerous more dangerous.
>
> Society has spent millions of dollars over the years to create and maintain the proven failure of prisons. Incarceration has failed in its two essential purposes—correcting the offender and providing permanent protection to society. (House of Commons Sub-Committee on the Penitentiary System in Canada, *Report to Parliament* [Ottawa: Minister of Supply and Services, 1977] [Chairman: Mark MacGuigan], cited in *Sentencing Reform* at 43)

What these (and many more) official reports suggest is that the experience of imprisonment, as a response to crime, is itself criminogenic: it actually produces and reproduces the very behaviour it seeks to control. There is another theme that runs the historical course of 150 years between the early days of the penitentiary and the cusp of the twenty-first century. It is that the experience of imprisonment, intended to inculcate respect for the law by punishing those who breach its commands, actually creates disrespect for the very legal order in whose name it is invoked.

The continuity of this theme is nowhere better illustrated than in events that have taken place on the shores of Lake Ontario, in the city of Kingston, where in 1835 Canada's first penitentiary received its first six prisoners. A sepia-toned photograph of the North Gate of Kingston Penitentiary shows a row of white Doric columns created from local limestone, announcing, to those who entered within, a new era in the treatment of prisoners, with reformation and moral recalibration fashioned along the Enlightenment ideals embraced by prison reformers on both sides of the Atlantic and reflected in the reform blueprints of John Howard. As legislative accompaniment to the new institution, Canada enacted its first *Penitentiary Act.* Borrowing from the preamble of the English *Penitentiary Act* of 1779, it set out the intentions behind Kingston: "If many offenders convicted of crimes were ordered to solitary imprisonment, accompanied by well-regulated labour and religious instruction, it might be the means under providence, not only of deterring others from the commission of like crimes, but also of reforming the individuals, and inuring them to habits of industry" (*An Act to Provide for the Maintenance by the Government of the Provincial Penitentiary,* [1834], 4 Will. IV, c. 37).

Yet in contrast to the promise of this preamble, the first decade at Kingston Penitentiary saw the establishment of a regime of cruel and escalating punishments which, while less public than the spectacle of the gallows, were unimagined by those who drafted the *Penitentiary Act.* The litany of abuses practised by Kingston's first warden are documented in the report of the Brown Commission, which was set up to investigate the penitentiary in 1848. In *Prisoners of Isolation,* my study of solitary confinement in Canada, I summarized the findings of that commission.

> For the first seven years of the penitentiary's operation the warden had relied exclusively upon flogging as the sole punishment for offences of all types. The Commissioners reported that many of these floggings were inflicted on children: during his first committal in Kingston, an eleven-year-old whose offences were talking, laughing, and idling was flogged, over a three-year period, thirty-eight times with the rawhide and six times with the cats; another boy whose "offences were of the most trifling description—such as were to be expected from a child of 10 or 11 . . . was stripped of the shirt and publicly lashed thirty-seven times in eight and a half months." The Commission referred to these and similar cases as examples of "barbarity, disgraceful to humanity." The Commission further

documented cases of men and women who had been flogged into a state of insanity. One prisoner was subject to "seven floggings with the cats in a fortnight, and fourteen floggings in four weeks with the cats or rawhide. It is very clear that if the man was deranged when he arrived, or had any tendency towards it, that the treatment he received was calculated to drive him into hopeless insanity." (Michael Jackson, *Prisoners of Isolation: Solitary Confinement in Canada* [Toronto: University of Toronto Press, 1983] at 28–29)

The Brown Commission's report condemned Warden Smith's regime not only as a living hell but as a catalogue of such arbitrariness and injustice that "must have obliterated from the minds of the unhappy men all perception of moral guilt and thoroughly brutalized their feelings" (*Second Report of the Commissioners Appointed to Investigate into the Conduct, Discipline, and Management of the Provincial Penitentiary* [1849], cited in Jackson, *Prisoners of Isolation* at 29). The commission, while condemning Warden Smith's individual sadism, reaffirmed that the purpose of the penitentiary was to restore the moral compass of the prisoner through contemplation, hard labour, and the teaching of honest trades. Its report also underscored the importance of fairness in the treatment of prisoners, both to re-establish the moral legitimacy of punishment and to allow the penitentiary experience to have a reformative effect.

A century and a half after Warden Smith's reign of terror, across the road from Kingston Penitentiary at the Prison for Women (opened in 1934), there was another series of events that drew the condemnation of a royal commission. Some of these events were captured in a dramatic Correctional Service of Canada videotape which, for the first time, in 1995 allowed the Canadian public to see deep inside the prison cells. The videotape and the 1996 report of the Arbour Commission documented how a small group of women, who were locked in their cells, had been descended upon by a male emergency response team from Kingston Penitentiary. The women, facing a phalanx of men outfitted in Darth Vader suits with full face visors, security shields, and batons, were forced to disrobe, and in some cases had their clothes literally cut off with razor tools. In her scathing report, Madam Justice Arbour commented that "upon viewing images taken from that videotape . . . members of the public have expressed reactions ranging from shock and disbelief, to horror and sorrow" (*Commission of Inquiry into Certain Events at the Prison for Women in Kingston* (Canada) [Ottawa: Public Works and Government Services Canada, 1996] [Commissioner: Louise Arbour] at 86). She concluded that "the process was intended to terrorize, and therefore subdue" (at 88). Terror in the name of the law, but in violation of the law, had also been the charge of the Brown Commission. Madam Justice Arbour saw the events at the Prison for Women not simply as examples of individual deviations from law and policy but as systemic failures demonstrating the absence of a culture that respected the Rule of Law and individual rights: "The Rule of Law is absent, although rules are everywhere" (at 181).

One of my students, Ori Kowarsky, in reviewing how Canadian prisons in every generation have generated a crisis, raised the question of whether "this habitual gearing down is analogous to a stock market 'correction,' a facile surface crisis which allows each generation the privilege of breathing new life into the institution and masking its unremoveable flaw by making its outward accoutrements according to the fashion of the times" (Ori Kowarsky, "Penitent and Penitentiary: The Problem of Situating Zones of Outlawry and Punishment" [University of British Columbia, Faculty of Law, 1998] [unpublished] at 8). The Canadian Sentencing Commission, in its 1987 summary of the succession of official inquiries, concluded that these inquiries were "more of a tribute to the resiliency of the criminal justice system than a chronicle of change" (*Sentencing Reform* at 40). At the end of his year-long study in my Penal Policy seminar, Ori Kowarsky concluded that "the story of the penitentiary in the 20th century may be the story of a system straining *against* the law in order to remain true to its nature . . . [T]he ideology of the penitentiary is like DNA, it is encoded in every brick, in every bar and every report" (Kowarsky at 58).

The remarkable resiliency the system of imprisonment has demonstrated despite a continuous stream of criticism runs alongside the equally remarkable ability of the system to absorb a succession of theories about the causes of criminality and the purposes of criminal law. When Kingston Penitentiary opened, the prevailing theory, as described by J. M. Beattie, was that crime was a social disease characteristic of the poor, the origins of which lay in indolence and a lack of moral sense.

> Since crime was thought to be the product of a criminal class that lived in destitution and ignorance, that lived without the restraints of morality and religion, . . . crime could only be prevented and society protected if the habits and behaviour of the lower orders of the population were changed . . . Internal discipline and good work habits would succeed in protecting property from the envy of the low orders where the horrors of the gallows had failed. (J. M. Beattie, *Attitudes towards Crime and Punishment in Upper Canada, 1830–1850: A Documentary Study* [Toronto: University of Toronto, Centre of Criminology, 1977] at 12–13)

The expectation of those who designed the regime at Kingston Penitentiary was that with a basic diet of hard work and religious instruction, outlaws would become law-abiding. As the penitentiary's official historians have noted, "At least this was the hope at a time when criminal behaviour was equated with sinfulness. It later would be called a sickness, and still later a disorder of the social environment, but the penitentiary would prove equal to all the theories" (Dennis Curtis et al., *Kingston Penitentiary: The First 150 Years, 1835–1985* [Ottawa: Correctional Service of Canada, 1985] at 4).

The penitentiary has been equally accommodating to shifting emphasis on the purpose of criminal sanctions, be that retribution, deterrence, reformation, or incapacitation. This facility of correctional regimes to accommodate themselves to shifts in basic assumptions about crime and criminals may, as Ori Kowarsky suggests, be caused by a deep-seated imprint that transcends theories. There is, however, another explanation, offered by criminologist Peter MacNaughton-Smith: that the assumptions underlying the theories not only change with the times but are inherently contradictory, although they share the common feature of justifying the practice of imprisonment and of dividing society into those who are criminals (and therefore deserving of imprisonment) and those who are not. In this parody of the assumptions that have driven penal policy, MacNaughton-Smith writes:

> Criminals are wicked (and we are rather good) but they are not really wicked, they're sick (so I suppose that we are not really good, we're just healthy) and in any case it doesn't matter which they are because the things they do are dangerous and inconvenient (and what everyone else does is always safer and more convenient) and we have to teach them a lesson, which they won't learn because they're incorrigible, and we have to integrate them back into the community, and also symbolize society's rejection of them. The young ones are the worst and we must spare them the shame of being treated like real criminals. Now some of these clichés may well be true, or may well not be, but they cannot all be true at once; we shall not believe anyone who asserts too many of them together. They are rather like proverbs: you can find whatever you want. Which ones the powerful members of the society believe are true will surely make a difference to what that society does; yet human society as a whole, over nearly all of its geography and history, has done very similar things in the name of the law and has offered whichever reasons happen to be in fashion at the time. When the reasons change and the activity remains, the reasons begin to look like excuses . . . In our own age (perhaps it is the age of mystification) the reasons are advanced almost proudly in self-contradictory pairs such as justice and rehabilitation. But as George Bernard Shaw says,
>
> > now if you are to punish a man retributively you must injure him. If you are to reform him you must improve him. And men are not improved by injuries. To propose to punish and reform by the same operation is exactly as if you were to take

a man suffering from pneumonia and attempt to combine punitive and curative treatments. Arguing that a man with pneumonia is a danger to community, and that he need not catch it if he takes proper care of his health, you resolve that he shall have a severe lesson, both to punish him for his negligence and pulmonary weakness and to deter others from following his example. You therefore strip him naked, and in that condition stand him all night in the snow. But as you admit the duty of restoring him to health if possible, and discharging him with sound lungs, you engage a doctor to superintend the punishment and administer cough lozenges made as unpleasant to the taste as possible so as not to pamper the culprit. A board of commissioners ordering such treatment would prove thereby that either they were imbeciles or else that they were hotly in earnest about punishing the patient and not in the least in earnest about curing him. (P. MacNaughton-Smith, *Permission to be Slightly Free* [Ottawa: Minister of Supply and Services Canada, 1976] at 30–32)

With so many contradictory assumptions supporting penal policy, is it so strange that the institution of imprisonment has, chameleon-like, developed the ability to present itself in many different colours over time, from Revenge to Restraint, from Restraint to Reformation, and from Reformation to Reintegration?

It is not only theories and attitudes that have vied for ascendancy within the penitentiary; there are competing histories of the penitentiary itself and of its role as an institution of punishment. As Stanley Cohen has observed in his masterful summary of these histories—broadly divided into the categories "traditional" and "revisionist"—"these are not just competing versions of what may or may not have happened nearly 200 years ago. They are informed by fundamentally different views about the nature of ideology and hence quite different ways of making sense of current policies and change" (Stanley Cohen, *Visions of Social Control: Crime, Punishment and Classification* [Cambridge, Mass.: Polity Press, 1985] at 50).

The dominant "traditional" historical accounts are essentially the history of progressive reform. As described by Cohen:

The conventional view of correctional change in general and of the emergence of the prison in the early 19th-century crime control system in particular, is based upon a simple-minded idealist view of history . . . All change constitutes "reform" (a word with no negative connotations); all reform is motivated by benevolence, altruism, philanthropy and humanitarianism, and the eventual record of success of reforms must be read as an incremental story of progress. Criminology and other such disciplines provide the scientific theory (the "knowledge base") for guiding and implementing the reform program. Thus, the birth of the prison in the late 18th century, as well as concurrent and subsequent changes, are seen in terms of the victory of humanitarianism over barbarity, of scientific knowledge over prejudice and irrationality. Early forms of punishment, based on vengeance, cruelty and ignorance give way to informed, professional and expert intervention . . .

Not that this vision is at all complacent. The system is seen as practically and even morally flawed. Bad mistakes are often made and there are abuses such as overcrowding in prisons, police brutality, unfair sentencing and other such remnants of irrationality. But in the course of time, with goodwill and enough resources (more money, better trained staff, newer buildings and more research), the system is capable of being humanized by good intentions and made more efficient by the application of scientific principles. As a view of history and a rationale of the present policies [this] is by far the most important story of all. (S. Cohen at 15, 18)

In contrast to the traditional and largely administrative histories stand the "revisionist" accounts that Stanley Cohen has divided into two models, one being the "we blew it" version of history and the other the "it's all a con" view of correctional change. Cohen summarizes the "we blew it" version (under the subtitle "Good [but Complicated] Intentions—Disastrous Consequences") in this way:

Roughly from the mid-1960's onwards, a sour voice of disillusionment, disenchantment and cynicism, at first hesitant and now strident, has appeared within the liberal reform camp. The message was that the reform vision itself is potentially suspect. The record is not just one of good intentions going wrong now and then, but of continual and disastrous failure. The gap between rhetoric and reality is so vast, that either the rhetoric itself is deeply flawed or social reality resists all such reform attempts. (S. Cohen at 19)

The best-known exposition of this model is in the work of the American historian David J. Rothman. In his books *The Discovery of the Asylum: Social Order and Disorder in the New Republic* (Boston: Little Brown, 1971) and *Conscience and Convenience: The Asylum and Its Alternatives in Progressive America* (Boston: Little Brown, 1980), Rothman tracks the history of prison reform and its organization around a cyclical pattern of brief inspirational reforms, led by dedicated individuals, followed by a slow process of displacement of the originating ideals by more mundane organizational imperatives. This revisionist view does not deny the possibility of or the necessity for reform, but suggests that the warning from history is that benevolence itself must be distrusted. In understanding the historical process of "reform," it is necessary to bear in mind the ways in which "convenience" can—and, if history teaches us anything, will—undermine a reform vision based upon "conscience."

The other, more radical and more pessimistic, model, subtitled "Discipline and Mystification" by Cohen, presents a very different historical trajectory:

> The original transformation of the system was not what it appeared to be, nor should the subsequent history of institutions like the reformed 19th-century prison be explained as stories of "failure." Contrary to Rothman's sad tale, the system was and is continuously "successful," not, of course, in line with the progress story, but in the sense of fulfilling quite other than its declared function. The new control system served the requirements of the emerging capitalist order for continual repression of the recalcitrant members of the working class and, at the same time, continued to mystify everyone (including the reformers themselves) into thinking that these changes were fair, humane and progressive.
>
> This is what the reformed prison does. It renders docile the recalcitrant members of the working class, it deters others, it teaches habits of discipline and order, it reproduces the lost hierarchy. It repairs defective humans to compete in the market place. Not just the prison but the crime system as a whole, is part of the larger rationalisation of social relations in nascent capitalism. (S. Cohen at 23)

In this model of revisionism, there are several variations. By far the most influential one in the scholarly literature is that of Michel Foucault. Cohen suggests that Foucault's influence is so pervasive that "to write today about punishment and classification without Foucault, is like talking about the unconscious without Freud" (S. Cohen at 10). Foucault's seminal book *Discipline and Punish: The Birth of the Prison* (trans. Alan Sheridan. New York: Pantheon, 1978) is part of a larger body of work that traverses the issues of madness, medicine, and sexuality, and traces the principles of surveillance and discipline that underpin modern penal institutions, focussing upon the technologies of penal power and the language in which they operate. In many respects Foucault's work, to use the analogy of Ori Kowarsky, sets out to describe the DNA of modern punishment. Stanley Cohen offers this summary of Foucault's thesis:

The "Great Incarcerations" of the 19th century—thieves into prisons, lunatics into asylums, conscripts into barracks, workers into factories, children into school—are to be seen as part of a grand design. Property had to be protected, production had to be standardized by regulations, the young segregated and inculcated with the ideology of thrift and success, the deviant subjected to discipline and surveillance. (at 25)

Foucault's account of the disappearance of punishment as a public, theatrical spectacle of violence applied against the body, and of the emergence of the prison as the general form of modern punishment, which is applied in places removed from the public gaze, is captured in this passage from David Garland, whose book *Punishment and Modern Society: A Study in Social Theory* (Chicago: University of Chicago Press, 1990) is a finely wrought analysis of the history and social theory of punishment.

This change in penal styles, which, according to Foucault, took place throughout Europe and the US between about 1750 and 1820, is to be understood as a qualitative shift rather than a mere decrease in the quantity or intensity of punishment. The target of punishment is shifted so that measures are now aimed to affect the "soul" of the offender rather than to just strike his body. At the same time the objective of punishment undergoes a change so that the concern is now less to avenge the crime than to transform the criminal who stands behind it.

This change in penal technology—from the scaffold to the penitentiary—signifies for Foucault a deeper change in the character of justice itself. In particular the new concern—which the prison introduced—to know the criminal, to understand the sources of his criminality, and to intervene to correct them wherever possible, had profound implications for the whole system of criminal justice. In this modern system the focus of judgement shifts away from the offence itself towards questions of character, of family background, and of the individual's history and environment. This will ultimately involve the introduction of experts—psychiatrists, criminologists, social workers, etc.—into the judicial process, with the aim of forming a knowledge of the individual, identifying his or her abnormalities and bringing about the reformation. The result of these changes is a system of dealing with offenders that is not so much punitive as corrective, more intent upon producing normal, conforming individuals than upon dispensing punishments: a penal system that the Americans named best when they called it, simply, "corrections." (at 136)

Just as David Rothman's revisionist history introduced into the scholarly literature of punishment the concepts of "convenience" and "conscience," Michel Foucault's work coined a number of conceptual phrases that have become part of the modern vocabulary of criminology. To describe how the disciplinary techniques employed in the prison were also applied in hospitals, schools, asylums, factories, and military academies, Foucault created the concepts of the ever-expanding "carceral continuum" and of the "carceral archipelago," which adds islands to the empire of punishment. Both have proven to be powerful images in describing modern developments in corrections.

David Garland's *Punishment and Modern Society,* drawing upon the principal tributaries of social theory concerning punishment, is perhaps the most important scholarly contribution to understanding both the changes that have taken place in the conception and practice of punishment and the reasons why conception and practice remain beset with contradictions. Utilizing Norbert Elias' account of *The Civilizing Process: The History of Manners and State Formation and Civilization* (trans. Edmund Jephcott. Oxford: Blackwell, 1994 [original publication 1939]), Garland adopts the concept of "civilization curves" to explain the general developmental pattern in the nature and experience of punishment over the last two hundred years. He prefaces his discussion with the observation that throughout this history there has been a well-developed link between the broad notion of "civilization" and a society's penal system, particularly its prisons. That link has been most clearly expressed in Winston Churchill's declaration that "the mood and temper of the public in regard to the treatment of crime and criminals is one of the most unfailing tests of the civilisation of any country" (U.K., H.C., *Parliamentary Debates,* 5th ser., vol. 19, col. 1354 (20 July 1910)), and in Dostoevsky's assertion that the standards of a nation's civilisation can be judged by opening the doors of its prisons.

One of the "civilization curves" Elias identifies is "the process of privatization whereby certain aspects of life disappear from the public arena to become hidden behind the scenes of social life. Sex, violence, bodily functions, illness, suffering and death gradually become a source of embarrassment and distaste and are more and more removed to various private domains" (Garland at 222). The history of punishment is a primary illustration of this pattern.

> In the early modern period capital and corporal executions were conducted in public, and both the ritual of judicial killing and the offender's display of suffering formed an open part of social life. Later, in the 17th and 18th centuries, the sight of this spectacle became redefined as distasteful, particularly among the social elite and executions are gradually removed "behind the scenes"—usually behind the walls of prisons. Subsequently, the idea of doing violence to offenders becomes repugnant in itself, and corporal and capital

punishments are largely abolished, to be replaced by other sanctions such as imprisonment. By the late 20th century, punishment has become a rather shameful social activity, undertaken by specialists and professionals in enclaves (such as prisons and reformatories) which are, by and large, removed from the sight of the public. (Garland at 224)

It is not only the forms and sites of punishment that change; these are accompanied by a whole new vocabulary that either literally or euphemistically "civilizes" what is done in the name of punishment:

The civilizing process in punishment is also apparent in the sanitization of penal practice and penal language. Pain is no longer delivered in brutal, physical form. Corporal punishment has virtually disappeared, to be replaced by more abstract forms of suffering, such as the deprivation of liberty or the removal of financial resources . . . [T]he aggression and hostility implicit in punishment are concealed and denied by the administrative routines of dispassionate professionals, who see themselves as "running institutions" rather than delivering pain and suffering. Similarly, the language of punishment has been stripped of its plain brutality of meaning and reformulated in euphemistic terms, so that prisons become "correctional facilities," guards become "officers," and prisoners become "inmates" or even "residents," all of which tends to sublimate a rather distasteful activity and render it more tolerable to public and professional sensibilities. (Garland at 235)

In the context of punishment, Elias' "civilization curves" have to contend with the contemporary escalation in the scale of punishment reflected in most western societies by increasing prison populations, longer prison terms, and an extended, more finely meshed net of corrections. In explaining the limited impact that the civilizing process appears to have on public perceptions of crime and punishment, Garland offers us an explanation drawing upon the analysis of George Herbert Mead and Sigmund Freud.

In the course of the civilizing process, at both the social and individual levels—human beings are led to repress (or to sublimate) their instinctual drives and particularly their aggressions. This process of repression, however, does not lead to the total disappearance of such drives—civilization does not succeed in abolishing the instincts or legislating them out of existence, as the wars and holocausts of the

20th century show all too clearly. Instead, they are banned from the sphere of proper conduct and consciousness and forced down into the realm of the unconscious . . . Civilization thus sets up a fundamental conflict within the individual between instinctual desires and internalized super ego controls, a conflict which has profound consequences for psychological and social life. Thus while social prohibitions may demand the renunciation of certain pleasures—such as aggression or sadism—this may be only ever a partial renunciation, since the unconscious wish remains . . . Civilization thus makes unconscious hypocrites of us all, and ensures that certain issues will often arouse highly charged emotions which are rooted in unconscious conflict, rather than single minded, rationally considered attitudes . . .

The "threat" posed by the criminal—and the fear and hostility which this threat provokes—thus have a deep, unconscious dimension, beyond the actual danger to society which the criminal represents. "Fear of crime" can thus exhibit irrational roots, and often leads to disproportionate (or "counter phobic") demands for punishment. (Ironically, our psychological capacity to *enjoy* crime—at least in the form of crime stories—leads the media to highlight the most vicious, horror-laden tales, which in turn serve to enhance the fears which crime evokes. The linked emotions of fascination and fear thus reinforce each other through the medium of crime news and crime thrillers.) . . .

In a society where instinctual aggressions are strictly controlled and individuals are often self-punishing, the legal punishment of the offenders offers a channel for the open expression of aggressions and sanctions and a measure of pleasure in the suffering of others . . . The view of James Fitzjames Stephens that it was the duty of the citizen to hate the criminal is nowadays considered reactionary and distasteful, and is normally cited to show how far we have come since the late 19th century . . . Nevertheless, there remains an underlying emotional ambivalence which shapes our attitudes towards punishment and which has so far prevented the civilizing effects of transformed sensibilities from being fully registered within the penal sphere. (Garland at 238–40)

The language of modern corrections is not framed as moral discourse. "Prison officials, in so far as they are being professional, tend to suspend moral judgement and treat prisoners in purely neutral terms. Typically, the evaluative terms which are used relate to administrative criteria rather than moral worth . . . hence the much quoted formula that offenders come to prison as punishment and not *for* punishment . . . In effect, penal professionals tend to orientate themselves towards institutionally defined managerial goals rather than socially derived punitive ones" (Garland at 183). But while this can be accomplished by changing the language of punishment to that of risk management, the men and women in the correctional bureaucracy, when they leave home to assume their posts as guards, case managers, or administrators, cannot so easily shed, like some reptilian skin, the cultural inheritance that the rest of us share. Correctional bureaucrats they may be, but as Michael Ignatieff, himself one of the revisionist historians, has reminded correctional workers, they are "bureaucrats of good and evil" (Michael Ignatieff, "Imprisonment and the Need for Justice" [Presentation to the Criminal Justice Congress, Toronto, 1987] [unpublished]). The fact that the official language of corrections does not acknowledge these concepts cannot change the fact that they inhabit our minds, consciously or unconsciously. In this way correctional workers bear the burden of sorting out their own ambivalence about punishment and that of the larger society, not as philosophical or existential angst but in carrying out the routines of their daily work.

Although it might help us to achieve a fuller understanding, we do not need to dig deep into the realm of the unconscious or debate the merits of psychoanalytical insights in a post-Freudian world to recognize the conflicts inherent in the practice of punishment. As I have explained, the idea and the practice of punishment are driven by conflict and contradiction, most of which is close to the surface and needs little excavation. At the end of his historical and sociological analysis, David Garland concludes with this sobering reflection:

> [Punishment is] an institution which has a last resort necessity in any society—authority must in the end be sanctioned if it is to be authoritative, and offenders who are sufficiently dangerous or recalcitrant must be dealt with forcibly in some degree. But however necessary it sometimes is, and however useful in certain respects, punishment is always beset by irresolvable tensions. However well it is organized, and however humanely administered, punishment is inescapably marked by moral contradiction and unwanted irony—as when it seeks to uphold freedom by means of its deprivation, or condemns private violence using a violence which is publicly authorized. Despite the claims of reforming enthusiasts, the interests of state, society, victim, and offender can never be "harmonized," whether by rehabilitation or anything else. The infliction of punishment by a state upon its citizens bears the character of a civil war in miniature—it depicts a society engaged in a struggle with itself. And though this may sometimes be necessary, it is never anything other than a necessary evil. (at 292)

The image of the practice of imprisonment as a form of civil war is not a comforting one. But then, and this is Garland's point, we should never be comforted or complacent about our prisons. Even though this imagery is far removed from the professional language of corrections, increasingly it is the preferred language of governments and law enforcement agencies in describing and seeking public vindication of their crime control policies. The "war on crime" is not an ambiguous rally to arms. As Canadian criminologist Laureen Snider has observed, "Note the language employed: who could take the side of 'enemies,' or advocate half-measures in a war?" (Laureen Snider, "Understanding the Second Great Confinement" [Spring 1998] 105 *Queen's Quarterly* at 39). But even in wars there are rules of engagement, and there are international human rights standards designed to protect those who are captured and imprisoned. Even in war—and perhaps especially in war—the law provides a bulwark against the abuse of human rights.

## CHAPTER 2

# "Good Corrections": Organizational Renewal and the Mission Document

In the late 1980s the Correctional Service of Canada (CSC) underwent a major reorganization. What distinguished this reorganization from earlier ones was its description, by those who animated it, as more than just a contemporary analogue to the restructuring taking place in the private sector, where the goals were primarily efficiency and economy. CSC's reorganization was conceived on a plane of higher principles. In the metaphorical language of a journey, what CSC embarked upon was a "journey of organizational renewal . . . motivated by a desire to 'do good corrections'" (Jim Vantour, "Foreword," in Jim Vantour, ed., *Our Story: Organizational Renewal in Federal Corrections* [Ottawa: Correctional Service of Canada, 1991] at i).

Published a year before the 1992 proclamation of the *Corrections and Conditional Release Act, Our Story,* published by the CSC itself, provides an internal, self-defined reference point against which to assess the actual practices of corrections in Canada in the 1990s.

Before tracking the official statement of progressive reform, it is worth reading the cautionary words of Stanley Cohen regarding the way in which "social-control talk" is designed to give the appearance of change:

> The language which the powerful use to deal with chronic social problems like crime is very special in its banality. Invariably, it tries to convey choice, change, progress, and rational decision-making. Even if things stay much the same, social-control talk has to convey a dramatic picture of breakthroughs, departures, innovations,

milestones, turning points—continually changing strategies in the war against crime. All social-policy talk has to give the impression of change even if nothing new is happening at all . . .

All this is to give the impression that social problems . . . are somehow not totally out of control . . . So magical is the power of the new languages of systems theory, applied-behaviour analysis and psycho-babble, that they can convey (even to their users) an effect opposite to the truth. (at 157–58)

Cohen's further comment that the language of social control may represent a "form of shamanism: a series of conjuring tricks in which agencies are shuffled, new names invented, incantations recited, commissions, committees, laws, programs and campaigns announced" (at 158) is particularly relevant in the Canadian context, where all of these activities have proceeded at an accelerated pace since the early 1990s.

In Canada, the official csc history provides us with this account of the motivation for organizational renewal and its culmination in the "Mission Document":

The business of federal corrections is widely regarded as one of drama and suffering. It is also one that touches at the very core of two of our society's most fundamental values: human freedom and public safety. Consequently, the Correctional Service of Canada must frequently respond to political and public demands for assurance that we are doing what is needed.

Given this situation, it seems that it would be difficult for us, the managers and employees of the Correctional Service of Canada, to do any more than to simply cope or to focus the bulk of our energy on just administering the prison system. Indeed, it appears that it would be easy for us to fall into the trap of believing that our fundamental object is to "stay out of trouble."

Yet for many of us, simply staying out of trouble is not enough. We really want to do the best job we possibly can. We want to do good corrections—to serve our Minister (the Solicitor General of Canada), the government, and the people of Canada well. It is evident to us that we have to do more than just administer the prison system. We believe that we have to take the initiative to define what good corrections is and to chart a course to make sure that good corrections is what we do. The predominance of this sentiment among a significant number of us prompted us to develop a clearly stated and highly integrated set of goals for the Correctional Service of Canada. This set of goals became our Mission Document. (*Our Story* at 3)

According to *Our Story,* the intellectual and organizational leadership for the Mission-related reforms came with the arrival on the Canadian correctional stage of Ole Ingstrup. "A lawyer and prison administrator in his native Denmark, Ingstrup had immigrated to Canada in 1984 and had immediately begun work in an advisory capacity to Donald Yeomans who was then the Commissioner of Corrections. Beginning in 1984, he studied many aspects of the Service and proposed a course for it to become a value-based, results-driven organization" (*Our Story* at 19). That initiative was not pursued, and in 1986 Mr. Ingstrup was appointed Chairman of the National Parole Board. However, with his return to CSC in 1988 as the new Commissioner of Corrections, he gained the authority to bring to fruition his "value-based, results-driven" model of organizational change. In a chapter of *Our Story* written by the Commissioner himself, he describes his vision of "good corrections."

> When we decided that we wanted to do good corrections, it became evident that such a concept meant many things. It meant aligning ourselves with the best current thinking in correctional research and practice. It meant abiding by the values entrenched in the *Canadian Charter of Rights and Freedoms* and related documents which reflect the attitudes of Canadians with respect to freedom, safety and human dignity. It meant doing well all the things that we commit ourselves to doing. In the most narrow sense, it meant doing those things well which have to do with the professional management of the offender's risk to society. (Ole Ingstrup, "Deciding to Change" in *Our Story* at 20–22)

The importance of the "mission" to CSC's organizational renewal is articulated in these inspirational and aspirational terms:

> The purpose of a mission is to lead. We wanted a declaration that would not simply describe what federal corrections is but rather what it should strive to become in the future. Such a declaration had to define the very reasons for our organization's existence and, most importantly, our ambitions—our ultimate organizational objectives. Furthermore, we wanted to clearly articulate the most important overall strategies required to achieve our ultimate objectives. At the same time we had to "bite the bullet" on the realities of the social institution that we manage. To us, then, a mission statement was to be a vision for the future, a blueprint for development, change and improvement . . .
>
> The Mission Statement is about people—their potential and our role in tapping that potential. It moves from the individual to the

organizational to the wider collectives of Canadian society, the justice system, and national and international corrections. It recognizes the past, but moves towards the future. It grounds the Service in its wider world. (*Our Story* at 46, 50)

The Mission Document was reviewed by CSC's senior managers at a conference in Banff in November 1988, and in February 1989 it was signed by then Solicitor General Pierre Blais. The Mission Document has four components: Mission Statement, Core Values, Guiding Principles, and Strategic Objectives. The first element, the Mission Statement, sets out the ultimate objective of the organization. According to that Mission Statement,

> The Correctional Service of Canada (CSC), as part of the criminal justice system *and respecting the rule of law,* contributes to the protection of society by actively encouraging and assisting offenders to become law-abiding citizens, while exercising reasonable, safe, secure and humane control. (Correctional Service of Canada, "Our Mission," online: <http://www.csc-scc.gc.ca/text/organi/organe01_e.shtml> [last modified: 22 October 1999])

The italicized words "and respecting the rule of law" did not appear in the original 1989 version of the Mission Statement, but were added when the Statement was revised in 1996.

The Core Values are intended to outline the basic and enduring ideals of the CSC and to serve as guides in the fulfillment of the Mission. There are five Core Values:

> Core Value 1
>> We respect the dignity of individuals, the rights of all members of society, and the potential for human growth and development.
>
> Core Value 2
>> We recognize that the offender has the potential to live as a law-abiding citizen.
>
> Core Value 3
>> We believe that our strength and our major resource in achieving our objectives is our staff and that human relationships are the cornerstone of our endeavour.
>
> Core Value 4
>> We believe that the sharing of ideas, knowledge, values and experience, nationally and internationally, is essential to the achievement of our Mission.

Core Value 5

> We believe in managing the Service with openness and integrity and we are accountable to the Solicitor General.

The third element of the Mission Document, Guiding Principles, states the key assumptions that direct the CSC in its daily actions. The Strategic Objectives, the fourth element, "translate the values and principles into action-oriented objectives—which operationalize the philosophy" (*Our Story* at 47). For each of the five Core Values there is a separate set of Guiding Principles and Strategic Objectives.

The adoption of the Mission Document in 1989 coincided with the implementation of a new model of correctional management. Although the decision to implement "Unit Management" preceded the development of the document, the model was endorsed as being consistent with Core Value 3, which "emphasizes the importance of human relationships in our endeavours and the need for all our staff to be correctional staff—active and visible participants in the correctional process" (*Our Story* at 91). The historical evolution of the concept of unit management, and in particular the transition from "guards" to "correctional officers," is tracked in *Our Story.*

> The history of penitentiaries has been long but the evolution of correctional management did not begin until the late 1960's. Until then, there were a few individuals in each penitentiary who worked towards the rehabilitation of the prisoner. Essentially, though, there were "guards" and "convicts," with the guards guarding and the convicts doing what they were told. Indeed, it was only a few decades ago that it was accepted that inmates should normally remain silent. Where conversations between staff members and inmates were necessary, they were minimal. Prisoners had no responsibilities but to follow the rules and regulations imposed upon them. If they "played the game" there was less conflict with the authorities; if they didn't, they did "hard time" . . . The penitentiary did not view itself as a correctional institution so if an inmate began to behave in a more socially acceptable manner, it was largely a result of his own initiative and not because of the system.
>
> In the 1960's, ideas about correctional management began to develop. One innovation was the Living Unit approach which was applied in many, but not all, of the federal correctional institutions. With this approach to managing institutions, the inmate population was divided into smaller groups (based on the proximity of their cells) and a group of staff members were assigned to work with them on a continual basis. These staff members, known as "Living Unit

Officers," had a dual role, to act as custodial officers and to serve as first-line case management officers. As guards, they observed the behaviour of a specific group of inmates in the living area, recreation or work areas, watching for changing patterns of behaviour . . . Although the intent of the Living Unit approach was good, it divided staff members into two groups: those who worked directly with inmates; and those who did not have any meaningful interaction with inmates, that is, those who only looked after what is called static security—walls, barbed wire, weapons and barriers.

A number of studies in the early 1980's, focusing on the operations of the penitentiaries and the management of inmates, highlighted a need to change. Specifically, concerns were raised about the number of staff members, particularly those entrusted with the security of institutions, who had almost no interaction with inmates . . . The reports of the 1980's had several common recommendations of particular relevance to the creation of a new management model. These recommendations focused on the need for an organizational structure that would facilitate extensive and meaningful interaction between staff and inmates—improved dynamic security and delegation of authority to the operational level.

As a result of wide-based consultation and detailed analysis of contemporary correctional practices, "Unit Management" evolved as the model for the Correctional Service of Canada Institutions. This meant dividing institutions into smaller units, with *all* staff sharing responsibility for interaction with offenders and participation in inmate programming, whether through formal or informal means. (*Our Story* at 92–94)

Kent and Matsqui Institutions, like all other federal penitentiaries, are now organized according to the principles of unit management. The overall responsibility for management of each institution rests with the warden, its chief executive officer. Reporting to the warden is the deputy warden, who is charged with the responsibilities for security operations and inmate management. Under the unit management model, each institution is divided into units, typically centred around a distinct cell block area, each under the direction of a unit manager. For example, at Kent Institution there are three unit managers, one for the general population ranges, one for the protective custody ranges, and a third whose responsibility is for the segregation unit. At Matsqui, there are unit managers for each of the three floors of the main cell block and a fourth for the segregation unit, whose responsibilities also extend to the Regional Reception Centre. Each unit manager has responsibility not only for a designated cell block area and the prisoners who live there but for a specific program area, such as Visits and Correspondence. The unit managers are supported by a team of correctional supervisors, correctional officers, and case management officers. (This latter group was redesignated in 1998 as "institutional parole officers.") The general responsibilities of these team members are described in *Our Story:*

> Two levels of line correctional officers are required in Unit Management. Both levels are responsible for basic security functions. The majority of the duties of the Correctional Officer I are comprised of the more traditional static security duties (such as movement control, tool control, searching, frisking, counting, etc.). The Correctional Officer II, the more senior of the two, is also tasked with these duties but has a greater involvement in case management and thus more contact with inmates.
>
> The Correctional Officer II is assigned a small inmate caseload and is expected to play a critical role in the development and monitoring of an inmate's correctional treatment plan . . . Although Correctional Officers I do not have an assigned caseload, they are required to report and record information on inmate behaviour, based upon their interaction with, and surveillance of, inmates.
>
> The case management officers are ultimately responsible for the management of all inmates' cases and provide functional support to the Correctional Officers II in their work with their inmate caseloads.
>
> The correctional supervisor is responsible for the supervision of correctional officers in the day-to-day operations in the unit. Although not carrying a caseload, the correctional supervisor is responsible for the assignment of caseloads and is expected to be knowledgeable about, and actively involved in, the case management process. (at 96–97)

The CSC, in its official literature, sees the introduction of unit management and the dissemination of the Mission Document as having changed the nature of staff-prisoner relationships, from one based upon "authority" to one of "interaction." In the words of one warden:

> Relations between staff and inmates are characterized less by power and authority than they were a few years ago; instead they are oriented towards contact of a professional nature. The control that we exercise over the inmates is now being experienced more as the helping relationship we are trying to create.
>
> A team approach to case management, in which the expertise of specialists is augmented by the assessments of correctional officers,

certainly helps to improve the quality of the work with the inmate and increases the understanding of correctional intervention . . . The principal party concerned, the inmate, is constantly involved in the process. Inmates are normally present at discussions and receive a copy of the reports written on their case. Such a practice fully corresponds with a policy of openness which the Correctional Service is trying to apply. In addition, this openness in our procedures accurately reflects the spirit of the Canadian *Charter of Rights and Freedoms*. (In this regard, we can even assert that the Mission and the policies of the correctional service harmonize so well with the *Charter of Rights and Freedoms* that they constitute its extension in penal and correctional matters.)

We consider our approach to dealing with the inmates to be proactive in nature. We lead the way for them by helping them choose an appropriate path—their correctional treatment plan; by sharing with them our opinions and expectations; and by indicating the possible consequences of their behaviour and attitudes. This new approach contrasts favourably with our practice of a few years ago which was more reactive . . . Generally speaking, the living and work atmosphere inside penitentiaries is more pleasant, and less strained than previously—evidence of improved relations between staff and inmates. (*Our Story* at 153–56)

Unit management is the front line of CSC's model of correctional management. Correctional institutions, from the super-maximum-security Special Handling Unit to community-based correctional centres, are linked through a corporate hierarchy of regional and national headquarters. Canada is divided into five regional areas, and for each region there is a Regional Deputy Commissioner to whom the wardens of institutions within the region report; the Regional Deputy Commissioners in turn report to the Commissioner of Corrections, who heads operations at national headquarters. Within national headquarters there is a management team which includes the Senior Deputy Commissioner, a Deputy Commissioner for Women, and five other assistant commissioners responsible for different divisions (for example, correctional operations and programs, performance assurance, and corporate services).

There is a third part to the "reorganization and renewal" of the Correctional Service of Canada in the 1990s. As well as producing the Mission Document and introducing the unit management structure, the CSC also adopted as the basis for its correctional programming a cognitive model of correctional intervention:

Our overall strategy focuses on programs that not only change behaviour, but also ensure that beliefs and attitudes change so that the change is more durable. The strategy focuses on the personal development of offenders so that they may acquire the skills and abilities required for the pro-social adaptation necessary for successful reintegration as law-abiding citizens . . .

The cognitive model attempts to teach offenders how to think logically, objectively and rationally without over-generalizing or externalizing blame. It is based on methods of changing the way offenders think because their thinking patterns seem to be instrumental in propelling them towards involvement in criminal activities. The model, a fairly recent innovation in correctional treatment, is founded on a substantial body of research indicating that many offenders lack a number of cognitive skills essential for social adaptation. For example, many lack self-control, tending to be action-oriented, non-reflective and impulsive. They often seem unable to look at the world from another person's perspective. They act without adequately considering the consequences of their actions. They are lacking in inter-personal problem-solving, critical reasoning and planning skills. The end result is that offenders become caught in a cycle of thinking errors—the situation that programs based on the cognitive model attempt to change. (*Our Story* at 70)

Just as unit management provides the foundation for the way in which correctional staff are organized, correctional planning for prisoners is founded on the cognitive model of behavioural change. Every prisoner who receives a federal sentence goes through an assessment process. Over the course of several months, information about the prisoner is collected from various sources, including the court's reasons for sentence, police reports, and correctional files (in cases where the prisoner has previously been imprisoned or on probation). In addition, the prisoner is interviewed by a team of correctional staff, including case management officers (now institutional parole officers) and prison psychologists. The purpose of this intake assessment is to provide "a complete profile of the offender's criminal and social history, including offence cycles, treatment outcomes and victim impacts; a rating of the static factors related to criminal re-offending; a prioritised listing of dynamic factors relating to reducing the risk of re-offending; a sentence-wide Correctional Plan; and a security classification and initial placement recommendation" (*Offender Intake Assessment and Correctional Planning, Standard Operating Practices*—700-04 [Ottawa: Correctional Service of Canada, January 29, 2001] [hereafter referred to as the *Offender Intake Assessment* manual] at 2).

From the perspective of case management, the most important document prepared as a result of the intake assessment process is the Correctional Plan. As described by the Service,

The objectives of sentence planning are as follows:
- To employ the most effective intervention technique and supervision approach;
- To address dynamic factors that contributed to criminal behaviour;
- To ensure consistency and continuity in case management throughout an offender's sentence; and
- To establish a base line from which to measure progress. (*Offender Intake Assessment* manual at 25)

Earlier formulations of the correctional planning process focussed primarily on "criminogenic factors," but the current emphasis is upon "reintegration potential." Thus,

A Correctional Plan is designed to address the factors which have been identified as contributing to a safe and timely reintegration. These factors must be prioritized so that interventions can be logical, sequenced and effective and ensure that the offender's progress can be evaluated during the offender's sentence. (*Offender Intake Assessment* manual at 25)

The correctional plan typically will identify which of the "menu" of cognitive-based programs are necessary to address the prisoner's criminogenic needs, risk factors, and reintegration potential. (Articles on the cognitive model of correctional intervention and risk/needs assessment can be found in CSC's *Forum on Corrections Research*. The *Forum* is also posted in the "Research" area on CSC's Website online: <http://www.csc-scc.gc.ca>.)

It is apparent from even these brief extracts that correctional planning, as presently articulated by the Correctional Service of Canada, is conceived as a rational and logical system, based upon a scientific theory of needs analysis and risk assessment. This is situated within an integrated and interactive staff structure and is overarched by the vision of the Mission Document. Its core values commit the correctional establishment to respect the dignity of individuals, recognize that offenders have the potential to live as law-abiding individuals, acknowledge that human relationships are a cornerstone of the enterprise, and manage the correctional service with openness and integrity. From all of this, it would appear that the Canadian promise of a kinder, gentler, and more just society has indeed been achieved by the end of the twentieth century, and nowhere more so than inside its federal penitentiaries. Indeed, one would be hard-pressed to find another organization that has proclaimed its commitment to so many ideals and values. Certainly the law school in which I work makes no such commitment to my colleagues and me, our students, or the public.

In the chapters that follow, I will describe cases and events that measure the distance between the rhetoric and the reality, the ideology and the practice, the talk and the walk. The vital importance of stepping inside penitentiaries and proceeding beyond the framed copy of the Mission Statement, of probing deep into the daily operations of the practice of imprisonment and not just clicking through the pages of the *Offender Intake Assessment* manual, is well captured by David Garland:

> If we wish to understand the cultural messages conveyed by punishment we need to study not just the grandiloquent public statements which are occasionally made but also the pragmatic repetitive routines of daily practice, for these routines contain within them distinctive patterns of meaning and symbolic forms which are enacted and expressed every time a particular procedure is adopted, a technical language used, or a specific sanction imposed. Despite the attention given to policy documents, commission reports, and philosophical statements, it is the daily routine of sanctioning and institutional practice which does the most to create a particular framework of meaning (Foucault would say a "regime of truth") in the penal realm, and it is to these practical routines that we should look first of all to discover the values, meanings, and conceptions which are embodied and expressed in penality. (at 255)

Some critics of the modern practice of punishment suggest that official statements professing a new correctional ideology are nothing more than rhetoric and should be treated as such. Andrew Scull, with reference to community corrections, has written, "The ideological proclamations of the proponents of current reforms are about as reliable a guide to the antecedents, characteristics and significance of what is happening in the real world as the collected works of the Brothers Grimm" (Andrew Scull, "Community Corrections: Panacea, Progress or Pretence?" in R. Abel, ed., *The Politics of Informal Justice: Vol. 1. The American Experience* [New York: Academic Press, 1982] at 100).

Stanley Cohen is a little more charitable in his assessment, classifying the official rhetoric of "social-control talk" as "good stories":

> These "good stories" stand for or signify what the system likes to think it is doing, justify or rationalize what it has already done and indicate what it would like to be doing (if only given the chance and the resources). This talk also has other functions: to maintain and increase the self-confidence, worth and interests of those who work in the system, to protect them from criticism and to suggest that they are doing alright in a difficult world. These stories constitute sociological data as much as the motivational accounts of individuals . . .

This is the theoretical double-bind: to take these stories seriously (seldom are they based on total delusion, fantasy or fabrication), but also to explore their connections with the reality they are meant to signify. (at 157)

Cohen's last point—the need to explore the connection between the talk and the reality—has been acknowledged by some who work within the Correctional Service of Canada. Pierre Allard, then Director of Chaplaincy, in a section he authored for *Our Story*, offers these well-phrased words of advice in his endorsement of the Mission:

Having a Mission clearly spelled out has great and many advantages. It also has some dangers. For example, we have committed ourselves to *respect the dignity of individuals* . . . These are nice words but words are not enough. We need to internalize the attitudes that the words call forth. The challenge is to learn to create the quality relationships that are called for by our nice words . . . we need wisdom to work with offenders, to care for them as unique individuals. We must go beyond the nice words.

The second value enunciated in the Mission, that *the offender has the potential to live as a law-abiding citizen,* brings with it the dangers of the weight of evil and what evil will do to us. Being involved with prisoners is touching closely the greed, the jealousy, the hatred, the pride, the violence, and all the other ugly faces of evil. Michael Ignatieff, addressing correctional workers, said: "You people are the bureaucrats of good and evil. Even bureaucrats of good and evil burn out; they lose their way; they wonder what they are doing sometimes" . . . Unless we realize the weight of evil and what it does to us, we cannot be honest in saying that we believe that the offender can live as a law-abiding citizen. If we fall into the grips of evil, it is going to lead us to cynicism . . .

The danger of the fourth core value—*the sharing of ideas . . .*—is that, in corrections, a formula for cure without care is useless. As we discover better tools to unveil the darkness in people, we must, at the same time, make commitments to accompany them in these valleys of darkness. What would be the consequences if our tools get so sophisticated that we can, from a distance, tell offenders how ugly they are, what kind of scum they are but this is not accompanied by a similar commitment to help them deal with these dark sides of their lives? . . . As we share our tools, and our knowledge and our new understanding, it has to be not that we can talk better *about* prisoners but that we can talk better *with* them. It has to be not that we stand back and know how badly they are going to fall but that we learn to walk with them so they will not fall. (Pierre Allard, "Beyond the Words" in *Our Story* at 167–71)

These cautionary words sit uneasily with the risk-management language of modern corrections, yet they resonate with the tones of the early history of the penitentiary. That they have an unfamiliar ring in the ears of contemporary correctional administrators reflects an important aspect of modern corrections, which David Garland has identified:

> It is a characteristic of bureaucratic organizations that they operate in a passionless, routinized, matter of fact kind of way. No matter in what field of social life they operate, whether in health care or social work or punishment—bureaucracies strive to act *sine ira ac studio* (without anger or enthusiasm), performing their tasks with studied neutrality and objectivity. As Weber puts it, such organizations become deliberately "dehumanized" and, to the extent that they approach this ideal, they succeed "in eliminating from official business love, hatred and all . . . irrational and emotional elements." We can see this very clearly if we consider the way in which penal administrators regard the offenders with whom they have to deal . . . Instead of seeking to convey moral outrage, punitive passions, or vengeful settings, these agencies tend to neutralize the effect of the penal process, to do their job in a professional manner, leaving the tones of moral opprobrium to the court and to the public. (at 183–84)

Even if the everyday language of correctional planning, in contrast to the high-flying language of the Mission Document, no longer carries the traditional message of virtue and morality, that does not mean the everyday practices of the penitentiary regime convey no moral message or lessons. The significance of the latent pedagogy of institutional practice is well captured by Garland:

> Institutions do inevitably address a specific rhetoric to their inmate audiences, even if it is only the amoral and dehumanizing rhetoric of a regime which treats prisoners primarily as bodies to be counted and objects to be administered. For the daily practices of an institution, no matter how mundane, tend to take on a definite meaning for those who are subject to them. And whatever meanings the judge, or the public, or the penitentiary reformers meant to convey by sending offenders to prison, it is the day-to-day actualities of the internal regime which do most to fix the meaning of imprisonment for those

inside. If this regime is just, fairly administered, caring, and humane, it is possible that its recipients will learn some of the lessons of citizenship, though prison inmates usually form a formidably sceptical audience. However, if, as is more usual, the prison regime belies its good intentions, and in the name of administrative convenience allows a measure of injustice, or arbitrariness, or indifference, or brutality, then it is likely to inspire nothing but resentment and opposition from this particular audience. Any moral message which the authorities may wish to hold out will be spoiled by the signs of hypocrisy, by self-contradiction or simply by the extent to which inmates are already alienated from the legal system and all that it stands for. (at 261–62)

In the chapters that follow, the voices of Canadian prisoners, expressed in rather less measured prose than that of Professor Garland, will speak no less eloquently of the lessons of modern corrections as learned through its administrative practices.

## CHAPTER 3

# Corrections, the Courts, and the Constitution

The legal architecture of imprisonment has changed more over the last two hundred years than any other part of the carceral landscape. Penal philosophy has oscillated, and correctional models have changed their shape and language, but these variations pale in comparison to the recasting of the role of the law inside prison. In *Prisoners of Isolation,* I summarized how, in the nineteenth century, a prisoner sentenced to imprisonment by a court of law was regarded by the law as a person largely outside a framework of legal rights.

> At common law, the person convicted of felony and sentenced to imprisonment was regarded as being devoid of rights. A Virginia court declared just over a century ago that a prisoner "has, as a consequence of his crime, not only forfeited his liberty, but all his personal rights except those which the law in its humanity accords to him. He is for the time being the slave of the State" (*Ruffin* v. *Commonwealth,* 62 Va. 790 (1871)). This view flowed historically from the old English practices of outlawry and attaint, the consequences of which were that the convicted felon lost all civil and proprietary rights and was regarded in law as dead. The warden of Kingston Penitentiary was properly reflecting the traditional status of the felon when in 1867 he wrote, "So long as a convict is confined here I regard him as dead to all transactions of the outer world." (Jackson, *Prisoners of Isolation* at 82)

Although by the end of the nineteenth century the concept of "civil death" had largely disappeared, the legislative framework governing penitentiaries in Canada was concerned mainly with assigning responsibilities for the management of institutions. Within this framework, the distribution of prisoners' entitlements was as austere as the regime under which prisoners served their sentences. Thus, the *Penitentiary Act* of 1886 stated,

> 51 The following general rules shall be observed in the treatment of convicts in a penitentiary:
>
> (a) every convict shall, during the term of his confinement, be clothed, at the expense of the penitentiary, in suitable prison garments;
>
> (b) he shall be fed on a sufficient quantity of wholesome food;
>
> (c) he shall be provided with a bed and pillow and sufficient covering, varied according to the season; and
>
> (d) he shall, except in case of sickness, be kept in a cell by himself at night, and during the day when not employed.
>
> (*Penitentiary Act*, R.S.C. 1886, c. 182)

The contours of the legislative landscape of imprisonment, dominated by the *Penitentiary Act*, remained relatively unchanged throughout the twentieth century, until the enactment of the *Corrections and Conditional Release Act* in 1992. In the most critical areas affecting the lives of prisoners, the *Penitentiary Act* in its various amended forms said very little about the legal regime, delegating to the Governor-in-Council (in practical terms, the Cabinet) the power to make regulations. Thus it was left to the regulations to set out what constituted a disciplinary offence and to establish the criteria under which a prisoner could be placed in segregation. But under the pre-1992 legal regime, even the combination of provisions in the *Penitentiary Act* and the *Penitentiary Service Regulations* represented only a small part of the labyrinth of rules governing the lives of prisoners. Under these *Regulations*, the Commissioner of Penitentiaries was delegated the authority to issue directives "for the organization, training, discipline, efficiency, administration and good government of the service and for the custody, treatment, training, employment and discipline of inmates and the good government of penitentiaries" (*Penitentiary Service Regulations*, S.O.R./62-90, s. 29.3). Prior to 1992, it was within the multivolumed binders of Commissioner's Directives that the official rules of prison justice were fleshed out. In a way symbolic of the extent to which prisoners remained outside the protective umbrella of the law, Canadian courts ruled that the Commissioner's Directives did not have the force of law, in contrast to the provisions of the *Penitentiary Act* and the *Penitentiary Service Regulations*. Therefore, there was no legal duty owed by a staff member of the Penitentiary Service to a prisoner to adhere to the directives

(*R.* v. *Institutional Head of Beaver Creek Correctional Camp ex parte McCaud* (1969), 2 D.L.R. (3d) 545; *Martineau* v. *Matsqui Institution Inmate Disciplinary Board,* [1978] 1 S.C.R. 118). But, as if to drive home the asymmetrical relationship between the keeper and the kept, the *Penitentiary Service Regulations* made it a disciplinary offence for a prisoner to contravene a directive (s. 2.29(n)).

## Beyond the Ken of the Courts

The statutory framework in which responsibility for the conditions of confinement and the treatment of prisoners was broadly delegated to penitentiary officials was buttressed by the reluctance of the courts in Canada (as in the United States and England) to review the decisions of prison officials in response to challenges by prisoners to inhumane conditions or unfair treatment. The court's role was to enforce legal rights; since prisoners were seen as persons without rights, their complaints were necessarily beyond the ken of the courts. This rationale for what has been called the "hands-off" doctrine was later supplemented by an additional argument, that "judicial review of such administrative decisions [would] subvert the authority of prison officials, the discipline of prisoners, and the efforts of prison administrators to accomplish the objectives of the system which is entrusted to their care and management" (Note, "Beyond the Ken of the Courts: A Critique of Judicial Refusal to Review the Complaints of Convicts" [1963] 72 *Yale Law Journal* 506 at 509).

The persistence of the hands-off doctrine in the United States has been described in this way by John Dilulio:

> As late as 1970, judges played a negligible role in the administration of prisons. For most of the previous two centuries, prisoners were "slaves of the state." A prisoner was beaten for minor rule infractions, worked mercilessly, starved, forced to live in filth, and made to suffer cruelties and hardships. Little or no help could be expected from the bench. Wardens were the sovereigns of the cell blocks, free to do pretty much as they wished with the incarcerated citizens in their charge. For prisoners, the Constitution was a locked door, and the protections of the Bill of Rights were hidden from sight. (John J. Dilulio, Jr., "Introduction: Enhancing Judicial Capacity," in John J. Dilulio, Jr., ed., *Courts, Corrections, and the Constitution: The Impact of Judicial Intervention on Prisons and Jails* [New York: Oxford University Press, 1990] at 3)

In *Prisoners of Isolation,* I suggested that the effect of this hands-off approach was "to immunize the prison from public scrutiny through the judicial process and to place prison officials in a position of virtual invulnerability and absolute power over the persons committed to their institutions" (at 82). It is a telling commentary on the state of prisoners' rights in Canada that in my first study on prison discipline, conducted in 1972 at Matsqui Institution, I could cite only a single case in which a Canadian court had ruled that prison disciplinary proceedings, under certain restrictive conditions, could be subject to judicial review.

By the early 1970s, the insulation of prison justice from public and legal scrutiny was increasingly showing serious fault lines. These lines made their appearance in a series of escalating episodes of individual and collective violence, the product of both deteriorating prison conditions and a rising expectation by prisoners, as human rights became increasingly important outside the prison, that they could no longer be treated as persons without rights. In 1971, Kingston Penitentiary experienced one of the bloodiest riots in its history. Five staff were taken hostage, and a small group of prisoners, mostly sex offenders, were placed in a circle in the prison dome and brutally tortured; two of the prisoners died, and part of the institution was destroyed. Mr. Justice Swackhamer, in his anatomy of the riot, identified the absence of meaningful rehabilitation, the lack of any effective prisoner grievance system, and the entrenched hostility between staff and prisoners. The depth of that hostility was reflected in the aftermath of the Kingston Riot. Because of the extent of the destruction at Kingston, the newly constructed Millhaven Institution opened prematurely in May 1971, and over four days (instead of the planned six months) a large number of prisoners were transferred to Millhaven. The reception they received there was equally unplanned. As described by Mr. Justice Swackhamer:

> We find that on [Wednesday] 10 to 12 custodial officers had been stationed in the southerly portion of P corridor, each armed with a riot stick . . . The officers positioned in P corridor were directed to stand some five feet east of the westerly corridor wall and approximately eight feet apart. We can only conclude that the objective and the result of such positioning of staff was to ensure that no inmate could pass through the corridor out of range of a riot stick. We find that on Wednesday, when the inmates left the buses and proceeded down P corridor, either singly or in pairs, substantial numbers of them were assaulted by officers standing either on the platform or in the corridor. In short, we find the inmates in the course of admission to the penitentiary were in this way required to run "the gauntlet." (*Report of the Commission of Inquiry into Certain Disturbances at Kingston Penitentiary during April 1971* [Ottawa: Information Canada, 1973] [Chairman: J. W. Swackhamer] at 34)

With such an induction ceremony, it was hardly surprising that Millhaven Institution, then the newest jewel in the correctional crown, went on to experience nineteen major incidents over the next six years.

Millhaven was not the only Canadian penitentiary to feel the volatile mix of deteriorating prison conditions and rising prisoner expectations. In the fall of 1976, the British Columbia Penitentiary experienced the most destructive riot in its hundred-year history. When the smoke cleared, damage of over $1.6 million had been sustained; a whole cell block had been destroyed, with the interior walls dividing the cells completely smashed. In the course of the riot, nine prisoners seized two staff hostages in the penitentiary kitchen. The B.C. Penitentiary riot came just nine months after another major incident in which three prisoners had seized sixteen hostages, both correctional officers and classification staff, and held them for three days. The hostage-taking ended when a tactical squad burst into the room in which the hostages were confined and opened fire, killing one of the hostages and severely injuring one of the prisoners.

As the main dome of the B.C. Penitentiary was being destroyed, another major disturbance broke out three thousand miles away, at Laval Institution in Quebec; a week later Millhaven erupted again. This unprecedented trilogy of riots resulted in the appointment of a House of Commons subcommittee to undertake a major inquiry. The subcommittee's report provided a dramatic account of the crisis that engulfed the Canadian penitentiary system in the mid-1970s.

> Seven years of comparative peace in the Canadian penitentiary system ended in 1970 with a series of upheavals (riots, strikes, murders and hostage-takings) that grew in numbers and size with each passing year. By 1976 the prison explosions were almost constant; hardly a week passed without another violent incident. The majority were in Canada's maximum security institutions. In the 42 years between 1932 and 1974, there was a total of 65 major incidents in federal penitentiaries. Yet in two years—1975 and 1976—there was a total of 69 major incidents, including 35 hostage-takings involving 92 victims, one of whom (a prison officer) was killed. (House of Commons Sub-Committee on the Penitentiary System in Canada, *Report to Parliament* [Ottawa: Minister of Supply and Services, 1977] [Chairman: Mark MacGuigan] at 5)

In page after page of the report, parliamentarians catalogued the continuing failure of the prison system to either reform prisoners or protect society. The Sub-Committee stated that it "saw and heard in both open and closed sessions in Millhaven, the Correctional Development Centre, Laval and British Columbia Penitentiary, the truth of the concept that 'prisons are the living graves of crime'" (at 10). For the purposes of this book, the most important chapter of the report is the one entitled "Justice within the Walls." In its very first paragraph, the Sub-Committee pronounced judgement on the state of prison justice.

There is a great deal of irony in the fact that imprisonment—the ultimate product of our system of criminal justice—itself epitomizes injustice. We have in mind the general absence within penitentiaries of a system of justice that protects the victim as well as punishes the transgressor; a system of justice that provides a rational basis for order in a community—including a prison community—according to decent standards and rules known in advance; a system of justice that is manifested by fair and impartial procedures that are strictly observed; a system of justice that proceeds from rules that cannot be avoided at will; a system of justice to which all are subject without fear or favour. In other words, we mean justice according to Canadian law. In penitentiaries, some of these constituents of justice simply do not exist. Others are only a matter of degree—a situation which is hardly consistent with any understandable or coherent concept of justice. (at 85)

To redress this situation, the Sub-Committee advocated that two principles be accepted. The first was that the Rule of Law must prevail inside Canadian penitentiaries.

The Rule of Law establishes rights and interests under law and protects them against the illicit or illegal use of any power, private or official, by providing recourse to the courts through the legal process. The administrative process, however, may or may not protect these things, or may itself interfere with them, depending on the discretion of those who are given statutory administrative powers. In penitentiaries, almost all elements of the life and experience of inmates are governed by administrative authority rather than law. We have concluded that such a situation is neither necessary for, nor has it resulted in, the protection of society through sound correctional practice. It is essential that the Rule of Law prevail in Canadian penitentiaries. (at 86)

The second principle was that

Justice for inmates is a personal right and also an essential condition of their socialization and personal reformation. It implies both respect for the person and property of others and fairness in treatment. The arbitrariness traditionally associated with prison life must be replaced by clear rules, fair disciplinary procedures and the providing of reasons for all decisions affecting inmates. (at 87)

In a perceptive analysis, the Sub-Committee reflected on the relationship between the judicial "hands-off" doctrine and the lawlessness of prison life.

> The gross irregularities, lack of standards and other arbitrariness that exists in our penitentiaries, by their very quantity, make, and always have made, the possibility of judicial intervention into prison matters a rather impracticable, time-consuming and dismaying prospect, as the judges themselves have pointed out. To open the courts to redress of these conditions would invite inmates to continue to increase the levels of their confrontation with prison staff and management, using the courts for purposes that, just like the present running battle between the opposing sides, are largely unassociated with any genuine interest in improving the operation of the system. By the same argument, however, the present judicial policy invites the perpetuation by the authorities of a system that is so far removed from normal standards of justice that it remains safely within the class of matters in which the imposition of judicial or quasi-judicial procedures would clearly be, in most instances, inconceivable. Further, this would ensure that the sheer immensity of the task of straightening it out is enough to discourage even the most committed members of the judiciary. The worse things are in the penitentiary system, therefore, the more self-evident it is to the courts that Parliament could not possibly have intended for them to intervene. *Injustice, as well as virtue, can be its own reward.* (at 86, emphasis added)

To bring the Rule of Law into prisons, the Sub-Committee made a series of recommendations: that the Commissioner's Directives be consolidated into a consistent code of regulations having the force of law for both prisoners and staff; that independent chairpersons be appointed in all institutions to preside over disciplinary hearings; and that an inmate grievance procedure be established in which prisoners had a substantial role. With these legislative and administrative reforms in place, the Sub-Committee envisaged a vital but focussed role for the courts.

> It should then lie with the courts to ensure that those individuals and agencies involved in the management and administration of the revised system adhere to general standards of natural justice and due process of law as they substantially exist elsewhere in the criminal justice system . . .
>
> We suggest that it would be both reasonable and appropriate to proceed in such a way as to allow a much greater scope for judicial

control over official activity and the conditions of correction in a reformed penitentiary system than is now feasible. Assuming that the system is definitive in its commitment, clear in its intentions, and effective in its prescription, then the nature of the task remaining to be done by the courts in ensuring that the Rule of Law prevails within penitentiaries should not be disproportionate to what they do outside prison walls on an on-going basis. Abuse of power and denial of justice are always possible under any system, no matter how well conceived or organized it may be. These things are felt no less keenly in prisons than elsewhere, and their consequences in a penitentiary setting are often far more severe. (at 87)

## The Duty to Act Fairly

At the time the House of Commons Sub-Committee's report was published, Canadian prisoners who sought redress in the courts faced a Catch-22. The only decisions subject to judicial review under prevailing principles of administrative law were those the courts classified as "judicial" or "quasi-judicial," as opposed to "administrative." Broadly speaking, the decisions of bodies given the authority to administer institutions or agencies, with a broad discretion as to how the statutory mandate should be exercised, were classified as administrative. Decisions affecting privileges or interests, as opposed to rights, were also classified as administrative and not subject to judicial review. Within this scheme of classification, with very limited exceptions, decisions made by correctional officials were deemed administrative and non-reviewable.

Any expectation that the creation in 1970 of the new Federal Court would open a wider window of redress for prisoners in federal penitentiaries was confounded. Jurisdictional interpretation of the provisions of the 1970 *Federal Court Act* (R.S.C. 1970, c. 10 (2d Supp.)) charted new depths of obscurantism, even for a profession used to such excesses. (For a review of the tortured jurisprudence of this era, see Jackson, *Prisoners of Isolation* at 125–33, and David P. Cole and Allan Manson, *Release from Imprisonment: The Law of Sentencing, Parole and Judicial Review* [Toronto: Carswell, 1990] at 46ff.).

It was not until 1979 that a historic breakthrough in expanding the scope of judicial review for prisoners came to pass. That year, the Supreme Court of Canada, in *Martineau* v. *Matsqui Institution Inmate Disciplinary Board*, provided relief from the conceptual impasse created by the dichotomy between "judicial" and "administrative" and the interpretative confusion surrounding the *Federal Court Act*. The *Martineau* case was first before the courts in 1975, following the conviction of Mr. Martineau and Mr. Butters, both prisoners at Matsqui Institution, of two disciplinary offences for which they were sentenced to fifteen days in solitary confinement. The prisoners' case was based upon alleged violations of the requirements of the Commissioner's Directive dealing with disciplinary hearings. It was a measure of the jurisdictional confusion surrounding the *Federal Court Act* that the prisoners' lawyer, John Conroy, in the first of his many legal forays on behalf of prisoners, filed proceedings challenging the convictions under both section 28 and section 18 of the *Act*. The section 28 application before the Federal Court of Appeal was denied, and this denial was affirmed by the Supreme Court of Canada in a 5:4 decision. The decision was a narrow, technical one based upon the wording of section 28. It involved a finding that, because the Commissioner's Directives did not have the force of law, a prison disciplinary board's decision was not "required by law to be made on a judicial or quasi-judicial basis" (*Martineau* v. *Matsqui Institution Inmate Disciplinary Board*, [1978] I S.C.R. 118).

While successful in his application before the Federal Court Trial Division under section 18 of the *Federal Court Act*, Mr. Martineau was again stymied by the Federal Court of Appeal, which ruled that a section 18 remedy was no more available than the section 28 one, in the case of a decision not required to be made on a judicial or quasi-judicial basis. In an appendix to the court's judgement, Chief Justice Jackett, while acknowledging that correctional officials should act on a fair and just basis, stated that any remedy for their failure to do so lay not with the judiciary but in the political arena. As I observed in *Prisoners of Isolation*, for federal prisoners, who at the time of the decision did not have the right to vote in federal elections, Chief Justice Jackett's decision "appeared as a mockery of their asserted legal rights" (at 130).

When the *Martineau* case returned to the Supreme Court of Canada for the second time, the jurisprudential ground proved more fertile. In 1979, in a decision involving the dismissal of a probationary police officer (*Nicholson and Haldimand* v. *Norfolk Regional Board of Police Commissioners*, [1979] I S.C.R. 311), the Supreme Court had held that judicial review through *certiorari* was not limited to decisions classified as judicial or quasi-judicial. The court ruled that there was a general administrative law duty to act fairly, and that police disciplinary decisions were subject to that duty and therefore subject to the superintendency of the courts to ensure compliance with it. In its ruling in the second *Martineau* case, the Supreme Court applied these principles to prison disciplinary decisions. After tracing the development of a parallel line of jurisprudence in the English courts, in which a general duty of fairness had been acknowledged, Mr. Justice Dickson rendered this critique of the legalistic doctrine in which only decisions affecting "rights" could trigger judicial review:

> There has been an unfortunate tendency to treat "rights" in the narrow sense of rights to which correlative legal duties are attached. In this sense, "rights" are frequently contrasted with "privileges," in a mistaken belief that only the former can ground judicial review of

decision-makers' actions . . . When concerned with individual cases and aggrieved persons, there is a tendency to forget that one is dealing with public law remedies which, when granted by the courts, not only set aright individual injustice but also ensure the public bodies exercising powers affecting citizens heed the jurisdiction granted them. *Certiorari* stems from the assumption by the courts of supervisory powers over certain tribunals in order to ensure the proper functioning of the machinery of government. To give a narrow or technical interpretation to "rights" in an individual sense is to misconceive the broader purpose of judicial review of administrative action. (*Martineau* v. *Matsqui Institution Inmate Disciplinary Board,* [1980] 1 S.C.R. 602 [hereafter referred to as *Martineau (No. 2)*])

In the particular context of prison disciplinary decisions, Mr. Justice Dickson unequivocally laid the groundwork for the modern theory and practice of judicial review of correctional decisions.

In the case at bar, the Disciplinary Board was not under either an express or implied duty to follow a judicial type of procedure, but the Board was obliged to find the facts affecting the subject and exercise a form of discretion in pronouncing judgement and penalty. Moreover, the Board's decision had the effect of depriving an individual of his liberty by committing him to a "prison within a prison." In these circumstances, elementary justice requires some procedural protection. *The Rule of Law must run within penitentiary walls.*

In my opinion, *certiorari* avails us a remedy wherever a public body has power to decide any matter affecting the rights, interest, property, privileges or liberties of any person. (*Martineau (No. 2)*, at 622)

The judgement of Mr. Justice Pigeon, while affirming a disciplinary board's duty to act fairly, amenable to review by the Federal Court, emphasized that such judicial review should be exercised with regard to "the requirements of prison discipline." He added the caveat that "it is specially important that the remedy be granted only in cases of serious injustice and the proper care be taken to prevent such proceedings from being used to delay deserved punishment so long that it is made ineffective, if not altogether avoided" (*Martineau (No. 2)*, at 636–37). Mr. Justice Dickson also emphasized that "interference would not be justified in the case of trivial or merely technical incidents. The question is not whether there has been a breach of the prison rules, but whether there has been a breach of the duty to act fairly in all the circumstances" (*Martineau (No. 2)*, at 630).

As to what exactly fairness requires in the prison context, Mr. Justice Dickson described the concept of fairness as a flexible one, fully capable of responding to the spectrum of administrative decisions which ranged from those of a policy-oriented nature to those approaching a judicial function. In the case of a decision approaching the latter end of the spectrum, "substantial procedural safeguards" may be required.

In the wake of *Martineau (No. 2)*, David Cole and Allan Manson, both legal pioneers in the era of prisoners' rights, have offered this definition of the requirements of fairness:

> At a minimum, the duty to act fairly means an obligation to provide notice of allegations and an opportunity to respond . . . Notice of allegations must be sufficiently clear and precise to enable the prisoner to know the case he has to meet . . . One can conceive of a variety of techniques by which an opportunity to respond can be provided. The least sophisticated may involve a response in writing or an oral response to an official who reports to the decision-maker. No matter how skeletal, the essential question will always be, in light of the circumstances, whether the prisoner has had an adequate opportunity to respond. As one progresses along the spectrum, some processes will require hearings perhaps even approximating the procedural trappings usually associated with the judicial model. (at 61)

The judgement of the Supreme Court in *Martineau (No. 2)* marks the beginning of a coherent and principled body of correctional law in Canada. Cole and Manson have described the significance of the case:

> *Martineau (No. 2)* opened the modern era of prison law in Canada and exposed internal parole and prison processes to judicial scrutiny. As a result, some procedures have been found wanting and decision-makers have been compelled to revise their processes to conform with the notion of fairness. But the impact of *Martineau (No. 2)* transcends questions of procedure. The opportunity for judicial scrutiny now compels judges to begin to examine the dynamics of internal decision-making with due regard to the competing tensions of liberty, self-interest and administrative exigency . . . A related product of expanded judicial review flows from the ability to challenge decisions on non-procedural grounds. For example, an application raising excess of jurisdiction as the ground for review requires the court to consider the appropriate scope of decision-making, including questions of acceptable criteria and extraneous considerations. Thus, the new era of judicial scrutiny represents not only the development of fair procedures but has also enhanced the evolution of substantive prison and parole law. (at 63–64)

Subsequent decisions of the Supreme Court of Canada contributed to that evolution. A year after *Martineau (No. 2)*, the Supreme Court took a significant step in the *Solosky* case, by expressly endorsing the proposition that "a person confined to prison retains all of his civil rights, other than those expressly or impliedly taken away from him by law" (*Solosky* v. *The Queen,* [1980] 1 S.C.R. 821 at 823). In the same case, the court stated that the courts had a balancing role to play in ensuring that any interference with the rights of prisoners by institutional authorities is for a valid correctional goal; it must also be the least restrictive means available and no greater than is essential to the maintenance of security and the rehabilitation of the prisoner.

The Supreme Court of Canada laid another important milestone in correctional law in a trilogy of cases decided in 1985. In *Cardinal and Oswald, Miller,* and *Morin,* which involved challenges by prisoners to their confinement in administrative segregation and their transfer to the Special Handling Units, the highest level of security in the federal penitentiary system, the court ruled that prisoners have a right not to be deprived, unlawfully or unfairly, of the relative or "residual" liberty they retain as members of the general prison population; and that any significant deprivation of that liberty—such as being placed in administrative segregation or a Special Handling Unit—could be challenged through *habeas corpus.* Mr. Justice LeDain, mirroring the caution first expressed in *Martineau (No. 2)*, observed that *habeas corpus* should not be invoked to question "all conditions of confinement," but does lie in respect of any "distinct form of confinement or detention in which the actual physical constraint or deprivation of liberty . . . is more restrictive or severe than the normal one in an institution," something different from simply the loss of privileges (*Morin* v. *National Special Handling Unit Review Committee,* [1985] 2 S.C.R. 662 at 641. See also *Cardinal and Oswald* v. *Director of Kent Institution,* [1985] 2 S.C.R. 643 and *R.* v. *Miller,* [1985] 2 S.C.R. 613). In subsequent cases, the courts have held that *habeas corpus* is available to review not only placement in segregation or transfer to a Special Handling Unit, but any involuntary transfer to higher security where the regime of confinement is significantly more onerous and restrictive of liberty.

## The *Charter of Rights and Freedoms*

The recognition of a common-law duty of fairness represents the first flag in the expanded role of the judiciary "in mapping the contours of powers, rights and privileges which characterize imprisonment in Canada" (Cole and Manson, at 40). The second flag was the enactment in 1982 of the *Canadian Charter of Rights and Freedoms* (Part I of the *Constitution Act, 1982,* being Schedule B to the *Canada Act 1982* (U.K.), 1982, c. 11). By constitutionally entrenching human and democratic rights and freedoms, the *Charter* has accelerated both the number and the nature of challenges by prisoners to the process and conditions of their confinement. That the *Charter* would become a lightning rod for prisoners and prisoners' rights lawyers is hardly surprising, given that it was conceived as a Canadian response to international human rights standards. As stated in a passage from a judgement by Chief Justice Dickson:

> Since the close of the Second World War, the protection of the fundamental rights and freedoms of groups and individuals has become a matter of international concern. A body of treaties (or conventions) and customary norms now constitutes an international law of human rights under which the nations of the world have undertaken to adhere to the standards and principles necessary for ensuring freedom, dignity and social justice for their citizens. The *Charter* conforms to the spirit of this contemporary international human rights movement, and it incorporates many of the policies and prescriptions of the various international documents pertaining to human rights. The various sources of international human rights law—declarations, covenants, conventions, judicial and quasi-judicial decisions of international tribunals, customary norms—must, in my opinion, be relevant and persuasive sources for interpretation of the *Charter's* provisions. (Reference *Re Public Service Employee Relations Act (Alberta)*, [1987] 1 S.C.R. 313 at 348)

While the analogy of the *Charter* as a lightning rod—sitting atop the edifice of Canadian law as a constitutional protector of human rights—is an evocative one, the body of jurisprudence which has emerged from Canadian courts since 1982 presents a much less dramatic picture of the recognition of human rights for prisoners. In what Mary Campbell has described as "the golden age of the revolution in Canadian prisoners' rights," the courts have clearly affirmed that prisoners do not by virtue of their imprisonment lose the guarantee of basic human rights, including freedom of conscience and religion, and freedom of expression, nor does their imprisonment remove their protection from unreasonable search and seizure and cruel and unusual punishment treatment (Mary E. Campbell, "Revolution and Counter-Revolution in Canadian Prisoners' Rights" [1996] 2 *Canadian Criminal Law Review* 285).

However, the prospect of a golden age has been somewhat dulled by several factors. First, the courts have held in some cases that the nature of the interest protected by a specific *Charter* right or freedom is, in the case of prisoners, attenuated. For example, in response to challenges to routine searches for contraband and weapons, and to random urinalysis for detecting drug use, the courts have ruled that the expectation of privacy, which underlies the protection of section 8 of the *Charter* against unreasonable search and seizure, has a much lower threshold in prison than in the outside community (*Weatherall* v. *Canada (Attorney*

*General)*, [1993] 2 s.c.r. 872; *Fieldhouse v. Canada* (1995), 40 c.r. (4th) 263 (b.c.c.a.)). The second limitation on the human rights of prisoners has been derived from the provisions of section 1 of the *Charter* itself. This states:

> The *Canadian Charter of Rights and Freedoms* guarantees the rights and freedoms set out in it subject only to such reasonable limits prescribed by law as can be demonstrably justified in a free and democratic society.

The Supreme Court of Canada, beginning with its decision in *R. v. Oakes*, [1986] 50 s.c.r. (3d) 1, has established a critical line of inquiry for the state to justify, as a reasonable limit, an intrusion into fundamental rights and freedoms. For a law to be deemed a reasonable law, it must serve the interests of societal concerns which are "pressing and substantial" and "of sufficient importance to warrant overriding a constitutionally protected right or freedom" (*Oakes*, at 30). Furthermore, the means chosen for achieving the objective must meet a proportionality test which has three components: the means must be "rationally connected to the objective"; the means should impair the right or freedom in question "as little as possible"; and the effect of the impairment of the right or freedom must be proportionate to the objective (*Oakes*, at 30–31). Unfortunately, some judges have found this critical pathway easily navigated when it comes to circumscribing the rights of prisoners.

Of all the sections of the *Charter*, it is section 7, which guarantees that the right to "life, liberty and security of the person" cannot be denied "except in accordance with the principles of fundamental justice," that has been most frequently the subject of prisoner litigation. In their application of section 7, the courts, paralleling the jurisprudence on the scope of *habeas corpus*, have recognized that the concept of liberty is not an all-or-nothing proposition. A prisoner, despite the loss of the most important form of liberty—that of moving in society as a free person—still retains a spectrum of liberty interests within the context of institutional life. Decisions affecting discipline, segregation, and transfer may affect these residual liberty interests and must therefore be made in accordance with "fundamental principles of justice." As with the concept of fairness, the content of these principles depends upon the extent to which the liberty interest is impaired, and therefore the degree of procedural protection must be commensurate and proportionate to that impairment.

While there is a close correspondence in the jurisprudence between the common-law concept of "fairness" and the *Charter's* "principles of fundamental justice," the constitutional nature of the section 7 guarantee has had a significant impact on enhancing the rights of prisoners to procedural protections. This enhancing effect is best illustrated by the decision of the Federal Court of Appeal in *Howard.* The issue in that case was whether a prisoner was entitled to be represented by counsel at a disciplinary hearing. Under the pre-*Charter* jurisprudence on the duty to act fairly, the courts had held that the chairperson at a disciplinary hearing had a discretion to permit representation by counsel where it was necessary to ensure a fair hearing. The Federal Court of Appeal in *Howard* held that where a prisoner's liberty interest was at stake (and depending on the particular circumstances of the case), section 7 gave rise to a right to be represented by counsel. Mr. Justice MacGuigan in his judgement commented on the new perspective the *Charter* had introduced in the context of prisoners' rights and suggested that "the right-enhancing effect of the *Charter* thus greatly increases the ambit of protection afforded" (*Howard* v. *Presiding Officer of the Inmate Disciplinary Court of Stony Mountain Institution,* [1984] 2 F.C. 642 at 688).

Prior to his appointment to the Federal Court, Mr. Justice MacGuigan had, as a Member of Parliament, chaired the House of Commons Sub-Committee on the Penitentiary System in Canada. His judgement in *Howard* also addressed the nature of the judicial inquiry in determining what fundamental justice required in the context of penitentiaries.

> What both the Canadian and the American cases indicate is that there are degrees of liberty, all protected in some way by a rule of due process of natural justice or fundamental justice, but not in the same ways. What there must always be is an opportunity to state a case which is adequate for fundamental justice in the circumstances. In other words, there is a sliding standard of adequacy which can be defined only in reference to the particular degree of liberty at stake and the particular procedural safeguard in question. The resolution may involve the balancing of competing interests. Here, the penitentiary setting is of capital importance in sorting out the interests in competition.
>
> In such an atmosphere of discord and hatred, minor spats can set off major conflagrations of the most incendiary sort. Order is both more necessary and more fragile than in even military and police contexts, and its restoration when disturbed, becomes a matter of frightening immediacy. It would be an ill-informed court that was not aware of the necessity for immediate response by prison authorities to breaches of prison order and it would be a rash one that would deny them the means to react effectively. But not every feature of present disciplinary practice is objectively necessary for immediate disciplinary purposes. The mere convenience of the authorities will serve as no justification; as Lord Atkin put it in *General Medical Consulate Council* v. *Spackman,* "Convenience and

justice are often not on speaking terms . . ." All that is not immediately necessary must certainly yield to the fullest exigencies of liberty.
(*Howard,* at 681–82)

## The Correctional Law Review and the CCRA

Although it is not commonly recognized, the principal benefit flowing from a
constitutionally entrenched *Charter of Rights and Freedoms* is not to be found in
the litigation it spawns, but rather in the climate and culture of respect it creates
amongst both governments and citizens for fundamental human rights and freedoms. It would be wrong, therefore, to register a judgement about the *Charter*'s
impact based simply on the volume of prisoner litigation or a checklist of issues
won and lost in the ongoing struggle between the keeper and the kept. This
point should be held in mind, because the post-*Charter* era has not been punctuated by landmark victories for prisoners' rights; indeed, some of the major
advances—for example, the expansion of *habeas corpus* in the *Miller, Cardinal
and Oswald,* and *Morin* trilogy—were made with reference to the common law
and not the *Charter*.

In assessing the developments in correctional law since 1982, a strong case can
be made that the most significant impact of the *Charter* has been in the development of new correctional legislation, culminating in the *Corrections and Conditional Release Act* in 1992. The genesis of this legislation was the Federal
Department of Justice's publication in 1982 of *The Criminal Law in Canadian
Society* (Ottawa: Government of Canada, 1982), which set out a comprehensive
vision of the federal government's policy on the purpose and principles of criminal and correctional law. Along with the publication, the Department of Justice
launched the Criminal Law Review, which included as a component the
Correctional Law Review (CLR) conducted by the Ministry of the Solicitor
General. Over the course of several years, the CLR published a series of working
papers which were widely circulated and the subject of public consultation. In its
working papers, the CLR specifically addressed the need for new correctional legislation that would incorporate the values of the *Charter* and work out the appropriate balance between correctional authority and prisoners' rights as mandated
by the *Charter*. In its fifth working paper, appropriately entitled "Correctional
Authority and Inmate Rights," the Working Group of the CLR explained the
rationale for a new legislative framework.

> The second Working Paper entitled "A Framework for the Correc-
> tional Law Review," examined, among other questions, whether
> inmate rights, although protected through the Constitution and
> common law, should nonetheless be further specified in statute or

regulation . . . There are a number of reasons why matters governing inmate rights should now be placed in law.

One is that legislated provisions are particularly important where the *Charter* is concerned. Because the *Charter* is drafted in general, abstract terms, legislative provisions play a crucial role in articulating and clarifying *Charter* rights and any restrictions on them that are necessary in the corrections context . . . In addition, development of legislative provisions at this time appears vastly preferable to a future of incremental and potentially inconsistent change forced upon the correctional system by the courts. Although judicial intervention plays an important role in providing outside inspection and scrutiny, the courts should be relied on as a last resort, rather than a first measure. In short, there is a need for legislative provisions to be developed in a way which does justice to all participants, in an effort to improve their collective enterprise. Litigation, in contrast, results in a win or loss for one side or the other, and often results in maximizing polarity.

In considering long term solutions, the need for resort to the courts should be avoided by developing legislative rules that recognize yet structure discretion consistent with principles that are understandable to inmates, prison staff and administrators, and the public. Legislative rules that are based on clearly stated principles and objectives would structure discretion to allow for the necessary degree of flexibility while ensuring the greatest possible degree of accountability. Development of legislative provisions to govern inmate rights and staff powers, with input from all those affected by the correction system, is necessary to strike the appropriate balance. In addition, legislative rules which reflect the interests of staff, offenders and the public are critical if they are to be fair and voluntarily complied with. (Correctional Law Review, Working Group, "Correctional Authority and Inmate Rights" [Working Paper No. 5] [Ottawa: Solicitor General, Canada, 1987] [hereafter referred to as CLR Working Paper No. 5] at 2–4)

The working papers of the CLR were designed to provide a comprehensive, coherent, and principled legislative framework which would embody the modern philosophy of corrections and incorporate the rights and guarantees of the *Charter*. Early in its work, the CLR identified the importance of articulating in new legislation a statement of both the purpose and the principles of corrections. The absence of any such statement in either the *Penitentiary Act* or correctional practice had been identified by the 1977 report of the House of

Commons Sub-Committee on the Penitentiary System in Canada as a corrosive flaw. The statement of purpose and guiding principles articulated by the CLR were intended to emphasize the multifaceted nature of corrections in modern society, particularly the need to balance the criminal justice goals of justice and security. The CLR explained the conceptual and practical links between its principles and statement of purpose in the following way:

> Of major significance to rights of inmates is the first principle of our correctional philosophy which states that inmates retain all the rights of a member of society, except for those that are necessarily removed or restricted by the fact of incarceration. This principle recognizes that offenders are sent to prison *as* punishment, not *for* punishment, and therefore, while in prison, retain the rights of an ordinary citizen, subject only to necessary limitations or restrictions . . . In effect, the "retained rights" principle means that it is not giving rights to inmates which requires justification, but rather, it is *restricting* them which does. Undoubtedly, some individual rights of inmates, such as liberty, must be limited by the nature of incarceration, in the same way that the rights of non-inmates in open society must be limited in certain situations. The important point, however, is that it is limitations on inmate rights which must be justified, and that the only justifiable limitations are those that are necessary to achieve a legitimate correctional goal, and that are the least restrictive possible.
>
> There are also very significant policy reasons, flowing from our statement of purpose, for recognizing and protecting the rights of inmates. As practically all inmates eventually get out of prison, society's long term interests are best protected if the correctional system influences them to begin or resume law abiding lives. According rights and responsibilities to inmates supports and furthers this goal. On the other hand, lack of respect for individual rights in the corrections context can build up resentments and frustrations on the part of inmates and undermine the system's short term and long term security goals. Arbitrary treatment may lead not only to resentment on the part of inmates who are sent to prison for breaking the law, but the ensuing tension could create an atmosphere of mistrust, which could lead to violence, and which is contrary not only to the interests of inmates, but to staff, management and the larger community as well. Thus the Working Group is firmly of the view that humane treatment of inmates and the recognition of their rights while they are in prison aids in their successful reintegration into the community. (CLR Working Paper No. 5 at 5–6)

Having articulated a statement of purpose and a set of principles, the CLR next addressed the crucial task of balancing prisoners' rights with institutional interests.

> Of major significance in balancing the various factors involved is the recognition that prison practices and programs vary in degree of intrusiveness on inmate rights, and that as the level of intrusiveness increases, the objective must be increasingly important and protections and safeguards must correspondingly increase. Finding the proper balance necessary to protect inmate rights while maintaining a safe, secure institution through a sliding scale approach is one of the primary concerns of this paper. (CLR Working Paper No. 5 at 12–15)

The CLR applied this balancing test in the areas of prison discipline, segregation, transfer, search, visiting, and correspondence. These are the areas which have generated most of the litigation, and they canvas the full spectrum of the prisoner and institutional interests at stake.

The recommendations of the CLR were the subject of extensive consultation with organizations such as the John Howard and Elizabeth Fry Societies and the Canadian Bar Association. Following public consultations, the Departments of Justice and the Solicitor General produced a draft of a new Corrections Act and a set of draft regulations. Although the reform package was presented as a refinement of the work of the CLR, there were substantial differences between the two sets of proposals. Most significantly, criteria and procedures recommended by the CLR to control the exercise of correctional discretion, particularly in the area of administrative segregation, were either removed or watered down. As a result, the Canadian Bar Association, in its submission to the House of Commons Committee on Legal and Governmental Affairs, concluded:

> The proposed Corrections Act and draft regulations have diluted, and in some cases eviscerated, the Correctional Law Review proposals. In our opinion, the Correctional Law Review proposals constitute a necessary, although not entirely sufficient, blueprint for law reform. The proposed Corrections Act and draft regulations fall below the minimum threshold for law reform and are therefore unacceptable. (Canadian Bar Association, "Submission on the Directions for Reform and the Green Paper on Sentencing, Corrections and Conditional Release" [Submission to the House of Commons Committee on Legal and Governmental Affairs, April 1991] at 62)

Most of the Canadian Bar Association's recommendations for strengthening the protection of prisoners' rights and for reinstating the substantive and procedural protections set out in the CLR proposals did not result in amendments to the legislative package, which eventually was passed by Parliament as the *Corrections and Conditional Release Act* of 1992 (*CCRA*). The new legislation, although falling short of the expectations raised by the Correctional Law Review, nevertheless was a significant advance in the field of correctional law. Mary Campbell, a senior official with the Secretariat of the Department of the Solicitor General, has suggested that the enactment of the *CCRA* "marked the pinnacle of reform in the modern era" (Campbell at 320). She highlights the statutory recognition of three principles of corrections which are of particular relevance to the protection of prisoner rights: that "the Service use the least restrictive measures consistent with the protection of the public, staff members and offenders" [section 4(d)]; that "offenders retain the rights and privileges of all members of society, except those rights and privileges that are necessarily removed or restricted as a consequence of the sentence" [section 4(e)]; and that "correctional decisions be made in a forthright and fair manner, with access by the offender to an effective grievance procedure" [section 4(g)]. In Campbell's assessment, "these statements reflect a truly fundamental, indeed revolutionary turning point in statutory protection of inmates' rights. Just these restatements on their own sent a clear and unequivocal message to all players in the system, whether legislators, judges or correctional authorities" (at 321).

Significant substantive changes were introduced in the area of the power to search. The *CCRA* replaced the very broad and untrammelled power contained in the *Penitentiary Service Regulations* with a detailed set of provisions which distinguished among routine, investigative, and emergency search powers, establishing threshold criteria for each and differentiating among non-intrusive, strip, and body cavity searches. The statutory scheme was specifically structured to reflect the jurisprudence of the Supreme Court on the interpretation of the guarantee in the *Charter of Rights and Freedoms* against unreasonable search. The *CCRA* also marks a legally significant shift from the pre-1992 regime, in which visiting was a privilege, to one in which prisoners have a right to maintain contact with the community, subject to reasonable limits.

In many other areas the *CCRA* did not alter either the substance or the procedure of decision-making affecting prisoners. However, it did change these from their previous status as policy guidelines in the Commissioner's Directives to legally binding provisions of the legislation and regulations, which is significant in increasing not only their visibility but also their enforceability. There are other provisions in the *CCRA* which enlarge the scope of prisoners' rights as they had been recognized by the courts under the *Charter*. The best example of this is the recognition of a prisoner's right to be represented by counsel at a hearing of a serious disciplinary offence. The Federal Court of Appeal in *Howard*, while recognizing a right to counsel as a principle of fundamental justice within section 7 of the *Charter*, had ruled that this right was dependent upon such factors as the complexity of the case and the capacity of the particular prisoner. The CCRA removed these limitations and gave the prisoner an unqualified right to counsel—although, as I will describe, the limited availability of legal aid has made this right illusory for most prisoners in Canada.

Significantly, the CCRA also moved beyond what the courts had established as baseline entitlements under the *Charter* in relation to Aboriginal prisoners. One of the principles in the CCRA is that "correctional policies, programs and practices respect gender, ethnic, cultural and linguistic differences and be responsive to the special needs of women and Aboriginal peoples, as well as to the needs of other groups of offenders with special requirements" [section 4(h)]. In implementing this general principle, the CCRA specifically recognizes that "Aboriginal spirituality and Aboriginal spiritual leaders and elders have the same status as other religions and other religious leaders" and authorizes the Solicitor General "to enter into agreements with Aboriginal communities to provide for the provision of correctional services for Aboriginal offenders" (sections 83 and 81).

In tracing the history of prisoners' rights from a time in which prisoners were "slaves of the state" and "dead to all transactions of the outer world," the lines of progressive reform are clear. Mary Campbell, after noting that prisoners' rights are "not the conferring of special entitlements so much as simply the prevention of abuse," summarizes the main features of the reform movement.

> The history of prisoners' rights in Canada demonstrates two key elements in this prevention: first, a necessity of creating and engendering respect for a culture of prisoners' rights as human rights, and second, the availability of adequate remedies. In tracing the evolution of prisoners' rights, it can be seen that reformation depended not only upon statutory reform, but also on providing means for inmates to express their concerns, as well as ways for the outside world to scrutinize life behind bars. Progress in each of these areas has been remarkable: the statute has gone from being a brief description of management structure to a comprehensive code of inmate and staff rights and responsibilities; inmates who at one time had almost no way of voicing their views and concerns now have a wide range of administrative and legal avenues of redress; and the outside world has an unprecedented window on prison life. (at 286–87)

In the chapters that follow, drawing on my research at Kent and Matsqui Institutions, I will take the measure of prisoners' rights in Canada as reflected not in the text of the CCRA and the values of the Mission Document but in the daily practices of correctional administrators. These practices, and the voices of prisoners who have experienced them, reveal the extent to which the terms "revolution" and "counter-revolution" vie for ascendancy in the contemporary prison.

## The Prisoner Grievance Process and
## the Office of the Correctional Investigator

It should not come as a surprise that in this review of the law I have focussed heavily on the role of the courts, the *Charter,* and correctional legislation in bringing prisoners within the protective umbrella of human rights. Resolving the competing interests of the keeper and the kept within the framework of a "due process" model is part of the natural order of things for those who are legally trained. This model proceeds on the assumption that the principal way to legitimize state power and prevent its abuse is to pour specificity into the criteria for decisions and gird the making of these decisions with rules that ensure fairness. Professor Fred Cohen, a thoughtful American commentator on developments in correctional law, has suggested that the adoption of due process as the strategy of choice for controlling discretion of prison officials is an example of the umbilical tie lawyers have to the use of analogy: since due process is required in other areas of the criminal justice system to ensure fairness, it is necessary also in the area of prison justice. Cohen suggests that one of the traps of "excessive reliance on analogy is the limitation it imposes on the development of more creative solutions to the problem and the apparent tendency to accept on faith the inherent worth of the missing fact" (Fred Cohen, "The Discovery of Prison Reform" [1971] 21 *Buffalo Law Review* 855 at 868).

One of the other problems with excessive reliance on a due process model, ultimately superintended by the courts through judicial review, is that it is subject to the vagaries of litigation and the limited access prisoners have to legal aid. This results in few cases reaching the courts and, for those that do, a heightened adversarial tension between the parties. For all these reasons, the development of alternatives to litigation, emphasizing non-adversarial and more informal dispute-resolution processes, has been identified as a necessary part of an effective system of prison justice. The Archambault Commission in 1938 observed:

> A serious feature in the penitentiaries is that a prisoner has no outlet whatsoever for his grievances . . . with the result that the prisoner feels that he has no access to a fair administration of justice and is absolutely removed from the protection of his fellow man. (at 344)

Some thirty years later the report of the Swackhamer Commission, in addressing the causes of the 1971 riot at Kingston Penitentiary, also identified the lack of an effective form of redress:

> Grievances of all types are bound to exist among the prison population. Whether those grievances are justified or not, they require to

be dealt with so that order and morale of the institution can be maintained. At present, we heard that such grievances can only be resolved, if at all, when an inmate's only avenue of complaint is the very administration which is frequently the source of his dissatisfaction. It is perfectly evident that at Kingston Penitentiary the total absence of any formula by which such matters could be effectively aired was a factor in the disturbance itself. (at 62)

Largely as a result of this report, the Office of the Correctional Investigator was created in 1973, and the following year an internal grievance system was established for federal prisoners. These two features, while quite distinct, have important points of intersection and together constitute the primary non-judicial mechanisms for prisoner redress.

The Office of the Correctional Investigator (CI) was created by an Order-in-Council under Part II of the *Inquiries Act* (R.S.C. 1970, c. I-13), rather than by special legislation. The Order-in-Council mechanism, which allowed a quick response in the aftermath of the Kingston riot, was intended to be a temporary measure until legislation could be drafted. However, it was not until 1992, nineteen years later, that the mandate of the CI found its proper place in correctional legislation in the *Corrections and Conditional Release Act*. The mandate of the first Correctional Investigator, Inger Hansen, was to "investigate, on her own initiative or on complaint from or on behalf of inmates as defined in the *Penitentiary Act*, and report upon problems of inmates that come within the responsibility of the Solicitor General" (P.C. 1973-1431: June 5, 1973). However, excluded from the mandate were complaints "where the person complaining has not, in the opinion of the Correctional Investigator, taken all reasonable steps to exhaust available legal or administrative remedies," a provision designed to encourage prisoners to first use the internal grievance system. The CI was given unrestricted access to prisoners in federal penitentiaries, and correctional officials were directed to provide "full co-operation" to the CI's office. Although the concept of the CI was derived from that of the ombudsman, one of the criticisms of the Canadian initiative was that, unlike most other ombudsmen's offices, the CI did not report directly to Parliament but rather to the Solicitor General. This limitation notwithstanding, the appearance of the CI on the correctional horizon opened up an important window for prisoner redress. In its first year of operation, the CI's office received complaints from 595 prisoners, and in her opinion "none of their complaints was frivolous" (*Annual Report of the Correctional Investigator, 1973–1974* [Ottawa: Information Canada, 1974] at 3).

The value of the CI's office was also seen in its ability to conduct inquiries into allegations of abuse. Early in its history, the CI conducted an inquiry into the use of gas and force at Millhaven Institution. As described by Mary Campbell:

Without the existence of the CI, this would likely have gone unnoticed as just "routine business" at that institution. The incident itself stemmed from a seemingly innocuous event, the early termination of the shower period one evening. Missed showers had, however, become a frequent occurrence and meant that some inmates were going several weeks without bathing. On the night in question, the inmates began shouting and banging on cell doors. When they refused to stop, staff decided to move the ring leaders to segregation, eventually using gas in the process. The inmates were left naked in segregation over night without mattresses or bedding. None of the rules regarding the use of gas and its decontamination, or regarding use of force, were followed. Even prior to this incident, specific instances of abuse of inmates were not uncommon.

> Through evidence from correctional officers as well as inmates it was established beyond question the inmates have, from time to time, been restrained by being handcuffed behind their backs, shackled with their legs bent backwards and upwards in order that the chain between the legs could be pulled through the chain on the handcuffs. It was also established the inmates had been left in their cells for hours in this position and a number of officers agreed that they had witnessed inmates left lying in their own excrement . . . When questioned about these methods of restraint, the Director of Millhaven Institution stated that he was not aware that this was taking place. (Correctional Investigator, *Report of Inquiry—Millhaven Incident, 3rd of November, 1975* (Ottawa 1975) at 15)

The significance of the Millhaven Inquiry is the emphasis on (1) the vulnerability of the prisoners in the hands of the system, and (2) what can happen where there is a complete absence of a climate of rights. Moreover, given that there wasn't a widespread riot and no lives were lost, it is questionable whether this incident would have ever been held up to public scrutiny if the CI had not existed. (Campbell at 300–301)

Mary Campbell suggests that another important aspect of the CI's office was "the consequent pressure it put on other parts of the system to become more visible and accountable in dealing with inmates—the terms of the appointment required that all other legal or administrative avenues of redress were normally to be exhausted first, which created systemic pressure for such alternative mechanisms to be created and to function effectively" (at 300). Although the internal grievance procedure was created in 1974, the House of Commons Sub-

Committee on the Penitentiary System in Canada, in its 1977 report, was very critical of its effectiveness.

> At present, the grievance procedure is so unwieldy and ineffective that it might well be creating more problems than it solves. An inmate with a grievance must fill out a form which may be dealt with by one or all of the four levels of authority from the keeper at the institution, on to the institutional director, to the regional director, and finally up to the office of the Commissioner. If the grievance passes through all these channels, the inmate may have to wait many months for a reply which, very often, leaves him no better satisfied than when he began. (*Report to Parliament,* at 97)

Following the *Report to Parliament,* the grievance mechanism was streamlined by reducing the number of levels of review from four to three. However, the procedures continued to suffer from a number of serious shortcomings which were identified by Joan Nuffield, a government researcher, just two years after the *Report to Parliament.*

> First, unlike an appeal to a court, for example, this procedure does not subject the dispute to a review by an authority independent of the present system. Apart from missing the benefit which can accrue from an impartial view of the matter, this type of mechanism runs the risk of becoming a system of almost routine ratification of one level's decision-making by the next level in the hierarchy. Each appeal level may to some extent share both the same perceptions of the dispute and the perceived need to provide support and reassurance to staff at other levels, whose jobs are difficult at the best of times. Even where such a "ratifying" function is not in fact the case, it may easily be perceived as such by inmates, thereby reducing almost to a nullity the essential credibility of the procedure in the eyes of inmates. Second, this type of internal mechanism does not provide for legally binding orders to be issued as to the matter in dispute. At most, a grievance filed through this system would result in a directive from the Commissioner of Corrections. This constitutes a lesser assurance of either awareness on the part of staff, or compliance, particularly troubling in view of the Sub-Committee's finding that the Directives are "confusing, poorly organized, difficult to understand and interpret, and generally unsatisfactory as a proper framework for ordering the prison community." (Joan Nuffield, *Inmate Grievance Procedure Pilot Project (Saskatchewan Penitentiary):*

*An Evaluation* [Ottawa: Solicitor General of Canada, 1979] at 4–5.
See also the *Annual Report of the Correctional Investigator, 1977–1978*
[Ottawa: Information Canada, 1978] at 25)

The House of Commons Sub-Committee had also faulted the grievance procedures on the ground that prisoners had no voice in the process. "So long as the inmate feels he has no input into the system which is governing his life, he will remain frustrated and embittered and the result of this frustration and bitterness inevitably results in the kind of violence presently plaguing our penitentiaries" (*Report to Parliament* at 98). The Sub-Committee, based on evidence it heard on the operation of a successful grievance model used in several United States' prisons, recommended a reformed process for Canadian prisons, one that would give prisoners a greater role and also provide for binding outside mediation.

The Correctional Law Review also recommended changes to the existing procedures, particularly adding a provision for binding arbitration. Under the CLR's proposal, a prisoner would have the right to have a grievance referred to an independent arbitrator. The decision of this arbitrator would be binding on the institutional authorities unless it was established to the satisfaction of the Federal Court that the decision would be contrary to law, would represent a clear danger to any individual or group of individuals, or would require funds not available in the current budget. In the latter case, the Commissioner of Corrections would be required to present to the court a plan for the implementation of the decision in future fiscal years (CLR Working Paper No. 5 at 115–16). As the CLR pointed out, experience in the United States with successful grievance procedures had shown that provision for independent review, even though used in only 1 to 5 per cent of all cases, was a critical element in establishing the credibility of the process in the eyes of prisoners. However, this element of the CLR's recommendation, one endorsed by the Canadian Bar Association, was not incorporated into the CCRA. Instead, the basic shape of the existing procedures was retained, although their status was elevated from policy to law by inclusion in regulations.

The CCRA, in keeping with its professed aims of codifying and integrating the essential legislative elements of correctional law, sets out in Part III the function and powers of the Office of the Correctional Investigator. Section 167(1) sets out the CI's mandate in these terms:

To conduct investigations into the problems of offenders related to decisions, recommendations, acts, omissions of the Commissioner [of Corrections] or any person under the control and management of, while performing services for or on behalf of the Commissioner, that affects offenders either individually or as a group.

Despite the often repeated criticism of the 1973 provisions establishing the Correctional Investigator's office that the CI did not report directly to Parliament but to the Solicitor General, the *CCRA* maintained this reporting relationship, although it did establish a time frame and structure within which the Minister must present reports from the CI to Parliament.

In his *Annual Report* for 1992–93, the Correctional Investigator summarized his experience, in the pre-*CCRA* era, with the Commissioner of Corrections' responses to his office's recommendations on a whole range of issues, including the effectiveness of the internal grievance system, by lamenting that they "continued to be excessively delayed, defensive and non-committal." However, he went on to express his hope that "as the appreciation and understanding of the new legislation increases, all parties involved in the correctional process will accept their responsibility in ensuring that offender concerns are addressed in a thorough, timely and objective fashion" (*Annual Report of the Correctional Investigator,* 1992–1993 [Ottawa: Supply and Services Canada, 1993] at 45). Later in this book I will examine, through the vehicle of the annual reports of the CI, whether the *CCRA* has in fact generated a climate characterized by respect not only for the Rule of Law and human rights but also for the recommendations of Canada's prison ombudsman.

The *CCRA* provided that after five years a comprehensive review of the *Act*'s provisions and operations would be undertaken by Parliament. In May 2000, a subcommittee of the House of Commons Committee on Justice and Human Rights tabled its report on the *CCRA* (Sub-committee on *Corrections and Conditional Release Act* of the Standing Committee on Justice and Human Rights, *A Work in Progress: The Corrections and Conditional Release Act* [Ottawa: Public Works and Government Services, 2000]. Online: <http://www.parl.gc.ca/infocomdoc/36/2/SCRA/studies/reports/just01-e.html>). Prison justice was not the primary focus of the report. That focus, in keeping with the temper of the times, was public protection. My research for this book began shortly after the enactment of the *CCRA*. Its focus has been justice and human rights behind the walls. Placed in the context of over thirty years of research and advocacy, the chapters that follow represent my own evaluation of Canada's correctional legislation and the state of prison justice as we begin the twenty-first century.

# SECTOR 2

## CHAPTER 1

# Life inside a Kaleidoscope

It is tempting to present prison life in black and white terms. In the wake of high-profile and violent crimes, politicians call for longer sentences and a toughening up of regimes to re-inject the rigours of punishment into what is perceived to be the "Club Med" atmosphere of modern prisons. At the same time, the public is drawn to films such as *The Shawshank Redemption* and *Murder in the First,* in which corrupt, violent wardens and guards vie for ascendancy over prisoners struggling against cruel and oppressive conditions. These stereotypes may make for good political rhetoric and even better movies; prison life, however, no less than life on the outside, rarely conforms to extremes.

Looking inside a federal penitentiary is like looking through a kaleidoscope; the images are viewed within a confined space, yet what we see is multifaceted, with colours that continually change and shift. The events I observed and the people I interviewed during my research at Matsqui and Kent brought many facets of the spectrum into sharp relief. Those events and interviews also shed light on the nature of change and continuity in the Canadian penitentiary.

## The Measure of Change

Some of the staff and prisoners I interviewed for this book were young children when I first entered the gates of Matsqui Institution in 1972. Some had just entered the federal correctional system when *Prisoners of Isolation* was published in 1983. Others had prison careers spanning a quarter of a century and had experienced the changes in life inside prison during that time up close, day by day.

From my perspective, one of the principal changes since I began my research and advocacy work in prisons in the 1970s is the ease with which many officers will now talk about events and experiences that were once hidden behind a veil of silence. During one of my 1993 interviews, a now-retired staff member confided that when he was working in the B.C. Penitentiary in the 1970s, there was, among a very influential group of guards, a visceral hatred of all that I represented as an advocate of prisoners' rights. He told me that officers in gun towers would track me with their rifles as I walked from the front gate on my way to the segregation unit atop B-7 Cell Block, hoping I would do something that might justify them getting a shot off. Some of these officers in their after-hours conversations would apparently take great pleasure in imagining ways to make the world a safer place by eliminating people like me. Although I never experienced any slashed tires or broken windshields (sanctions visited upon some staff members who broke ranks with the officers' code of silence), my picture identification at the front gate was disfigured with cigarette burns strategically placed between my eyes. For many years I kept that disfigured memento in a box along with a small section of the bars of one of the cells at the B.C. Penitentiary, mounted on a wooden base, which was given to invited guests at the ceremony marking the official closing of the Pen in 1980. As Correctional Supervisor Jim Mackie observed during my interview with him at Kent in 1998, it took a long time before staff at Kent felt comfortable opening up to me. As he put it, "It took years for people to decide what side of the fence you play on, where did you come from, were the staff getting a fair shot?" In response to my question about what side of the fence staff thought I was on, he stated diplomatically, "Sometimes inmate-slanted, but being very truthful." I can return the last part of the compliment as I reflect how forthright correctional staff have been in my many interviews with them.

The nature of change in the Canadian penitentiary was brought home to me early in my research for this book by an encounter in the staff dining room at Matsqui Institution. A young correctional officer came over to my table and introduced himself. He said he had been speaking to some of the older staff, who remembered me from the B.C. Penitentiary days. They told him that then I had been a radical lawyer with all kinds of wild, unrealistic ideas. However, from their conversations with me over the last few months, they felt I had mellowed; my ideas seemed more reasonable, and instead of shunning contact with me they were eager to share their experiences.

My reaction to his words took several turns. Initially I was startled that I was no longer regarded as a radical lawyer. As someone whose legal education coincided with the rise of the civil rights movement and whose professional life has always been in support of greater recognition of human rights, I regarded the label "radical" as a badge of honour. If I wasn't radical, did that mean I had become mainstream? I did not believe that I had lost the fire of my convictions, nor that my ideas for justice behind the walls had been compromised as my career had matured.

As I reflected further on why my image and my message were now seen in a different light, I was able to offer the young officer something more than a pained expression. When I first met with the young officer's colleagues, prisoners had no rights. When lawyers like John Conroy and myself argued that prison officials had a duty to act fairly in making decisions about prisoners, our arguments were seen as subversive. The idea that Aboriginal prisoners should have the right to practise their own spirituality was viewed in almost apocalyptic terms as either a return to "barbarity" or the leading edge of a revolution based on Red Power. Yet by the time this young officer went through his basic training in 1993, prisoners had legal rights guaranteed by the CCRA and the *Charter of Rights and Freedoms;* the duty to act fairly was an integral part of the correctional mandate; and the right of Aboriginal prisoners to practise their distinct forms of spirituality was recognized as a vital part of their journey towards healing and rehabilitation. Principles that in the temper of the times had been viewed as radical were now embedded in the law and the Constitution of Canada; indeed, they were now part of this young officer's training and job description.

There was another important level to understanding why officers who had once hated my guts would now sit and talk with me, almost as in a confessional, often decrying practices they had seen or participated in. Could they be right that I had mellowed? They were right to believe that over the years I had become more knowledgeable about prison as a social and cultural institution, and that I better understood both the pressures under which correctional staff and administrators worked and the difficulties of translating law and policy into operational reality. While I remained an advocate for the rights of prisoners, I took seriously the concerns of correctional staff and administrators that their rights to safety and dignity should not be undermined in the process of respecting those same rights for prisoners.

## The Keepers

Case Management Officer Dave Sinclair began working in the federal penitentiary system in 1969. He worked in the B.C. Penitentiary for four years and then moved to Australia, where he worked in probation and parole. Upon returning to Canada in 1980, he resumed his career with the Correctional Service of Canada, first as line staff and then as a case management officer. In a 1993 interview, he described his experiences in the B.C. Penitentiary as "an absolute nightmare, although I didn't realize it at the time." In those days, the battle lines were clearly drawn not just between guards and prisoners but between guards and the administration:

The communication lines between management and the operational staff were not good because the senior officers had a vested interest to keep the rest of us angry at the administration and they did that very effectively. So far as the rest of us were concerned, the senior officers were the real bosses. The management, the warden, the assistant warden and all of those people were just interlopers that didn't know what the hell they were doing. That was the prevailing attitude. It was a terribly unhealthy attitude. (Interview with Dave Sinclair, Matsqui Institution, August 16, 1993)

Mr. Sinclair also remembered his induction into life as a guard at the B.C. Penitentiary:

I walked into the institution and I had civilian clothes on, a sports jacket and a tie, and I was put on the ranges. My training was that for three days while I was in civilian clothes, I observed and assisted another correctional officer do the job. That was awful. You were a target, not only for the staff, you were a target for the inmates. But it sure desensitized you in the long run. The down side was that desensitization really gave you a need to give it back and when the opportunity presented to give it back, you did. Because of this attitude it was very easy to shift into a man-handling kind of attitude. Somebody gives you a hard time, wham, boot, slam the cell door and go on to the next one. In those days, violence was part of the job. Cons were beat up. There were no checks, no balances. If somebody pissed you off, you grabbed them and marched them up to the hole. At the end of the shift, you gave the list to your supervisor, and he took it over to the keeper and those guys might stay up in the hole for five or six months. There's no way that you could do time in the B.C. Pen in that era and get released from there without being really, really angry. I often think back to the horrible, horrible things that we did and how much we contributed to the violence in the community.

Dave Sinclair told me a story I had heard from several other officers who worked in the B.C. Penitentiary at a time when Clifford Olson was in segregation, prior to going on to become Canada's most infamous serial killer.

Olson was in the rat hole at B.C. Pen, which was a hell hole underneath the East Wing. The cells down there were these old English cells with the latch that goes around the corner and then the padlock, the old padlock. I can still see those cells and that bar going around that corner just like it was yesterday. Olson used to shoot his mouth off. He got beat quite badly. I know of an incident (thank God I wasn't involved) where two garbage cans were set up in the hallway and a game of football ensued and Clifford Olson was the football.

According to Mr. Sinclair, the dynamic at the B.C. Penitentiary was such that even if correctional staff felt what they were doing was wrong, a momentum carried them along with the flow. He recalled that some staff would actually try to provoke prisoners in segregation to hang themselves by kicking on their doors over a prolonged period of time and then one day throwing a towel torn up into strips into the cell. He knew of one occasion where this strategy was successful, although he was not on shift when it happened.

Recoiling from these accounts of the B.C. Penitentiary, Mr. Sinclair described the energy and enthusiasm he brought to his work at Matsqui as a case management officer twenty years later.

> God help me, I love dealing with these guys. I think it's one hell of a challenge. Give me a guy that says he won't do something and I'll be happier than hell to spend the next two or three months trying to convince him that that's what he should do. I really love it, but I love it in the sense that if that guy does make it, he can look back and say hey, I'm glad Dave Sinclair was there because he got me to do this.

Although Dave Sinclair appreciated the changes that had come about in the life of a correctional officer, he was concerned about other developments that had taken place in the bureaucratization of prison work. When he first became a case management officer, there was more scope for individual initiative within the system. When I interviewed him in 1993, there was a much greater emphasis on correctional staff conforming to a systems approach, in which detailed documentation and review by endless boards were the order of the day. Mr. Sinclair's sense was that much of the work he did was designed to meet the needs of the system rather than those of prisoners.

Like Dave Sinclair, Jesse Sexsmith began his correctional career as a guard in the 1960s. When I interviewed him, Mr. Sexsmith was the assistant deputy warden of Matsqui, and he later became the deputy warden at Kent prior to his retirement in 1995. He told me that in the early days, "The guards brought with them what the prisoners brought: hatred. It wasn't a surface thing. It came from the gut. When I went into the service I was twenty-five years old and I went in thinking that I was being a correctional officer, but I got caught up in the hatred like everybody else" (Interview with Jesse Sexsmith, Matsqui Institution, August 17, 1993). He remembered the old keepers at the B.C. Pen, who stood in the dome and all day hurled abuse at prisoners. Guards would take government supplies for personal use, and violence against prisoners was routine. For Jesse Sexsmith, as for Dave Sinclair, remembering those days was like recalling a nightmare. Some of the guards were extremely disturbed and dangerous men. He referred in particular to one officer about whom I had heard many chilling stories. One of these even found its way into the 1977 *Report to Parliament* by the House of Commons Sub-Committee on the Penitentiary System in Canada. Months after the 1976 riot in the B.C. Penitentiary, when only a few prisoners remained, this officer went down the ranges on Christmas Eve handing out razor blades and wishing prisoners a Merry Christmas and "a slashing New Year."

Attitudes characteristic of an ongoing war against prisoners were not confined to the B.C. Penitentiary. On Mr. Sexsmith's first day at Matsqui, he was taken on a tour of the institution by a veteran correctional officer. After entering the kitchen, the officer said loudly, "Look at this bunch of fucking animals. We should take them all out into the field, dig a hole, fill it with lime and put them in it." On Mr. Sexsmith's first shift in the unit, as he was preparing to do his range walk, he was told by a supervisor about a particular prisoner who was a source of problems and given this invitation: "If he mouths off, drive that fucker between the eyes and I'll back you up." In his more reflective moments, Jesse Sexsmith had trouble understanding why he had remained in the Service. But he welcomed the changes which had taken place as he moved up the career ladder: the greater professionalism of correctional officers, the increased standards of education, the introduction of women officers, and the legal recognition and protection of prisoners' rights. He saw the release of the Mission Document and the enactment of the *Corrections and Conditional Release Act* as the marks of a progressive system.

Jim Mackie began his career as a guard in the B.C. Penitentiary in 1977. In 1979, he was among the first group of staff to receive inmates at the newly opened Kent Institution. He worked initially as a living unit officer, was promoted to a living unit supervisor, and then in 1987 became a correctional supervisor, a position he has retained ever since. At the time of my interview with him in October 1998, Mackie had held the position of correctional supervisor for twelve years, was the senior keeper at Kent, and was one of the few staff who had been there since the day it was opened. He had served under the six wardens that spanned Kent's history.

In explaining the differences between the environment of the B.C. Penitentiary and that of Kent twenty years later, Jim Mackie attributed many positive changes, particularly the lessening of violent confrontation, to increased communication across the divide.

> In the 1970s at B.C. Pen there was a very militaristic regime towards the security staff and almost as severe towards the inmate population.

At the Pen the ability for officers to walk amongst the inmates, to walk into the exercise yards wasn't there. Staff were as frightened of the most violent inmates as the other inmates were. They hid in cages up above them. So the interaction amongst the inmates and the guards was very poor . . . The con code in those days was almost a code of silence with staff. You told staff nothing. You imparted nothing. If you were friendly with staff it wasn't even a verbal gesture, it was sort of a nod as you walk by, like "you're alive, I'm alive" . . . I know that the prisons when I first walked in the door at B.C. Pen were so damn dangerous that you were glad to be home any given day. I know now when I walk in the door I expect to be home . . . At the B.C. Pen there were excesses in force. There was no such thing as use-of-force documents, you didn't record anything. You were told to go deal with the person and drag him to the hole. If the guy went hard so be it, if he went easy so be it. We've learned to do things better and it is paying a dividend to us now. Possibly there are some people that are saying there are too many rights for inmates, but if they lose those rights then possibly we lose the same rights. Because when they take away their rights, they take away our rights. (Interview with Jim Mackie, Kent Institution, October 7, 1998)

Matt Brown is another correctional supervisor who had a long history at Kent Institution and who remembered the attitude some B.C. Pen officers brought with them when they transferred there. When I asked him to identify the most significant changes he had observed since he began work at Kent in 1981, he focussed primarily on the changes in staff attitudes.

One way to relate the changes is a story that I recall when I first arrived here and started working. The majority of the staff were ex-B.C. Pen who had the old attitudes, and I can remember distinctly standing in the courtyard talking to some of these officers and, of course, we'd normally talk about inmates, which ones were bad, which ones were good. The old attitude was pretty well how we'd get rid of this inmate, how do we "hurricane" him. How do we bug him, and if there ever was a riot, which one were we going to shoot and kill? I remember those days and I remember distinctly about a couple of months ago talking to staff in the same courtyard and we were discussing inmates again, about their attitudes and how they are working, but the change was that staff were discussing which programs would help them, which would best suit them, how do we deal with an attitude problem with an inmate, where do we direct him on how to get motivated. I kept thinking people didn't talk this way in the old days. Now it's a whole different attitude.

A lot of people complain about the *Charter of Rights,* how it has relaxed the rules and allowed the inmates to get more things. Well, true, it has, but it has made our job easier in ways, too. It is a little bit difficult discipline-wise but inmates that are motivated are easy to deal with. We still have the problems with unmotivated inmates but we are always going to have that problem. Inmates are more willing to listen to me now, too. In the old days if an inmate talked to you it was "Hey, you fucking pig." Now they either call you by your first name or your last name. I remember distinctly the first time an inmate said "please" to me. I was shocked. Now it is common for inmates to say please and they are polite. That is a critical factor, being civil. (Interview with Matt Brown, Kent Institution, July 1995)

Doug Cassin, like Jim Mackie, was one of the first living unit officers to work at Kent Institution. He stayed until 1985 as a living unit supervisor. After several years at Mission and Elbow Lake Institutions, he returned to Kent in 1988 and worked there as a correctional supervisor until 1995. Mr. Cassin had a reputation as the toughest of the correctional supervisors at Kent, a reputation reinforced in no small measure by his physique. In the maximum security world, where weightlifting and physical strength are highly respected attributes, the fact that Doug Cassin was an accomplished weightlifter and could probably bench-press more than any prisoner had a certain cachet. In light of his reputation as a hard-rock officer, I asked Mr. Cassin how he responded to the Club Med view of prisons so prevalent in the media. The prisoners had television, they had Nintendo games, they could watch videos and get private family visits; did he believe that these changes were coddling prisoners? This is how he responded to that question:

I think I've said the same thing in my day, too, but when I take a realistic view, we don't have as many hostage-takings or smash-ups and assaults. But it is still a maximum security prison, and if an inmate causes too many problems he is still segregated. He may not be on a punishment diet and his cigarettes may not be taken away, but he is still put away from the main population. You know, I wouldn't want to be living here having my meals delivered on a cart and locked up for twenty-three hours a day. I've been through my share of the ruckus in prison, and I think for the most part it is a safer place for an officer to work now because of a lot of these things. I don't think the inmates are any better guys or less inclined to violence, but it doesn't erupt as much.

The other part of my answer is that one of our mandates is to protect society. Protecting society, a lot of people think, is just keeping
the inmates in the fence, but 99 per cent of these inmates are going
back to the street. Now I'm not guaranteeing that because you let
him watch television he's going to be a model citizen, but if you've
got a guy where you've had him chained to a bed or locked up or you
are fighting with him every day and you send him out on the street
in that condition, and we've seen instances like that, you are not
actually protecting anybody. (Interview with Doug Cassin, Kent
Institution, September 1995)

The assessment that the recognition of prisoners' rights and the liberalization
of prison regimes were hallmarks of a progressive system was not a unanimous
one among correctional staff at Matsqui. Rick Cregg had spent thirteen years
working in corrections, the first six in the provincial system at the now-
demolished Oakalla jail and the last seven years in the federal system. At Matsqui
his assignment as a correctional officer was a rotating shift in the Regional
Reception and Assessment Centre (RRAC) and the segregation unit. Mr. Cregg
described himself as a hard-liner when it came to prisons and prisoners, and he
believed that the correctional system was now completely out of balance, with
priority given to the rights and concerns of prisoners to the detriment of staff
safety and morale. He saw the CCRA as a "pernicious" piece of legislation foisted
on an unknowing public. As he characterized it, "It protects the rights of a bunch
of low-life degenerates and the general public would be scandalized if they
realized what the *Act* did in their name." In particular, Mr. Cregg faulted the
manner in which the legislation had cast in stone matters previously left to
administrative and operational discretion. He cited the daily requirement of one-
hour yard time for prisoners in segregation. This had been policy under the
Commissioner's Directives and staff had tried to do their best to provide it, he
said, but there were circumstances in which it was not possible to do so; for
example, if the segregation unit was understaffed or if there was an incident on
the tier and prisoners were acting out. Under the CCRA, staff were required to give
the one-hour exercise, even if in the process it compromised their safety. Mr.
Cregg made no bones about the fact that, when faced with such a conflict, he
favoured the safety of staff over the rights of prisoners.

The new legislation places the staff in handcuffs. They're not physically restrained but they are emotionally restrained in that the *Act* has
put the fear in them that if they use violence against prisoners, they
will face strong measures. They are likely to be subject to disciplinary
action or court action by some lawyer using his *Charter* and the legislation against the staff. It used to be that we couldn't beat the cons

> enough, now it seems that we can't kiss their asses enough. (Interview with Rick Cregg, Matsqui Institution, August 12, 1993)

One theme of my interviews with senior correctional administrators was the impact of developments outside of prison, in the larger society, on the culture inside. Roger Brock, the warden of Matsqui Institution, began his correctional career at Matsqui as a summer student. After working in the Pilot Treatment Unit there, one of the first correctional programs to introduce intensive group and individual psychotherapy, he left the Correctional Service and completed a Master's degree in Social Work, specializing in social administration, social planning, and community development. He worked as a social worker in the Northwest Territories for a year but then returned to correctional work.

> I was kind of a chronic recidivist; I missed working in institutions. There is something about them that gets in your blood . . . There is a certain intriguing thing about institutions that once you become aware that they are very much living, dynamic places where some of the worst things that you will ever see happen, but also some of the most profoundly moving things that I've ever seen have happened in institutions. I guess what I find about institutions is that everything I've ever learned in my life somehow I see played out on the stage in terms of this community. It is small enough that you can actually see the whole dynamic unfolding. There is a place that if you do understand the theory you really do get a clear understanding about what is going on. (Interview with Roger Brock, Matsqui Institution, September 6, 1995)

Mr. Brock identified the introduction of the Rule of Law and greater public accountability as the most profound changes in his twenty-five years in corrections:

> I don't think there is any doubt that the introduction of the Rule of Law into the institutions has had probably the most profound effect. The work of lawyers like yourself and John Conroy forced CSC and anybody within it to have to consider that we were not above the law, that we didn't create our own law, that we were subject to law, and that whether we liked it or not the courts of the land were not going to give us an unfettered run at the inmates . . . The Mission Document tried to capture where we should be as an organization, and then you had the codification of the Mission Document in terms of the new legislation [the CCRA] which, I think, most people would observe is probably one of the most advanced pieces of correctional

legislation anywhere in the world. It is probably the envy of most correctional jurisdictions. If there is any criticism of that legislation it is that it is probably way in advance of where the mentality of the Canadian public is today . . . Today the Service is trying to contend with the problems of a very angry, hostile reactive public that demands 100 per cent perfection. There is no tolerance with any kind of what is perceived to be bureaucratic bungling or mistakes. Throughout the process it has its effects on staff, particularly on management staff. We are a political organization, I am not going to apologize for that. It is run by the shareholders or the public and we have to be responsive to that, but within that is always the problem of balancing science, correctional wisdom, and sound correctional practice with what the public mood is at the time, and along with other government priorities. Despite all that, it still comes down to this basic premise that legally there is just some stuff you can't do in this country, no matter whether you passionately believe that the inmate ought to be hung, drawn, and quartered.

In reflecting on the change in public mood towards prisoners, Warden Brock related it to shifting attitudes towards authority and "deviance."

In the early seventies we were still very much into the Vietnam War. There was a lot of distrust of government, and society was far more prepared to accept the poor old inmate; after all, "but for the grace of God." The public tolerance of drug activity was far greater than it is today. The policing community was almost ridiculed by large numbers of members of society, and today I think the policing community is now seen, judging by all these programs on TV, as white knights. They certainly weren't seen as white knights in those days, they were seen as the "narcs." They weren't terribly sophisticated. In terms of community interaction, the general openness of society and tolerance of deviance in society in those days was far greater than it is today.

I asked Warden Brock what he saw as the main changes in correctional staff over the period of his career.

The staff that work the line, the staff that have come on in the past ten years particularly, they are far more sophisticated, worldly, and their communication skill levels and a whole variety of things are just head and shoulders above some of the staff that existed a number of years ago. Then this was not a very attractive job. Jobs were generally fairly plentiful. The last ten years as peoples' options have shrunk they've looked to businesses and organizations where there are in fact careers and some stability. By these standards CSC line jobs are not bad jobs at all. You get a CO-II [Correctional Officer II] job and with the overtime you are making at least as good money as a teacher and even some of the lawyers that are struggling when they first get out practising. The other thing is that there is a greater acceptance of people that are in this business, from policing to prisons.

One of the most visible changes in Canadian prisons, apart from the physical architecture, is the presence of women, working as everything from line staff to wardens up to, as of September 2000, the Commissioner of Corrections. In the early 1970s the job of a line correctional officer was strictly a man's world. A few women worked as classification officers, but the only other women in the system were clerical staff in the front office, whose contact with prisoners was carefully limited. As my research came to an end, women occupied the position of warden at Kent, Mission, and Ferndale Institutions. Over the six years of my research, three of the unit managers of the segregation unit at Kent were women, and women officers were regularly part of the segregation line staff, something unimaginable in the days of the penthouse at B.C. Pen or H unit at Kent in the early 1980s. The push to have more women working within federal corrections was part of a larger government initiative towards gender equality in the work-force. And paradoxically it was in corrections—in some ways the most macho of career paths—that some of the greatest gains were made in the 1980s. Although the move towards greater participation by women in the prison workplace was not conceived as a correctional strategy, it has definitely had correctional impacts. Many of the people I interviewed felt that the presence of women in federal institutions, as line staff and administrators, had changed the nature of interaction between prisoners and staff. The conventional wisdom, along the lines of "men are from Mars, women are from Venus," is that the value women place on communication has improved the quality of interaction between prisoners and staff, and that the presence of women has had a tendency to reduce both the volume and the harsh edge of the verbal abuse that parades as communication. I asked Warden Roger Brock for his views.

I don't think the fact that there's women in prisons creates less problems or more problems. They are just different problems and different issues. I don't think there is any doubt that having women in the place does tone down things, but there are a couple of corollaries to that; that is, if you can get the women not to jump into a macho mode. Some of the women become jocks and macho with all the bravado and the tough-guy stuff as much as any man. We have almost a kind of stereotyping of women as soft. Well, in this environment—I'm not sure what it has been like in the police community—that is somewhat naive and doesn't reflect the full range and dimensions of women. Here we have everything from gay and feminist women through to some that are very soft and some that are, quite frankly, so traditional in terms of their relationships with men that I fear for them because I don't think they stand on their own two feet. They always have to have a man backing them up. But on the other hand, you've also got men in here that always have to have a woman backing them up. The bottom line, I think, is that these places are far more natural and richer, but I wonder whether ultimately the simple fact of having women in the place has reduced violence. If the simple fact of having women working in institutions was to make them softer places, then the Prison for Women ought to be the quietest joint in the country, and it's not.

Ending his career as the warden of a federal penitentiary was the last thing Ken Peterson contemplated when he graduated from university with an education degree and enrolled in a doctoral program. Mr. Peterson first walked through the gates of the B.C. Penitentiary as a summer intern teacher in 1972. He decided to extend his summer job into the next year, and, as he told me, "Now it's 1999, that was 1972, and a lot of time has passed." The 1970s were tempestuous years in the B.C. Penitentiary, and Ken Peterson worked through a series of hostage-takings, one of which resulted in the death of his friend and colleague Mary Steinhauser in June of 1975. Then came the full-scale riot in September 1976. Mr. Peterson had good reason to remember the riot, because he found himself in the position of Acting Warden as the Penitentiary came under intense public scrutiny.

> You had the civil rights movements in the latter part of the sixties and the beginning of the seventies, and the uprising against the Vietnam War and some degree of anti-authoritarianism that existed in the States that was also expressed in a less violent way—there were no Kent States here—in Canada. There was a revolution of rising expectations, and those echoed or mirrored themselves inside the penitentiaries in Canada. At the same time there were prisoners' rights movements in the community, and they certainly had an impact, not the least of which was to bring what was going on in the prisons to the newspapers and televisions, and as a result it became a profile issue for a number of years. (Interview with Ken Peterson, Mission Institution, July 25, 1999)

There was also a link in Ken Peterson's mind between the unrest of the seventies and the cultural distance between the people who worked in the B.C. Penitentiary and the prisoners who served their sentences there during these years.

> When I started, most of the people working in the B.C. Penitentiary were veterans. At quite a young age they had gone through the Second World War or through the Korean War, and from the military they went into government service. There was a lot of the old New Westminster Regiment in the B.C. Penitentiary. So you had basically a paramilitary organization with militarily trained people, disciplined people, people who believed that orders were orders and you followed them and that's the way it is. So you have on the one hand an organization that is essentially paramilitary and that expects obedience and you come into a situation where the offenders are part of the new age of Better Living through Chemistry, so you have a tremendous clash of cultures; the expectation of a dumb, heel-clucking obedience and a society that is saying the world is changing, and whose expectations are rising. In those days, the offenders weren't allowed to have rings or watches, they weren't allowed to have this, that, and the next thing. Not because the rules were rational rules, but because irrational authoritarianism was the key.

In addressing the principal lines of change over the course of his career, Ken Peterson picked up the common thread of the Rule of Law.

> Since the mid-seventies it has been well recognized that the Rule of Law has to be what runs these places, regardless of the culture or the history that heretofore had said that the warden was the law, which of course meant that if you had fifty different prisons you had fifty different laws. It also meant that the principles and purposes of the organization would not be set internally, they would be set externally for us through a number of cases, some of which you were involved in, that would create the parameters by which we would run the Service. First and foremost it is the Rule of Law that will run it, and we will test everything against the Rule of Law. That takes a long time. Policy-makers are in little motor torpedo boats or ski-doos, and they can just do pirouettes and figure-8's in three minutes. The Service is like a battleship. It's moving at full steam; to turn it around is going to take a long time. But what I see is that there is a convergence going on regarding the Rule of Law and people are cleaving to the course, and when there are aberrations the courts are not reluc-

tant to step in, whereas they were in the past. It was, "This was out of sight and out of mind, and it's very nice if it stays that way, thank you. This is the warden's business." There is also an evolving understanding on the part of staff. They understand much better that the Rule of Law is not an impediment to running the prison. The feeling in the past was that if prisoners have rights then we won't be able to do anything and all hell will break loose. That's not the fact.

In the course of our interview, Ken Peterson addressed the other major change since the 1970s: the increased conservatism brought about by law-and-order politics and the impact this had had on the Service.

> I think we are in a highly defensive mode in our case management. There is a little bit of a cookie-cutter corrections when it comes to this. I have to cross every "t" and dot every "i," because everything can go to court. There isn't a single thing that can't go to court. So if you are living in that hyper-defensive way it is almost like a marriage that has gone wrong. Love keeps no records, but when holy wedlock turns to unholy deadlock records are kept, and so we know that every single thing we say we have to be prepared to defend in court. And if there is supposed to be a piece of paper and there isn't a piece of paper then there are problems. If the piece of paper isn't completed correctly there are problems. Now if we have to go down to chapter and verse, line and phrase, and where the punctuation mark is, that's all very fine, but it will get you a different kind of person as a case manager. The person who rises in a situation like that will be the person who can best survive, and the person who best survives will be the person who really deals with the paperwork very well and is foolproof. There's no question that it gets to be CYA because your ass is right out there with every decision.

There are also forces inside prison that have taken a heavy toll. Ken Peterson identified the growing strength of the drug culture in the lives of prisoners.

> In this institution, as in all institutions, there is a drug subculture. It carries on feeding those who have a habit and it brings new people in. It is responsible for an undercurrent of violence that exists in all institutions. It is something to which you have to pay a lot of attention if you are an offender, because there is no neutral ground in here. I can see why inmates use drugs . . . it is to sedate themselves from what is going on. I don't think they use it to get high, I think they use it to get normal, whatever normal may be. It is to relieve

that undercurrent of fear, tension, angst, whatever it may be. It's mood-altering, and when you get down to the mood in here, the mood in any prison is not good.

I first met Doug McGregor in 1972 when, as the superintendent of Matsqui Institution, he conducted disciplinary hearings, reviewed segregation cases, and triggered involuntary transfers to the B.C. Penitentiary. Mr. McGregor's signature was on the many unescorted temporary-absence passes given to prisoners in those years to enable them to participate in a wide range of community programs, before that power was taken away from wardens and given to the National Parole Board. Mr. McGregor started his correctional life at Kingston Penitentiary in 1963, and a year later he returned to university and took a Master's degree in California. His thesis focussed on a California correctional institution and, as he observed in our interview, in those days California prisons were seen as leading the way in modern corrections. He noted with dismay the changes that had taken place in California since then; by 1996, the state was spending more of its budget dollars on prison construction than on higher education. From 1965 until his retirement in 1997, Mr. McGregor held a variety of positions, including being the warden of both Mission and Matsqui Institutions, as well as doing a stint as Assistant Deputy Commissioner for the Pacific Region.

In our interview, Doug McGregor reflected on the changes that had come about in furtherance of what was now called "good corrections." He quickly focussed on the changes in case management since the advent of the computer-based Offender Management System and the detailed policies and procedures that were now built into security classification. This prompted a discussion of how technology was changing the face of corrections and the nature of the relationship between prisoners and staff.

> The advent of the computer really causes great concern to me, because it has a voracious appetite. The Offender Management System demands tremendous amounts of data and information, and staff are spending a lot of time attending to that requirement. There are people at regional and national headquarters who are watching it all the time and they are quick to tell you that you haven't filled in a certain amount of data on a security classification or that you haven't met these deadlines. This system is the tail wagging the dog as it stands now. One time late last fall on one of those foggy days I looked out of the window of my office late in the afternoon. It was getting very foggy and it was getting fairly dark at that point, and I went in to the Co-ordinator of Correctional Operations' office and I said, "Norm, don't you think it's about time you should be giving some thought

to locking the jail down?" He was busy working at his computer and he looked out of the window and said, "Oh my God." I have jokingly said to people that since that time I've had visions that one day I'll be sitting in my office watching inmates jumping the fences and I'll be the only person noticing it because everyone else is dutifully working away at their computer, putting information into it, and I'll be screaming out the window, "Does anybody care?" (Interview with Doug McGregor, Mission Institution, May 13, 1996)

Doug McGregor was not alone in his misgivings about a "Windows" approach to offender management. Don McDonnell began his career in corrections as a classification officer at the Prison for Women. He worked for about a year and then left the Service for adventures abroad, returned in 1975 and began work again as a living unit development officer at Mission Institution. In 1980 he became the head living unit officer, and from 1983 until 1993 he worked in the community as a parole officer. He then returned to work at Matsqui as a case management officer. In our interview, he decried the loss of interpersonal dynamics that gave his job as a case management officer much of its juice. As he described it, the transition was from the conception of a case manager as a professional bringing independent judgement to bear to being "just another cog in the wheel of the bureaucracy working around offender management." Paradoxically, Don McDonnell felt that the changes in the structure of the Service, which encouraged staff to see themselves as having rewarding long-term careers in corrections, actually undermined individual advocacy.

Under the present system we have everybody entering the correctional process as a staff person at the bottom, as an entry-level uniformed officer, and then you work through your uniformed career to then maybe going to case management. That changes the actual role of the case manager, because you have formed your values and attitude in uniform and you have come to have a particular view of prisoners, which is as likely as not pessimistic and sceptical of the potential for change. The impact of computers in case management has also had major effects. The actual reality of interpersonal dynamics starts to become minimalized and the reality you deal with is not how the offender deals with you personally but how that offender looks on paper. The other problem is that the Offender Management System causes people to think in standardized ways, and while there is nothing wrong with a systematic approach, that is not the same thing as a standardized technocratic approach to human affairs. (Interview with Don McDonnell, Matsqui Institution, July 13, 1995)

Don McDonnell also identified a more general change in the corrections system, one related to the larger society within which corrections operated.

> Coming out of a sixties mentality, there was a sort of belief out there that people can make a difference, and when you work with people, be it in the health care system, any kind of system where you are working with people, then you believe that an individual professional could make a difference in the lives of people. Like everything else, when you take on self-responsibility and if you want to get something done you do what it takes to give your best. When it comes to managing offenders, if you were in a judging situation as a case manager and you felt that something wasn't being done properly, you would do your best to make it right. So advocacy was built into the system, and as the system has changed, so the role has changed. We're not advocates. It's just not part of the job description. If you are an advocate you are viewed with distrust.

Barry Owen and Randy Voth began their careers in corrections fifteen years after Don McDonnell did, and they represented a later generation of case management. In my interviews with them, as the senior case management officers during my research at Kent, they reflected on both the changing nature of their responsibilities and the attitudes and values of the latest generation of case management officers, with their new title of "institutional parole officers," most of whom had been recruited since the passage of the CCRA. Barry Owen summarized his response to the computerized Offender Management System:

> It is more and more case management by numbers. We are attached to those computers. It is almost like as long as we feed that machine and keep it happy then we are okay. We have done our job. But we don't have to go down to the units and see the inmates, or rather we can't because of the time constraints imposed by all the reports we have to write. You end up spending the vast majority of your day typing reports. It is more like we are technicians operating numbers and scales. The human side is going out of it more and more, and I think that was where the advocacy role came into it. You could relate to this person as a human being. You could see if there was an injustice and say, "This isn't fair. I've got to get something straightened out for this guy. The prisoner might be a total jerk, but still he doesn't deserve this." (Interview with Barry Owen, Kent Institution, August 12, 1999)

For Randy Voth, the demand for more and more data and progress reports had taken a toll on his ability to work at a personal level with offenders.

One big part of the job that has really been lost in the last ten years is the whole aspect of counselling. Somewhere in the neighbourhood of 25–30 per cent of our job is supposed to be counselling offenders. However, counselling does not happen between institutional parole officers and offenders at any level. New initiatives such as the streamlining of the Offender Management System have actually taken away from the quality time where you can actually sit down with an inmate and develop some kind of plan with him. That is where the real challenge is. When you go home at the end of the day and you have talked to half a dozen guys, and maybe there are three or four of them that involve very intense, heated discussions, and a couple of them were very positive, you feel like you have accomplished something. And you might even have developed some rapport with that person. But the computers have taken us away from that. It doesn't matter if an IPO [institutional parole officer] doesn't have social skills because they can hide behind the computer screen. (Interview with Randy Voth, Kent Institution, August 12, 1999)

Both Mr. Owen and Mr. Voth expressed grave reservations about the attitudes of the newest practitioners of "good corrections," the young institutional parole officers who had been hired as part of the move to strengthen the reintegration strategy of the Service. Ironically, said Mr. Voth, the Correctional Service's efforts to carve out career paths for employees had given rise to a narrow corporate mentality among new recruits.

A lot of these people are very highly career-motivated. They will toe the company line at all costs. They do not want to offend management. They do not want to disagree with management, because they are concerned that it is going to impact upon their career aspirations. It is almost like these people have suspended their own personal value system when they come into the Service and they have sold themselves out and basically whatever management wants they will do. If that means writing somebody up for the Special Handling Unit, they'll do it even if in their hearts they believe that the guy should not be transferred. They will not sit there and argue with a unit manager or deputy warden that this is not a legitimate case. They will just write it up the way management wants it. There is no conscience there.

Randy Voth's criticisms of the technologically driven corporate approach to modern corrections demonstrated the continuing relevance, at the end of the twentieth century, of David Rothman's characterization of correctional history as a process in which conscience is repeatedly subordinated to convenience.

## The Kept

Many of the conversations I had with prisoners in the course of my research also centred on changes within the system. Steve Fifer came into the federal system in 1972 and was at Matsqui when I did my initial study there. I asked him what had changed in the twenty years since we first met. He said the changes were quite dramatic in terms of both staff and prisoners. The profile of the prisoner population was completely different, he said. The old "con code" was dead, and prisoners today regularly ratted on each other without being concerned about it. Mr. Fifer attributed this to a number of factors. One was that there were now far fewer career criminals among the prisoners than those for whom crime was the consequence of their victimization through childhood abuse. He distinguished between people like himself who had been "arrested" for their crimes and other prisoners who had been "rescued." The former group, when they came to prison, saw themselves as outlaws—a breed of people who operated outside lawful society. There were very few people like this left, he said, and the respect they once had evoked among other prisoners and staff was no longer there. He expressed his feelings vividly by saying, "I'm ashamed to be here. I look at this place as living in a sewer," and added, "in fact, it's what's retiring a lot of guys like me." He also pointed to some of the changes in the institutional regime as contributing to the breakdown of the old con code. The introduction of the "living unit" concept, in which staff interact with prisoners on the ranges, made it easier for prisoners to pass on information. He accepted that communication between prisoners and guards was a good thing, because it made for less violence and anger in the living environment, but at the same time it was bad because it increased the number of informants and encouraged acceptance of ratting (Interview with Steve Fifer, Matsqui Institution, September 1, 1993).

Steve Fifer believed changes in the staff had been even more marked. Just as the con's code had been broken, so had the "bull's" code. The employment of women had softened the whole system up, and that contributed to making it more humane. Line staff now had far more promotion possibilities, were better trained, and were therefore more motivated towards programs and rehabilitation. He thought that the Mission Document had been important and that it was being followed as far as human nature permitted. He summed up the changes by saying, "Most of the staff got rehabilitation on their mind instead of slamming you up and telling you to shut the fuck up."

I asked Steve Fifer whether the contemporary programs at Matsqui were different from those twenty years ago and whether the prisoners who participated in them were better motivated. His response was that, in most cases, prisoners participated for the same reasons as before—"the hustle for parole or transfer to lower security"—but that it was possible some of the prisoners did benefit from these programs. He gave as an example the substance abuse program; he did not find it very useful, but he was amazed at how much misinformation the younger prisoners had about the physical and psychological effects of drugs and alcohol. In addition, he said that the Violent Offender Program at the Regional Psychiatric Centre had had a profound impact on him. He had been made to hold up a mirror to his face day after day and to ask questions of himself he had always managed to evade. He came to accept that for twenty years he had been building a legend of himself based on false premises. It was the only program that had brought tears to his eyes and over which he had lost sleep.

In reflecting on his years in prison, Steve Fifer proudly pointed to the landscaping around Matsqui Institution. He had planted a lot of the flower beds just inside the front gate, and his job now was to take care of them. He said, "I've always tried to leave my mark wherever I've been." He added that he had such a low profile in the institution, people almost didn't notice him as he worked in his garden with a flower in his hair. I told him about the story I read to my children, Shane and Melissa, of an imaginary world in which all the wild animals, including the tigers, were the size of butterflies and lived inside the petals of giant flowers, the reversal of the natural predatory order. Mr. Fifer liked that image and said it reflected where he saw his life going once he finished his sentence.

Dave Humphries was serving a life sentence for manslaughter and had spent much of his adult life in federal penitentiaries. He was also a heroin addict. He told me it is difficult for non-addicts to understand the tremendous investment of energy that goes into making drug connections. Giving up drugs requires finding something else in which you can invest all that energy, he said. Mr. Humphries told me he had been very affected by what I had written in *Prisoners of Isolation* about slashing being the only way some prisoners could focus the pain in their lives. By seeing their own blood, they could at least identify a source of their hurt. Dave Humphries said that for him, sticking a needle into his arm was how he dealt with the pain that had filled his life from the time he was a physically and emotionally abused child. By using heroin, he obtained a release from the pain for a few moments. He knew that heroin would always provide that release; hence its great attraction (Interview with Dave Humphries, Matsqui Institution, August 9, 1993).

A month after our first interview, Dave Humphries was granted a parole which, like some of his earlier releases, proved to be short-lived. He came back to prison with a further five years added to his sentence, for a robbery committed to obtain money for heroin. Mr. Humphries had been optimistic about his release, in large measure because he would have the joys and challenges of a new family—his wife had borne him a son while he was in prison, conceived through family visiting—and his highly acclaimed wildlife paintings were bringing good prices. When he returned to Matsqui, I asked him why these things had not enabled him to succeed. His response was that he had not made as much money as he had hoped from his artwork, and the work he was able to secure in construction had been limited. His wife was working double shifts to pay the bills. His not being able to fill the function of provider gnawed away at his self-esteem, and his experience of family life again became painful.

In describing the changes in the system since 1973, Dave Humphries, like Steve Fifer, focussed on the changes within prisoner culture.

> It's the cons themselves. It's a state of mind, an attitude. Back in the early seventies, there was a strong sense of unity, fellowship, support for one another that you don't see today. A guy can be thrown in the hole today and nobody bats an eye. Prison was a community when I came into the federal system, but today it's more of an individual thing. People are just like lost shadows scurrying about here and there, and you don't even know your neighbour any more. The loss of unity, the loss of solidarity, a loss of a common sense of values and purpose and direction. Back then criminal activity was a way of life. That's what we chose, as other people would choose something else as a career. Drugs were secondary. Now for many of the young guys in Matsqui, the drugs are the main thing, and they become criminals because of the drugs. (Humphries interview, August 9, 1993)

When Dave Humphries commented on changes among the correctional staff, he identified the genuine compassion he had seen in some individuals, particularly when he was in the Violent Offender Program. Compassion was not a quality he had seen much of in his early days of imprisonment, but it had given him an additional reason to try to succeed, he said, so as not to let down those who had extended themselves for him.

## The Spaces of Punishment and Healing

Continuity, change, and the competing visions of the proper balance between punishment and rehabilitation were reflected not just in the language of my interviews; they also had their mirror image in the physical architecture and interior spaces of the contemporary prison.

The most punishing space at Matsqui is the segregation unit—officially identified as the "Special Correctional Unit (scu)" and unofficially known as "the hole." Although the cells are no smaller than those in the main living unit, the austerity of the cell fittings—a steel sink and toilet, a metal double bunk, shelf, desk, and stool bolted to the wall and floor—contrive to squeeze out any semblance of "house," as prisoners call their cells in the living units. On the inside of the cell, in front of a sliding glass window, is a grid of iron bars. A foot beyond the window are the horizontal concrete slabs which form the exterior framework of all the cells in Matsqui; however, in the segregation unit a densely woven steel grill is bolted to the outside of the slabs to prevent prisoners in segregation from throwing contraband items through the window or from passing items from one cell to the next. From inside the segregation cell, the view outside is therefore both fragmented and distorted.

Two cells in the segregation unit are specifically designated, one as a dry cell and the other an observation cell. The dry cell is devoid of any furnishings except a portable toilet. The observation cell has a combined stainless steel sink/toilet and, above the door, a video camera covered with a heavy plexiglas screen to prevent it from being broken. Neither cell has a bed or bunk, only a slightly raised pallet on which a mattress is placed. Attached to the pallet are metal restraint bracelets. Both cells have an additional finely meshed steel grill on the inside of the window, limiting even further the amount of light coming in, and increasing the distortion of the view out.

The exercise yard for segregated prisoners is as bleak as a yard can possibly be; it is enclosed by concrete walls with a wire mesh over top and offers a view of nothing but a sky broken into a thousand pieces. The yard is devoid of any amenities except a chin bar. The already small space is made smaller by a chain link fence that separates protective-custody from general-population prisoners.

If the segregation unit represents the continuity of repressive elements in the carceral landscape, other spaces within Matsqui represent positive change. One of the most significant developments in Canada's federal prison system over the past twenty years has been the emergence, or rather the renaissance, of Aboriginal spirituality as a source of strength and healing for Aboriginal prisoners. The journey towards healing is referred to both inside and outside the prison as the "Red Road." In the middle of Matsqui, surrounded by and in contrast to the architecture of what Aboriginal people call "the Iron Houses" of the colonizers, are a tepee and a sweat lodge. Although the most visible landmarks on the Red Road, these are not the only spaces within the prison that Aboriginal people have made their own. The same day in August 1993 that I toured the segregation unit, I was invited to a meeting of the Native Brotherhood. The meeting, like most Brotherhood meetings, was arranged in the form of a "talking circle." The circle was convened in an area of the prison where most of the industrial workshops are located. The Brotherhood had been given one of these large warehouse-like spaces so that its members could carry on Aboriginal arts and crafts such as wood carving, drum-making, and painting. What distinguished the space in which the Brotherhood met were the large murals painted on the walls. Their distinction lies not only in their artistry but in their symbolic content. Joe Manitopes, the prisoner who painted most of them, helped me understand the imagery. It was a guided tour unlike any other I have taken inside prison.

On the right wall is a painting of a women's sweat lodge with a group of women about to enter. This represents those who carry within them the beginning of new life and the nurturing of the Great Mother. The painting next to it represents a medicine wheel with the colours of the Four Directions. The medicine wheel is an ancient and powerful symbol of the universe; it shows the ways in which all things are interconnected. When the medicine wheel is used as a mirror, it shows human beings that within them are hidden many gifts that have not yet been developed. These must be discovered and nurtured and held in balance. Each of the four directions also holds gifts that point the way along this journey of discovery. The East is the direction from which the new day comes into the world. It is the place of all beginnings. It is also the direction of illumination, the place from which light comes into the world. Hence it is the direction of guidance and leadership. The South is the direction of the sun at its highest point. It is the place of summer, of fullness, of youth, of physical strength and vigour. It is also the place of the heart, of generosity, of sensitivity to the feelings of others, of loyalty, of noble passions, and of love. The West is the direction from which darkness comes and where people go when they die. This is the direction of the unknown, of dreams, prayer, and meditation. It is also the place of testing, where the will is stretched to its outer limits so that the gift of perseverance may be won. The North is the place of winter, of white snows that recall the white hair of the elders. It is the dawning place of true wisdom. Here dwell the bestowers of intellectual gifts. The North can also be seen as a direction of completion and fulfilment.

One of the great lessons of the medicine wheel is that all human beings can acquire gifts in all of the symbolic directions. At the top of the painting, framing part of the circle, are a number of buffalo, representing the source of sustenance for the prairie people when their communities and spirits were strong. The message here is the need for the Brothers to recreate their own source of sustenance and strength through their spiritual practices.

The third painting is a portrait of three brothers participating in a Sundance. In the centre of the painting is a pole representing the tree of life, to which are attached thongs that are embedded in the skin of the dancers. One of the brothers has just pulled himself free from the thongs and is on his knees in a state of exhaustion. The dancers in the Sundance ceremony have previously made a vow to honour the Great Spirit and to walk in the way of their ancestors; the Sundance is a cleansing and healing ceremony to make atonement for deviations from the path and to give them strength to renew their vows. The dancers will usually fast for four days, and on the last day will attach ropes to their chests as reflected in the painting. Some Sundancers remain tied in this way for the whole four days, but it takes a very strong man and a very strong spirit to do this.

The last painting on this side of the wall is of a death lodge in which, atop a wooden platform, is the body of a departed elder wrapped in hides, awaiting his passage on the great journey. On one side of the lodge are the heads of his two favourite horses, who will accompany him on that final journey. This is the ceremony of the dead as practised in olden times, but its message in the sequence of paintings is that if you respect the rhythms of birth and life and practise the spiritual ways of your people, then the ultimate journey is nothing to be feared.

On the left side of the room is a beautiful landscape depicting a mountain, tall evergreen trees, and a circling bald eagle. The colours are calm and muted and are meant to give Brothers a sense of peace and tranquillity. Next to this landscape is a painting of the double-headed sea serpent celebrated in West-Coast Salish and Kwagiulth masks and dances.

The next painting, in the style of the Ojibway peoples of the East, depicts a man transforming into a wolf, reflecting the interconnections between human beings and animals. It also symbolizes the transformation Brothers can make from their previous lives of abuse and violence to a life in which they are at peace with themselves and with the communities to which they return. The final painting draws upon the history of the Iroquois Confederacy, the Haudenausanee, showing the great fire which in Iroquois symbolism is rekindled on the occasion of any important meeting. The mural also shows a series of masks used by members of the Iroquois "False Face" societies. Like the Koshare clowns of the Navajo Nation in the United States, the false faces of the Iroquois mock the foolishness of humankind. The Brothers, in their talking circles, look up to these images and reflect upon the false faces which have brought them to prison. By continuing their journey along the "Red Road," they can return to their true selves.

As I listened in the talking circle, surrounded by these murals, Brothers retraced the violent upbringings which had resulted in their coming to prison and searched for a pathway back to their spiritual centre and away from the life of imprisonment. The energy, although charged with pain and suffering, was essentially positive and full of promise for these men.

Although they were separated by no more than a few hundred feet, there was a vast conceptual and emotional distance between the Brotherhood's meeting place and the segregation unit. In that unit, which constitutes the darkest place in the "Iron House," prisoners are literally "boxed" in cells that distort their view of the outside world. Men's minds are also distorted here by the negative energy which characterizes what passes for communication between the keeper and the kept. If the segregation unit can be seen as representing the poison of bitterness which the prison can inject into a human being, the Aboriginal structures and the talking circle represent the antidote, which can make that same human being whole.

During my first weeks at Matsqui, the Aboriginal Elder Pat Henrickson, who like me had just begun his work there, commented that Matsqui was "a powerful and forceful place." There are powerful people who work and live within the prison, with attitudes about crime and punishment, criminals and corrections, expressed in forceful language; there are also powerful spaces within the prison, which in very different ways seek to change the minds and bodies of the prisoners who enter them. Embedded in the prison regime are well-trodden pathways calculated to strengthen only negative attitudes towards lawful authority. However, there are also avenues through which prisoners, with the support of prison staff and members of the community, can develop the strength to live within the lawful boundaries of civil society. The law, also a powerful force, has an important strategic role to play in providing the framework to support the positive elements of corrections and to protect against the abuse that flows from negative ones. In my first month at Matsqui, I participated in and observed events which highlighted these competing elements. In the next two chapters, I trace the paths of two very different journeys.

## CHAPTER 2

# Along the Red Road

Although Aboriginal peoples did not traditionally have the institution of imprisonment in their conceptual or architectural landscapes, they have, more than any other group in Canada, experienced its impact. Comprising less than 2 per cent of Canada's population, they make up 13 per cent of its federal prison population. In 1988, in a study prepared for the Canadian Bar Association, I wrote:

> Prison has become for young Native men the promise of a just society which high school and college represents for the rest of us. Placing this in a historical context, the prison has become for many young Native people the contemporary equivalent of what the Indian residential school represented for their parents. (Canadian Bar Association Committee on Imprisonment and Release, *Locking up Natives in Canada,* by Michael Jackson [Ottawa: Canadian Bar Association, 1988]. Reprinted in [1989] 23 *U.B.C. Law Review* 215. See also Royal Commission on Aboriginal Peoples, *Bridging the Cultural Divide: A Report on Aboriginal People and Criminal Justice in Canada* [Ottawa: Canada Communications Group, 1996].)

In 1999 the Supreme Court of Canada cited this passage in the *Gladue* case, stating, "These findings cry out for recognition of the magnitude and gravity of the problem and for responses to alleviate it. The figures are stark and reflect what may fairly be termed a crisis in the Canadian criminal justice system" (*R. v. Gladue,* [1999] 1 s.c.r. 688 at para. 64).

Over the past twenty-five years, Aboriginal prisoners have become increasingly critical of the lack of recognition by correctional authorities of the distinctive cluster of problems facing them and of the irrelevance to them of many correctional programs. In 1983, members of the Native Brotherhood at Kent Institution went on a hunger strike, maintaining that they had the right to practise their spirituality, including participation in spiritual and healing ceremonies, and that this was both an existing Aboriginal right under section 35 of the *Constitution Act, 1982* and a right of freedom of religion protected by the *Canadian Charter of Rights and Freedoms*. Beyond these arguments, they maintained that practising culturally relevant ceremonies directed to healing was more appropriate in their journey towards rehabilitation and reintegration into the community than programs that lacked Aboriginal cultural or spiritual content.

In the years that followed, the Red Road and Aboriginal spirituality became increasingly powerful influences in the lives of many Aboriginal prisoners, who discovered, often for the first time, a sense of identity, self-worth and community. Because the path must be taught by those who have special knowledge and who are respected for their spiritual strength and wisdom, the practice of Aboriginal spirituality requires that prisoners communicate with Elders drawn from outside the prison. Some prisoners, by virtue of prior training or the training they undergo in prison, are able to lead certain ceremonies and provide spiritual counselling to other prisoners. There has developed, therefore, a continuum in which those who are more experienced in spiritual ways are able to help those less experienced. From this a sense of community emerges, based not on the common element of criminality or membership in a gang but rather on the search for spiritual truth. In place of the alienation that prison typically engenders, Aboriginal prisoners are able to experience a sense of belonging and sharing in a set of indigenous values. Aboriginal spirituality therefore provides prisoners with constructive links not only to each other but with Aboriginal people outside of prison and with their collective heritage. Charting a path along the Red Road is seen by many Aboriginal people, both inside and outside the prison, as an important element in dealing with problems of alcohol and drug dependency, violence, and other forms of anti-social behaviour (James Waldram, *The Way of the Pipe: Aboriginal Spirituality and Symbolic Healing in Canadian Prisons* [Peterborough: Broadview Press, 1997]).

However, the distinctiveness of Aboriginal spirituality and the historical undermining of Aboriginal cultures have made it difficult for non-Aboriginal correctional staff to accord these spiritual ways due respect. Although there are Aboriginal men and women who have special training, powers, and responsibilities in spiritual matters, they are not distinguished by clerical collars or degrees from schools of divinity. Although Aboriginal spirituality has its own ceremonies and rituals, these are unfamiliar to both Western and Eastern religious orthodoxy. While there are places of special spiritual significance for Aboriginal peoples in North America, cathedrals, churches, and temples of worship were not part of Aboriginal physical architecture.

In the context of the prison system, the ceremony of the sacred pipe and the sweat lodge are two of the distinctive ways in which Aboriginal prisoners have sought to express their traditions. The sacred pipe ceremony, common to many Aboriginal nations, represents the unifying bonds of the Aboriginal ethos. Through smoking the pipe within a ritual circle, the prayers of Aboriginal supplicants rise with the smoke and mingle with all living creatures. The Great Spirit evoked by the pipe enters and connects Aboriginal people with all their relations in the living world. The different materials used in the ceremony—sweetgrass, sagebrush, red willow, and cedar bark—all have symbolic importance. In the same way, the use of eagle feathers in these ceremonies is integrally related to matters of the spirit. The sweat lodge ceremony, like the pipe, is widely distributed across Aboriginal cultural and geographic lines and is primarily an act of ritual purification. Each component of the sweat lodge structure symbolizes the elemental forces of the universe and the cycles of nature.

The 1992 *Corrections and Conditional Release Act* contains provisions which require the Correctional Service of Canada to "provide programs designed particularly to address the needs of Aboriginal offenders" (section 80). The *Act* also authorizes the Solicitor General to enter into agreements with Aboriginal communities to provide correctional services to Aboriginal offenders (section 81); it mandates the establishment of a National Aboriginal Advisory Committee and permits the creation of regional and local advisory committees to advise CSC on the provision of correctional services to Aboriginal offenders (section 82). Section 83 provides that:

(1) For greater certainty, Aboriginal spirituality and Aboriginal spiritual leaders and elders have the same status as other religions and other religious leaders.

(2) The service shall take all reasonable steps to make available to Aboriginal inmates the services of an Aboriginal spiritual leader or elder.

Legislating respect and recognition is one thing; its achievement in the reality of everyday prison life is another. But the warden of Matsqui, Roger Brock, was committed throughout his tenure to translating law into operational practice, and he lent his full support to a variety of Aboriginal initiatives. One of those initiatives was a series of escorted temporary-absence passes that enabled Aboriginal prisoners to make a one-day journey, accompanied by correctional staff, for the purpose of gathering lava rock and plant materials for use in the sweat lodge and other Aboriginal ceremonies within the prison. Lava rock, because it does not crack under the heat of the sweat lodge fire, is a prized resource. On August

19, 1993, four members of the Native Brotherhood, Dennis Bigsky, John Ironchild, Cory Bitternose, and Cheam Nanaquetung, left Matsqui on one of these
passes. They were escorted by two staff members: Jill Hummerstone, a non-
Aboriginal Native liaison worker, and Ken Poirier, a correctional supervisor of
Metis descent. I accompanied the group and chronicled the remarkable events
of that day.

We left the institution shortly after 7:00 a.m. in two vehicles, an eight-
passenger van normally used by the Emergency Response Team and a dump
truck in which the lava rock was to be brought back. We headed down Highway 1, crossing over the Fraser River on the Agassiz road until we got to the
Seabird Island Reserve, where we stopped to buy tobacco. The tobacco would be
used as a reciprocal offering for the lava rock, sagebrush, yarrow, and willow
gathered later in the day. I asked the Brothers when they had last been on the
street; the periods ranged from nine months to over two years.

After leaving the reserve, we drove along the Trans-Canada Highway through
Hope and into the Fraser Canyon. Of the group, only John Ironchild was from
British Columbia, and the three other prisoners had never been through the
canyon. At Hell's Gate we stopped to look down at the awesome sight of the
Fraser exploding through the constricted river channel. I recounted the history
of Hell's Gate: the landslide in 1914 during the construction of the railway that
turned the river into a raging torrent; how as a result, until the construction of
the fish ladders in 1946, the upriver First Nations fishers were deprived of access
to salmon at their traditional fishing stations; how this had given rise to arrangements between the upriver and the downriver First Nations that permitted the
upriver fishers to fish at stations in the lower canyon, an example of First
Nations' treaties of economic co-operation. All of this was completely new to the
three Brothers from the prairies, and in this way the journey began to take on
the character of both cultural and geographical discovery.

From Hell's Gate we drove to Lillooet. On the way, Jill Hummerstone
pointed out several areas with extensive sagebrush that we could gather on the
way back for use in Aboriginal ceremonies. Several miles north of Lillooet we
turned off onto the gravel road to Bridge River. From the turn-off we could look
down to where the Fraser narrows into a series of canyons with literally hundreds
of fishing camps dotting the banks of the river, proclaiming the First Nations'
presence in this territory. The camps were shielded by brightly coloured tarps to
protect people from the intense sun and drying fish from the rain. I shared with
the Brothers the history of the Lillooet peoples' resistance to efforts by the
Department of Fisheries to restrict Aboriginal fisheries to compensate for over-
fishing by the commercial fleet.

The Fraser and the tarps of the fish camps grew smaller as the vista of river
canyon, alpine benches, and mountain peaks grew larger. Cory Bitternose and
Cheam Nanaquetung, the youngest of the Brothers, exclaimed they had never

seen anything like this, that it was quite beyond anything they had anticipated as part of their day of freedom from the routine of prison life. Their smiles grew wider and wider, matching the broadening horizon thousands of feet below them.

Around 1:30 we arrived at the area where the lava rock was to be collected. The site had originally been pointed out on a trip several months earlier by a Lillooet Elder, and the gathering of rock was done with the permission of the Lillooet Nation. Dennis Bigsky and the other Brothers climbed up the rock face, and Dennis placed strings of tobacco ties in the rocks as an offering, together with a prayer, to acknowledge that what was being taken from the earth would be treated with respect.

After the men returned to the road, Ken Poirier moved the dump truck closer to the rock face. While the Brothers and Ken loaded the lava rock, I took an axe and split wood for the fire we needed for our lunch of hot dogs. The work of gathering the lava rock was shared equally between the Brothers and Ken as they formed a chain, passing pieces of rock from one to the other. To a stranger passing by, the sight of five men hefting rocks along a line into a truck against the backdrop of a grey cliff face might have evoked the harsh scene of a prison chain gang in the American Deep South. However, the reality behind this picture illustrated the difference the Matsqui Aboriginal spiritual program brought to the experience of imprisonment. The Brothers, through their physical labour, were providing the raw material for sweat lodges, not only for the use of their Brothers inside Matsqui Institution but also for Brothers imprisoned in other institutions across Canada. Jill and Ken, the two staff escorts, had been invited to attend an Aboriginal Programs conference in Saskatchewan and had agreed to drive their own vehicles the fifteen hundred miles in order to take some of the lava rock to prisoners in Saskatchewan Penitentiary. The prisoners at Matsqui Institution, by making this gift to their Saskatchewan Brothers, would be physically and symbolically acknowledging the common experience of all Brothers in prison and their shared search along the Red Road. That contribution and sharing would be made possible with the direct assistance of these correctional officers, who, both metaphorically and literally, would be part of that Red Road.

After lunch, it was time to start back. Along the way to Lillooet we stopped twice, the first time to gather yarrow, which is used by the Elders for making medicines, and then to gather willow for use in the sweat lodge. On both occasions the Brothers left tobacco as an offering. The willow would be used to construct an altar in the sweat lodge, where Dennis Bigsky himself would be undergoing a four-day fast.

In Lillooet we stopped briefly to get a punctured tire repaired. As we waited outside the shop in the intense heat, John Ironchild squatted down on his haunches and responded in kind to a dog barking about a hundred yards away. The interchange caused Cory Bitternose to reflect that since going to prison two years ago he had not seen or heard a dog. The comment brought into sharp relief how disconnected prisoners are from the world and how different this day was from yesterday and would be from tomorrow.

By the time the tire was fixed, we were all tired, greyed with road dust, and ready for a swim. We pulled off at a campsite next to Cayoosh Creek, a fast-flowing stream that enters the Fraser River just below Lillooet. It was not deep enough for swimming, but that did not discourage Ken, who waded into the water in his runners and socks, only to have his feet knocked out from under him by the current. We all laughed at the absurdity of this macho correctional supervisor sitting fully clothed in Cayoosh Creek being watched by four Matsqui prisoners, one woman liaison officer, and a law professor. However, we were not to remain observers for long. John quickly stripped down to a pair of swimming shorts and soon he too was sitting in the water. Caught up in the spirit of things, Cory and I stripped down to our underwear and joined the other two in the water. As I tentatively stepped across the slippery rocks, Ken and John splashed me from head to foot. Jill and Cheam maintained the dignity of the group by limiting their disrobing to their feet.

Thus refreshed, we returned to the road. Outside Lytton we stopped at a field of sagebrush and all gathered armfuls. The sun had dipped to the other side of the mountain, and its refracted rays cast a blue glow over the alpine forest that contrasted with the pale green of the sagebrush. The Brothers moved quietly amongst the waist-high brush, gathering what would be needed in the weeks ahead—and, I suspected, stocking up on the feel and smell of freedom that would be theirs for only a few more hours.

During the drive through the Fraser Canyon to Boston Bar, I reviewed for Cory and Cheam the history of the struggle for recognition of Aboriginal spirituality in federal institutions, a history new to them. The discussion traced the rise of the American Indian Movement, the events at Wounded Knee (which took place when Cory was still an infant), and the relationship between Aboriginal political struggles outside of prison and those inside.

We stopped for dinner and then again for dessert at a Dairy Queen, where Jill bought everyone an ice-cream cone. From there, the two vehicles moved down Highway 1 back to Abbotsford and "the Squi." We got to the gates at about 10:50 p.m. The original plan was that Ken would drive the dump truck into the institution and together we would unload the lava rock. However, everyone was so tired that, instead, the dump truck was left outside the gates overnight, the unloading to await the morrow. Ken told the men he would go inside with them and try to make arrangements for them to have a shower before they went back to their cells. I shook hands with everybody and, and as the four Brothers headed back into prison, headed down freedom's highway to my home in Vancouver.

Cory Bitternose, in a letter he later wrote to Warden Brock, explained what the day had meant to him.

I would like to thank you for giving me the chance to go out and collect the spiritual supplies needed for the sweat lodge area.

It was almost two years since I walked outside the wall without handcuffs and shackles. The experience was really overwhelming. I looked at the world in such a different way. Before, because of the drugs and alcohol and my troublesome upbringing, I never looked at the world that way. The two men, Mike and Ken, treated us like human beings, with respect and also with sensitivity towards our spiritual needs and towards our spiritual healing. The sweat lodge has become an important part of my life. It's not easy mind you. I am young and I make mistakes but I keep pushing myself.

The one thing that I am most assured of is my sobriety. I have been sober and drug-free for almost two years. When I first sobered up it was inside prison. I went through the DTs for about six weeks and then it really hit me, the things I had done. I hurt a lot of people in my life and took so much.

Now while following the direction of the elders, spiritual advisors, pipe carriers, I have found a way of life which has been there all along. I have replaced and changed that irresponsible hurt young man that I used to be, to be a responsible hard-working, eager, giving, loving, young man that I am now.

I can never undo the things that I've done. I wish I could but I can't. I look at it in a more positive attitude though, I now know where it (drugs, alcohol, violence, selfishness, gambling) all leads to because I lived through it. I'm only 23 years old, my peers laugh at me because I act and sound like an old man, but I call it growing up, I call it doing something about my life.

All these things went through my mind on that day of the temporary absence, especially on that mountain. There is a lot more but my letter has kinda got long. There is another person I would like to acknowledge, and that is Jill. I never met a lady like that before, so willing to help. I don't know if she knows it but it's that sensitivity that helps us grow and it's that sensitivity which reflects to all your staff, a lot of the Brothers look at them as human beings.

Again, I would like to thank you. (Letter from Cory Bitternose to Warden Roger Brock, Matsqui Institution, August 30, 1993)

This remarkable day achieved even more significance when, two months later, in October 1993, I participated in the Second International Symposium on the Future of Corrections, held in Popowa, Poland. The Symposium was jointly sponsored by the Correctional Service of Canada and the Polish Ministry of Justice, and it was a follow-up to a 1991 conference held in Ottawa. The purpose of the second conference was to develop a strategic framework for correctional policy and practice, and the delegates included representatives from many of the former Soviet Republics, Poland, the Czech Republic, the Slovak Republic, and Hungary, together with representatives from the Scandinavian countries, Western Europe, England and Scotland, South Africa, Australia, the United States, and Canada. Although I was 7,000 miles from Matsqui, my presence at the Popowa conference was very much informed by the work I had been doing there. I had been asked to prepare a paper for the opening session designed to look at prison systems from different perspectives. My presentation was entitled "The Experience and Perspectives of Canada's Indigenous Peoples," and its centrepiece was a description of the Red Road—a term which had a very different resonance in an Eastern Europe emerging from the grip of Communism. Through the use of slides that depicted my journey with the four Brothers gathering lava rock and the remarkable wall paintings in the Brotherhood's meeting room at Matsqui, I endeavoured to explain the healing journey of indigenous prisoners, which formed the foundation of an individual and collective strategic framework of their own making. In a way I could never have predicted, the images, voices, and experiences of indigenous prisoners from Matsqui were shared with delegates from around the world in a common search for correctional initiatives that support the development of a just, peaceful, and safe society.

## CHAPTER 3

# Operation Big Scoop

The journey along the Red Road in which I had participated on Friday, August 20, 1993, could not have stood in starker relief to the events that unfolded at Matsqui the following Monday, August 23. Those events set in motion another correctional journey, which ended with thirteen prisoners being taken to the segregation unit. This operation—code-named "Operation Big Scoop"—took place under the imprimatur of the same warden who had authorized the escorted temporary passes for the Aboriginal prisoners, and was carried out under the authority of the same legal framework, the *Corrections and Conditional Release Act.* Friday's journey, although taking place along public roads, was a private one, the full significance and effects of which were known only to those who participated; by contrast, Operation Big Scoop, while taking place within the private world of the prison, was a public event, and its significance and effects within the prison community were far more pervasive.

## Monday, August 23—Officer Down!

On Monday, August 23, I spent the day at Matsqui interviewing prisoners in the case management building, and just before 4:00 p.m. went to review some files in the records room. I heard some shouting at the other end of the corridor and came out into the hall to see one of the case management officers, Mike Boileau, slumped on the floor with blood streaming down his face. Mr. Boileau had been interviewing a prisoner, Dennis McLaren, who had six months earlier been returned to Matsqui from Elbow Lake minimum security camp. Mr. McLaren had appeared before the Parole Board in June, and although he was denied parole at that time because he did not have a suitable release plan, the Parole Board set a further review date for August 1993, with the expectation that a proper plan would then be placed before them. The paperwork necessary for Mr. McLaren's parole hearing had not been prepared, and Mr. Boileau, who had recently taken over Mr. McLaren's case, was explaining the reasons for the delay. Mr. McLaren, dissatisfied with the explanation and the consequence that his August hearing would have to be postponed, became very angry and punched Mr. Boileau in the face, knocking him to the ground. Another staff member, Tony Gagné, intervened and wrestled Mr. McLaren down. Someone pressed the emergency button, and other officers rushed to the case management building, where Mr. McLaren was taken into custody and escorted to the segregation unit. A nurse from the prison hospital was called to attend to Mr. Boileau, who was taken by wheelchair first to the prison hospital and then to the outside hospital in Abbotsford. All of this happened just minutes before the staff in the case management building normally leave at the end of the day. Because there was no psychologist in the institution, the normal debriefing for staff who had witnessed a major incident could not be carried out. However, the warden asked all of the case management people to meet in the Visiting and Correspondence area to give everyone a chance to catch their breath before going home. He indicated that a full debriefing would be held the next day.

(Unless otherwise indicated, the source of material presented in this chapter is my research notes made contemporaneously with the events described.)

## Tuesday, August 24—A Warden Takes Charge

The harsh reality of Mike Boileau's broken face was in the forefront of Warden Brock's agenda at the morning briefing the next day, August 24. He referred to "a deteriorating climate" at Matsqui, the attack on Mike Boileau being the most recent and serious example. He pointed to the incident the previous week in which a prisoner had been attacked with a weight bar by another prisoner on one of the breezeways, and stated that he had become increasingly concerned about reports of disrespectful behaviour by prisoners towards staff. Warden Brock informed his senior staff (the briefing was attended by the deputy warden, unit managers, heads of divisions, and some correctional supervisors, as well as myself) that it was time to take immediate and firm measures. Doug Richmond, Acting Deputy Warden, informed the group that on Thursday there would be a strategy meeting with the institutional preventive security officers (IPSOs) and selected staff to share information and to identify those prisoners who were the instigators regarding drugs, muscling, home brew, and other problems in the institution. As Mr. Richmond put it, "It's only 5 per cent of the inmates who cause 95 per cent of all the problems." Warden Brock added, "The power we have over the inmates is in information and organization." He hoped the strategy identified by Doug Richmond would ensure that the institution used its information sources more effectively. He concluded with this comment: "There are certain times when you make decisions based upon gut reaction, and now is the time at Matsqui to take the institution by the scruff of its neck in order to get its problems under control."

A correctional supervisor briefed the meeting on events subsequent to the Boileau assault and reported that five prisoners had been "boxed"—placed in segregation—after they were heard by staff to make derogatory remarks suggesting their approval of the assault. The night before, in segregation, these prisoners had been loud and disruptive. Warden Brock stated, "They will not come out [of segregation] quickly and I want them charged." He also observed that, as a result of the planned crackdown on instigators, the institution would be needing all the space they could get in segregation, and therefore there was to be no tolerance of any disruptive activity there. If the five men kept it up, he wanted transfer packages written so they could be shipped to Kent. "There is to be zero tolerance for mouthing off in the institution." The warden ended his plan of action by stating that, in asking staff to come forward with information they had regarding troublemakers, he did not expect them to act as lawyers, with clear proof of guilt. In due course, the gist of this information would be shared with prisoners. Warden Brock, looking in my direction, characterized his approach as acting "in accordance with the duty to act fairly, quickly."

Following the morning briefing, I attended a further debriefing by an institutional psychologist for those who had been involved in the incident on Monday. The session provided me with important insights into the staff response to the events. Statements from the staff who had directly observed the confrontation between Dennis McLaren and Mike Boileau traced the following trajectory of events. Mr. McLaren had come into the case management building on a number of occasions earlier in the afternoon asking to see Mr. Boileau about his parole. He appeared to be getting increasingly worked up, and eventually the receptionist asked Mr. Boileau if he would see him. Mr. Boileau took Mr. McLaren into his office. Brian Furman, another case management officer, heard Mr. McLaren raise his voice several times, and so he kept his door open in case his assistance was needed. However, things seemed to calm down, and Mr. Furman closed his door to better concentrate on a report he was preparing. This was shortly after 3:00 p.m. After seeing Mr. McLaren, Mike Boileau left his office and went to the front of the case management building, followed by Mr. McLaren. There was a heated exchange between the two. Some papers that should have been prepared for a parole hearing had not been prepared, with the result that Mr. McLaren was not going to appear before the Parole Board at its next sitting at Matsqui. Mr. Boileau had taken over Mr. McLaren's case just three weeks before, and he was trying to explain that it was not his fault the paperwork had not been done. Mr. McLaren, for his part, was trying to explain his frustration that nothing had been done. Mr. McLaren became increasingly angry and was standing inches away from Mr. Boileau's face.

Tony Gagné, who was dictating a report in the interview room, came out upon hearing the raised voices, went up to Mr. McLaren, took him by the arm and told him to calm down, step outside and discuss what was happening. Mr. Gagné thought that Mr. McLaren was going to come with him. Instead Mr. McLaren ran at Mr. Boileau and hit him hard enough to knock him to the ground, splitting his nose open. Several of the clerks heard the sickening sound of bone crunching; the next thing they saw was blood all over the place. While Mr. Boileau was on the floor, Mr. McLaren kept punching him. Mr. Gagné jumped on Mr. McLaren and tried to drag him off. Eventually Mr. Gagné grabbed Mr. McLaren's hair, pulled him off Mr. Boileau, and ended up landing on his back with Mr. McLaren on top of him. At that point, Mr. Gagné told the debriefing, he and Mr. McLaren locked eyes, and Mr. Gagné thought that it was his turn to get hit. Mr. McLaren, however, made no move to hit him, allowed himself to be restrained, and was held over by the front desk until other security came onto the scene. In the course of the scuffle Mr. Gagné was hit on the cheek, but thought that this was done not by Mr. McLaren but by Mr. Boileau's knee.

Mr. Boileau had staggered out of the room where he had fallen, bleeding extensively from the nose. Maria Parton, another of the case management officers, explained that when she went into the washroom looking for paper towels to stem the flow of blood, she remembered that you could stop blood flow by pinching the nose. She tried to apply this technique, but Mr. Boileau, who by this time was sitting on the floor, recoiled in pain. This was the point at which I had first seen Mr. Boileau after hearing the commotion. Several other security staff came into the building and sat down by Mr. Boileau, trying to comfort him. He was still bleeding profusely and was clearly in a state of shock. A nurse was called and eventually he was placed in a wheelchair and taken to the prison hospital. The staff there called for an ambulance, and he was taken to the MSA Hospital in Abbotsford. He was treated for a fractured nose and cuts to his cheek and the bridge of his nose.

The discussion in the second round of the debriefing centred on the helplessness felt by a number of staff. The female clerks and receptionist talked about their vulnerability. "What would have happened," they asked, "had Mr. McLaren gone after one of us?" The receptionist, who was employed as a temporary worker through an agency and had no special training for the job, talked about her concerns as the person who often had to tell prisoners that they could not see their case management officer, either because the officer did not want to see the prisoner or because the officer was unavailable. There had been another incident the year previous in which a prisoner came over the desk at the entrance;

although the receptionist at the time had escaped injury, the assault of Mr. Boileau clearly revived concerns about staff vulnerability.

I was impressed by the fact that debriefing had become a regular procedure for staff who experienced incidents that could give rise to post-traumatic stress. The opportunity for the staff to revisit their experiences and hear others express their feelings had a reassuring impact. The solicitude for staff welfare must, however, be contrasted with the response to those prisoners who observed, from their cells, Mr. Boileau being wheeled out, bleeding, and were alleged to have made remarks suggesting they derived pleasure from the fact that an officer had been assaulted. These comments were met with the immediate response of placing the men in segregation.

The comments made by the prisoners were clearly insensitive. As an example, one of the prisoners was heard to say, "It looks good on you." In trying to understand such callousness, it should be remembered that more than a few of the prisoners I interviewed at Matsqui had bitter memories of being the subject of what they viewed as unprovoked assaults by prison officers and police officers; seeing a staff member suffer the same fate may have revived some of these memories. Post-traumatic stress works both ways. Yet the response of the institutional authorities was not to involve the prisoners in debriefing but to place them in segregation. While this might be justified on the basis of trying to prevent the spread of anti-authoritarian sentiment among the prison population at a critical moment, the more understandable explanation is that the staff were genuinely incensed at the insensitivity demonstrated by the prisoners. The decision to segregate these prisoners was not so much a principled decision based upon the need to prevent further violence but rather a visceral reaction based upon anger.

In the course of the debriefing, I heard that one of the prisoners taken to segregation after the assault was Dave Humphries. I was surprised to hear this, because I had interviewed Mr. Humphries the previous week, and he had emphasized that he was impressed with how many staff had demonstrated real compassion for his situation and had gone out of their way to help him. Moreover, he had just been granted a day parole to Sumas Centre, which was due to go into effect the following week. Why would someone who spoke so respectfully about staff and was on the verge of leaving the institution commit an act likely to jeopardize any chance of release? On my way up to segregation to interview Mr. Humphries again, I was stopped by another prisoner who told me that the remark the staff had attributed to Mr. Humphries—"It looks good on you"— had actually been made by him and that he was prepared to go to the warden and tell him that, because it was not fair that Mr. Humphries had been "scooped" for something he had not done.

When I interviewed Mr. Humphries, he seemed genuinely shocked to find himself placed in segregation on the eve of being paroled. He explained that on

Monday afternoon he had been told by another prisoner that a staff member had been assaulted and that there was going to be a lock-down. Mr. Humphries went to his cell before this occurred. This was his normal pattern, because he did not like to have the doors closed on him—he preferred to do it himself. He watched a television program, and then at about 5:00 p.m. his door flew open and a bunch of officers came in, told him to stand up, pushed him against the wall, had him spread his legs, and handcuffed him behind his back. He asked why and was told he would learn that soon enough. On the way down to segregation he asked again why he was being taken to the hole. He was told that "diarrhoea of the mouth is just as bad" and that he would be notified of the reasons for his being in segregation in due course. At around 10:00 p.m. he was given a segregation review notice, which stated that he had been heard making a derogatory remark after a staff member had been hurt.

On my way down from the segregation unit on Tuesday I spoke briefly with Mike Csoka, the correctional supervisor for the segregation unit. Mr. Csoka stated that he had some reservations about Dave Humphries' involvement and that he, too, had heard another prisoner was volunteering he was the culprit. Mike Csoka thought this was believable, since the other prisoner was the type of person who would make that kind of comment. I then met with Darryl Ghostkeeper, the chairman of the Inmate Committee (elected by the prison population, with a mandate to represent the interests of prisoners in dealing with CSC management), who told me that he had already had a meeting with the warden and had raised the Committee's concern that Mr. Humphries was being unfairly kept in segregation. He had also raised with the warden the fact that Mr. Badari, one of the other prisoners taken to segregation, alleged that the guards who took him to segregation used unnecessary force and after he was handcuffed had smashed him into one of the barriers.

I went to the correctional operations room in search of Acting Deputy Warden Doug Richmond, and on my way met Warden Brock heading in the same direction for an end-of-the-day briefing. He invited me to attend. At the meeting the Warden brought up the Inmate Committee's concern that unreasonable force had been used against prisoner Badari in taking him to segregation, and reported that he had requested a senior staff member from the Regional Psychiatric Centre be sent over to conduct an internal investigation into the allegation. Mr. Richmond, in reviewing the information received during the day, commented that although he had been told that the prisoner who made the derogatory remark was not Mr. Humphries, the staff member who had reported it, the hobby officer, was quite clear in her mind that following the derogatory statement someone had laughed out loud, that it was a deep laugh, and that it was Mr. Humphries'. Before leaving the institution I went to the walkway outside the case management building and looked up to the third floor, the floor where Dave Humphries' cell was located. I had difficulty seeing how anyone standing on the walkway could identify who had made a statement or laughed on the third floor, particularly at a time when emotions were heated.

## Wednesday, August 25—A Prisoner's Perspective

The next day, Wednesday, August 25, Warden Brock gave staff an update on Mike Boileau's condition. Although his nose was broken and he had been in great pain initially, there appeared to be no major damage to his face and he was resting at home. It would likely be some weeks before he could return to work. Later in the day, I spoke with Ron Tessier, the other prisoner representative on the Inmate Committee. Mr. Tessier gave me his view of the assault. It had become apparent to a number of prisoners that Mr. McLaren was wound up and extremely frustrated by the lack of progress on the paperwork for his parole, and Mr. Tessier found it difficult to believe that the staff had not been aware of this. (As I have pointed out, the receptionist in the case management building had noticed Mr. McLaren's increasingly agitated behaviour.) Mr. Tessier doubted Dennis McLaren had it in for Mike Boileau in particular. It was probably a generalized frustration at the system that caused Mr. McLaren to strike out. He was not trying to justify what Mr. McLaren had done, but said the institution should understand that for a guy who was "hanging on the gate to be told that the paperwork had not been done, even if it is not the particular officer's fault, doesn't cut much ice when it means the prisoner may have to spend unnecessarily another month or two in prison."

Revealingly, Ron Tessier pointed to a systemic problem in case management—the lack of timely preparation of reports—as the principal cause for this incident. Staff, on the other hand, identified the principal cause as the inherently violent propensities of many of the prisoners at Matsqui and the lack of effective protection for the staff against them.

## Thursday, August 26, 8:30 a.m.—The Morning Briefing

On Thursday, August 26, I attended the morning briefing. The first issue raised was that two prisoners now alleged they had been subject to excessive force while being taken to segregation after the assault on Mike Boileau. Acting Deputy Warden Richmond reported that he had spoken to the two prisoners. The first, Mr. Barry, admitted that he had mouthed off at the guards and probably deserved what had happened to him, and he did not wish to lay charges against the officers or have the police involved. The second prisoner, Mr. Badari, said that he did want to lay charges; he had asked to talk to someone at Prisoners' Legal Services but had been told by the officer on duty in segregation that he could phone the next day. Mr. Richmond told Mr. Badari that he could phone right then and there. This gave rise to a direction by Warden Brock that he did not want anyone in segregation who asked to contact a lawyer to be told to wait until the next day; they were to be given telephone access immediately, because the institution would be "raked over the coals" if they denied access to lawyers. Warden Brock stated that he ran "an open show" and wanted the institution itself to contact the RCMP and let them interview the two prisoners; in the long run it was in the best interests of the institution to show that they had nothing to hide. In relation to the Badari allegations, the warden said he understood that Mr. Badari was videotaped while being taken up to segregation and therefore the tape would be important evidence. He was advised, however, that the staff member operating the video camera was inexperienced and there had been no film in the camera. Warden Brock became visibly upset and asked if anyone remembered what had happened to Richard Nixon.

The tracking meeting to identify the troublemakers in Matsqui was scheduled for 1:30 that afternoon, and all available staff were encouraged to attend. The warden, in characterizing his strategy, said that while there was a need to maintain balance and the prisoners had to feel that they were being dealt with fairly, decisions necessary to maintain control in the institution must be taken.

## 9:30 a.m.—The Segregation Review Board

Following the morning debriefing, the Segregation Review Board convened. The first cases reviewed were those of the prisoners taken to segregation for making derogatory remarks after the assault of Mike Boileau. Mr. Barry had been segregated the day after the assault on Mr. Boileau. He had been late for work and, when challenged by a staff member, remarked, "Maybe more of you guys should get it." Mike Csoka, the correctional supervisor for segregation, informed the Board that Mr. Barry had apologized and admitted it was a stupid remark. The Board agreed that he should be returned to the population.

Mr. Slater, who had been taken to segregation immediately after the incident, had told Mr. Csoka he thought it was a sex offender who had been assaulted and not a staff member. Although Mr. Csoka did not buy this story, he advised the Board that Mr. Slater had agreed to write a personal letter of apology to Mr. Boileau. The Board agreed that he also should be released to the population.

The Board was advised there had been a mix-up regarding Mr. Elgin, a third prisoner taken to segregation. Although staff had initially thought he was involved in making derogatory remarks, it turned out that this was not the case. The charges that had been written up against Mr. Elgin would be withdrawn. That left two other prisoners, Mr. Humphries and Mr. Badari. In Mr. Humphries' case, it was determined that since there was some uncertainty about whether he had made the remarks attributed to him, it would not be appropriate to interfere with his day parole plans. The Board agreed that Mr. Humphries should be released from segregation.

Mr. Csoka advised the Board that Mr. Badari was the only one of the men who had fought with the staff when being taken up to segregation, and that he understood Mr. Badari was being considered for an involuntary transfer to Kent. This version contrasted with what I had previously heard, that it was Mr. Badari who, while handcuffed, had been pushed against the barriers by the staff. The Board determined that Mr. Badari would remain in segregation pending a decision on whether an involuntary transfer would be initiated.

## 1:30 p.m.—The Tracking Meeting

In the afternoon I met with Warden Brock to confirm that it would be appropriate for me to come to the tracking meeting. He said he had no difficulty with this, as he recognized that the more I knew about institutional life, the more informed my assessment of the overall situation would be. Some lawyers he had dealt with heard only the prisoner's side of the story, he said, and so they never had anything to balance it against. He believed that the traditional way of looking at prison society as "them and us" was outdated. Within the prison community there were diverse interests both among prisoners and among staff; as warden, he saw himself in the role of a mayor, making political decisions in the context of competing choices, although he acknowledged that the warden of a federal penitentiary had an enormous amount of power, probably more than most mayors. His objective this particular week was to change the culture of Matsqui, particularly the lack of respect being shown staff and the high levels of drug and alcohol use. His strategy was to identify and remove from the general population the 5 to 10 per cent of prisoners who caused most of the problems; this strategy had been successful at Mission, when he was warden there, in changing the climate of the prison. After removing the troublemakers, there had been a noticeable reduction of tension, he said; people smiled more and there was a general easing of relationships.

The outstanding questions for me were whether this strategy would be carried out in a way consistent with the law and the duty to act fairly, and whether it would properly balance the institutional interest in maintaining a peaceful institution with the rights of prisoners. The meeting that afternoon would provide the answers.

The tracking meeting convened at 1:30 p.m. in the Officers' Trailer. There were about forty staff members, with a very heavy concentration of correctional supervisors and correctional officers (CO-II's and CO-I's). Only three of nine case management officers attended—one from each unit—together with the coordinator of case management. Also attending were a number of senior administrators, including the warden, the acting deputy warden, and some heads of divisions.

Warden Brock started the meeting by explaining the purpose of the afternoon's session. He talked about the "biorhythm" of an institution, its ups and downs, and said that he wanted to "take the head off" an arrhythmic cycle to reduce tension. There had been lately at Matsqui an increase in assaults on staff and on prisoners. The level of mouthing off by prisoners to staff had increased, and he wanted to cut this off before it reached a crescendo. Every six to nine months the anti-social part of the prison population established a highly negative influence on the culture of the institution, he said. He was not interested in hard evidentiary proof of anything; he was more interested in the gut reactions and instincts of the participants as experienced officers who dealt directly with prisoners and were aware of their associations. Their collective task was to see what they could put together on the people who were identified as troublemakers.

The IPSOs had taped to the walls some large pieces of paper bearing prisoners' names. These were the prisoners the IPSOs had identified from their files as the "wheels"—those who had the most influence and caused the most problems at Matsqui. The purpose of the exercise, as described by the warden, was to get everyone's input into whether these were indeed the problem prisoners, to list their associates, and to identify other troublemakers. This would create a large list of names that later could be whittled down to the maybe twenty prisoners about which there was agreement. A staff member asked whether the purpose of the exercise was to identify the twenty most influential or most disruptive prisoners. Although Warden Brock did not give a clear answer, he did talk about the need to identify those prisoners who raised the tension level in the institution. As he put it, "Who are those people who, when they walk down the range, there is a chill?"

The warden, in elaborating on his strategy, said that individual plans would be developed in relation to these twenty or so prisoners. In some cases, the best way to respond would be to remove the leader of a group by a transfer. In other cases it might be better to go to the second or third man in the group because, if the leader was removed, the person or persons who replaced him might be even worse. Another factor to be considered was getting "the best bang for your buck." As he put it, "We will have to spend a lot of resources in order to transfer someone to higher security, particularly in terms of the case management staff who would have to prepare the packages." However, transfer was not the only option. Some people might be "boxed" in segregation. Once there, they could be told that the institution knew what they were up to, and that might be enough to bring them around. In other cases, warning them could be combined with a behavioural contract prior to their release to the population. As to the segregation strategy, Warden Brock said, "Our people upstairs [in the segregation unit] have obliged us by making thirteen beds available, so that is not a problem." It became clear to me that the decision of the Segregation Review Board earlier in the day to release a number of prisoners from segregation had been made in order to create room for the anticipated new arrivals.

For the next half hour or so staff members peppered the IPSOs with names of the associates of the men identified on the walls. It was a free-wheeling affair in which some prisoners were identified not by their name but by the range they were on and what they looked like. In some cases, a prisoner was identified by one staff member, and then information about him was confirmed by other staff. In other cases, staff members disagreed among themselves about the involvement of prisoners. This did not, however, prevent those prisoners' names from being placed on the lists. One correctional officer made the point that none of the prisoners identified initially by the IPSOs were members of the "French Connection," and a separate list was created for francophone prisoners. Another list was then put up for white supremacists, and this list included a couple of Asian prisoners. This raised a query from one staff member about how an Asian person could be part of the white supremacist group. The answer given was that it was "a business relationship." Another group identified was referred to as the punks or "shitheads." I asked Mike Csoka, who was sitting next to me, what the difference was; he said that shitheads did not take care of their appearance or their cells. A number of inmates were quickly added to this list.

Although the purpose of the exercise was to get a pool of information, a number of the prisoners whose names were posted were identified principally by one staff member. For example, Greg Hanson was identified by a correctional supervisor based on his behaviour in segregation the previous week. The prisoner was described as "smooth as butter" in his dealings face to face with staff but "when your back is turned he is completely different." Richard Ambrose was identified by a staff member as someone who was involved in handling money in the institution and who had a lot of influence.

"Influence" was also the basis for targeting other prisoners. Art Winters was identified by several staff members as the very influential leader of an Edmonton group who had transferred to Matsqui several months earlier and taken over the Lifers' canteen. This group was said to be waiting in the wings to take over the institution; they had little time for drug users. There was a lot of discussion regarding Darryl Ghostkeeper and Ron Tessier, members of the Inmate Committee. Mr. Ghostkeeper was believed to be heavily involved in drug use, and his position as president of both the Inmate Committee and the Native Brotherhood was seen as a conflict of interest. The Native Liaison Officer observed that Mr. Ghostkeeper's drug problem was well known to the Brothers and that the Native Elder, Pat Henrickson, was spending a lot of time with him trying to address it. Ron Tessier was identified as being influential also in the francophone group and with the drug group.

Within half an hour there were fifty to sixty names on the lists. The warden announced that there would be only two minutes more for listing names and commented that it was interesting that the whole population (some four hundred prisoners) did not appear on the wall but only selected prisoners. He saw this as confirmation of the fact that only a minority of prisoners were the real problem. In my view, however, the limitation to only fifty or sixty names was purely a product of the amount of time allowed for the exercise.

The warden then explained that the second stage of the exercise would identify a smaller group who merited specific strategies. However, the only strategy he mentioned was putting the members of this group in segregation. One staff member said that the punks should be taken off the list because they could be handled in the population one on one. Another staff member said that the Edmonton group should be taken off the list because they had not yet made their move. If Mr. Ghostkeeper and Mr. Tessier were removed from the Inmate Committee and put in segregation, the leaders of the Edmonton group would probably take their place, he said; that group would be easier to deal with and would have a more positive influence on the population.

One staff member very pointedly asked the warden, "How are you going to do this legally?" Warden Brock's response was, "We have information on a lot of these guys. Once we have got them upstairs [in segregation], we don't have to follow through with involuntary transfers. When they are sitting upstairs knowing that they could face transfers, they may turn around. If they don't, then we'll follow through." The warden was also asked the question, "Are we going to throw out all the rules?" His answer was that no one had any confidence in the intelligence system through which the IPSOs currently gathered information; what was going on that afternoon was a different process. The question of the legality of the exercise was not really answered.

As three o'clock drew near, attention focussed on drawing up the final list of individuals who would be segregated. This list was assembled quickly, in a quite extraordinary way: staff would shout out the name of a particular prisoner, and the name would then be written on a flip chart. There was no attempt to see if there was consensus on any particular name. In the case of one prisoner—Mike Miller—his case management officer clearly stated that he ought not to be on the list, but he remained on it anyway. Another prisoner, Peter Paquette, was more fortunate. A number of security staff identified Mr. Paquette as a negative influence. The Native Liaison Officer managed to persuade people that Mr. Paquette was not active, however, and was interested only in getting out of prison. His name, therefore, was not included. The last two names were added in the final moments of the meeting.

There was no attempt during the meeting to determine whether information was reliable, corroborated, or recent. Indeed, several prisoners initially identified as troublemakers were no longer in the institution; in one case, the prisoner had not been in the institution for several months. To my mind, this cast doubt on the credibility of the staff members' sense of who the movers and shakers were and who had current influence in the institution. The final list of eleven included seven prisoners I had previously interviewed. The other four prisoners I did not know. The meeting broke up with the indication that these eleven prisoners would be scooped the next day.

One remarkable feature of the tracking meeting was the minimal participation of the three case management officers present. Case management officers are responsible for preparing progress summaries relating to parole and transfer, critical documents in determining a prisoner's future. CMOs participate in the Performance Boards and present cases for Escorted Temporary Absences (ETAS) at the Temporary Absence Board. Within the system, they are the key players in terms of synthesizing information and reflecting it in documents for decision-makers. The tracking meeting was designed to improve the flow of information, with the maximum involvement of all staff. Yet CMOs were underrepresented, and even though the IPSOs had identified ten high-profile individuals at the outset, no effort was made to ensure that the CMOs for those prisoners were present. The final list was compiled without any effective contribution from the CMOs, and, in the case of one prisoner, in the face of the CMO's opposition.

At the end of the tracking meeting, the warden announced that, in order to implement the strategy, he would be meeting further with the unit managers. At 3:30 p.m., that meeting was convened in the warden's office. Unit Manager Irv Hammond observed that the final list of eleven men had emerged very late in the meeting and did not bear much relationship to the original list of ten prisoners selected by the IPSOs. The final list included two prisoners from the francophone group, two from the Lifers, two from the white supremacists, and two from the Native Brotherhood, and he said "off the top" that there were at least three men on the list for whom the institution had no file material to justify either segregation or transfer. Mr. Csoka did not see this as a problem, since the point of the exercise was to identify who was causing problems. From his perspective, the list had correctly identified the most influential individuals in the main groups. He strongly disagreed that the list should be changed in any way, because the staff who had participated in the tracking meeting expected that those prisoners would be taken out of the population. The warden replied that he was not concerned about changing the final composition of the list and believed the staff would understand if it was explained to them that, after further consideration, some prisoners were not included. The meeting concluded with a discussion on the timing of the removal of the men from the population. A consensus emerged among the unit managers that the best time to do the removal would be at lunch the next day, when the prisoners were back in their cells.

I found the afternoon's events remarkable; had I not been there and seen how the decision to segregate the eleven prisoners was made, I would not have believed it. The process was as far removed from principled decision-making as one could conceive. What I saw that afternoon were collective and generalized gut reactions forming the basis for making major decisions affecting prisoners' lives. Yet this strategy was designed and approved by a progressive and thoughtful warden who clearly accepted the duty to act fairly as a general principle and sought to encourage his staff to act in accordance with it. Based on my conversations with him, I knew the warden saw the afternoon's decisions as consistent with that principle, because prisoners would be told the basis upon which they had been segregated or were being recommended for transfer. The bottom line, however, was that the decision to segregate was not based on a careful assessment of the evidence available, not properly corroborated from reliable sources, and not evaluated against the criteria of the *Corrections and Conditional Release Act.* The segregation decision was the product of a group consciousness, the "voltgeist" of the particular group of staff assembled in the Officers' Trailer. As the tracking meeting progressed, I had had the uneasy feeling I was witnessing a military operation that violated almost every principle of fundamental fairness. Once these eleven men were segregated, the duty to act fairly would be deployed to sanitize decisions based upon the afternoon's exchange of information; further documentation and file information, far from being the basis for the decision, would be the *ex post facto* rationalization. In other words, the law and the fundamental principles of fairness, instead of channelling decisions, were to be used as screens to legitimize decisions made upon entirely different grounds and through an entirely different process than that envisaged by the legislation.

The extent of my unease had become manifest when, between the tracking meeting and the meeting in the warden's office, I went back to the case management building to pick up my briefcase. Along the walkway I passed four of the men whose names were among those to be segregated the next day. I knew that they were going to be segregated; I also felt that the process by which the decision had been made was fundamentally flawed. However, my position as researcher and my undertaking that any information I heard in the course of the meeting would not be shared with individual prisoners prevented me from telling them that by this time the next day they would be in the hole. In the notes I dictated later that evening, I observed that even recalling the moment when I passed the four prisoners was painful. Conducting my research and temporarily withdrawing from my normal role as an advocate for prisoners required that I make difficult compromises. I reflected that this particular compromise would ultimately be justified by the publication of what had happened that day, and that such publication might protect other prisoners from the same arbitrary imprisonment.

## Friday, August 27—The Scoop

On Friday, August 27, when I arrived at Matsqui at 8:20 a.m., the institution was in a lock-down position. I went to the correctional operations building for a briefing and was told that the segregation of prisoners was just beginning. The boardroom in the operations building had been set aside as the command centre, and I was told that only designated individuals were to be admitted; the warden had named me as one of those select few. I was advised that the exercise had been assigned the code name "Operation Big Scoop." I asked whether the list of prisoners to be segregated had changed since yesterday. I was told that the unit managers and the IPSOs had met the previous evening and revised the list. Three men had been taken off the list on the basis that there was no information to justify their segregation. However, one of them had subsequently been restored to the list when the IPSOs provided new information. Three other men were added to the list on the basis of this further discussion, resulting in a final list of twelve prisoners. The beginning of the operation had also been pushed forward, from noon to 8:30 a.m.

Two squads had been formed to remove the prisoners from the living unit to segregation. Each squad had a video camera operator; and tear gas, which was under the exclusive control of the squad leader, had been issued. All prisoners were to remain locked in their cells until the operation was completed, which meant no breakfast. The operation was carried out in a military fashion; as each prisoner was taken to segregation, a message was radioed to the command centre that the prisoner had been removed. Darryl Ghostkeeper was the first person taken, followed by Ron Tessier. Mike Csoka, who was in command of one of the squads, came in during the operation and reported that the living unit was quiet; there had been no cat-calling, and it was clear that the population knew what was happening. The only problem occurred when Mr. Hurst, who was one of the ten prisoners originally designated by the IPSOs but was not on the final list, had mouthed off at the guards and said that he would get "the institution rocking." He was also taken to segregation. The whole operation took from about 8:30 to 10:00.

At the completion of the operation, there was a meeting in the warden's office. The warden announced that he wanted to restore the institution to normal as soon as possible. Staff should be talking to prisoners, smiling, asking them how they were doing, because, in his experience, prisoners took their cues from the staff, and if staff acted as if everything was back to normal, prisoners would follow suit. However, if the staff withdrew or demonstrated that they were apprehensive and fearful, this would quickly spread to the population. The warden also announced that he was going to meet with a small group of selected prisoners to explain to them what he had done. He had prepared a letter to be distributed to all prisoners and staff, setting out the reasons for his actions and his expectations for the future.

The warden then held a briefing meeting with a number of staff to thank them for their successful completion of the operation. Shortly thereafter, he convened the meeting with the selected prisoners. He briefly explained that his preemptive move had been made to reduce tension before matters got out of hand. Prisoner Tom Elton asked some very pointed questions of Warden Brock:

I can understand what's happened as a power thing. You've got to show that this is your prison and you're in control and we're just doing time here, but what I don't understand is why you had to use segregation. You said that you're going to do an investigation on these guys in the next week before you decide what you're going to do with them. My question is why you couldn't do that investigation first and then segregate them afterwards. I didn't think that you could use segregation unless guys had done something which represented an immediate threat, and it doesn't seem that these guys do.

The warden responded that this was a judgement call on his part and that he had no intention of keeping prisoners in segregation indefinitely. He stated that the IPSOs and the case management people would be reviewing the cases of all of these men individually, starting the following Monday.

During the course of the day, I made several observations that underlined the arbitrariness of the selection process for the prisoners who had been segregated. Art Winters, who had been identified by some staff members as the most influential of the Edmonton group, and therefore a troublemaker in waiting, was one of the prisoners selected to meet with the warden regarding the purpose of Operation Big Scoop. Rick Ambrose had been on the list of prisoners to be segregated at the conclusion of the tracking meeting, but after further discussions among the unit managers, his name was taken off the list. Mr. Ambrose was one of several prisoners brought down from the living unit before the general release of the population to start stocking up the canteen items in the Lifers' store. I saw him chatting amiably with the warden in the walkway; twelve hours before he had been designated a prime candidate for Operation Big Scoop.

Once the prisoners from the general population had been released from the living unit, it was clear their concerns were not limited to ensuring they could find supplies at the Lifers' store. As I moved along walkways and stopped to talk to prisoners, the primary question asked of me was whether what had been done was lawful. People told me that telephone calls had been made to Prisoners' Legal Services to secure the release of the men taken to segregation. The first challenge to the process came later in the afternoon when Beth Parkinson, a paralegal worker from Prisoners' Legal Services, phoned the warden, questioning the sufficiency of the notices of segregation served on the prisoners. Earlier in the day, when I was observing the implementation of Operation Big Scoop from the administration building, the question had arisen as to who would prepare the segregation notices to be served on the prisoners. Kevin Morgan, the acting unit manager for the segregation unit, was designated to do this. Another senior officer offered to help because he knew how to write these forms "creatively."

Initially, all the segregation notices gave the same reason for segregation: "You have been placed in segregation pending an investigation of inappropriate activity/behaviour within Matsqui Institution." When these notices were shown to the warden, he sent them back, saying that they did not contain enough detail. Revised notices were written, with added wording that varied from prisoner to prisoner. About half the notices were amended to read as follows: "You have been placed in segregation pending an investigation of inappropriate activity/behaviour within Matsqui Institution and your involvement in illegal drugs." Other notices also bore the words "and/or extortion."

I was in the warden's office when Beth Parkinson phoned him, and he invited me to stay and listen on the speaker phone to their conversation. Ms. Parkinson read out the segregation notices of three of the prisoners, Darryl Ghostkeeper, Ron Tessier, and Mike Miller. Mr. Tessier's and Mr. Ghostkeeper's notices contained exactly the same wording: "alleged involvement in illegal drugs and/or extortion." Mike Miller's referred merely to illegal drugs. In Ms. Parkinson's opinion, these notices did not meet the requirements of the CCRA, as they did not give the prisoner sufficient information to meet the case against him. As she put it, "All a prisoner can say in relation to these allegations is that they're not true." In her view, what the institution should have provided in relation to any prisoner's alleged involvement with drugs was the date on which the incident was supposed to have happened and the information on the type of drugs, the amount of drugs, and things of that nature. Warden Brock explained that the action had been taken because there were indications of rising tension in the institution in the form of assaults on staff and prisoners and the increased use of brew and drugs; he had segregated these prisoners on the basis of information that they were the principal instigators. He told her that the allegations would be evaluated individually and that this work would start on Monday.

Ms. Parkinson reminded him that under the CCR *Regulations,* segregation review notices with sufficient information had to be served within one working day of prisoners being placed in segregation (which was the following Monday). If the men in question were to be seen by the Segregation Review Board on the following Thursday for their mandatory five-day reviews, the *Regulations* required prisoners to receive three working days' notice of any material to which the Segregation Review Board would refer; this meant that that information also must be provided by the following Monday. She asked the warden to confirm that the information would be given to the prisoners on Monday; the warden said it would.

After this telephone conversation, the warden talked to me about the difficulty of balancing legal requirements with the responsibility to manage a safe institution. He said that if dynamic security—information flow and effective communication between staff and administration—had been operating properly, the IPSOs would have had properly documented files to provide information to these prisoners as to why they were being segregated. The reality was that this work had not been done, and clearly there was a gap in the information-collection process at Matsqui Institution. In effect, the warden was confirming my impression of the method used at the tracking meeting, which was to identify the prisoners first, then ask questions to fill in the gaps later.

Another observation I would make in assessing the warden's perception that Matsqui was in a phase of escalating tension and increasing violence is that the two major incidents he cited could be seen more appropriately as evidence of a different phenomenon: that is, the breakdown of some operational systems of staff and management. Following the attack by one prisoner on another with a weight bar, which had occurred the week before the Boileau incident, it was revealed that the staff had received information that this prisoner, while on parole, had assaulted the common-law wife of the prisoner who was alleged now to have assaulted him; this first prisoner should, therefore, never have been placed in the living unit. Had this preventive action been taken, there would have been no assault. One of the institutional psychologists shed further light on the attack on Mr. Boileau by Mr. McLaren. The psychologist told me that Mr. McLaren had had three different case management officers in the last two months, all of whom were supposed to do the paperwork necessary for his parole hearing. The first was someone who had just been made a case management officer and had proved not up to the task. He was replaced by someone in an acting position who had also not done the necessary work. She in turn was replaced by Mike Boileau, who had been in the job for only three weeks when the incident took place. Mike Boileau himself told the psychologist that he could well understand why Mr. McLaren was upset and that he had good reason for being so. This, of course, did not justify Mr. McLaren's assault. But if the system had operated the way it was supposed to, Mr. McLaren's paperwork would have been done in a timely manner, and the assault would not have taken place. Both incidents, in other words, were preventable and isolated, and really did not speak directly to the level of violence at Matsqui Institution as a general phenomenon. Yet both incidents had been used as evidence of the heightening of the biorhythm, to use the warden's metaphor, which had to be topped to reduce it to a lower and more tolerable level.

## Sunday, August 29—Dancing in the Shadow of Razor Wire

The events culminating in Operation Big Scoop stood in sharp contrast to those I described in the correctional journey along the Red Road one week before. In the weekend after Operation Big Scoop, there was another event at Matsqui which provided a unique opportunity to reflect on the conflicting objectives and ideals permeating contemporary imprisonment. Well before Operation Big Scoop was conceived, the Native Brotherhood had been given approval to hold a pow-wow on Sunday, August 29. Because Operation Big Scoop was seen as successful, with no violence or other resistance from the general population, the Warden determined that the powwow should go ahead as planned. Prior to his segregation, Darryl Ghostkeeper, as President of the Brotherhood, had asked that I come as one of the guests.

The powwow was held in the back field of the prison and was attended by 150 guests and 70 prisoners, mostly members of the Brotherhood but also some non-Aboriginal prisoners. Powwows are held all over western Canada during the summer months, with Aboriginal communities hosting their relatives and friends from other places. Like other powwows, the Matsqui powwow was a blend of formal presentations, informal gatherings with elders, dancing and drumming, the sharing of private time with family and loved ones, and a splendid barbecued meal of salmon, deer, buffalo, hamburgers, and hot dogs.

An important part of any powwow is the giving away of gifts. The Matsqui powwow was no different; included in the gift receivers were Ken Poirier and Jill Hummerstone. I was honoured to be given a drum made by Cory Bitternose. He told me it was one of the first drums he had made, and he wanted to share it with me because on the day of his temporary absence pass I had treated him with respect, as a human being and not as a prisoner.

A group of Brothers formed a drumming circle, and throughout the afternoon their drumming and singing provided the accompaniment for the festivities. The four men who had been on the pass to gather lava rock were part of this drumming circle. The relationship between their participation in the powwow and their work outside the prison was symbolically represented in the act of giving to all the guests, in the shadow of Mount Baker, the bundles of sagebrush they had gathered in the shadow of the mountains outside Lillooet. When the sagebrush was being harvested, the Brothers had said prayers thanking Mother Earth for giving up her bountiful gifts. Today, the Brothers passed on those gifts to be used by their families and friends in ceremonies that would link them in a circle with the Brothers within Matsqui.

At one point Dennis Bigsky and Cory Bitternose danced around the drumming circle. Dennis, an accomplished dancer, had borrowed a costume from one of the members of the dance group that had come in from the community. Cory did not have a costume, so he danced in his sweats, also displaying the joy and spirit of a dancer. Although they were physically dancing within a hundred feet of a high barbed wire fence and a gun tower, it seemed to me that these Brothers had spiritually escaped the confines of prison and renewed their connection with an inheritance that had never needed places of confinement.

My optimism at seeing Aboriginal prisoners throw off the mantle of imprisonment was tempered by my scepticism regarding correctional authority. One of the first people I saw at the powwow was Rick Ambrose, who had been on the original list of prisoners to be segregated in Operation Big Scoop. He had escaped this fate as a result of discussions among the unit managers, in which Irv Hammond had said he was confident there was no negative file information on

Mr. Ambrose. Given that the same could be said for other prisoners who were scooped, Mr. Ambrose's exclusion from the list was almost happenstance. The afternoon of the powwow, I watched him hold his three-month-old daughter and embrace his wife with a tenderness and serenity that few staff members had likely observed during his lengthy imprisonment.

That afternoon in many ways encapsulated the competing themes of change and continuity in the nature of imprisonment. There clearly had been enormous changes. Ten years earlier, when the first hunger strikes were carried out by the Brotherhood at Kent Institution for the right to exercise Aboriginal spirituality, it would have been difficult to imagine holding a powwow inside a federal prison. Yet now that this had become a reality, the President of the Native Brotherhood, instead of welcoming participants to the celebration, found himself in a segregation cell, placed there through a process that he rightly perceived as the arbitrary exercise of authority—no different in kind from the arbitrary exercises of power that had been part of correctional practice ten years before.

The commitment and sensitivity displayed by Jill Hummerstone and Ken Poirier, the staff supervisors of the powwow, were by any standards a model of professionalism tempered with cross-cultural understanding, a combination that was seen rarely a decade before. Yet that also had its negative counterpoint. During the course of the afternoon, I heard from several people that their visitors had been given a hard time at the front gate by some of the staff, who seemed to feel it was a mistake to allow the powwow to proceed in the wake of the previous week's events. One visitor with two children, a baby in arms and a toddler in a stroller, had been told she could not bring the stroller into the prison, but would have to carry the children the 400 yards or so to where the powwow was taking place. When Ken Poirier heard about this, he not only walked to the front gate to approve the entry of the stroller but personally pushed it and the child back to the gathering.

In the bigger picture, however, the mean-spirited interpretation of rules by a few staff could not change the fact that the Matsqui powwow provided a much-needed space in which prisoners, their families, and members of their communities could celebrate their common humanity.

## Monday, August 30—Operation Fizz?

On Monday, August 30, Matsqui got back to the business of dealing with the prisoners who had been the object of Operation Big Scoop. At the morning briefing, the Warden referred to Beth Parkinson's telephone call on Friday afternoon and stated that, to give prisoners three days' notice before the meeting of the Segregation Review Board, it would be necessary for everyone to complete the process before day's end by providing sufficient details of the reasons for segregation. It was agreed that Dianne Livesly, as the co-ordinator of case management, would review the cases with a committee of case management officers and the IPSOS.

Diane Livesly's committee spent the rest of the morning going over the files of the thirteen prisoners and considering their case histories. It was an embarrassing experience. In nine cases it became evident there was no information that could justify segregation under the CCRA. Case management officers provided glowing reports on several prisoners, stating that their positive behaviour in recent months had led to recommendations for transfers to lower security or the granting of parole; they were at a loss to understand why these prisoners had been identified as troublemakers. Even in cases where there was information on file regarding drug-related activities, it quickly transpired that this information was dated, in one instance going back over a year.

The review of the first prisoner on the list set the tone for the rest of the committee's discussion. The IPSOS said they had nothing at all on Mr. Amey, and CMO Brian Furman reported that his review of the files did not reveal any behaviour justifying segregation or transfer. The IPSOS suggested that the thing to do with Mr. Amey was to "sit him down, let him know about how he is perceived in the institution, and that we will be watching him." Ms. Livesly said that Mr. Amey should be counselled and that he should enter into a behavioural contract. Mr. Furman questioned the justification for either a behavioural contract or counselling and made specific reference to the duty to act fairly. As he put it, "If we do not have enough on him to justify segregation or transfer, what is the purpose of counselling or having him enter a behavioural contract? If I'm going to write a behavioural contract and he asks me what it is that he has done that justifies the contract, what am I supposed to say?" Mr. Furman pointedly asked the IPSOS, "There is no identifiable behaviour, right? Is our concern just that he is being too influential?" At the end of the discussion about Mr. Amey, there was a number of speculative comments around the table as to why his name had been added to the list of prisoners to be segregated. The only specific reason given was that he had an intimidating physical presence, highlighted by a Mohawk haircut. Ms. Livesly's minutes of that part of the meeting stated: "Left wondering why he was segregated." The decision taken was to warn Mr. Amey, then release him from segregation.

The failure of Mr. Amey's review to yield any information to justify segregation led one of the IPSOS to make this comment: "We had no knowledge that the guys would be boxed. We had been asked to prepare profiles on the high flyers in the institution, in order to discuss them with other staff and to start having these men tracked. However, we are now in a situation where these guys got boxed and what we are doing today is trying to justify the boxing. That to me is backwards." With these words, the IPSO was accurately describing the "shoot first and ask questions later" character of Operation Big Scoop. Several of the case management officers had not been aware of the code name of the operation; when it was shared with them, they suggested that it should be renamed "Operation Fizz."

By the end of the review of the thirteen prisoners, it was determined that nine of them should be released back to the population. In some of these cases, like Mr. Amey's, there was nothing on file to justify a behavioural contract; in others, negative file information, typically relating to drug involvement, was seized upon to justify a recommendation for a behavioural contract. This left four of the thirteen men whose cases were recommended for further review.

The meeting also addressed the timing of the release for those prisoners who had been recommended for release from segregation. One case management officer felt that they should all remain there until the Segregation Review Board met on Thursday. Unit Manager Irv Hammond believed they should be released as soon as possible; those who would be only counselled should be released the next morning, and those who were to have behavioural contracts should be released later the next day, assuming that the contracts could be prepared within twenty-four hours. Another case management officer suggested that if the prisoners were released that day, Monday, there would be a very negative staff reaction, because the staff would not understand why these men were scooped in a big operation on Friday and yet, three days later, were back in the population. She felt it was important to brief the staff on what had happened, so that they were fully aware why most of these prisoners were now coming back to the living unit. Everyone agreed with this. However, it meant that those prisoners for whom there had been no reasonable grounds for being placed in segregation in the first place, and for whom no behavioural contracts were necessary, would be spending another night in segregation without lawful justification. As it turned out, even though the release of the prisoners was delayed until the next day specifically to permit a briefing, the release took place *without* the staff being briefed.

Before the meeting broke up, there was some general discussion about the events of the last few days. Mr. Hammond tried to put a positive face on the experience by suggesting it demonstrated an important systemic deficiency: information which was important for decision-making was not being documented in the files. "When we looked to the staff to help us identify the top ten troublemakers, we came up with particular inmates. When we checked their files, we find nothing. That says something about our intelligence systems and our documentation." While that was one explanation, there is another, which says something else about prison decision-making: a process in which staff members are invited to express their opinions based upon rumour and reputation, without supporting evidence, is inherently unreliable and is an unprincipled basis for making decisions about prisoners' lives.

## Tuesday, August 31—Release from Segregation

At the morning briefing on Tuesday, August 31, Warden Brock reported that on Monday afternoon he had spent about two hours in segregation, interviewing the prisoners who had been taken there as part of Operation Big Scoop and explaining to them why he had taken the action he had: "If I've taken the steps to put them up in segregation, I should at least have the guts to face them and tell them myself why I have done it." He told his staff that he was particularly moved by his interview with Darryl Ghostkeeper; at the end of it Warden Brock had tears in his eyes and was satisfied that Mr. Ghostkeeper was serious about trying to address his drug problem.

Following the morning briefing the warden met with Ms. Lively's review committee. He went through the cases individually and approved the release of nine prisoners. The first group of five prisoners was released at 10:40 a.m. Two other prisoners were released at 1:00 p.m., and the last two were released at 3:35 p.m. The different times of release reflected the arbitrariness of the whole operation. In the cases of Darryl Ghostkeeper, one of the first to be released, and Ron Tessier, one of the last, they had been sharing the same cell.

## A Legal Analysis of Operation Big Scoop

Operation Big Scoop may be seen as a preliminary litmus test for the critical questions with which this book is concerned. First, and perhaps most importantly, were the decisions to place these men in segregation made in a manner that would convey the message, both to the prisoners concerned and to the general population of Matsqui, that justice and fairness were essential and integral elements of the correctional mission? Second, were decisions made in conformity with the law, specifically the *Corrections and Conditional Release Act?* The final question is, were segregation decisions in the 1990s made in a significantly different way than those in the 1970s and 1980s, as described in my previous studies?

At this preliminary stage I want to focus on the second question: whether the decisions in Operation Big Scoop were made in conformity with the law as reflected in s. 31(3) of the *CCRA,* which sets out the grounds for confining a prisoner in administrative segregation. The section reads:

> The institutional head may order that an inmate be confined in administrative segregation if the institutional head believes on reasonable grounds:
> (a) that
>   (i) the inmate has acted, has attempted to act or intends to act

> in a manner that jeopardizes the security of the penitentiary
> or the safety of any person, and
>
> (ii) the continued presence of the inmate in the general inmate
> population will jeopardize the security of the penitentiary
> or the safety of any person,
>
> (b) that the continued presence of the inmate in the general inmate
> population will interfere with an investigation that could lead to
> a criminal charge or a charge under subsection 41(2) of a serious
> disciplinary offence or,
>
> (c) that the continued presence of the inmate in the general inmate
> population will jeopardize the inmate's own safety,
>
> and the institutional head is satisfied that there is no reasonable
> alternative to administrative segregation.

I would first observe that at no time during any of the discussions and meetings surrounding Operation Big Scoop was there any specific mention of, or reference to, s. 31(3). There are a number of possible reasons for this. The first might be that the law is so well etched in peoples' minds that it requires no articulation but is referentially incorporated into any decision through institutional osmosis. A second reason, much less charitable, might be that in situations of perceived institutional crisis the law is not a primary consideration. A third possible explanation is that the law is so broadly written it enables an institutional decision-maker to use segregation in accordance with his or her best judgement, with the law's requirements seen principally as procedural ones, in terms of providing notice and a review system. Based upon my participation in Operation Big Scoop, the second and third explanations came closest to representing the operating reality in Matsqui Institution.

Regardless of which reason best explains what happened, was the segregation of the thirteen men justified by s. 31(3)? Ground (c), that the inmate's own safety would be prejudiced by his remaining in the population, was not an issue in any case, and so we need not consider it further. Ground (b), that the continued presence of an inmate in the population would interfere with an investigation that could lead to a criminal charge or a serious disciplinary offence, was also not an issue; in no instance was there any suggestion that fact-finding or evidence-gathering to lay charges was dependent upon the prisoners being removed from the population to prevent their interfering with potential witnesses.

This leaves ground (a), which requires that the institutional head believes on reasonable grounds that the prisoner has acted, attempted to act, or intends to act in a manner that jeopardizes the security of the penitentiary or the safety of any person, and the continued presence of that prisoner in the population would jeopardize such security or safety. This ground is very generally worded and has been subject to serious criticism for not providing substantive control on segregation decisions. But even given its very broad contours, it still requires the presence of reasonable grounds directed to actions, actual or intended, that jeopardize the security of the institution or personal safety. A number of the prisoners targeted in Operation Big Scoop were believed to be involved in extortion, which does fall within the parameters of jeopardizing the safety of any person. A number of other prisoners, however, were identified as being involved in drugs, absent any extortion or trafficking. This allegation lacks the link with jeopardizing personal safety and is not clearly referable to jeopardizing the security of an institution. It could be argued that "security" refers to "dynamic security," and that anything that raises the tension in an institution therefore constitutes an interference with institutional security. This certainly underpins Warden Brock's biorhythm theory. If the security of the institution is given this very broad meaning, however, then almost any action, actual or intended, of any prisoner could be brought within s. 31(3)(a).

But even assuming that we give the term "security" this almost meaningless interpretation—meaningless in the sense that it places no real limitations or constraints on institutional decision-making—there is still the question of reasonable grounds. Could it be said that the information-gathering process reflected in the tracking meeting, upon which the warden relied, constituted reasonable grounds? Would a judge, contemplating the issue of a search warrant or determining the legality for a police arrest, find reasonable grounds to believe that an offence had been committed and that relevant evidence was located in a particular place, based upon a process in which a group of police officers swapped information about their perceptions of suspects, without identifying whether this information was based upon direct observation, reliable informant information, or simply general reputation? The unequivocal answer is that such a process would not constitute reasonable grounds under the existing jurisprudence. It no more provides reasonable grounds to justify segregation under the *CCRA*.

Leaving that point aside, s. 31(3) also requires that if the institutional head has reasonable grounds, he must still be "satisfied that there is no reasonable alternative to administrative segregation." In the case of Operation Big Scoop, there was no consideration given to this question. From my interviews with the acting deputy warden, it was clear he and several other administrators had anticipated that the tracking meeting would identify the principal troublemakers and then determine individual strategies directed to each of them, precisely to see if there were alternative ways of dealing with these prisoners and changing their behaviour and influence, without resorting to segregation and/or transfer. Such a process would have been in conformity with s. 31(3), because only after completion of such a process could it be said that there was no reasonable alternative to segregation. The warden's decision to resort to immediate segregation bypassed this critical part of the process. In my judgement, Operation Big Scoop was carried out in blatant violation of s. 31(3).

## Friday, September 3—Reflections on Operation Big Scoop

On Friday, September 3, I interviewed three of the prisoners who had been part of Operation Big Scoop, now released back into the population. I also touched base with some of the staff to get their reflections on what had happened. Mike Miller was the first prisoner to whom I spoke. He told me that in the past, and in other institutions, he had been a major player in the drug trade, but that since his transfer from Kent in May, his only involvement was in using heroin on a very limited basis. As he put it, "I've been cool as a cucumber." He gave me a copy of the assessment he had received from Officer Gagné in the substance abuse program, which showed he had received consistently high marks with very positive comments from the instructor. I asked Mr. Miller what he made of Operation Big Scoop. He told me, "Given a little bit of time, I figure that I can explain almost anything, but how can you explain what happened the other day? So far as I'm concerned, the only thing I could say is that my reputation preceded me, because there was absolutely nothing else upon which they could have justified putting me in seg."

I asked Mr. Miller whether, in his opinion, the warden had captured the players in the institution in relation to drugs and muscling when he segregated the thirteen prisoners in Operation Big Scoop. Mr. Miller went through the twelve other prisoners, one by one, explaining, as only another prisoner can, their personal and business profiles in the institution, and concluded that the real players were not among those caught in the net. He could name fifteen to twenty prisoners who were main players in the drug scene, and they had not been part of Operation Big Scoop.

I also interviewed Darryl Ghostkeeper and Ron Tessier, being interested particularly in how their segregation affected them as individuals and as members of the Inmate Committee. Ron Tessier admitted to being a consumer of drugs, but said he was not a player or a dealer, and that that should be fairly evident to anyone who looked in his cell. He barely made it from canteen day to canteen day keeping himself in tobacco. He was convinced the real reason he had been placed in segregation was because he and Darryl Ghostkeeper were on the Committee; the administration had anticipated that if a large number of men were segregated, the Committee would naturally become involved and somehow agitate the population to participate in a protest such as a sit-down. He felt this assumption was unfair because, in the year he had been on the Committee, he had demonstrated his commitment to negotiation rather than confrontation. On a number of occasions he and Darryl had intervened in tense situations and had cooled things down rather than stirred them up. Mr. Ghostkeeper pointed to the hypocrisy of the warden telling the Committee at a recent meeting that it was important to sit down and talk things out, that the CCRA indeed required wardens to involve prisoners in decisions, and then, when there were some real problems in the institution, of the warden scooping the Committee before doing anything else.

In reflecting on what had happened and comparing it to prison regimes a decade earlier, Ron Tessier said the only difference was that ten years earlier the prisoners would have all been shipped to Kent the same day. In describing Operation Big Scoop, he summed it up this way: "The same struggle, just different faces."

Warden Brock's justification for Operation Big Scoop had been grounded in his desire to change the criminalized culture of Matsqui. Based upon my interviews with the prisoners who were the immediate subjects of the operation, the irony was that, far from undermining the criminalized element of the population, Operation Big Scoop reinforced a sense of the lawlessness and arbitrariness of the system and of the men and women who operate it.

Before leaving the institution that day, I went up to the segregation unit to get Rick Cregg and Mike Csoka's impressions about what had been achieved by the events of the last week. In response to my question, "How is Matsqui Institution different this Friday than last Friday?," they agreed that nothing had really changed and that Operation Big Scoop had achieved very little. In fact, Rick Cregg was of the view that it may have made matters worse; prisoners were laughing at the staff because they had had to let most of the guys out within a few days. Mike Csoka suggested it was all a question of perspective. If the guys who were boxed realized they were walking on thin ice, then maybe for a while they would keep a low profile. On the other hand, if they were seen by the other inmates as heroes, then their influence and power in the institution would be even greater than it was before. I asked each of them why they thought the operation had gone sideways, and their answers were quite different. Rick Cregg said he did not blame it on Warden Brock; in fact, "after the tracking meeting on Thursday, I went to the warden and shook the man's hand." Rather, he blamed it on the *Charter of Rights and Freedoms,* the CCRA, and all the legislators and lawyers with their bleeding hearts protecting the rights of prisoners. As he saw it, the CCRA put the warden in a legal straitjacket, and that was why he was unable to transfer these prisoners out of the institution. As for the *Charter,* "The warden's power has been chartered to death." Mr. Csoka also did not fault Warden Brock, but felt that middle management were the ones to blame "in not getting their act together." I asked both officers whether they thought most of Operation Big Scoop's targets had been released because they were not really the players in the institution or because the documented information was not on file. Not surprisingly, both felt the latter interpretation was correct. The problem with official files was that they were prepared for the most part by case management officers, yet these people did not know who the prisoners really were. CMOs saw the prisoners in their offices during the day, when they were putting on their best face and doing all the programs the institution had set up for them. However, the correctional officers and the correctional supervisors saw the real people back in the unit in the evening when, in Mike Csoka's graphic words, "The beast comes out. If you want to see what the prisoners are really like, just see how they relate to the staff in the living unit. It's totally different from how they relate to their CMO, but it's a far more reliable indicator of who these men are: violent criminals rather than smooth-talking rehabilitated cons."

## Sunday, September 5—The Forces of Matsqui

Pat Henrickson's description of Matsqui as "a powerful and forceful place— full of different forces," proved an evocative and accurate description of what I saw and experienced in my first month of research there. Operation Big Scoop had been premised upon the fact that the forces of evil, or, as the warden described it, the small but influential group of prisoners "who were criminaliz- ing the culture at Matsqui," had to be restrained by institutional power to enable the positive, rehabilitative forces of institutional programming to be maintained. Contrasted with this negative application of physical force was the powerful influence of Aboriginal spirituality reflected in the powwow and the day spent with the four Brothers gathering lava rock. These activities were charged with spiritual, not physical, power, and were conducted in an atmosphere of elevation rather than one of degradation.

Matsqui was also a forceful place in terms of the individuals who inhabited it. Rick Cregg and Mike Csoka, in describing their views on the true nature of criminals, talked of the "beast" in the hearts of men which revealed itself to them and their colleagues on the afternoon shift as darkness descended on the prison. These images were not far removed from those used by prisoners in relating their opinions of institutional staff, not only in relation to this most recent disregard of fairness but to accumulated experiences of previous disregard in other, even more forceful prisons than Matsqui.

But if the forces at work in Matsqui were at one level expressed in visceral lan- guage, at another level they were described in abstract and even metaphorical terms by people further removed from the everyday encounters of the keeper and the kept. Roger Brock, the urbane, sophisticated warden and self-described politician, explained the dynamics of power in terms of social and criminologi- cal theory, of operations designed to change the culture of the prison. Here was a warden who firmly believed that by demonstrating a management style of openness and accountability, he could influence the culture not only of his staff but also of the prisoners. Other important forces had over the years caused dra- matic changes in the men and women who work in Matsqui. Jesse Sexsmith, a man whose early days as a guard were, in his own words, characterized "by hatred at the gut level," identified, while drinking herbal tea, the forces of change that have made him proud to be a member of the Correctional Service of Canada.

For Ken Poirier, once an advocate and participant in "thump therapy," those same forces had enabled him to participate in a group pass with Aboriginal Brothers to gather lava rock for a sweat lodge.

The events of August 1993 showed me that Matsqui was a forceful place in the way people usually associate that term with prisons. Under my eyes, Mike Boileau was the victim of a violent assault that left him, and the walls around him, covered in blood. Barely fifty yards from where I conducted my interviews, a prisoner luckily escaped permanent injury when he was attacked with a weight bar by another prisoner. These are images of a force which the public expects in a prison. The other forces I have described are not so visible, but their impact on the lives of those who live and work inside prisons, whether as prisoners, administrators, case managers, or correctional officers, is essential to understanding the many faces of imprisonment at the beginning of the twenty-first century.

## CHAPTER 4

# The Life and Death
# of the Electric Man

Six months after Operation Big Scoop, on February 22, 1994, at the beginning of my research at Kent Institution, a prisoner named Gary Allen was fatally stabbed in the courtyard by another prisoner, Hughie MacDonald. The circumstances surrounding the death of Gary Allen provide a window on the forces of life and death in maximum security, which is all but beyond the comprehension of those of us who live our lives outside of prison. Those circumstances, as they were related at Hughie MacDonald's murder trial, describe a reality in which the threat of violence permeates the fabric of existence, shaping prisoners' conceptions of who they are, informing their perceptions of other prisoners, and conditioning their interpretations of the gestures, walk, and talk of those around them.

## The Protagonists

I had first met Gary Allen in 1991, at one of the meetings I regularly arranged between students in the Faculty of Law at the University of British Columbia and prisoners at Kent. I started the meeting by challenging the prisoners to explain why the students, when they became lawyers, should have concern for the lives and rights of prisoners. After all, there are many disadvantaged groups who have not offended against the law and have a strong claim upon the time and energy of lawyers concerned with social justice. Gary Allen, in rising to this challenge, explained the effects of living through years of imprisonment marked by the daily practice of injustice. He told the students he was nearing the end of a decade of being locked up and he would be leaving Kent with a raging anger that would imperil everyone with whom he came into contact. Lawyers, he said, should be active in protecting the rights of prisoners if only to protect themselves, their families, and their friends from becoming victims of the anger and violence prison generated in men like him. He explained that when he felt his anger rising, it was as if an electrical energy pulsed through his veins, and there were times when that force was so great it seemed the electricity flowing out of his hands and feet would have the power to electrocute anyone standing close to him. On these occasions, although wearing runners and standing on a concrete floor, he would feel his toes curl and grasp the concrete as the anger coursed through his body. He felt as if he were literally transfixed to the floor.

Gary Allen was a giant of a man, with an upper body toned by years of working out with heavy weights. His description of the anger flowing through and out of his body, and of the danger that this could generate for the public when the steel and wire insulation of a maximum security prison was removed, was truly frightening.

I saw Gary Allen again three years later, in February 1994. He had received a new sentence and was in segregation in Kent. I told him I wanted to interview him after he was out of segregation, but that interview never took place. A few hours after he was released from segregation on February 22, he was stabbed by Hughie MacDonald in the courtyard of Kent Institution in front of prisoners and guards, and he later died of his injuries. I was in Kent that day, although at the time of the stabbing I was interviewing prisoners in segregation. What I did see later was the trail Gary Allen's blood had left as he was taken from the courtyard to the Health Care Unit. A trail of blood was what Gary Allen had predicted would be the product of his long imprisonment: either someone else's or, as it came to pass, his own.

Hughie MacDonald was charged with the first-degree murder of Gary Allen. The following account of the events leading to Gary Allen's death is drawn from the evidence in Mr. MacDonald's trial, court exhibits, my own notes on the trial, and the judge's charge to the jury. The MacDonald trial serves to introduce not only the dynamics of maximum security but also many of the cast of characters who feature in later chapters of this book.

The protagonists in the courtyard at Kent Institution on February 22, 1994, were no strangers to violence. Hughie MacDonald was the older of the two men by eleven years. His criminal record dated back to 1958 and prior to 1977 consisted principally of property offences. In 1977 he was convicted of manslaughter and received a sentence of three and a half years. In 1978, while at Collins Bay Institution, he fatally stabbed two staff members and wounded a third, as a result of which he was convicted in 1980 of two counts of first-degree murder, receiving the mandatory sentence of life imprisonment with a minimum of twenty-five years before parole eligibility. Gary Allen's adult criminal career dated back to 1974; in addition to property offences such as theft, breaking and entering, and possession of narcotics and stolen property, it included convictions for assault, assault with a weapon, robbery, and one conviction for manslaughter.

Gary Allen and Hughie MacDonald first met in Edmonton Maximum Security Institution in 1983. Hughie MacDonald came to Edmonton from the Special Handling Unit, where he had spent almost four years as a result of his deadly assault on the two correctional officers at Collins Bay. Gary Allen had been in Edmonton since 1981 and was halfway through his four-year manslaughter sentence. On January 23, 1984, Gary Allen and his younger brother, Tony, were involved in a violent confrontation with Hughie MacDonald and Howie McInroy in the courtyard of Edmonton Institution. Edmonton and Kent Institutions were built around the same time on the same architectural model, with the living units in both institutions opening up into a central courtyard. But there was more than architectural symmetry connecting Edmonton and Kent in this case. Although the events were separated by a decade, what took place in the courtyard at Edmonton Max in 1984 had profound significance for what was played out in 1994 in the courtyard at Kent Institution.

At his trial in B.C. Supreme Court in Chilliwack in May 1996, Hughie Mac-Donald testified about the circumstances which led up to the confrontation in Edmonton. He described how Gary Allen and two of Allen's brothers had been involved in strong-arming and intimidating other prisoners in connection with drugs, and he said that the Allens seemed to have been granted relative immunity from sanctions by the prison administration. Hughie MacDonald gave as one example a case where Gary Allen and one of his brothers laid a beating on another prisoner using hockey sticks. Even though the authorities knew about this, no disciplinary or other action was taken against the Allen brothers. Hughie MacDonald's account of his and other prisoners' experience of the influence of the Allen brothers at Edmonton Institution was corroborated by CSC's internal documents. According to one report:

> The Allens over an extended period of time had by the use of force, threats, and blackmail placed themselves in an untenable position to some of the other inmates who viewed them as receiving extra privileges and protection from the administration of the institution and as such it was only logical to the other inmates that the Allens were selling out the inmate population in some fashion.
>
> The beating of [name blanked out here in report] by the Allens with no reaction by the administrative authorities was viewed by certain factions in the population, that the Allens were protected and had special statute [status] in the institution. (CSC Security Investigation Report, February 3, 1984)

Against this backdrop, Hughie MacDonald described how in January 1984 his partner, Howie McInroy, informed him that the Allens had made threats against Howie McInroy and that he was going to square off with them. Hughie MacDonald volunteered to go along to ensure that the odds were even. During the fight in the courtyard, Howie McInroy took on Gary Allen and Hughie MacDonald, Tony Allen. Knives were involved, and by the end of the fight both Allens had been stabbed and Hughie MacDonald had sustained a deep cut to his finger. The Allens were the clear losers in this fight. Gary Allen sustained puncture wounds in the chest and stomach area. His brother, Tony, was more seriously injured, receiving stabs in the shoulder and neck area. No criminal charges were laid as a result of this incident, the Allens refusing to give any statement incriminating Hughie MacDonald or Howie McInroy. However, following the fight, Mr. MacDonald and Mr. McInroy were transferred back to the Special Handling Unit, where Mr. MacDonald spent a further four years. The Allens were transferred to lower security institutions in the Pacific Region.

For the next decade, until January 1994, Gary Allen and Hughie MacDonald served their time at opposite ends of the country. After spending four years in the Special Handling Unit and a period in Millhaven Institution, in 1992 Mr. MacDonald was transferred to the Regional Psychiatric Centre (RPC). For eight months he participated in the Violent Offender Program there. He did not complete all phases of the program, and he was advised to come back and complete it at a later time. He was transferred to Matsqui Institution briefly and then to Mission Medium Security Institution in June 1993. In July 1993, he returned to the RPC and was there until December of that year. At the RPC he was a member of the Inmate Committee at the time a home brew was found hidden in the Inmate Committee office. He was also found to be in possession of a small exacto blade knife used for hobby purposes. He was charged with possession of contraband and received a sentence of 30 days' segregation, suspended for 60 days, for the brew, and a $25 fine for the knife. The offences led to his being transferred out of the RPC to Kent on December 15, 1993. He remained in segregation at Kent until bed space became available in the general population on January 17, 1994. In a meeting with his case management officer, he requested that he be readmitted to the RPC to complete the Violent Offender Program and was advised that he should reapply after four months. At this stage in his sentence, Hughie MacDonald had served the fifteen years required under a sentence for first-degree murder after which he could, pursuant to the provisions of s. 745 of the *Criminal Code,* apply for a hearing in the Supreme Court before a jury for a determination that his parole eligibility be reduced from 25 years.

Just one week before Hughie MacDonald was transferred from the RPC to Kent, on December 8, 1993, Gary Allen was sentenced to the term of 2 years less a day for possession of narcotics, possession of an unregistered and restricted weapon, and possession of property obtained by crime. As he was serving a sentence of less than 2 years, he was sent to a provincial institution, the Fraser Regional Correctional Centre. The initial entry in his provincial sentence management file read, "Well known offender in provincial and federal gaols. Extremely violent history." The degree to which provincial authorities viewed Mr. Allen as potentially dangerous, both to prisoners and to staff, was reflected in an entry in the Inmate Progress Log on December 12, 1993. "Inmate Allen is to be in belly chains when being transported by staff members, and three staff must be present when inmate is let out of cell or not in belly chains." A decision was made that Mr. Allen would be placed in "separate custody" (administrative segregation) under s. 38.1 of the *Provincial Correctional Centre Rules and Regulations.* The reason for this is set out in a memorandum written by Mr. A. E. Riou, Director of Operations for the Fraser Regional Correctional Centre (FRCC), who was later called as a witness for the defence in the trial of Hughie MacDonald.

> Mr. Allen continues to pose a threat to the management, operation, discipline and security of the Correctional Centre; therefore, it is advised that he continue to serve his sentence in separate custody. A lot of documentation has been submitted regarding Mr. Allen. He is described by the FRCC psychologist as "a true psychopath," and is fully capable of violence with or without provocation. Throughout his period in segregation, Mr. Allen has made numerous threats to staff and inmates within the Centre. In my view, he is not an inmate that can be trusted in either general population or protective custody to abide by all rules and regulations of the Centre. His potentially violent nature is ever present even though there may be periods of apparent co-operation on his part. The continuation of separate custody status for Mr. Allen is requested. (Memorandum from A. E. Riou to R. Williams, District Director, Fraser Regional Correctional Centre, January 13, 1994)

The Fraser Regional Correctional Centre's consulting psychologist, Dr. Myron Schimpf, was also called as a witness for the defence in the MacDonald trial. He gave evidence that he saw Gary Allen on four or five occasions in January and February of 1994 and reviewed for the court the clinical notes he had made following his interview with Mr. Allen on January 18. Those notes contained the following entries:

> Today we discussed the term "predator" and the degree to which it applies to him. He was very disclosive and reflective, showing considerable willingness to discuss controversial material. He shared that usually he was controlled, studied, and very aware, engaging in violence only when necessary for self-protection, i.e., not random or

gratuitous. However, he acknowledges that he occasionally experiences a type of altered consciousness, at which time he withdraws into himself and eschews interaction with others. Interestingly, he feels that his actual facial countenance changes, and he does not like to look at himself. Consequently, at such times he removes mirrors from his room. He becomes hyper-sensitive to physical stimuli (sounds, smells) and his focus of attention becomes very narrow. Obsesses upon one situation or individual with little or no awareness of anything outside the narrow range. His mood becomes intense and bellicose, and he lashes out, sometimes indiscriminately. He admits that during such dark periods he is predatory and dangerous, and may injure essentially innocent parties. (Clinical notes on Gary Allen, Dr. Myron Schimpf, January 18, 1994)

Gary Allen, faced with the prospect of serving his full sentence in a provincial prison in administrative segregation, sought to transfer to a federal penitentiary, something that can be arranged pursuant to a federal-provincial transfer agreement. That request was reviewed by the warden of Kent Institution. In a letter from Bob Lusk, Warden of Kent Institution, to Ron Williams, Director of the Fraser Regional Correctional Centre, Mr. Lusk indicated that Kent was prepared to accept Mr. Allen under certain circumstances. In the course of the letter Mr. Lusk expressed concern that Gary Allen "not enter into a transfer to Kent Institution under any illusions" and pointed out that "currently, all new intake is being housed in segregation until general accommodation cell space can be found for them. Cells are allotted on a first come, first serve basis. Our current waiting list is eleven and it should be approximately six weeks before a cell can be found for him" (Letter from Warden Bob Lusk to Ron Williams, January 6, 1994).

Dave Dick, the institutional preventive security officer (IPSO) at Kent, went to Fraser Regional Correctional Centre on January 12 to interview Gary Allen. The subject matter of that interview is reflected in a detailed memorandum Mr. Dick prepared for the deputy warden of Kent Institution, dated January 13, 1994. It read:

1. Gary Allen requested an ESA [Exchange of Services Agreement] transfer to Kent from the Fraser Regional Correctional Centre where he is currently being housed in their segregation unit . . . The Warden has agreed to accept Allen provided he signed an understanding he would participate in programs and that, should he require long-term segregation at Kent, he could be returned to the provincial system.

2. I interviewed Allen yesterday morning at FRCC. He refused to sign the understanding as presented, objecting to the wording which

implied he might be segregated for his own protection. He wanted that changed and said he would sign if it stated segregation "for any reason." He emphasized he had never requested protection and never would.

3. He made the point several times that he had never run from any confrontation and would never go to staff with any problems. If someone had a problem with him, he would deal with it on his own terms. He said this was the way he was taught years ago when he entered the system and he was not going to change now.

4. I gave him a list of our current inmates, asking if he had any particular problems with anyone. He started to go through it, making comments on one or two of them but very quickly gave the list back to me, saying he had never done that before and would not start now. The brief comments he did make confirmed one previously identified incompatible . . . [A prisoner is then named.] In addition, there are certain others which should be regarded as likely sources of conflict . . . [A number of prisoners are then named.]

5. Finally, there is a serious and previously unidentified incompatibility with Hugh MacDonald who is currently in J unit GP segregation. Allen became extremely agitated when seeing this name on the list, saying he had not encountered him in many years but that he had "fucked him over badly" when he was a new kid in the system. He noted that MacDonald was now much older and he, Allen, was in his prime and "what goes around, comes around!" Allen noted that MacDonald had killed two guards and suggested this was a good reason for me to put them together on the same range and Allen would "look after him for you."

6. When his suggestion was rejected out of hand he seemed to realize what he had said and backtracked somewhat. He did not withdraw his threats, however. He only wanted to keep the conversation private, "between you and me."

7. Given this interview, I feel more strongly than ever that Allen represents a serious risk to our institutional security and he is unlikely to ever be released to our general population. He will be both a potential target and aggressor and I would anticipate a violent incident within days, if not hours, of his arrival in an open unit. In segregation he would be manageable—but even there we would constantly need to monitor who he comes into contact with on his range.

8. I have told Allen my concerns and my recommendation that he not be accepted at Kent. I have also told him he would likely not

be released to population though this would, of course, be reviewed on a regular basis. Given our discussion, he is reconsidering his request for transfer but has asked that a revised letter be given to him for signature.

Somewhat surprisingly in light of Mr. Dick's strong recommendation against it, the warden of Kent confirmed with his provincial counterpart that he was prepared to accept Mr. Allen.

At the preliminary inquiry of Hughie MacDonald—in serious cases, the first stage of the criminal trial process—Jesse Sexsmith, who had left Matsqui in late 1993 to become the deputy warden of Kent Institution, was questioned by defence counsel as to how he interpreted the threats made by Gary Allen against Mr. MacDonald as reported in Mr. Dick's memorandum. Mr. Sexsmith responded:

> I knew this fellow, Allen, well. He was a braggart . . . He loved to sit and brag. He loved to sit and talk violent. He loved to believe that he was the toughest guy on the block, and he consistently spoke in terms like that. In my experience, my personal experience with Allen, the experience of others on the management team . . . provided us with a . . . considered opinion that the man was a braggart and that it really didn't mean a lot . . . because there was no record that we were aware of any incident. No-one had ever told me of previous incidents or anything in particular . . . There was nothing on case management files. There was nothing on our offender management system in terms of our computer files for incidents. There was nothing there, or as I was told, there was nothing there. (Proceedings at the Preliminary Inquiry of Hughie MacDonald, November 17, 1995, at 58–59)

On February 7, 1994, Gary Allen was transferred from Fraser Regional Correctional Centre to Kent Institution and was placed in segregation pending available bed space in the general population. On February 22, Gary Allen was released from segregation. In his memo of January 13, Mr. Dick had predicted that Gary Allen "will be both a potential target and aggressor and I would anticipate a violent incident within days, if not hours, of his arrival in an open unit." In fact, it was only hours from the time Gary Allen left segregation that he was carried, fatally wounded, from the courtyard of Kent Institution.

The events which led to the death of Gary Allen in February 1994 were the subject of much evidence in the four-week trial of Hughie MacDonald on a charge of first-degree murder. While the Crown's evidence focussed almost exclusively on what correctional officers observed during the few minutes of the confrontation in the courtyard, the evidence of the Defence, principally though not exclusively the evidence of prisoners, framed those same events within a broader context, taking the jury deep inside the interior spaces of maximum security and the culture of a prisoner society.

The Crown's theory was that Hughie MacDonald deliberately planned to kill Gary Allen. When Hughie MacDonald learned that Gary Allen was coming out of segregation, he obtained a knife and came into the courtyard where he confronted and attacked him. Gary Allen was unarmed and retreated, but he was pursued by Mr. MacDonald, who repeatedly tried to, and eventually did, stab Mr. Allen.

The Defence's theory was that Hughie MacDonald had been told by other prisoners that Gary Allen intended to kill him as soon as he was released from segregation. On the day of Mr. Allen's release from segregation, the prisoners who had spoken with Gary Allen advised Hughie MacDonald that Gary Allen intended to carry out his threat and that he was armed with a knife. Hughie MacDonald obtained his own knife and went into the courtyard with the intention of talking to Gary Allen. Mr. Allen punched and kicked Mr. MacDonald, and Mr. MacDonald then drew his knife. In the ensuing struggle Hughie MacDonald stabbed Gary Allen, believing that his own life was in danger. In the words of Defence counsel, Hughie MacDonald acted in self-defence in a situation where it was "kill or be killed" and his stabbing of Gary Allen was justified homicide.

## The Crown's Case

Crown Counsel Jack Gibson called a number of correctional officers in support of the prosecution's case. Officer Chicoyne, who was in charge of B unit on February 22, 1994, testified that Unit Manager Dewar asked him to go to J unit to see if Mr. Allen was ready to come out to general population. Mr. Chicoyne met with Mr. Allen, who was agitated and asked a lot of questions about the mood of the general population with reference to his coming out. Mr. Chicoyne told Mr. Allen that he was not aware of any particular dangers, but that there were rumours. Mr. Allen asked, "Where is it coming from? What am I going to be looking at?" Mr. Chicoyne asked Mr. Allen if he was prepared to come out. Gary Allen "hemmed and hawed," threw his hands up, and said, "Okay. Let's do it." When Mr. Allen was released to B unit he asked for and received a parka. The units were unlocked for lunch at around 12:10 p.m. Mr. Chicoyne stayed in the office of B unit, looked out the window, and saw Gary Allen conversing with a group of prisoners. He did not, however, see the fight.

Officer Titus was working in B unit on the morning Mr. Allen was released from segregation. Gary Allen arrived in B unit at 10:30 a.m. During his range walk, which he did once an hour, Mr. Titus noticed Gary Allen keeping to himself in his cell, which was somewhat unusual because he had free access to other prisoners in the unit. Darryl Bates was Mr. Allen's only visitor. Mr. Titus was in the courtyard during the lunch hour as part of his normal duties. He noticed a number of prisoners going over to Gary Allen and talking with him. He testified that he found the manner of these conversations unusual, indicating trouble. He attempted to contact the IPSO by phone and, failing to get an answer, he contacted Correctional Supervisor Greer, who advised him that there were no special monitoring orders on Mr. Allen but that he should keep observing the situation.

Mr. Titus saw Hughie MacDonald come out of either C or D unit and quickly go down the steps leading to the courtyard. Hughie MacDonald and Gary Allen came close together, and Mr. Titus observed Gary Allen backing up rapidly, moving side to side, across the courtyard. In cross-examination, he said he did not see any blows struck and could recall no initial physical contact. He testified that Hughie MacDonald came forward with his arms moving in a punching fashion. Hughie MacDonald moved at a fast pace and Gary Allen was stepping backward, side to side, fending off blows. Mr. MacDonald's jabbing motions were numerous and continuous. Mr. Titus stepped into the A unit office, told the officer there what was happening, and then returned to the scene. By that time the incident was over, and Mr. MacDonald was restrained face down on the ground. In cross-examination, Mr. Titus stated that when Mr. MacDonald first came out into the courtyard Mr. Titus was also watching other prisoners, because he had suspected trouble.

Officer Gordon testified that he was in the courtyard when another officer yelled, "Fight." He turned around and saw Gary Allen running or moving quickly, backwards, being pursued by Hughie MacDonald. Mr. Allen was protecting himself with his hands up and Mr. MacDonald was thrusting. As the officers approached him, Mr. Gordon could see that Mr. MacDonald had a "shank." Mr. Allen ended up on the ground on his back, at which point Mr. Gordon was two to three feet from his head. Mr. MacDonald knelt down, right knee to right knee; he still had the knife and was making thrusting motions with it towards Mr. Allen's chest. Mr. Gordon saw it contact Mr. Allen's parka in the upper chest area. He testified that he saw Mr. Allen kick the knife from Mr. MacDonald's hand and it fell between Mr. Allen's legs. Mr. Gordon moved to Mr. Allen's left side, thinking that he could grab the knife. However, Mr. MacDonald retrieved the knife. Someone yelled, "Kick the shank," and Mr. Gordon kicked at Mr. MacDonald's elbow area to distract him. The knife flew out of Mr. MacDonald's hand and landed near Mr. Gordon's feet. Mr. Gordon grabbed the knife, took it to the window of F unit, and passed it to another officer. He then returned to the fight and held down Mr. MacDonald's legs. Mr. MacDonald was face down on the grass with other officers on top of him. Mr. Gordon testified that he never saw Mr. Allen strike Mr. MacDonald, but in cross-examination he conceded that he did not see the start of the fight.

Officer Beacon was working in the F unit office on February 22 during lunch time. He was sitting at the desk, facing away from the window. He heard a loud noise, turned, looked out and saw two prisoners struggling. At the same time he heard "A fight in the courtyard" over the radio. He saw a shank in Hughie MacDonald's right hand. At this point the prisoners were twenty to thirty feet away from Mr. Beacon and Mr. Allen was backing up, trying to ward Mr. MacDonald off. When Mr. Beacon saw the weapon, he left his office and went out into the courtyard. He got within two to three feet of the two prisoners; Mr. MacDonald still had the shank in his hand. Mr. MacDonald was trying to stab Mr. Allen, who was trying to fend Mr. MacDonald off. The shank was kicked out of Mr. MacDonald's hand, then retrieved by Mr. MacDonald but almost immediately kicked out of his hand again. After Mr. MacDonald was restrained, Mr. Beacon asked Mr. Allen, "Are you okay?" Mr. Allen said, "No," and opened his parka. There was a spot of blood the size of a large coin on his chest. Mr. Beacon and Mr. Titus picked Mr. Allen up. Mr. Allen was losing a lot of blood. Mr. Beacon pressed his left hand to Mr. Allen's chest to stem the flow of blood; but this did not seem to have much effect. The two men then carried Mr. Allen into the Health Care Unit. Mr. Beacon testified that it was "the most [blood] I'd ever seen." (Although no mention of this was made at the trial, it is important to recognize that Officer Beacon's effort to stem the flow of blood was a sponta-neous humanitarian action that placed him at considerable risk, in light of the fact that Gary Allen was a known drug user.)

Ms. Dinn, a registered nurse who worked at Kent Institution, gave evidence that when Gary Allen was brought into the Health Care Unit, he was pale but conscious. She could not feel his pulse and there was no blood pressure. She ap-plied a pressure dressing until the ambulance arrived. Another nurse attempted intravenous but was unsuccessful. The ambulance attendants testified that when they arrived they noticed "an enormous amount of blood." It was bright red, which indicated blood from an artery. Mr. Allen was white as a ghost and "just about bled out."

Gary Allen died on February 28, 1994, six days after he was stabbed in the courtyard at Kent. Dr. Ferris, the pathologist who performed the autopsy, testified that Gary Allen died of multi-organ failure from blood loss through a stab wound in the right shoulder. The stab cut the subclavian artery, a large, high-pressure blood vessel which can bleed massively unless direct pressure is applied to the wound. From this artery, a man can "bleed out" within two to five minutes.

The Crown also called Dave Dick, the IPSO from Kent, at the request of the Defence. Mr. Dick described his interview with Gary Allen at Fraser Regional Correctional Centre, leading to his memo of January 13 recommending against the admission of Gary Allen to Kent. Crown counsel, in his questioning of Mr. Dick, asked him to review the options that a prisoner would have where he has a dispute with another prisoner. Mr. Dick suggested seven options: (1) Deal with the problem himself without bringing it to staff attention. (2) Go to the chaplain or a Native Elder to mediate the problem; these people are not obliged to report or document such requests. (3) Go to a staff member to ask them to intervene or mediate; most staff members will report the incident. (4) Request to see the IPSO and have him deal with it; this might attract the attention of other prisoners, unless the prisoner concocts a reasonable excuse for talking to the officer. (5) Get friends together and plan some form of direct action, which may lead to a physical confrontation. (6) Get himself removed from the population, for example, by letting himself get caught with contraband. (7) Physically confront a staff member and get himself sent to segregation. Mr. Dick expressed the opinion that a prisoner could use either option 6 or 7 and still maintain the image of a "solid con" in the eyes of other prisoners.

## The Defence's Case

John Conroy, counsel for Hughie MacDonald, opened the Defence by calling Mr. MacDonald to the stand. Mr. MacDonald was taken through his criminal record, then described in detail the events leading up to his confrontation with the Allen brothers in Edmonton in 1984. He also explained his efforts to rehabilitate himself by participating in the Violent Offender Program at the Regional Psychiatric Centre in 1992–93. In February 1994, following his transfer from the RPC to Kent and his release into the general population, he learned that Gary Allen had been admitted to Kent and was in segregation.

Mr. MacDonald stated that Dennis Smith, a member of the Inmate Committee, had advised him that Gary Allen planned to kill Hughie MacDonald as soon as he got out of segregation. Mr. MacDonald asked Mr. Smith to find out why this was. The next week Dennis Smith and another member of the Committee, Jean-Louis Tremblay, told Hughie MacDonald that Gary Allen was intent on carrying out his threat and "there was no talking to him." Mr. MacDonald did not believe the institution would release Mr. Allen into the general population, however, as he assumed they were fully aware of the incident in Edmonton Institution back in 1984. He based this assumption on the fact that the incident was always being thrown in his face by CSC staff and was well known among prisoners.

On the morning of Mr. Allen's release from segregation, Mr. MacDonald went to work as usual in the kitchen and stayed there until 12:00 p.m. On his way back to his unit, another prisoner, Walter Sinclair, informed him, "Your worst nightmare has come true. Allen has been released from segregation." Hughie MacDonald obtained a knife from another prisoner and took it to his cell, where he placed it in his bed. He then went to the dining room. He sat two tables away from Gary Allen and watched as a number of prisoners came up and spoke to Mr. Allen. After Mr. Allen left the dining room, Dennis Smith and Jean-Louis Tremblay came to tell Mr. MacDonald that Mr. Allen was out in the yard, that he was armed and that he intended to kill Mr. MacDonald. Shortly afterwards Mr. MacDonald was given the same information by a third prisoner, Jimmy Whitmore. Mr. MacDonald watched through the window of the dining room to see what was happening in the courtyard and observed Mr. Allen talking with a number of prisoners. Mr. MacDonald left the dining room and went back to his cell, where he retrieved the knife, and then went out into the courtyard.

Mr. MacDonald testified that because he wanted to hear from Mr. Allen himself what his intentions were, he went over to the other man in the courtyard and said he would meet him later that evening in the gym. He explained to the jury that his intention was to try and talk things out to avoid further problems. Mr. Allen's response was, "What for? I'm going to fucking kill you right now." According to Mr. MacDonald, Mr. Allen then hit him in the face and kicked him in the knee, causing Mr. MacDonald to fall to the ground. Believing that Mr. Allen was armed and that his own life was in danger, Mr. MacDonald reached for the knife he had in the leg of his pants. He waved it at Mr. Allen in a to and fro motion. Mr. MacDonald testified that his intention was to keep Mr. Allen preoccupied so that he could not get at his own knife, which Mr. Mac-Donald believed him to have under his parka. Mr. Allen backed up, slipped, and fell down. A scuffle ensued. Three times during the scuffle the knife was knocked out of Mr. MacDonald's hands, but on each occasion he managed to retrieve it. He was concerned that Mr. Allen might grab it. The fight ended when Mr. Allen, on the ground, grabbed Mr. MacDonald's wrists in an attempt to throw him over his head. Mr. MacDonald attempted to stab Mr. Allen, aiming for his chest. Mr. Allen succeeded in flipping Mr. MacDonald into the air, so the blow was deflected into Mr. Allen's upper chest and shoulder area. As Mr. MacDonald flew over Mr. Allen's head, his body went in one direction and the knife in the other. At that point the guards jumped on Mr. MacDonald and restrained him. Hughie MacDonald testified that because he was convinced Gary Allen was armed and intended to kill him, his purpose in using his knife was to stop Mr. Allen or "at least to put a hole in him," and if it meant killing him he was prepared to do that. "I did not want to die that day."

Under cross-examination, Crown counsel suggested to Hughie MacDonald that it had been he who was chasing Gary Allen and that Gary Allen was backing up. Mr. MacDonald responded, "I would have chased him to hell that day." It was put to Mr. MacDonald that, as suggested during the evidence of IPSO Dick, there were alternative ways he could have dealt with the problem. He could have sought the intervention of the Inmate Committee. Mr. MacDonald said that that was not an option, because it was the Inmate Committee who had come to him in the first place to tell him there was a problem with Mr. Allen.

Clearly their intervention had not helped deflect Mr. Allen's intentions. The second alternative suggested by Crown counsel was going to a staff member and telling that person of the bad blood between Mr. Allen and himself. Mr. MacDonald responded that he believed the administration already knew about the incompatibility. The third alternative suggested was that Mr. MacDonald could have informed a guard that he had some contraband in his cell, as a result of which he would be taken to segregation and thereby avoid any confrontation with Mr. Allen. Mr. MacDonald indignantly responded to this by saying, "Why should I get myself locked up because this piece of—gentleman—wants to kill me?" In response to the further suggestion that he could have told staff he had a knife in his cell, which also would have led to his being segregated, Mr. MacDonald replied even more indignantly that this would probably have resulted in his being sent back to the Special Handling Unit for another four years. The final suggestion put to Mr. MacDonald was that he could have sought protective custody (PC) status. Mr. MacDonald said that was not an option for him, because he had lots of incompatibles in PC and if he had checked in, he would have become involved in an ongoing war with these individuals, including some of Gary Allen's friends.

During cross-examination, Crown counsel asked Mr. MacDonald to name the prisoner who had supplied him with the knife on February 22. Mr. MacDonald declined to answer, saying it would place this prisoner in jeopardy. The judge then instructed the jury that they could take the accused's refusal to answer to account in assessing his credibility. On redirect examination by Mr. Conroy, Mr. MacDonald was asked what the consequences would be if he named the prisoner. He said he would be labelled an informer and run the risk of being stabbed or beaten by other prisoners.

Hughie MacDonald's evidence was followed by that of another prisoner, Marty Hornell, whose criminal record consisted of numerous counts of bad cheques, false pretences, and several robberies. Mr. Hornell explained that he had been a junkie for twenty years, and all of these offences had been committed to support his habit. He had known Gary Allen back in the late 1970s when they were both scoring heroin on Granville Street in Vancouver. During that time Gary Allen was known as a "muscle head," meaning that he was very intimidating and used his strength to get drugs from other guys. Mr. Hornell said he himself had been robbed by Mr. Allen and that on another occasion he observed Mr. Allen beat a person up to get dope from him. He did not see Mr. Allen for another fifteen years, until he met him in Kent. Mr. Hornell was in segregation at Kent early in 1994 following an involuntary transfer from Mission Institution. He was the food server, and therefore had the free run of the J segregation unit. He testified that Gary Allen was constantly badmouthing Hughie MacDonald and that he used Mr. Hornell to pass papers of heroin to other prisoners as part of what Mr. Hornell understood to be Mr. Allen's "building an army" who would support him when he was released into the population. As Mr. Hornell explained, "If you supply prisoners with heroin then you have a lot of influence. It's like bees to a flower." He testified that Mr. Allen bribed other prisoners who had numbers lower than his—and therefore would normally be released to population before him—by giving them heroin in return for refusing to leave segregation when their number came up. In this way Gary Allen was able to accelerate his own release.

Meva Gill was the next witness. Mr. Gill was serving three life sentences, two of which were imposed in 1978 for the murder of his uncle and aunt and the third in 1983 for the murder of another prisoner at Kent Institution. Mr. Gill had been described by a Federal Court judge, in a case in which Mr. Gill challenged his transfer to the Special Handling Unit (SHU), as one of the "barbarian princes" of the Canadian prison system. Although not a tall man, Mr. Gill had the physique of a well-disciplined weightlifter. His evidence was that he had met Gary Allen in Kent in 1991–92 and had met Hughie MacDonald earlier, when they were both in the Special Handling Unit. Mr. Gill's relationship with Mr. Allen had begun when they were working out together in the gym. Subsequently, Mr. Gill had asked Mr. Allen for some favours, in the form of enforcement services for the collection of drug debts. Mr. Gill testified that he had had a conversation with Gary Allen shortly after Mr. Allen returned to Kent from the Special Handling Unit in 1991. Mr. Allen asked him for news about guys in the SHU, and when he mentioned Hughie MacDonald's name, Mr. Allen got visibly upset. On another occasion, when Mr. Gill asked him what the problem was with Hughie MacDonald, Mr. Allen's response was "He's dead." Mr. Gill said Mr. Allen had told him that he had it in for Hughie MacDonald "because of what he and his friends did to me in Edmonton." Mr. Gill eventually withdrew from his association with Gary Allen because, as he put it, Mr. Allen "was a heat score," and Mr. Gill was trying to lower his own profile and move to lower security.

Meva Gill described Gary Allen as a big man, strong and intimidating. When asked to describe Hughie MacDonald, he laughed and immediately apologized to the court for doing so: "I'm sorry, I was laughing because he reminds me of Santa Claus." I noticed that several jury members smiled at this. At the beginning of the trial, I'm sure they could not have imagined Hughie MacDonald, with his convictions for manslaughter and double first-degree murder, as Santa Claus. Having since compared the demeanour and the physical appearance of this fifty-two-year-old, 185-pound man, bulging more at the waist than the biceps, with the photograph of Gary Allen, 6'2" and 275 pounds, stripped to the waist, with his 58-inch chest and massive biceps, and now with the imposing physique of Meva Gill, the association was not so far-fetched.

The third prisoner witness was Jimmy Whitmore. Mr. Whitmore was serving a life sentence for murder. He too had the narrow waist and the upper body contours of a weightlifter, and as he crossed the courtroom to the witness box, his musculature and attitude were highlighted by the distinctive swagger developed in maximum and some medium security prisons. The prisoners testifying at this trial were in leg irons, which had the effect of accentuating the prison walk. Mr. Whitmore was also wearing large black sunglasses, which increased the intimidation factor by several notches. The intensity of his physical presence was further charged by his very soft speaking voice, which required the judge on several occasions to ask him to speak louder.

Mr. Whitmore had met both Gary Allen and Hughie MacDonald in Kent Institution. On the morning Mr. Allen was released into the population from segregation, Mr. Whitmore was living in A unit. Mr. Allen had been released to B unit. Mr. Allen approached Mr. Whitmore at the door which separates A and B units and asked him for a knife. Mr. Whitmore "sloughed him off." He had heard there were bad feelings between Mr. Allen and Mr. MacDonald and that Mr. Allen was going to kill Mr. MacDonald. Ten minutes later Mr. Allen told Mr. Whitmore he had obtained a knife from someone else. Mr. Whitmore said that he went to talk to Mr. Tremblay, the chairman of the Inmate Committee: "I was really pissed off because this great big guy was going to take out this old man." Following that, Mr. Whitmore went to the dining room where Hughie MacDonald was having his lunch, related what had transpired between him and Gary Allen, and asked Mr. MacDonald what he was going to do. Mr. MacDonald said he was going to suggest to Mr. Allen that they settle it in the gym that night. Mr. Whitmore asked Mr. MacDonald whether he needed some help; Mr. MacDonald declined his offer.

Mr. Whitmore's evidence ended the day on a dramatic note. His examination-in-chief finished at 4:00 p.m. and Crown counsel indicated that he would need at least twenty minutes, perhaps half an hour, for cross-examination. Since the judge had promised the jury that he would accommodate one juror's problems with daycare by not sitting much beyond 4:00 p.m., he adjourned the day's hearing. Mr. Whitmore got visibly upset, urging that the cross-examination be completed that day because "I'm sitting downstairs in one of those fucking animal cages and I don't want to have to come back again." The sharpness of Mr. Whitmore's tone and the sudden rise in the volume of his voice caused both the court reporter and the court clerk to freeze. The sheriffs braced themselves, but the incident was over in a moment, and counsel explained to Mr. Whitmore that he would be back on the stand first thing next morning and therefore would not have to wait very long downstairs. Mr. Whitmore completed his cross-examination the next day, maintaining his soft-spoken answers as a counterpoint to the physical tension he generated.

The next witness was Shawn Preddy. Mr. Preddy's first federal sentence was in 1986, when he received 7 years for three robberies and possession of weapons. After being released straight to the street from Kent's segregation unit, he had been rearrested and had been brought to court today from the Kamloops provincial jail, where he was awaiting trial on new charges of robbery and assault. In describing Hughie MacDonald's reputation Mr. Preddy testified, "He's an older convict who does his own time and doesn't get in anyone else's face." As to Gary Allen, "he was regarded as a dangerous man, very aggressive, intimidating, who muscled other prisoners for drugs or whatever else he wanted." Mr. Preddy described Kent as a "cliquey" institution in which prisoners formed partnerships for reasons of both friendship and survival.

> Kent is a very dangerous place and having partners is part of surviving. Living in such a place you are putting your life in your partner's hands on a regular basis. For example, when you're taking a shower and you've got shampoo all over your hair, you can't see. One of your enemies can just pull the shower curtain aside and plunge you with a blade. Your partner is there to make sure that doesn't happen. Your partner is someone who will take your life into their hands and hold it dearly.

Shawn Preddy related how Gary Allen, when he came into the institution in 1992, quickly formed a partnership with Wayne Bellegarde. "Bellegarde is also a big man who liked to think of himself as dangerous, but when push came to shove he always backed down." However, when Mr. Allen and Mr. Bellegarde teamed up, Mr. Bellegarde's worst characteristics came out. The two of them were constantly muscling prisoners for drugs, canteen, deodorant (which could be used in making home brew, by squeezing the deodorant stick for its alcohol content), or anything else they could use to get high. Mr. Preddy described how this muscling activity, bitterly resented by most prisoners, led to a major incident. It had started one evening when Wayne Bellegarde told Mike Tyson, Shawn Preddy's partner, that he could not play floor hockey in the gym. Mr. Preddy confronted Mr. Bellegarde and told him that Mr. Tyson was going to play: "Bellegarde backed down and Mike had his game." Several weeks later, Mr. Preddy was going out to the yard on a Saturday morning and had just entered what he described as a "blind spot," meaning a place which could not be seen from either of the two adjacent guard towers. As he walked through the door he saw Gary Allen and Wayne Bellegarde sitting at a table. As Mr. Preddy got closer Mr. Bellegarde moved to block access to the yard and Mr. Allen circled around behind him. Both drew knives. Mr. Preddy was not armed, and Mr. Bellegarde berated him for what had happened in the gym. With knives being flashed in his face, Mr. Preddy was forced to back down and give Mr. Bellegarde an apology. Shawn Preddy testified, "It was a very dangerous situation. I thought I was going to die that day."

Mr. Preddy described how the activities of Mr. Allen and Mr. Bellegarde continued to escalate. To Mr. Preddy and his friends this behaviour constituted outlaw behaviour even in a society of outlaws. He testified that he had a reputation as someone who would stand up against wrongdoing by the administration or among the prisoners: "I'm a bit of a policeman within our own society." This prison policeman role was played out in 1992 when Shawn Preddy, Mike Tyson, and a few other prisoners decided that they were tired of the predatory behaviour of Gary Allen and Wayne Bellegarde. They invited them to come to a meeting in the gym. The purpose of the meeting was to present Mr. Allen and Mr. Bellegarde with two options: to leave the population, meaning that they should ask to go to the hole, or to face the wrath of the whole institution. Mr. Preddy testified that, knowing Mr. Allen, it was not likely he would go for this first option, and therefore Mr. Preddy and his friends would probably have to "take these guys out"—to kill them.

By the time Mr. Preddy and his friends went down to the gym, Mr. Allen and his associates had already arrived and taken over the weight pit, where they had strategically arranged weight bars and baseball bats. Shawn Preddy and his associates were armed mainly with knives. However, this confrontation, what Mr. Preddy described as "a Mexican stand-off, because everyone realized that if this was played out, it could end up as a blood bath," had the desired result. Mr. Allen and Mr. Bellegarde were taken to segregation with the other prisoners involved, and were kept there when it was made clear to the administration that their presence in the population would not be tolerated again.

The next time Shawn Preddy saw Gary Allen was over a year later, the morning Mr. Allen was released from segregation on February 22, 1994. In the courtyard after lunch that day, Mr. Preddy and his partner, Mike Tyson, approached Mr. Allen, who was standing with his partner, Mark Biega. Mr. Preddy and Mr. Allen did several laps around the courtyard, Mr. Preddy making it clear that he would not put any road blocks in Mr. Allen's way as long as Mr. Allen did not get into the "garbage" that had led to the 1992 incident. He also made it clear that he would not tolerate having Mr. Allen in the same unit. At the end of the conversation the two men shook hands and Mr. Preddy left the courtyard. Mr. Preddy testified that he had tucked a knife inside his waistband before the meeting with Mr. Allen, since he was fearful of what Mr. Allen might do if there was a fight. Though he was 6'2" and was in the best physical condition of his life, weighing 195 pounds and regularly working out, Shawn Preddy doubted whether he could take Gary Allen in a straight fight.

Shawn Preddy was asked how Gary Allen compared to other prisoners at Kent, in terms of his potential danger to the public. Mr. Preddy prefaced his remarks by saying, "Not everyone at Kent is dangerous but there are many dangerous men." Mr. Preddy said that he would rate Gary Allen among the most dangerous. Asked how he would rate Hughie MacDonald, he replied that he did not see him as a dangerous man. Crown counsel put it to him that Hughie

MacDonald had two first-degree murder sentences on his record, and surely, therefore, must be viewed as dangerous. Mr. Preddy replied that from a prisoner's perspective, how dangerous someone is "is measured by your relationship with the person and what you can expect in your dealings with that person." Mr. Preddy had never had any problems with Hughie MacDonald, his reputation being that of an older prisoner doing his own time, and therefore had no reason to think Mr. MacDonald would be dangerous in the context of daily interaction.

From the moment the next witness, Dale Curran, came into the courtroom, his presence was charged with the electric energy Gary Allen himself had spoken about. Although he was half the size of Mr. Allen, in spirit and attitude the two men were very similar. Unlike Mr. Allen, however, Dale Curran did not seem to be speaking out of anger; rather, his experiences in prison over a very long period of time had imprinted in him a way of seeing the world, reflecting how he believed the world saw him. Mr. Curran was thirty-five years old and had been on the street for only about thirty months since 1978. His youth was punctuated by stints in foster homes, group homes, juvenile detention facilities, and then provincial and federal prisons. He was a heroin addict with convictions for narcotic offences, breaking and entering, robberies, and escapes. While on statutory release in 1994, he spent nineteen months on the street, the longest continuous period in almost twenty years. He then became readdicted and went to his parole officer to turn himself in. His statutory release was suspended and he was returned to Kent Institution.

Mr. Curran's evidence had the unmistakable footprint of a maximum security prisoner, and his candour was almost alarming. He described how he and Gary Allen became partners at Matsqui. Mr. Curran would have drugs sent into the institution and would sell them to various prisoners, whose names he would then give to Gary Allen. Mr. Allen would muscle those prisoners for the drugs they had obtained and the drugs would be returned to Mr. Curran for resale to other prisoners, with the proceeds split between Mr. Allen and Mr. Curran. Of Gary Allen, Mr. Curran said, "Gary was an enforcer. He liked weapons but he didn't need them."

Mr. Curran made it very clear that he had been willing to stand up for his friend Gary Allen, no matter what. He testified that he knew Mr. Allen had a beef with Mr. MacDonald and that Mr. Allen was going to settle the score when he came out of segregation. When Mr. Curran heard that Mr. Allen had been released from segregation, he went back to his unit, retrieved a four-foot chain, placed it under his parka, returned to the courtyard, and offered the chain to Mr. Allen for use in his confrontation with Mr. MacDonald. Mr. Allen showed Mr. Curran a shank made from a small kitchen knife that had been sharpened and placed in a homemade handle. The blade and the handle were each about four inches in length. When Mr. Allen told Mr. Curran, "I'm going to seriously fuck him up," Mr. Curran responded that he would need a bigger blade to carry out his intention. He took the knife from Mr. Allen, and it was agreed that another prisoner, Ralph Moore, would get Mr. Allen a bigger one.

Mr. Curran testified that he saw Mr. MacDonald come out of C unit and walk over to Mr. Allen in the courtyard. Mr. Allen put out his hand as if in a handshake and then sucker-punched Mr. MacDonald.

> It's the oldest trick in the book. Gary offered to shake his hand and then smoked him in the head and threw a couple of kicks at him. Hughie fell and then pulled a knife. Gary grabbed him on the wrists and he then slipped and went down. It looked like he was trying to toss Hughie over his head. The next thing I see is Gary goes limp and I realize my friend is down. As the bulls started to move in, I moved over to try and retrieve Gary's knife but there was nothing there. It turned out that Gary didn't have a knife. Ralph Moore never got a chance to give him another blade.

Mr. Curran was asked by Defence counsel John Conroy to come out of the witness box to demonstrate the way in which Gary Allen had sucker-punched Hughie MacDonald. Mr. Curran left the witness box and the two sheriffs who had been sitting next to him quickly got to their feet. He stretched out his hand, then withdrew it and rapidly completed a right hook. Still standing up, out of the witness box, Mr. Curran continued with his description of how Mr. Allen had grabbed Mr. MacDonald's wrists. Turning to one of the sheriffs as if to demonstrate, he reached for the sheriff's wrists. The sheriff, a much bigger man than Mr. Curran, recoiled; Mr. Curran stopped and returned to the witness box. The sheriff was visibly shaken and remained so for the rest of the afternoon. Recalling Gary Allen's words, I thought that it was as if Dale Curran sent a powerful electrical charge through the sheriff without even touching him.

In his cross-examination, Crown counsel Jack Gibson asked each of the prisoners in turn a series of questions designed to establish that there was a rigid convicts' code, two of its rules being that you never informed on another prisoner and that when you did a favour you expected a favour in return. In relation to the first rule, it was put to the prisoners that if Gary Allen had survived the attack, they would not have come forward in a courtroom to testify regarding his muscling and other outlaw activities. In relation to the second rule, Mr. Gibson suggested the prisoners had an interest in saying whatever was necessary to get Hughie MacDonald acquitted, because then he would be indebted to them and they could expect something in return. All of the prisoners rejected these suggestions. Shawn Preddy admitted that if Gary Allen killed Hughie MacDonald but was still alive himself, he would not have given evidence pointing the finger at Mr. Allen. If Mr. Allen had survived the attack by Mr. MacDonald and Mr. MacDonald was on trial for attempted murder, Mr. Preddy admitted that would be a dilemma for him; however, he thought he would have given the same evidence. Shawn Preddy thus drew a distinction between providing information to the authorities that could be used to convict a prisoner and giving evidence that could exonerate a prisoner.

When the same questions were put to Dale Curran, he questioned the whole concept of a convict code. "You think there's a convict code? Let me give you a reality check. The code you've got in your mind is a hypothetical one. It's a theory of the way we're supposed to act. There are no rules when you are sitting in a maximum security institution. It's chaos." As if to emphasize his point, Dale Curran was wearing a T-shirt designed by Ralph Moore that bore the initials C.A.O.S.: "Convicts against Oppressed Society."

By the time Mr. Curran was finished giving his evidence, it was 3:30 p.m. on Friday afternoon. It had been a long week for the jury. What they had learned about life in a Canadian prison was far removed from the experiences they shared as law-abiding citizens of British Columbia's Fraser Valley. In addition to the evidence of what happened in the courtyard at Kent, they had also heard about Mexican stand-offs in the gymnasium in which armed camps of prisoners stared each other down. They themselves had come face to face with the prisoners involved in these events, with men who carried the physical and psychological freight of maximum security with them into the witness box—not simply the tattoos and the bulging muscles but the attitude, the uncompromising look of the Big House. At a time when the jury was likely thinking of the weekend ahead and returning to the peaceful rhythms of their own lives, they were to hear the evidence of a prisoner who would leave them with no reasonable doubt that violence in prison has its own distinctive beat.

In the half-hour remaining, one more prisoner, Darryl Bates, gave evidence for the Defence. Mr. Bates was taken through his criminal record and was asked to describe, in particular, the circumstances leading to his latest conviction for unlawful confinement arising out of a hostage-taking at Surrey Pre-trial Centre. The Crown, as part of its case, had earlier called the nurse from Surrey Pre-trial who had been taken hostage by Darryl Bates to give evidence that Gary Allen had been influential in persuading Mr. Bates to release her unharmed. In this way, the Crown meant to demonstrate that the evidence given by Defence witnesses, which depicted Gary Allen's character as that of a psychopathic aggressor, was one concocted to secure Hughie MacDonald's acquittal. The Defence had called Mr. Bates' evidence, in part, to rebut the suggestion that Mr. Allen had been instrumental in bringing the hostage-taking to a peaceable end. Defence counsel anticipated that Mr. Bates' evidence would be relatively brief. However, as Mr. Bates explained what led to the hostage-taking, he began to relive each moment for the jury, his breathless images filling the courtroom: a desperate addict in withdrawal seizing a nurse and demanding drugs in return for her release. Mr. Bates described Gary Allen as a friend who had helped him negotiate with the authorities but said he had made his own decision to release the nurse unharmed.

Darryl Bates continued his evidence on Monday morning. He described Gary Allen as "no one to mess with." Regarding the events of February 22, 1994, Mr. Bates testified he had seen Mr. Allen that morning, following his release from segregation. Mr. Allen told Mr. Bates that he had a couple of beefs to deal with, one with Shawn Preddy and a more immediate one with Hughie MacDonald. Mr. Bates said that Mr. Allen appeared to be in withdrawal and asked Mr. Bates for drugs. Mr. Bates got him some heroin and "fixed" him. Even though Mr. Bates was on Mr. Allen's side in any beef, Mr. Bates said that he went to Mr. MacDonald and advised him, "You better watch your back because he's going to come for you."

The next witness, Walter Sinclair, was the only Aboriginal prisoner to give evidence in the trial. Like Mr. MacDonald, Mr. Sinclair was serving a life sentence for the murder of two prison guards. Mr. Sinclair said he had heard from other prisoners that Gary Allen was intent on killing Hughie MacDonald as soon as he came out of the hole. Because Mr. Sinclair had done time with Mr. MacDonald in the Special Handling Unit, he said he felt obliged to warn Mr. MacDonald that Mr. Allen was in the population and was going to kill him.

Mr. Sinclair was asked what he had observed in the courtyard that day regarding the fight between Mr. Allen and Mr. MacDonald. His answers were vague, and he expressed a great reluctance to give details about who or what he had seen. At one point, when Crown counsel asked him about an answer he had given to a question put to him by Defence counsel, Mr. Sinclair said he didn't understand what the Crown was getting at. Crown counsel asked, "What don't you understand?" Mr. Sinclair angrily responded with several words in Cree followed by the statement, "*You* don't understand what *I* just said; that's why *I* don't understand what *you* said," effectively making the point that in many respects he was appearing in a forum and a language foreign to him.

The issue of cultural distance was revisited when Crown counsel questioned Mr. Sinclair about his lengthy criminal record. Mr. Sinclair politely said he did not want to talk about it. When Crown counsel asked him why, he replied that he was trying to heal himself from all the harm he had done to others, and to bring it up in the courtroom would not help him along that path, and indeed would set him back. Since the jury did not know that over the past several years Mr. Sinclair had been participating in Aboriginal ceremonies and working with Aboriginal Elders in a healing journey, it is likely jury members were left with the impression that he was being evasive, thus placing his credibility on the line.

Evasive was not a word that could ever be used to describe the next witness, Jean-Louis Tremblay. He entered the courtroom wearing a black sweatshirt with the words "Murder Incorporated" emblazoned on the front. At the time of Gary Allen's death and for some time before and after, Mr. Tremblay was chairman of the Inmate Committee of the general population side of Kent Institution. While doing my research at Kent I had met regularly with Mr. Tremblay, or Cacane, as he is known to prisoners, and he filled me in on the politics of the prison. Mr. Tremblay had a passion for tropical fish and in both the Inmate Committee room and his own cell there were large fish tanks filled with exotic fish, which he kept in immaculate condition.

Mr. Tremblay was serving a life sentence for first-degree murder, together with a 10-year sentence for attempted murder. In his examination-in-chief, he was asked to describe Gary Allen's reputation and his own relationship with him.

> He was a bully, a man who had his own way in jail. I met him when we were both in Matsqui Institution. I had come from Kent and had asked some people who I trusted at Kent for some contacts at Matsqui. They told me about Gary Allen. I saw him again when we were both in Pre-trial. It's good to have a bully on your side in prison, someone who can rock. I didn't like a lot of the things Gary did to other prisoners, still I liked the guy.

When Mr. Tremblay first visited him in segregation, Mr. Allen told him he had beefs with two guys in the population, Shawn Preddy and Hughie MacDonald, and that he intended to kill Hughie MacDonald when he got out of the hole. Mr. Tremblay testified that he was taken off guard by how committed Mr. Allen seemed to this course of action and discussed it with his fellow committee member Dennis Smith. As chairman of Kent's Inmate Committee, his job was to resolve differences and to avoid problems in the population. Mr. Tremblay and Mr. Smith went to see Mr. MacDonald, who asked them to find out why Mr. Allen wanted to kill him. On his next visit to segregation, Mr. Tremblay conveyed Mr. MacDonald's question. Mr. Allen replied: "He stabbed my brother. It's payback time." Mr. Allen told Mr. Tremblay that he planned to do the killing in front of the entire population. Mr. Tremblay testified that he asked Mr. Allen to reconsider this course of action. "There was no need to do it in front of everybody. He could do it in his cell, in the showers, anywhere but not in the courtyard in front of the cameras and in front of the guards." Mr. Allen responded that he had made a commitment and meant to keep it. Mr. Tremblay calculated that he would have more time to work on Mr. Allen to get him to change his mind, because it would be at least a month, if not two, before Mr. Allen was released from segregation to the population.

Mr. Tremblay testified that on the morning of February 22 the Inmate Committee had a meeting with Unit Manager Gerry Dewar. Mr. Dewar asked Mr. Tremblay and Mr. Smith whether Mr. Allen would have any problems in the population. Mr. Tremblay said no, because the issues between Mr. Allen and other prisoners were prisoner business, not the institution's. Mr. Tremblay then went back to his cell and, in accordance with his regular routine, went to sleep. He was woken up just before noon by Mr. Smith, who told him that Mr. Allen was in the courtyard waiting for Mr. MacDonald to come out of the dining room. Mr. Tremblay had a hard time believing that Mr. Allen was out of segregation. He got dressed and went out to the courtyard to talk to Mr. Allen. He put it to Mr. Allen that Mr. MacDonald was an old man and that it was an old beef, but Mr. Allen was determined that it go down. As chairman of the committee, Mr. Tremblay said it was his responsibility to go and speak to Mr. MacDonald. Together with Mr. Smith, he went to the dining room and told Mr. MacDonald that Mr. Allen was planning to kill him in the yard in front of everybody.

Mr. Tremblay was asked by Defence counsel whether he knew if Mr. Allen was armed at the time he spoke to him in the courtyard. Mr. Tremblay testified that Mr. Allen had showed him a small butter knife, taken from the staff dining room, which had been sharpened and mounted in a handle. Mr. Tremblay recounted his efforts to dissuade Mr. Allen from doing this: "We have other enemies to deal with who are young, strong and healthy." In the course of this discussion, Dale Curran came over and told Mr. Tremblay that he should let Mr. Allen deal with this in his own way. Since it was now clear that Mr. Allen would not back away, it was suggested that "to do the job" he would need a bigger knife than the one he had. Mr. Tremblay testified that at this point he asked Ralph Moore, who had joined the conversation, to go get "the chopper." The chopper was a twelve-inch blade from a heavy-duty paper cutter, sharpened and stashed in the prison grounds. Mr. Allen then handed over the small knife he had, and Mr. Tremblay and Mr. Moore went into C unit. While they were there, the confrontation between Mr. Allen and Mr. MacDonald took place. The doors to the courtyard were locked, and Mr. Tremblay was trapped inside and did not see the fight.

Mr. Tremblay was asked for his reaction when he found out that Mr. Allen had been stabbed and was on his way to hospital.

> I was shocked. No one could convince me that that guy could kill Gary Allen. Gary Allen was a good fighter, he always trained and he was good with his legs and he was very strong. I didn't believe that a fifty-two-year-old guy with a pot [belly] could do that. But for me and most of the guys I know, even with two or three shanks, we couldn't win a fight with Gary Allen. I was also disappointed. I hoped he would win. He was my friend.

Under cross-examination Mr. Tremblay was taken through his long record, and Crown counsel made much of the fact that his record included three charges of conspiracy to commit various crimes. The Crown's theory was that just as Mr. Tremblay had conspired with others to commit criminal offences, so had he conspired with the prisoners who were testifying to concoct a common story in order to help Mr. MacDonald. Mr. Tremblay's response revealed the enormous gulf between the reality of a Crown counsel and that of Jean-Louis Tremblay.

Q: This conspiracy, what was that a conspiracy to do?
A: To rob banks. I have robbed banks since I was fourteen. That's what I do. I rob banks. I have conspirated all my life. I have planned to do crime all of my life.
Q: You mean that's your job?
A: Yes, that's my job.

As to the specific suggestion that he was in court to do Mr. MacDonald a favour, in the expectation of receiving a favour in return, Mr. Tremblay responded:

I don't need any favours from that guy. I spend my whole life in jail. I have been in the toughest and most dangerous penitentiaries in the country. I have seen all that there is to see. I do not need to do this to get favours. I have my own club. I have my own people. I have nothing to prove to no one. To come here and lie to help Hughie MacDonald will not help me. No one is going to say Tremblay came to court and lied and that he's a good guy. It would do nothing to increase my reputation as a tough guy. I don't need to be here. I hate courts. If I had my way this morning I would be in Kent smoking a spliff and taking it easy. I would not be here.

Mr. Tremblay also threw off the suggestion that he had an interest in helping Mr. MacDonald. "That man killed my friend. That day he was supposed to die." Crown counsel also put to Mr. Tremblay the standard suggestion that if Mr. Allen had survived and Mr. MacDonald had died, Mr. Tremblay would not have come to court to testify. His response was immediate:

If Gary Allen were here I would not have to give evidence. He would say to the judge, "Your Honour I killed MacDonald. I did it in front of everybody. Give me the life sentence. I don't care."

Jean-Louis Tremblay's testimony vividly described what life is reduced to in a maximum security penitentiary in the 1990s.

I have to survive in jail. Every day you wake up you don't know whether you will go to sleep that night. All my life is to survive.

Ralph Moore followed Jean-Louis Tremblay on the witness stand. Mr. Moore also wore the black colours of "Murder Incorporated," but he was a little more discreet: the logo was on the back of his T-shirt. His evidence broadly followed the contours of Mr. Tremblay's, although he made a particular point of emphasizing the nature of his activities as representing "his people." Shawn Preddy, in the course of his evidence, had said that Kent was a "cliquey kind of place." Mr. Moore began his evidence by making it clear that his clique was among the most powerful in terms of influence in the institution. Mr. Moore also made it clear that he had regarded Gary Allen as a friend and that he and his people stood behind Mr. Allen. He described how he had learned through the committee that Mr. Allen intended to kill Hughie MacDonald and had made arrangements for a knife to be ready for Mr. Allen when he was released to the population. Like Mr. Tremblay, he was surprised when Mr. Allen was released so early. He met with Mr. Allen in the courtyard that morning, trying to persuade him to take his revenge against Mr. Macdonald in a place secluded from official view. While they were talking, Mr. Moore saw Mr. MacDonald leave the dining room and go into D unit. Mr. Moore told Mr. Allen that he should go into D unit and deal with Mr. MacDonald there. But Mr. Allen wanted to get more heroin first. While they were talking Dale Curran came over with a chain wrapped around his neck and under his parka and offered it to Mr. Allen. Mr. Allen declined and showed the group the knife he had. They all agreed it was not big enough for the job at hand. Mr. Tremblay told Mr. Moore to go and get the big blade, and the small knife was passed to Mr. Curran, who placed it in his pants. Mr. Moore said that he again suggested to Mr. Allen that, if he was committed to this course of action, he should do it in D unit. Mr. Allen remained adamant that he was going to do it in the courtyard, and Mr. Curran at this point told the others to back off. Mr. Moore then went back into C unit, got the heroin, and put it in a condom. He retrieved the big blade and put his weight belt on. As he was preparing to go back into the courtyard the doors started to close and he, like Mr. Tremblay, missed the "play."

In cross-examination, Mr. Moore was asked to describe the circumstances of his last offence, when he was convicted of damaging property through criminal negligence and received a 5-year sentence. He told the jury he had previously been charged with first-degree murder arising from a killing at Kent Institution. He had been kept in segregation for two years until the charge was stayed by the Crown, and then released straight to the street from segregation. He described the experience this way:

You are at the end of the earth. Your life is worth nothing. They feed you through a slot. After keeping me locked up for two years I'm

released straight to the street. They yelled at me on the street and I
shot sixteen bullets into the parole office.

When Mr. Moore was asked the standard question, "Isn't it true that you and
other prisoners got together and came up with this story to help MacDonald?"
he fired back, "This case does not need a story to be concocted."

The next witness was Tim Staller. Whereas Mr. Whitmore and Mr. Curran
had come into the courtroom radiating energy, and Mr. Tremblay and Mr.
Moore were almost defiant in their outlawry, by contrast Mr. Staller crossed the
courtroom almost lazily. To the extent that anyone can be so wearing leg irons,
he was laid-back. That phrase aptly characterizes the manner in which he gave
his evidence. Mr. Staller explained that he was a loner at Kent, that he belonged
to no group and preferred to do his time by himself, unto himself. He had less
hassles that way. He had been at Kent since 1988 on a charge of second-degree
murder although his record predated that, and, like so many prisoners, he had
spent most of his adult life locked up. In describing Gary Allen he said, "I found
the guy to be pretty brutal." He described an occasion when Gary Allen and
Wayne Bellegarde had run out of home brew and "were running around the
units grabbing guys' deodorant" for its alcohol content—the incident previously
described by Shawn Preddy. Mr. Staller corroborated Mr. Preddy's evidence that
when one prisoner objected, he was given a bad beating by Mr. Allen.

Because he had done time with Gary Allen previously, when Mr. Staller found
himself in segregation with Mr. Allen in February 1994, he struck up a conversation. Mr. Allen asked if Mr. Staller knew where Hughie MacDonald was. Mr.
Staller said that he did not know Mr. MacDonald. Mr. Allen's response was to
slam his fist into the wall and say, "I'm doing him." Mr. Staller testified that he
understood this to mean Mr. Allen was going to kill the man. That conversation
was the last time Mr. Staller saw or spoke to Mr. Allen.

If Tim Staller's laid-back walk into the courtroom reflected the way he did
time at Kent, Gary Weaver's assertive, heads-up approach to the witness box exhibited his attitude to imprisonment. Only twenty-seven years old, Gary Weaver
had spent all but eleven months locked up since the age of fourteen. He had
received a life sentence for second-degree murder in 1989 and had done every day
of the past seven years in either maximum security or the Special Handling Unit.
He was asked what effect doing time in maximum and super-maximum security
had on a prisoner.

You become accustomed to a violent and volatile atmosphere. The
Special Handling Unit is a much more intense place where you have
to fortify yourself. You have to train yourself to be mentally strong in
order to survive. When you go out into a common room with other
prisoners if you make a mistake you could be dead. You don't have

the choice of being wrong. If you are, you fall. After doing time in the Special Handling Unit it becomes a part of you. You have a more rigid attitude to life and to doing time. You do not lose traits like this and throw them out the window, even when you leave.

Mr. Weaver testified that he had never met Gary Allen before February 1994. On February 17 of that year Mr. Weaver was placed in segregation, based upon allegations that he was involved in the importation of drugs into Kent. He had heard of Gary Allen and he assumed that Mr. Allen had heard of him. Mr. Weaver testified that he had heard stories about Mr. Allen as "a rock and roll guy. A stand-up guy."

On February 18 Mr. Weaver was moved into Mr. Allen's cell and spent the next five days double-bunked with him. He learned that Mr. Allen had been using heroin and had only a little left. Mr. Allen demanded medication from the nursing staff, as he was going through withdrawal, and they gave him some Ativan. Usually a prisoner just is given just one or two pills, but on this occasion Mr. Allen was given almost a whole card of Ativan, about twenty-one pills, which was very unusual. Mr. Weaver testified, "We split them up and ate them. It was a party." During the time they spent together the two men shared war stories.

Mr. Weaver was asked whether Mr. Allen talked during these five days about his problems with Mr. MacDonald. He testified that Mr. Allen had told him he had a beef with Mr. MacDonald. Mr. Weaver testified Mr. Allen had told him, " 'I'm going to take that old cocksucker's head off.' He was pretty agitated and kept on about it." Asked if there was any discussion of weapons, Mr. Weaver responded, "Sure, I asked him if he was going to beef, whether he was ready. He told me that he had something worked out for him." Mr. Weaver testified that on the morning of February 22, Mr. Allen had gone to see the Segregation Review Board and been told that he was being released that morning. He came back to his cell and began preparing himself for a fight by doing sets of push-ups. Mr. Allen disparagingly referred to his antagonist, Mr. MacDonald, as "a sawed-off little fuck." That dismissive view of Hughie MacDonald was to haunt Gary Allen to his grave.

Mr. Weaver was asked whether he thought there would have been any way to avoid this particular "beef":

When someone says there's going to be a beef, the word gets around and people tell other people and you are committed to it. If you don't follow through you're in trouble. Given what Allen had said to people in the hole, it was clear to him that he had no choice but to do the beef, because that's what other people expected of him. It would have been the wrong thing to say he was going to kill MacDonald and not do anything.

Under cross-examination, Mr. Weaver was asked the standard question about why he was giving evidence in the trial, and the standard suggestion was put forward that it was as a favour to Hughie MacDonald. His answer was emphatic.

> As a favour? I'm telling these people [the jury] the truth. Sending a man to prison for twenty-five years for defending himself in a fight in which he could have been killed is not right. I'm obligated to be here to tell the truth.

The last prisoner called for the Defence was Dennis Smith, who at the time of the stabbing was vice-chair of the Inmate Committee. Since then he had left general population and checked into protective custody. He was the only PC to give evidence in the trial. Mr. Smith was forty-seven years old and serving a life sentence, with a minimum of twenty years before parole, imposed in 1985. He had a long previous record, and by his own estimate had spent about thirty days on the street in the last twenty-six years. He had no association with Hughie MacDonald before meeting him in the segregation unit in his capacity as a member of the Inmate Committee. However, he had heard of Mr. MacDonald over the years and his best friend spoke highly of the man. He therefore "took him at face value." Mr. Smith knew of Gary Allen's reputation from having served time with him and also through the prison grapevine. As he put it, "When you have the reputation as mean as his, word travels." He described Mr. Allen as "a large man with an attitude to go with it. He was an extremely violent man and I've seen him squeeze people for dope." Asked to explain what that "attitude" was, Mr. Smith replied, "Give it to me or I'll take it."

Mr. Smith testified that his most recent encounters with Mr. Allen had been in the segregation unit, in February 1994. Mr. Smith and Jean-Louis Tremblay saw Mr. Allen on one of their regular visits to the hole. Mr. Smith spoke to Mr. Allen through the food slot and they exchanged the usual formalities. Mr. Allen asked who was in Kent, and Mr. Smith rattled off a list of the people he knew who were Mr. Allen's associates or people he would have done time with. Hughie MacDonald's name came up and Mr. Allen responded, "He is dead." Mr. Smith explained, "Gary had that look about him. It's difficult to explain, but Gary gets a certain look about his face when he's serious."

After they left segregation, Mr. Smith and Mr. Tremblay talked about what Mr. Allen had said, because "when a prisoner like Gary Allen makes a statement like that you have to take it seriously." They agreed that Mr. MacDonald should be told about the threat, but for the time being they would not tell other prisoners. They felt if the word got out about what Mr. Allen had said, he would be obliged to carry through on the threat. As Mr. Smith expressed it, "Rumours fly faster than e-mail in prison."

Mr. Smith described what happened when he told Hughie MacDonald about what Gary Allen had said.

> Hughie was in his housecoat in his cell. I told him that I'd got a mes-sage from Gary Allen and it was that Gary was going to kill him. Hughie told me to sit down and offered me a coffee. He had this look of surprise, perplexed. He told me that he had had a problem with Gary Allen in Edmonton ten years ago, but he didn't think that it warranted a statement like that. He asked me to talk to Gary the next time I was in the hole to tell him that Hughie didn't want any problem and that they should talk about it.

The next time Mr. Smith was in segregation he conveyed Mr. MacDonald's message, and Mr. Allen's response was simply, "It's done. Hughie dies; there is no getting around it."

Shortly afterwards Mr. Allen was released into the population. The first Mr. Smith knew of this was when he was leaving C unit and saw Mr. Allen standing in the courtyard. He immediately went to see Mr. Tremblay and had to wake him up. He told Mr. Tremblay that Mr. Allen was standing in the courtyard with his parka on. Mr. Smith explained that there are only two reasons a prisoner wears a parka in the courtyard: one is to keep the rain off, and the other is to conceal a weapon. Even though it had been raining, Mr. Smith had no doubt that the second reason was why Mr. Allen was wearing his parka that day. Mr. Smith watched as other prisoners went up to Mr. Allen, and then he made his approach. He asked whether there was anything that could be done to prevent the incident. Mr. Allen responded, "It's going to come to an end. I've got what it takes." Mr. Smith understood this to confirm that Mr. Allen had a weapon. He explained to the jury, "You have got to know Gary Allen to know what he's about. That look, that parka, you knew that he was armed and that he was serious."

Mr. Smith went on to describe how he and Mr. Tremblay had gone into the dining room to tell Mr. MacDonald that Mr. Allen was waiting in the courtyard for him. Mr. Smith told him, "There's no time to talk. He's going to kill you. You had better get armed up, otherwise you're going to die." Mr. Smith described the expression on Mr. MacDonald's face at this point: "It's difficult to explain but it was a look of a man who stood between a rock and a hard place through no fault of his own." Mr. Smith said that he and Mr. Tremblay went back into the courtyard and made one last-ditch effort to dissuade Mr. Allen. Mr. Allen said, "It's done."

Mr. Smith went back to C unit and up the stairs into the Inmate Committee room. He heard the doors slamming shut. He remembered that moment well because he turned around and looked at Mr. Tremblay, thinking, "Hughie is either dead or is dying."

Asked about his reaction to learning that Mr. Allen had been stabbed and was on his way to hospital, Mr. Smith testified,

> Disbelief. Disbelief that the whole event could take place in the first place. Things are usually settled here privately, not in front of the population and under the cameras. Disbelief that Gary was down. I would have assumed that Gary Allen would just break Hughie up and squash him like a bug. Gary Allen didn't need a weapon.

Mr. Smith explained that he was now in protective custody because he had run up drug debts he could not pay. As a result of his last escape from William Head Institution, he had effectively thrown away ten years of his life. When he came back to Kent he started using drugs again, and that had led to the debts. It had also led to a crisis in his life. "I was hoping that if I didn't do myself, some-one else would kill me. I was sent to RPC. While I was there I made a conscious decision to break with my past life and here I am."

Mr. Smith was asked whether protective custody would have been an option for Hughie MacDonald. He replied, "Knowing Hughie's problem, PC would not have helped him." He explained that protection is a relative term, and that your safety in protective custody depended upon "who wants you and how badly they want you." If someone wanted you badly enough, there were ways they could get to you through other prisoners even in protective custody. In Hughie MacDonald's case going PC would not have put him beyond Gary Allen's reach.

Under cross-examination, Mr. Smith stated, "Gary Allen had a way about him that made it better to be a friend of his than to be on the outs." He was asked about his motives for coming to court to give evidence, since earlier that month he had sent a note to Defence counsel stating, "Gary's got too many friends and Hugh's got too many enemies. I don't want anything to do with this." Mr. Smith said that the first statement in the note was not true and that he had written the note as an excuse not to testify, because "I was trying to wash my hands of all this, of everything to do with that part of my life." Asked why he had changed his mind, he replied, "My conscience had a big part in it. It's my belief that what has happened to Hughie MacDonald is not right."

During the course of cross-examination, Mr. Smith had his record put to him. Included in that record was a series of escapes. The Crown's theory was that these escapes were planned affairs, in much the same way Mr. Smith's evidence in court was a planned affair to help Mr. MacDonald. Mr. Smith pointed out that all of his escapes had been spur-of-the-moment affairs. "Every time I see a crack in the door I try to get a look on the other side. I figure I'm never going to get out of prison and so the days I take are the only days I'm ever going to get."

To my mind there was a sadness in Dennis Smith's evidence, a reflection of the burden of his years of imprisonment. Dennis Smith was never to see another crack in the door. He died in custody in Mission Institution of a heart attack in 1997.

In addition to the oral evidence given by correctional officers and prisoners, there was a further thread in the evidentiary reconstruction of the death of Gary Allen referred to by both the Crown and the Defence: videotape evidence. The Crown played for the jury a composite tape. The first part showed the images recorded by a camera mounted at one end of the courtyard. It suffered from several critical deficiencies: not only was it recording events from a distance of some sixty yards, but it picked up only the action close to the end of the fight, when Hughie MacDonald and Gary Allen were on the ground. The tape included images of staff moving in and then of two officers helping Gary Allen across the courtyard on his way to the hospital, followed by two other officers escorting Hughie MacDonald across the courtyard on his way to segregation.

The second part of the video recording showed images taken with hand-held cameras operated by prison officers. It showed Hughie MacDonald being taken to the segregation unit, strip-searched, and placed in his cell. It tracked the trail of blood that Gary Allen left as he was taken from the courtyard to the hospital. It then recorded the scene in the hospital with the medical staff attending Gary Allen, concluding with his being taken out of the hospital area by ambulance attendants.

The Defence, shortly before the beginning of the trial, had obtained copies of both the master tape—which included the images from the courtyard camera—and a tape from a camera in the prisoner dining room. The Defence played the dining-room tape during the evidence of Hughie MacDonald. Using the tape as a reference, Mr. MacDonald showed the jury where he had been sitting in the dining room, where Gary Allen had been sitting, how Gary Allen left the dining room, how Jean-Louis Tremblay and Dennis Smith came back in and spoke with Mr. MacDonald, and how, a little later, Jimmy Whitmore came over. Broadly speaking, this part of the videotape corroborated Mr. MacDonald's account of the events immediately preceding the confrontation in the courtyard. The images played by Defence counsel from the master recording showed staff and prisoners in the courtyard in the period prior to the confrontation. The tape then jumped to the images showing Mr. Allen and Mr. MacDonald struggling on the ground near the end of their fight.

John Conroy, for the Defence, directed the jury's attention to the lack of recorded images showing what happened when Hughie MacDonald and Gary Allen first came together in the courtyard. He suggested that while this may have been a function of technical problems or of the various cameras in the courtyard automatically switching over at the critical point (although the Crown witnesses never explained this), it raised a question: given that the cameras were there precisely for the purpose of recording events in the courtyard, why in this case were there no images available that showed one way or the other what took place between the two men?

## The Closing Addresses

In their closing addresses to the jury, both the Defence and Crown counsel focussed on the critical issue of self-defence. Defence counsel John Conroy submitted that the jury must answer two questions in their deliberations. The first question was, Did Hughie MacDonald have reasonable grounds to believe that Gary Allen was going to kill him, or at least cause him serious bodily harm? The second question was, Did Hughie MacDonald have reasonable grounds to believe that, in order to save his own life, he had no alternative but to kill Gary Allen?

On the first question, Mr. Conroy reviewed the evidence of the prisoners regarding Gary Allen's determination, indeed obsession, to kill Hughie MacDonald. He suggested that the serious reality of this threat could be found also in the evidence of the correctional authorities. He reminded the jury of the evidence of Dave Dick, to whom Gary Allen had suggested that, if the institution put him on the same range as Hughie MacDonald, he would "look after him" for the institution. Mr. Conroy also reviewed the evidence of Dr. Schimpf, the psychologist who had seen Gary Allen on a number of occasions at Fraser. Mr. Allen had talked to Dr. Schimpf about entering into "dark periods" in which he developed a narrow, almost obsessive, focus, and Mr. Conroy suggested that this is exactly what had happened in February 1994 when Mr. Allen determined that he was going to kill Mr. MacDonald in full view of the population, the staff, and the surveillance cameras. Counsel reminded the jury of Dennis Smith's evidence that when Gary Allen told Mr. Smith he was going to kill Hughie MacDonald, he had that "look about him" which meant that he was serious.

In addressing the second question, Mr. Conroy pointed out that although Mr. Allen had not been armed, there was ample evidence to ground Mr. MacDonald's belief that Mr. Allen was armed and was intent on carrying out his threat. He reviewed the evidence of the discussions in the dining room confirming that Mr. Allen was armed and the exchange in the courtyard in which Mr. Allen gave up his small knife in anticipation of being supplied with a larger weapon. Defence counsel reviewed the evidence of Mr. MacDonald and some of the other prisoners that it was Mr. Allen who threw the first punch, suggesting that there were reasonable grounds for Mr. MacDonald to believe that it was a situation of "kill or be killed."

Mr. Conroy also submitted that even if the jury did not believe the prisoner witnesses as to who threw the first punch, this would still leave open a plea of self-defence for Hughie MacDonald. He submitted that the law of self-defence, under certain circumstances, permitted a person to take preventive action to protect his or her life against a perceived aggressor even before the aggressor attacked. Fortunately for Mr. MacDonald, the Supreme Court of Canada (*R. v. McConnell*, [1996] 1 S.C.R. 1075) had just weeks earlier endorsed the dissenting judgement of Madam Justice Conrad of the Alberta Court of Appeal, who, in a prison case involving self-defence, had referred to the "prison environment syndrome" as somewhat analogous to the battered wife syndrome (*R. v. McConnell and Letendre* (1995), 32 Alta. L.R. (3d) 1 (Alta. C.A.)). Mr. Conroy advanced a similar argument. Just as a spouse who has experienced a history of abuse, if she reasonably fears another attack, may strike out against her abuser without having to wait until the first blow is struck, in "prison environment syndrome" a prisoner may be justified in taking similar preventive action. And just as battered wife syndrome takes into account the imbalance of power in relationships, Mr. Conroy said, so "prison environment syndrome" should take into account the imbalance of power between particular prisoners. In this case, the jury should have regard to the fact that Mr. Allen at the time of his death was 6'2", weighed 275 pounds, and was a muscle man in his physical prime. Counsel asked the jury to compare Mr. Allen to Mr. MacDonald, who at the time was fifty-two years old, described by one of the prisoners as "an old man with a pot," well past his prime and much smaller than Mr. Allen.

Crown Counsel Jack Gibson, in his address to the jury, focussed on the issue of witness credibility. He suggested that the evidence of the correctional officers suggested a fight in which Mr. MacDonald, armed with a knife, was the aggressor, with Mr. Allen, unarmed, retreating in a zigzag fashion to defend himself. There was no evidence from the guards that Mr. Allen hit Mr. MacDonald or in any other way initiated the confrontation. Mr. Gibson argued that the prisoners had manufactured a story consistent with self-defence in order to help Mr. MacDonald. In assessing the credibility of the prisoners, he said to the jury, "You saw them come into this courtroom in chains, and you heard their records, you saw the T-shirts with 'Murder Incorporated.' I ask you, if these men were on the street, having seen them in this courtroom and knowing of their records, would you accept their word?" Mr. Gibson suggested that there could be no room for self-defence in this case. Even assuming that there was a threat to Hughie MacDonald's life, and even if Gary Allen had thrown the first punch, at the point when Mr. MacDonald had lost possession of the knife, he lost the benefit of any argument of self-defence. At that point, with the guards right there, he knew that he and Mr. Allen would never be placed in the same population again, yet he retrieved the knife and lunged after Mr. Allen. At that point, Mr. Gibson concluded, Mr. MacDonald could have no reasonable grounds to believe that the only way to save his own life was to kill Mr. Allen. At that point there was blood on his mind and his actions constituted first-degree murder.

## The Judge's Charge to the Jury

Mr. Justice Singh, in his charge to the jury, reviewed the evidence they had heard and instructed them on the law applicable to the charge against Hughie MacDonald. The centrepiece of that charge was the law of self-defence. In accordance with well-established principles of criminal law, his Lordship explained that the burden of proving the guilt of the accused lay with the Crown and that this burden included not only proving that Mr. MacDonald had the necessary intention ("*mens rea*")—either intending to kill Mr. Allen or intending to cause him serious bodily harm knowing that death was likely and being reckless as to that death—but also proving beyond a reasonable doubt that the elements of the defence of self-defence were not established. If, at the end of their deliberations, the jury entertained a reasonable doubt on the issue of self-defence, then the Crown had not proved its case and Mr. MacDonald was entitled to be acquitted.

In light of the primary function of the *Criminal Code* of Canada—to provide a clear articulation of the behaviour society condemns on pain of official punishment—one might reasonably expect that the principles governing the circumstances under which persons can invoke self-defence, as a justification for what otherwise would be criminal conduct, would be clearly set out in the *Code*. However, as the Chief Justice of Canada has observed, the law on self-defence has often been criticized for its "complexity and lack of coherence" (*R. v. Petel*, [1994] 1 S.C.R. 3 at 12). Despite this complexity, the basic elements of a claim of self-defence are the accused's apprehension of harm and the proportionality of the accused's response to that harm. The law, as set out in the *Criminal Code* and interpreted by the courts, is a blend of subjective and objective considerations. Unlike areas of the law where the sole inquiry is directed to what the accused person honestly believed to be the state of affairs, the law on self-defence, while giving important weight to what the accused thought to be the facts, also requires that there be an objective reasonable basis for that belief. The reason for this limitation is not difficult to fathom. As articulated by the New York Court of Appeals, in one of the most publicized cases in which self-defence was raised—that of Bernie Goetz, who shot several young black men on the New York subway—to base self-defence solely on the subjective beliefs of the accused "would allow citizens to set their own standards of permissible use of force" and risk acquitting an individual who resorts to violence "no matter how aberrational or bizarre his thought patterns" (*People* v. *Goetz*, 497 N.E.2d 41 at 50 (N.Y.Ct.App. 1986)).

The *Criminal Code* provisions governing self-defence draw a distinction between a situation in which the accused person intended to cause death or grievous bodily harm and one in which he or she had no such intent. Section 34(2) is the section engaged by the facts in Hughie MacDonald's case. It reads:

> 34(2) Everyone who is unlawfully assaulted and who causes death or grievous bodily harm in repelling the assault is justified if
>  (a) he causes it under reasonable apprehension of death or grievous bodily harm from the violence with which the assault was originally made or with which the assailant pursues his purposes; and
>  (b) he believes, on reasonable grounds, that he cannot otherwise preserve himself from death or grievous bodily harm.

The Supreme Court has held that there are three constituent elements for self-defence under this subsection: (1) the existence of an unlawful assault; (2) a reasonable apprehension of a risk of death or grievous bodily harm; and (3) a reasonable belief that it is not possible to preserve oneself from harm except by killing the adversary. With all three elements, the jury must determine how the accused perceived the relevant facts and whether that perception was reasonable. The test, therefore, is a blend of subjective and objective factors. A mistake by the accused as to the harm threatened or force needed does not destroy a claim of self-defence so long as the mistake was reasonable.

The Supreme Court, in its 1990 decision in *Lavallee* (*R. v. Lavallee*, [1990] 1 s.c.r. 852), made some pronouncements that significantly enlarged the scope for a claim of self-defence. In *Lavallee*, the accused was a woman who had a history of experiencing abuse from her partner and who shot him in the back of the head after he threatened on one occasion that she would be harmed when their guests had left the house. The Crown argued that self-defence was not available because at the time Ms. Lavallee shot her partner she was not facing an "imminent attack." The Supreme Court rejected any rule requiring that the apprehended danger be imminent. Madam Justice Wilson held that expert evidence about the effects of battering on women cast doubt on the view expressed in a previous case that it was "inherently unreasonable to apprehend death or grievous bodily harm unless or until the physical assault is actually in progress" (*Lavallee*, at 877). Rather, "it may in fact be possible for a battered spouse to accurately predict the onset of violence before the first blow is struck, even if an outsider to the relationship cannot" (*Lavallee*, at 880–81). As Madam Justice Wilson stated,

> The issue is not, however, what an outsider would reasonably perceive but what the accused would have reasonably perceived, given her situation and her experience. I do not think it is an unwarranted generalization to say usually the size, strength, socialization, and lack

of training of women are typically no match for men in hand-to-hand combat. The requirement . . . that a battered woman wait until the physical assault is "under way" before her apprehensions can be validated in law would . . . be tantamount to sentencing her to "murder by instalment." (*Lavallee,* at 883)

Madam Justice Wilson, in the context of spousal battering, made it clear in *Lavallee* that "the definition of what is reasonable must be adapted to circumstances which are, by and large, foreign to the world inhabited by the hypothetical 'reasonable man'" (*Lavallee,* at 874).

The Supreme Court also held in *Lavallee* that this contextual approach to reasonableness was relevant in determining whether the accused had a reasonable belief in the lack of alternatives to deadly force. Madam Justice Wilson stated, "I think the question the jury must ask itself is whether, given the history, circumstances, and perceptions of [the accused], her belief that she could not preserve herself from being killed by [the deceased] that night except by killing him first was reasonable" (*Lavallee,* at 889). *Lavallee* affirmed that there is no requirement that the accused retreat in order to qualify for self-defence under section 34(2) of the *Criminal Code.* Madam Justice Wilson, with reference to the origins of this concept in the notion that "a man's home is his castle," pointedly observed that "a man's home may be his castle, but it is also the woman's home even if it seems to her more like a prison in the circumstances" (*Lavallee,* at 888–89).

Hughie MacDonald's home at the time of the death of Gary Allen *was* a prison, and a maximum security one at that. Applying the contextual approach endorsed by the Supreme Court in *Lavallee,* Mr. Justice Singh instructed the jury that in determining whether Hughie MacDonald had reasonable grounds for apprehending that an assault from Gary Allen was likely to cause his death or grievous bodily harm, and whether Hughie MacDonald had reasonable grounds to believe he had no alternative but to kill Gary Allen to preserve himself from such harm, they must consider Mr. MacDonald's situation and experience as a prisoner in a maximum security institution.

The jury in the MacDonald trial began their deliberations after lunch on Thursday, May 30, 1996. They deliberated for the rest of the day and for an hour on Friday morning before coming back with their unanimous verdict: not guilty.

## Not Guilty in Criminal Law, but Guilty in Prison Customary Law

Although the verdict signalled a cardinal change in Hughie MacDonald's status—from that of a man accused of first-degree murder to one declared by a jury of his peers to be innocent of such a charge—it was not to have the same significance with relation to his status as a prisoner. Just as the events leading up to the stabbing of Gary Allen took us deep into "the belly of the beast" of maximum security, the response of correctional authorities to the acquittal of Hughie MacDonald takes us to the heart of the difference between legal and institutional perspectives on the Rule of Law.

The videotape the Crown had played for the jury documented Hughie MacDonald being taken out of the courtyard, then being strip-searched and placed in a cell in the segregation unit. He remained in segregation from the day of the stabbing, February 22, 1994, until his trial in May 1996. Following his being charged with first-degree murder, the warden of Kent Institution recommended Mr. MacDonald's involuntary transfer to the Special Handling Unit, the highest level of security in the Canadian system. That recommendation was upheld in a decision by the Deputy Commissioner for the Pacific Region on December 20, 1994. In the end, however, the transfer was not implemented because it would interfere with the ability of Mr. MacDonald's counsel to meet with his client and prepare for the trial. By May 31, 1996, the day of his acquittal, Hughie MacDonald had been in administrative segregation for two years and three months, a total of 830 days. During that time, a decision to continue his segregation was made at each monthly meeting of the Segregation Review Board. Initially, the reason given was that Mr. MacDonald was being considered for transfer to the Special Handling Unit. Once the transfer was authorized, that authorization itself became the basis for maintaining his segregation. The written monthly notice of the review of his segregated status given to Mr. MacDonald during this period was to the following effect: "You were segregated following the assault and murder of another inmate. You are approved for the transfer to the SHU Quebec pending completion of your court proceedings. You anticipate trial issues to be concluded in May 1996." In light of his acquittal on all criminal charges, it was not unreasonable for Hughie MacDonald to expect both the reversal of the Correctional Service of Canada decision to transfer him to the SHU and his release from segregation.

The Kent Segregation Review Board met on Monday, June 3, 1996, the first working day after Hughie MacDonald's acquittal. I attended the meeting on that day as part of my ongoing research. Mr. MacDonald also attended the meeting, requesting that he be released from segregation. However, he was advised by the chairman, Mr. Lin Wallin, that he would not be released from segregation until the SHU transfer had been reviewed by both the warden and regional headquarters. Mr. Wallin also said that because the transfer was not based exclusively upon the court proceedings, Mr. MacDonald's acquittal would not necessarily result in his release from segregation.

After Mr. MacDonald left the room, I asked Mr. Wallin about the basis for his last statement, given that the transfer documents had clearly focussed on the alleged murder of Gary Allen. He responded that Mr. MacDonald had pursued Mr. Allen across the courtyard and knifed him in front of a dozen correctional officers. I pointed out that Mr. MacDonald's acquittal amounted to a finding that he was legally justified in killing Mr. Allen to defend his own life. As such, it was a justifiable homicide, not a criminal or an unlawful act.

The airing of this issue at the Segregation Review Board proved to be an early warning sign of the different interpretations that would be placed on the acquittal by institutional authorities. In the week following his acquittal, Mr. MacDonald received a letter from the warden of Kent Institution informing him that his transfer to the SHU was being reviewed and that he would be advised shortly of the results of that review. On June 13 I interviewed Mr. MacDonald in segregation, and he had not yet heard back from the warden. He was nonetheless in very good spirits, confident that he would soon be returned to the general population.

After I left the segregation unit that day I saw Dave Dick. (As outlined earlier in this chapter, Mr. Dick, in his capacity as an IPSO, had interviewed Gary Allen at the Fraser Regional Correctional Centre in February 1994, and had at that time recommended that Allen not be accepted at Kent. His subsequent memo to Deputy Warden Sexsmith prophetically stated that if Allen were released into the general population at Kent, there would be a major incident within days, if not hours, of that release. Mr. Dick had since then become Co-ordinator of Programs at Kent, and he was about to take up a new assignment as a unit manager at William Head Institution on Vancouver Island.) I asked Mr. Dick whether a decision had been made regarding Hughie MacDonald's transfer to the SHU. He said he understood meetings were in progress that day, but he was not part of the decision-making loop. When I said it was difficult to see what justification there could be for proceeding with the transfer, Mr. Dick responded by giving me what he understood to be the institutional perspective on the issues. The acquittal on the basis of self-defence represented a finding by the jury that Hughie MacDonald believed that it was a kill-or-be-killed situation. However, from the institution's perspective, there had been other options open to Mr. MacDonald, as presented in Mr. Dick's court testimony. The fact that Hughie MacDonald had resorted to a confrontation with Gary Allen instead demonstrated something wrong with his approach to solving problems, which in turn raised questions about whether his risk was manageable in a maximum security institution.

There was another important thread in the institutional perspective. Mr. Dick told me that both he and the warden were extremely concerned about the implications of legitimizing self-defence in these circumstances. Hughie MacDonald's was the third such acquittal. From the institution's perspective, this was sending the wrong message to the population: that is, if you solved problems with violence, you had a good chance of being acquitted of any criminal charges. I reminded Mr. Dick that Mr. MacDonald's lawyer, John Conroy, had even before the trial filed a *habeas corpus* challenging Kent Institution's decision to keep Mr.

MacDonald in segregation, and that he would certainly bring that application on for a hearing if the institution kept Mr. MacDonald in segregation or transferred him to the Special Handling Unit. I offered my opinion that such an application would likely be successful and that the court would order Hughie MacDonald's release from segregation. Dave Dick commented, "There are some cases which you have to fight in court even if you know that you might lose. And this is one of them." Later that afternoon I spoke with Wayne Culbert, the current IPSO. He too was concerned about the power of the precedent in the MacDonald case and the implications of not proceeding with the SHU package: "He killed a guy in front of everybody. That's a fact, self-defence or not."

What was missing from both Mr. Dick's and Mr. Culbert's analyses was an understanding of the legal basis for self-defence. For Mr. Culbert, the public nature of the killing was the most significant factor, overshadowing the legal principle that a killing in self-defence, whether committed publicly or privately, is a justified homicide and not criminally or even morally culpable. In Mr. Dick's case, he misunderstood self-defence to be based only upon what Hughie MacDonald himself had believed necessary to save his life. Yet as Mr. Justice Singh had explained to the jury, self-defence requires that there be *reasonable grounds,* as assessed by the jury, to believe both that your life is in danger and that killing is the only way to avoid death or serious bodily harm. The law therefore has a built-in safeguard that prevents the defence from being advanced by someone who simply believes his life is in danger.

The difference between the institutional perspective and the legal perspective in this case could not have been more dramatic. From a legal perspective, Hughie MacDonald was justified in killing Gary Allen, and his act deserved no legal censure. From the institutional perspective, his actions represented "criminal thinking," standing in need of both censure and correction. The censure, which would take the form of segregation and a transfer to the Special Handling Unit, was intended to send a strong message to other prisoners. The correction, designed to reshape the prisoner's "warped" thinking, would be the programming of anywhere from one to four years in the Special Handling Unit. The conflict between these two perspectives can be expressed in this way. A prisoner who defends himself by using deadly force where he believes, on reasonable grounds, that he is facing a threat of death or serious bodily harm, is acting within his legal rights and responsibilities as a citizen of Canada under the *Criminal Code* of Canada. Those same circumstances, which entitle him to a finding of not guilty of criminal culpability, subject him, as a prisoner of Canada, to a finding that he is among the most dangerous of men and thus deserving of the most severe and restrictive form of imprisonment in the Canadian correctional system.

Is there *any* view of corrections that could justify exculpation under the *Criminal Code* and condemnation under the penitentiary code? There are situations in which prisoners, while acting within their legal rights and responsibilities as Canadian citizens, nevertheless may be in breach of their obligations and responsibilities as prisoners or parolees. The myriad of rules and regulations governing the lives of prisoners, for breach of which they can be disciplined and transferred to higher security, do not typically give rise to sanctions when committed by non-prisoners. For example, except in special situations, the citizen who is not a prisoner cannot be required on pain of punishment to give a urine sample as part of a random scheme to deter the use of drugs; a prisoner can. Except under special circumstances, citizens not undergoing a sentence of imprisonment have rights of mobility that enable them to move from one part of the country to another without leave or licence of state authorities; a citizen serving a sentence of imprisonment who is in the community on parole or statutory release may be subject to restrictions on mobility, so that the otherwise lawful act of driving from one place to another can be the subject of disciplinary action, including the return to prison, if that act is done without the permission of a parole officer. In both examples, the special legal regime governing the lives of prisoners and those on parole is justified by the principle that the control and correction of those subject to sentences of imprisonment require additional restrictions on freedom and liberty—in the one case to control drug use within the volatile environment of a prison, and in the other to facilitate the supervision of parolees.

In such cases, there is a coherent theory for the special restrictions and obligations placed upon prisoners and parolees. In Hughie MacDonald's case, what coherent theory would justify limiting the right of a prisoner to act in self-defence in the face of a threat to his life? There is nothing in the legal regime governing prisons or prisoners that restricts access to defences and justifications under the *Criminal Code*. The fact that the violent environment of maximum security prisons is more likely to give rise to threats of bodily harm is hardly sufficient basis to limit a prisoner's right to resort to justified self-defence. Indeed, the argument is compelling that, if maximum security is an environment which, more so than any other, generates violent threats and actions, it is essential that prisoners required to live in that environment should be able to act in self-defence, within the constraints of the law. To limit the right of prisoners to resort to self-defence would be to withdraw the protection of the law precisely at the point where that protection is most relevant and necessary.

The institutional perspective in this case, which points to the power of the precedent in allowing prisoners to resort to violence in maximum security, and which seeks to encourage prisoners to use nonviolent ways of responding to threats, does not require a different legal regime or justify special additional responses. The legal requirement for acquittal on self-defence, a reasonable belief by the accused that it is not possible to preserve himself from harm except by the infliction of death or grievous bodily harm, permits and requires a consideration of alternatives. The essential difference between the legal and the institutional perspectives on this question is that, under the law, the reasonableness of the belief is assessed by either a judge or a jury, taking into account the special circumstances of the accused; in the institutional perspective, that determination is made by the correctional authorities, who in determining reasonableness assess not only the special circumstances of the accused but also the correctional agenda of prison administrators. From that perspective Hughie MacDonald's response is not deemed to be reasonable, because he struck out rather than going to talk to a staff member, or checking into protection, or adopting one of the other alternatives suggested by Dave Dick as a means to avoid confrontation with Gary Allen. The institutional perspective changes the legal test of self-defence so that it is viewed through the eyes of correctional authorities rather than the eyes of the prisoner.

On June 17, 1996, approximately two weeks after his acquittal, Mr. MacDonald received a letter from Warden Lusk, which read in part:

> We are aware that you have been found to not be criminally responsible, by reason of self-defence, in the death of inmate Gary Allen. However, our recommendation for placement in the Special Handling Unit was based on information that we presented to you in a progress summary report dated 25 April 1994, that dealt with your ongoing institutional behaviour since 1977. We concluded at that time that placement in a Special Handling Unit was appropriate given your ongoing violent behaviour, and continuing stated belief that pre-emptive violent action is justified, and in fact your only recourse for dealing with conflict in certain situations . . . I can find no reason to conclude you are any less dangerous than at the time of our original submission. Therefore, I am not prepared to alter my original recommendation. (Letter from Warden Bob Lusk to Hugh MacDonald, Kent Institution, June 17, 1996)

Following receipt of this letter, Mr. MacDonald's lawyer, John Conroy, set down the *habeas corpus* application for a hearing in the B.C. Supreme Court. In a decision dated August 21, 1996, Mr. Justice Wilson ruled that Mr. MacDonald's detention in segregation was unlawful and that the decision to transfer him to the Special Handling Unit was "patently unreasonable and could not take place." As a result, the judge ordered that Hughie MacDonald be released from segregation to the general population at Kent Institution. In arriving at his decision, Mr. Justice Wilson reviewed and rejected the institution's arguments that Mr. MacDonald, notwithstanding incarceration virtually throughout his entire adult life, had learned nothing; that he insisted on resolving his disputes by resorting to violence; that he had a vigilante attitude; and that the manifestation of that attitude, reflected in the death of Mr. Allen, rendered him an unacceptable risk in a maximum security institution.

> What that submission, in my judgement, fails to recognize, is that following a jury trial, in which the defence of self-defence, under the appropriate provisions of the *Criminal Code,* was placed before a jury, the jury decided that Mr. MacDonald was not guilty of either murder, in any degree, or manslaughter. In the jury's verdict, I take it to be a confirmation that the force used, under the circumstances, by Mr. MacDonald, was proportionate to the risk he was facing . . . The authorities had taken the decision to bring Mr. Allen into the institution. Mr. MacDonald received information from inmates that the late Mr. Allen intended him harm. He acted in the way that he did, facing that risk, and the jury found that he was justified in doing so.
>
> I think the majority reasons in *Dridic* v. *The Queen* (1985) 19 c.c.c. (3d) 289, contain the principle governing my disposition of this aspect of this case. Mr. Justice Lamer . . . writing for the majority [on the issue of the legal effect of an acquittal in subsequent criminal proceedings] said:
>
>> . . . It does mean that any issue, the resolution of which had to be in favour of the accused as a prerequisite to the acquittal, is irrevocably deemed to have been found conclusively in favour of the accused.
>
> [Counsel for the warden] has not persuaded me that that test is not applicable in this case. I agree with her that the issue for the jury was: was Mr. MacDonald guilty or not guilty of the murder or manslaughter of the late Mr. Allen?, while the issue for resolution by the warden is: is Mr. MacDonald a risk which cannot be managed at a maximum security institution such as Kent? Or to put it another way: is Mr. MacDonald such a dangerous offender that special handling is required?
>
> In my opinion that reasoning proceeds from the basis that Mr. MacDonald did, as the warden appears to have understood when he made his initial determination, resolve in his mind that he would bring an end to the apparent threat from Mr. Allen by arming himself with a knife, running up to Mr. Allen in the courtyard in broad daylight, subject to video camera surveillance, in the presence of other inmates and guards, and repeatedly stab him.
>
> What that decision does not take into consideration is the jury's finding that, in all the circumstances, Mr. MacDonald's reaction to the risk presented by Mr. Allen, which I might say was a risk clearly

identified by Mr. Dick, the preventive security officer, before Mr. Allen's arrival, was proportionate.

That, in my judgement, is not evidence of a propensity to resort to violence to solve all problems, so as to constitute Mr. MacDonald a dangerous offender, and a risk to any other persons in the general population, or indeed any officer of the Correction Service in the institution. The matter of the Allen/MacDonald hostilities was a specifically identifiable, predictable problem. No such evidence is available with respect to the balance of the population. I find that the decision to send Mr. MacDonald to a Special Handling Unit is patently unreasonable under those circumstances. (*MacDonald* v. *Warden of Kent Institution*, Vancouver Registry, cc951235)

Hughie MacDonald was finally returned to the general population at Kent on August 23, 1996. In the concluding paragraph of his reasons for judgement, Mr. Justice Wilson had stated, "I would like to add that I would certainly encourage the Service to endeavour with all deliberate speed to get Mr. MacDonald to the Regional Health Centre." However, it would take than more than judicial encouragement to get Hughie MacDonald to the Regional Health Centre. He remained at Kent for almost two years after Mr. Justice Wilson's judgement. And in July 1998, even when the Correctional Service finally agreed to transfer him, it was not to the RHC but to Matsqui Institution. In August 1999, almost three years to the day after the court's exhortation to CSC to get Mr. MacDonald to RHC "with all deliberate speed," I spoke with him at Matsqui. He had just been told he was not sufficiently motivated to benefit from the Violent Offender Program and therefore would remain at Matsqui. In July 2001, over five years after his acquittal, I again interviewed Mr. MacDonald. He was still warehoused at Matsqui, having served twenty-two years of his life sentence. He was not transferred to the RHC until October 2001. The Correctional Service's interpretation of "all deliberate speed," while inviting comparison with civil rights violations in the American Deep South, hardly stands as a model of respect for the Rule of Law.

# SECTOR 3

## CHAPTER 1

# The Disciplinary Process 1972–92: Warden's Court to Independent Chairpersons

When I began my research in Canadian prisons in 1972, I set out to understand how the administration of prisons related to the overall administration of criminal justice. In my first year of teaching criminal law in the Faculty of Law at the University of British Columbia, I had come across a book with the evocative title *Military Justice Is to Justice as Military Music Is to Music* (Robert Sherrill [New York: Harper and Row, 1970]). Did prison justice have the same asymmetrical relationship to justice? Certainly some American scholars had drawn that conclusion in characterizing the U.S. prison as a "lawless agency" (David Greenberg and Fay Stender, "The Prison as a Lawless Agency" [1971–72] 21 *Buffalo Law Review* 799).

My focus initially was on the internal disciplinary process. I chose that area because it represents the private criminal law of the prison; as in the larger public system, the disciplinary system in the prison defines the limits of behaviour which will be accepted without official intervention, sets out procedures for dealing with those suspected of violating these limits, and prescribes sanctions for those convicted of violations.

In comparing this private system with the public system of criminal justice, I sought to identify differences, whether of principle or process, and to evaluate those differences in light of the overall goals of criminal law, the particular goals of corrections, and the exigencies of prison administration. My dominant concern was "to see if prison justice is a fair system, and if not, how it can be made fair" (Michael Jackson, "Justice behind the Walls: A Study of the Disciplinary Process in a Canadian Penitentiary" [1974] 12 *Osgoode Hall Law Journal* 1 at 2).

When I began my research at Matsqui Institution in 1972, disciplinary hearings were the prerogative of prison wardens or their delegates. It had been this way since Kingston Penitentiary opened in 1835. During my first few days I heard from both prisoners and prison staff of the way discipline was handed out by the warden of the B.C. Penitentiary. On the floor in front of the warden's desk were two footprints where prisoners were required to stand. They were escorted into his office accompanied by the refrain, "March the guilty bastard in." Initially I thought these stories to be folkloric, but the footprints were real enough, and the stories were repeated often enough by both groups to make it clear that this "kangaroo court" was indeed part of the B.C. Pen's history.

When it came to the disciplinary process at Matsqui Institution, however, I heard conflicting stories from the keepers and the kept. Prison administrators assured me that the differences between the B.C. Pen and Matsqui went far beyond the thirty miles that separated the two institutions. The traditions of the B.C. Pen were, like its architecture, based in the nineteenth century. Placed high on a hill overlooking the Royal City of New Westminster, the B.C. Pen was intended, through its Bastille-like appearance, to warn the populace of the wages of sin and the pains of punishment for those who violated the Queen's peace. For almost a hundred years the B.C. Penitentiary was as elemental a part of the lexicon of crime and punishment as the *Criminal Code*. Indeed, its hold on the public imagination was more visceral.

By contrast, Matsqui was a modern institution. It had opened in 1966, and from the beginning it was organized around the philosophy and principles of correction and rehabilitation, not punishment and deterrence. I was assured I would find no footprints in the warden's office there. But prisoners suggested that the absence of those footprints, like the absence of high, forbidding walls, did not mean prison justice was more benevolent at Matsqui. They insisted that the warden's court there, no less than its counterpart at the B.C. Penitentiary, was a kangaroo court.

## The Warden's Court: 1972

As I explained in Sector 1, in 1972 the *Penitentiary Act* and the *Penitentiary Service Regulations* provided only a skeletal framework for the prison disciplinary process in Canada. The fleshing out of that skeleton was left to Commissioner's Directives, and it was in these directives, the subsidiary divisional instructions, and institutional standing orders that the detailed procedures for disciplinary hearings were to be found.

Under these procedures, serious disciplinary charges were to be adjudicated by the prison warden or his deputy. The Commissioner's Directives elaborated a framework designed to ensure procedural fairness. Thus it was provided that no finding should be made against a prisoner unless he had received, in advance, a written notice of the charge and a summary of the evidence alleged against him; had appeared personally at the disciplinary hearing; and had been given an opportunity to make his full answer and defence to the charge, including the questioning of witnesses and the introduction of witnesses or written material, either in denial of the offence or in mitigation of punishment. (Details of the 1972 procedures can be found in Jackson, "Justice" at 30.)

My first impression on reading the rules was that disciplinary proceedings in the federal prison system were surrounded by substantial due process protections, and at least their procedural aspects were a fair approximation of the basic elements of a criminal trial. However, after four months of observing disciplinary proceedings at Matsqui, I concluded there were vast differences between a criminal trial and a disciplinary hearing. I summarized those differences in this way:

> The dominant features of the disciplinary proceedings were that there was a general presumption of guilt as opposed to a presumption of innocence; a confusion of the issue of guilt or innocence and that of appropriate disposition; a reliance on informal discussion concerning these issues, much of it based on hearsay and rumour, carried on out of the presence of the inmate accused; and a lack of concern for uniformity of sentences for offences of similar nature. (Jackson, "Justice" at 31)

I found also that prison administrators did not place a high priority on due process values, and that adjudication was concerned mostly with maintaining the goals of the rehabilitative ideal or reinforcing institutional interests relating to security and staff morale. The superintendent of Matsqui, who presided over most of the disciplinary proceedings, expressly linked his handling of them to the individualized treatment model he saw as underlying the overall rehabilitative plan at Matsqui.

> As he explained it, his purpose in the disciplinary proceedings was to force the inmate to accept responsibility for his own actions and to participate in the appropriate disposition to ensure better behaviour in future . . .
>
> The effect of this kind of philosophy on the operation of the disciplinary hearing was to focus attention on the disposition of the case rather than the issue of guilt, since by presuming guilt and minimizing any real issue as to innocence, the inmate is fairly effectively denied an opportunity to play the "cops and robbers" game. Thus the presumption of guilt, which is the dominant impression of the

proceedings, is functionally related to the basic assumption behind the proceedings. (Jackson, "Justice" at 32)

Although the procedural rules required that prisoners be provided with written notice of the charge and a summary of the evidence alleged against them, I found that these requirements were not met at Matsqui. Typically, prisoners were told of their impending appearance in warden's court on the morning of the hearing. The evidence against the prisoner was presented at the hearing itself, and in no cases were prior written summaries of evidence provided. Given the treatment theory of discipline, this non-compliance was not seen as a major issue, "because if the inmate [was] not aware of the evidence that would be given against him, he clearly [was] not in a good position to make up a story and therefore [was] less able to play the 'cops and robbers' game" (Jackson, "Justice" at 34).

From my direct observation of disciplinary proceedings and from interviews with prisoners tried in warden's court, I concluded that the disciplinary process at Matsqui lacked the essential attributes of objective and fair adjudication. This conclusion was based in part upon the lack of proper notice, the confusion of the issues of guilt and disposition, and the extensive discussion of the case that took place in the absence of the prisoner, but it was also related to a more fundamental concern. The overarching flaw in the warden's court system was that the very people responsible for maintaining the good order of the institution were the ones judging whether prisoners had committed offences against that good order. The judges, in other words, were the offended parties. Furthermore, in most cases these adjudicators brought to the hearings considerable personal knowledge of the prisoners, based on previous dealings, and it was therefore impossible for them to approach a particular case free of that bias. A further source of bias prejudicing objective judgement was a perceived need of prison administrators to maintain staff morale by accepting the testimony of guards where it conflicted with that of prisoners.

My analysis of the underlying sources for the unfairness of the disciplinary process led directly to the reforms I advocated at the conclusion of my early research, the centrepiece of which was the appointment of an Independent Chairperson to the disciplinary board.

> This study suggests that prison administrators and staff have perceptions of the nature of disciplinary proceedings that place a low priority on the value of due process and the procedural protections which give it meaning, and that the mere provision of such protections without ensuring the implementation by officials imbued with a sense of their value is likely to result in their being circumvented . . .
>
> The crux of any real reform lies therefore in an impartial disciplinary tribunal, in the sense of one which will approach cases free

from bias based upon prior knowledge of the inmate and which will handle the task of discipline in a spirit of maximizing rather than undermining the procedural protections designed to ensure a fair hearing . . .

. . . [T]he proper response to the need for an impartial tribunal is to have a truly Independent Chairman of the disciplinary board, that is, someone who has no particular ties or allegiance to the administration of the prison or to the federal penitentiary service. Not only would such an Independent Chairman avoid the bias of personal knowledge of the parties involved but also the bias of institutional pressures. He would not be threatened, as is the present administration, by the prospect of disrupting staff morale, and his examination of the facts would not be encumbered by an automatic presumption against the inmates' credibility. (Jackson, "Justice" at 63–65)

I also recommended that Independent Chairpersons be legally trained and therefore familiar with the elements of a fair hearing. Since part of the work of a disciplinary board, like that of an outside court, is an educative one, the Chairperson would be involved in legitimating due process values in the eyes of all participants, and a legally trained Chairperson would be better equipped for this role. In response to the concern that having an outside person presiding over disciplinary hearings would undermine the flexibility of the warden's court system, as part of the institutional decision-making fabric, I suggested that prison staff could become involved at the sentencing stage. The Independent Chairperson would deal with the adjudication of guilt or innocence, but a panel of advisors drawn from the institutional staff could advise the Chairperson in a non-binding way on what constituted a fair sentence.

My recommendation that Independent Chairpersons adjudicate serious disciplinary offences was endorsed in 1975 in the report of the Study Group on Dissociation established by the Solicitor General to review the use of punitive and administrative segregation. That group concluded: "The present composition of the disciplinary board prohibits the appearance of justice. This will continue to be the case as long as the director or assistant director . . . chairs the board" (*Report of the Study Group on Dissociation* [Ottawa: Solicitor General of Canada, 1975] [Chairman: James A. Vantour] at 76).

The Study Group on Dissociation recommended that independent disciplinary board chairpersons should be employed on a one-year experimental basis in two of the five regions of the Penitentiary Service. No action, however, was taken by the Solicitor General. Two years later, the House of Commons Sub-Committee on the Penitentiary System in Canada strongly recommended that "Independent Chairpersons are required immediately in all institutions to preside over disciplinary hearings" (*Report to Parliament*, recommendation 30 at 91). The Sub-Committee observed, "It is especially unsuitable that the director of an institution should be in charge of the proceedings, since he is an interested party in a case. Moreover, he is in an extremely difficult situation if he acquits an inmate against staff testimony, when he must later rely on the same staff to control the same inmate" (*Report to Parliament* at 90). The Sub-Committee expressed its view that the *Report of the Study Group on Dissociation* did not go far enough by recommending the gradual implementation of Independent Chairpersons; rather, "Independent Chairpersons for disciplinary hearings are required immediately as a basic demand of justice in all penitentiary institutions in Canada" (*Report to Parliament* at 91).

The Solicitor General acted upon the House of Commons Sub-Committee's recommendation, but only to the extent of appointing Independent Chairpersons in maximum security institutions. The first such appointments were made in December 1977. Subsequently, in June 1980, Independent Chairpersons were appointed in medium security institutions. Amendments were made to the *Penitentiary Service Regulations* to provide the necessary legal authority for the appointment of Independent Chairpersons and to clothe them with the jurisdiction to adjudicate serious disciplinary offences. The amended regulations also made provision for institutional staff advisors and required the Independent Chairperson to consult with those advisors in the presence of the accused prisoner (s.o.r./79-625, s. 36(1)).

## The Independent Chairperson's Court: 1983

In 1983 I returned to Matsqui Institution, and over a six-month period observed the disciplinary hearings presided over by the Independent Chairperson. I expanded the scope of my original study by also observing, over the same period, the disciplinary proceedings at Kent, a maximum security institution. At Matsqui a single Chairperson conducted all hearings, but at Kent the docket was handled by two Chairpersons on a weekly rotational basis. As with most Independent Chairpersons appointed across the country, the three Chairpersons at Matsqui and Kent were members of the legal community. The Matsqui Chairperson had recently retired from a long career as general counsel to the B.C. Telephone Company. One Chairperson at Kent was a retired provincial court judge and the other was a retired lawyer who had practised as a criminal defence counsel.

The primary purpose of my 1983 study was to investigate whether the changes to the federal disciplinary process had resulted in a system which exhibited the hallmarks of fairness and accorded with principles of fundamental justice. The independence of the Chairperson was the single most important feature distinguishing between the disciplinary processes of the 1980s and the 1970s. I therefore set out to compare the conduct of cases before the Independent Chairpersons at Matsqui and Kent with similar types of cases I had observed in warden's court in my 1972 study. At the end of my research period, I concluded that there had been a significant number of acquittals before the Independent Chairpersons in circumstances where, under the old regime, convictions would almost certainly have been entered; the difference was attributable to the Chairperson's being prepared to render a decision based upon a reasonable doubt, notwithstanding strong institutional pressures for conviction. My conclusion that the independence of the Chairperson played a significant part in the outcome of cases was supported by a comparative analysis of the rate of acquittals. In 1972, under the warden's court system, the acquittal rate at Matsqui Institution was less than 10 per cent. For the years 1981, 1982, and 1983, under the Independent Chairperson system, the rates ranged from a low of 22 per cent to a high of 29 per cent, the 1983 figures therefore representing almost a tripling of the 1972 acquittal rate.

In 1972, the prisoners I spoke to about their experiences in warden's court called it "a kangaroo court." Eleven years later, halfway through my six-month research period at Matsqui and Kent, I questioned prisoners through interviews and a questionnaire about their experiences of the Independent Chairpersons. Here is a sampling of their responses:

> There is no difference between the Independent Chairperson and the warden's court. The institution controls the judge.

> The ICs are not fair, but they are better. The warden was totally biased. The problem with the hearings is that the Chairperson may have all the best intentions in the world, but the advisors are biased. They should be from the street. At first the Chairperson's decisions seemed fairer than they are now. It seems that the more times he is here, the less objective he becomes.

> I don't look at it as fair or unfair. Just the way it is. I know one thing: if they want, they'll get you sooner or later.

While falling short of condemning the Independent Chairperson process, these comments clearly are less than fulsome in their praise. How were they to be explained in light of my own judgement, based on both observation and an analysis of acquittal rates, that Independent Chairpersons acquitted prisoners on a regular basis in circumstances where wardens would almost certainly have convicted them? Did this difference suggest that, whatever reforms are introduced, prisoners will always see the system as unfair and biased against their interests, or were there good reasons, grounded in prisoners' experience of the process, to explain their criticism? During my six months of observations at Matsqui and Kent, I discovered elements of the disciplinary process as administered by

Independent Chairpersons which justifiably undermined prisoners' confidence in the independence of the process.

At Matsqui, every prisoner I interviewed said that, in his experience, it was the staff advisors, and not the Chairperson, who determined the outcome of a case. Regulations and Commissioner's Directives, in setting out the respective roles of the Independent Chairperson and the staff advisors, focussed on the advisors' role of recommending the most appropriate punishment. At Matsqui in 1983, the standard practice of the Independent Chairperson was to ask the advisors for their recommendation; if both of them agreed on a sentence, which they usually did, he adopted that sentence as the sentence of the court without further discussion. As recorded in my research notes, the following exchange, which came after the conviction of a prisoner on a charge of using abusive language, reflects this practice:

> CHAIRPERSON: Okay, advisors—what's your recommendation for sentence on this one?
> FIRST ADVISOR: There have been too many cases of abusive language. I recommend 10 days in SCU and 10 days' loss of remission.
> SECOND ADVISOR: I agree.
> CHAIRPERSON: That's the sentence.

The Independent Chairperson at Matsqui held the view that his decisions should not be made in an institutional vacuum. Since the staff advisors knew exactly what was happening in the prison, he felt that by adopting their recommendations on a sentence he could ensure that his decision was woven into the fabric of institutional life. While this practice was certainly appreciated by prison staff, it predictably had quite the opposite impact on prisoners. Given that most prisoners charged with disciplinary offences either pleaded guilty or were found guilty (a situation which parallels that of accused persons in the criminal justice system outside of prison), the fairness of the sentence is the critical issue. To find that this element of the case was decided by institutional advisors, as prisoners did at Matsqui, made it difficult for them to see the Chairperson as anything more than a figurehead. That perception was expressed by several prisoners who, as they left the hearing room, disdainfully commented, "I thought *you* were the judge."

At Kent Institution, the advisors' recommendations on sentence were not automatically adopted by the Independent Chairpersons. However, at Kent another practice undermined the perceived independence of the Chairpersons just as drastically. That practice, adopted by one of the Chairpersons, required the prisoner, after a finding of guilty, to leave the hearing room so that the advisors could make their recommendations about sentence in the absence of the accused. This meant the prisoner had no way of knowing what the advisors said to the chairperson and, therefore, no way of knowing whether the chairperson had exercised independence of judgement in determining the sentence.

One of my criticisms of warden's court proceedings had been the inconsistency in sentencing. I observed that the disciplinary board at Matsqui in 1972 "was simply fixing a sentence which they felt 'appropriate' without placing any particular value on the concept of treating like cases alike" (Jackson, "Justice" at 54). Legally trained Independent Chairpersons, I argued, would bring with them an understanding of the importance of treating like cases alike and be in a better position to develop a consistent set of sentencing principles and practices. A necessary focus of my inquiry in 1983 was, therefore, how well the Independent Chairpersons met these expectations.

The disappointing conclusion I drew was that sentencing by the Independent Chairpersons at both Matsqui and Kent still lacked the hallmarks of a fair, consistent, and coherent system of justice. At Matsqui, I identified three reasons for the lack of consistency. First, it was the advisors at Matsqui who determined the sentence, yet senior staff acted as advisors on a rotating basis. A second reason for disparity was related to overcrowding in the segregation unit. There were many weeks when the segregation unit was full, and at such times the advisors recommended sentences that involved a suspended period of dissociation and/or loss of remission. When there was room in the segregation unit, the same advisors would recommend, for the same offence, a dissociation sentence which was *not* to be suspended. From the staff's point of view, one can argue they had little choice; however, the need to manipulate the sentence to accommodate space in segregation inevitably imparted an arbitrary aspect to sentencing. The third reason for disparity in sentencing brings us back to a question of principle or, perhaps more correctly, a lack of principle. There was no more commitment at Matsqui in 1983 to treating like cases alike than there had been under the warden's court system. Although the disciplinary records that provided a bird's-eye view of broad trends in sentencing for particular offences were available, neither the staff nor the Independent Chairperson saw fit to review these records. Rather, they developed what might be termed the custom of individual cases: each advisor brought to bear his sense of what the right sentence should be. Even those advisors who articulated some understanding of the need to be fair, in terms of consistency, did not seek out the information to make that a reality. In addition, the need for recommendations to accommodate the practical pressures of overcrowding often made the idea of principled recommendations seem futile.

Life in the prison must go on, and most prisoners do not spend much time trying to figure out why some of them are sent to the hole for five days for an offence and others end up there for ten or fifteen days—or serve no segregation time at all—for doing the same thing. But like waves on a beach, this knowledge washes through the prison every day, continually eroding prisoners' respect for the authority that imprisons them.

How did things compare at Kent Institution in 1983? The problems of over-crowding, while present, were not so pressing, and while sentences in some cases were influenced by the fact that the segregation unit was full, this was less of an issue. However, based upon my observations at Kent and a review of the disci-plinary records for the previous year, my conclusions regarding the sentencing process by the Independent Chairpersons there were virtually the same as at Matsqui. One searched in vain to find evidence of any principle of treating like cases alike, or indeed, any coherent principles of sentencing at all.

In 1991, a comprehensive evaluation of the Independent Chairperson's pro-gram undertaken by the Correctional Service of Canada confirmed my observa-tions. After conducting a national survey, the csc evaluation team concluded that the system of Independent Chairpersons overall was providing "guarantees of impartiality and fairness." However, they noted that there was a need for the development of clearer principles and procedures as to the role of advisors, and that the appearance of justice would be reinforced if the decisions of Indepen-dent Chairpersons were accompanied by reasons (Correctional Service of Can-ada, *Independent Chairperson Program: Evaluation Report* by Benoît Boulerice and Michel Prosseau [Ottawa: Correctional Service of Canada, 1992] [hereafter referred to as the csc's *Evaluation Report*] at vii).

## The *Corrections and Conditional Release Act*

The *Corrections and Conditional Release Act* (s.c. 1992, c. 20) was passed in June 1992. The *Act* and the related *Regulations* (s.o.r./92-620) introduced a number of changes to the prison disciplinary system. The most significant of these was that most of the provisions dealing with the disciplinary process are now set out in the *Act* and *Regulations,* thereby having the force of law, rather than being left to the Commissioner's Directives. Another important change was to the list of disciplinary offences: several offences were removed, some were amended, and several others were added. The principal deletion was s. 39(k) of the *Penitentiary Service Regulations,* which made it an offence to do "any act that is calculated to prejudice the discipline or good order of the institution." In my 1972 study, and again in 1983, I had criticized this offence as offending against the principle of legality: that penal statutes be defined with precision. Furthermore, this was the offence that Chief Justice Thurlow in the *Howard* case had described as "a noto-riously vague and difficult charge for anyone to defend" (*Howard,* at 665).

The *Corrections and Conditional Release Act* (ccra) introduced for the first time a legal obligation on a staff member to "take all reasonable steps to resolve [a disciplinary] matter informally where possible" (s. 41(1)). Section 43 legally entrenches the presumption of innocence by requiring that "the person conducting the hearing shall not find the inmate guilty unless satisfied beyond a reasonable doubt, based on the evidence presented at the hearing, that the inmate committed the disciplinary offence in question." The CCRA also affirms the right of the prisoner to be present for all phases of the hearing unless he is disruptive or there are reasonable grounds to believe he would jeopardize the safety of any person present. Further important changes were introduced by the *Corrections and Conditional Release Regulations* (*CCR Regulations*). Section 31(2) recognizes a prisoner's right to counsel for a serious disciplinary offence.

> The service shall ensure that an inmate who is charged with a serious disciplinary offence is given a reasonable opportunity to retain and instruct legal counsel for the hearing, and that the inmate's legal counsel is permitted to participate in the proceedings to the same extent as an inmate.

This provision removed from the Independent Chairpersons the responsibility for determining whether a prisoner required the assistance of counsel to ensure a fair hearing, a determination the CSC's *Evaluation Report* found had resulted in significant regional differences.

Another important change introduced by the *CCR Regulations*, which was responsive to my own criticisms of sentence disparity and to the recommendations of the CSC's *Evaluation Report*, is the provision for legally binding guidelines to determine sanctions for disciplinary offences. Section 34 provides:

> Before imposing a sanction described in section 44 of the Act, the person conducting a hearing of a disciplinary offence shall consider
> (a) the seriousness of the offence and the degree of responsibility the inmate bears for its commission;
> (b) the least restrictive measure that would be appropriate in the circumstances;
> (c) all relevant aggravating and mitigating circumstances, including the inmate's behaviour in the penitentiary;
> (d) the sanctions that have been imposed on other inmates for similar disciplinary offences committed in similar circumstances;
> (e) the nature and duration of any other sanction described in section 44 of the Act that has been imposed on the inmate, to ensure that the combination of the sanctions is not excessive;
> (f) any measures taken by the Service in connection with the offence before the disposition of the disciplinary charge; and
> (g) any recommendations respecting the appropriate sanctions made during the hearing.

The most significant change in the range of sanctions flowed from the abolition of the scheme of earned remission. Until the CCRA was passed, a prisoner could earn up to fifteen days a month in remission. If a prisoner earned the maximum remission, he or she would be entitled to release from imprisonment, subject to parole supervision, at the two-thirds point in the sentence, assuming he or she had not been paroled earlier. However, if a prisoner was convicted of a serious disciplinary offence, loss of remission could be imposed by the Independent Chairperson as one of the sanctions. The CCRA abolished the system of remission, in part because of the complexities of administering it, and replaced it with the system of statutory release. (This creates a presumptive entitlement for a prisoner to be released at the two-thirds point in his or her sentence, again subject to parole supervision. That presumptive release is subject to a determination by the Parole Board that the prisoner is likely to commit either an offence involving death or serious harm or a serious drug offence prior to the expiry of the sentence. The Board can then order that the prisoner remain in prison for the full duration of the sentence or serve the last third at a community residential facility.) With the abolition of remission, the sanction of forfeiture of remission passed into correctional history.

The CCR Regulations introduce restrictions on the use of other sanctions. Under the CCRA, the maximum period of segregation that can be imposed for a single disciplinary offence is 30 days. Section 40(2) of the Regulations provides that, where a prisoner is ordered to serve a sentence of segregation for one offence while subject to a sanction of segregation for another serious offence, the total period of segregation shall not exceed 45 days. Section 40(3) provides that a prisoner serving a period of segregation as a sanction for a disciplinary offence be accorded the same conditions of confinement as would be accorded a prisoner in administrative segregation. Under s. 37, the maximum fine that may be ordered is $25 for a minor offence and $50 for a serious one, and s. 38 requires that no fine shall be imposed unless the prisoner's financial means have been considered. Section 36 places the ceiling on the sanction of restitution at $50 for a minor offence and $500 for a serious offence. Section 41 authorizes the imposition of a suspended sentence and limits the period of suspension to 21 days for a minor offence and to 90 days for a serious offence.

The CCR Regulations contain a further provision which, like the sentencing guidelines, is intended to provide a mechanism for addressing the issue of disparity and providing greater co-ordination among the activities of Independent Chairpersons. Based upon the recommendation of the Correctional Law Review, s. 24 of the Regulations provides for the appointment of "a Senior Independent Chairperson," whose duties are to "train the Independent Chairpersons in the Senior Independent Chairperson's region" and "promote the principle among the Independent Chairpersons in the Senior Independent Chairperson's region that similar sanctions should be imposed for similar disciplinary offences committed in similar circumstances."

Several aspects of the disciplinary process are not dealt with either in the *CCRA* or the *CCR Regulations*. First, no mention is made of the role of institutional advisors. This is surprising, given that both my research and the CSC's *Evaluation Report* found considerable institutional and regional disparity regarding the role of advisors and their influence on Independent Chairpersons. The provisions dealing with advisors are left instead to the Commissioner's Directive on Discipline. Commssioner's Directive 580 provides that the institutional head should designate a member of the CSC, at the level of correctional supervisor or higher, "to provide continuity and facilitate the disciplinary process. This member shall provide assistance and any details or documents requested by the Chairperson to facilitate the hearing" (C.D. 580, January 24, 1997, para. 19). The Commissioner's Directive also provides that "at the request of the Chairperson, the member designated to assist may, in consultation with the inmate's unit staff or other concerned staff, provide recommendations to the Chairperson on the appropriate sanction" (C.D. 580, para. 44).

The second matter left to the Commissioner's Directives are the definitions of "serious" and "minor" charges. Under the new legislation, as under the old, serious charges are heard by the Independent Chairperson and minor charges are dealt with by a staff member; also, more severe sanctions can be imposed following conviction on a serious charge. Commissioner's Directive 580 defines "serious offence" as a situation in which an inmate commits a serious breach of security; exhibits violent behaviour; or, commits, or attempts to commit, an act that could generate such behaviour on the part of others or could cause harmful consequences to staff members or inmates. "Minor offence" is defined as a situation in which an inmate "exhibits negative or non-productive behaviour towards institutional rules governing the conduct of inmates" (C.D. 580, para. 8).

The scattering of the provisions governing the disciplinary process among the *CCRA, CCR Regulations,* and Commissioner's Directives leaves much to be desired. Although more is now contained in the *CCRA* and the *CCR Regulations,* gaining an understanding of the totality of the federal disciplinary process still involves referring to three different documents, when the process is simple enough that it could easily be codified in a single document. Indeed, that was one of the recommendations included in the Canadian Bar Association's commentary on the *CCRA* when the *Act* was introduced into Parliament. Notwithstanding these criticisms, the 1992 changes have infused the disciplinary process with greater legality, have unequivocally recognized a prisoner's right to counsel when faced with a serious charge, have affirmed a prisoner's right to be present throughout all phases of the hearing (except where the prisoner is disruptive or poses a threat to the safety of others), and have introduced, through sentencing guidelines and the establishment of the office of Senior Independent Chairperson, measures to address sentence disparity.

The question that presents itself today, as we move into the twenty-first century, is the question with which I began my studies of the Canadian prison almost thirty years ago: does the federal disciplinary process, in practice, operate fairly and in accordance with fundamental principles of justice? The following chapters are directed to providing an answer.

## CHAPTER 2

# The Disciplinary Process at Matsqui

Unlike the criminal courts of this country, disciplinary hearings in prisons are not open to the public, nor are they the subject of media accounts. While the courtroom scene is a familiar and sometime central feature of movies (the riveting court-martial clash between Jack Nicholson and Tom Cruise in *A Few Good Men* [1992] springs to mind), even prison movies focus on events that have more dramatic potential than disciplinary hearings. While sex, drugs, and rock and roll do feature in some hearings, the great majority of cases are routine, and many involve behaviour—for example, a charge of being disrespectful—which is not the subject of state intervention when it occurs outside of prison. Over the six years of my research, from 1993 to 1999, I observed more than five hundred disciplinary hearings. In the next two chapters I endeavour to give readers a sense of what takes place in prison courtrooms not by highlighting exceptional cases but by presenting the everyday reality of the practice of discipline. In this way, I hope to create a foundation upon which readers can form judgements about the experience of justice.

## July 1993: Mr. Routley's Court

Mr. Keith Routley has been the Independent Chairperson at Matsqui Institution since 1988. In 1994 he was appointed the Senior Independent Chairperson for the Pacific Region. For many years Mr. Routley maintained his own law practice, which included criminal defence work. He then left the practice of law to assume executive responsibilities in the aviation industry. During the course of my research, in his capacity as the Senior Independent Chairperson Mr. Routley organized meetings with other Independent Chairpersons in the region and with Senior Chairpersons from other regions to address issues of common concern, particularly achieving consistency in the interpretation of the law and in procedure.

Disciplinary hearings at Matsqui were generally held once a week in one of the two boardrooms in the visiting area. The room is also used for meetings of the Segregation Review Board. Mr. Routley sat on one side of a square table with the court clerk to his left. The institutional advisor sat on the right side of the table, and on the opposite side sat any witnesses who testified, be they institutional staff or other prisoners. There were usually one or two officers in the room who served as sheriffs, co-ordinating the appearance of prisoners and escorting them into the hearing room. The accused prisoner sat at the other side of the table, facing the Independent Chairperson and the court clerk. There was no Canadian flag, raised dais, or other symbolic indicator of a courtroom.

On my first day of observation, July 14, 1993, the court docket included the most serious charge in the disciplinary code—assault on a staff member. The accused prisoner, Mr. Wagner, responded with "Not really" when asked whether he understood the charge. He explained that a number of different charges had been laid and he was not sure which one he was now facing. Mr. Routley read out some details of the incident from the officers' reports and asked the prisoner whether he had seen these reports. Mr. Wagner replied that he had not, although he had asked for them. In response, Mr. Routley stated that he was going to put the matter over to the next court session and asked the clerk to make sure Mr. Wagner got copies of all incident reports attached to the charge before then. Mr. Wagner said he wanted to get the hearing over with as soon as possible and asked, "If I plead guilty, what will I be looking at? I've never been convicted of assaulting anyone before." Mr. Routley replied, "I won't entertain that," and adjourned the case to the next court day, telling Mr. Wagner that once he had read the incident reports, he should consider his position and, if necessary, get legal advice; he should then come to the next hearing prepared with whatever he wanted to say. Mr. Wagner replied, "It doesn't matter what I say. It won't make any difference."

Mr. Routley's adjournment of the case to ensure that Mr. Wagner received full disclosure of the officers' incident reports marked a significant change from the days of warden's court where the notice requirements were regularly ignored. This proved to be Mr. Routley's consistent practice (along with that of the other Independent Chairpersons I observed), demonstrating a concern for compliance with the procedural requirements of the law.

There was no court session on either July 21 or July 28, and there were only two cases on the docket on August 11. This did not signify that the prisoner body had gone on a summer good-behaviour vacation; rather, it reflected an institutional decision to classify most charges as minor ones, so that their adjudication would come before "minor courts" presided over by Correctional Supervisors and not the Independent Chairperson. With what results, we will see shortly.

## August 1993: The Wagner Case— The Disciplinary Process in Context

The adjourned hearing of Mr. Wagner's case was held on August 11. At the beginning of the hearing, Mr. Wagner complained to Mr. Routley that he had been kept in segregation since he was charged with this offence over a month ago, pending the court hearing, and questioned whether that was lawful. Mr. Routley responded:

> Well, I'm not looking at the particular paperwork that you're looking at, but I can tell you that the warden has the authority under the law to hold an inmate in administrative segregation, and the reasons for that are threefold: either protection of the inmate from parties in general population or protection of general population from that particular inmate or, thirdly, for the general security of the institution . . . There is no fourth reason that says pending the hearing of charges. It's a lot like being held without bail. When you told me that that's why you thought you were in segregation, I knew that couldn't be, because they can't by law hold somebody for that reason.

While Mr. Routley correctly stated that the *Corrections and Conditional Release Act* does not authorize detention in segregation based solely upon a pending disciplinary hearing, one of the important questions of my research was whether prisoners were detained in segregation for precisely this reason. That had been part of the customary law of Matsqui at the time of my 1972 study. Certainly Mr. Wagner was under the impression that it remained the case and his apparent willingness to plead guilty on his first appearance in July had been based upon his belief that he would thereby shorten his time in segregation.

Mr. Wagner's hearing moved to address the specific charge of which he stood accused. The following excerpt from the transcript of the tape recording of the hearing gives the flavour of prison disciplinary hearings and illustrates some further connections between the disciplinary process and other critical features of the correctional system that affect the rights and interests of prisoners.

> ICP [Independent Chairperson]: We're looking at the events here of some one month ago back on the 7th of July. Inmate Wagner's been charged on the 7th of July under subsection (h) of the *Corrections and Conditional Release Act*, "fights with, assaults or threatens to assault another person," and this relates to an activity in the cell

3 South at 2030 hours. I wonder if you can pick up your recollection of the tale there and tell me what was said and done.

IW [Institutional Witness]: I don't have my notes with me so where it began, Officer Laker and myself . . .

ICP: If I can just, before you start . . . Mr. Wagner, are you listening to what this officer says? Listen carefully. At the conclusion, if you can frame polite questions to the officer relevant to his testimony and the circumstance, I'd invite you to ask him those questions. If not, you can flag me to the areas that you wish to have examined. But while Officer Tate is giving his evidence I'd ask you sit quietly. Go ahead.

IW: Okay. That evening Officer Laker and myself were doing range walks as per standing orders and I was proceeding down 2 South and it was approximately cell number 21. I may be mistaken on the number. It was inmate Kwok's cell. I heard a buzzing noise, which is familiar to myself as being a tattoo gun. I looked in the cell and I observed inmate Wagner tattooing inmate Kwok's shoulder. He was sitting on the bed at the far back of the cell. I opened the door and there was another inmate sitting in the doorway, inmate Valenzuela, and they were all shocked and I believe some of the words were "ah, fuck." I asked them to step out of the cell and there was a bit of an argument between myself and inmate Valenzuela, who didn't want to leave the cell right away. He was sort of blocking my entrance into the cell. During this time I noticed inmate Wagner stick something down the front of his pants. Once I got inmate Valenzuela out of the cell I went into the cell and inmates Kwok and Wagner were still in there and I told inmate Wagner to turn over the tattoo gun, which he did. I then picked up . . . there was a wire that they were running the power off of a stereo, so I took the wire off that at the time and I informed all three that they were being placed on lock-up. About that time Officer Laker observed Wagner put something into his back pocket. I didn't know what it was at that time, and she told him to hand it over, which he didn't. We began locking up inmate Kwok and inmate Valenzuela, who both reside on 2 South. At that time inmate Wagner left the range while we were locking up. We followed him up to the third floor. He was in the third range south washroom with another inmate. I think he was washing off some ink on his hands. I'm not exactly positive of that. I told him he was going to be placed on lock-up and charged and the argument began at that time, that you either charge me or . . . He'd rather just be charged and not locked up, and I told him he was going to be locked up too. The argument began to get hostile at that point.

ICP: You're in the washroom on the third floor now?

IW: Yeah, he came out of the washroom and we were proceeding to his cell and the argument was continuing. He was walking into his cell at that time. He went into his cell and then I told him to hand over what he had in his pocket. He said it was ink. Well, at that time I knew it was ink from Officer Laker. So he was saying he had permits for it, and when I told him that as far as I was concerned he was using it as contraband and that I was going to remove it off him, he was arguing that fact and he didn't want to hand it over. The argument was getting quite verbal.

ICP: Now, paint a picture if you can for me of the surrounding circumstances. I know that we're in this 3 South cell area now and it's about 8:30 in the evening. Are there other inmates around?

IW: Yes, all the inmates are loose. The phone calls were being made at that time. There was a congregation of inmates outside the control room.

ICP: How far is that away? Seventy feet?

IW: No, it wouldn't even be that. I would say maybe twenty feet to the common area there, and there were inmates congregating at the far end of the range.

ICP: You guys were arguing about this bottle of ink? Laker's still with you, though?

IW: Yeah, she is. I'm in the doorway at the cell and she was outside the doorway to my left and behind me. I felt the situation was beginning to escalate, and I made the decision and I told him he was going to the hole. He wasn't handing over the contraband, and I felt in the situation that he should be removed out of the unit.

ICP: You told him, I'm going to take you from the cell now.

IW: Yeah. I told him, you're going to segregation. At the same time he handed me the ink, and then he sort of stepped back and then he came towards me like a rushing motion. That's when I decided I felt I had to push him back into the cell to contain him in that cell. I pushed him and I believe I grabbed somewhere on his arms. I had the tattoo gun in my one hand and I had a punch clock, which is a wand that's got a wrist strap.

ICP: Where's the ink bottle?

IW: I had that in my hand too. So I had everything in my hands. At that time I pushed him back in the cell. The wand ended up on his floor and the tattoo gun ended up on the floor outside the cell, and I think I ended up with the ink. I think it's the only thing I did have in my hand. At that time, when I grabbed hold of him to push him back in the cell, he also grabbed hold of my arms, and somehow he spun me and I bumped into the locker to my right and to his left in the cell. I pushed him back, and it was still verbal at that time. I was saying stuff to him. I couldn't tell you what was being said. We sort of held each other for a second and looked at each other, then both realized we were in a situation that shouldn't be going down and we both let go of each other. He backed off, and I just backed out and I locked the door. Officer Laker had already called for assistance from the bubble, and Officer Prue was coming outside the door and he was just outside the bubble area, and I yelled for him to get gas and restraints, to get handcuffs, which he did. We went right back. This was within thirty seconds, and I looked in the cell and saw inmate Wagner was packing up his tobacco and his papers and whatever he was gonna need. So we just opened up the door and I placed restraint equipment on him and we escorted him up to the hole. There was no more physical altercations. There was verbal stuff on the walkway, but that was it.

ICP: Now, you refer to a rushing motion. I want you to direct your mind to that.

IW: I don't know if he was going to try to push me out of the cell. My assumption was he was going to block me from closing the door. That's why I pushed him back, so I could lock the door.

ICP: He was going to block you from . . .

IW: Well, I think he was going to block . . . hold the door. That's what it appeared to me. I don't think he was rushing to hit me or anything at that time. I think he was coming to the door to stop me from closing the door [emphasis added]. Whether to argue the fact or whatever . . .

ICP: You perceived he was going to block you from closing the door, i.e., he wanted the door left open?

IW: Yeah.

ICP: So then you went into the cell and he grabbed you?

IW: Yeah, it was basically at the same time. You know, when I made the motion. *I would assume that I got a hold of him first. Because I made the first grabbing motion* [emphasis added]. He made the motion towards me and I made the grabbing motion.

ICP: Mr. Wagner, anything arising on that? Is that substantially what happened? It's always difficult.

P [Prisoner]: Can I make a comment on a few of those things?

ICP: Well, tell me what areas you want to look at here. I made notes on what the officer said.

P: It's pretty accurate on the second range down there. Yeah, I was tattooing. There's no doubt about that. When I was up I was washing my hands on the 3 South range washroom. He did tell me that I was gonna be going to the hole if I didn't co-operate and stuff, and I did tell him that either he could lock me up, I mean, do one or the other. Either lock me up but don't charge me, or if you're going to charge me don't lock me up. I just went to my room, right? And then he asked me to hand over the ink. I didn't hand him the ink. I told him I had a permit for it and he told me I was gonna be charged and I handed him the ink. He started closing the door and said you'll be charged anyways, I guess for being stubborn or whatever.

ICP: For tattooing, perhaps.

P: Yeah. And I wanted to talk to him. Like he said, I just wanted to talk, so I did, I made a quick motion towards the door and I grabbed the door and pulled the door open. But Officer—what's her name?

ICP: Laker.

P: Yeah. I think she's blowing this thing a little more out of proportion . . . in her statements. She says in her statement that I ran for the door, I grabbed the door and I opened the door and pulled him inside the room by both arms.

ICP: That's not this officer's recollection either.

P: No. And the only way that he could escape was by pushing me into my desk and then escaping out the doorway. That wasn't the case. I didn't want no conflict. I would rather just avoid the whole thing. I was verbal, I was kind of mad.

ICP: Anything further, Mr. Wagner?

P: I just didn't want a confrontation with anybody. I got no assaults on my record.

ICP: Well, just give me a moment here. I want to review this. We're not going to hear from Officer Laker, apparently.

IW: She's writing an exam.

P: It's pretty accurate of when I was on the second range, and his statements I can tell you are more accurate than hers.

ICP: You're referring to the officers' statements, copies of which you were provided. You've had time to study them both . . . You've heard his evidence, and you're referring now to Officer Laker's statement which you think isn't as accurate as what we've heard here today.

P: Yeah.

ICP: Okay. Officer Tate, you can stay if you wish. I'm just going to review these notes here.

Well, Mr. Wagner, I know you'll agree we've listened carefully and looked thoroughly at the events here of July 7, and I can tell you that I find both your evidence and the evidence of Officer Tate to be quite candid and quite frank. The charge that I have to address is one of "fights with, assaults or threatens to assault another person." Now, the "assaults or threatens to assault" usually follows a completely different pattern, so I'm looking here at what is the nature of a fight. In looking at the evidence, it clearly boils down to the events in your cell, involving what I would call a bit of a push and shove. Whatever the mistaken motivations of the parties, whether you were trying to open the door or close the door or what your intention was, I do find that in the circumstances a fight took place. *I do not find that there was a threat by you to assault* [emphasis added]. I think that the fight speaks for itself. Now, having found that, it follows that a guilty finding will ensue, *but I want to note as well that clearly you were no sooner engaged in this shoving than you realized that this obviously was not appropriate and clearly this officer reached the same conclusion and that as a fight it sort of stopped the moment it started, or very soon thereafter. So in the circumstances I find that the charge is made out, but it is in fact of a lesser degree* [emphasis added]. I mean, I can envision a conviction under this [section] with a lot more activity and confrontation than took place here. So with that in mind, I'm going to defer here to Mr. Gerl [the institutional advisor] and ask if you have any inquiries to make of this inmate, and then I'd like to hear a little bit about how long you've been here and what you've been doing while you've been here. Mr. Gerl, any comments or inquiries?

IA [Institutional Advisor]: I have a comment, that you indicated in your testimony that you didn't want a confrontation. It seems to me from the testimony here that very clearly you escalated the matter by not dealing with it when Mr. Tate initially asked you to turn it over, and you could have resolved it there. I think that by forcing the exchange you sort of escalated the situation to where you're in court here, and I think as Mr. Routley has indicated you both more or less realized at that time that this is a mistake, you shouldn't be doing what you're doing, and that's good. I just wish you hadn't pressed the matter. You should have co-operated with Mr. Tate and we wouldn't be here today.

ICP: Now, what by way of sanction? I can tell you, I've sent people to the bucket here for 30 days and put a $50 fine on fighting charges. I'm not inclined to do that in this circumstance. But I want you to tell me how long you've been in Matsqui.

P: About six months now.

ICP: How long a sentence are you doing?

P: Twenty-eight months.

ICP: Well, I'm inclined to put some time over this inmate's head [give him a suspended sentence].

IA: I would recommend time over his head and an upper-end fine.

ICP: Do you have a job here right now?

P: Yes, I do.

ICP: What are you doing?

P: I go to school.

ICP: Well, I'm going to put 30 days over your head for 90. [That is, if the prisoner remained charge-free for the 90 days, he would not have to serve the 30 days in segregation; conversely, if he was charged within that time frame and convicted before the Independent Chairperson, he would have to serve the 30 days together with any further sanction imposed for the new charge.] And I'm going to take into account actually the immediate way this fight was broken off. I think that indicates that to some extent you were aware this was inappropriate, and Officer Tate as a result suffered no further prejudice to himself. That being the case, I'm going to impose a fine. Mr. Gerl, I can't agree on an upper-end fine on this. I'm going to put a mid-range fine in place and I'm going to impose a fine of $25.

P: May I add something further? I'm due for parole on the 16th of August. This, what I'm being charged for now, was already written up on my file. It was already wrote up that I assaulted Mr. Tate and I grabbed him by both arms and pulled him...

ICP: I don't mean to cut you off, but I can tell you there's very complex rules in law regarding what goes in the file that a Parole Board looks at. You can be represented, and you'll have an opportunity at the time at any Parole Board hearing to address the charge and the results of that charge. I don't know if I can note here . . . I think a Parole Board looking at this, really, realizing that you didn't draw any hole time immediately, would realize that there were certain mitigating factors to the facts of the charge and you'll have an opportunity to tell them that. But I don't want to comment any further on anything to do with parole.

P: All right.

ICP: All right, thanks very much then.

Mr. Routley, during his last exchange with Mr. Wagner, clearly intended to reassure the prisoner that the Independent Chairperson's findings regarding the nature of the "fight," and the mitigating circumstances which in Mr. Routley's view placed it at the low end of the scale of seriousness, would be readily understood by the Parole Board since the sentence did not involve segregation. However, Mr. Routley's genuine expectation that this would be the case was not reflected in Matsqui's paper trail. The documentation on Mr. Wagner's disciplinary file would reflect only the fact that he was found guilty of a charge of "fights with, assaults or threatens to assault another person" and that he had received a suspended sentence of 30 days' segregation together with a fine of $25. None of Mr. Routley's findings of fact would be recorded on the disciplinary charge sheet, and the only individuals who would have knowledge of the hearing were those present—which did not include either Mr. Wagner's case management officer or the correctional officer specifically assigned to his case. The only way those officers could find out what had actually happened at the hearing would be to listen to the tape of the proceedings. This is a time-consuming process, and in my experience at Matsqui no staff member ever requested the tape of a disciplinary hearing. The only transcripts produced were those generated by lawyers in the very rare cases where judicial review was sought of the Independent Chairperson's decision. (The other exception, of course, was the transcripts I prepared for the purposes of my research.)

A case management or correctional officer required to prepare a progress or assessment report on a prisoner convicted of a disciplinary offence has recourse to the disciplinary face sheet prepared for each hearing. This contains a brief description of the offence, the subsection of the CCRA under which the charge was brought, whether the offence was designated as serious or minor, the finding of guilt or acquittal, and, if the finding is guilty, the sanction. Attached to the face sheet are reports prepared by the charging or witnessing officers. These reports are analogous to police or witness statements prepared during the course of a police investigation into a criminal offence outside of prison. In most cases, officers who give evidence at a disciplinary hearing give an approximation of what they have written in the offence reports. However, even where the Independent Chairperson finds a prisoner guilty of the offence as charged, the Chairperson does not necessarily accept everything in the offence reports or agree with the charging or witnessing officers' evaluation of the seriousness of the offence.

Mr. Wagner's is a case in point. Officer Laker's report described the incident as being more serious than did the evidence given by Officer Tate, the primary officer involved. Officer Laker was not called upon to give evidence, and Mr. Routley based his decision on the evidence of Officer Tate, with which Mr. Wagner basically agreed. This was the factual matrix Mr. Routley characterized as a "push and shove" incident rather than an assault on an officer. However, prior to the disciplinary hearing, Mr. Wagner's case management officer had prepared a progress summary in support of a recommendation that Mr. Wagner be transferred from Matsqui to Kent, on the grounds that his behaviour at Matsqui merited a maximum security classification. The progress summary referred to five minor disciplinary convictions, all of which involved Mr. Wagner's activities in tattooing other prisoners and his failure to be at his cell for lock-up. However, the summary placed the greatest reliance on the serious charge of assaulting Officer Tate. The alleged offence is described in these terms:

The purpose of this report is to address Mr. Wagner's involuntary transfer to Kent institution as a result of his recent assault on a staff member . . .

His current situation has arisen as a result of his being caught in [another prisoner's] cell by security staff while doing a tattoo on another inmate. His reaction was at first co-operative but turned sour when he was ordered to give up his tattooing ink. He began swearing and drawing more attention to his plight on the tier, eventually giving up the ink when told he would be placed in s.c.u. The report dated 93/07/07 indicates Mr. Wagner became more aggressive, threatening and intimidating. Upon returning to his cell, Mr. Wagner grabbed the officer who was locking him in his cell by the arm with both hands. The officer was drawn into the cell and a pushing match ensued in the cell until the officer was able to exit. Mr. Wagner was immediately segregated as a result. Although there were no weapons used or blood drawn, there is a deliberate attempt on Mr. Wagner's part to fight with the officer . . .

Mr. Wagner's criminal history has no violence. However, he has displayed increasing willingness to use violence within the institution against staff. (Progress Summary, Matsqui Insitution, July 13, 1993)

Since this progress summary was prepared prior to the disciplinary hearing, it was based on the incident reports, including that of Officer Laker. The characterization of the incident as "an assault" on an officer was specifically negated by Mr. Routley's findings. Furthermore, the statement in the progress summary that there was "a deliberate attempt . . . to fight with the officer" is contrary to the evidence given by Officer Tate. Nonetheless, a copy of the progress summary would be provided to the Parole Board as a matter of course, and any attempt by Mr. Wagner at a parole hearing to explain the circumstances of the incident as a "push and shove" would likely be viewed by Board members as rationalization or minimization of the seriousness of the incident. Mr. Wagner would not have the benefit of a transcript of the disciplinary hearing to demonstrate that his characterization accorded with that of the Independent Chairperson, and the expectation expressed by Mr. Routley, that the Parole Board would realize the offence was not serious from the fact that Mr. Wagner did not get segregation time, would not be borne out by the correctional reality.

## August 1993: Brew Parties—Different Strokes for Different Folks

On August 18 I attended my third session of the disciplinary court. The six cases on the docket involved charges of possession of contraband in the form of home brew. Three of the prisoners had been charged following a "brew party" on August 11 and the other three following another party on August 12.

At the disciplinary hearing on August 18, the three prisoners charged on August 12 appeared first. Mr. Hanson, Mr. Loucks, and Mr. Jones had been kept in segregation since August 12 and appeared in the courtroom in handcuffs. Each pleaded guilty to the charge. None of the prisoners had previous convictions for possession of brew, and all received what Mr. Routley described as his normal sentence for a first contraband conviction: 30 days' segregation suspended for 90 days. The institutional advisor expressed no disagreement with this standard sentence. However, after the third prisoner was dismissed from the room, the advisor informed Mr. Routley that the three had caused problems for the institution over the weekend while in segregation by threatening to kill staff members and throwing food out of their cells onto the range. Mr. Routley asked rhetorically, why, if this was so, they had not been charged with these incidents.

The next three cases involved the prisoners charged following the brew party on August 11. These prisoners had also been taken to segregation, but, unlike the first three, they had been released the next day; at the Segregation Review Board held that morning, the decision had been made that the prisoners be released from segregation since they had sobered up, the segregation unit was overcrowded, and cells were needed for other prisoners. After the August 12 meeting, which I had attended, I asked the Chairperson of the Segregation Review Board whether, if segregation cell space had not been at a premium, the three prisoners would have been kept in segregation. He said the normal practice was to release prisoners sent to segregation on brew charges the next day, provided they had sobered up. This second group of prisoners had therefore spent the last week in the general population and appeared in court without handcuffs. Like the previous three prisoners, they pleaded guilty and received the standard 30 days' segregation, suspended for 90 days.

That all six prisoners received the standard sentence for a first conviction for possession of contraband was entirely appropriate, given that their offences were virtually identical. However, from the prisoners' point of view, viewing the disciplinary process as one which began with their being charged for the offence and ended with their guilty pleas and the imposition of punishment, there was unequal treatment. The prisoners charged on August 11 spent only one day in segregation prior to their court hearing, but those charged on August 12 spent six days in segregation after being charged with exactly the same offence. The reason for the difference lay in a decision made by the warden on Friday, August 13. Responding to the fact that there had been brew parties in the institution on two consecutive nights, he informed his staff that it was important to demonstrate the zero tolerance policy of Matsqui towards brew. To crack down, prisoners charged with brew offences would be detained in administrative segregation until their court appearances. The prisoners charged on August 12 had been the first to feel the brunt of this crackdown. Mr. Routley, in his response to Mr. Wagner the previous week, had correctly stated that under the *Corrections and Conditional Release Act* there was no authority to keep a prisoner in segregation based solely on the ground that he was facing a disciplinary charge. A week later, the warden at Matsqui concluded that, to indicate zero tolerance of brew offences, such detention was justified.

The three prisoners charged on August 12 were thus the subject of unfair treatment, and I wondered if their disruptive behaviour in segregation had been related to their sense of that unfairness. To answer this question, I decided to interview the three. Before doing that, I spoke to one of the staff involved in the cases. His response, like the responses of the prisoners, revealed not only the relationship between disciplinary and administrative decision-making but also the critical importance of perception. In the prison, as outside, justice and fairness oftentimes lie in the eyes of the beholder.

The first person I spoke to after the disciplinary hearings was Rick Cregg, who had been in charge of the segregation unit over the weekend in question. He said Mr. Hanson, Mr. Loucks, and Mr. Jones had caused problems for the staff there. When I asked why he had not laid charges against them, he responded that it was futile to do this in light of the way the charges would be dealt with by the Independent Chairperson. In support of this position, he cited the fact that the men had received suspended sentences for the brew charges. I explained that Mr. Routley had not been made aware of any aggravating circumstances in the cases of these three men, and therefore he had followed his previous precedent, to which no objection had been raised by the staff advisor.

I then interviewed Greg Hanson, Randy Loucks, and Ron Jones. Mr. Hanson told me that he and Mr. Loucks had obtained some brew in order to have a little celebration for Mr. Jones, who had just arrived in Matsqui. They had known each other in Drumheller Institution and, as Mr. Jones put it, it was a "coming to Matsqui party." They were sitting reminiscing about old times in the recreation yard when some guards came up to them. Even though they had emptied their cups, the guards smelled the liquor, and the men were charged with possession of contraband and taken to the hole. Mr. Hanson said that this was the first brew he had ever taken in jail and "it was definitely not Glenfiddich"; he was quite drunk, and when he got to the hole he could barely stand up. When he awoke the next day he was extremely embarrassed, both for being caught and because he had thrown up all over his cell. He hit the buzzer in his cell and asked when he was going to get out, assuming he was in segregation only until he sobered up. Instead, he was told by the keeper that "the warden was pissed off" with him and that he and the other two were going to be made an example of because of the increasing use of brew in the institution. They would be kept in segregation for the weekend and let out Monday. On Monday, they were told they would be kept in segregation until the court dealt with their cases. Mr.

Hanson was told this was because he and the other two prisoners had been heard talking to each other about taking staff hostages and "kicking pig ass."

The prisoners were informed that incident reports had been filed by Officer Cregg, the keeper on duty over the weekend. When Mr. Cregg returned on shift on Tuesday, the prisoners asked him what he had written. He said he had reported an exchange among four prisoners, including the three of them, that involved talk about taking hostages. The prisoners were told that although they would not be charged with any offence, these incident reports would be on their records. The men expressed concern that they were not shown copies of incident reports and therefore had no way to challenge the truth of what was written in them.

Mr. Hanson, in describing what had happened over the weekend, told me the comments about "kicking butt" were made more in the nature of bravado. If the men had been serious about taking hostages, he said, they would hardly have proclaimed their intentions in the segregation range for all to hear. Their talk was also prompted by being singled out by the warden for especially harsh treatment; instead of being released the next day, like the three prisoners charged with the same offence the night before, they had to spend the weekend in segregation. Yet their drinking had been no more serious than anyone else's; they had not created an incident when arrested nor challenged staff when they were taken to segregation. Mr. Jones and Mr. Loucks told me this kind of unfair treatment would not help them change what the administration viewed as their "bad attitude" towards authority. Mr. Hanson was rather more stoic. He said that ten years earlier he would have been really angry about this kind of treatment, but now he had come to accept it as part of doing time. As he put it, "I've come to accept that in prison anyone with a red pen can fuck up your day."

## August 1993: Mr. Wagner's Second Appearance

The six cases of contraband brew were the only cases dealt with at the disciplinary court on August 18. At 10:15, court was ended abruptly when the Independent Chairperson was informed that all prisoners were being returned to their cells because of an assault by one prisoner on another in a walkway.

We later learned the victim of the assault was Mr. Conte. He had been attacked with a weight bar and had suffered a skull fracture and severe bruising across his stomach. He had been taken to the MSA Hospital in Abbotsford but brought back to Matsqui the next day and was now in stable condition in the prison hospital. Mr. Wagner was accused of the attack; he was taken to segregation after the attack occurred and later charged with the disciplinary offence of assault.

The involuntary transfer of Mr. Wagner to Kent Institution initiated in July, following the alleged assault on Officer Tate, had not been pursued on condition that Mr. Wagner sign a behavioural contract agreeing to participate in certain programs. Following the attack on Mr. Conte and the further disciplinary charge of assault, a second involuntary transfer package was prepared. The progress summary supporting the transfer asserted that Mr. Wagner "was recently convicted in disciplinary court for assaulting an officer in the living unit following a frisk of his cell." The report went on to state:

> His current situation has arisen as a result of his attack on another inmate in the walkway. He attacked this inmate with a weight bar and hit him twice on the skull resulting in profuse bleeding. He then ran to the gym to return the bar and then showered. Mr. Wagner was located in his cell and immediately segregated as a result. (Progress Summary, Matsqui Institution, August 24, 1993)

The principal observation report relating to the assault on Mr. Conte was that of Correctional Supervisor Ford, the only officer who saw the attack. His report stated:

> At approximately 09:20 a.m. I was returning from the exercise yard from a conversation with CO-II Ginger. As I approached the walkway area I observed through the chain-link fence an inmate being assaulted by another inmate with what appeared to be a metal bar approximately 15 to 20 inches long. I immediately yelled to the assailant to stop and I then proceeded to the scene. As I was approaching the scene, the inmate assailant again struck the victim to the shoulder area. I called central control and requested medical and staff assistance immediately to the S.I.S. [Stores and Institutional Supplies] area. When I arrived at the S.I.S. area, the victim was beginning to fall towards the ground so I directed him to the ground to prevent further injury. As this inmate came to rest on the ground I yelled to the assailant to remain where he was standing. When I looked back to see the assailant he was just going out of sight into the gym area. I instructed Officer Ginger to watch over the victim and I proceeded to the gym area. As I approached the gym I indicated to Correctional Supervisor Furst to enter the gym at the door nearest him while I entered at the second door. When I entered the gym, I took a look around and found two possible suspects that resembled the assailant. I asked Officer London to identify the two inmates and he stated that one was inmate Wagner and the second was inmate DaSilva. I approached the universal gym area to find the weapon that was used on inmate Conte. I found the weapon on the floor in front of the universal gym. Another inmate was just about to pick this weapon

up so I removed it from the area. The weapon appears to be a handle from the universal gym. I then proceeded outside the gym and
asked an inmate his name. This inmate stated his name was inmate
Wagner and he continued walking towards the kitchen. I was now
pretty sure that inmate Wagner was the assailant . . . A lock-down
was ordered by Unit Manager Irv Hammond and then a count was
done. During the count in the living unit, I assisted in the removal
of inmate Wagner from his cell to the special management unit.
Inmate Wagner was observed prior to the count taking a shower and
then changed his clothes. Inmate Wagner stated several times during
his escort to the s.c.u. area that he was always being blamed for
something and pleaded that he had done no wrong. (Officer Observation Report, Matsqui Institution, August 18, 1993)

None of the other officers who filed observation reports had observed the
attack, and they were therefore not able to identify the assailant.

In his response to the involuntary transfer package, Mr. Wagner had denied
any involvement in the attack on Mr. Conte. He claimed he was in the gym
when the attack happened and saw the staff running about and went to investigate. Two staff members approached him and told him and the other prisoners
to stay in the gym. He questioned why, if the staff were sure he was the person
involved in the assault, he was not grabbed at that time and taken to segregation.
He acknowledged taking a shower after he left the gym; his explanation was that
he had not taken a shower that morning and, having been in lock-down situations before, he knew it might be several days before he got another one.

Mr. Wagner's case appeared on the docket of the disciplinary court in August
and was adjourned several times to enable him to obtain legal counsel. A further
adjournment was granted at the institution's request in September because of the
unavailability of Officer Ford. A hearing date was finally scheduled for October
13 and was made "pre-emptory" on Matsqui. This meant that there would be no
further adjournments granted to the institution.

Meanwhile, the involuntary transfer process proceeded. Having received Mr.
Wagner's written response, Warden Brock affirmed the recommendation for
involuntary transfer. In his reasons, he stated:

Following the investigation by security staff, you were positively
identified as the individual who attacked inmate Conte. This attack
resulted in a skull fracture and inter-cranial haemorrhage requiring
emergency medical attention. This unprovoked attack confirms that
you continue to show violent tendencies and are not appropriate for
a medium security institution. (Notification of Review and Recom-

mendation Relative to Transfer, Matsqui Institution, September 7, 1993)

That recommendation was upheld by the Assistant Deputy Commissioner in a decision dated September 22. The decision stated:

> Given Mr. Wagner's continued problematic behaviour and his recent assault of another inmate, transfer to maximum security is warranted.

Following that decision—and prior to October 13, the hearing date set for the disciplinary charge—Mr. Wagner was transferred to Kent. On October 12, his counsel was informed by Matsqui that the disciplinary charge against Mr. Wagner would be administratively withdrawn at the hearing, because Mr. Ford was on annual leave and would not be available for the hearing.

On the day of the hearing, I was shown a copy of an earlier memorandum sent to Mr. Ford advising him that his appearance in court was imperative on October 13, because the Independent Chairperson had made the case pre-emptory and, if Mr. Ford was not there, the case would be thrown out of court. Mr. Ford had responded, "You might as well dismiss this case and save time and money. I'll be on annual leave on October 13, 1993." After the administrative withdrawal of the charge at the hearing, I asked Mr. Gerl, the institutional advisor, what effect this withdrawal would have on Mr. Wagner's transfer, given that the alleged assault was the principal basis for it. Mr. Gerl said it would not have any impact. Mr. Wagner's record showed that over a period of time he had been unable to conform to the rules at Matsqui. And since the charge had been withdrawn administratively rather than dismissed by the Independent Chairperson, the incident could still be relied upon as a basis for the transfer. In other words, the administrative withdrawal denied Mr. Wagner the opportunity to establish his innocence of the charge, the proof of which was the central element in his involuntary transfer.

The case against Mr. Wagner was far from overwhelming. Officer Ford, in his observation report, had stated that upon entering the gym he saw "two possible suspects that resembled the assailant." On the basis of a further discussion with Mr. Wagner, he became "pretty sure" that Mr. Wagner was the assailant. A cross-examination of Mr. Ford would have been critical at the disciplinary hearing. The questioning would have addressed such issues as the distance Mr. Ford was from the assault at the time it occurred; his description of the assailant; and his observations about whether Mr. Wagner's body or clothes had blood on them. This last point was extremely relevant, because the inference the institution had drawn against Mr. Wagner was that he had taken a shower and changed his clothes to get rid of telltale signs of the assault. Since the assault had caused profuse bleeding, it was likely that some of the blood would have splattered onto the assailant. Yet Mr. Ford's observation report did not note any incriminating presence of blood on Mr. Wagner or his clothes. In the absence of a hearing, there was no testing of Mr. Ford's observations, and Mr. Wagner had no opportunity to explain his actions before or after the attack. While there was no conviction on his disciplinary record for this assault, he was nonetheless treated for all correctional purposes as if he had been convicted. Subsequently, he remained at Kent for the balance of his sentence.

## September 1993: Minor Disciplinary Court— Due Process Gets a Rough Ride

As discussed, the legal framework governing prison discipline draws a distinction between serious and minor offences. Under s. 27 of the *Corrections and Conditional Release Regulations,* a disciplinary offence which is designated serious must be heard by an Independent Chairperson. Section 27(1) specifies that the hearing of a minor charge is to be conducted by the institutional head or a staff member designated by the institutional head. A further difference between serious and minor charges lies in the sanctions consequent upon conviction. Only following conviction of a serious offence can a sentence of punitive segregation be imposed, and the maximum fines, orders of restitution, and loss of privileges are greater for serious offences. However, the procedural code set out in the *CCRA* and the *CCR Regulations* regarding such matters as notice of the offence, conduct of the hearing, calling of evidence, burden of proof, and recording of the proceedings are common to both serious and minor offences. In other words, the legislative framework assumes a model of due process applicable to all disciplinary offences. It therefore becomes possible, through observing how minor offences are adjudicated, to see if the institutional staff conducting this adjudication interpret the due process of law in qualitatively different ways from Independent Chairpersons.

At Matsqui (and other federal institutions), the hearing of minor charges is delegated to correctional supervisors. The hearings are not held according to a regular schedule, like the Independent Chairperson's court, but are scheduled at times convenient to the correctional supervisor. By September 1993 a significant backlog of minor charges had built up, and on September 23 Correctional Supervisor Mike Csoka was given the daunting task of trying to clear this. The disciplinary docket consisted of thirty-eight cases. The hearings were conducted beginning at 1:00 p.m. in the office of one of the unit managers in the main living unit. With Mr. Csoka were two co-IIs, although the role of these two officers was not clear to me (nor was it indicated to any prisoner). Whereas the Commissioner's Directives specifically provide that the institutional head shall designate a staff member to assist the Independent Chairperson in the hearing of serious charges, there is no similar provision for any assistant role for minor charges.

The first case heard by Mr. Csoka involved Mr. Hurst, who was charged with contravention of s. 40(p) of the *Corrections and Conditional Release Act;* this section covers refusing to work or leaving work without reasonable excuse. The gist of the offence, as set out in the offence report, was that when told to lock up (go back to his cell), Mr. Hurst said to Officer Logan, "You can kiss my ass." Mr. Csoka did not ask for a plea but instead asked Mr. Hurst for his explanation. Mr. Hurst responded that he was not aware that if he was not working he had to stay in his cell. He had a morning job, and this incident had occurred in the afternoon; if the officer had told him first that the rule was he had to lock up if he wasn't working, he said there would have been no problem. Mr. Csoka replied, "I have known Officer Logan for ten years. He does the job the way it should be done. He doesn't have any attitude problem." Mr. Hurst was then asked to leave the room. In his absence, Officer Laker, one of the CO-IIs, said that Mr. Hurst had apologized to Officer Logan the next day. The other CO-II added that this was Mr. Hurst's standard practice: he mouthed off and then felt bad about it afterwards. Mr. Csoka said, "The bottom line is that he admitted saying to an officer, 'You can kiss my ass,' so he's guilty." The discussion then turned to the appropriate sentence. A fine of $10 was agreed upon. Mr. Hurst was brought back into the room and Mr. Csoka said, "I'm not all that familiar with the law and I forgot to take your plea. I'm marking it down as not guilty and I'm finding you guilty." Mr. Hurst asked what he was guilty of, and Mr. Csoka replied, "Swearing at the officer."

There are a number of comments to be made about this first hearing. As Mr. Csoka himself observed, there was no plea taken, as is required by s. 30 of the Commissioner's Directives. Nor was the procedure set out in s. 31 of the Directives followed. Section 31 requires that, where the plea is not guilty, "the accused inmate shall be given a reasonable opportunity to question witnesses, through the Chairperson, introduce evidence, call witnesses on his or her own behalf, and examine exhibits and documents relied upon. The inmate shall be afforded the opportunity to make relevant submissions, including submissions regarding the appropriate sanction, during all phases of the hearing." In Mr. Hurst's case, the charging officer was not called upon to give evidence, and Mr. Hurst was not invited to make submissions regarding the appropriate sanction. In addition, s. 43(2) of the CCRA provides that "a hearing shall be conducted with the inmate present unless (a) the inmate is voluntarily absent; (b) the person conducting the hearing believes on reasonable grounds that the inmate's presence would jeopardize the safety of any person present at the hearing; (c) the inmate seriously disrupts the hearing." In Mr. Hurst's case, he was told to leave the hearing during important stages of the deliberations—determination of whether he had committed the offence and discussion of the appropriate sentence—although there were no grounds to justify his exclusion. The final problem with Mr. Hurst's hearing was that the statement set out in the offence report, if proven by evidence, might have supported a charge under s. 40(f)—"being disrespectful or abusive towards a staff member in a manner that would undermine the staff member's authority"—but it clearly did not support the offence with which Mr. Hurst was charged: without reasonable excuse, "refuses to work or leaves work." Mr. Hurst was charged under the wrong section of the *Act* and should have been found not guilty.

In the next case, Mr. Clark was charged with wilfully disobeying a written rule governing the conduct of inmates, contrary to s. 40(r) of the *CCRA*. The allegation was that he had forced open the barrier at the end of 1 South range. He pleaded not guilty. In response, Mr. Csoka said, "Give us your explanation of why you're not guilty." Mr. Clark said, "I didn't push the barrier." Mr. Csoka continued, "Why did the officer think it was you, then?" Mr. Clark replied, "I may have been the first one out of the barrier and he may have thought that I pushed it." Officer Moran was then called into the hearing to give evidence, and Mr. Csoka asked him, "Is this the inmate you saw force open the barrier?" Officer Moran said it was. Mr. Clark asked Officer Moran, "How did you know it was me?" Officer Moran responded, "Because I called you back and you gave me the finger." Mr. Clark was then asked to leave the room. Mr. Csoka announced, "Well, he's obviously guilty." Officer Moran suggested that this was not a minor matter, because when prisoners force the barrier they could end up breaking it. There was a consensus that an appropriate fine was $10.

Mr. Clark was brought back into the room and told he was being fined $10. He responded, "I'm not working, how can you fine me?" Mr. Csoka responded, "Thanks for telling me. Do you have any money in your account?" Mr. Clark said no. A discussion ensued between the officers about whether it would be appropriate to impose early lock-up as the penalty. Mr. Clark said, "I'm on lock-up already." He was reminded that his lock-up was during working hours; early lock-up would mean he'd be locked up during leisure hours as well. Mr. Clark was then sentenced to two weekends' lock-up; Mr. Csoka explained that on Friday night Mr. Clark would be locked in his cell until Monday morning. Mr. Clark responded bitterly, "How about I do it in the hole?"

As Mr. Clark left the room, he had no idea that his sarcastic suggestion would be taken seriously. Early lock-up posed problems for staff in keeping track of prisoners, particularly on a range where there were no toilets in the cells. In such cases, the prisoner would have to be let out of his cell to use the common washroom at the end of the range, and it was difficult for the officer in the control bubble to ensure the prisoner went back to his cell. The alternative was to have early lock-up on weekends served in segregation, where there were no such administrative problems. After Mr. Clark had left the room, Mr. Csoka and the other officers agreed that this new policy would be implemented starting with

Mr. Clark. He would be taken to segregation at 4:00 on Friday afternoon and let out at 8:00 Monday morning.

There were some serious flaws in Mr. Csoka's handling of the Clark hearing. First of all, the CCRA, in setting out the disciplinary procedure for both serious and minor offences, clearly preserves the presumption of innocence by providing that:

> The person conducting the hearing shall not find the inmate guilty unless satisfied beyond a reasonable doubt, based on the evidence presented at the hearing, that the inmate committed the disciplinary offence in question. (s. 43(3))

That Mr. Csoka's operational assumption was a presumption of guilt, not innocence, was exemplified in his opening remarks to Mr. Clark: "Give us your explanation of why you're not guilty." Even though in this case the charging officer was called to give evidence, Mr. Csoka left no doubt about his preference for the officer's evidence over that of the prisoner. As in Mr. Hurst's case, there was also some question as to whether Mr. Clark was charged under the right section of the CCRA. During the hearing, there was no reference made to the written rule Mr. Clark was alleged to have broken, and the proper charge would seem to have been an attempt to wilfully damage property. Third, as with Mr. Hurst, the discussion regarding sentence took place in Mr. Clark's absence. Finally, the sentence imposed, that of two weekends' lock-up to be served, in accordance with the "new policy," in segregation, translated into a sentence of punitive segregation; such a sentence can only be imposed by an Independent Chairperson for conviction of a serious disciplinary offence. The sentence, however administratively convenient, was therefore illegal.

Mr. Longtin, the third prisoner on the docket, faced a charge of being "disrespectful or abusive towards a staff member in a manner that would undermine a staff member's authority," contrary to s. 40(f) of the CCRA. The allegation was that when told by an officer he was coming onto the range too often during the day, Mr. Longtin responded, "Fuck you, you can't tell me what to do." He pleaded not guilty and said he did not use those words. The charging officer was not called to give evidence. Mr. Longtin was asked to leave the room, and Officer Moran, who had remained in the room after Mr. Clark's hearing, stated, "The charging officer is a pretty straight guy." It was agreed that a fine of $5 was appropriate. Mr. Longtin was brought back into the room, and Mr. Csoka advised him, "We find you guilty. We don't believe your story. The officer has no reason to lie." Mr. Longtin responded, "How do you know that? Maybe he has a thing in for me."

In my 1972 study of the disciplinary process, I had concluded that two dominant features of the warden's court were the presumption of guilt and the presumption that officers do not lie and so their evidence is to be preferred to that of prisoners. Mr. Csoka's comments in Mr. Longtin's case make it clear that these presumptions continued to animate decision-making in minor court.

The fourth man to appear, Mr. Tschritter, faced a charge of "without reasonable excuse, refuses to work or leaves work," contrary to s. 40(p) of the *CCRA*. Mr. Tschritter pleaded guilty. When asked for an explanation, he said, "I was tired," to which Mr. Csoka responded, "So you took the day off." Mr. Tschritter was then asked to leave the room. Mr. Csoka reviewed Mr. Tschritter's record and noted a previous conviction on the serious charge of possession of brew, for which he had received 30 days' segregation suspended for 90 days. Mr. Csoka expressed the view that conviction for the minor charge would activate the 30 days' segregation. Officer Laker suggested (correctly) that only a serious charge could do that. Mr. Csoka phoned Norm Gerl, Co-ordinator of Correctional Operations and advisor to the Independent Chairperson, to get some clarification of the issue, but Mr. Gerl was not in his office. The prisoner was brought back in and told that his sentence was a $5 fine. He was then asked about his previous suspended sentence. He said it had occurred in 1992. A closer review of the file showed this to be the case, so there was nothing to activate.

The next prisoner was Mr. Robie, who was also charged under s. 40(p). The offence report alleged that he had failed to report for work. Mr. Robie too pleaded guilty. He said that the staffperson who was his boss had recently been on two weeks' holiday, and during that time Mr. Robie got into a routine of sleeping late. After Mr. Robie was asked to leave the room, there was a discussion about him being a "chronic sleeper." Mr. Csoka noted that Mr. Robie had been convicted on a serious charge the previous month and had "30 days over his head." One of the co-IIs asked, "Should we give him early lock-up?" The response was, "He likes being locked up." It was agreed that he should get a $5 fine, but it was unclear to everyone what to do about the 30 days' suspended sentence. Officer Laker said again that she had never seen a suspended sentence activated for a minor offence. Mr. Csoka phoned Mr. Gerl again, got through this time, and then reported to those present that Mr. Gerl had confirmed the 30 days was automatically activated by conviction in minor court. Officer Laker reacted with "That blows me away." Mr. Robie was then brought back into the room. When he was told he was being given a $5 fine for this offence and that he would also have to serve the 30 days in the hole which had been suspended, he was visibly shaken by the news. As a result of sleeping in—the seriousness of which justified only a $5 fine—Mr. Robie would now spend the next 30 days in segregation.

Mr. Jones, the next prisoner on the docket, faced a charge of being disrespectful towards staff. When questioned about having a pass, he was alleged to have become abusive and called the officer a "fucking goof" and a "power-tripper." Mr. Jones asked for a remand so that he could speak to his lawyer. Officer Moran replied that lawyers were not allowed in minor court. Mr. Jones then said, "I asked to have a witness and he's not here." At this point Mr. Csoka, who was reading through the documents, stated, "I see why you want to have this case remanded. You've got 30 days over your head, haven't you?" Mr. Csoka told Mr. Jones that he was going to proceed with the case and asked for his plea. Mr. Jones pleaded not guilty. Mr. Csoka said, "Do you have any explanation?" Mr. Jones said no and was then asked to leave the room. During the brief discussion that followed, it was determined that Mr. Jones was guilty of the charge, that he should be fined $5, and that the 30 days' segregation would be automatically activated. Mr. Jones was brought back into the room and told that he would be going to the hole to serve his 30 days. He looked at Mr. Csoka incredulously. Officer Moran took out handcuffs and said to Mr. Jones, "Do you want me to put these on you, or will you be going quietly?" Mr. Jones, his voice shaking, said, "You had better put them on me as I don't feel quiet right now." Officer Moran then left to escort Mr. Jones to segregation. Mr. Csoka radioed up to say that Mr. Jones was on his way and suggested there be two staff waiting for him because the prisoner might cause some problems.

When Mr. Jones' hearing is reviewed within the legal framework for disciplinary hearings, it is clear he should have been granted an adjournment. Adjournments are a regular feature of hearings for serious charges, and a prisoner's request for an adjournment at a first appearance to consult with counsel or Prisoners' Legal Services is granted by the Independent Chairperson as a matter of course. Although Officer Moran was correct in stating that the right to be represented by counsel is recognized in the *CCR Regulations* only for hearings on serious charges, this does not apply to the issue of seeking an adjournment to consult with counsel in order to prepare a proper answer and defence to a disciplinary charge. Mr. Jones' hearing also proceeded in violation of the *CCR Regulations* and the Commissioner's Directives. A decision was made about his guilt in the absence of evidence presented by the charging officer and without giving Mr. Jones an opportunity to question witnesses, and he was not allowed to make any submission regarding the appropriate sentence.

A vast distance between legal principle and administrative practice was further demonstrated when Mr. Lloyd's case was considered. Mr. Lloyd faced two charges of being abusive and disrespectful to a staff member, contrary to s. 40(f). In the first offence report, the allegation was that he was yelling out his cell to the officer in the bubble and then came up to the bubble and pounded on it, calling the officer an "f-ing cunt." Mr. Lloyd pleaded not guilty and said the guard in the bubble was being an asshole. Mr. Csoka responded, "Do you remember me last week in Segregation Review? You gave us a different explanation there. You said you didn't mean it, you were sorry and you just lost your cool." (After the incident in question, Mr. Lloyd had been taken to segregation; he was there for three days until he appeared before the Segregation Review Board, which recommended that he be released.)

Mr. Lloyd was then asked to leave the room. One of the officers reported that

Mr. Lloyd was always abusive to staff and had a real attitude problem. His file showed four previous minor charges; he had received warnings on two of them, a fine of $5 for a contraband tattoo gun, and three nights' lock-up on his last appearance. The recommendation this time around was that he be given a fine of $10. When Mr. Lloyd was brought back into the room and told he was being sentenced to a $10 fine, he responded, "I don't want the fine. I did three days in the hole for this and that should be enough. I've just got back to work and I've got no money. Do you want me to go back doing tattooing? I've been keeping out of that. I just can't take the fine."

Mr. Csoka then read the second charge Mr. Lloyd was facing, in which it was alleged that he appeared for breakfast inappropriately dressed, was told to go back and change, and then became "abusive with the staff, loud and aggressive and anti-authoritarian." Mr. Lloyd pleaded not guilty. He said that he had not been anti-authoritarian and he probably had a very different idea of what that meant than the officer did. In any event, Mr. Lloyd said that the incident had happened before he started going to work and so there was no requirement for him to be in work clothes. Again, no officer was called to give evidence before Mr. Lloyd was asked to leave the room. His guilt was assumed, because the discussion immediately focussed on what the appropriate sentence should be. It was recommended that, since he had had difficulty with the first fine of $10, he should be given a weekend of lock-up in the hole for this offence instead.

Mr. Lloyd was brought back into the room and told that he had been found guilty but would not be fined for the second offence; instead, he would be on weekend lock-up, to be served in segregation. Mr. Lloyd immediately responded, "How do you find me guilty—where is the evidence?" Mr. Csoka read the description of the offence written by Officer Charles and commented, "I know Officer Charles, and he is not going to lay a charge unnecessarily." Mr. Lloyd then got up and started swearing, calling Mr. Csoka "You fucking piece of shit." Just as he was at the door, Officer Moran blocked him and said, "You are very close to going up to the hole right now." Mr. Lloyd replied, "Just let me get out of here before I lose my cool." He was allowed to leave the room. As soon as he was outside, Mr. Csoka said, "I want him in the hole now." When Officer Moran suggested that they get him at the 4:00 p.m. lock-up, Mr. Csoka responded, "I don't want him running around getting all steamed up, so they should go and take him up right now." The two officers then left and went down to Mr. Lloyd's cell, where he was handcuffed behind his back and taken up to segregation. I accompanied them to observe this. There were about a dozen prisoners gathered around the control bubble watching, and I heard comments to the effect, "They're throwing everyone up in the hole this afternoon."

Even though Mr. Lloyd had pleaded not guilty to both charges and disputed the allegations, neither of the charging officers was called to give evidence, and Mr. Lloyd, like the other prisoners, was denied the opportunity to question witnesses. In assessing Mr. Lloyd's plea of not guilty in the first instance, Mr. Csoka rejected the plea's credibility by reference to what Mr. Lloyd had told the Segregation Review Board the week before. However, Mr. Lloyd's statements at that time, in which he apologized for losing his cool, did not necessarily amount to an admission of guilt. In any event, they were likely made to facilitate his early release from segregation. In the cases of Mr. Lloyd and Mr. Jones, Mr. Csoka's responses *after* the hearing left no doubt that, in discharging his adjudication function in minor disciplinary court, he was acting first and foremost as a keeper. As a result, not only were two prisoners sent to segregation but the due process of law was also banished.

Mr. Csoka next dealt in swift succession with a number of cases in which prisoners were charged with refusing to work or leaving work without reasonable excuse; the offence reports stated only that the prisoners were still in their cells after the 8:30 a.m. labour count. Most of the prisoners pleaded guilty and were given either a warning or a small fine, depending upon whether or not they had any prior disciplinary record. Because 3:00 p.m. marks a shift change in the prison, the officers who had been assisting Mr. Csoka left the institution at that time. Normally Mr. Csoka too would have gone off shift, but he decided to continue with the disciplinary court in order to clear the backlog. He was joined by Officer Van Vugt, who had just come on shift. I left the hearings for about half an hour to attend to some other business, and by the time I returned the docket had been cleared except for the final case involving Mr. Johnson.

Mr. Johnson faced several charges of refusing to work or leaving work, all of which involved allegations of sleeping in. He requested an adjournment in order to get medical certificates; these would show that his offences had resulted from stress due to the recent death of his mother and the loss of his appeal against his conviction. Mr. Csoka told Mr. Johnson that there was no need for an adjournment, because he could take Mr. Johnson's stress into account in his sentencing. Mr. Johnson said he was not prepared to go ahead because he had asked to have his CO-II present. Mr. Csoka responded, "That's a good reason for an adjournment," although he did not indicate that he was prepared to grant it. Officer Van Vugt then said to Mr. Johnson, "Look at this from a corrective, not a punitive, point of view. How can we get you to go to work? I know about your mother and about the appeal, but lots of guys lose their appeal, and you still have to go to work." Mr. Johnson responded that he had been in Matsqui six months but still had not received a correctional plan, which was required to be completed within forty-five days of his admission. That was the reason he wanted his CO-II there, because she was the one who was supposed to have prepared his plan and as of yet he had not seen her. Officer Van Vugt responded, "You're always minimizing the problem." Mr. Csoka interjected at this point, "The bottom line is we are going to deal with these charges today." Mr. Johnson said he was not going to enter a plea, to which Mr. Csoka replied, "We've got a box even for that"—referring to the fact that, on the face of the disciplinary sheet, there are three boxes under the general heading of "Plea," one of which is "Refuses to plead." Commissioner's Directive 580 provides that where a prisoner refuses to plead, the hearing shall be conducted as if the plea was not guilty.

Mr. Csoka read out the first charge and asked Mr. Johnson whether he had any explanation in response. Mr. Johnson gave every indication at first that he was standing mute to the charge. However, within a short period of time he again began complaining that his CO-II was at fault in not preparing his correctional plan. Officer Van Vugt advised him that he should put in an official complaint. Mr. Csoka became visibly upset at this point and exclaimed, "You're not dealing with the charges." He then read out the second charge. Mr. Johnson pleaded not guilty to this charge, saying he was at work on the day in question. A third charge of not working was then read to him, to which he entered no plea but pointed out that there was no officer present to give evidence. Mr. Csoka responded, "You did not request a witness." Eventually, Mr. Johnson said, "Fuck, I'll plead guilty to all of the charges." He again pointed out that all three charges arose because of the stress he was under, which was aggravated by not receiving his correctional plan. When he had gone to see his case management officer about this, he was told to see his CO-II, and yet she was not available to him. In support of his explanation that the charges were stress-related, he said, "Look at my institutional record over the last five years. I haven't missed a day of work until this." Following the usual procedure, Mr. Johnson was asked to leave the room, and a fine of $20 was agreed upon as his sentence.

Mr. Csoka's denial of an adjournment in this case was unreasonable, because Mr. Johnson wished to show medical certificates not simply to mitigate his culpability but to present a defence that he did not refuse to work or leave work "without reasonable excuse." Furthermore, it was apparent that Mr. Csoka did *not* take Mr. Johnson's stress into account in his sentencing, because Mr. Johnson received the heaviest fine of any of the prisoners whose cases were heard that afternoon—including those who, like him, faced multiple charges stemming from sleeping in during the labour count. As in the other cases, no witnesses were called to substantiate the charges, and when Mr. Johnson requested the presence of a charging officer, Mr. Csoka's response was that Mr. Johnson had not requested the witness be present. This represented a complete reversal of the legal onus upon the institution to call witnesses to substantiate a charge when a prisoner pleads not guilty or is deemed to have pleaded not guilty because he refuses to enter a plea. It was not Mr. Johnson's responsibility to ensure the attendance of the charging officer. This reversal of onus, while inconsistent with the CCR *Regulations* and the Commissioner's Directives, was consistent with Mr. Csoka's presumption of guilt.

In the course of a three-hour session, Mr. Csoka had disposed of thirty-eight minor disciplinary charges. Pleas of guilty had been made in twenty-three of these cases. However, as in Mr. Johnson's case, some of the guilty pleas were the result of resignation or exasperation. Of the fifteen cases in which not guilty pleas were entered, only two cases resulted in not guilty decisions.

Before the afternoon session started, I had spoken with Mike Csoka about his experiences to date with CSC. Mr. Csoka was not a product of the old B.C. Penitentiary mentality. Young, ambitious, and well-educated, with a degree in criminology, he represented the new breed of correctional officer, who sees corrections as a challenging career with real prospects of advancement to senior management. The particular challenge he faced—and met—that afternoon was to clear a large backlog of minor disciplinary cases. In terms of administrative efficiency, it was a veritable tour de force which only enhanced his reputation as a tough, no-nonsense correctional supervisor who could get the job done. However, the job of conducting hearings on minor disciplinary offences is not bounded only by the limits of administrative efficiency; it is bounded also by a legal framework designed to ensure that the hearing process is fair and just. Mr. Justice MacGuigan of the Federal Court of Appeal, in the *Howard* case, observed that "convenience and justice are often not on speaking terms" (*Howard*, at 681–82). On that September afternoon, justice, in the form of the rules and procedures of the *Corrections and Conditional Release Act* and *Regulations*, could not get a word in edgewise. Yet in the rough ride justice took that day, the reins were held by a correctional supervisor whose career had begun at around the same time the *Charter of Rights and Freedoms* became entrenched in the Canadian Constitution. The important lesson to be taken from these proceedings was that the balance between correctional efficiency and justice remained a precarious one. There are well-trained practitioners and advocates of correctional efficiency, but in the absence of equally well-trained practitioners and advocates of the due process of law, a legal framework cannot ensure that justice will be given a fair hearing in the prison.

A review that evening of the legislation and the *CCR Regulations* confirmed my opinion that the sentence of weekend lock-up in segregation was an illegal one, beyond the power of a minor court. I also came to the conclusion that a suspended sentence imposed by an Independent Chairperson could not legally be activated by a subsequent conviction in minor court. The next day I conveyed these concerns to Norm Gerl, Co-ordinator of Correctional Operations. Mr. Gerl consulted with Regional Headquarters and also with CSC's legal counsel in Ottawa, Charles Haskell. Mr. Haskell confirmed my opinion that minor court had no power to impose punitive lock-up to be served in segregation and that only a conviction for another serious offence before the Independent Chairperson could activate a suspended sentence imposed by the Independent Chairperson. As a result, the prisoners who had been sentenced to weekend lock-up did not have to serve it in the hole, and the three prisoners who had begun to serve their suspended sentences were released from the hole the following Monday.

## November 1993: The Borasso Case—Threatening to Take Hostages

A primary reason for my original recommendation that serious disciplinary offences be adjudicated by Independent Chairpersons rather than by the warden's court was that in cases where the charge involved threats or disrespectful behaviour towards staff members, or where there was a conflict between prisoner and staff evidence, wardens showed a clear bias towards staff evidence. The marathon minor court hearing conducted at Matsqui in September 1993 demonstrated in spades that this quite natural bias remained a feature of institutional decision-making. In November 1993, a hearing conducted by Mr. Routley demonstrated, by contrast, how having an Independent Chairperson does make a difference to the assessment of both evidence and the gravity of a charge.

Mr. Borasso was charged with fighting, assaulting, or threatening to assault. Officer Wales gave evidence that, at around 6:30 p.m. one evening, Mr. Borasso had approached the first-floor control bubble to obtain permission to take a book to a friend in hospital. Officer Wales called the Health Care Unit about this and then informed Mr. Borasso he could go to see his friend at 9:00 p.m. According to the officer, Mr. Borasso got very angry and said, "What is their fucking problem? If I could get down there I would take them hostage. It is just a fucking book." Mr. Routley asked Officer Wales if he had taken Mr. Borasso seriously or felt the prisoner was just mouthing off. The officer said, "I thought possibly some of it was show. There were other inmates around. The thing I took seriously was the words 'hostage taking.' Any time it is mentioned it has to be taken seriously." Officer Wales testified that after Mr. Borasso left, he phoned the Health Care Unit to advise them of what had happened and then phoned Correctional Supervisor Wren, who asked that Mr. Borasso be escorted up to the "inmate waiting room" so that she could talk with him. (The inmate waiting room is an area adjacent to Central Control that contains a number of holding cells. This area provides greater security for conducting interviews because of the presence of other officers and the absence of other prisoners. It is also a geographical halfway point between the living unit and the segregation unit.)

Following this testimony, Mr. Borasso asked Officer Wales whether it was possible that the words he had used were actually, "If I was forced to live like them, I would take hostages." The officer said that was not how he had heard it. Mr. Borasso then gave his recollection of what had happened. It had started when he tried to take tobacco down to his friend in the hospital and was stopped. But another prisoner who went down to Health Care Unit to give a prisoner tobacco had no problems. Mr. Borasso's sick friend needed an atlas for his school work, and that was the book Mr. Borasso was trying to get to him. He had gone first to the third-floor security bubble to get permission and was told to check with the first-floor bubble, so he did that. He admitted he had told

Officer Wales that he would take hostages but said his comment was made in the context of a hypothetical situation: "If I was forced to live in the hospital." It was not intended as a threat to take hostages, and in his eyes the whole incident had been blown out of proportion. He had already spent three days in segregation as a result.

Mr. Routley said he wanted to hear from Correctional Supervisor Wren. After a short adjournment she appeared and gave evidence. She stated that upon receiving a report about a confrontation with Mr. Borasso, she had ordered him to be brought to the waiting room. He told her that he had wanted to take the book to his friend in the hospital and that he got very upset at the delay. Officer Wren asked the prisoner about his reported comment that if he were allowed down to the hospital he would take hostages. Mr. Borasso responded that he had said rather that if he was in the hospital as a patient he would take hostages. The officer explained to him that, in prison, any mention of taking hostages was considered very serious, as it was at airports, and that she was going to put him in segregation overnight so he could think about how he dealt with his problems.

Upon completion of Ms. Wren's evidence, Mr. Routley, without hearing any further submissions from Mr. Borasso, found him not guilty. His decision was made on the grounds that, to sustain the charge of assault or threatening to assault, there needed to be a focus for the assault or threat. While Mr. Borasso's words, "If I was forced to live like them, I would take hostages," could give rise to different interpretations, Mr. Routley was not satisfied beyond a reasonable doubt that a threat was intended.

## November 1993: Mr. Walters' Court

In the middle of November 1993, Keith Routley took a four-month leave of absence from his duties as Independent Chairperson. During that period, Matsqui disciplinary court was presided over by Mr. Rory Walters. Mr. Walters was a criminal defence lawyer who had previously presided over several disciplinary hearings conducted in French.

During November and December of 1993, Mr. Walters developed his own rhythm as Independent Chairperson. His pattern of decision-making demonstrated to me that he brought his own judgement to bear on each case. However, the comments I increasingly began to hear from the institutional advisor and other staff suggested they were not similarly impressed with Mr. Walters' demonstration of independence. In fact, following a series of decisions in which prisoners were acquitted of charges for which staff believed they should have been convicted, Mr. Walters came to be seen by many staff as "pro-prisoner" and out of touch with the realities of a federal penitentiary. By reviewing some of these cases, I hope to illuminate what lies behind these differences in perception.

## November 1993: The Gordon Case—Whose Brew?

Mr. Gordon found himself in Mr. Walters' court on a charge of possessing contraband and pleaded not guilty. Officer Randle testified that while doing routine security rounds, he had detected the odour of brew on the range. The smell seemed to be coming from Mr. Hartman's cell. The cell was locked, so he had the officer in the bubble "crack" the cell. When the cell door opened, the odour of brew was very strong. As the officer walked into the cell, he saw Mr. Gordon in an area of the cell not visible through the door window. He asked both Mr. Hartman and Mr. Gordon to leave the cell. He then saw on the floor, next to where Mr. Gordon had been, numerous bags of a brew-like substance. The two prisoners were taken up to segregation. Officer Randle took the brew-like substance to the office, where two samples tested positive for alcohol. He then wrote up an offence report charging both Mr. Hartman and Mr. Gordon with possession of contraband. According to Officer Randle, Mr. Gordon was charged both because he had been in an area in the cell where brew was found and because, on the way up to segregation, Mr. Gordon had made the statement, "Well, you got me this time before I got it on myself." Mr. Walters asked Officer Randle whether there was any odour of brew on Mr. Gordon's breath at this time, and the officer replied, "No, I believe they were in the process of straining the brew." Mr. Walters asked Officer Randle whether he had seen the prisoners straining the brew. He replied that he had not, but that the brew was in two groups, one clear and the other with sediment in it.

Mr. Hartman was then called as a witness. He testified that the brew was his and that he was in the process of straining it when Mr. Gordon came into the cell for a coffee. Mr. Hartman had already been charged, found guilty, and sentenced to 30 days' segregation suspended for 90 for the offence. That should be the end of the matter, he said, because Mr. Gordon had nothing to do with it; he had simply been in the wrong place at the wrong time. Mr. Gordon then gave evidence that he had had the flu for a week and had just woken up before he went into Mr. Hartman's cell for coffee. Because of his flu, he could not smell the brew. Mr. Gordon candidly admitted that, had he not been feeling sick, he probably would have drunk the brew, but he came into the cell for coffee and was not there for more than a minute before the officer arrested him.

Mr. Walters acquitted Mr. Gordon, saying he was not satisfied beyond a reasonable doubt that Mr. Gordon was in legal possession of the brew found in Mr. Hartman's cell. The evidence of Officer Randle did not support any inference of legal possession, which required not only knowledge of the presence of the prohibited substance but also consent and control.

Officer Randle came back into the courtroom, very upset, after he heard about the acquittal. He explained to Mr. Walters how small the cell was and how Mr. Gordon had been right on top of the brew and must have known it was there. He asked Mr. Walters what an officer was supposed to do in this situation. Mr. Walters said if there was no evidence that the second prisoner had physical control of the brew (for example, was holding a cup containing brew) or evidence that he was associated with its manufacture or consumption sufficient to infer consent, then probably all the institution could do was charge the prisoner whose cell it was and confiscate the brew.

## December 1993: The Longtin Case—Whose Brew This Time?

The last disciplinary court of 1993 had a very uncharitable docket consisting of twenty-three cases. The day's hearings were unusual in that every prisoner who pleaded not guilty was found not guilty. The first hearing involved Mr. Longtin on a charge of possession of contraband. Evidence was given by Officer Shannon that while conducting a search of the range she noticed Mr. Longtin return to his cell and go over to where his locker was. She asked him to leave the cell and went to the locker area, where she found a leather pouch containing a yeast-like substance. At the bottom of the locker, under a pair of jeans, she found a bag of yeast in a commercial packet. She could not remember the brand name.

Mr. Longtin, in his defence, stated the yeast was not his and he had not put it there. The yeast belonged to Mr. Gordon, who had recently been transferred to Kent and so could not be called as a witness that day. Mr. Longtin said he had only discovered it was Mr. Gordon's yeast the previous week, when he and Mr. Gordon were in the hole together. Mr. Walters did not find Mr. Longtin's evidence credible and found him guilty. Mr. Longtin angrily challenged Mr. Walters as to how he could conclude that his story was not credible, particularly since his witness had been shipped out of the institution. Mr. Walters then reversed himself, adjourning the case to allow Mr. Longtin to call Mr. Gordon as a witness and striking his finding of guilt.

In explaining his position after the hearing to Mr. Gerl, the institutional advisor, Mr. Walters said that even though he had not found Mr. Longtin a credible witness, Mr. Longtin was entitled to present his defence, and since Mr. Gordon was an important witness, he should be given the opportunity to call him. If the matter ever came before Federal Court, Mr. Walters said, he had little doubt that a judge would conclude that denying Mr. Longtin the right to call Mr. Gordon also denied his right to present a full answer and defence to the charge.

## December 1993: The Miller Case—Can Prison Hospitals Make Mistakes?

Prisoner Mike Miller was charged with taking an intoxicant into his body, based upon a positive result from a urine sample. Mr. Miller, when asked to plead to the charge, said he had voluntarily given the urine sample; the test indicated the presence of Serax in his body, but he could not explain how it got there because he had not taken it. Mr. Walters replied he could not take a guilty plea, because it was a necessary part of the charge that the person must knowingly have taken an intoxicant into his body, and Mr. Miller seemed to be saying he had not done this. Mr. Miller confirmed that he had not knowingly taken Serax.

Officer Buxton, the co-ordinator of the urine analysis program, testified that after staff noticed fresh needle tracks on Mr. Miller's arm, Mr. Miller was asked to provide a urine sample. Mr. Miller complied with this request, and the sample tested positive for Oxypan, generically known as Serax. Health care records indicated that Serax was not a prescribed drug for Mr. Miller.

At the conclusion of Officer Buxton's testimony, Mr. Miller offered his explanation of events. Before the testing was done, he told an officer that the sample might come back positive for marijuana. It did not, but this showed he was not trying to hide anything. He also said that the reference to needle marks did not make much sense, since Serax was taken orally, not injected. Officer Buxton confirmed this. After getting the test results, Mr. Miller had spoken to several staff members and consulted pharmacological references in the library to see if any of the approved medications he was on could test positive for Serax. He had satisfied himself that none of them would so test, and he was at a loss to explain the results. He pointed out, however, that in the report from the Health Care Unit regarding Mr. Miller's medications, they had failed to include one medication which he had been taking for over a year. He produced a card with a number of these pills still in their gelatin cases; he had been given the drug in January 1993 to be taken as necessary, and the prescription did not expire until the following month. This medication would not explain the positive Serax reading, but it showed that the prison hospital could make mistakes. Maybe he had been given the wrong medication in another instance, resulting in the positive test.

Section 69 of the *CCR Regulations* provides that, in hearing a disciplinary charge of taking an intoxicant, a positive urinalysis certificate "establishes, in the absence of evidence to the contrary, that the inmate who provided the sample has committed the offence." Mr. Walters found Mr. Miller not guilty, on the basis that his evidence was "evidence to the contrary" and raised a reasonable doubt about Mr. Miller's knowledge of taking Serax.

## December 1993: The Nicholas Case—The Difference a Lawyer Makes

The last case of 1993 was also the first one in my five months of observation where a prisoner was represented by legal counsel. Mr. Nicholas had been transferred to Kent Institution on the basis of three disciplinary charges and other allegations that he was involved in drug trafficking within Matsqui. He had been brought back from Kent to deal with the charges. The first charge was possession of contraband. Officer Shannon testified that during a lock-down she and Officer Stuart had conducted a search of Mr. Nicholas' cell. In a desk drawer she found a brown pill-like item, together with a similar item which had been broken in two. Officer Stuart discovered a light bulb with a crystal-like substance on the end of it. Officer Stuart then took these items to have them tested.

The Independent Chairperson, Mr. Walters, asked Officer Shannon if she had seen a copy of the certificate of analysis; she had not, so it was then shown to her. Mr. Zipp, counsel for Mr. Nicholas, stated that he was somewhat confused, because the certificate of analysis indicated the items seized were pieces of cotton wool; there was no reference to any pill-like substance or a light bulb. Mr. Gerl explained that some cotton balls found in the cell had also been tested and were found to be impregnated with heroin. That was the basis for the charge of contraband. The pills had been tested but did not register positive for any of the prohibited drugs. Mr. Seran, the institutional preventive security officer, testified next that the material he had tested as positive for heroin was in the form of a white powder. Officer Stuart was not called to give evidence, because just before the start of the hearing Mr. Gerl had discovered the officer was on the first of his rest days.

Mr. Walters then said that without calling upon Mr. Nicholas to answer to the charge, he was satisfied that a finding of not guilty should be entered. Officer Shannon's evidence had no bearing on the drug on the cotton balls, which had tested positive for heroin; her evidence referred to pills and a light bulb. In the absence of any evidence by the institution linking the substance seized from Mr. Nicholas' cell with that analyzed by Mr. Seran, this was self-evidently the only conclusion Mr. Walters could have drawn. Had Officer Stuart given evidence, as the charging officer who had taken the alleged contraband from Mr. Nicholas' cell to Mr. Seran for analysis, the necessary relationship could perhaps have been established. However, the institution made no application for an adjournment to ensure that this evidence was given.

The second charge against Mr. Nicholas was refusing to provide a urine sample. Officer Buxton testified that the day after a lock-down, he was asked to have Mr. Nicholas provide a urine sample because the prisoner was suspected of being under the influence of drugs. Mr. Nicholas said he would provide a sample but could not at that moment, so Officer Buxton gave him the two hours allowed by the *CCR Regulations*. Mr. Nicholas was placed in a room and Officer Buxton checked back with him on several occasions. At the end of two hours, when Mr. Nicholas had not complied, he was charged.

Mr. Walters asked Officer Buxton the reason for requesting the sample. Officer Buxton replied that during the lock-down it was noticed that Mr. Nicholas had fresh needle marks on his arm. Mr. Walters asked the officer whether he had noticed this personally. Officer Buxton said that other staff members had observed it and written a report. The report was sent to Mr. Gerl, and on the basis of that Mr. Buxton was asked to make a demand of Mr. Nicholas. That was reasonable and probable grounds, and it was the standard procedure. Mr. Walters asked the officer whether he had seen the report himself, and he said he had not. The staff member who had made the observation was Officer Stuart, who was not available to give evidence. In the course of Mr. Walters' questioning, Officer Buxton stated that Mr. Nicholas had actually provided a sample of urine but that it only contained 25 ml and test procedures required a minimum of 40 ml.

Mr. Zipp then cross-examined Officer Buxton, establishing that at 3:00 p.m. Mr. Nicholas had provided a sample. Officer Buxton said the sample was inadequate because it was neither the necessary quantity nor in the necessary temperature range. Mr. Zipp asked him how he knew the temperature, and Officer Buxton replied that the bottles used for collecting samples have a built-in thermometer. Mr. Zipp also asked Officer Buxton whether he was aware that the federal Department of Health and Welfare had sophisticated devices which could detect drugs in urine samples of far less than 25 ml. Officer Buxton said that he was not aware of those but the test at Matsqui required 40 ml. Following the cross-examination, Mr. Walters remarked that the basis for the charge was not that Mr. Nicholas had refused to provide a sample but that he had failed to provide what the institution regarded as a valid sample for testing purposes. Mr. Zipp then submitted that, because there was evidence he provided a sample, Mr. Nicholas' conduct did not fit within the ambit of the section under which he was charged.

Mr. Walters stated he was satisfied the institutional case had not been made. First of all, the evidence showed that Mr. Nicholas did provide a sample, and the section required a deliberate failure to provide it; "For want of 15 ml of urine, I am not prepared to convict Mr. Nicholas of a serious charge," he said. Second, the institutional witnesses failed to give evidence of reasonable grounds for making the demand in the first place. The legislation authorizes a staff member to demand that a prisoner submit to urine analysis where the staff member believes, on reasonable grounds, that the prisoner has committed or is committing the disciplinary offence of taking an intoxicant into his body. In this case, there was no evidence from the staff member alleged to have seen needle tracks in Mr. Nicholas' arms, Officer Stuart, to provide the necessary evidentiary foundation for the demand.

The third charge against Mr. Nicholas was another one of contraband. Officer Duran testified that he had been asked to conduct a search of Mr. Nicholas' cell. Mr. Nicholas, who had been sleeping, was asked to leave the cell, and, upon searching, Officer Duran discovered a drug outfit in the form of a syringe under Mr. Nicholas' mattress. The officer produced the exhibit envelope, tagged by him, and testified as to the various components of the syringe: a plastic vial with a needle on the end, an orange plastic cup to protect the needle, and a nail inserted into a small piece of sponge. Officer Duran explained that the syringe was all in one piece when he found it and that he had taken it apart when placing it in the exhibit envelope. In his experience, it was typical of the kind of outfit used to inject drugs. He also testified that he had not had the outfit tested for the presence of drugs. In cross-examination, Mr. Zipp established that, at Matsqui, prisoners are free to visit each other during certain hours.

Mr. Nicholas, giving evidence on his own behalf, was asked by Mr. Zipp whether he knew that the device was in his cell. Mr. Nicholas answered that he did not, and that the first time he had seen it was in the courtroom. He was asked whether he had ever used this outfit, and he said he had not. He testified that Mr. Kellough, Mr. Hancock, and a few other prisoners had been in his cell the night before the outfit was discovered. During the period they were in his cell, Mr. Nicholas left on several occasions. When asked by Mr. Walters why the item would be under his mattress, he replied as follows:

> Well, I found out later that Mitch [Mr. Kellough] had left it there because security was coming up and he got paranoid because he kept getting searched. A few days prior to this he had been searched, and he thought he was going to be getting searched again, so his first reaction was to take it out and stash it in my house so that he wouldn't get busted with it, because he didn't think they'd be searching my house. He left it there. So, lock-up came and he never said anything to me about it, because maybe he'd used before and forgot about it.

Mr. Kellough was then called in to give evidence. At first, he had some difficulty focussing on the incident in question. However, he went on to testify that he had just finished fixing before he went over to Mr. Nicholas' cell. He took the outfit with him because he did not want it found during a search of his cell. He was in Mr. Nicholas' cell when he saw the guards coming up the back way. He quickly put the outfit under the mattress and then went out into the corridor so that the guards would see him; if they had any suspicion about him, they would search him there and not find the syringe. Mr. Walters asked him why, when he was not searched, he had not gone back to retrieve the syringe. Mr. Kellough said he got side-tracked because he was high. The next day he slept in until noon, and by that time Mr. Nicholas had been arrested. Mr. Walters asked Mr. Kellough to describe the syringe, and his subsequent account was very credible in both its detail and its spontaneity. Mr. Walters asked again why Mr. Kellough did not go back and retrieve the syringe, knowing that he was putting another prisoner in jeopardy. Mr. Kellough replied, "When you're high you're not thinking about things like that."

Mr. Zipp submitted that there was a reasonable doubt about Mr. Nicholas' possession of the syringe. He had given evidence that he did not know it was in his cell, and Mr. Kellough had come forward to state he had placed it there without Mr. Nicholas' knowledge. Since knowledge was an essential element of possession, Mr. Nicholas should be found not guilty.

Mr. Walters ruled that the case turned on credibility:

> In regards to Mr. Kellough's evidence, his evidence basically leaves me with reasonable doubt. I thought his evidence was very weak at first and still, at the end of the day, I don't know that I believe his evidence. But his evidence is such that I could not say that he was lying or that it's not true. Without having any opportunity to view the syringe in question here, he was able to describe it very carefully and exactly. He described the orange cap, the plunger, how it was made, and it could well have been his. It could have been in Mr. Nicholas' possession, too, but I don't know. It leaves me with doubt and I find you not guilty. Mr. Nicholas, you're getting in a position where people are going to say lightning may strike once, it may strike twice, but it's pretty rare that it strikes three times. You've had a good day.

At the conclusion of the hearing, Mr. Gerl raised some concerns. He could not understand why Mr. Walters had, in dismissing the second charge, dealt with the question of whether there were reasonable grounds for making the demand, since this was not raised by Mr. Zipp. Mr. Walters responded that, in his role as Independent Chairperson, he should deal with any defence made out on the evidence, and he was not limited to those raised by counsel. He felt this was the only way to proceed, since in most cases counsel was not present, and the role of Independent Chairperson should not be significantly different in the two situations.

From their comments, it was clear the staff officers felt Mr. Nicholas had been found not guilty because of the presence of Mr. Zipp. In my judgement, he would likely have been found not guilty by Mr. Walters even if unrepresented, given the nature of the institution's evidence. Mr. Zipp's presence did ensure that the Independent Chairperson was directed to the relevant issues, however, and he identified weaknesses in the institution's case in his cross-examination. Furthermore, Mr. Zipp ensured that the prisoners' evidence was presented in a focussed way and he incorporated that evidence into his final submissions.

## The Disciplinary Process at Year's End— Perception and Perspective

The next day, when I stopped in to wish Warden Brock a happy Christmas, he asked me my views of the previous day's disciplinary hearing. He explained that the staff were so agitated by the lack of results that he felt he had to take some corrective action. He had sent a memo to Regional Headquarters, with a tape of the previous day's proceedings, indicating the staff's displeasure with the way disciplinary court was being handled by Mr. Walters. The staff sensed that the prisoners were laughing at them for having lost so many cases, he said. I offered my opinion that Mr. Walters' decisions were justified on the evidence and that, in several cases, the institutional case was nonexistent.

My conversation with Warden Brock underlined how great a role perception plays whenever the correctional enterprise and its contending objectives are evaluated. A day of decision-making which, from my perspective, had been a model of due process of law was seen by staff and management at Matsqui as undermining institutional order.

## January 1994: Due Process Visits the Principal's Office

The first disciplinary hearing of 1994 took place on January 5. The docket was a long one, and the proceedings were interrupted by a remarkable "time out" in the middle of the morning.

First on the docket was the case of Mr. Longtin, which had been adjourned so that Mr. Gordon could be brought from Kent Institution to give evidence for the defence. Mr. Gordon testified that the contraband yeast discovered in Mr. Longtin's cell belonged to him and had been placed there without Mr. Longtin's knowledge. When asked by Mr. Walters why he had access to Mr. Longtin's cell, he replied that the two of them worked out together and he spent a lot of time in Mr. Longtin's cell. He had been transferred to Kent for possession of contraband brew, he said. Questioned about why he had not come forward earlier, he replied that he learned of Mr. Longtin's charge only a few days before he was transferred to Kent, when he met up with Mr. Longtin in the hole.

Mr. Gordon was dismissed from the hearing room, and Mr. Walters reviewed his notes from two weeks earlier, in particular the evidence of Officer Shannon. Having done that, he asked to have Mr. Gordon brought back into the courtroom and proceeded with some further questions. In response, Mr. Gordon said that he had put the yeast in a pair of pants at the bottom of Mr. Longtin's locker, that the yeast was in its original packet and that it was wrapped in plastic. He couldn't remember the brand name on the packet, although he had swiped it from the kitchen. He also said the packet was about one-third full. Finally, he was asked whether he had had any communication with Mr. Longtin since his transfer to Kent. He said he had not; he gone straight from the hole in Matsqui to the hole in Kent and remained there ever since.

Mr. Walters found Mr. Longtin not guilty, on the basis that Mr. Gordon's evidence raised a reasonable doubt in his mind as to whether Mr. Longtin was in possession of contraband. He said that his questions had been designed to test

Mr. Gordon's story against the evidence of Officer Shannon and, in his opinion, Mr. Gordon's evidence could reasonably be true. Mr. Gerl, the institutional advisor, was clearly upset by this decision.

The next case involved Mr. Hill, who was charged with possession of contraband and pleaded not guilty. Officer Tate testified that while doing security rounds he had seen another prisoner, Mr. Campbell, in Mr. Hill's cell, and they were smoking what he believed to be marijuana, judging by its smell. He entered the cell and told them to "huck the butt" out the window, giving them the benefit of the doubt. He then observed a piece of what he believed to be hashish on the table near where Mr. Hill was standing. He seized it and placed it in an envelope which was sent for analysis. He produced the envelope during the hearing. Also attached to the charge sheet was a certificate indicating that the material analyzed contained THC (the active ingredient in hashish).

In cross-examination, Mr. Hill asked Officer Tate whether he was aware that prisoners grew their own tobacco in Matsqui and that when smoked the home-grown product gave off a smell similar to that of marijuana. Officer Tate said that was why he had at first given the men the benefit of the doubt. Mr. Hill then said he wanted to call Mr. Campbell as a witness, to testify that the hashish was his. Officer Tate conceded that Mr. Campbell had admitted the drug was his the day after the incident. When Mr. Walters asked why the other prisoner had not been charged, Officer Tate responded that Mr. Hill was responsible for what was in his cell, and the drug had been lying in the open very close to him. Mr. Walters then asked Mr. Hill why Mr. Campbell had not owned up to the drug at the time it was seized. Mr. Hill replied that after the officer left, Mr. Campbell told him he would go to staff the next day and admit that the drug was his. That was precisely what he did.

Mr. Walters found Mr. Hill not guilty, on the basis that he had a reasonable doubt as to whether Mr. Hill was legally in possession of the drug. At this point, Mr. Gerl asked if the court could be stood down and we moved to Mr. Gerl's office. He said he had a real problem with the two decisions that morning. He could not understand why Mr. Hill was acquitted; he knew the law required that there be knowledge, control, and consent, but as far as he was concerned those had been proved. The hashish had been found in Mr. Hill's cell, so he had control, and it was out in the open, so he had consent and knowledge. Mr. Gerl was particularly concerned about Mr. Hill's statement that he was not responsible for everything in his cell or for what other people brought into it. Under institutional policy, prisoners *were* responsible for what was in their cell. Otherwise, it would be impossible to ever bring a charge of contraband against a prisoner. Mr. Gerl also challenged Mr. Walters' acceptance of Mr. Gordon's evidence. The man had a record of brew-related offences as long as his arm, he said, and could hardly be seen as a credible witness. He had probably described the location of the yeast after seeing the offence reports and having Longtin tell him what to say. Mr. Gerl concluded, "There is a real credibility issue in the institution. In light of today's acquittals and the ones from the previous hearings, the staff might start giving up laying charges because they would see it as being a complete waste of time."

Mr. Walters addressed Mr. Gerl's points regarding the two acquittals. He felt that Mr. Gordon's evidence was sufficient to raise a reasonable doubt as to whose yeast it was and whether Mr. Longtin had any knowledge of it. Mr. Gordon's evidence was detailed, precise, and consistent with the evidence of Officer Shannon. From observing Mr. Gordon on the two or three occasions he had been in court, Mr. Walters doubted the prisoner could keep that kind of detail in his head unless he was speaking about matters of which he had personal knowledge. The fact that Mr. Gordon had a record of brew-related charges *added* to his credibility, because it illustrated his propensity for this kind of offence.

Mr. Gerl clearly was not persuaded. For him, evidence given by Mr. Gordon would always be suspect. Mr. Walters, for his part, tested the weight of Mr. Gordon's evidence against other evidence to determine its credibility. The differences between the two approaches can be characterized as assuming guilt (or disbelieving evidence) based on reputation, as opposed to finding guilt only on the basis of credible evidence proved beyond a reasonable doubt.

In addressing the Hill case, Mr. Walters said that while Mr. Gerl was right that the elements of legal possession were knowledge, consent, and control, he was not prepared to find these elements proven simply because an item was found in one prisoner's cell. As he understood the law, something more had to be shown. In particular, there had to be knowledge by Mr. Hill that he knew the substance was there and that it was a drug. He also had to be satisfied that Mr. Hill had control, and this could not necessarily be assumed if another prisoner had brought the substance into his cell. Mr. Gerl reiterated that it would be impossible to operate the institution if prisoners were not responsible for things found in their cells or brought into them when they were present. If Mr. Hill had wanted to avoid being charged, he should have told Mr. Campbell to take the drug out of his cell.

I suggested that there were two different realities operating here: the institutional reality, under which Mr. Gerl operated, and the legal reality, under which Mr. Walters was required to operate. The institutional reality was reflected in the customary rule that a prisoner is responsible for things in his cell. However, in terms of the legal reality of the elements of possession necessary to found a charge, the institutional reality did not automatically translate into proof of possession. While in many circumstances it would be permissible to infer that a prisoner had knowledge, consent, and control of things in his cell and therefore was legally in possession of them, this was not an inference that could always be drawn. In other words, there could be no irrebuttable presumption of possession simply because an item was found in a prisoner's cell.

At this point Warden Brock and Deputy Warden Wiebe joined the discussion.

The warden talked about the importance of maintaining an institutional strategy to clean up the drug scene. He portrayed the disciplinary process as a pivotal part of this, and suggested that if staff lost confidence in the disciplinary process and stopped laying charges for possession of contraband or taking an intoxicant, this would undermine his goal of stopping the flow of drugs into Matsqui and thus of avoiding the violence and loss of life to which drug use ultimately led. If there were too many acquittals under circumstances the staff could not understand or respect, then the disciplinary process would be undermining, not contributing to, public policy inside the institution. Warden Brock suggested that prison discipline, as part of administrative decision-making, was not the same as criminal law, although some criminal law principles were applicable. It was crucial that the disciplinary process be sensitive to the special situations faced in an institution. Mr. Walters made a pointed response to the warden's suggestion that the principles of administrative law be tailored to the needs of the prison by stating, "Intellectually, I can't tailor my understanding of reasonable doubt to the needs of my customers."

When I discussed this "time out" with Mr. Walters at the end of the day, he referred to it as "a visit to the principal's room," clearly conveying his perception that he was being taken to task for how he was running the disciplinary court. Mr. Walters' "visit" was not unprecedented in Matsqui's history. In 1989, two years after Mr. Routley had taken over the position of Independent Chairperson, he was invited to meet with Warden McGregor for a discussion about the conduct of disciplinary hearings. As a result of that "discussion," Mr. Routley received the following letter from the warden:

> I am disappointed, to say the least, that our conversation of three weeks ago with reference to your approach to the role of Independent Chairperson has had little impact. You will recall in my capacity at Regional Headquarters that I had serious concerns about your overly legalistic approach to what is an administrative hearing. In my view this has now gone too far and the simple fact is that you are now undermining the authority of my staff.
>
> The complaints coming to me range from the poor treatment of the court clerks, berating the staff in front of inmates, to your unrealistic requirements for evidence on contraband. Numerous examples have been brought to me by the Advisors and by staff who have been subject to this treatment in court. I find this unacceptable and feel that we must review your approach again. My concerns are serious enough that I have asked for and received a substitute Independent Chairperson for the next two weeks so that we have time to try and resolve these problems.

I must tell you, Keith, that if we cannot reach a compromise, I will have no alternative but to ask the Deputy Commissioner to seek approval for a replacement. I will arrange for us all to sit down with the relevant staff so that you can get detailed and accurate feedback again about our concerns. I look forward to hearing from you. (Letter from Doug McGregor to Keith Routley, Matsqui Institution, September 5, 1989)

Warden McGregor's letter evoked a strong response from Mr. Routley.

The letter takes me completely by surprise, the contents of which strike right to the root of the mandated legal independence of the Chairperson.

My notes of the "conversation of three weeks ago" indicated that it was a meeting in your office prior to the commencement of the regular Wednesday session, and that it lasted for fifty-five minutes. You indicated at the outset that it was for the purpose of making known to me your unhappiness with my decisions, notably the one involving inmate Bates. No mention was made by you at that time of any shortcoming in my personal behaviour in the discharge of my duties. I have no knowledge of any "poor treatment of the court clerks," or "berating the staff in front of inmates," at any time during the preceding two and one-half years. You will recall that at the meeting you refer to I specifically invited you to attend sessions of the Discipline Court to learn first-hand the facts. I am confident that had you taken up that invitation, a more considered response to staff complaints would be apparent to you.

In regard to your first paragraph, I have no idea what you mean when you talk about "serious concerns" or "overly legalistic" or "administrative hearings" or "authority of my staff." Perhaps when you get the facts straight on a particular case-in-point, we might discuss this to some benefit. In the absence of this, or meetings with advance agenda, I fear little constructive interchange can take place.

As a result of the foregoing, I must respectfully resist your asserted authority to unilaterally substitute my person with that of another Independent Chairperson of your preference. I say this with the greatest reluctance, but I sincerely believe that your chosen course of action will give rise to great future difficulty in both of our tasks. For you, it will place you under constant pressure to manipulate the operation of the Institution Discipline Court in the future. For me, it will permanently compromise my ability to function as an actual

and perceived independent adjudicator. Further, I believe it undermines the role of all Independent Chairpersons in Canada, and is
contrary to the thrust of the legislation, if not unlawful.

As a result of the foregoing I can confirm my intention to attend
to my duties as Independent Chairperson on this and further Wednesday mornings. (Letter from Keith Routley to Doug McGregor,
Matsqui Institution, September 11, 1989)

The discussion five years later between Warden Brock and Mr. Walters was
much more diplomatic, as befits Roger Brock's style of management, but it still
conveyed the same message of measured disapproval of the Independent Chairperson's conduct of disciplinary court.

## July 1998: Postscript

Almost five years after my observation of Mike Csoka's marathon session in
minor court at Matsqui, I conducted a lengthy interview with him at Kent
Institution. In the intervening time, his career had taken off; from his position
as a correctional supervisor at Matsqui he had been assigned to the Staff Training
College, where he taught new recruits the full spectrum of courses, including
case management, interpersonal skills, self-defence, and weapons training. After
a two-year stint there, he transferred to Kent Institution, where he was the acting co-ordinator of case management. After winning a competition for that permanent position, he became acting unit manager for segregation at Kent. He
wrote and passed the competition for unit managers in 1998.

Mike Csoka's career progression was a reflection of the high regard in which
he was held by both staff and senior management. Over the course of my
research I spent many hours with him, and developed a healthy respect for the
way he discharged his onerous responsibilities. On several occasions I invited Mr.
Csoka to U.B.C.'s Faculty of Law to address my seminar on Penal Law and
Policy.

As I came to know him better, and as he shared more and more of his experiences, I became increasingly uneasy about how Mike Csoka would react to the
critical account I had written of his handling of the Matsqui minor court docket
in 1993. I worried that when he read it he would feel betrayed. In research presented later in this book, I also voice criticisms of his conduct of segregation
review hearings. Although these criticisms apply to segregation reviews conducted by other unit managers as well, Mr. Csoka is the featured player because
he was the acting unit manager for segregation during some of the major events
that occurred. I decided to explain to Mr. Csoka what I had written about his
handling of the minor court proceedings at Matsqui and his handling of segre-

gation reviews at Kent in 1997 so I could get his reaction to my analysis. That exchange took place in July 1998.

I began by characterizing my description of the minor court marathon as a classic conflict between efficiency and due process and explained how, in my judgement, due process took a back seat that day. Mr. Csoka had no difficulty understanding why I might come to that conclusion, but he offered me his perspective on his conduct of the court hearings.

> I look at it a little differently. I started my career working with inmates, first as a correctional officer, again as a case management officer, and then a correctional supervisor. I worked at Matsqui for seven and a half years. I knew the inmates I was dealing with, they were my responsibility. I get to know inmates. I don't know how— it's a knack, an ability, or experience. I know the inmates that are going to lie to me and I know the inmates that are going to tell the truth. How I do that, I don't know, but I've been successful. I've never had an inmate charge me with harassment. I've never had an inmate come back at me. I've never had an inmate get mad at me after a court hearing because generally when they're caught and they know they're caught and you're fair, they walk away, even though they lied to you.
>
> With respect to the officers, same thing. I know the officers that just charge for the sake of charging, half the time they didn't really hear what they heard. And I know the officers that charge only when there is something significant.
>
> I agree that efficiency did prevail that afternoon, but there's a couple of reasons why it prevailed. One was I was told to get the job done and I did. Two, there was a large number of those inmates who were getting screwed out of transfers [to lower security] because these minor court hearings were hanging over their heads. I gave them a $5 fine or a warning, we'd move on; the inmate gets transferred. So a lot of times when we look at this, in your case when you're sitting there watching us, it almost looks like there's a bit of "let's just throw the law out." I guess maybe there is, but at the same time, it's also to benefit the inmates, not always to screw them.
>
> The other aspect of that whole afternoon is that you probably assumed that as a correctional supervisor I had been trained to run minor court. The reality is I had never been trained to run minor court. In fact, at that point I did not even know that there were specific rules I had to follow based in the law, and that they were similar to those in major court hearings. Nobody ever told us that. As

correctional supervisors we thought we go in, we hear the inmate, we look at the charge, so the officer's not on duty, I know the officer, I trust his offence report, and so we go ahead. Was that a miscarriage of justice? Maybe it was, but at the same time, I still view myself as fair and so do the inmates. It may have been efficiency on my part but at the same time some of those guys were able to get their transfers because their charges were no longer hanging over their head . . .

On this issue of training, it was not until the fall of 1997 that Ottawa established any staff training in Corrections and the Law, and even then that was very general and didn't give any guidance to correctional supervisors holding minor court hearings. (Interview with Mike Csoka, Kent Institution, July 1998)

In the course of our conversation, I asked Mike Csoka for his current assessment of the *CCRA,* first reminding him of the opinions he had expressed during my first weeks of work at Matsqui in 1993; he had been quite sceptical then about the new legislation and concerned it would handcuff staff in their dealings with prisoners.

I will be honest with you, it does handcuff me, but at the same time it has its place and it has its purpose. If someone could tell me or show me that all managers and staff in the Service could be trustworthy to the point that they would do the job the way they're supposed to do it, we never would have needed the *CCRA,* but you can't. Does it handcuff me? Yes. Do I need it? No. Because I won't screw an inmate, I won't take advantage of something. There are times when I want to do certain things that the *CCRA* gets in my way, but it doesn't get in my way in the sense of what I'd be doing was wrong or different, it just makes me go a big circle to get where I need to get and you've seen me, I'm task-orientated. I want to go from A to B. It drives me nuts to go from A to C to E to F and then finally get to B, even though I know I could just go there and the inmates would understand that and they wouldn't scream and yell and say I was doing something wrong.

In Sector 4 I will return to my 1998 interview with Mike Csoka to review his comments on the *CCRA* provisions in relation to administrative segregation.

## CHAPTER 3

# The Disciplinary Process at Kent

I began my observations of the disciplinary court at Kent Institution on January 25, 1994. Dean Fox, a lawyer specializing in civil litigation, had been the Independent Chairperson at Kent since 1987. In the 1970s, before he went to law school, Mr. Fox worked for a brief period at Mission Institution as a living unit officer. Because of his involvement in an extended civil trial in January 1994, he had taken a three-month leave of absence, and Independent Chairpersons from other institutions sat in for him during this period. For the first two months of my observations, Rory Walters, the acting Chairperson from Matsqui, also conducted the hearings at Kent. When Keith Routley resumed his position as Independent Chairperson at Matsqui, he and Mr. Walters rotated as Independent Chairperson at Kent until Dean Fox's return to the institution in April 1994.

The hearings at Kent were held in a boardroom off the corridor leading to the segregation unit. The Chairperson sat at the head of a large rectangular table, with the accused prisoner seated at the other end. The court clerk and the institutional advisor sat along one side of the table, with the institutional advisor closest to the prisoner. Witnesses sat on the other side of the table. Usually one officer stood by the door, acting as the sheriff. The designated institutional advisor to the disciplinary court at Kent, as at Matsqui, was the co-ordinator of correctional operations.

## January 1994: The Knight Case—A Brew of Excellent Quality

One of the major differences between Kent and Matsqui, reflecting Kent's maximum security status, is much greater control of prisoner movement. Prisoners spend more time locked on their ranges, and during such times, when they are not in their cells, they can be found in either the large pool room or the smaller TV room. The fact that these are "common" recreational areas gives rise to legal issues when prisoners are charged with possession of forbidden items. One such case involved Mr. Knight, who was charged with possession of contraband.

Officer Tyler testified that he had come on shift around 3:00 one afternoon and heard laughter coming from the TV room. The lights were off when he and Officer Chicoyne entered the room, where they detected the smell of brew. Mr. Knight and two other prisoners were present, and there were a variety of containers on the coffee table. These included a large jug half-full of orange juice, a small Maalox bottle half-full of clear liquid with the odour of brew, a cup half to three-quarters full of a substance which smelled of brew, a container holding a brew-like liquid and mash, and a black plastic bag full of mash and brew. The cup and the jug were within arm's length of all three prisoners. After seizing the items Officer Tyler had phoned the correctional supervisor, who asked whether the prisoners seemed to be under the influence. Upon his confirmation that they were not, the prisoners were allowed to go back to their cells. They were observed during the rest of the shift, and Mr. Knight and a second prisoner were not seen to be in any abnormal state; however, the third prisoner was. Mr. Routley asked whether the contraband alleged to be brew had been tested for alcohol content. Officer Tyler said it had not. Mr. Routley asked Officer Tyler how, in the absence of a test, he could tell it was alcohol. He replied, "My experience with brew."

Officer Chicoyne then gave his evidence. As he was identifying the various items that had been seized, he referred to a bag of "brew mash." Mr. Routley asked him whether he had ever made a brew, and Officer Chicoyne said he had. At the conclusion of Officer Chicoyne's evidence, Mr. Routley asked him, "Is there anything that could satisfy me that what we are dealing with here is an intoxicant? At other institutions the practice is to test the sample to confirm that it is alcohol. In the absence of that test, how am I to conclude that it is an intoxicant?" Officer Chicoyne responded, "You could take a drink of it. I did. I took a sip of it in the cup. The reason I did that is that there was a jug of orange juice on the table and I wanted to see what we were dealing with. I suspected that the orange juice was being used to dilute the brew." Mr. Routley asked Officer Chicoyne what he was able to determine from sampling the liquid, and the officer responded with the appreciation of a connoisseur, "It was a brew of excellent quality. It took my breath away." Mr. Knight tried to hide a smile at this unexpected compliment for prisoners' brew-making skills.

Mr. Knight then asked Officer Chicoyne, "Did I appear to be under the influence of anything? I was not taken to the hospital, was I?" Officer Chicoyne confirmed that Mr. Knight was not taken to the hospital. The staff's purpose was to control and diffuse the situation, he said, and they had been successful in doing that. Mr. Knight went on to argue that the TV room was open to all prisoners on the range and that he had been in the room for only a couple of minutes when the officers arrived. Officer Chicoyne confirmed that the room was open to other prisoners.

Mr. Routley then proceeded to give his judgement, stating, "I don't need to hear from you, Mr. Knight. I accept that this material is contraband but I don't see anything linking you to it, and therefore I'm finding you not guilty."

After Mr. Knight had left the room, the institutional advisor, Diane Knopf, asked Mr. Routley, "What do we need to establish possession in a common room?" Some evidence linking the prisoner to the material, Mr. Routley replied; for example, that the cup in which the brew was found belonged to him or that he was impaired. In this instance, there was no evidence of Mr. Knight being impaired, and physical presence alone was not enough to establish the necessary elements of possession. Ms. Knopf was obviously upset at the turn of events, and she asked Mr. Routley, "Have you ever walked into a room where a brew party is going on?" Mr. Routley acknowledged that he had not, and Ms. Knopf advised him that it was "a tense, emotional, and very difficult situation for staff." Mr. Routley responded, "That may be so, but a tense, emotional atmosphere can't justify a charge."

Mr. Routley asked Ms. Knopf whether it was the practice at Kent to do an analysis of contraband believed to be alcohol. She said that it was not, and that Mr. Fox did not require such proof. Mr. Routley advised her that the issue had been raised at the meeting of Independent Chairpersons in November 1993 and it was agreed then that an analysis would be required as necessary proof. He suggested that the court clerk get a copy of the certificate of analysis used at Matsqui. (The necessity for evidence indicating the level of alcohol content—in order to prove that a substance had the potential to impair or alter judgement and behaviour—and the insufficiency of an officer's testimony as to the texture and odour given off by the substance were later affirmed by the Federal Court, in the judgement of *Mineau* v. *Besnier,* [1997] F.C.J. No. 459).

There was a further discussion initiated by Ms. Knopf as to the difficulty of making recommendations on an appropriate sentence, because of the different sentencing practices of each Independent Chairperson. She said this was a real problem when it came to suggesting an appropriate fine. One Chairperson would think that $15 was a reasonable fine, and in exactly the same circumstances another would impose $30. Mr. Routley said one of his functions as Senior Independent Chairperson was to try to ensure consistency. Ms. Knopf responded that when it came to sentencing, there did not seem to be much evidence of that.

Ironically, as I would discover, one of the major contributors to sentence disparity at Kent was that, in contrast to at Matsqui, there were frequent changes in the institutional advisor. I observed significant differences in the sentencing recommendations individual advisors made to the Independent Chairperson.

## Similar Acts, Different Sentences—Kent and Matsqui Compared

I would also come to observe disparities between the sentences imposed at Matsqui and Kent for similar offences. The most glaring of these was in the standard sentence for a first offence of possession of brew. At Matsqui, Mr. Routley's standard sentence was 30 days' segregation suspended for 90 days; at Kent it was 30 days' hole time, with no suspension. Yet even though the sentence was more severe at Kent, the institutional practice there upon discovering a brew was more lenient, insofar as prisoners were not taken to the hole unless they were threatening, out of control, or unstable in some way. A lighter sentence was imposed at Matsqui, yet the response upon detection and apprehension of the prisoner was more severe, with prisoners automatically being placed in segregation until the next day and, in a good number of cases, until they made their first appearance in disciplinary court. This was the very reverse of the practice one would expect. To the extent that possession of brew was perceived to be a less serious concern to institutional security at Matsqui than at Kent, because Matsqui is medium security, it would seem logical that placing prisoners in segregation upon the discovery of a brew would be done on a very selective basis. In fact, at Matsqui, the placement of prisoners in segregation was a punitive "administrative" response inconsistent with the ultimate "disciplinary" response, which in the absence of a previous record was a non-segregation sentence.

## February to April 1994: The Unger, Ratcliff, and McKay Cases—Fighting, Assaults, or Threats to Assault

Of all the offences in the prison disciplinary code, the offence of "fights with, assaults or threatens to assault another person" covers the broadest spectrum of behaviour, ranging from two prisoners squaring off in a "fair fight" involving no injuries to assault causing bodily harm. It is also the offence which, at the most serious end of the spectrum, carries with it the most dire consequences for a prisoner, including transfer to the Special Handling Unit. The offence can be committed in three ways, each of which involves different considerations. The first mode, fighting, would seem to be the least problematic. During my research, all three Independent Chairpersons, whether at Matsqui or at Kent, were consistent in ruling that a prisoner who had not initiated a fight but was defending himself from an attack had a good defence to a charge of fighting. Notwithstanding this correct legal interpretation (affirmed in the Federal Court judgement of *Clark* v. *Fox,* [1998] F.C.J. No. 459), prisoners at Kent were regularly charged with the offence of fighting even when it was clear that one of them was acting in self-defence.

In March 1994, Mr. Unger faced a charge of fighting arising from an incident with Mr. Mohamoud. He pleaded not guilty, testifying that Mr. Mohamoud had thrown his coffee at him and then started swinging. When he grabbed Mr. Mohamoud's hands, the two of them slipped on the coffee and fell to the floor. Mr. Mohamoud grabbed hold of Mr. Unger's hair, and it was at this point that Officer Howard came on the scene. Mr. Unger told Mr. Walters he had no idea what started the fight. He had been talking to Mr. Mohamoud and then, all of a sudden, Mr. Mohamoud threw his coffee. Mr. Unger said, "I was just trying to avoid being hit and was defending myself. I never hit Mr. Mohamoud."

Officer Howard essentially corroborated Mr. Unger's account. Her observations were that Mr. Mohamoud was the aggressor. She said she never saw Mr. Unger striking Mr. Mohamoud, only defending himself. Mr. Walters found Mr. Unger not guilty.

The fact that this case ever got to disciplinary court was of some concern. Officer Howard, in her offence report, had written, "Inmate Unger was involved in a fight. However I did not observe him strike out but rather defend himself." In light of the unequivocal evidence that Mr. Unger's actions were purely in self-defence, why was a charge written up on Mr. Unger, and why was it designated a serious charge by the unit manager? After Mr. Unger had left the courtroom I spoke to him briefly, and he told me that following this incident he was taken to segregation and kept there for five and a half days until he was released back to his unit. When I spoke to the unit manager for segregation about this later in the day, she said it was standard policy that both prisoners involved in a fight were taken to segregation, because it was usually difficult at the time to determine who was responsible. However, Officer Howard had been quite clear in her report that Mr. Unger was defending himself, and it should not have taken five and a half days to confirm this fact.

The issue of what constitutes a threat to assault—a second mode of committing this offence—came up in a case in February 1994 involving Mr. Ratcliff. Officer Howson testified that when he was doing the count he had told Mr. Ratcliff to lock up and Mr. Ratcliff responded by saying, "I wish I had a shotgun, I'd blow your fucking head away." Later that day the officer went to Mr. Ratcliff's cell and told him he was going to be charged for what he had said, to which Mr. Ratcliff replied, "If I had a shotgun I would shove it up your nose." Mr. Ratcliff had no questions of Officer Howson but testified he had not said what the officer claimed he had. He explained that, after being told to lock up, he was going back to his cell when saw the guard in the control bubble and thought to himself, "It's only by the barrel of a gun that I'm being locked up." While he was thinking this, he said to Officer Howson, "If I had a shotgun you sure as hell wouldn't be locking me up." Mr. Walters then asked Officer Howson if he could have misunderstood what Mr. Ratcliff said. Officer Howson replied, "That's not the way I heard it."

Speaking in his own defence, Mr. Ratcliff made a statement that the whole incident had happened because he was frustrated about having been on cell lock-up for six weeks after being suspended from work. He argued that if this was a "street charge," it would be thrown out, because it was not a threat. As he understood the law, a threat had to be perceived as real, and there was no way this one could be, because it was impossible for him to get a shotgun in prison. "It was an off-the-wall comment that you make when you feel that you've been done wrong," he said. Officer Howson replied that he had been in the institution for five years and this was the first time he had laid a charge against a prisoner.

Mr. Walters said he was satisfied that the statements had been as the officer testified and that they did make out the charge. In his view, the comments were so inflammatory that, even if Mr. Ratcliff could not get hold of a shotgun, it was to be inferred that if he would use something else as a weapon if it came his way, and in that sense he had definitely made a threat. Ms. Knopf said that normally she would ask for a period of segregation for a threat to assault, but because of overcrowding in segregation she would recommend a fine of substantial proportions. Mr. Walters imposed a fine of $25.

The *Corrections and Conditional Release Act* provides no interpretive guidance on the definition of a threat, but s. 265(b) of the *Criminal Code* of Canada (R.S.C. 1970, c. C-34) provides that:

> A person commits an assault when:
> he attempts or threatens, by an act or a gesture, to apply force to another person, if he has, or causes that other person to believe on reasonable grounds that he has, present ability to effect his purpose.

This definition of assault therefore includes a threat to assault, and as such the threat must meet the criteria set out in the balance of the section. Under this definition, Mr. Ratcliff's submission that his behaviour would not constitute a criminal offence of assault has some merit, given the lack of any reasonable grounds to believe that he had the present ability to effect his purpose, because he did not have a shotgun. However, using this same definition, Mr. Walters could reasonably draw the inference from the nature of his comments that Mr. Ratcliff was prepared to make good on his threat, using whatever alternative might be at hand. Given that there was no physical barrier separating Mr. Ratcliff from the officer, he did have the present ability to carry out the threat.

The third way in which the offence of fighting, assaulting, or threatening to assault can be committed is the way most people understand the meaning of assault—the application of force by one person to another without that person's consent. But here also there are important issues of legal interpretation, as reflected in a case involving Mr. McKay that came before Mr. Routley on April 5, 1994.

Ron McKay was the first prisoner whose case I had observed during my 1983 research at Kent. At that time, aged nineteen, he was serving a two-year sentence for breaking and entering. I predicted that unless the system responded differently to this angry young Aboriginal prisoner, the system would be seeing more of him in the future. Not long after that he was sent to the Special Handling Unit in Millhaven for his involvement in an assault on a guard at Matsqui. Mr. McKay had put on a good deal of weight since I'd last seen him, and, I suspect, a few more tattoos.

Officer Noon-Ward testified that he had been doing a search of a unit pursuant to a lock-down, and Mr. McKay was asked to strip prior to leaving his cell. He became verbally abusive and called the officer an "f-ing goof." He then pulled his sweatpants and underwear down to his knees and then pulled them up again. Upon being told that he had to take everything off, he again swore at the officer. He removed his sweatpants and tossed them into the officer's arms, then pulled down his underpants, took them off and threw them in the officer's face. The officer stated that Mr. McKay had come literally face to face with him, and his right fist was cocked back. The officer pressed his personal alarm and pushed Mr. McKay back with the flat of his hands. Mr. McKay was then restrained.

Mr. Routley asked the officer whether Mr. McKay had said anything when he had his fist cocked back. The officer responded that although he had not, he thought Mr. McKay was going to assault him. Mr. McKay then suggested to the officer that the first words the officer had said when he opened the cell were "We're tired of putting up with your bullshit." Officer Noon-Ward denied this and stated that Mr. McKay had simply been asked to take his clothes off. Mr. Routley asked if there was any other witnessing officer, and Officer Morrison was called. He testified that he was in the control bubble at the time of the incident. He cracked open Mr. McKay's cell prior to the search and switched his intercom on so he could monitor the situation. He heard Mr. McKay "become verbal" to Mr. Noon-Ward and make the usual remarks prisoners make when they are asked to do something they dislike. He then saw something fly out of the cell, although he could not tell what it was. He saw Officer Noon-Ward go into the cell and after that he heard the sounds of a scuffle, but he was not able to observe anything from where he was. Mr. McKay, in his defence, said that Officer Noon-Ward was exaggerating what had happened and that he had had both his hands by the side of his body and had not cocked his fist. He acknowledged throwing his underwear but said he had no intention of striking the officer; he was angry at being made to strip for no good reason. Mr. McKay concluded by saying that given the way the officers subsequently jumped on him, he should charge *them* with assault.

Mr. Routley expressed concern that the evidence of the two officers did not quite reconcile. And while he would have no difficulty convicting Mr. McKay of a charge of being disrespectful or abusive, he said, he had a reasonable doubt on the charge which had been laid, and he was therefore finding Mr. McKay not guilty of the charge of assault.

Later in the morning Officer Noon-Ward came back into the courtroom and asked Mr. Routley why Mr. McKay had been acquitted. Mr. Routley said Mr. McKay had been charged under the wrong section. Officer Noon-Ward questioned how Mr. McKay could be not guilty of assault when he had thrown his underwear in an officer's face. Mr. Routley responded that he was not satisfied Mr. McKay had the necessary intent to commit an assault. Officer Noon-Ward then turned to the institutional advisor and said, "I'm never going to charge another inmate at Kent Institution." (To the chagrin of many prisoners, Officer Noon-Ward later reconsidered his position.)

Mr. Routley's comment about the "necessary intent to commit an assault" was a reference to a basic legal principle in the interpretation of criminal or penal offences. As a general rule, in order to be guilty of an offence, an accused person must not only commit the prohibited act—which lawyers call the *actus reus,* the guilty act—but must also have the necessary intent, reflected in the legal language of *mens rea,* which translated from the Latin means a guilty mind. Such a guilty mind requires that the accused meant to cause the prohibited harm, or, while not meaning to cause it, was sufficiently aware of the risk that such harm would be caused but proceeded to act disregarding that risk. Mr. Routley had judged that while Mr. McKay's flinging of his underwear did involve the application of force to the officer, he had not meant to strike the officer but was throwing his clothes as an expression of frustration at being made to submit to a strip search and, in the circumstances, he was not reckless.

Mr. McKay had already been kept in segregation for three weeks pending his court hearing. He was seen by the Segregation Review Board the next day and told he would be released to the living unit when there was bed space. He was released one week later, having served twenty-nine days in segregation—only one day less than the maximum sentence he could have received had he been found guilty of the charge.

## March 1994: The Fuson Case—A Set-up?

Mr. McKay's was not the only case at Kent in which a prisoner had been kept in segregation for what seemed an unreasonably lengthy period prior to the disposition of his charge. Mr. Fuson was charged with contraband in the form of "a metal rod approximately six or seven inches long sharpened to a point at one end." The offence report stated that the item had been found in a small cardboard box beside his toilet on the floor of his cell.

Mr. Fuson, after indicating he was going to plead not guilty, told Mr. Walters he hoped to raise a reasonable doubt regarding his possession, on the basis that his cell was open and any other prisoner could have put the homemade knife in his cell. Officer Mead gave evidence that he and two of his colleagues did random cell searches on Mr. Fuson's range. One of his partners had found a five-inch piece of solid-core wire about 3/16" in diameter, sharpened to a point, in Mr. Fuson's cell. The rod was retrieved about two feet inside the cell door. Officer Mead then produced the contraband and showed it to Mr. Walters. Mr. Walters asked whether Mr. Fuson had been present during the search, and Officer Mead said he was in the area but not in the cell. Mr. Walters also inquired whether Mr. Fuson had been asked about the rod, and Officer Mead stated he had not.

Mr. Fuson gave evidence that his job, as the unit maintenance man, required that his cell be open most of the time; only when he went out of the unit did he close it. He denied any knowledge of the rod and said the only way it could have been in his cell, which he did not dispute, was that someone else had put it there. Mr. Walters asked why someone would put the rod in his cell. Mr. Fuson responded that he tried to be helpful to new prisoners who came onto the range and lent them tobacco and other items until they got their first canteen. He felt that some prisoner who owed him, and could not pay him back, figured out that if a weapon was found in his cell he would be taken to segregation and would lose his cell in the unit; therefore, the other prisoner would not have to pay back his debt. He also stated he was not the kind of person who carried a weapon. In the six and a half years he had been in prison, he had never been charged with any violence, nor had he ever been charged with having a weapon. He prided himself on always being able to settle disputes without violence or threats of violence. Mr. Walters asked Mr. Fuson what had happened to him since he was charged. He replied that he had been in the hole since February 24—some twenty-one days.

Mr. Walters found Mr. Fuson not guilty, stating, "The explanation that you have given me is not one that I can say I disbelieve. Your explanation is one that could reasonably be true. The fact that you have been segregated for the last twenty-one days supports your explanation that one of the reasons why someone may have placed this weapon in your cell was to get you out of the unit."

After Mr. Fuson left the room, the advisor, Mr. Demers, stated that the search had been based on information that Mr. Fuson was going to stab his case management officer, Randy Voth, because he was going to be recommended for detention until warrant expiry. However, Mr. Demers said he had discussed this issue with Mr. Voth, who felt Mr. Fuson had been set up by some other prisoner. If Mr. Voth, as the staff member most familiar with Mr. Fuson, believed that Mr. Fuson did not have knowledge of the knife in his cell, this raised two questions in my mind: why was the charge laid and proceeded with, and why was Mr. Fuson kept in segregation for three weeks before the hearing?

The Fuson and McKay cases reflected the institutional reality at Kent in 1994–95, and indeed up until the Segregation Task Force Review in August 1996, that prisoners often spent as long, or longer, in segregation pending their disciplinary hearings than they would serve if found guilty. Part of the reason for this was that even where prisoners were cleared for release by the Segregation Review Board, they remained in segregation until bed space was available in the population. The other part of the reason had nothing to do with the dynamics of overcrowding. It reflected the continuation of prison customary law—the CCRA notwithstanding—that prisoners charged with assault or possession of weapons were kept in administrative segregation pending their disciplinary hearings, the equivalent of being detained without bail. Therefore prisoners suffered "administrative" consequences of conviction that overshadowed their acquittal in the "disciplinary" process.

## May 1994: The Chartrand Case—A Correctional Video and The Eye of the Beholder

On May 24, 1994, Mr. Chartrand appeared before Mr. Fox facing two charges which originated in the Regional Psychiatric Centre (RPC). I arrived for court early that day. Standing outside the courtroom were two officers from the RPC, who, together with half a dozen officers from Kent, were reviewing a video of the incident on a television monitor. The RPC officer showing the video immediately shut it off when he saw me, thinking I was Mr. Chartrand's lawyer. Correctional Supervisor Knopf explained to him that I was doing research, and the tape was switched back on.

The video showed Mr. Chartrand in his own cell being told by three officers to go to the RPC segregation area. He was frisked by one officer and handcuffs were applied behind his back. Mr. Chartrand was then escorted out of his cell and out of his unit. While being escorted, he was swearing at the officers, and about halfway along the corridor he suddenly turned around, as a result of which he fell to the ground. It was not clear whether he was pushed or slipped. He was then made to walk backwards, with the officer pulling him along by the cuffs. At this point Mr. Chartrand's shirt was off his shoulders. The video showed Mr. Chartrand being placed in the segregation cell. He was placed face down on the bed, and while one officer removed his handcuffs, the other knelt on his lower torso. There was nothing in the video to indicate why Mr. Chartrand should be held down like this; there was no indication of his struggling with the officer removing the cuffs. After the cuffs were removed, Mr. Chartrand was told to strip. While doing so he angrily asked one of the officers for his name and went on to state, "I will deal with you in my own way on the street and that's not a threat, it's a promise." Mr. Chartrand also requested a telephone call to his lawyer and was told by one of the officers that while he was acting up he would get nothing, but if he calmed down he would be allowed to make a phone call. After stripping, Mr. Chartrand was told to place all his clothes in a bag. He complied, putting his boots on the top of the bag. He then picked up the bag and threw it at one of the officers standing by the door. It was evidently the action of a very frustrated and angry man. At this time Mr. Chartrand was completely naked; he made no other movement towards the officer, nor did he say anything. The immediate reaction of one of the officers, however, was to rush at Mr. Chartrand and throw him onto the bed with his hand around Mr. Chartrand's throat, at which time he squirted Mace into Mr. Chartrand's mouth and face. Mr. Chartrand is seen face down on the mattress making choking sounds. While he was still choking, the officer put handcuffs on him. Mr. Chartrand was then left in his cell completely naked, handcuffed behind his back.

The next images in the video show events some time later, when another officer came to the cell and Mr. Chartrand was asked whether he had calmed down enough that the handcuffs could be taken off him. He again asked to call a lawyer and also to see a nurse, because his face was burning from the gas. The officer removed the handcuffs and told Mr. Chartrand to wash his face under the tap. Mr. Chartrand repeated his request for a lawyer and a nurse and requested a Valium for the pain the gas had caused him. The officer again told him to wash his face under the tap. Mr. Chartrand refused to do that until he had seen a nurse. At this point one of the Kent officers watching the video commented sarcastically that Mr. Chartrand's refusal to wash his face indicated how seriously hurt he was by the gas.

From my perspective, the video showed a prisoner subjected to gratuitous force, overpowered by strength of numbers, left without a shred of dignity and yet expected to somehow control his rage in the aftermath. The officers watching this video clearly saw staff doing their job and following standard procedures.

Mr. Fox arrived and the hearing began. The offence report, written by Officer Strum, gave the following account of the first charge, an alleged assault. "Did at 1205 hours yell at the writer, 'I will kill you when I get onto the street.' At this time he had his fist in front of my face with a finger pointed at me. After saying this the subject continued to yell and scream at staff when his cell door was locked. The inmate also referred to myself as 'being dead meat when I get out.'" Officer Strum testified that on April 18, Mr. Chartrand had approached him and was verbally abusive, saying, "You are my f-ing CO-II and it is up to you to take care of my requests." Officer Strum told Mr. Chartrand to lock up. He initially refused to do so, then complied when given a direct order. Subsequently, Officer Strum went to Mr. Chartrand's cell with a nurse, and Mr. Chartrand told him he would kill him when he got onto the street. Asked by Mr. Fox if he saw this as a serious threat, Officer Strum replied, "I perceived these threats to be real, and if I ever see him in my own neighbourhood I will deal with him accordingly."

Mr. Chartrand was asked whether he had any questions of this officer. He stated that he never used the word "kill," what he had said was, "I will have you dealt with in my own f-ing fashion." Mr. Fox asked Mr. Chartrand what he meant by that. Mr. Chartrand responded, "It doesn't matter." To this, Mr. Fox replied, "It does matter. It's important that I know your intention at the time you made this statement." Mr. Chartrand responded, "I did not mean anything. I was just angry."

On the second charge of assault, Officer Strum testified that while Mr. Chartrand was being placed in a screened cell, he again threatened him and this time threw his clothes and boots at him, hitting him with the boots. Then Officer Strum suggested the video of the incident be played. The video was stopped just after the other officer is shown taking Mr. Chartrand down onto the bed and holding him by the throat, but before he is gassed. Mr. Fox had the segment showing Mr. Chartrand throwing his clothes played back three times. Mr. Chartrand was then asked if he had any questions of Officer Strum or any comments he wanted to make. He said, "You could see in the video that I was not trying to assault Officer Strum. I threw my personals at him like a basketball toss—no way did I assault him."

Mr. Fox then gave his judgement. "As to the first charge, I am satisfied that the charge is made out. The words and the way you said them can only be taken to be a threat. On the second charge, I am not satisfied that an assault was made. You were clearly upset, and while you did throw your clothes at the officer, I don't think you intended to assault him."

Mr. Chartrand was asked if he had anything to say before punishment was imposed. He responded that he had already spent one month in segregation because of this offence. After the incident, he had been kept in the screened cell overnight and then was released back to general population at RPC. Four days later he was transferred to Kent and had been in segregation ever since. He had been told by the Segregation Review Board that he was being kept in segregation only because of these outstanding charges. The court advisor confirmed this.

Mr. Fox asked the court advisor for the institution's recommendation. She recommended 45 days' segregation but felt that the 30 days already served in segregation should be taken into account, which would result in a sentence of 15 days' segregation. Saying that he was taking this earlier segregation time into account, Mr. Fox imposed a sentence of 20 days' segregation.

I found this sentence to be unjustifiably severe, and it did not comport with the requirement of the legislation that any sanction take into account administrative measures imposed as a result of the offence. Mr. Chartrand had spent thirty-two days in segregation solely as a result of these charges. He was found not guilty of one of the charges, and under the CCRA, the other charge carried a maximum of 30 days' segregation. Yet he was now required to serve a further 20 days. The impact of this sentence was that Mr. Chartrand would serve a total fifty-two days in segregation for the single offence of threatening to assault: twenty-two days more than the permitted maximum, and seven days more than the maximum permitted for multiple offences. Even at that point his sentence would not be over, because he would have to await his turn for bed space in the general population.

Mr. Chartrand's case was one where representation by counsel would likely have made a significant difference to the outcome. While Mr. Fox correctly applied the law to the evidence in convicting Mr. Chartrand of one charge and acquitting him of the other, counsel's submissions would have focussed on the appropriate sentence. One of my findings in my 1972 and 1983 studies was that prisoners were given credit for their pre-trial segregation on a haphazard basis, if at all. Yet the CCR *Regulations* contain specific provisions designed to ensure that pre-trial segregation is taken into account in determining a disciplinary sanction. The sentencing guidelines require that, in determining a sanction, the Independent Chairperson consider any measures taken as a result of the commission of the offence and, even more importantly, provide that "an inmate who is serving a period of segregation as a sanction for a disciplinary offence shall be accorded the same conditions of confinement as would be accorded to an inmate in administrative segregation" (s. 40(3)). In other words, prisoners in administrative and disciplinary segregation are to be treated equally so far as their rights and privileges are concerned. And so they should be, since the operational reality at both Kent and Matsqui was that a prisoner serving a disciplinary segregation sentence could find himself sharing a cell—and a legal regime—with a prisoner serving administrative segregation. The clear implication of these provisions is that a prisoner confined in administrative segregation as a result of a disciplinary charge should, if convicted, be given credit for every day served in administrative segregation. Had Mr. Chartrand been represented by counsel, this argument could have been presented, coupled with the submission that Mr. Chartrand had already served more than the maximum time that can be imposed for a disciplinary offence and therefore no further segregation should be imposed. Furthermore, counsel would have ensured that when the videotape was played for Mr. Fox, it was not stopped after Mr. Chartrand threw his boots but continued rolling to show the level of force used against Mr. Chartrand, including the spraying of Mace into his mouth at point-blank range. As it was, Mr. Fox never saw this and therefore was not able to take it into account in determining a fair sanction.

## August and September 1994: Rumble in the Jungle— The Mike Tyson Fight at Kent

In the world outside of prison, talk of "a brew party" may conjure up images of good-looking people chugging beer in a sports bar. The idea of people getting together to have a few drinks is not necessarily loaded with the potential for violence. It is a very different story inside a prison. In my many conversations with experienced correctional officers, when I asked what they saw as the most dangerous situation they encountered in the course of their work, the one which caused them the most fear for their safety, it was not the high-profile hostage-taking that punctuates the history of Canadian corrections but, as one officer described it, "a brew party that goes sideways." Even though the consumption of prison home brew, manufactured in a variety of ingenious stills, does not typically result in prisoners going on a rampage, there is enough oral history about such incidents to generate a realistic fear among staff. In August 1994, that oral history had another chapter added to it.

On the evening of August 16, 1994, Officers Cole and Durand were working in C unit. They became suspicious that a brew party might be taking place when two prisoners called down for minor court hearings, James Doherty and Shawn Preddy, appeared to be under the influence. Shortly afterwards, the officers decided to investigate further. They observed four prisoners inside cell 3: Shawn Preddy, Rick DaSilva, Mike Tyson, and Mark Biega. According to a tape-recorded statement from Office Cole, the following events unfolded:

> The four inmates all stopped what they were doing and looked at me. I stated to them, "Fellows, you know why I'm down here, but you guys have the option right now to dump out the brew that you have in your cups, no paperwork will be done, and to lock up." At that time Shawn Preddy agreed with that, turned to his fellow inmates and said, "That's a good idea." Preddy dumped out his cup full of homemade brew, walked down the range and walked up to his cell. At that time Mark Biega followed Preddy out of the cell. He still had a cup full of brew. I asked him to dump it out, he refused, stating that he is going to drink it on the way to the cell. At the time inmate Tyson and inmate DaSilva were hugging. Tyson then left the cell, went towards his cell, which was 002, and entered his cell. He ended up stepping backwards out of his cell, removed his front teeth and his glasses, stepped towards the officer, hit myself in the top part of my left side of the cheek and at the time the fight ensued. It took approximately ten seconds for myself to control inmate Tyson. At that time inmate DaSilva realized what was going on. We were unable to get his door closed at that time. Inmate DaSilva charged at myself. My partner, Maurice Durand, ended up jumping on DaSilva's back. We were able to take DaSilva down and at that time both my partner and myself pushed our PPAS [portable personal alarms] to summon extra staff. At that time extra staff did attend. When they did attend I ended up going down to the end of the range where the correctional supervisor, Matt Brown, ordered me to Health Care to check my wounds. I ended up going to the hospital with Maurice Durand and we were checked out. Maurice had a very sore back. Myself,

I had a broken little finger in my right hand, a cut below my left eye, a bruising under my left eye, and a swollen chin on my left side.

Officer Dain, who arrived on the scene when officers Cole and Durand were "facing off" with Mr. Tyson and Mr. DaSilva, wrote in his incident report:

Tyson was trying to hold back DaSilva from getting at the officers. DaSilva was swinging at anybody over the shoulder of Tyson. When I closed in to try and subdue DaSilva he punched me in the right cheek. Correctional Supervisor Brown called for a shield and gas. When it arrived he warned the two inmates that gas would be used if they did not cooperate. At this time DaSilva just flipped out and tried to get at staff. Gas was used on both inmates and they were handcuffed.

All of the prisoners involved in this incident were taken to segregation, and disciplinary charges were laid. In addition, instructions were given to Mr. Tyson and Mr. DaSilva's case management officers to prepare transfer packages for the Special Handling Unit.

Disciplinary court appearances took place on August 30. The first prisoner was Mr. Doherty, whose appearance in minor court had triggered the officers' suspicion that a party was in progress. The charge against Mr. Doherty was one I had not seen before at Kent or Matsqui: *CCRA* s. 40(s), "attempts to do or assists another person to do anything referred to in paragraphs (a) to (r)." The offence report signed by Officer Durand read:

On 94-08-16 Doherty attended a minor court hearing in the office in C Unit at which I was present. Doherty appeared to be under the influence of an intoxicant because his gait was unsteady and his eyes seemed slightly unfocused. The subsequent inmate who appeared at the minor court hearing seemed substantially more impaired. Therefore my partner and I proceeded to investigate down the range and interrupted a brew party in cell C 003. My partner ordered the four inmates involved to dump the brew and go back to their own cells. I attempted to isolate Doherty and two other inmates by locking them into cell C 005. My partner at this time was being assaulted by one of the inmates involved in the brew party. Inmate Doherty resisted by trying to obstruct the cell door from closing.

Mr. Doherty came into the hearing room wearing a baseball hat. Correctional Supervisor Logan, the court advisor, asked him to take his hat off. Mr. Doherty refused, saying his hair would fall over his eyes. Mr. Logan told him again to take his hat off and stood up to make his point. Mr. Doherty said, "Are you going to get violent with me for keeping my hat on?" Mr. Fox told Mr. Doherty to go back to his cell until he was prepared to show the appropriate respect for the court. Mr. Doherty again explained that if he took his hat off, his hair would fall over his eyes, and he wanted to see what was happening. Mr. Fox responded, "That is your choice." Mr. Doherty then took his hat off, revealing a mass of long curly hair that did flop down over his eyes, requiring him to brush it back. (What seemed to escape everyone in the room was that the duty officer standing by the door of the courtroom was wearing a baseball hat of the type sported by Mr. Doherty. There was no suggestion that the officer should take his hat off or that his failure to do so showed disrespect for the court.)

Mr. Doherty pleaded not guilty, and Mr. Fox proceeded to read over the offence report. Having done so, he said it was not clear to him from the description of the offence which particular things in s. 40 (a) to (r) of the CCRA the charges referred to. He said it was important a charge such as this be specific so the prisoner knew what he had to defend himself against.

Mr. Doherty said he had been in segregation for almost two weeks, and the charge had not been laid until ten days after the incident. Mr. Fox asked Mr. Logan if there was some reason for the unusually long period between the date of the incident and the date of the offence report. Mr. Logan said that the initial investigation had been directed to prisoners DaSilva and Tyson, who were involved in the assault on the officers. Only after that investigation had been completed was the involvement of Mr. Doherty reviewed, and it was decided then to lay a charge against him.

Mr. Fox reviewed the various officers' statements attached to the offence report, two of which were written the day after the incident, and found that these did implicate Mr. Doherty in one way or another from the outset. On the basis of that information, he said, an appropriate charge to lay against Mr. Doherty might have been participating in a disturbance. However, he found that the ten-day delay between the incident and the time the charge was finally served on Mr. Doherty was unreasonable, and the charge against him was therefore dismissed.

The next prisoner, Mr. Tyson, pleaded not guilty to the charge of assault and requested an adjournment to retain counsel. A hearing date was set for September 27. The third prisoner seen was Mr. Preddy, who faced a charge of taking an intoxicant into his body. He also requested an adjournment to retain legal counsel, and his new hearing date was also set for September 27.

There were further developments arising from the August brew party. The charge against Mr. Biega was withdrawn after he was transferred to Surrey Pretrial to await the execution of a deportation order back to Poland. The assault charge against Mr. DaSilva was dismissed on the grounds of unreasonable delay when, on the date scheduled for his hearing, the institutional witnesses were not available. Neither the dismissal of the charge against Mr. DaSilva, nor the fact that Mr. Tyson's hearing had not yet taken place, prevented the completion of transfer packages to the Special Handling Unit, which were served on both prisoners on September 7.

At the September 27 hearing, Mr. Tyson appeared without legal representation and changed his plea to guilty of the assault on the two officers. When asked by Mr. Fox whether he wanted to add anything to what was written in the officer incident reports, he said that he did not and commented, "I'm going to the SHU, so let's get this over with." Mr. Fox asked Officer Wallin, the institutional advisor, whether the staff involved had ongoing injuries. He said Officer Cole was on sick leave after the incident with a broken finger and contusions to his head but had just begun work again. Officer Wallin recommended a sentence of 30 days' segregation, and that was the sentence Mr. Fox imposed. No credit was given for time in the hole since the incident, which in Mr. Tyson's case amounted to forty-five days.

I have already pointed out that punishment inflicted through the formal disciplinary process is only one of the consequences that may be visited upon a prisoner charged with an offence. In Mr. Tyson and Mr. DaSilva's cases, by far the gravest consequence they suffered was their transfer to the Special Handling Unit. Reviewing the process through which Mr. Tyson was deemed to be such a serious risk to staff safety and institutional security reveals how a prisoner's history can be re-characterized to support a particular correctional outcome.

In February 1986, Mr. Tyson had been convicted of attempted murder and the use of a firearm during the commission of an offence, for which he was sentenced to 11 years. Following a statutory release in May 1993, he was returned to prison in October of that year after incurring new charges of possession of stolen property and theft of an auto, for which he received an additional sentence of 4 months. On August 3, 1994, two weeks before the brew party, Mr. Tyson's case management team recommended that his security classification be reduced to medium security and that he be transferred to William Head Institution. That report stated:

> Mr. Tyson has not been a discipline problem in C Unit. Mr. Tyson is co-operative to deal with and he obeys the rules and regulations and gets along with other inmates. He has a friendly attitude towards staff. Mr. Tyson has not received any institutional charges and has been drug free since his return to Kent institution. Mr. Tyson has completed some programming in substance abuse and life skills while at Kent institution. (Progress Summary, Kent Institution, August 3, 1994)

The case management team rated Mr. Tyson's public safety concern to be moderate, concluding:

> This subject has a lengthy history of criminal behaviour and his current offence of attempted murder involved him shooting another individual with a shotgun. However, that offence occurred nine years ago. Since then he has not displayed any aggressive or violent behaviour while incarcerated at Kent institution and he has displayed a more mature and responsible attitude over all.

On August 24, 1994, a week after the brew party and the assault, Mr. Tyson's case management officer prepared a new progress summary in support of his transfer to the Special Handling Unit. That summary emphasized Mr. Tyson's disruptive behaviour in the remand centre nine years previously and during his initial admission to the federal system. It noted that his behaviour then showed a marked improvement, and he was transferred to Matsqui in 1991. The report asserts that this improvement in behaviour was shortlived and that Mr. Tyson "reverted back to his previous violent behaviour . . . when the subject was involved in a serious stabbing attack on another inmate. This attack almost caused the death of this victim, consequently Tyson was involuntarily transferred back to Kent Institution." What the new progress summary did not note was that three other prisoners were alleged to be involved in this stabbing; Mr. Tyson denied any responsibility for it, was never charged under either the *Criminal Code* or the prison disciplinary code, and was not recommended for transfer to the Special Handling Unit. Indeed, he was released into the population at Kent Institution less than three weeks after the stabbing, which suggests that the authorities had serious doubts about his involvement. The summary observes that there were no further problems with Mr. Tyson's behaviour. His security was again reduced to medium, and that was his status at the time of his statutory release.

In describing the assault on August 16, the progress summary stated:

> The correctional officer that was attacked by inmate Tyson suffered a broken finger, and bruising and cuts to his facial area. The second officer suffered bruising, strained muscles and a sore back . . . Fortunately, more serious or life threatening injuries did not occur as a result of this attack, but the attack is viewed as extremely serious regardless, especially inmate Tyson's actions. After being shown significant leniency (just dump the brew and return to his cell), he made a very clear and conscious decision to violently attack correctional staff. This is demonstrated by the fact that he did proceed to

his cell as requested at which point the matter would have ended. However he, instead, planned and acted out a violent attack. He obviously knew what he was doing when he removed his glasses and false teeth, and he clearly prepared himself for what he must have thought would be a violent fight. In essence, he prepared himself for a serious battle as opposed to a spur of the moment act of anger.

In view of his actions it is clear that inmate Tyson has really gained little or no benefit whatsoever from his period of incarceration. Instead, his violent past behaviour has clearly resurfaced and he has shown by his actions he is prepared to violently attack staff with little or no provocation. (Progress Summary, Kent Institution, August 23, 1994)

In his response to the institution's recommendation that he be transferred to the Special Handling Unit, supplemented by a further submission from Prisoners' Legal Services, Mr. Tyson challenged both the description and the characterization of what took place on August 16. He pointed out that this was one of the rare times he had consumed alcohol in prison in recent years, and on the night in question he had become extremely intoxicated. He remembered that when Officers Cole and Durand ordered the prisoners to get rid of their brew and lock up, he proceeded to "chug-a-lug" the brew in his cup. By the time he reached his cell, the alcohol had "hit him like a ton of bricks," and thereafter he remembered very little of what took place. He denied any previous plan to attack the officers, saying he had a good prior relationship with them and could offer no rational explanation for his actions beyond the fact of his extreme intoxication. (The irrationality of what he had done was substantiated when one considered that Officer Cole was six inches taller and a hundred pounds heavier than Mr. Tyson.) While he acknowledged that he had removed his glasses and teeth, he stated that in any potentially aggressive situation this was almost a reflex action, learned from the years he had spent in maximum security, and it did not reflect a planned attack on the officers.

The submission from Prisoners' Legal Services noted that the progress summary did not refer to Officer Dain's statement that Mr. Tyson tried to prevent Mr. DaSilva from attacking Officer Cole up until the time both prisoners were gassed. These actions supported the contention that Mr. Tyson's assault on Officer Cole was caused by a momentary bout of irrationality due to his intoxication, which he then endeavoured to rectify. Ultimately, Mr. Tyson argued that the attack on Officer Cole was unplanned and out of character; it was the result of his intoxication, and as such he did not represent a continuing and serious risk to staff. Mr. Tyson's rebuttal notwithstanding, the warden of Kent upheld the recommendation for his transfer to the Special Handling Unit, and that recommendation was affirmed by the deputy commissioner. After spending more than three months in segregation, Mr. Tyson was transferred to the Special Handling Unit in Prince Albert, Saskatchewan, where he would spend the next two years.

## January 1995: The Merk and Jago Cases—The Indelible Mark of Maximum Security

The morning of January 3, 1995, was bitter but bright. As I drove to Kent I encountered the strong Arctic outflow winds I had heard about on the radio weather forecast. But if these winds were going to usher in a year of change, the cases that appeared on the docket of the first disciplinary court at Kent gave no hint of it, because they bore the unmistakable mark of maximum security.

Mr. Merk and Mr. Jago were both charged with offences based upon an incident on December 17, 1994. Mr. Merk was charged with threatening to assault. The offence report of that date stated, "At the beginning of the meal line CO Clark and I overheard a portion of a conversation between Merk and Jago. Merk said, 'Yeah, then we'll take them hostage, torture 'em and cut their throats.' We were on post next to the kitchen control bubble and heard them as they walked into the dining room." Mr. Merk pleaded not guilty, stating that he and Mr. Jago were talking about the video game Street Fighter which they had just been playing in the common room. Their references had not been to staff or other prisoners. The hearing was adjourned to the following week, when the officers in question would be available to give evidence.

Mr. Jago was charged with disobeying a justifiable order. The offence report stated, "Refused to go to segregation when ordered. Physical force and gas used to subdue Jago. The inmate refused a direct order to go to segregation." Mr. Jago said he was going to plead not guilty but first wanted to know what Mr. Fox was thinking of giving him if he was convicted. If he was going to be segregated, he would fight the charge. He stated that if Mr. Fox had been in the institution the previous week, he would have seen that as a result of this incident Mr. Jago had a shiner, his lip was bleeding, and his eyes were burning from pepper spray.

Mr. Fox said he could not give Mr. Jago any assurance he would not get segregation time if he was found guilty, because it would depend on the circumstances, but at the moment Mr. Jago was presumed to be innocent. Mr. Fox did, however, ask Officer Wallin whether the institution was prepared to indicate what its recommendation might be. Officer Wallin said he did not want to prejudice Mr. Jago's right to a fair hearing. Mr. Jago said that his hearing would not be prejudiced, because he was in control of what he did, but he was concerned that his cognitive living skills course not be interrupted, and he had sixteen days to go on that. One of the reasons he would plead not guilty was to avoid going to segregation so as not to interrupt that program. Officer Wallin stated that if Mr. Jago was found guilty he would recommend a suspended sentence so as not to interfere with his program. Mr. Jago then said he was prepared to plead guilty. Officer Wallin recommended 15 days' segregation, suspended for 60 days, which Mr. Fox imposed.

Two days after these hearings, I observed the videotape of the removal of Mr. Merk and Mr. Jago from their cells to segregation. The removal of Mr. Merk was uneventful. Correctional Supervisor Logan informed him that he was going to segregation for comments he had made outside the kitchen regarding taking hostages. Mr. Merk co-operated, allowing himself to be handcuffed behind his back, and was then escorted to segregation, where he was strip-searched and placed in a cell.

The removal of Mr. Jago followed a very different trajectory. Mr. Logan informed Mr. Jago that he was going to segregation. Mr. Jago responded, "What are you talking about, what for?" Mr. Logan told him that earlier in the day threats had been made about taking hostages and cutting throats; although Mr. Jago had not made the statements, he was implicated in them. Mr. Jago continued to question why he was being taken to segregation, and Mr. Logan said his orders were to take him there. Mr. Jago, still seated at his desk, stated, "I won't go easy," at which point Mr. Logan, accompanied by four or five other officers, moved into the cell very quickly and forced Mr. Jago onto the bed. It is not clear from the video whether it was at this time or a few seconds later that Mr. Jago was pepper-sprayed in the face by Mr. Logan. In any event, four of the officers were quickly on top of Mr. Jago, holding him down. Mr. Jago could be heard screaming. He was subsequently escorted out of the cell, complaining that his face was burning and asking for his tobacco.

On my first viewing of the tape I was shocked at the immediacy of Mr. Logan's resort to force and gas. Mr. Jago had not adopted an aggressive physical stance—indeed, he was still sitting at his desk. He had not become verbally abusive to Mr. Logan. His statement that he would not go easy had not been accompanied by any threatening gesture or attempt to pick up a weapon. Mr. Jago was not a big man; Mr. Logan was an extremely strong and physically fit officer, an expert weightlifter with biceps the size of Mr. Jago's head, and he was accompanied by four or five other staff members. My assessment of the situation was that the use of force was premature.

I rewound the tape to view it a second time. Correctional Supervisor Knopf came into the room, and I asked her whether she had seen the tape. She had. I gave her my first impressions and also suggested that if she had been the correctional supervisor at the time, the matter would have been handled differently, without resort to the use of gas. We looked at the tape again together. I asked her why Mr. Logan had moved in on Mr. Jago and used the gas without further efforts to persuade him to go without resistance. Ms. Knopf said these situations were judgement calls, and what we could not see from the videotape was Mr. Jago's body language. Furthermore, Mr. Logan had a wealth of experience and an intuitive sense of when it was appropriate to move in quickly. She acknowledged, however, that different officers approached situations in different ways. She suggested a video I might want to review, entitled "Verbal Judo," which she used in staff training to illustrate how it is often better to resolve a situation by coming at it from a variety of angles rather than through direct confrontation. This was her preferred approach, but it was not everybody's. She ended her comments by saying I was right in thinking she would not have used gas on Mr. Jago.

I also discussed the Jago videotape with another unit manager who had seen it. She had spoken to Mr. Jago about the incident, and he had admitted it was stupid for him to say, "I won't go easy," even if it was just an act of verbal bravado. She made the further comment that a swift and forceful response is the best way to make an impression on some kinds of prisoners. Particularly in relation to someone like Mr. Jago, who fit into the category of "young punk," an experience like this would "make him smell the coffee," so that the next time he was asked to go to segregation he would realize the smart thing to do was go quietly and ask questions later. In her view, a pre-emptive action like Mr. Logan's could make a greater impression and thus have a greater influence on the prisoner's future behaviour.

This approach was not far removed from a statement I'd heard a B.C. Penitentiary officer make in 1973; he admitted to gassing a prisoner by mistake but sought to justify it on the basis that it would be "a lesson for the future." Mr. Jago's gassing was quite intentional, but the action may have had more to do with making an impression on Mr. Jago by conveying to him the need for instant compliance than with any real threat he presented.

Mr. Merk's case resumed on January 10, 1995. Officer Cove gave evidence regarding the portion of the conversation he overheard between Mr. Merk and Mr. Jago, in which Mr. Merk stated, "Yeah, then we'll take them hostage, torture 'em, and cut their throats." Mr. Fox asked the officer whether he knew the context of the conversation. He said he did not; he overheard the prisoners talking as they walked past him and his co-worker. Mr. Fox asked whether the prisoners seemed to be in good humour. The officer said they were. Mr. Fox asked if the officer had observed anything sinister about their conversation; for example, were they looking around to see if anyone was listening, or were they whispering? The officer said there was nothing of that nature.

Mr. Merk, in his own evidence, admitted making the statements but said he and Mr. Jago were talking about the video game they had been playing for a couple of weeks and joking about what kind of game they would make up themselves, specifically for prisoners. He said he had no institutional record for violence, and he was shocked when he was thrown in the hole that night and told he had been overheard talking about taking hostages. He had spent Friday to Monday in the hole and was then released.

Mr. Fox asked Officer Cove whether he had anything to add to his statement, particularly about the context of the conversation. The officer said the conversation had taken place on the day before increased double-bunking was going into effect, and a number of prisoners were commenting about resisting this move. The comments overheard between Mr. Merk and Mr. Jago were extremely disturbing and threatening given the hostile environment at Kent at the time, and that was why they were written up.

Mr. Fox said he was dismissing the charge, not because it had been inappropriate to log the statements or to lay the charges but because there was no evidence of a threat to assault any individual. While it may have been a fair assumption of the officers that the threats were directed against them, there was no evidence beyond a reasonable doubt that Mr. Merk was directing his threats to a person rather than speaking in reference to a video game.

Even given the legitimate staff concern regarding prisoner discontent with increased double-bunking (although double-bunking had been implemented at Kent thus far without incident), it is difficult to understand why there was not some investigation prior to the decision to segregate the two men. Had there simply been an inquiry of Mr. Merk or Mr. Jago about the conversation, Mr. Jago would not have been gassed, the men would not have spent the weekend in segregation, and charges against them would not have been laid. Any concern that approaching the two men could have provoked an incident, if they had been serious about taking hostages, could have been addressed easily by questioning them in the presence of several officers. Indeed, Mr. Logan did appear with a full cohort of support. However, those officers were deployed to segregate first, leaving it to others to ask the questions later. That may be the maximum security way, at least for some correctional supervisors, but it can result in very rough justice.

There is a postscript to Mr. Jago's case. In November 1997, together with Jared Sharp, an Australian student spending the semester at U.B.C.'s Faculty of Law, I interviewed Mr. Jago. The interview was one of several conducted at Kent as research for a paper Mr. Sharp was writing on the effects of juvenile incarceration on future violent conduct. Interestingly, Jared Sharp and Keith Jago were born within months of each other. Mr. Jago had first been imprisoned in "juvie" when he was thirteen years old. He had spent most of his teenage life locked up, primarily in maximum security juvenile institutions. In his interview, Mr. Jago described a level of violence in those institutions, both between staff and prisoners and among prisoners themselves, which far exceeded the violence he had experienced at Kent Institution. Those years had created in him a deep hatred for correctional authority and reinforced a value system based on a "violence works" rationale. I asked Mr. Jago if he had learned anything from his years in juvenile institutions. Reflecting on his time at the Boulder Bay maximum security camp, he told us:

The only thing I learned is that in freezing cold weather standing in the middle of a lake trying to make a helicopter pad, your hands tend to freeze to the sledgehammer. Other than that there was nothing to learn in Boulder Bay. (Interview with Keith Jago, Kent Institution, November 1997)

Mr. Jago told me he had no problem with a system of discipline. "Discipline's good; just don't go to the excessive like throwing me in a little rubber room and start spraying me with hoses. That's too much. I'm not an animal, I'm a human being." When, ten years after his experiences in juvenile detention, Mr. Jago was gassed at Kent Institution while sitting at his desk, it was not a signal that he should smarten up but a painful reminder that he had not yet outdistanced his reasons for hating correctional authority.

## CHAPTER 4

# Bringing Justice to the Disciplinary Process

## Views from the Trenches

In describing the practice of prison justice at Matsqui and Kent, I have reflected on features which both demonstrate and compromise its claim to be a fair and effective process. Another dimension to my understanding of the disciplinary process came from a series of meetings held at Kent in the summer of 1994, in which prison administrators, line staff, prisoners, and the Independent Chairperson engaged in a discussion of the disciplinary process and made constructive recommendations for improving the system. These recommendations illustrate the different perceptions prison staff and prisoners have of the process, but they also reveal pathways to greater justice in the disciplinary process.

The primary area of concern to correctional staff and administrators was the lack of legal education relating to the disciplinary process. Unlike police officers, who routinely write reports to Crown counsel on the basis of which charges can be laid, most correctional officers write few offence reports, and they receive little or no training in how to do this. Independent Chairperson Dean Fox corroborated my observations that some offence reports left a great deal to be desired in terms of both specificity and clarity. The laying and designation of the charge was also an area in which lack of proper legal training created recurring problems. As Mr. Fox pointed out, it was important that the person who reviewed the offence reports to determine whether a charge should be laid, what the charge should be, and whether it should be designated as serious or minor, be conversant with the legal and factual elements required to prove particular offences.

Cases were dismissed at both Matsqui and Kent because the wrong charge had been laid, although the facts would have supported a conviction on a different charge. This occurred most frequently in relation to charges of possession of contraband in situations where possession of an unauthorized object would be the appropriate charge, and to charges of assault in circumstances where the evidence supported only the charge of being disrespectful or abusive. The necessary elements of an offence are matters of legal definition and interpretation, and it is unreasonable to expect correctional staff to perform functions of this kind in the absence of proper legal training.

Correctional staff would also be well served by better training in preparing and giving evidence at a disciplinary hearing. Mr. Fox, in explaining his expectations to the staff at Kent, stressed how important it was for the charging officer to review the offence report and any observation reports before giving evidence. Not infrequently, an officer was called to the hearing room directly from his or her post and, on arrival, gave the impression of taking a deep breath, then giving evidence without thinking too much about what he or she was going to say. In some cases the officer, as he or she was about to give evidence, asked to review the offence report. It was Mr. Fox's practice not to permit this, because he believed it resulted in the officer simply reading what was in the report rather than giving oral evidence. Mr. Routley did allow officers to refresh their memories in this way, although typically it resulted in the kind of testimony Mr. Fox's practice was intended to avoid.

Two suggestions were made to address these issues. Mr. Fox suggested that a book of precedents be maintained at each institution; it would include well-written offence reports dealing with the most common situations that gave rise to charges. Another suggestion, made by staff members, was that a series of videos be produced from actual disciplinary hearings; these could be shown to new staff during training. Both initiatives could be implemented easily, and, in conjunction with continuing legal education about the *Charter of Rights and Freedoms* and administrative law, would provide line staff and correctional administrators with the knowledge and skills to discharge their responsibilities in the disciplinary process.

Line staff were also concerned about the lack of feedback in cases where a prisoner was acquitted even though the officer believed that evidence had established the basis for conviction. Under current procedures, institutional staff were excused from the courtroom after giving their evidence. In some cases, the news of acquittal came from the prisoner himself, in the form of "I beat the charge." The officer then had to find out from the institutional advisor what had happened; in many cases, the explanation was both delayed and imperfect. The result was predictable: the officer was left frustrated and with a lack of respect for the process. In the absence of a rational explanation, staff tended to interpret an acquittal either as arbitrary or as a demonstration of the Chairperson's pro-prisoner bias.

One recommended solution to this problem was that the charging officer come back into the hearing room to hear the Chairperson's decision. This way, the officer would not be left to speculate on the basis for an acquittal, and the Chairperson's reasons might prove instructive where the acquittal resulted from deficiencies in the institutional case. Another recommendation was that the Independent Chairperson provide detailed reasons for his decision in writing. As I have explained, the sheet which constituted the principal disciplinary record provided room only for a check against three boxes, "guilty," "not guilty," and "refuses to plead." In my observations, written reasons were rendered only where legal arguments had been raised, almost always by legal counsel for a prisoner, and the Independent Chairperson deemed it advisable to respond in writing to the submissions. At a meeting of Independent Chairpersons for the Pacific Region, I had been advised that this was extremely rare and that some Chairpersons never prepared written reasons. The Independent Chairpersons I observed at Matsqui and Kent always gave reasons for their decisions and, in many cases, quite detailed ones. But while these were part of the taped proceedings, they were not transcribed by the institution. It would not be difficult to transcribe them, although it would involve additional work for the court clerk.

The transcribing of the Independent Chairperson's reasons would likely have another impact. Mr. Routley had commented to me that upon seeing his oral reasons reduced to writing, in the few cases where a prisoner had appealed his decision to Federal Court, he was less than impressed with either the clarity of his reasoning or the felicity of its expression. The knowledge that the Independent Chairperson's reasons for decision would be distributed in writing to both staff and the prisoner would no doubt have a salutary effect on the quality of those reasons.

## The Case for Institutional Representation

Given my analysis of institutional hegemony, it was initially surprising to hear correctional staff express their sense of being disadvantaged in a disciplinary hearing. The concern voiced during one focus group discussion was along the lines: "When staff come to court they feel intimidated by the process. They are on their own, with no one representing them. The Independent Chairperson gets to ask them questions, the prisoner gets to ask them questions, and then they leave." This problem was aggravated when the prisoner was represented by a lawyer who conducted a cross-examination of the officer. Staff felt this imbalance should be remedied by having someone at the hearing whose role it was to represent institutional and staff interests.

It is easy to dismiss this concern on the grounds that it misconceives the purpose of a disciplinary hearing. Mr. Fox pointed out, quite rightly in my view, that it is the prisoner who is charged with an offence, and it is the prisoner who will be subject to punishment if found guilty. The prisoner is granted rights for this fundamental reason. If the hearing seems slanted in favour of the prisoner, it is because the prisoner's interests are in jeopardy, and his guilt must be proved beyond a reasonable doubt.

From a purely legal perspective, it is possible to end analysis of the issue here. However, a more extended discussion is necessary to distinguish real from imagined concerns. When I first advocated twenty-five years ago that prisoners should have a right to counsel in serious disciplinary cases, correctional administrators and staff recoiled at the idea. They imagined criminal lawyers coming into the prison and demeaning them in front of prisoners through aggressive and intimidating cross-examination. That spectre arose mainly from television and film dramatizations of the role of counsel, which are a far cry from the normal operations of criminal counsel. The charges on the typical docket of disciplinary court are not the stuff of which dramatic cross-examination is made. Even though the appearance of counsel at either Kent or Matsqui was a relatively rare event, and in no case I observed did counsel conduct anything approaching an aggressive cross-examination (indeed, by their own admission counsel were usually far less aggressive than in criminal cases), this spectre still loomed large in the minds of some staff. This unfounded concern by itself would not justify staff representation at a disciplinary hearing.

Nonetheless, there is a serious case to be made for more effective institutional representation at disciplinary hearings. Under existing law and policy, as reflected in practice at Kent and Matsqui, the institutional advisor's role is limited principally to making recommendations on sentences in the event of a guilty plea or a finding of guilt. Even though advisors at both Matsqui and Kent did intercede on occasion to clarify a point of institutional policy or practice, it is fair to say that the advisors often felt stifled, and in their view their inability to participate more fully in the hearing limited the Independent Chairperson's fact-finding.

Appointing a formal representative for the institution, analogous to a Crown counsel, would create a larger role than that presently envisaged for the institutional advisor. Such a position would also change some functions of the Independent Chairperson. Under present procedures, the Chairperson asks most of the questions, both of staff witnesses and of the prisoner, and in this respect he plays the simultaneous roles of Crown counsel, defence counsel, and judge. Indeed, in the focus group discussion, staff suggested this was an impossible confusion of roles. In most cases I observed, the Independent Chairpersons at Kent and Matsqui managed to juggle these roles with some success. In my judgement, however, too much of a prosecutorial role was played in some cases, and I am sure there were many others in which staff perceived the Chairperson as too defence-oriented. If a prosecuting officer were established, the Independent Chairperson would be relieved of the primary responsibility of questioning witnesses, leaving a residual role of raising questions arising from the examination or cross-examination.

A number of other benefits would flow from a designated prosecuting officer. As with Crown counsel, such an officer would be responsible for reviewing the offence and observation reports to ensure that there was sufficient evidentiary basis to justify a charge and that the appropriate charge had been laid. In preparation for the hearing, the officer would interview and prepare witnesses and ensure that evidence was presented in an orderly fashion. The proper discharge of these responsibilities would go a long way to resolve many of the problems that lead to staff dissatisfaction with the process, a dissatisfaction which in many cases they direct towards the Independent Chairperson or, exceptionally, to the clever talk of a lawyer. In several of my case studies I have shown how acquittals were entered because the wrong charge was laid or the manner in which the evidence was presented failed to establish a case against the prisoner. In a number of cases, witnesses were summoned directly from their security posts, and the order in which they appeared corresponded to the order in which they arrived at the courtroom door. Predictably, this resulted in a disruption of the chronology of events, which militated against the Chairperson gaining a full understanding of the incident. Not infrequently, an officer giving evidence would omit important details because he or she assumed incorrectly that another officer had covered that material in prior testimony. Thus critical elements in the institution's case failed to be proved. The acquittal of a prisoner under these circumstances inevitably led to considerable bitterness on the part of the staff.

The presence of an institutional representative would also address the problematic issue of adjournments. Though many staff voiced the view that the main reason for lengthy adjournments was prisoners' requests to consult with counsel, in reality adjournments more often were requested by the institutional advisor to accommodate staff scheduling and rotation (a finding certified by the csc's *Evaluation Report*). I observed a good number of cases in which prisoners were prepared to proceed with the hearing but staff were unavailable, and this became apparent only on the day of the hearing. An institutional representative with responsibilities for the conduct of the case would do a much better job of avoiding adjournments due to the absence of witnesses and, in those cases where a prisoner has counsel, of arranging a speedy date for the hearing.

An institutional representative would also act as the principal institutional voice on appropriate sentence. Since the role of institutional representative would be specialized, requiring particular knowledge and skills, the position could not be easily reassigned, a characteristic of the existing process. For example, there

were a significant number of occasions at Kent in which there were three different advisors in as many weeks, with noticeable shifts in the sentencing recommendations made for similar offences.

My case studies on the process illustrate that many legal issues of definition
and interpretation are raised in the course of disciplinary hearings. These result
in prisoners or legal counsel making arguments that require determination by the
Independent Chairperson. An institutional representative would ensure that
the institutional perspective was taken into account in any decision of this kind.
In addition, submissions prepared by that representative would likely be based
on consultation with CSC's counsel in Ottawa, particularly in cases which raised
general legal principles that might affect the interpretation of the CCRA in other
institutions.

Two further questions arise from the proposal for an institutional representative at disciplinary hearings. First, should such a representative be a lawyer, or
at least legally trained? Second, would the presence of such a representative
increase the adversarial nature of the process, thus undermining some functions
presently served by disciplinary court?

On the first question, a number of staff at Kent suggested that the institution
be represented by a lawyer at disciplinary hearings, to counterbalance the fact
that prisoners were represented by lawyers. However, it is rare that lawyers actually appear for prisoners and, unless this situation changes (I will later specifically
address this issue), having a lawyer represent the institution in all cases would
decidedly imbalance the process. Another argument in favour of having a lawyer
is that a lawyer would best be able to conduct examination and cross-examination
of witnesses and to make legal submissions. Yet given the nature of the evidence
at most disciplinary hearings, and bearing in mind that the legal issues tend to
be quite specialized, it would be feasible for the function of an institutional representative to be fulfilled by a non-lawyer who undertook a course of training
and study in the field.

There would be significant advantages for the Correctional Service of Canada
if its own staff were equipped to take on these new responsibilities. The Service
has already moved along this path in areas involving program delivery; for example, correctional officers are specially trained to be facilitators in substance abuse
and cognitive skills programs. The advantages of a staff person representing the
institution in disciplinary cases are several: a staff person would be well positioned to decide whether a charge should be laid, to assess adequate alternatives
to the disciplinary process, to determine the seriousness of the charge, and to recommend the appropriate sanction.

There is a more overarching advantage to having a legally trained officer in
this position. One of the fundamental issues facing the Correctional Service of
Canada is how it can adapt its corporate culture to demonstrate respect for the
law and the *Charter*. The establishment of a legal officer at the institutional level

could be an important part of meeting this challenge. In addition to serving as institutional representative at disciplinary hearings, such an officer could assume more general responsibilities for ensuring compliance with the law.

The second question raised by the proposal to establish an institutional representative relates to its impact on the adversarial nature of disciplinary proceedings. In the Federal Court of Appeal decision in *Howard,* Mr. Justice MacGuigan pointed out that recognition of the prisoner's right to counsel in disciplinary hearings could lead to the introduction of a prosecuting officer, the disappearance of any inquisitorial aspect of the process, and the full acceptance of an adversarial system. He concluded:

> I accept this as an accurate estimate of the likely consequences, but not as an argument in *terrorem.* If that is what fundamental justice requires, it is a step forward rather than a limitation. (*Howard,* at 684)

Based upon my observations of disciplinary hearings in the 1970s, 1980s, and 1990s, the reality is that disciplinary hearings are inherently adversarial in nature and practice. This reality derives from both the power dynamics between prisoners and guards and the structure and format of the proceedings. The legal framework provides for a trial-like process, in which the institution's case is presented with an opportunity for the prisoner to cross-examine witnesses and give evidence in his own defence. Kent correctional staff supported the idea of someone performing the functions of prosecuting counsel in recognition that the proceedings were adversarial and trial-like. For their part, prisoners had no doubt that what was being invoked against them in disciplinary court was the same authority that had sent them to "the pen." The process was more intense and pervasive but no less adversarial.

## The Case for Prisoner Representation

I have described how the Federal Court of Appeal in the 1985 *Howard* case held that, under certain circumstances, prisoners had a constitutionally protected right to counsel in prison disciplinary hearings. The CSC attempted to get around this ruling by introducing a new "intermediary" category of offence, which, they argued, did not attract a right to counsel. This evasionary tactic ultimately failed when the Federal Court ruled that the right to counsel could not be discounted by a definitional sleight of hand (*Engen* v. *Canada (Kingston Penitentiary),* [1987] F.C.J. No. 641). In British Columbia, however, the *Howard* decision was muted in another way. Since most prisoners in federal penitentiaries do not have the financial ability to retain counsel, their ability to access their right to representation is dependent upon legal aid. B.C.'s Legal Services Society took the position that the *Legal Services Society Act* (R.S.B.C. 1979, c. 227) placed them under no legal obligation to extend legal aid to prisoners facing disciplinary hearings, regardless of the category of offence.

Under this *Act,* a person qualifies for legal aid if he or she (a) is the defendant in criminal proceedings that could lead to his or her imprisonment, (b) might be imprisoned or confined through civil proceedings, or (c) has a legal problem that threatens his or her livelihood. Following his denial of eligibility by the Legal Services Society, Mr. Landry, a prisoner charged with the serious offence of doing an act with intent to escape, initiated a court challenge that came before the B.C. Supreme Court. That court ruled the proceedings were neither criminal nor civil but "disciplinary." While *Howard* might give a prisoner the right to counsel, "nothing is said of any reciprocal obligation to provide and pay for counsel" (*Landry* v. *Legal Services Society,* [1986] B.C.J. No. 336). That position was affirmed by the B.C. Court of Appeal ((1987) 28 C.C.C. (3d) 138).

A number of consequences flowed from this decision. Prisoners ineligible for legal aid were forced to find lawyers who would represent them based either upon some moral obligation, arising from their having represented the prisoner during a criminal trial, or on the basis of a future promise to pay. Prisoners therefore often sought adjournments in order to locate counsel who would represent them. The result was a sense of frustration shared by everyone involved in the process. Prisoners were frustrated by not being able to realize the right they were said to have, the staff by what they saw as the games prisoners played in seeking adjournments, and the administration by not having the ability to resolve disciplinary problems quickly.

In 1992, the CCR *Regulations* translated the *Howard* decision into a legislated right by providing that "the Service shall ensure that an inmate who is charged with a serious disciplinary defence is given a reasonable opportunity to retain and instruct legal counsel for the hearing" (s. 31(2)). However, the CSC was not prepared to recognize the argument that, since representation by counsel is an essential part of the disciplinary process, its cost is an integral part of running a prison system. Although the CCR *Regulations* recognized that prisoners had an unqualified right to be represented by counsel, the CSC took the position that it had no obligation to pay for that representation; the implementation of the right remained dependent upon prisoners either paying for counsel themselves or obtaining provincial legal aid.

In the years following the enactment of the CCRA, the Legal Services Society of B.C. maintained its position that prisoners facing disciplinary hearings were not eligible for legal aid. Prisoners' Legal Services, which is funded by the Legal Services Society, had a staff of one full-time lawyer and two paralegals for their mandate to respond to issues raised by some two thousand federal prisoners. The enormous responsibilities and limited staffing made it impossible for them to represent prisoners at disciplinary hearings. For over ten years the University of

Victoria's Faculty of Law operated a legal clinic which provided services to federal prisoners at the William Head medium security institution, and the clinic's staff lawyer, on a very selective basis, provided representation at disciplinary hearings. In June 1997, as a result of funding cuts, the staff lawyer's position was terminated.

The operating reality during the period of my study from 1993 to 1999 was that for the overwhelming majority of prisoners, the right to counsel affirmed by the Federal Court of Appeal and recognized in the *CCRA* was a mirage. Based on personal observation and discussions with Independent Chairpersons and Prisoners' Legal Services, I estimate that in less than 1 per cent of all cases during that time was a prisoner represented by counsel.

The situation in British Columbia is replicated in other provinces housing federal institutions with the exception of Quebec and, to a lesser extent, Ontario. Only in Quebec does the provincial legal aid plan provide for routine representation of prisoners at disciplinary hearings. This relative advantage is offset by the standard tariff of $200 per case (including preparation time), which means very few lawyers are prepared to undertake the work. Legal aid certificates for representation on disciplinary hearings are available in Ontario, although the process for receiving one is so cumbersome and bureaucratic that for all practical purposes they are nonexistent. The legal aid scheme does provide for a system of duty counsel at some federal institutions in the Kingston area, which, together with some representation by law students at the Correctional Law Project of the Faculty of Law at Queen's University, results in a greater degree of prisoner representation than exists anywhere in the country outside of Quebec. This patchwork arrangement has the invidious consequence that a federal prisoner, who can be imprisoned in any federal institution, can find himself facing a charge in Ontario or Quebec for which he can obtain legal representation, and then find himself the following month in an institution in Atlantic Canada, British Columbia, or Saskatchewan where, faced with exactly the same charge and facing the same possible punishment, he would effectively be deprived of that right. This serendipitous quality of prison justice, administered across the board under the same federal statute by the same federal department, certainly does not go unrecognized in the judgements prisoners make regarding the inconsistent application of the Rule of Law within Canadian prisons.

During the course of my study, the issue of the Legal Services Society of British Columbia's lawful obligations to fund counsel in serious disciplinary cases was relitigated. The case involved a prisoner at Matsqui, Art Winters, who in November 1993 was charged with assaulting another prisoner. He was placed in segregation and an involuntary transfer package to Kent Institution was prepared, based primarily upon the allegation of assault. When Mr. Winters first appeared in disciplinary court, he sought and was granted an adjournment to retain counsel. He had a lot at stake. There was not only the threat of transfer to higher security and the punishment of segregation if he were convicted of the offence. Mr. Winters was serving a sentence for first-degree murder; under the provisions of s. 745 of the *Criminal Code,* having served fifteen years, he would be eligible in 1998 for a judicial review at which a jury would determine whether his parole eligibility should be reduced from 25 years. One of the considerations juries are required to take into account in making this determination is the conduct of the prisoner during his incarceration. A conviction for an assault on a prisoner would be a serious blot on Mr. Winters' record. He consulted with counsel and was advised that, in light of the implications of conviction, it was important that he be represented by counsel at the hearing. However, the fee for such representation was beyond Mr. Winters' means. He approached Prisoners' Legal Services, who advised him that since legal aid did not cover disciplinary hearings they were unable to represent him. He then approached John Conroy, the lawyer who had argued the *Landry* case. Mr. Conroy determined that Mr. Winters' case was an appropriate test case to re-argue *Landry.* Mr. Winters was transferred from Matsqui to Kent, and in the process exchanged one segregation cell for another. When the *Winters* case came before Mr. Justice Fraser, he ruled that he was bound by the decision of the Court of Appeal in *Landry* (*Winters* v. *Legal Services Society,* [1995] B.C.J. No. 1001). The B.C. Court of Appeal dismissed Mr. Winters' appeal, seeing no reason to depart from its interpretation in *Landry* that prison disciplinary hearings were not covered by s. 3 of the *Legal Services Society Act* ([1997] B.C.J. No. 1280).

The *Winters* case was then appealed to the Supreme Court of Canada. In December 1998, John Conroy and I presented the oral argument before the Court as co-counsel. We argued that an interpretation of the *Legal Services Society Act* which enables and facilitates the legal representation of prisoners in disciplinary proceedings that could result in solitary confinement would contribute to the establishment of a correctional culture that encourages respect for the Rule of Law behind prison walls. We also sought to impress upon the Court the very real penal consequences that could flow from a disciplinary conviction. We urged the Court to adopt a remedial interpretation of the *Legal Services Society Act* that cast the protective umbrella of legal representation over those who faced a proceeding which can result in the most intrusive form of custody— solitary confinement—and which, in the words of the House of Commons Sub-Committee on the Penitentiary System in Canada, is the "most individually destructive, psychologically crippling and socially alienating that could conceivably exist within the borders of the country" (*Report to Parliament,* 1977 at 156).

The appeal was successful. The Supreme Court, in a judgement handed down on September 15, 1999, overturned the decision by the B.C. Court of Appeal and held that a prison disciplinary hearing that could result in the imposition of a term in solitary confinement was a "civil proceeding" within the definition of the *Legal Services Society Act.* Mr. Justice Cory cited a passage from my book *Prisoners of Isolation*—"Dostoevsky is a surer guide than Glanville Williams in understanding what is it that we do, in the name of the criminal law, when we send men to the solitary confinement cells"—and concluded that:

> It is clear that solitary confinement is not simply a different yet similar form of incarceration than that experienced by the general prison population. Its effects can be serious, debilitating and possibly permanent. They serve to both emphasize and support the conclusion that solitary confinement constitutes an additional and a severe restriction on a prisoner's liberty. (*Winters* v. *Legal Services Society and the Attorney General of British Columbia*, [1999] 3 S.C.R. 160 at para. 67)

While the court's judgement was unanimous that a prison disciplinary hearing which could result in the imposition of a term in solitary confinement was a civil proceeding within the meaning of the *Legal Services Society Act,* there was a division of opinion on whether that entitled a prisoner to representation by counsel in every case. Mr. Justice Cory held that it did; Mr. Justice Binnie, writing for the majority of the court, held that the obligation of the *Legal Services Society Act* was to ensure that "legal services are available"; that "legal services" was not synonymous with "legal representation"; and that the Society had the discretion to determine when legal services ought to rise to the level of legal representation by a lawyer. In making that decision, he wrote,

> the Society must consider all of the relevant circumstances of the application, including the nature of the charge, the procedure for its determination, the severity of the punishment of the applicant if convicted, and other potential indirect consequences such as . . . prejudice to a potential transfer to a lesser institution. (*Winters,* at para. 15)

The majority of the court provided some guidance in determining what legal services might mean in the context of prison disciplinary hearings:

> [They] would include a preliminary investigation of the facts giving rise to the disciplinary charges, and advice about the range of potential outcomes, and the chances of success. This is a function that could be performed by the Legal Services Society staff counsel, or even a non-lawyer staff person who is well versed in prison matters, provided that any advice given by that person is "under the supervision of a lawyer" (s. 9). It might be expected that in many cases the best advice would be to have a lawyer at the hearing. The prospect of

solitary confinement, if a plausible risk in the circumstances, would argue for such an outcome.

In some circumstances, however, the best advice might be that there is no useful role for a lawyer. The facts may not be in dispute. It may be apparent that solitary confinement, while theoretically available, is not a realistic possibility and that legal counsel at the hearing is unnecessary. The Society should not be required to provide more than a reasonable person of average means would provide for himself or herself. (*Winters,* at paras. 30–31)

As a direct consequence of the Supreme Court's judgement in *Winters,* the Legal Services Society allocated additional resources to Prisoners' Legal Services to enable them to hire an additional legal intake officer and a paralegal worker dedicated to providing advice and representation for prisoners at disciplinary hearings. A paralegal now provides the equivalent of duty counsel service for Kent and Matsqui Institutions and other institutions with heavy disciplinary dockets. Depending on the nature of the charge and the complexity of the case, representation is also provided in many cases by the paralegal, leaving a residual number of cases in which legal aid certificates are issued to members of the Bar. For institutions outside the geographical reach of Prisoners' Legal Services, for example, William Head Institution on Vancouver Island, representation is provided exclusively by members of the Bar.

## The Qualifications of an Independent Chairperson

Based upon my observations of approximately 500 cases at Matsqui and Kent, my judgement was that the three Independent Chairpersons who presided over disciplinary court conducted hearings fairly and in conformity with the law. However, the perception of many CSC staff and administrators that the Chairpersons demonstrated a bias in favour of prisoners was counterbalanced by an equally pervasive perception among prisoners that the Chairpersons preferred the evidence of staff. Although there could be considerable improvement in conveying the legitimacy of the disciplinary process to both staff and prisoners by implementing the reforms I have suggested—better communication of reasons for decisions, a properly trained institutional representative, and a more effective process for prisoner representation—the polarized atmosphere of the prison virtually ensures that the disciplinary process will be criticized from both ends of the pole. Indeed, Mr. Fox had commented to me at one point that if he heard criticisms from both staff and prisoners, it probably meant he was striking the right balance in his adjudication.

That having been said, some features of the existing disciplinary regime do serve to entrench a polarized view of the Independent Chairperson. Any practices that compromise the perceived independence of the Chairperson necessarily cast a long shadow over the legitimacy of the process. In my interviews with both prisoners and prisoners' advocates, the perception that some Independent Chairpersons were biased in favour of the institution was closely tied to the nature and continuity of the Chairpersons' relationship with that institution. Not surprisingly, prisoners feel that a Chairperson who has been assisted and, in effect, educated by institutional staff over a period of time might develop an approach which favours the institution. This would be the case particularly where an Independent Chairperson had a long tenure. For example, the same Independent Chairperson held office at William Head Institution on Vancouver Island from the early 1980s until his retirement in 1999, and his presence at the institution predated that of all but a few correctional staff.

There is a strong case to be made that an effective Independent Chairperson must understand the institutional context within which discipline takes place; developing a feel for the "pulse of the institution" is an important part of this. At Matsqui and Kent, Mr. Routley and Mr. Fox have had tenures of ten and fifteen years respectively, during which time each has developed a depth of experience but also taken pains to maintain a professional distance from institutional advisors and other correctional staff. Both amply demonstrate their independence in both substance and appearance. However, a vigorous grapevine maintained by both prisoners and staff questions the independence and competence of some Independent Chairpersons. It would be easy to dismiss the fruit of this vine as sour, reflecting perceptions which may not accord with actual experience. Yet while the Independent Chairperson occupies the pivotal position on the fulcrum of prison justice, neither the *CCRA* nor the *CCR Regulations* identify detailed criteria or qualifications for the position. The *Regulations* go no further than requiring the Commissioner to appoint "a person, other than a staff member or an offender, who has knowledge of the administrative decision-making process to be an Independent Chairperson to the purpose of conducting hearings of serious disciplinary offences" (s. 24(1)(a)). The problem is compounded by the low rate of remuneration authorized by the federal Treasury Board (until an increase to $350 per day in April 2001, the rate had remained at $300 for more than a decade), which means that in some parts of the country few candidates present themselves as being interested in the position. It is not altogether coincidental, therefore, that many Independent Chairpersons are drawn from the ranks of retired lawyers who accept the positions to "keep their hand in."

The absence of prescribed qualifications also explains the great distance separating the best from the worst Independent Chairpersons, in terms of the quality of their decision-making and their credibility with staff and prisoners. Although the Correctional Service has made some effort to provide training to Chairpersons, this responsibility is left largely in the hands of the Senior Independent Chairperson in each region, and there is significant regional variation in how seriously it is taken up. Mr. Routley, as Senior Independent Chairperson in the Pacific Region, has been particularly diligent in convening regular meetings with his colleagues to discuss issues of common concern, particularly relating to different legal interpretations and practices.

A consistently high standard in the work of the Independent Chairpersons depends on an articulation of the qualifications and qualities necessary for the position, an appropriate level of remuneration, and an active search for the best candidates. The understandable concern about a Chairperson losing independence through long association with a single institution could be addressed through the rotation of Chairpersons within a region, a practice the Senior Independent Chairperson in the Pacific Region has encouraged.

## Independent Adjudication: An Ideal or an Aberration?

Thus far, I have suggested that much of the dissatisfaction expressed by staff and prisoners about the disciplinary process can be traced to identifiable causes which can be addressed by making incremental rather than radical changes. Improving the staff's understanding of the process, making it more effective through better training of an institutional representative, ensuring greater legal representation of prisoners, and improving the competence and credibility of Independent Chairpersons through a set of prescribed qualifications and remuneration commensurate with the importance of the position should increase both staff and prisoner confidence in the legitimacy of the process.

There is, however, another quite different line of explanation for the dissatisfaction of prison administrators and staff. This line of explanation has the following elements. First, the decisions made by the Independent Chairperson are the only prison decisions affecting the rights and liberties of prisoners made by someone not a full-time employee of the csc. In all other significant areas, including administrative segregation, transfers, and visits, decisions are made by prison administrators. Although the evolution of administrative law, the advent of the *Charter*, the proclamation of the csc's Mission Statement, and the passage of the ccra have acknowledged and entrenched the duty to act fairly and the principles of fundamental justice, responsibility for the implementation of these principles, except in the area of disciplinary hearings, remains in the hands of prison administrators. Administrative practice in segregation and transfer decisions, areas over which they have exclusive control, is the standard prison administrators and staff use to arrive at the proper balance between maintaining security in the institution and being fair to prisoners. This practice, with its heavy reliance upon confidential information and informal decision-making, is in stark contrast to the process under which prison disciplinary hearings are held and the basis upon which adjudication of guilt or innocence is made by the Independent Chairperson. By the measure of current administrative practice in the areas of administrative segregation, transfers, and visits, the disciplinary process before the Independent Chairperson appears as aberrant. In this view, the features of that aberration are that the process is overly concerned with the rights of the prisoner—the presumption of innocence, the need for proof beyond reasonable doubt—and not sufficiently concerned with the rights of the staff who give evidence or the needs of the institution to maintain security and discipline.

In my 1974 study "Justice behind the Walls," one of the arguments I advanced for the introduction of Independent Chairpersons was that they could provide a role model for due process values in prison decision-making. In both that study and subsequent ones, I also argued that the case for independent decision-making was not limited to the formal disciplinary process but should extend to the other critical processes that affected the rights and liberties of prisoners. That extension has not happened. Although decisions in these other areas now take place within the legal and administrative framework of the duty to act fairly, they reflect a system in which the balance lies with the institutional interest of maintaining control and security. Fairness is a value subsidiary to operational reality.

This second line of explanation may not only better explain the dissatisfaction of prison administrators and staff with the formal disciplinary process, it may also explain why many prisoners express the opinion that the formal disciplinary process is still not fair. It could be argued that this belief stems from insufficient information about the process. Given my findings that the Independent Chairpersons at Kent and Matsqui do treat prisoners fairly and that findings of not guilty are a common feature of the system, providing better feedback to prisoners regarding the outcome of cases might seem a reasonable strategy to change their perceptions. However, the formal disciplinary process is but one area of prison decision-making, and in many cases decisions made by non-independent prison administrators regarding segregation and transfer may overshadow, even supersede, the formal disciplinary outcome. Consider the numerous cases I have described here in which prisoners awaiting a hearing on disciplinary offences were confined in administrative segregation for longer periods than those to which they could be sentenced if found guilty. In these cases, regardless of the outcome of the process, the administrative practice of segregation constituted the effective punishment. Consider also the cases in which not only were prisoners transferred to higher security on the basis of charges they were subsequently acquitted of, but those acquittals did not result in reversal of the transfers. It is therefore no surprise that prisoners view the disciplinary process as part of a seamless administrative web which they judge to be unfair.

In Sectors 4 and 5 of this book, where I focus on administrative segregation and the involuntary transfer process, I will return to the nature of the relationship between the "administrative" decisions and formal discipline and revisit the role of independent adjudication in bringing justice into the prison.

# SECTOR 4

## CHAPTER 1

# Administrative Segregation: The Litmus Test of Legitimacy

## Lessons from History

Many elements of the tension between rhetoric and reality in the contemporary prison can be found in the regime of administrative segregation. True to the rhetoric of corrections, the very term "administrative segregation" provides apparently benign semantic camouflage for the most intensive form of imprisonment. In *Prisoners of Isolation,* I charted the history of solitary confinement in Canada and described how its origins, like those of the penitentiary itself, lay not in the practice of torture and the abuse of state power but rather in a well-intentioned and reform-spirited reaction against such practices. John Howard, the pre-eminent prison reformer of his generation, was insistent in his blueprint for radical reform of eighteenth-century imprisonment that the legitimacy of punishment, in the eyes of both the public and the offender, was dependent upon its observance of the strictest standards of justice and morality. In the minds of early reformers, the abuses, cruelties, and corrupt administrative practices within the prison system were explained by the absence of rules and the lack of supervision by an outside authority; thus, their proposals for reform had two parts. The first was the imposition of an authority of rules to be applied to the keepers no less than the kept. The second was the determination to ensure that these rules were enforced through the superintendency of magistrates and by the democratic overview of the general public: "In place of the unwritten, customary, and corrupt division of power between criminals and custodians, the reformers proposed to subject both to the disciplines of a formal code enforced from the outside"

(Michael Ignatieff, *A Just Measure of Pain: The Penitentiary in the Industrial Revolution 1705–1850* [New York: Pantheon, 1978] at 77).

The authority of rules proposed by the eighteenth-century reformers had a dual purpose:

> They were an enumeration of the inmates' deprivations, but also a charter of their rights. They bound both sides of the institutional encounter in obedience to an impartial code enforced from outside. As such, they reconciled the interests of the state, the custodians, and the prisoners alike. (Ignatieff, *A Just Measure* at 78)

The regime of solitary confinement was the centrepiece of this new model of the prison; it was designed to be a punishment that was severe but humane, rational, and ultimately transformative. "In the silence of their cells, superintended by authority too systematic to be evaded, too rational to be resisted, prisoners would surrender to the lash of remorse" (Ignatieff, *A Just Measure* at 78). It was this theory that was embodied in Canada's first *Penitentiary Act* in 1834; it was this theory that Kingston Penitentiary was intended to translate into practice.

As I have described in Sector 1 of this book, the hope that the opening of Kingston Penitentiary would usher in a new era in the treatment of prisoners, with reformation and moral re-education replacing the spectacle of terror, was never realized. The means that Kingston's first warden chose to enforce discipline were characterized by the 1848 Brown Commission as "barbarous and inhumane." In its recommendations for the future management of Kingston Penitentiary, the Commission addressed the principle by which prison discipline was to be administered:

> All convicts should as far as possible be placed on a footing of perfect equality; each should know what he has to expect, and his rights and obligations should be strictly defined. If he breaks the prison rules, he should also have the quantum of punishment to which he becomes subject. He should not witness the spectacle of offences similar in enormity treated with different degrees of severity, unless in cases of frequent repetition. One of the most important lessons to be impressed on the convict's mind is the justice of his sentence, and the impartiality with which it is carried into execution. (cited in J. M. Beattie, *Attitudes towards Crime and Punishment in Upper Canada, 1830–1850: A Documentary Study* [Toronto: University of Toronto, Centre of Criminology, 1977] at 152)

The Brown Commission also addressed the principle of outside inspection. Although the *Penitentiary Act* of 1834 had established a local board of inspectors with general jurisdiction to superintend the administration of Kingston, the Commission found that this board had proved inadequate to the task of controlling the abuses and excesses of the warden. Having "pointed out how likely the unrestricted and continued exercise of arbitrary power is to degenerate into apathy or tyranny," the Commission recommended the appointment of national inspectors directly responsible to the government, with expanded authority to make rules and regulations and clearly defined duties to visit and inquire into the management of the penitentiary.

In *Prisoners of Isolation,* I commented on the parallels between the ideas of John Howard and the recommendations of the Brown Commission:

> What was to be sought in the carrying out of discipline within the prison walls, if it was to operate as a catalyst for moral transformation, was the re-establishment of the moral legitimacy of punishment. To Howard and the Brown Commission, this meant that the jailer, with his virtually unfettered discretion, had to be rendered accountable to the authority of rules and to outside supervision and that the punishment must meet the strictest standards of justice. To their European counterparts such as Decazes, commenting on French penal discipline, it meant that "the law must follow the convicted man into the prison where it has sent him." (Jackson, *Prisoners of Isolation* at 31)

In this and the following chapters, I will make the case that rendering the jailer accountable to a legally binding authority of rules and establishing an effective process of outside supervision are as yet unfulfilled preconditions to ensure that the practice of administrative segregation adheres to fundamental principles of justice.

## *McCann v. The Queen,* 1975—The "Cruel and Unusual Punishment" Case

At the core of *Prisoners of Isolation* were the experiences of a group of prisoners who, in 1974, had asked for my help in challenging the conditions of their solitary confinement in the notorious "Penthouse" of the B.C. Penitentiary; they had been detained there in some cases for years at a time. That challenge took the form of a Statement of Claim filed in the Federal Court of Canada in the name of Jack McCann and six other plaintiffs (filed June 4, 1974; No. T-2343-74). It asserted that the conditions of their confinement in "administrative segregation" constituted cruel and unusual treatment or punishment under section 2(b) of the *Canadian Bill of Rights* (R.S.C. 1960, c. 44), and that their solitary confinement, without notice of any charges laid against them and without a hearing before an impartial decision-maker, deprived them of their right to a fair hearing in accordance with the principles of fundamental justice, guaranteed to them under sections 1(a) and 2(e) of the *Bill of Rights*.

The conditions in the "Penthouse" were appalling:

> The cells measured 11 feet by 6½ feet and consisted of three solid concrete walls and a solid steel door with a 5-inch-square window which could only be opened from outside the cell. Inside the cell, there was no proper bed. The prisoners slept on a cement slab four inches off the floor; the slab was covered by a sheet of plywood upon which was laid a four-inch-thick foam pad. Prisoners were provided with blankets, sheets and a foam-rubber pillow. About 2 feet from the end of the sleeping platform against the back wall was a combination toilet and wash-basin. An institutional rule required that the prisoner sleep with his head away from the door and next to the toilet bowl to facilitate inspection of the prisoners by the guards. Failure to comply with this rule would result in guards throwing water on the bedding or kicking the cell door. There were no other furnishings in the cell. One of the expert witnesses described the physical space as "one step above a strip cell . . . a concrete vault in which people are buried."
>
> The cell was illuminated by a light that burned 24 hours a day. The 100-watt bulb was dimmed to 25 watts at night. The light was too bright to permit comfortable sleep and too dim to provide adequate illumination . . . Prisoners only had cold water in their cells. Twice a week they were given a cup of what was supposed to be hot water for shaving but which, they testified, was usually lukewarm. They were not permitted to have their own razors, and one razor was shared among all the prisoners on the tier . . .
>
> The prisoners were confined in their concrete vaults for 23½ hours a day. They were allowed out of their cells briefly to pick up their meals from the tray at the entrance to the tier and for exercise. That exercise was limited to walking up and down the 75-foot corridor in front of their cells. Exercise was taken under the continuous supervision of an armed guard who patrolled on the elevated catwalk. For the rest of the day prisoners were locked up in their cells.
>
> Prisoners spoke to visitors through a screen and conversations were monitored by the staff. Standard procedure governing the movement of prisoners from the unit to the visiting area decreed that they be handcuffed to a restraining belt around their waist and that leg-irons be placed on them. Upon returning from the visit, prisoners were subjected to skin-frisks, even though they may never have left

the sight of the escorting officer or had any physical contact with their visitors. (Jackson, *Prisoners of Isolation* at 48–49)

Harsh as they were, it was not just the physical conditions in the solitary confinement unit that constituted the principal basis for pain and suffering. The prisoner, upon climbing the stairs to the unit and entering the doors that isolated it from the rest of the prison, both literally and symbolically entered a different world. In the Penthouse, the worst things about prison—the humiliation and degradation, the frustration, the despair, the loneliness, and the deep sense of antagonism between prisoners and guards—were intensified. In my interviews with prisoners, and in their testimony before the court, they talked about how that antagonism often reached the point of gratuitous cruelty. Jack McCann testified that after a prisoner in solitary had slashed himself, an officer offered him (Mr. McCann) a razor blade so he, too, could "slash up." Evidence was given of mentally unstable prisoners being goaded by guards and beaten when they reacted. Even medical treatment became disguised punishment. In one incident, a prisoner who had refused oral medication from a hospital officer and would not allow himself to be injected was tear-gassed so that the medication could be administered. Tear-gassings were a ritualistic part of the regime, and even prisoners not primarily targetted suffered ill effects and received no subsequent change of clothing or bedding.

During my interviews in preparation for the *McCann* trial, I heard many stories about encounters between prisoners and guards that strained the limits of my belief. In subsequent years, and indeed during my research for this book, officers who had worked in the Penthouse during the seventies told me stories even more horrific. In *Prisoners of Isolation,* I portrayed this relationship between the keeper and the kept as follows:

> There is a perverse symbiotic relationship between guards and prisoners in [the Penthouse]. The guards, by perceiving the prisoners as the most dangerous and violent of men, can justify to themselves the intensity of the surveillance and the rigours of detention. Prisoners, by responding to that perception of dangerousness with acts of defiance, have at least one avenue of asserting their individuality and their autonomy, of making manifest their refusal to submit. The treadwheels of the 19th-century penitentiaries are no longer with us, but in [the Penthouse] we have created a psychological treadwheel put into motion and maintained by ever-increasing hostility and recrimination. (at 53–54)

There were two prisoners who did not give evidence at the *McCann* trial but whose experiences in the Penthouse nonetheless loomed large in the testimony before the court. Tommy McCaulley was one of these men. I had heard Mr. McCaulley screaming in his solitary confinement cell on many occasions. Prisoners believed he had been driven mad by his extended imprisonment in the Penthouse, and the guards viewed him as extremely violent and unpredictable. Mr. McCaulley was so out of touch with reality when I interviewed him that he could not be included as a plaintiff in the lawsuit. Jacques Bellemaire, the other prisoner, believed there was a machine in his cell that controlled his life. Although he set fire to his cell to rid himself of it, the machine did not leave, and a week after I last interviewed Mr. Bellemaire he hanged himself.

The terror of life in the solitary confinement unit of the B.C. Penitentiary was not limited to the machine imagined by Jacques Bellemaire. Dr. Stephen Fox, a psychologist and expert witness called by the prisoners in the *McCann* trial, explained to Mr. Justice Heald how Tommy McCaulley's insanity and Jacques Bellemaire's suicide were the living and dying proof to other prisoners of their own vulnerability. In his chilling words:

> When McCaulley becomes insane to your face, they are McCaulley, that is all there is to it. There is not one of them who will tell you anything different. Each one of them is part of McCaulley, and it was a part of them that had gone to that place where McCaulley is, exactly to that place where McCaulley is, where all rationality has left them and they have come back from that place only by some freak accident of their own prior upbringing. But there is not one of them that does not hear their own voices screaming when McCaulley screams. They are McCaulley's insanity and in them is McCaulley's insanity. When he becomes insane and moves towards death, like Bellemaire did, when they see insanity approaching self-extinction, they know that part of them is moving to that place and they have to live with their own insanity and it is in front of them . . . When the blood runs in front of their cells, it is their blood . . . when they see death approach, it is their death that approaches. (cited in Jackson, *Prisoners of Isolation* at 73–74)

Between 1970 and 1974, the seven plaintiffs in the *McCann* case had spent a total of eleven and a half years in solitary confinement. Jack McCann had spent 1,471 days in solitary; the longest continuous periods of that total were 754 and 342 days. Donald Oag was in solitary for 682 days, including one period of 573 days; Andy Bruce had been locked up for 793 days, including one period of 338 and another of 258 days. The prisoners maintained that the injustice of their confinement was not limited to its physical and psychological dimensions; it included the process by which they had been placed in solitary and through which they were—in some cases years later—released. At the time of the *McCann* case, and up until the enactment of the *Corrections and Conditional Release Act* in 1992, administrative dissociation was governed by the *Penitentiary Service Regulations.* (The pre-1992 term was "dissociation"; the CCRA refers to "segregation." The terms are synonymous and are used interchangeably here.) Section 2.30 of the *Penitentiary Service Regulations* provided:

(1) Where the institutional head is satisfied that
(a) for the maintenance of good order and discipline in the institution, or
(b) in the best interests of an inmate
it is necessary or desirable that the inmate should be kept from associating with other inmates, he may order the inmate to be dissociated accordingly, but the case of every inmate so dissociated shall be considered, not less than once each month, by the Classification Board for the purpose of recommending to the institutional head whether or not the inmate should be returned to association with other inmates.
(2) An inmate who has been dissociated is not considered under punishment unless he has been sentenced as such and he shall not be deprived of any of his privileges and amenities by reason thereof, except those privileges and amenities that
(a) can only be enjoyed in association with other inmates, or
(b) cannot reasonably be granted, having regard to the limitations of the dissociation area and the necessity for the effective operation thereof.

In *McCann,* prisoners gave evidence of being placed in dissociation without notice of the grounds and without a hearing at which they could challenge the case against them or make representations. They also testified that they had no knowledge of a monthly review of their cases. The evidence given by the B.C. Penitentiary's warden and its head of security regarding their interpretation of "the maintenance of good order and discipline" revealed no consistent standards for determining what constituted sufficient grounds for dissociation. Rather, it suggested that decisions to place prisoners on dissociation were made on the basis of rumours, hunches, and intangible feelings grounded on a prisoner's past reputation or his present attitude. Dr. Richard Korn, one of the plaintiffs' expert witnesses and himself the former warden of an American penitentiary, described the process of admission to and release from dissociation as "highly capricious, arbitrary and in its design and effect . . . mystifying, and to me [failing] to satisfy any human criterion of predictable process" (cited in Jackson, *Prisoners of Isolation* at 57). Dr. Korn compared this with the way a prisoner enters prison:

He enters the general prison society as a result of a hearing in a court of law. The charges are specific, he has an opportunity to present his own case, to cross-examine witnesses, all of the rights and amenities that are provided under the presumption of innocence . . . In general, if a prisoner has had a fair trial, he will accept the process of getting to prison. (cited in Jackson, *Prisoners of Isolation* at 56–57)

In recounting their experiences, all of the plaintiffs in *McCann* expressed their sense of the injustice and illegitimacy of entering administrative segregation. Andy Bruce described the differences between serving a sentence of 30 days' segregation for a disciplinary offence and being placed indefinitely in administrative segregation.

[Punitive dissociation]'s easier. It's a hell of a lot easier when you know when you're getting out, you've got a date in your mind and you know that's when you're going to be released and you're going to go to the population. When you're doing indefinite seg it just hangs over your head. You don't know what you're supposed to do to get out of there because there is nothing you can do. It's entirely up to them. They say it depends on your behaviour but there's nothing you can do. You can't do nothing except get worse, and when you do get worse, they say that's why you're up there. (cited in Jackson, *Prisoners of Isolation* at 62–63)

The B.C. Pen's head of security testified that he received a weekly report from the officer in charge of the Penthouse, which he forwarded to the Inmate Training Board. That board met weekly to review the report, and any comments made about a particular prisoner were entered in that prisoner's file to constitute what was termed at the trial "the running score." There was, however, no formal monthly review of each case. Jack McCann, for example, was confined in solitary from July 1970 until August 1972. For much of that time, his running score indicated that he was "quiet and co-operative." The July, August, September, October, November, December, and January reports of 1970–71 all used that terminology. However, Mr. McCann was not released, and his behaviour was even seen as having a dark underside; a January 1971 entry said he was "quiet and co-operative but his attitude might belie the mental activity which could take a devious route" (cited in Jackson, *Prisoners of Isolation* at 58).

Mr. Justice Heald, in his judgement in *McCann*, held that the confinement of the plaintiffs in the Penthouse constituted cruel and unusual punishment and was unlawful. However, he rejected the plaintiffs' claims that the placement of prisoners in administrative dissociation must be surrounded by a procedural framework, including personal hearings at which grounds for dissociation were presented and prisoners given an opportunity to make representations. Using the pre-*Martineau* legal framework, he held that the decision to place a prisoner in administrative dissociation was an "administrative" one not subject to judicial review, and that because a warden "must have the power to act decisively and expeditiously to quell disturbances and isolate the offenders," to require "due process before administrative dissociation would render the administration powerless and a chaotic situation would result" (*McCann* v. *The Queen*, [1976] 1 F.C. 570 at 612, cited in Jackson, *Prisoners of Isolation* at 124).

Within a week of Mr. Justice Heald's decision on December 30, 1975, prisoners were moved out of the Penthouse and placed in regular cells equipped with standard beds and built-in desks/bookcases. The warden said that the change was made "to live up to the spirit of the judgement" (*The* [*Vancouver*] *Province,* January 9, 1976). The press was invited in to see the new cells. However, in April 1976, after a hostage-taking incident by prisoners in segregation and in the face of guards' increasing hostility to the move (they demanded that the warden resign), prisoners were moved back to the Penthouse, the name of which had been changed to the Super-Maximum Unit.

> The only change that had been made to the unit was that the 5-inch-square window in the steel doors had been enlarged to 18 inches by 30 inches. Only two changes were made in the regime of the unit: the light in the cell was turned off from midnight until six a.m. and prisoners now exercised in the central control area instead of the corridor outside the cells. This move was viewed as constituting "fresh air" exercise since the roof of the central control area was, at its extreme ends, open to the outside. There were no other changes. An editorial in the *Vancouver Sun* entitled "The Window of Contempt" reflected the views of prisoners on the extent to which the penitentiary had responded to the spirit of Mr. Justice Heald's decision. (Jackson, *Prisoners of Isolation* at 141)

## The Study Group on Dissociation and the Report to Parliament

Several months after the *McCann* trial began, the Solicitor General established the Study Group on Dissociation, under the chairmanship of James Vantour, to review the use of both punitive and administrative dissociation. The Study Group presented its report a week before Mr. Justice Heald handed down his decision. I have explained in Sector 3 that the report of the Vantour Study Group endorsed my own recommendations that Independent Chairpersons be appointed to adjudicate serious disciplinary offences, albeit on an experimental basis. The Study Group recognized that prolonged segregation "enhances the inmate's antisocial attitude and, in general, constitutes a self-fulfilling prophecy" (*Report of the*

*Study Group on Dissociation* at 24). The Study Group also pointed to the Canadian Penitentiary Service's lack of compliance with existing law, regulations, and policy dealing with dissociation.

> The failure to pay strict attention to the [Commissioner's] Directives reflects the philosophy of the Canadian Penitentiary Service toward dissociated inmates . . . We agree with the claims of many inmates that those in dissociation are "forgotten" or "ignored". . . This means that [a prisoner] may be deprived of privileges to which he is entitled according to the *Penitentiary Service Regulations* . . . We encountered many situations in which regulations were ignored by staff in charge of dissociation facilities. (*Report of the Study Group on Dissociation* at 16–17)

The Study Group, in its proposals for reform of administrative segregation, recommended the establishment of a Segregation Review Board chaired by the Director (warden) of the institution. The Segregation Review Board would review a prisoner's case within five working days of the warden's decision to segregate, and at least once every two weeks thereafter. The Board would be required to develop a plan to reintegrate the prisoner into the population as soon as possible, to monitor that plan during subsequent reviews, to maintain written records on the substance of each review, and to forward such reports to the Regional Classification Board. The Study Group did not recommend changes to the broad criteria justifying segregation, nor did it address the issue of independent adjudicators for the Segregation Review Boards, despite recommending that disciplinary hearings be run by Independent Chairpersons.

Independent adjudication and a reformed disciplinary and administrative segregation process were the subjects of further recommendations by the House of Commons Sub-Committee on the Penitentiary System in Canada in its 1977 *Report to Parliament* (Ottawa: Minister of Supply and Services, 1977). The Sub-Committee endorsed both the concept of Independent Chairpersons for disciplinary hearings and the Study Group's recommendation that a Segregation Review Board be set up in each institution to review cases after five days and every two weeks thereafter. On the question of independent adjudication, the Sub-Committee had this to say:

> We have debated with ourselves whether such an internal review provides adequate protection for inmates, and in particular whether the chairman of the Review Board should be the same kind of independent person we recommend for Disciplinary Boards. Our present conclusion is that the proposal we have described, which is based upon the thorough study of the Vantour Committee, should not be

judged and found wanting until it has been tried. The adequacy of
the protections should be reconsidered after two years of experience.
(*Report to Parliament* at 92)

It was not until the *Report to Parliament* was filed that the Canadian Penitentiary
Service began implementing the Vantour Study Group's recommendations
regarding the appointment of Independent Chairpersons for disciplinary boards
and the establishment of Segregation Review Boards—a full two years after those
recommendations had first been made.

## Administrative Segregation in the 1980s

Despite the recommendations of the House of Commons Sub-Committee, the
Service did not conduct an internal evaluation of the new segregation review
process after two years. However, as part of my 1983 study of the disciplinary process at Matsqui and Kent Institutions, I reviewed a series of cases of prisoners
who had been placed in administrative segregation. In this way, I hoped to assess
whether the "new, reformed" process had been successful in ensuring that segregation decisions were made fairly and that prisoners were not subject to inhumane and degrading conditions. During this pre-1992 period, the power to place
a prisoner in administrative segregation continued to rest in the broadly worded
authority of the *Penitentiary Service Regulations,* although Commissioner's Directives now provided a much more detailed decision-making structure. Written
reasons had to be given within twenty-four hours of a prisoner's placement in
segregation and the placement confirmed by the warden on the following working day; a hearing before a Segregation Review Board consisting of an assistant
warden and two other staff members had to take place within three days of the
prisoner's segregation; a weekly review by the Board was required for the first two
months of segregation and a monthly review thereafter. In addition, monthly
reviews were required by Regional Headquarters for prisoners segregated for
more than sixty days and by National Headquarters for prisoners segregated
for more than ninety days. The prisoner was given the right to appear before the
Review Board at his initial review and at the subsequent monthly reviews. After
spending thirty days in segregation, he was, subject to his co-operation, to be
given a psychological assessment. It is within this procedural context that the
following two case studies are set.

## The Isabelle Case

Mr. Isabelle was placed in segregation at Kent Institution on July 26, 1983. He
was told only that he was being detained "pending a security investigation."
Three days later, he was charged with doing "any act with intent to escape" and

"damaging government property." He remained in segregation until August 22, when he appeared before the Independent Chairperson for a disciplinary hearing on these charges. The primary evidence relied upon by the institution was a partially completed plexiglas key, three sets of wire cutters, and a 3/8" drill bit— all discovered in a heating pipe in an area to which many prisoners had access— and the presence of a plexiglas shelf in Mr. Isabelle's cell, one corner of which had been cut out. The institution's claim was that the key had been cut from the shelf and that Mr. Isabelle was responsible for this. Mr. Isabelle said he had not cut the key and denied any knowledge of it or the other tools. He testified that he had found the shelf in a washroom with a piece already missing from it and had made no effort to hide this shelf in his cell. The Independent Chairperson acquitted Mr. Isabelle on both charges.

Mr. Isabelle was not released from the segregation unit, however. Staff expressed great displeasure with his acquittal, since they saw this prisoner, who had arrived at Kent Institution from the Special Handling Unit, as a serious escape risk. They had planned to use his conviction on the charge of intent to escape to support an application for his transfer back to the Special Handling Unit.

Mr. Isabelle's case was reviewed by the Segregation Review Board on September 2, twelve days after his acquittal. At the hearing, he asked why he had not been released to the population. He was informed that the institutional preventive security officer was still investigating the case and the plexiglas key and shelf had been sent to the RCMP crime lab for further analysis. The Board stated that until this RCMP analysis was received, Mr. Isabelle was to remain in segregation. He protested that it could take months for the RCMP to complete an analysis, given the low priority the case would have. And even if they confirmed that the key had been cut from the shelf, he argued, that did not show he was the person responsible for making the key. As he had told the Independent Chairperson, he had found the shelf in the washroom with the piece already missing, and the Chairperson, in acquitting him of the charge of damaging government property, had believed him.

Following each review, the Segregation Review Board forwarded its recommendation to the warden. In response to the Board's review on September 2, the warden made the following comments.

> As Mr. Isabelle was found not guilty, we would have to have some rather compelling reason to keep him in segregation. It is agreed to keep him in segregation pending the next review where above factors should be taken into consideration. (Segregation Review Board Hearing Minutes, Kent Institution, September 2, 1983)

The next review was conducted on September 9, and the written record of that meeting stated:

> The situation has now been reviewed by the Warden and it was
> decided that there was not sufficient justification to proceed
> with this matter. Accordingly Isabelle has been interviewed by
> the Head of the Living Unit and advised of the behavioural
> expectations the living unit staff have for him. He has agreed
> that he will abide by these expectations. The Segregation
> Review Board recommends that Isabelle be released from H
> Unit to the Induction Unit pending cell space in general pop-
> ulation. (Segregation Review Board Hearing Minutes, Kent
> Institution, September 9, 1983)

Accordingly, after almost seven weeks in segregation, and almost three weeks
after he had been acquitted of the charges, Mr. Isabelle was released from H unit.
Nearly a month later, on October 7, he was released from the Induction Unit,
where he had been double-bunked, and returned to a single cell in the general
population.

This case reveals how the same facts are viewed in a quite different manner by
an independent adjudicator and correctional administrators. The Independent
Chairperson concluded that Mr. Isabelle was not responsible for damaging government property and that there was no evidentiary basis connecting him to the
key or the other items secreted in the heating pipe. The Segregation Review
Board disbelieved the prisoner's story, resulting in a further three weeks of segregation after his acquittal on the charges. Had an independent adjudicator been
involved in the segregation review process, the institution's argument for continuing segregation would have been given short shrift.

Mr. Isabelle's return to the general population proved fleeting. At approximately 8:00 a.m. on October 13, two prisoners, Willy Blake and Stuart Stonechild, slipped through a window in the institutional schoolroom and, under
cover of heavy fog, made their way to the perimeter fences of Kent, where they
snipped their way through to the outside using wire cutters. They were recap-
tured later that day. Mr. Isabelle and two other French-Canadian prisoners
had been in the schoolroom at the time of the escape, although they had not
attempted to utilize the escape route.

One week later, on October 20, a pair of pliers went missing from the electrical shop. A massive search was conducted; every prisoner was strip-searched,
and all areas accessible to prisoners were checked. The pliers were not found. The
warden informed the Inmate Committee that until the pliers were found, all
programs would be put on hold.

Less than an hour after this meeting, five French-Canadian prisoners were
taken from the population and placed in segregation. Among the five were Mr.
Isabelle and the two other prisoners who had been in the schoolroom during the
escape the week before. None of the five worked in the electrical shop. The five

prisoners were told they were being placed in segregation for a review of their security classification. Subsequently, they were informed by staff that they were suspected of being involved in an escape plot.

On October 24, a petition signed by nearly every prisoner at Kent was submitted to the warden. It alleged that the warden was using the segregation process improperly to bring peer pressure on the prisoner population to yield up the pliers. They further alleged that the warden was responding in an unjust way to the criticism levelled at him by the community and police in the wake of the recent escape. Copies of the petition were sent to the Solicitor General, government Opposition critics, and the media. On October 25, the Segregation Review Board met, and following this review three of the five prisoners were released from segregation. The reasons for their release were similar and are reflected in the following excerpt from the minutes:

> [Prisoner D] was segregated because of his suspected involvement in an escape plot with four other inmates. Prisoner D was interviewed by the Board at his request. During this interview he stated that he was not involved in any escape plot and that he in fact had passed up the opportunity to escape when two other inmates had escaped on 13th October. He also emphasized that he was working toward transfer to lesser security and that he was not intending to escape with only four and a half years left in his sentence. The Board was of the unanimous opinion that there is a strong possibility that prisoner D was not involved in any escape plan at this time. It was recommended that he be given the benefit of the doubt and that he be released to the general population. (Segregation Review Board Hearing Minutes, Kent Institution, October 26, 1983)

Mr. Isabelle, at his review, also submitted that he was not involved in an escape plot and had proved this by not escaping with the two prisoners from the schoolroom. He pointed out that he was within five months of his parole eligibility date and hoped to receive a recommendation for transfer to lesser security. He was not about to do anything to jeopardize his chances before the Parole Board after serving almost five years of a 15-year sentence, he said. Yet despite the similarity of Mr. Isabelle's arguments to those of other prisoners, he was not released from segregation. The reasons are contained in the minutes of the Review Board:

> Isabelle was segregated because of suspicion that he and four other inmates were involved in an escape plot. Isabelle was recently released from segregation after charges linking him to possession of escape tools (wire cutters and a Folger Adams key blank) were dis-

missed by the Independent Chairperson at institutional court. Prior to his release, he was counselled by the head living unit officer as to the expectations that would be put on him by living unit staff. Despite this counsel, there are serious indications that Isabelle may have been involved in an escape plan. Due to the above circumstance, the members of the Segregation Review Board unanimously recommend that Isabelle be held in segregation until a transfer to another maximum security institution can be effected. Hopefully such a move will diffuse any plot that he is involved in at this time. (Segregation Review Board Hearing Minutes, Kent Institution, October 26, 1983)

Thus, the primary reason for keeping Mr. Isabelle in segregation was the staff's belief that he had been trying to escape earlier in the year, notwithstanding the dismissal of those charges in disciplinary court. Mr. Isabelle remained in segregation for another two weeks, until November 10. On that date the Segregation Review Board reconsidered his case, and the minutes reflect the results:

Isabelle was segregated because of suspicion that he was involved in an escape plot. However, despite past indications of this type of activity, there is no solid evidence to presently indicate his involvement in an escape plot. The Board recommends that the option of releasing Isabelle to the Induction Unit pending decision on transfer to another maximum security institution be considered by the Warden. It is proposed to have Isabelle remain in Induction until transferred. (Segregation Review Board Hearing Minutes, Kent Institution, November 8, 1983)

That proposal was accepted by the warden. Mr. Isabelle was transferred to Induction where, because of overcrowding, he was required to double-bunk.

Perhaps no better case could be found to illustrate the capriciousness of the administrative segregation process; suspicion is layered upon suspicion to yield "serious indications" that a prisoner is involved in an escape plot, and yet three weeks later the suspicion evaporates to reveal "no solid evidence" of any such involvement. However, the case does not end here. Mr. Isabelle requested that he be released from Induction back into the general population. Since the institution had conceded there was no case against him, he argued, there was no justification for keeping him there, particularly since he was double-bunked, was confined to the unit most of the day, and had no access to the work or hobby programs available to the rest of the population. His argument went unheeded.

Mr. Isabelle was joined in the Induction Unit in late December and early January by first one, then the other prisoner who had escaped from the schoolroom in October. Both had been placed in segregation at the time of their recapture and remained there until their conviction on criminal charges arising from the escape. As in the case of Mr. Isabelle, the warden had decided that the two escapees would be transferred to another maximum security institution. However, unlike Mr. Isabelle, both escapees were released from Induction into the general population prior to their transfers being effected.

When these two prisoners left the Induction Unit, Mr. Isabelle renewed his efforts to be allowed to return to the population. His argument at this point seemed overwhelming, and no doubt an independent adjudicator would have seen it that way. Here were two prisoners who had recently been convicted of criminal charges of escape. They were viewed by the institution as sufficiently serious threats to the good order of Kent to justify their transfer to other maximum security prisons. One of them had also served time in a Special Handling Unit. In light of these facts, how could the warden justify releasing them back into the general population but keeping Mr. Isabelle in the Induction Unit? How could he conceivably be more of an escape risk than two prisoners who had *actually* escaped?

I was mystified by the administration's continued refusal to release Mr. Isabelle to the population. Indeed, I found the inherent arbitrariness in the three cases so blatant that I asked the Warden if there was some factor I was missing which would explain the different treatment afforded Mr. Isabelle. His response was that his staff continued to express serious concerns about Mr. Isabelle and, in his view, Mr. Isabelle was a risk if left in the general population. The basis for that staff concern went back to preventive security sources, he said, and was ultimately a judgement call.

This is what Mr. Isabelle had to say about the warden's judgement call in a letter he sent to me shortly before he was transferred from Kent's Induction Unit to another maximum security penitentiary:

> All I ask is to be treated fairly, like everybody else here. Some guys actually do things here, like escape on the street, or stabbing or fighting, and they get back in the population. But me, I don't do anything and get here on suspicion over nothing. It is cruel and unusual punishment and it's got to end somewhere. (Letter from Marcel Isabelle to Michael Jackson, November 1, 1983)

## The Blake Case

The second example of the 1980s segregation process at Kent involves the two prisoners who escaped in October 1983, Stuart Stonechild and Willy Blake. They were apprehended without incident the same day and were returned to Kent, where they were immediately placed in segregation. They were formally charged under the *Criminal Code* with escape, and told at their first Segregation Review Board hearing that they would remain in segregation pending disposition of these charges. On December 7, 1983, both prisoners were convicted of escape. Two weeks later, on December 21, Stuart Stonechild was released from segregation into the Induction Unit to await his transfer to another maximum security institution. His co-accused, Willy Blake, was not released at that time. The Review Board minutes state that "whilst in segregation Stonechild has been generally co-operative with all staff"; in relation to Mr. Blake, however, "members of the Board felt that his attitude towards staff has been hostile and abrasive during his time in H Unit. Given this attitude plus his recent escape, it was felt by the Board that release to the general population would be inappropriate as he has not earned this privilege" (Segregation Review Board Hearing Minutes, Kent Institution, December 21, 1983).

Prior to his segregation, Mr. Blake had been involved with other Aboriginal prisoners at Kent in seeking recognition of the right to practise their distinctive spirituality. After the breakdown of initial negotiations with the administration, he and two other prisoners had gone on a hunger strike to obtain recognition of their right to perform the sacred pipe ceremony and to hold sweat lodges within prison walls. Their action brought national attention to the problem and precipitated more negotiation, as a result of which procedures were worked out which enabled these ceremonies to be introduced into Kent. The procedures also enabled Aboriginal prisoners to keep medicine bundles, which contain items used for prayer and often include sagebrush and sweetgrass, on their person and in their cells. When Mr. Stonechild and Mr. Blake escaped, they took their medicine bundles with them, and these were confiscated by RCMP officers upon the men's capture. An arresting officer asked Mr. Blake if the medicine bundle was a device to disguise human scent in case tracker dogs were used in the search. When Mr. Blake explained the spiritual significance of the medicine bundles, the RCMP returned them to the prisoners.

When the prisoners were placed in segregation at Kent, the medicine bundles were again taken from them. According to Mr. Blake, the staff desecrated the medicine bundles by opening them and dumping the contents on the floor. This he viewed as contrary to the negotiated procedures, which required that staff treat all spiritual items with the utmost respect. After several days in segregation, he asked for the return of his medicine bundle and was told by security staff that it was being retained as evidence at the request of the RCMP. Mr. Blake heard this with some disbelief, given that the bundle had been returned to him by the arresting RCMP. Through the intervention of Sasha Pawliuk, a lawyer with Prisoners' Legal Services, it was established that the RCMP had *not* requested that the bundles be retained as evidence. However, it was six weeks before the administration conceded that there had been a mistake.

During this time Mr. Blake continued to press for the return of his articles and also requested visits from two Aboriginal spiritual advisors who came into the institution to participate in the pipe ceremony and sweat lodges. He was interviewed each week by one of a number of assistant wardens who visited the segregation unit; each time he requested the return of his medicine bundle, he was told the assistant warden would inquire into the matter. The bundle was not returned to him, however, nor did his repeated requests to see the spiritual advisors lead to a meeting with them. On December 12, a member of the security staff informed Mr. Blake that he was returning to him those effects he was permitted to have in the segregation unit, and Mr. Blake was handed a brown paper bag that contained what was left of his medicines. In a letter of protest to the warden, Willy Blake stated, "They appear to have been put through a blender of some sort. The desecration was so complete that in the list compiled by your office my medicines were referred to as 'miscellaneous plant-like debris'" (undated). Mr. Blake protested that the handling of his effects showed disrespect for his religious rights. He also maintained that his "attitude," which staff cited as the reason for keeping him in segregation, was a justifiable response to the cavalier "attitude" demonstrated by staff towards his constitutional right to practise his religion.

Many issues in this case would have been addressed differently had there been an independent adjudicator chairing the Segregation Review Board. First was the institution's justification for keeping the two prisoners in segregation until the disposition of the escape charges. Certainly an initial period of segregation was justified, as the administration completed an investigation to see if any other prisoners had been involved. But beyond that there was no legal justification for keeping the two men there. Given that no violence was associated with the escape and that the prisoners had not resisted recapture, there was no question of their being transferred to a Special Handling Unit, and it was not seriously argued that if they were in the population they would try to escape again. They were kept in segregation because the "customary law" at a maximum security institution is that if you escape, you remain in segregation until your charges are dealt with. That customary law is not supported by the legislative framework for segregation, however. An independent adjudicator would have compelled the institution to demonstrate reasonable grounds for believing the two men would constitute a threat to the security of the institution if returned to the general population.

Independent adjudication would also have addressed the denial of Mr. Blake's medicine bundle and access to the elders. Had this been done in a timely fashion, Mr. Blake would not have had to engage in verbal protests, or at least those protests would have been placed in their proper context. Where prison officials are armed with the widest administrative discretion to segregate "for the good order and discipline of the institution," this kind of legitimate protest against the abrogation of constitutional rights is easily converted into a "negative attitude" towards authority, justifying continued segregation. Mr. Blake's hunger strike had brought significant media attention to the institution, and his escape had been extremely embarrassing to the administration. Keeping him in segregation, therefore, created significant dividends in terms of a "payback." Yet this concept, however understandable within the human dynamics of a maximum security prison, is not a justifiable or lawful basis for segregation.

## "My Home Is Hell"

In *Prisoners of Isolation,* I described how the solitary confinement unit at the British Columbia Penitentiary was a world unto itself, a place where the unimaginable became a reality, a place where the worst nightmares penetrated the light of day. In September 1983 (literally on the eve of the book's publication), prisoners and staff in H unit, the segregation unit at Kent Institution, lived through just such a nightmare.

I had been alerted to trouble in H unit during one of my visits to the institution. A number of prisoners had flooded their cells and were being extremely disruptive. I requested interviews with some of these prisoners to find out what lay behind the disturbances, but I was told this was impossible until after the disturbance was settled. Almost ten days passed before I was allowed into H unit. During that time, rumours flew that prisoners were being fire-hosed and denied exercise or contact with lawyers and that they were reciprocating by throwing excrement and urine at the guards.

One of the prisoners I interviewed was Bill "Shotgun" Frederick. Mr. Frederick had been placed in segregation in May on suspicion of being involved in an escape plot. Kent's recommendation that he be transferred to a Special Handling Unit was rejected in late August by the SHU National Review Committee. Nevertheless, on September 8, the Segregation Review Board had determined that he should remain in segregation pending his transfer to the general population of another maximum security institution.

I spent the better part of September 23 interviewing Mr. Frederick. He told me that problems in H unit had developed early in September because of inconsistency in the way segregation unit staff were applying the rules. At the time, one of the prisoners was employed as the unit cleaner, and that prisoner, in addition to leaving his cell to fulfil cleaning responsibilities during the day, was allowed out during the evening for minor cleaning jobs; it was also customary to allow the cleaner to serve coffee to other prisoners through the food slots. Early in September, on some shifts, staff had cut short this activity and ordered the cleaner back to his cell. There had been no official change in the rules; some officers simply were not prepared to allow the cleaner to fulfil his customary duties. This inconsistency led three prisoners to resign as unit cleaner in quick succession, leaving the unit without a cleaner. As Mr. Frederick explained, the response of Mr. Jones, the correctional supervisor in charge of H unit, set off a rapidly escalating chain of events:

> What happened then was that Jones threatened us. He said, "There *will* be a cleaner, and if there isn't a cleaner, you guys are getting stripped cells." Now, there was no justification for this, because when I was the unit representative, I had had a meeting with the warden, the deputy warden, and Jones, and the warden had made it very clear that the cleaner in the segregation unit was on a volunteer basis and no one could be forced to be the cleaner. On Monday Ron McKay resigned as the cleaner and on Tuesday morning Jones came down and asked certain people if they were willing to be cleaners. They told him to jam it. At that point he proceeded to take us all into the yard three at a time and the guards went into our cells and boxed up everything. Now that got us hot, because he took away our legal papers which is something he shouldn't be doing, specially when there were people in the hole who were going to trial on outside beefs and other guys, including myself, who had our complaints and grievance forms. They also took away our envelopes and stamps, and for some guys they took away all their pens and their address books. The idea was to hold us more or less without access to the outside. We were told we could not make phone calls even to lawyers. When we came back in our cells we find them empty. We got a mattress, blankets, and the clothes on our backs. We were locked in our cells all day Tuesday with no exercise, no showers. We discussed amongst ourselves what we were going to do and we decided to kick back, waiting to see what the warden would do to resolve the problem.
>
> We never heard anything from the warden on Tuesday, and everything was cool Tuesday night. All day Wednesday, we're kicking back waiting to see if anything is going to happen. Nothing happens on Wednesday, and so on Wednesday night some of us proceeded to flood our cells. It was strictly a protest about the way they were jerking us around over the cleaners and then retaliating against us by taking away our rights and privileges. When the guards came on shift in the morning, they were pretty upset because they had to clean the ranges up. At that time, there was only water on the range, because it was intended to be a peaceful demonstration. On Thursday, Jones decided to crack down and started taking away the rest of our rights and privileges. We were told there would be no more showers, no more yard, no more medical staff. Lawyers would not be allowed to interview us. We would not be able to send any mail out because all

our writing materials and address books were taken away. At this point things are getting uncomfortable, but it was not the discomfort that was the problem. What Jones was doing was in direct contravention of the *Penitentiary Service Regulations,* and that is what was getting guys choked up. The *Regulations* say that we are supposed to get showers on a periodic basis, the *Regulations* say that we are supposed to get yard at least one hour per day. The only way they can be suspended is if there is an emergency situation. But there was no emergency situation. All the cons are locked in cages and it was just a demonstration.

It was at this point that things started to go sideways. The first thing that happened was that the guards decided to clean up the ranges using the firehoses. So they came down the range with the firehose and there's cracks at the side of the cell doors. They put the firehose in there and it's got enough pressure that it ricochets of the wall—it just covers your whole house. So now we're getting extremely upset because we are sitting in our cells soaking wet and the thermostats aren't working and because it was raining that week it was pretty cold. In the case of some of the guys who they singled out as troublemakers, the guards opened up their food slots and fired the hose into the cell. They did this with one of the guys near to me. They fired that hose for a good sixty seconds, putting it on his face, and when he covered his face they aimed for his testicles and they literally drove him into the corner. They did that to a couple of guys, and at that point it became a straight hate score. They had stripped our cells and so the only weapons that we had was excrement and urine, I mean our toilets were plugged up anyway and we did not want to keep our body wastes in our cell, and so we are firing it out the door onto the range. That takes some difficulty, given that the doors are solid and the food slots are closed. That only leaves the gap between the door and the floor. Because our toilets are blocked up and they have turned the water off, you can't wash your hands afterwards, so this whole thing is a very heavy trip. To think that you are reduced to that as the only way to get back at the guards for what you believe to be their illegal behaviour keeps you totally choked.

Over the weekend things quieted down a bit because the keeper who was on duty was pretty reasonable, and while they used the firehoses to clean the ranges, he made sure that nobody put the hose in the cracks of the door or hosed us down. So because we weren't being attacked, things were pretty cool over that weekend. When Monday comes around and Jones comes down and starts in again with his ultimatums about us having to clean our cells or we're not going to get anything, the whole thing starts up again. On Tuesday, there is another incident with the guards firing the hose through the cracks and getting everybody going. That was when one of the guys spat on an officer. The guard opened up the food slot and tried to fire the hose into the cell, but the prisoner took his mattress and held it up against the slot to prevent this from happening. So the guard cracks open the cell and then the fight is on. Four guards came down the range and there is a big struggle and we could see through the crack in the door that they have got this prisoner on the ground, he's covered in excrement and they're standing over him with their shields and black sticks and this is really getting us choked to see one of us in that degraded state. So we started shouting and screaming and threatening the guards. They charged a number of us for threatening to assault, but the way we see it, it's the guards who are the ones who should be charged, not with threatening but with actually assaulting the prisoners. (Interview with Bill Frederick, Kent Institution, September 23, 1983)

Ten years before Mr. Frederick's experiences in H unit, Jack McCann, while confined in the Penthouse at the B.C. Penitentiary, had written a poem entitled "My Home Is Hell." He read it in open court to help Mr. Justice Heald understand the impact of months and years in segregation. The first stanza of the poem reads:

My home is hell in one small cell
That no man wants to own
For here I spend my life condemned
A man the world disowns.
(cited in Jackson, *Prisoners in Isolation* at 69)

Bill Frederick did not read me any poems about his life in solitary confinement. However, during our interview, he expressed the profound fear arising out of his experiences in segregation. At the age of nineteen he had been sentenced to life with 25 years before parole, following his plea of guilty to the charge of first-degree murder of a police officer. At the time of our interview, he was twenty-six years old. He insisted he had never intended to kill the officer and had never seen himself as a person capable of killing other human beings. However, his greatest fear was that if he was subjected long enough to the kinds of degradation he had just gone through in H unit, he would become the callous killer people believed him to be. When he looked at himself in the mirror, he did not see the eyes of a murderer. But he feared one day the eyes staring back at him would signal that fatal transformation: fatal because the compassion he believed he still had would be gone, and fatal because there would be nothing more left for him to lose.

"Freedom's just another word for nothing left to lose," Janis Joplin sang in the 1960s. When a maximum security prisoner has been reduced to this state, the "freedom" he experiences is the lack of caring for anybody, including himself, and with that comes the terrifying capacity for unleashing a whirlwind of violence against those he sees as his oppressors. As I spoke with Bill Frederick in September 1983, he could hear early warning signs of these whirlwinds, and he feared that without a speedy resolution to the crisis in H unit, Kent would experience a rock 'n' roll of violence which would shake it to its foundations.

## Administrative Segregation on the Eve of the CCRA

The Federal Court in the *McCann* case, applying the pre-*Martineau* judicial/administrative distinction, had ruled that the decision to place a prisoner in administrative segregation was by its nature administrative and not judicial, and therefore not subject to the rules of natural justice. A decade later, in *Cardinal and Oswald* v. *Director of Kent Institution,* the Supreme Court of Canada extended the procedural duty to act fairly to decisions concerning administrative segregation, stating:

> In *Martineau (No. 2)* the Court held that the duty of procedural fairness had been held to apply in principle to disciplinary proceedings within a penitentiary. Although administrative segregation is distinguished from punitive or disciplinary segregation under s. 40 of the *Penitentiary Service Regulations,* its effect on the prisoner in either case is the same and gives rise to the duty to act fairly. ([1985] 2 S.C.R. 643 at 653–54)

Also of great significance, the Supreme Court in *Cardinal and Oswald* ruled that the remedy of *habeas corpus* was available to determine the validity of confinement of a prisoner in administrative segregation and, if such confinement were found to be unlawful, to order the prisoner's release into the general population of the penitentiary.

The Commissioner's Directives dealing with administrative segregation were revised and streamlined in 1987. Segregation was authorized pursuant to s. 40(1) of the *Penitentiary Service Regulations* when no other reasonable alternative existed and:

(a) there are grounds to believe that the inmate has committed, attempted to commit, or plans to commit acts that represent a threat to the security of the institution or the safety of individuals;

(b) the presence of an inmate in normal association would interfere with the investigation of a criminal or serious disciplinary offence;

(c) there is reason to believe that an inmate's presence in normal association represents a risk to the good order of the institution; or

(d) there is concern for the inmate's safety. (C.D. 590)

The new directive seemed to identify criteria for segregation with greater specificity than the generic "good order and discipline" set out in the *Regulations*. However, there was only the *appearance* of change. Most significantly, clause (c) replicated the "good order of the institution" rationale. Granting prison officials this broad-based power made it unnecessary for them to give much consideration to the more focussed criteria of clauses (a) and (b). Predictably, the new directive brought about no substantive change in the resort to the power to segregate prisoners.

## The Model Segregation Code

My purpose in writing *Prisoners of Isolation* was not only to expose the serious injustices and abuses of power taking place in segregation units in Canadian penitentiaries but also to bring about fundamental changes in the law to ensure that these injustices would no longer be tolerated. My critique of existing law and practice focussed on three interrelated areas: the criteria justifying segregation, the process through which prisoners were segregated and their segregation reviewed, and the conditions under which prisoners were held in segregation. To encourage the creation of a principled and fair process through which segregation decisions were made and a system of checks and balances to protect against the abuse of the involuntary segregation power, I drafted a "Model Segregation Code" (Jackson, *Prisoners of Isolation*, Appendix A).

The first part of this code addresses the criteria which, in a principled system of corrections, would justify segregation. At the time, there were no legally binding criteria for segregation beyond "the maintenance of good order and discipline" or "the best interests of an inmate":

The failure of the 1975 Vantour *Study Group Report on Dissociation* to bring about any change in an arbitrary process is not in the least surprising in light of the *Report*'s refusal to require greater specificity in the criteria for administrative segregation. Without such criteria a review process, however elaborate, will fail to render an unprincipled

decision any more principled or fair. So long as the review is of a
decision that can be made without reference to principled criteria
and without any factual underpinning, the process will remain ille-
gitimate in the minds of those on whom it is imposed. (Jackson,
*Prisoners of Isolation* at 207)

The Model Code would justify segregation on several bases. First, it would
authorize segregation to facilitate an investigation of allegations that the prisoner
is implicated, on reasonable and probable grounds, in specified serious criminal
or disciplinary offences, where there is a substantial likelihood that either the
offence will be continued or the prisoner will intimidate potential witnesses to
the offence. The code thus recognizes the legitimate institutional interest in em-
powering prison administrators to segregate prisoners pending an investigation
under certain circumstances. However, because this is an exceptional power not
granted to law enforcement authorities outside of prison, and because segregation pending investigation has been abused within the penitentiary system, the
Model Code places time constraints on this basis for segregation, coupled with
an obligation on the investigating authority to exercise all due diligence in completing the investigation. Thus, segregation for investigative purposes is to be
limited to two weeks' duration, subject to an extension upon demonstration by
the authorities to an independent adjudicator that they have exercised such due
diligence and that the further time is required to complete the investigation.
Upon such demonstration, there is a one-month limit on the basis that, given
the relatively focussed nature of investigations into offences committed in prisons and the accessibility of people to be interviewed, a month is a reasonable
length of time for the completion of the investigation and the laying of charges.

The Model Code next deals with the situation in which charges, of either a
criminal or a disciplinary nature, have been laid against a prisoner. Outside of a
prison context, the detention of a person charged with an offence pending trial
is specifically dealt with in the *Criminal Code*. The Model Segregation Code
seeks to tailor the justifications for pre-trial detention in the larger criminal justice system to the special circumstances of prison life. Thus, pre-trial segregation
is permitted under the Model Code in the case of charges involving actual or
threatened violence, wilful destruction of property, or disobedience to orders,
where there is a substantial likelihood that the offence will be continued or
repeated.

The Model Code contemplates a further basis for segregation in a situation
where investigations have been completed but no formal disciplinary or criminal
charges have been laid. This is intended to deal with cases in which the primary
evidence against the suspected prisoner comes from prisoner informants whose
safety will be jeopardized if they are required to give evidence in a formal hearing. This exceptional power to restrict a prisoner's institutional liberty in the

absence of any charge is unknown to our criminal justice system outside of prison walls; its justification in a prison context must therefore be predicated upon a compelling correctional necessity. The Model Code proceeds on the assumption that such a compelling necessity can be made out in circumstances where the institution has credible information that a prisoner has committed, attempted to commit, or plans to commit acts which represent a serious and immediate threat to the physical security of the institution or the personal safety of the staff or prisoners. The code would seek to prevent the abuse of this exceptional power by circumscribing it with the requirement that the threat be serious and immediate, that it be established beyond a reasonable doubt, and that it be so established to the satisfaction of an independent adjudicator.

The Model Segregation Code also contains a segregation review process designed to ensure a fair and independent application and review of the criteria in individual cases. It proposes a process which would permit the warden to order segregation for up to seventy-two hours without a hearing providing that written reasons for the order are given to the prisoner within twenty-four hours. By the end of the seventy-two-hour period, a full hearing must be held, at which time the institution's case would be presented to an independent adjudicator in the presence of the prisoner unless there is a substantiated claim of the need to maintain confidentiality of particular evidence, in which case the adjudicator would summarize that evidence for the prisoner. The prisoner would have the right to cross-examine witnesses, save those to whom confidentiality was extended, and to present evidence on his own behalf, including the calling of witnesses. The prisoner would have the right to be represented by counsel at the hearing. The adjudicator would be required to provide detailed written reasons for the decision. If continued segregation was authorized, further reviews would be required every week, subject to the same procedural requirements. At these reviews an onus would be placed on the institution to develop a plan to reintegrate the prisoner into the population, and the adjudicator would monitor that plan at any subsequent reviews. Except under very limited circumstances, segregation would be terminated after a ninety-day period.

The third part of the Model Code addresses the conditions of segregation, particularly the fact that even though the *Penitentiary Service Regulations* provided that a segregated prisoner should not be deprived of any privileges or amenities, in most segregation units very few privileges and amenities were provided. This deprivation was based on an enormous qualification in the *Regulations*: "except [those privileges and amenities] that cannot reasonably be granted having regard to the limitations of the dissociation area and the necessity for the effective operation thereof" (s. 2.40(2)). The depressing reality in 1975 at the British Columbia Penitentiary, and at Kent Institution ten years later, was that this qualification was used to justify discriminatory and debilitating treatment of segregated prisoners.

The Model Segregation Code attempts to deal with this problem by setting out in affirmative terms the rights and privileges to which segregated prisoners are entitled and the specific bases upon which restrictions of these rights can be authorized. Where a prisoner is deprived of a right or privilege to which he is normally entitled, that deprivation must be reviewed at a segregation review hearing by an independent adjudicator and can only be continued with that adjudicator's written authorization. Similarly, the adjudicator is empowered to make findings regarding alleged violations of the Model Code in relation to the rights and privileges of segregated prisoners and may issue written directions to the warden to remedy those violations. In the event that there is non-compliance with these directions, the adjudicator is required to prepare a report detailing the nature and extent of the violations, the directions issued, and the circumstances of non-compliance; a copy of that report is to be provided to the warden and the prisoner and also forwarded to the Solicitor General.

The Model Segregation Code also requires that when a prisoner has been in segregation for more than thirty days, the adjudicator shall hear the evidence of two psychiatrists or psychologists on the effects of such continued segregation on the prisoner. One of these psychiatrists or psychologists is to be nominated by the warden and the other by the prisoner, although provision is made for a joint nomination. Where the adjudicator determines, based upon the expert evidence or other evidence, that continued segregation will cause the prisoner substantial psychological or physical harm, the adjudicator shall order the prisoner released into the general population.

It should be apparent that the role of the independent adjudicator is the linchpin in the Model Segregation Code. That role exists to ensure that there is a factual basis to justify segregation measured against specific criteria; to assess the reliability of confidential information which cannot be disclosed to the prisoner; to ensure that the prisoner receives a fair hearing and is able to present an answer and defence to any allegations made against him; and to ensure compliance with the time constraints placed upon segregation and with the law regarding the conditions of segregation.

Independent adjudication in the Model Segregation Code has four intersecting justifications. First, the issues surrounding involuntary segregation are such that the interests of prisoners and correctional administrators are in conflict and facts and allegations are often in dispute; fairness requires an independent and unbiased decision-maker. Second, the recommendations of the Study Group on Dissociation failed to bring about real change, and there is a continuing issue of non-compliance with the law when segregation decisions are left with correctional administrators. Third, the potential for abuse and the potentially debilitating effects of long-term segregation require that limits be placed upon segregation in the form of specific criteria for placement, review, and the length of time for which segregation can be maintained; effective application and enforcement of these limits requires an independent adjudicator. Fourth, there is a need for a process to ensure that the rights and privileges of prisoners in segregation are respected, and this will be better achieved through an independent adjudicator.

## The CCRA—Old Wine in New Bottles?

Independent adjudication of segregation decisions was not incorporated into the 1992 *Corrections and Conditional Release Act*. However, many pre-1992 features of the administrative segregation process were elevated from policy and procedures set out in Commissioner's Directives to legally binding provisions in the CCRA or the *Corrections and Conditional Release Regulations* (although some important provisions are still relegated to the Directives). A full understanding of the current legal and administrative framework within which the case studies in the following chapters are set necessitates reading together the provisions contained in the CCRA, the CCR *Regulations,* and the Commissioner's Directives. (These can be found in the Internet edition of this book.)

A comparison between the current legislative and administrative framework and the regime in place when I began my inquiry into prison justice in 1972 uncovers significant changes. The current framework sets out detailed, structured review and accountability mechanisms involving the Segregation Review Board, the warden, and Regional Headquarters. There are requirements for hearings at which a prisoner has the right to make representations; to make that right effective, the prisoner must be given three days' advance notice, in writing, of the hearing and the information that the Board will be considering at the hearing. There is a further requirement that a plan be developed to resolve the situation that led to the segregation and, in cases of extended segregation, that a plan be developed within sixty days which addresses in detail the schedule of activities regarding a prisoner's case management services and his access to spiritual support, recreation, psychological counselling, administrative education, and health care services.

If, as I have maintained, a critical part of preventing the abuse of segregation power is to circumscribe that power with legally binding rules, it would seem that the CCRA and the CCR *Regulations* provide that authority. Senior officials at National Headquarters, while acknowledging that the new provisions did not go as far as my Model Segregation Code, suggested shortly after the enactment of the legislation that I should take satisfaction from the fact that many features in the CCRA reflected ideas and proposals I have advocated over the years. It is important, therefore, to understand the principal differences between the current legislative framework and the Model Segregation Code.

The first difference is that the criteria for segregation in the CCRA are much more broadly based than those set out in the Model Code. For example, the power to segregate pending an investigation of a criminal charge or a serious disciplinary offence is not limited to cases where the charge involves actual or threatened violence, attempted escape, or offences where there is a substantial likelihood of a repetition or a continuation of the offence; neither are there any specific time limits on the duration of this form of segregation to ensure that the investigations are conducted in a timely manner.

The omnibus ground for segregation contained in the *CCRA,* s. 31(3)(a)—"that (i) the inmate has acted, has attempted to act or intends to act in a manner that jeopardizes the security of the penitentiary or the safety of any person, and (ii) the continued presence of the inmate in the general inmate population will jeopardize the security of the penitentiary or the safety of any person"—while loosely based upon a provision in the Model Code, significantly weakens the original language. The burden of proof has been reduced from "beyond a reasonable doubt" to "reasonable grounds to believe"; the need for proof of the immediacy of the jeopardy or threat is omitted, and that threat or jeopardy can be to the "security" of the institution rather than to the more narrowly drafted "physical security" of the institution in the Model Code, a term designed to refer to escape risks. One of my grave concerns with the broad sweep of s. 31(3)(a) was that it would become the general ground for segregation, providing little improvement over the "good order and security of the institution" contained in the old *Penitentiary Service Regulations.*

The second significant difference between the *CCRA* provisions and the Model Code is that under the *CCRA,* segregation decisions continue to be made and reviewed by correctional administrators with no element of independent decision-making. The third difference is that neither the *CCRA* nor the *CCR Regulations* detail the specific rights and privileges of segregated prisoners; the legislation continues the approach of the old *Penitentiary Service Regulations,* which declare that prisoners in segregation have the same rights, privileges, and conditions of confinement as the general population, except those that cannot reasonably be given owing to limitations specific to the administrative segregation area or security requirements. This is identical to the pre-1992 legal regime which supported the continuation of inhumane and debilitating conditions in segregation units. Although the Commissioner's Directives do set out some affirmative entitlements of prisoners to specific services, they are not as extensive as those set out in the Model Segregation Code. Furthermore, because there is no role for independent adjudication, there are no mechanisms built into the legal and administrative structure of the segregation process to ensure respect for and compliance with those entitlements, as exist in the Model Segregation Code. Rather, prisoners must rely on the internal grievance process and the general avenues for external review provided by the Correctional Investigator or the courts. The final difference between the *CCRA* provisions and the Model Segregation Code is that the *CCRA* places no limitation on how long a prisoner can be confined in administrative segregation. As outlined, the Model Segregation Code would, except under exceptional circumstances, limit this to a period of ninety days.

When I began my work at Matsqui and Kent in 1993, my agenda was to assess the reality of change in the use of segregation and in the conditions under which prisoners in segregation were confined. Had the new regime resulted in a principled and fair process? If not, did the fault lie with a failure to respect and implement the law or with deficiencies in the law itself?

Before rendering my judgement on the basis of my latest inquiries, I should highlight a distinction within the population of segregated prisoners which assumes a larger significance than is apparent in the current legislation. Under both the old *Penitentiary Service Regulations* and the *CCRA,* the power to segregate a prisoner is founded on two broad, alternative bases: one is the risk the prisoner represents to the safety of other persons or to the security of the institution, and the other is the risk to the prisoner himself from other prisoners if he remains in the general population. Although there are cases in which prisoners placed in segregation for their own protection argue there is no basis for this fear, most prisoners segregated on this ground acknowledge that the fear is well-founded, and in many cases the prisoners themselves have requested that they be removed from the general population or have precipitated an incident in which such removal is the inevitable result. Thus, within the population of segregated prisoners, there has arisen a distinction between "involuntary" and "voluntary" cases.

As I have described in the Introduction to this book, one of the major changes in the Canadian prison system in the twenty-five years since I began my studies is the large increase in the number of prisoners designated as "protective custody" prisoners. The response of the Correctional Service of Canada to this increase has been to designate specific institutions as protective custody facilities. In a few institutions, one of which is Kent, the prison itself has been split into two populations—general population and protective custody. However, even within a designated protective custody institution or the protective custody side of a larger institution, prisoners run into problems, often but not always of their own making, which pose a threat to their safety. These situations frequently result in a request from the prisoner to go into segregation, either until the problem is sufficiently resolved that a return to the population is safe or until a transfer to some other institution can be arranged. In a general population prison such as Matsqui, where prisoners encounter situations in which their lives or safety are endangered, often through the intersecting and conflicting lines of prison commerce, politics, and personalities, prisoners may find themselves with no choice but to request placement in segregation. From there, since protective custody prisoners are unwelcome in general population prisons, they are left with no choice but to move to an institution designated for protective custody prisoners, either within or outside the region.

In *Prisoners of Isolation,* my critical focus was on the cases of prisoners who were segregated involuntarily. In this book I have broadened my focus to cover both involuntary and voluntary segregations, not only to identify the common issues affecting them but also in recognition that the differences between the two groups pose special, often intractable problems for prisoners and prison administrators.

# Administrative Segregation at Matsqui and Kent, 1993–96: The Persistence of Customary Law

In many societies, customary law transmitted through an oral tradition provides the basis upon which social, economic, and political relationships are ordered and maintained. Efforts to change that basis through the introduction of written legal codes often meet with resistance and result in the development of parallel legal orders with an uneasy and distant relationship. "Uneasy and distant" is also an apt characterization of the relationship between the formal legal and administrative framework of administrative segregation under the CCRA and prison customary law and practice. From a reading of the formal statutory framework, there is the clear expectation of a process which has a uniform and consistent structure, with prison administrators making decisions by applying the same legislative criteria from institution to institution, region to region. Yet this legitimate expectation must compete with the reality that each prison is a distinct society with a unique character, rhythm, and way of ordering relationships between the keepers and the kept. For this reason, customary law and practice play a central part in each institution, particularly in those areas where the formal legal regime accords correctional administrators the greatest discretion. It is precisely *because* the formal legal criteria for administrative segregation are so broad that customary law and practice are the most significant force in determining why, when, and how prisoners are placed in segregation.

## Segregation Review at Matsqui: Non-compliance with the Law

Although the CCRA requires that the Segregation Review Board conduct a review of a segregated prisoner after five days and every thirty days thereafter, the practice at Matsqui Institution in 1993 was to conduct the five-day review and then review every case on a weekly basis. Prisoners were advised that they could attend these weekly reviews, and in this way administrative practice went beyond the legislative framework. However, in other significant ways the review process failed to meet the requirements of that framework. In Sector 2, Chapter 3, "Operation Big Scoop," I observed how during several meetings of the Matsqui Segregation Review Board conducted in August 1993 the Board failed to discharge its legislative mandate of reviewing cases for the purpose of making recommendations to the warden; segregation decisions were instead made directly by the warden as a matter of institutional policy. The prime example of this was the warden's decision that prisoners involved in brew parties be kept in segregation until their first court appearance notwithstanding that they had regained sobriety, they had not been disruptive in segregation, and their return to general population posed no risk to safety or security.

A second area of non-compliance with the law at Matsqui was that discussion and review of a prisoner's case took place without the participation of the prisoner; when prisoners who had requested that they be allowed to attend their review were seen, it was a postscript to the review which never changed the text of the decision. This administrative practice was seen to be in compliance with the law because s. 21(3)(b) of the *CCR Regulations* required only that the prisoner "is given an opportunity to be present and to make representations at the hearing." At Matsqui, the prisoner was present for at least part of the hearing and was allowed to make representations. However, the underlying purpose of the right to personal appearance at a hearing is to know the full extent of the factors that are being considered by the Review Board and to make representation that would influence the ultimate decision. Personal presence at the end of a hearing where a decision has already been made completely defeats the purpose of the legal requirement.

Section 21(2)(a) of the *CCR Regulations* also requires that the prisoner "is given, at least three working days before the hearing, notice in writing of the hearing and the information that the Board will be considering at the hearing." This requirement is integrally related to the prisoner's opportunity to be personally present at the hearing and to make representations; obviously, if a prisoner does not know what the Board will be considering at the review, it is impossible to prepare adequately for the hearing. In none of the cases I observed at Matsqui was the prisoner given anything in writing prior to the five-day review other than the segregation notice required to be served within twenty-four hours of the initial segregation. This notice was extremely brief, typically consisting of one or two sentences. For example, the segregation notice given to Mr. Wright on August 23, 1993, stated:

> You are being placed in segregation and will remain there pending an
> investigation into your behaviour in the living unit. Further, your
> case management team will be reviewing your program involvement
> and assess your progress in same. (Segregation Notice, Matsqui Insti-
> tution, August 23, 1993)

In several cases, prisoners appeared at their five-day reviews without having
received even the initial segregation notice. The requirement of three days' written notice detailing the information to be considered by the Segregation Review
Board was not met at any subsequent reviews. Notwithstanding the specific provisions in the CCR *Regulations,* the Matsqui Segregation Review Board continued
to operate according to the customary law of the prison, in which information
was shared with a prisoner only at the hearing itself. However, as explained, its
delivery served no useful purpose because it was received too late to affect the
shape and content of the prisoner's representations so as to influence the Board's
decision.

Finally, segregation reviews at Matsqui were conducted without regard for the
critical path of legal inquiry charted by the CCRA to justify segregation of a prisoner. There was no attempt to measure the specific activities or behaviour of the
prisoner against one of the grounds set out in s. 31(3) of the CCRA. There was no
determination on any reasonable alternatives to segregation. In those cases where
a prisoner was retained in segregation for more than thirty days, there was no
review of any written psychological or psychiatric opinion regarding the prisoner's capacity to remain in segregation, as required by s. 7(e) of Commissioner's
Directive 590. Although for prisoners who remained in segregation beyond sixty
days there would be a Review Board discussion of possible alternatives—which
almost always involved a transfer to another institution—I never once observed
the Board either developing or reviewing "a plan, addressing in detail the schedule of activities for the inmate," as required by s. 7(d) of the Commissioner's
Directive. Rather, the reviews were relatively shapeless discussions of individual
cases, the precise agenda of which depended on questions raised by individual
Board members. Any expectation I had had that the segregation review process at
Matsqui would be conducted within the framework of the CCRA, CCR *Regulations,*
and Commissioner's Directives was confounded during my initial observations.

The best evidence that the legal framework had not become part of the operational reality of decision-making at Matsqui was the execution of "Operation
Big Scoop." I have described how that operation was planned and implemented,
and how at no time was any reference made to or reliance placed upon the
provisions in the CCRA. As I have observed, in my judgement the operation was
carried out in violation of both the spirit and the letter of the law.

## Segregation Review at Kent: The Law and Operational Reality

Segregation cast an even longer shadow at Kent Institution during 1993–96 because of the exceptionally large numbers of prisoners who were segregated. During these years Kent had an average population of 280 prisoners. The division of the population into general population (GP) and protective custody (PC) was reflected during these years by a division of the segregation unit along the same lines, with J unit containing the GP prisoners and K unit the PC prisoners. The two units, while linked by a common control bubble, had their own separate exercise yards, common rooms, and interview rooms. Because of the pressures of overcrowding, most of the cells in K unit and many of those in J unit were double-bunked. There were months in which segregated prisoners represented almost 30 per cent of the total population, the highest percentage in the country. Segregation therefore came close to being the normal condition of imprisonment for a significant part of the population. Normalcy in this context involved confinement in an often double-bunked cell for twenty-three hours a day, with an hour out for exercise and a few more minutes for a shower, where life was shared in all its intimacies with another person and privacy reduced to the thickness of a curtain around a toilet standing only a few feet from your bed. Although the presence of televisions and Walkman radios suggested a degree of progress from the sterility of the Penthouse in the B.C. Penitentiary, for many prisoners long-term segregation under double-bunked conditions was seen as a regression. Certainly, judging by the length of time prisoners spent in segregation, it was difficult to see much progress from the days of the Penthouse. During 1993–95, one of the plaintiffs in the *McCann* case, who had spent 682 days in segregation at the B.C. Penitentiary in the early 1970s, came to spend almost 1,000 days in segregation in Kent Institution.

When I began my observations at Kent, it quickly became apparent that the segregation review process there was carried out differently than at Matsqui. At Kent, the Board maintained the five-day and thirty-day sequence of reviews set out in the legislation. There was also a separate designation for a sixty-day review, which reflected the requirement in the *CCR Regulations* that there be a regional review of any prisoner kept in segregation for sixty days. There were far more prisoners at Kent than at Matsqui who fell into that category, and this was recognized by the attendance at Kent's sixty-day reviews of a representative from Regional Headquarters.

The segregation review processes at Kent and Matsqui had several elements in common. Neither institution referred to the legislative criteria for segregation, nor was a conscious critical line of inquiry directed to whether the evidence or information available to the Board established legal justification for segregation or whether there were reasonable alternatives to segregation. In addition, there was no compliance with the legislative requirement that a prisoner receive, at least three working days prior to each review, a written copy of any documentation to be used. In no case I observed between 1993 and 1996 was a prisoner given documentation over and above the typically minimal segregation notice received when he was first placed in segregation or the notices provided following the thirty- and sixty-day reviews. Any information given to prisoners regarding the reasons for their segregation was conveyed at the segregation review and was given orally. The only exceptions to this were in cases of men being considered for involuntary transfer; they received a progress summary detailing the grounds for the recommended transfer.

The official record for segregated prisoners at Kent consisted of segregation review notices prepared following every review and placed on the prisoner's file, but the operational filing system was a set of index cards maintained by the unit manager for segregation. Every segregated prisoner had such a card, and on it were handwritten notations indicating the circumstances leading to segregation together with updates after each review. The cards were kept in a small recipe box as an accessible and transportable information base for segregation reviews.

As discussed, s. 31(3) of the *CCRA* sets out the lawful grounds for segregation. A further extra-legal ground was often used at Kent to justify continued segregation. A great number of prisoners received notices stating that they been approved for release to general population "pending available bed space." This was a result of the expansion of the federal prison population during those years and the transition of double-bunking from an emergency measure to an accepted long-term feature of correctional operations. This situation had cumulative effects at Kent. The pressures of overcrowding in lower security institutions resulted in more prisoners being deemed unmanageable and therefore subject to involuntary transfer to maximum security prisons. The stepping up of the war against drugs and of "zero tolerance" policies also increased the number of prisoners facing involuntary transfers to Kent, for reasons which at other times would not have been deemed sufficient to justify them. With GP and PC units full, and a ceiling placed on the number of cells that could be double-bunked, prisoners coming into Kent found themselves placed in the segregation unit until a cell opened up in the regular units. Kent prisoners in administrative or punitive segregation remained there until space became available in the units, even though the original grounds for placing them in segregation no longer existed or they had served their sentences. The segregation notice given to one prisoner read: "Your punitive time is expired. The Board has no reason to maintain your segregation at this time and will recommend your release pending bed space in general population." Segregated prisoners were assigned a number, indicating their priority for release, on a first-in, first-out basis. Depending on the number of prisoners in segregation at any one time, the duration of the period a prisoner spent in segregation for no reason grounded in law varied from a few days to two months. As I have described in Sector 3, Chapter 3, "The Disciplinary Process at

Kent," there were a significant number of cases in which the maximum punitive sentence of 30 days stretched into an actual sentence of 90 days, resulting in prisoners being released straight from segregation to the street on their statutory release or warrant expiry dates.

## The Rhythms of the Law (I): The Thirty-Day Review

Like other aspects of life in a prison, the law governing segregation has its own set of rhythms, and the thirty-day and sixty-day reviews are its basic metre. Within this legal and operational framework, however, the actual number of days a prisoner spends in segregation slides into the background. At one of the first thirty-day reviews I observed, thirty-four prisoners' cases were considered. Three of these prisoners had served more than 300 days in segregation, five more than 200 days, seven more than 100 days, and sixteen between 30 and 100 days. Only three prisoners had served between 20 and 30 days.

The legal model of segregation review envisages a process in which correctional administrators review each case against legal criteria to determine whether there are initial grounds to justify segregation and whether those or other grounds exist to justify continuing it. Part of the latter inquiry requires the Board to satisfy itself that there are no reasonable alternatives to segregation. The legislation clearly places the burden upon the correctional authorities to justify, on a continuing basis, detention in a prison within a prison. But the model of the law is one thing; the model of operational reality is another. That reality often reshapes the review so that there is a presumption, in some cases irrebuttable, that the prisoner will be retained in segregation.

The element of operational reality which, more than any other, eclipses the legal reality of an effective monthly review is the prospect of the prisoner's transfer to the general population of another prison. For many prisoners in segregation for their own protection, this is the only realistic avenue for their release. Yet because of their histories, finding another institution willing to accept them and where they do not have "incompatibles" is often a difficult process which drags on for months and even years. I observed that the frustrations experienced by prisoners facing this situation, coupled with other pressures such as being double-bunked and having restricted access to open visits and telephone calls, was reflected in ways ranging from depressive withdrawal to outspoken protests at segregation review hearings. Dwight Lowe, who in the course of his long imprisonment has spent many years in segregation, was one of those who consistently spoke out about the effects "operational reality" had on the lives of prisoners in segregation. When I first saw Mr. Lowe at his thirty-day segregation review on May 9, 1994, he had been in segregation for 392 days, dating from his transfer from Mountain Institution.

Unit Manager Shadbolt, who chaired the Segregation Review Board, asked

Mr. Lowe, "What do you have to tell us?" Mr. Lowe replied, "I want to know what's happening." He was informed that although Kent was trying to get him back to Mountain Institution, he was a hard sell. Mr. Lowe then asked angrily why there were only four open-visit slots for protective custody prisoners and why only two prisoners could go out at a time. He said this was causing problems, with some prisoners muscling others for visits. Psychologist Zender Katz said to Mr. Lowe, "Let's not talk about unit politics, let's talk about your case." Mr. Lowe got even angrier and said that the visit situation affected everybody's case: "When you push guys to the limit and then you fuck around with the visits you're asking for trouble." He went on to point out that this was his fourth summer in the hole. Mr. Lowe referred to a report he had prepared for the K unit correctional supervisor, which outlined complaints he had gathered from prisoners, and went on, "You guys are supposed to promote and foster family relationships under your correctional mandate. You don't do that with your visitors' policy." Ms. Shadbolt said the visit slots were not going to change, and Mr. Lowe's last comment before he left the room was "Well, if it doesn't change, it's going to lead to someone getting really hurt."

Dwight Lowe's report, although framed in very specific terms, raised issues that go to the heart of the different ways prisoners, particularly prisoners in segregation, experience time and space. These larger dimensions are eloquently captured in an essay by Dr. Richard Korn, who has interviewed hundreds of prisoners in solitary confinement, and who gave evidence before the Federal Court in the *McCann* case.

> These hostages of Time are its profoundest students. Mankind had to wait for an Einstein to prove that one cannot understand Time without dealing simultaneously with Space and Motion. Any Greek galley-slave could have proved to Socrates that ten days chained to an oar in the bilges lasts longer than ten days in a comfortable room chatting with friends. Time has a different duration in different places. Space has a different configuration over different times.
>
> Experienced prisoners can nicely calculate the impact of different spatial settings on the inner duration of the same unit of calendar time. How long does a calendar year last in the county jail? "Twice as long as a year in San Quentin," answers the ex-con from California. And a year in San Quentin? "Four times as long as a year on the street." And how long is a week in the "hole"? The respondent's eyes become dream-like. "A month, two months . . . limbo."
>
> Sensitive prison visitors are typically shocked by the dimensions of the cell. They are troubled by the restrictions on movement and activity. While valid, these concerns miss the heart of the problem. The problem is the impact of Time, Space, and Action on each other.

Solitary travellers in the desert sometimes report that the sky above them feels too close for comfort. The solitary, inactive prisoner often feels physically crushed between the walls, the ceiling and the floor. A jeweller working on the insides of a tiny watch is operating in a larger psychological space than the man immobilized in his cell. Constricting a man's space while simultaneously restricting his activities has a fantastically expansive effect on the crucial third dimension of Time. As space collapses inward toward the vanishing point, Time is ballooning out toward infinity. (Richard Korn, "Liberating the Future from the Past? Liberating the Past from the Future?" [1998; unpublished])

In *Prisoners of Isolation,* I wrote that the worst fear of prisoners in segregation was that they would be driven over the edge of sanity, that their worst experiences were having to see and hear the anguish of prisoners who had already been pushed into a place from which they might never return. At the May 9, 1994, Segregation Review Board hearing at Kent, two prisoners appeared perilously close to this brink. John Soane had been placed in segregation in December 1993 following his transfer from Mission Institution, based upon allegations of his involvement in drug trafficking. He denied this involvement and initiated court proceedings to challenge the transfer. His continued stay in segregation arose because of a problem with incompatibles in the protective custody open units. I had interviewed Mr. Soane earlier in May at Dwight Lowe's urging, and at that time he was extremely agitated, relating his history in disconnected fragments. It was clear he had all his hopes pinned on his lawyer's challenge to the transfer and the prospect of his returning to Mission Institution.

At the Segregation Review Board hearing, Mr. Soane proceeded to deny his involvement in the alleged activities that had brought him to Kent. He voiced frustration at being told by staff that they did not know what was going on with his case and could not comment on the validity of the allegations made by the Mission authorities. At his last review he had been told he would be contacted by the institutional preventive security officer, Mr. Dick, about complaints that erroneous information was in his file, but Mr. Dick, who had only come to see him the previous week, had not yet read the file. Although Mr. Soane's account was understandable, he stuttered repeatedly and quite deliberately avoided any eye contact. He was told by Ms. Shadbolt, the unit manager for segregation, that she would make sure Mr. Dick reviewed his file for inaccuracies. In the meantime, his segregation would be maintained until there was resolution of the problems preventing him from moving into the open protective custody units.

After Mr. Soane left the room, Ms. Shadbolt asked the psychologist, Mr. Katz, if the stuttering was part of an act to impress the Board. Mr. Katz responded,

"What you are seeing is pressured speech, which is the effect of segregation." After Mr. Soane's review, I spoke to Mr. Katz, and he readily conceded that long-term segregation was having a very negative impact on Mr. Soane. His role at the segregation review was, however, limited to bringing this to the Board's attention; he had no authority to recommend release from segregation.

The second prisoner close to the edge reviewed on May 9 was Mr. Smith. Mr. Smith had taken an overdose of heroin at the Regional Psychiatric Centre (RPC) with the intention of killing himself after having made previous attempts at slashing. The incident was logged by the RPC as drug-related, and Mr. Smith was transferred to Kent, where he was placed in segregation. He had been there since February 22. Mr. Smith said he wanted to go back to the RPC. Ms. Shadbolt reported that RPC staff felt the treatment program would be too intense for him right then, but efforts would be made to get him back there as soon as possible. Mr. Smith hardly participated in the review, answering questions in an impassive and abbreviated manner.

After the hearing, I asked Mr. Katz why a man who had tried to kill himself had been transferred out of the RPC—the place he clearly ought to be—into the segregation unit at Kent. Mr. Katz said that the RPC saw this as a drug-related case and, in a climate of zero tolerance, transfer was justifiable. He acknowledged that Mr. Smith was very depressed and agreed that segregation was not the appropriate place for him.

## The Madness of Segregation

In *Prisoners of Isolation,* I described how "the screams in the night" heard from the solitary confinement cells of England's Pentonville Prison and Canada's Kingston Penitentiary in the 1840s had not been stilled by the 1980s. The horror of prisoners who have slipped over the edge in segregation is carried forward in the oral history of maximum security prisons and captured here by Jerome Washington, in his description of a psychological observation room at Attica:

> Room Number 1—called "the space station"—is the prison hospital's psycho observation room. There is nothing in this room except a mattress on the floor, a bare bulb in the ceiling and ghosts of minds out of control. Every night, shrieks and howls from Room Number 1 sound across the empty yard. They remind us, caged in the cells, that going over the wall is not the only escape. As in a game of chance where every number is a potential winner, in prison every inmate is a potential space case. We all have an inside story waiting to be screamed across the yard. (Jerome Washington, *Iron House: Stories from the Yard* [New York: Vintage Books, 1994] at 97)

On May 25, 1994, I spent a deeply disturbing shift in the segregation unit at Kent interviewing prisoners, listening to their stories and to their screams, some issued aloud, others confined to prisoners' minds. These interviews bear testament to the ways in which long-term segregation undermines a person's psychological hold on reality and intensifies a sense of injustice and paranoia.

John Edwards set out his recent institutional history, which he claimed was filled with unfair treatment. This had generated within him a rage which, given that he was just three months away from statutory release, should have been—but did not seem to be—of great concern to the Segregation Review Board. Mr. Edwards was serving a 4-year sentence for robbery. He had been transferred from Alberta's Bowden Institution to Matsqui in November 1992, although he had requested Mission Institution as he had an incompatible at Matsqui. Within days of arriving at Matsqui, his incompatible left a note in his jacket to the effect, "Check in, goof, or you die." He passed this note on to staff, who told him to try to settle the issue on his own. The next day a prisoner wearing a hood came into the cell where Mr. Edwards was watching television and struck him on the head with a chair leg, opening a gash that required twenty-three stitches to close. After leaving hospital, Mr. Edwards was placed in segregation at Matsqui for his own protection. He was there for forty-seven days, until his transfer to Mission early in January 1993. He spent Christmas and New Year's Day in segregation.

In June of 1993, Mr. Edwards was transferred to Kent because of alleged negative and deteriorating behaviour, including a threat to set a fire by piling up a bunch of grievance papers and igniting them. He told me this was a protest against the inadequate responses he had received to the grievances and was not meant as a serious threat. He was in segregation at Kent for some two months before being transferred to the PC population. He remained there until April of 1994, when he was placed in segregation following being punched by another prisoner. He now refused to return to the population because he was "tired of dealing with the games out there." His statutory release date was September 1994, and he had applied for a transfer to Mountain Institution to try to get free from the anger and negativity of his last few years. He told me he had an offer of a job on the street but wanted to make sure he was able to take best advantage of it.

The last several weeks had been particularly difficult for Mr. Edwards. He was double-bunked with Mr. Pope, who had slashed himself in frustration at his own situation. He was placed in the observation cell for a day and then brought back into Mr. Edwards' cell. Mr. Edwards was extremely frightened by the situation, because he did not know whether Mr. Pope would try to slash again or might attack him. In fact, Mr. Pope did slash himself again, and this time he was taken to the Regional Psychiatric Centre. Mr. Edwards was left to clean up the blood himself. He had not spoken to anyone about the incident, although he admitted it had had a traumatic impact on him.

As I have explained in "Operation Big Scoop," there are procedures in place for dealing with possible post-traumatic stress among staff who experience incidents involving threats or violence to themselves or their colleagues. Had a staff member witnessed a slashing, it would have been the subject of a debriefing with the institutional psychologist. Yet Mr. Edwards had experienced, close up, two slashings by his cellmate and had received no counselling.

Mr. Edwards ended the interview by saying, "Recently my CO-II told me that I won't be leaving segregation before my statutory release except through the hospital or in a body bag. What do they expect when they release me on the street? That I'm going to be like a model citizen?"

Later that day I met with John Soane, who had just been told that the appeal against his transfer from Mission had been dismissed. He was beside himself and told me in front of two officers, "I just can't take it any more." In our interview, he fluctuated between voicing great anger and expressing despair. His stuttering increased. He said he asked only to leave K unit and go over to J unit; he would then at least be able to look out of his cell window and see people and cars moving. I relayed Mr. Soane's request to a correctional supervisor, who agreed to this. After Mr. Soane packed his stuff, it was brought over to J unit, checked, and then issued back to him. I went to talk with him in the observation cell. He was sitting on his bed with his face in his hands. As on many previous occasions at Kent, I found myself on my knees at the food slot of a segregation cell, endeavouring to reassure a man on the point of giving up that there were still people who cared about him and would try to redress the injustice he felt so keenly. Mr. Soane repeated over and over again, "How can they do this to me? I have done nothing wrong." I said I would talk to his lawyer in the morning to see if she was thinking about an appeal and promised to talk to the deputy warden about his alleged incompatible in the PC population. It was clear that John Soane could do no more time in the hole. He was at the point where further segregation could tip the balance from survival to self-destruction.

On this occasion the staff at Kent behaved in a caring way, demonstrating an understanding for what the prisoner was going through, in sharp contrast to the callous indifference I had observed years earlier in the Penthouse and H unit. But this could not change the reality that an extended stay in segregation ultimately dissolves the hope of the strongest person and generates a cycle of alternating rage and despair. As it always has, seeing men reduced to this state brings up my own scream of outrage that we can do this to our fellow human beings.

## The Rhythms of the Law (II): The Sixty-Day Review

At the sixty-day review of a prisoner in segregation, the *CCR Regulations* require that the case be reviewed by Regional Headquarters to determine whether the segregation of the prisoner continues to be justified. In light of this, it might be expected that the regional representative who attended the sixty-day Segregation Review Board hearings at Kent would play a significant role, if not a leading one. In practice, though, the regional representative resembled the invisible man (or woman). At the May 1994 sixty-day review, the first one I attended, the regional representative did not ask a single question or make any comment. The hearing showed no evidence of independent review or evaluation, and this remained the case throughout my observation period. Though the regional representative changed from time to time, his or her participation was limited to providing information on the progress of inter-regional transfers. This was not surprising given that the regional representative, usually the transfer co-ordinator for the region, occupied a place in the organizational hierarchy below the unit manager and deputy warden. Within such a context, to challenge conclusions or to suggest that all reasonable alternatives had not been explored would be not only difficult but ill-advised from a career perspective.

## The Worst of Times: Christmas in Segregation

Almost twenty years after Robert Martineau was placed in segregation at Matsqui Institution—under circumstances that resulted in the landmark judgement of the Supreme Court of Canada, in *Martineau (No. 2),* that the duty to act fairly applied to prison administrators—Mr. Martineau was placed in segregation at Kent Institution. Although no *Martineau (No. 3)* resulted from this placement, the case illustrates many of the systemic problems which still pervade the use of segregation.

In 1994, Robert Martineau was elected President of the Native Brotherhood of the PC population at Kent. Mr. Martineau is a vigorous long-time advocate not only of prisoners' rights but of the rights of Aboriginal prisoners to practise their spirituality. Although this right is recognized in the CCRA, there continues to be at Kent, as in many other institutions, an ongoing struggle to translate it into a culture of respect for Aboriginal spirituality. In the fall and early winter of 1994, a series of incidents highlighted the tension between Aboriginal perspectives on the Red Road and institutional demands for control of institutional programs. The issue came to a head at a meeting on November 25, 1994, when members of the Brotherhood attended a meeting with Theresa Nahanee, at that time Director of the Aboriginal Offenders Program at National Headquarters. Also at the meeting were members of the National and Regional Aboriginal Advisory Committees of CSC, together with a number of Aboriginal people involved in the managing of halfway houses and drug and alcohol counselling programs. The meeting was held as a forum for Aboriginal prisoners to identify the problems they faced in the prison system and in their efforts at reintegration upon release. In his presentation, Robert Martineau was highly critical of the manner in which the CCRA had been implemented at Kent. Although there was a regional budget for Aboriginal programming, a portion of which was allocated to Kent Institution, the Brotherhood had experienced great difficulty in accessing those monies. Mr. Martineau compared the process of getting approval for a project to that which prevailed under the old Indian Agent system, in which to get anything done on a reserve the Chief and council had to obtain a permit from the Indian Agent.

Mr. Martineau gave two recent examples of this "Indian Agent" mentality. The Brotherhood had drawn up two proposals to be funded out of the budget allocated for Aboriginal programs. One involved making gingerbread houses in the shape of West Coast longhouses to be given away as Christmas gifts to needy children through Indian Friendship Centres; the other involved bringing in an Elder to teach drumming and singing. Both proposals had initially been rejected by the unit manager on the grounds that they did not have a sufficiently distinctive Aboriginal focus. In response, the institutional Elder had explained that "give-aways" were an important part of Aboriginal cultural traditions, and that this particular give-away would allow the Brothers to reach out to children, the most vulnerable members of their communities. As for the singing and drumming, she explained that they were part of helping the Brothers to re-establish their spiritual and cultural connection to the Red Road, through a shared experience which wove together songs and dances of many different Aboriginal nations. However, even with these explanations, there had developed an impasse in accessing the money to bring the gingerbread house ingredients into Kent.

Mr. Martineau also itemized other problems, such as lengthy delays in providing honorariums and travel expenses for Elders coming into the institution and the Brotherhood executive's lack of access to segregated Aboriginal prisoners. In his usual way, he was outspoken in his comments, and there was little doubt that the Kent representatives were discomfited by being so openly criticized in front of regional and national Aboriginal representatives, particularly since Ms. Nahanee confirmed that she had heard many of these criticisms from other Brotherhoods across the country and that they demonstrated systemic problems in the implementation of the CCRA. By the end of the meeting, Mr. Martineau's criticisms of Kent had been given not only a larger circulation but a new degree of legitimacy.

In the weeks following this meeting, Mr. Martineau, together with the institutional Elder and the liaison worker, struggled to bring the gingerbread project to realization in time for Christmas; it was only after a direct appeal to the deputy warden and the warden that the impasse was broken and the Brothers could begin working on their give-away.

On December 9, 1994, Lorne Flamond, an Aboriginal prisoner at Kent, was knifed and taken to hospital. The PC population was locked down and remained in that status until December 13, while the RCMP were called in and, together with the IPSOs, conducted an investigation into what was believed to be a conspiracy to murder Mr. Flamond. Mr. Sherratt, the prisoner believed to be the assailant, and two other prisoners were placed in segregation; on December 15, Paul Brown, a close associate of Mr. Martineau and a member of the Brotherhood, was also placed in segregation. When Mr. Martineau questioned the PC unit manager about the reasons for Mr. Brown's segregation, he was told, "We're conducting an investigation and it takes many turns; as we make these turns, we're grabbing people." Mr. Martineau challenged the legitimacy of the segregation in light of the fact that Mr. Brown, like Mr. Martineau, was a close friend of Mr. Flamond and would be the last one to be involved in a conspiracy to harm him.

The Christmas social for the PC population was scheduled for Saturday, December 17. Mr. Martineau's wife was driving the 800 miles from Prince George to participate and intended to stay on for a three-day private family visit with her husband arranged for December 28, 29, and 30. From the time the lock-down ended on December 13, the Brothers worked long hours to complete the ginger-bread houses, and by Saturday morning the work was finished. But at around 11:00 a.m., Robert Martineau's expectation that he would be spending the rest of the day with his family and friends at the social was dashed. As he described:

> My door opened and Correctional Supervisor Greer was there with seven other staff members and they told me, "We have orders to take you to segregation for the investigation of the stabbing of Flamond." They got this spray with them and the camera and they looked like they were expecting a problem, so I thought it was a little insignificant to raise the issue of my guilt or innocence with them. It was going to happen one way or the other so I went along with them. I went down to segregation. I was demanding from the time they came to my cell until they locked me up, "What am I doing down here?" They were just saying an investigation. I immediately got hold of the keeper and told him to ask Mr. Cawsey if I could at least see my wife for half an hour on a screened visit to let her know why I'm in segregation. She drove all this way and it's Christmastime. At least let her know why she can't come in and why I'm in segregation. I wasn't allowed any visit. (Interview with Robert Martineau, Kent Institution, January 6, 1995)

The segregation notice given to Mr. Martineau stated that he was being segregated pending an investigation into the stabbing of Mr. Flamond. On December 20, Mr. Martineau was seen by the Segregation Review Board for his five-day review. Unit Manager Shadbolt said all she could tell him was that he was being segregated while the investigation continued because it was believed that his presence in the population would interfere with it. Mr. Martineau became very angry and demanded to know on what basis the institution believed him to be involved in the stabbing. Mr. Flamond was a good friend of his, and at the time of the stabbing (which took place in the unit) he was in the prison chapel at a Brotherhood meeting. If he had been aware Mr. Flamond was going to get hurt, he would have tried to stop it, although he said that what had happened was a "goof trip," meaning it did not make any sense and was not the kind of event you could anticipate or prevent. He reminded the Board that he had a private family visit with his wife coming up on December 28 and it was very important to him. To be in segregation at Christmas without any good reason was an injustice, and he demanded to be released. Ms. Shadbolt said he would not be released until the completion of the investigation, which could take several weeks.

When I spoke with Mr. Martineau after his review, he related in more detail what I had heard him tell the Board. Mr. Flamond was a close friend of his, more like a younger brother he had taken under his wing. The genesis of the stabbing, as best Mr. Martineau could understand, was drug-related and arose from a complicated chain of indebtedness involving Mr. Flamond, Mr. Sherratt, and another prisoner. Mr. Martineau had understood that the problems between Mr. Flamond and Mr. Sherratt had been resolved peacefully, so he was shocked when he heard that Mr. Flamond had been stabbed. (Mr. Sherratt was subsequently convicted of the attempted murder of Mr. Flamond.)

Mr. Martineau's account revealed a complex web of relationships which only insiders to the politics of the drug trade could fully understand. Someone only peripherally involved in those events, or who heard a second-hand account of them, could easily get important elements wrong. Many prisoners have told me over the years that informers are the source of much inaccurate information, since they have their own agendas and therefore deliberately make up stories. While this may well be the case, the intricacies of the account Robert Martineau gave me suggested that anyone not directly involved would likely give an inaccurate account of these events even with no deliberate intent to distort or fabricate.

Following our interview, Mr. Martineau contacted Prisoners' Legal Services and sought their assistance in securing his release from segregation. When Beth Parkinson phoned the institution on his behalf, she was informed that because Mr. Martineau was believed to be heavily involved in the underground drug economy, it was deemed necessary to segregate him to avoid his interference with the investigation. When Mr. Martineau learned about this, his anger only increased.

> I was really choked. I had been working hard on getting the Native Substance Abuse program off the ground and not only participating

in it myself but in baby-sitting the whole program and making sure that the other guys attended and maintained their commitment to it. I had been working to get the supplies for the gingerbread houses for the kids and we'd worked all week on that. And for all that work all I got was the same paranoia and suspicion about my involvement in the drug trade and the IPSOs' belief that if anything negative happened I must be behind it. (Interview with Robert Martineau, Kent Institution, January 6, 1995)

After my interview with Mr. Martineau on December 20, I met with Unit Manager Shadbolt and inquired about the ongoing investigation into the stabbing. She advised me she had received information that Mr. Martineau had persuaded Mr. Flamond to hand over the knives he used in his wood carving; one of these knives was given to another prisoner, who in turn gave it to Mr. Sherratt, and this was the knife with which Mr. Sherratt had stabbed Mr. Flamond. The inference was that Mr. Martineau had orchestrated the attack on Mr. Flamond, and she observed that Mr. Martineau "was conspicuously absent" at the time the attack took place.

Mr. Martineau remained in segregation until January 3, 1995. In an interview three days later, he described what had happened subsequent to his five-day review on December 20. He had received no further information from the institution regarding the state of the investigation, nor was he given any information in writing or orally regarding the basis for the institution's belief that he was involved. On December 29, Mr. Martineau was out of his cell getting a cup of coffee when he saw Deputy Warden Sexsmith and asked to speak with him. Mr. Sexsmith explained that the stabbing investigation had originally been assigned to a unit manager at Matsqui. However, that unit manager had been attacked with a baseball bat by a prisoner and so the preliminary investigation had been reassigned to Mr. Sexsmith himself. According to Mr. Martineau, Mr. Sexsmith told him:

> There's three inmates in the PC population that we consider are the drug traffickers and suppliers and one of them is you. We felt that this was a drug-related incident and therefore that the drug traffickers would be involved. The information that you were segregated on was information received that you were directly involved in that you gave a knife to another prisoner, that prisoner supplied the knife to Sherratt who did the stabbing, and you ensured that you were not in the area by establishing yourself visibly in another part of the institution. That was the information I received and I've now completed my investigation and it has not corroborated that you were involved in any conspiracy to stab Flamond and therefore you and Mr. Brown

will be released from segregation on January 3. (Interview with Robert Martineau, Kent Institution, January 6, 1995)

Mr. Martineau questioned why, if there was no justification for his segregation, he could not be released immediately. Mr. Sexsmith replied that unit managers normally made the recommendations for release, and Mr. Cawsey, the unit manager for the PC side, would not be back in the institution until January 3. Mr. Martineau raised the issue of having lost his single cell and not wanting to double-bunk on his return to the population, and mentioned the effect his segregation had had on his scheduled three-day family visit, the first two days of which had already passed. Mr. Sexsmith said that he would make sure Mr. Martineau got a single cell and would do his best to make arrangements to have the third day of his visit with his wife.

Mr. Sexsmith made good on the latter promise; Mr. Martineau spent the next day with his wife, and on January 3 he was released from segregation. However, as the following account describes, that release hardly represented his vindication in the eyes of Unit Manager Cawsey:

> On January 3 I saw Mr. Cawsey and he said to me, "You were talking to the Deputy Warden last week?" I said, "Yes." He said, "Well, you were told you were getting out today and I don't have any alternative, I have to act on that, but as far as I'm concerned you were directly responsible in this incident. I can't prove it but I know that. I have no choice but to let you go." When I asked about getting a single cell he said, "There is no single cell out there. You can either wait in segregation until we get a single cell or otherwise, if Brown agrees, I will release you into a double-bunk cell with him. That's it." I said, "Hey, listen, why are saying that I was directly involved in this? You know what you're telling me? You're telling me that this is going to affect everything I do. You're the unit manager where I am living. You're the man with all the juice here. This is going to affect my transfers, my parole applications, my security classification, everything, because of something you believe." So I get out of segregation but I'm in a double-bunk cell, I've lost the job I had for three years, and I'm told by the unit manager that he believes I'm guilty whatever the deputy warden thinks. (Interview with Robert Martineau, Kent Institution, January 6, 1995)

Following Mr. Martineau's release, I spoke with Unit Managers Cawsey and Shadbolt. Mr. Cawsey confirmed that while he had no concrete proof of Mr. Martineau's involvement in the Flamond stabbing, he still had serious reservations about his innocence. Both unit managers viewed Mr. Sexsmith's communication with Mr. Martineau on December 29, that he intended to have him released on January 3, as inappropriate. The staff were also upset about the reinstatement of the last day of the private family visit because, as it fell on a long weekend, staff were left to do a lot of scrambling to ensure the visit went ahead. Ms. Shadbolt shared with me another highly significant fact. She believed that part of the reason Mr. Martineau and Mr. Brown had been segregated before Christmas was to break down their power base within the institution. Their release from segregation so quickly, as a result of orders from Mr. Sexsmith, had undermined that objective.

I also interviewed both Mr. Martineau and Mr. Brown to record their views on how they were segregated and the circumstances under which they were released. This is what Mr. Brown told me:

> It was depressing and frustrating because we both knew that we had nothing to do with it. Moochie [Mr. Flamond] was a friend of ours and we were really pissed off about some of the things that were being said, some of the things that we were hearing. It was frustrating because we were asking to speak to the people who were supposedly in charge of the investigation and no one would speak to us, no one would give us any information of any kind, so we were kept completely in the dark. It's really depressing. Our friend's in the hospital with stab wounds, we are being investigated for it or dragged into the investigation for some reason unknown to us, and it was really kind of a helpless feeling. (Interview with Paul Brown, Kent Institution, January 6, 1995. In 1999, Paul Brown himself was fatally stabbed at Kent.)

Mr. Martineau summarized his feelings in this way:

> Whenever I've been segregated generally there's a reason. I get myself in situations that probably there's a reason for them putting me there, but in this instance, Moochie is somebody that I've known since he was a kid and I baby-sit him wherever I go. I was really upset about what happened because I know that had I been there it wouldn't have happened. There's no doubt in my mind that there was a hidden agenda. Some of the staff obviously didn't like the pressure I was putting on the institution as a result of the meeting with the national and regional Aboriginal representatives, and didn't like it that the warden and deputy warden had stepped in and ordered that the Christmas project should go ahead. They were looking for an excuse to undermine what I was doing even though I was trying

to do what was right for the Brothers. I'm really angry about what happened. If you wanted to remember a Christmas that was the worst one of your life, this is certainly one of them for me, in or out of prison. (Interview with Robert Martineau, Kent Institution, January 6, 1995)

Mr. Martineau's early release on this occasion was fortuitous, arising as it did because of the intervention of Deputy Warden Sexsmith. Ironically, it was only because of the assault on the officer originally designated to do the investigation that Mr. Sexsmith reviewed the facts and concluded there was no case against Mr. Martineau. Had the investigation taken its normal course, it would likely have been months before a decision was made. But even with Mr. Sexsmith's involvement, there was an element of arbitrariness to Mr. Martineau's release. As Mr. Sexsmith acknowledged, he had concluded by December 29 that there was no legal justification for keeping Mr. Martineau in segregation; the only reason for delaying his release until January 3 was to appease the unit managers. In other words, Mr. Martineau spent an extra five days in segregation for reasons of institutional politics.

Politics in a prison, on both sides of the keeper/kept divide, are complex. The essential difference is that prisoners usually assert their authority in ways that are characterized by the administration as unlawful. Yet the tools of institutional authority, particularly with regard to segregation, are deployed under the umbrella of apparent legality. In my judgement, Robert Martineau's assertion of authority as the President of the Native Brotherhood was honourable and in furtherance of the objectives of the *Corrections and Conditional Release Act* regarding Aboriginal programming. From the perspective of the unit managers, everything he did was viewed as having a sinister undercurrent; every agenda was seen as self-serving, every move inspired by a drug play rather than an endeavour to improve the situation of Aboriginal prisoners.

The umbrella of legality under which Kent Institution segregated Mr. Martineau in December 1994 would have provided scant protection had Mr. Martineau's segregation continued and a legal challenge been mounted in the form of a *Martineau (No. 3)*. Both the process and the substance of Mr. Martineau's segregation were deeply flawed. In terms of process, he was not given written notice prior to his five-day review of the information that the Segregation Review Board would be considering; indeed, at no time during his segregation, until December 29, was he personally told anything beyond the fact that there was an ongoing investigation. In terms of substance, the legal basis invoked by the institution for Mr. Martineau's segregation was s. 31(3)(b); this required the institutional head to believe on reasonable grounds that Mr. Martineau's continued presence in the general population would interfere with an investigation.

The basis for those reasonable grounds, as explained by Deputy Warden Sexsmith on December 29, thirteen days after Mr. Martineau had first been segregated, was received information that Mr. Martineau had arranged for the transmission of Mr. Flamond's carving knife through a prisoner intermediary to the prisoner who ultimately carried out the attack, coupled with Mr. Martineau's "conspicuous absence" from the unit when the attack took place. But in an environment where virtually every prisoner has access to a knife, for either defensive or offensive purposes, how reasonable is it that Mr. Martineau would construct a long chain of involvement to pass a knife along to the perpetrator of the offence? The issue of reasonableness must also be sifted in the context of the close personal relationship between Mr. Martineau and Mr. Flamond. As to Mr. Martineau's "conspicuous absence" from the unit at the time of the stabbing, how reasonable was the conclusion that this provided grounds to implicate him, given that he was in the prison chapel for the purposes of participating in a scheduled Brotherhood meeting? In any event, whatever reasonable grounds might have existed initially for believing that Mr. Martineau was implicated in the attack, or that his presence in the population would interfere with the investigation, had evaporated by December 29, on the Deputy Warden's own admission. The five-day delay in Mr. Martineau's release was to satisfy the dynamics of institutional politics; clearly, leaving a prisoner in segregation to avoid ruffling the feathers of unit managers is not authorized by the CCRA.

When the veils of legality are stripped away, the underlying rationale for Mr. Martineau's segregation becomes more apparent. As one of the unit managers candidly conceded, Mr. Martineau's power base in the institution was becoming a problem. He had openly called into question the unit managers' interpretations of CCRA provisions regarding Aboriginal prisoners and had held them to account in front of national and regional representatives. Furthermore, he had successfully invoked the assistance of the warden and the deputy warden to bring to fruition the Brotherhood's Christmas give-away plans. Placing Mr. Martineau in segregation for Christmas and New Year's Day, thereby precluding his participation in the Christmas social and all but eclipsing his long-awaited visit with his wife, was both a symbolic and a real message about who was in charge at Kent Institution. That message had little to do with the provisions of the CCRA or the pronouncements of the Supreme Court of Canada on the duty to act fairly.

## Segregation Review, 1996: New Cast, Same Script

Segregation review at Kent in 1996 involved some new players on the institutional side, but the players on the prisoners' side and the play itself remained much the same. As in 1994–95, the majority of the prisoners in K unit were in segregation because of incompatibles in the PC population and were seeking transfers to other institutions. These cases continued to drift from one review to the next. At times, it seemed to embarrass the administration and staff to realize how little had been done since the last review. Far from being seen as urgent, these long-term segregation cases seemed consistently to be lowest on the priority list for speedy resolution. This continued notwithstanding some changes in case management assignments designed to address this problem. In place of the previous practice where one or two case management officers were responsible for all segregated prisoners, the case load was now divided among all CMOs. As it was explained to me, the expectation was that the CMO assigned to each prisoner would be at the five-day review and would work on the development of a plan to reintegrate the prisoner into the population at Kent or at another institution; that plan would be monitored at the thirty- and sixty-day reviews with the active participation of the CMO. This expectation was confounded at the sixty-day review I attended on May 31 and at the thirty-day review on June 3, when only one CMO was in attendance. Indeed, on the list of sixty-day reviews, there were five cases in which the entry under "CMO" read "vacant," reflecting the fact that no CMO had yet been assigned to the prisoner. These five prisoners had been segregated for periods of 383, 153, 82, 81, and 42 days.

## Donnie Oag: Twenty Years after *McCann*

One of the prisoners whose case was reviewed at the thirty-day review on June 3 was Donald Oag. According to the review sheet, he had been in segregation for 638 days, although this belied the fact that, save for a four-month break when he was transferred to Mountain Institution, he had been in segregation at Kent for the last four years. I had first met Mr. Oag in 1973 when he was in solitary confinement in the B.C. Penitentiary, and he became one of the plaintiffs in the *McCann* case. Prior to his experience in the Penthouse, Mr. Oag had lived through other dark moments in Canadian penitentiary history. He was a prisoner in Kingston Penitentiary during its worst riot in 1970. From there, he was transferred to the newly opened Millhaven Institution, where he underwent a "reception and orientation" session which consisted of walking a gauntlet, handcuffed and shackled, while guards beat on him with riot sticks—an event documented in the Royal Commission Report on the Kingston riot (Swackhamer Commission at 34).

In *Prisoners of* Isolation, I described my first interview with Mr. Oag.

> When I interviewed Donnie Oag, I found a man who, after some nine months of continuous solitary confinement, appeared almost as a disembodied spirit. His face was ashen, his voice not much above a whisper. I saw on him the marks of his isolation; terrible scars across his neck and on his wrists and arms—the frightful evidence of his suicide attempts. (at 45)

Following the completion of the *McCann* trial, I did not see Mr. Oag again until February 22, 1994. Our interview at Kent Institution that day was memorable not only for what Mr. Oag told me about his experiences in the twenty-one years since we met but also because it took place late on the afternoon Gary Allen was fatally stabbed. When I first asked to see Mr. Oag, a staff member said she doubted he would see me, because he never came out of his cell and talked only to a woman visitor. I suggested she let me ask him myself. Mr. Oag's cell was at the end of the range, and as I knelt to talk to him through the food slot, I realized that nine years before I had knelt in this same place, pleading with a man not to blind himself with a razor blade as a protest against being sent to the Special Handling Unit. Thankfully, in this instance, I was only asking Mr. Oag if he wanted to talk. After getting over his surprise at seeing eyes from the past looking through the small opening in his door, Mr. Oag agreed to meet, and we spent the next two hours together.

Donnie Oag had been locked in segregation for the last ten months and, apart from a weekly visit with a longtime woman friend, he came out of his cell only to shower. His only interaction with other prisoners was as the recipient of verbal abuse.

He still bore the marks I had observed many years earlier: scar tissue around his neck and on his arms from the multiple slashings and mutilations he had imposed upon himself. Since then, he had endured beatings, gassings, and stabbings that had left more scars on his body. He showed me the blotches under his right eye from repeated tear-gassings in Millhaven Institution and a scar over his eye dating from a beating in which several clubs were broken over his head as he was dragged to the hole. That beating and several others had combined to leave him totally deaf in his left ear, and one side of his face was paralyzed. The scars on his left jaw and chest were the grim reminder of nineteen stab wounds he had received at the hands of two other prisoners in the Special Handling Unit. When I met Mr. Oag in 1973 he had already suffered a broken back, and his experiences over the past two decades had aggravated that injury.

Since the age of nine, when he was locked up in a juvenile detention facility, Donnie Oag had spent less than five of the intervening thirty-five years on the street. He calculated that he had served eleven years in solitary. He was only forty-four at the time of our 1994 interview, but what I saw was a man whose body had literally been broken on the anvil of imprisonment. When I had seen him in 1973, it seemed that his spirit had already suffered the same fate. Remarkably, though, Donnie Oag was more alive in 1994 than I had ever seen him. Our interview left me in little doubt that the principal reason for this was the relationship he had developed with his woman visitor; it had given him the will to survive his sentence of imprisonment and begin life anew.

I asked Mr. Oag to describe the changes he had seen in prison conditions since 1973. He prefaced his response by saying that he was "not an expert on prison generally but only on the prison within a prison," because he had spent so much of his sentence in segregation, and the little time he had spent in open population had always been in maximum security.

> Segregation is a physical and a mental thing; back then it was more physical, now it is more mental. At one time when I was in the "Chinese cell" back east in Millhaven after the riot, I was chained up for long periods of time with no clothes on. They would come in and dump buckets of cold water on me during the night just to wake me up. They would say, "We aren't afraid of you, you f-ing son of a bitch, because you aren't ever getting out of here." You don't see that stuff going on any more. One time they had me in the Chinese cell for about eight months and then they moved me to another cell. They brought a guy into the hole and put him in the Chinese cell for slashing up. He was in there five minutes and he was screaming. He couldn't handle it. He was burned. They took him out and he looked like a lobster. That's how much gassings they gave me. By then I was immune to the gas. Since I've been in segregation at Kent they've gassed a few guys, but as far as I know they give them a shower after. When they use gas they bring a medical nurse or somebody from the hospital to check it out. Back years ago they didn't do that. (Interview with Donald Oag, Kent Institution, February 22, 1994)

I asked Mr. Oag why he was not coming out of his cell to take his daily hour of exercise.

> If you know you are going to spend a long time in the hole and you keep on hoping that you will get out and keep thinking about what you are missing, it slowly drives you mad. Alternatively, it makes you so angry and desperate that you either run into problems with the guards or you take it out on yourself, which is what I used to do by slashing up. Now what I do is to withdraw from the world as you know it, so that the world is like wrapped in a fog, you can't see it and so you forget about it. Then it becomes possible to do the time because the world really stops.

"Every time you do this you always lose something," Mr. Oag said, "and when you do come back into the world [the general population in a maximum security prison], you never quite recover what you had before."

> Every time you're locked up you have to withdraw again. If I was to sit in my cell and contemplate everything what I'm missing and even

the yard, I would be going crazy and I'd slash. A guy just hung himself here two cells from me a little while ago. Killed himself. So you
have to let those things go. Just to keep your sanity when you are
locked up. It's hard to explain. But the more you are locked up, especially coming back and being locked up again, when you're released
it's harder to come back because it's harder to adjust. You can't talk
to people like you could years ago. You can't carry on a conversation
about everything because you've let those things go just to survive in
here. I guess it's like being in a coma and you are aware of things
going on but you're not there. You know what I'm saying? It's like
being put into an empty room and someone closing the door, then
opening the door a week later and saying, "Come on out." Well, you
don't know the week's gone by, it's blank. Imagine if you are in that
empty room for years on end, how would you be? Now you come
out and everybody you know is older. If you've got brothers or sisters
they've grown up and got families of their own. A person never fully
does come back. I could never do it.

Mr. Oag and I both remembered Jacques Bellemaire, the prisoner who hanged
himself in 1973 before he could become a plaintiff in the *McCann* case. Mr. Oag
told me that the callous way in which Jacques Bellemaire's body was dragged off
that tier was only marginally more insensitive than what he recently had seen at
Kent. In both cases, the dead man was a dead *prisoner;* that distinction explained
why callousness can be the response of even men and women who pride themselves on sensitivity in their normal relationships.

For Donnie Oag, the most significant change in the prison over two decades
was the change in the attitudes of prisoners themselves. Twenty years earlier, prisoners had cared for each other, and what happened to one man left a deep impression on others. "Back then, there was a different class of prisoner in every
way. Since the drugs came, that's when things changed inside. For a lot of prisoners drugs are the priority, and people themselves don't really matter any more."
Mr. Oag also felt that the system of "carrots," such as transfers to lower security
and earlier parole, had made prisoners more willing to sacrifice each other to
advance their own interests.

Although many prisoners at Kent believed that Mr. Oag's most recent
segregation was related to the carrots system, he said, the reality was quite the
opposite. In August 1992, he had become aware of an escape plan involving a helicopter, which would have been a repeat performance of an escape that had taken
place at Kent two years earlier. Mr. Oag had no problem with prisoners wanting
to escape—"I wish them all the best and send me a postcard"—but what concerned him was that the plan involved killing the helicopter pilot so there would

be no witnesses. He made the decision to pass the information on to the authorities and asked for nothing in return beyond the assurance that his information would remain confidential. The institution's response was to place the prisoners believed to be involved in segregation and to initiate their transfer to the Special Handling Unit; Mr. Oag was placed in isolation in the hospital area. Other prisoners put two and two together, and Mr. Oag was identified as an informer. As a result of providing information he felt would save an innocent person's life, he was paying a terrible price. Despite everything, he still believed he had done the right thing.

From August 1992 until April 1993, Mr. Oag was kept isolated in the hospital at Kent, where due to the set-up he had no access to the exercise yard. In April 1993, he was transferred to the Regional Psychiatric Centre, but he was harassed by other prisoners there from the very first day. One prisoner flashed a knife at him. Rather than match force with force, something he had proved quite capable of earlier in his sentence, he chose to remain locked in his cell for two weeks. During this time he went on a hunger strike in an attempt to speed up his transfer. Later that month he was transferred back to Kent. He refused to be placed in K unit, the protective custody unit, because he believed that what he had done was right, and he did not deserve ostracism for the duration of his sentence. He was placed therefore in J unit, where he remained in segregation for eleven months, bearing the brunt of continual verbal abuse from general population prisoners. He also received hate mail from prisoners in other institutions.

February 1994 was the tenth month of Mr. Oag's segregation. He had become physically ill and believed that foreign substances had been planted in his food, which was served to him by other prisoners. In March 1994 he was transferred to Mountain Institution. It was the first time he had moved below maximum security.

Mr. Oag agreed to a case management plan at Mountain Institution which included his participation in cognitive living skills, psychological intervention, and a substance abuse program. However, what remained of most importance to him was his relationship with his visitor. While at Kent he had applied for a private family visit with her, but this had not been approved. He had hoped, and indeed had been led to believe, that institutional approval at Mountain prison for this extended visit would be forthcoming. It was not. Mr. Oag lost confidence in his case management officer, although he did complete the cognitive living skills program.

On August 23, 1994, Mr. Oag's brief respite from solitary confinement came to an end. He was placed in segregation at Mountain Institution, and a decision was made to transfer him back to Kent. Because the segregation unit at Kent was full, he was transferred instead to the segregation unit at Mission Institution. There he was held in the observation strip cell, subject to twenty-four-hour camera observation, and was allowed no visitors. He remained in segregation at Mission for three weeks, then was transferred back to Kent and held in an observation cell in the segregation unit.

The reasons given for his being placed in segregation at Mountain and for his transfer back to Kent, via Mission, were outlined in a progress summary served on him in support of the involuntary transfer.

> This action resulted after it was noted that his cell has been stripped of all pictures, plants, etc., and these articles had either been given away or found already packed in his steel lockers under his bed. On discovering this, Mr. Oag was directed to the correctional supervisor's office. It was at this point Mr. Oag was noted to appear to be under the influence of an unknown substance and refused to provide answers to questions with regard as to why his cell articles were packed away, to whom he had given his plants and some salamanders that he had acquired. When requested to provide a urine analysis or see health care staff he refused and was therefore placed into administrative segregation. (Progress Summary, Mountain Institution, August 25, 1994, at 2)

This same progress summary, in assessing Mr. Oag's escape risk as high, went on to state:

> Mr. Oag has a history of escape lawful custody, the most recent date being 1985. Even while in a maximum security facility (Kent) Mr. Oag was actively involved in escape attempts, the latest resulting in his protective custody status.
>
> The fact that his cell had been stripped, personals being packed away, and other items being given away, with a refusal to provide just cause for this action, causes some concern. While the evidence is inconclusive, given his history, it would seem to indicate that Mr. Oag may very well have been involved in another escape attempt. This after being at Mountain Institution for only a short time. (at 5)

The escape allegation was dealt with in his lawyer's response to the involuntary transfer notice. Mr. Oag had been informed by a staff member at Mountain Institution that the authorities were going to transfer him again, and it was this knowledge that precipitated his giving away one of his pet lizards, although he kept the other. As for the allegation that he had packed away his cell effects, Mr. Oag had this explanation:

> The state of my cell on April 23, 1994, was that I had a number of articles in padlocked boxes under my bed. The boxes and the pad-

locks were provided by staff to keep some personal effects clean during maintenance of my cell. The maintenance of my cell was that a shelf for a television was being added which would require some drilling into the concrete, causing dust. The statement . . . that my cell effects were packed up in preparation of an escape attempt is false. At the time of the transfer, my cell had a television; a radio; a fan; track clothes; a hot water bottle; soap; a lamp; and shampoo. I had seen a picture taken of my cell by staff at Mountain after my visit to [Correctional Supervisor] Ellis' office. I noticed at the time that the picture of my cell was only that portion which had been stored due to the maintenance. (Affidavit of Donald Oag, May 17, 1995)

Mr. Oag's lawyer further submitted that the allegation of Mr. Oag's being involved in an escape attempt at Kent was perverse, given that he had provided information to the authorities which thwarted any such plans.

Back at Kent Institution, in another strip cell without personal possessions, canteen, or tobacco, Mr. Oag once more faced the despair of being treated as a non-person. To compound his agony, he found himself in a cell next to one of the men he had implicated in the escape plot years before. Death threats were made against him and the other prisoners kept up a constant verbal bombardment, urging Mr. Oag to kill himself. To encourage him, the food server threw razor blades through the food slot of the door of his cell. On September 12, 1994, Mr. Oag slashed the veins in his arms using one of these. He was taken to the prison hospital and then transported to Chilliwack Hospital via ambulance. He was returned to Kent the next day and placed in the cell from which he had been carried the day before. The blood had not yet been cleaned up, the razor blade was still imbedded in the floor, and Mr. Oag was placed on a suicide watch, with the light on twenty-four hours a day.

Mr. Oag remained locked in segregation for the rest of 1994 and the whole of 1995. He was still there on June 3, 1996, when I attended the thirty-day review of the Segregation Review Board. Over the course of his long segregation at Kent, his security classification had been reduced to "medium," and his case management team had recommended his transfer to either William Head or Mountain Institution. The wardens at both institutions had refused the transfer, and therefore Mr. Oag remained in maximum security segregation. The harassment by other prisoners never abated, and he lived in continual fear for his life. The only relief from twenty-four-hour lock-up was his weekly visit with his friend, supplemented by the private family visits finally approved after his return to Kent. In recent months he had also been given the job of cleaning up the yard, which he did in the evening after all other prisoners had taken their exercise.

The institution's psychologist told the Board that Mr. Oag's case was being reviewed by the Regional Health Centre with a view to his going there for an individualized program, the purpose of which would be "to detoxify him from segregation." Mr. Oag was only eight months away from his statutory release date, and the idea behind this plan was that once "detoxification" had been effected, he might be transferred to a medium or minimum security institution for the last few months before his release to the street. The psychologist emphasized, however, that RHC had not yet agreed to the plan. Mr. Oag told the Board he was not going to get his hopes up, because he had previously been recommended for lower security by Kent staff only to be refused by the other institutions. He was trying to focus his attention on his relationship and his life after prison; he said he had put in an application to the warden for permission to marry his friend in a ceremony in the chapel at Kent and was hoping that this could take place within the next few months. (The marriage took place quietly in August 1996.)

When I interviewed Mr. Oag later in June 1996, he reviewed the events of the previous two years without acrimony or indignation, though he had just cause for both. The prisoners against whom he had given his information were now either in general population at Kent or on the street, yet he remained entombed in solitary confinement. He had not asked for or expected any reward for bearing witness against his fellow prisoners, but neither did he deserve to spend four years in solitary confinement because he had taken a stand to protect a potential victim. If he had himself participated in the escape plan, he said, he would have been treated better than he was after trying to prevent it. He and his future wife had reconciled themselves to the likelihood that he would spend the last eight months of his sentence in segregation at Kent. He had always survived segregation by letting the world outside become obscured by the fog of imprisonment. Now he was trying to reimagine the world outside with a woman he loved, letting that same fog obscure the horrors of solitary confinement.

When I had taken up the cause inscribed in Jack McCann's hand-written writ in 1973, challenging the conditions of solitary confinement in the B.C. Penitentiary as cruel and unusual punishment, my purpose had been to end an inhumane and barbaric practice. Twenty-three years later, I heard no talk that 638 days in segregation was cruel and inhumane, no talk that it denied Donnie Oag his basic human dignity. In place of the language of respect for human rights, what I heard about was the need to "detoxify" Mr. Oag from his experience. Two years of solitary confinement was transformed from a systemic issue of injustice and abuse of human rights, calling out for redress, to an individual issue of psychological toxicity, which cried out for nothing more than decontamination through further correctional treatment.

It should not be thought that Mr. Oag's unrelieved segregation did not cause real concern among some staff at Kent. Mr. Ouellette, the institution's psychologist, told me that each time a plan was developed for getting Mr. Oag out of segregation and into the population of another institution, only for that plan to be rejected by the wardens of those other institutions, he found it more difficult to face Mr. Oag in an interview or at the Segregation Review Board. As he put it, he was "embarrassed" that the correctional system was treating Mr. Oag in this uncaring manner, given what he had sacrificed to protect an innocent life. Other individual staff did what they could to help Mr. Oag and were not shy about voicing their disagreement with his extended stay in segregation. But these voices were never strong enough to have an impact on the decision of the Segregation Review Board. The "Review of Inmate's Segregated Status" form, month after month, contained the same thin lines:

> You were involuntary transferred from Mountain. You have remained in segregation due to incompatibles. Your p.f.v.s have been approved. You were not approved for transfer to William Head or Mountain Institutions. (Review of Inmate's Segregation Status, Kent Institution, May 3, 1996)

Many of Mr. Oag's review notices also contained a further comment: "You waived your right to be seen by the Segregation Review Board." This waiver represented Mr. Oag's judgement that nothing he could say would alter the bottom line of the Review Board's decision—that he be maintained in segregation. That indeed was the literal bottom line in every one of Mr. Oag's notices: "The Board recommends your seg. status be maintained for your protection."

There are compelling reasons to see Mr. Oag's case as a measure—if not the litmus test—of the reality of change in the legal and administrative regime governing segregation. Over twenty-three years ago Donnie Oag spent 682 days in solitary confinement in the B.C. Penitentiary, where his case was reviewed every thirty days by an internal board that saw no alternative but to maintain his segregation for "the good order and discipline" of the institution. As of June 19, 1996, he had spent 638 days in segregation in Kent Institution, where his case was reviewed every thirty days by an internal board who could see no other alternative but to maintain his segregation "for his own protection." Although legal reforms now gave Mr. Oag a right to appear in person before the Board, the reality was that his appearances never made a difference to the Board's decision; Mr. Oag in fact elected to waive his right to appear, because it generated only frustration.

The conditions of Mr. Oag's confinement had marginally improved over those two decades. In the 1990s he was permitted to have a television in his cell, though this was a mixed blessing. While the TV alleviated the crashing boredom of his isolation, the images it brought were a constant reminder of a world from which he was dissociated. In the B.C. Penitentiary, his access to exercise had taken the form of walking up and down the tier in front of his cell, at all times under the surveillance of a guard armed with shotgun; in Kent, although there was an exercise yard, at thirty feet long and fifteen feet wide it was little more than an extension of a cell. A prisoner, whether walking around its perimeter or pacing back and forth, got little sense of movement beyond pursuing his own shadow. Indeed, shadows were the only things to pursue, given that the yard was dominated by twenty-foot walls with a ceiling of thick mesh wire. Even when the sun was sufficiently high to permit its penetration to the floor of the courtyard, its rays served more to remind those below of their exile than they did to warm their bodies. Segregation had removed them from summer itself.

In the B.C. Penitentiary, Mr. Oag had lived under a regime in which physical deprivation was aggravated by abuse and harassment perpetrated by guards. Official harassment and abuse had not loomed large in Mr. Oag's experience of segregation at Kent. However, this was small comfort, given that his fellow prisoners more than took up the slack.

The single element that distinguished Mr. Oag's segregation in Kent from that in the B.C. Penitentiary—and the element which literally kept him alive— was his access to open visits and, after two years' persistence, private family visits with the woman who was to become his wife. In 1975, the Canadian Penitentiary Service had responded to the Federal Court of Canada's judgement in the *McCann* case by enlarging the window in the steel door of the segregated cells in the Penthouse of the B.C. Penitentiary. The window of opportunity opened up for Mr. Oag by his visits provided a far greater vista on normality and humanity.

Mr. Oag's debilitating experiences in the 1990s demonstrate that new architecture, a new corps of correctional staff, and new correctional legislation have achieved little in limiting the abuses of segregation. I take no comfort in arriving at this conclusion. Because I am a reformer, not an ethnographer, it is important that I go on to grapple with the questions it raises. Why has so little changed? Are the fault lines in the substantive and procedural provisions of the correctional legislation itself; in their administration by correctional officials; or in a lack of effective enforcement of the legislative framework? In Mr. Oag's case, and in most of the other case studies that form my study, fault lines exist in all three areas.

Legislative provisions should have prevented Mr. Oag's long-term segregation after his return from Mountain Institution. Section 4(d) of the CCRA provides that "the Service use the least restrictive measures consistent with the protection of the public, staff members and offenders." This principle is reflected in s. 28, which sets out criteria for the selection of the penitentiary a prisoner is to be confined in and provides that "the Service shall take all reasonable steps to ensure that the penitentiary in which the person is confined is one that provides the least restrictive environment for that person." According to the face sheet of Mr.

Oag's "Review of Segregated Status," his security classification was "medium" on October 27, 1995. By no manner of interpretive leap can maintaining a prisoner in a segregation unit of a maximum security prison be deemed "the least restrictive environment" for that person. Indeed, it is the *most* restrictive environment short of the Special Handling Unit, and arguably, given the conditions under which Mr. Oag was confined, even more restrictive than the SHU. Kent Institution did recommend that Mr. Oag be transferred to medium security, but those recommendations were not accepted by the wardens of William Head or Mountain Institution. The process of transfer to lower security is not seen by the Correctional Service of Canada, at the operational level, as exclusively or even primarily one of lawful obligation; instead, the process is deeply coloured by the politics and preferences of the correctional bureaucracy.

In addition to the general principle enshrined in s. 4 and the criteria for transfers set out in s. 28, there is a further provision of the *CCRA* dealing specifically with administrative segregation which is relevant to Mr. Oag's case. His segregation was based upon s. 31(3)(c): that the institutional head believed on reasonable grounds "that the continued presence of the inmate in the general inmate population will jeopardize the inmate's own safety." That ground for segregation, like the others, is subject to the further qualification that "the institutional head is satisfied that there is no reasonable alternative to administrative segregation." In Mr. Oag's case, correctional authorities at Kent, including the institutional head, were satisfied that there *was* a reasonable alternative to segregation, in the form of a transfer to a medium security institution. Again, when the wardens of those institutions refused to accept the transfer, the politics and preferences of correctional administrators formed the unacceptable basis for concluding there was no reasonable alternative to segregation.

The provisions in the existing correctional legislation which should have prevented Mr. Oag's extended segregation would seem to pinpoint lack of effective enforcement of the law as the real problem in this case. Had a legal challenge been mounted following his reclassification to "medium security," Mr. Oag's rights might well have been respected. In my judgement, however, the issue of enforcement is linked to the larger issue of the sufficiency of the existing legal framework for segregation.

In the previous chapter I reviewed my recommendations for a Model Segregation Code. I observed that while some of those recommendations were incorporated into the *CCRA,* the most important features were either ignored or relegated to the Commissioner's Directives, which lack the force of law. Thus, the requirement in the Model Segregation Code that a plan be developed for the reintegration of the prisoner does not appear in either the *CCRA* or the *CCR Regulations.* The provision that segregation be ended where evidence is presented that its continuation will cause the prisoner substantial psychological and physical harm is not adopted in either the *CCRA* or the *CCR Regulations;* the

Commissioner's Directive requires only that at least once every thirty days there be a written psychological or psychiatric opinion respecting the prisoner's capacity to remain in segregation. In practice, even that limited provision has been further truncated by the adoption of a checklist approach by institutional psychologists, often in the absence of any personal interview with the prisoner. But over and above these limitations of the existing legal and administrative framework, there are two vital elements of my Segregation Code which would have prevented the abuses evident in Mr. Oag's case. The first element relates to the nature of the decision-maker in the segregation process; the second relates to the limitations on the duration of segregation.

Effective reform requires that the person making decisions regarding segregation to be independent from the correctional authorities administering the institution, along the lines of the Independent Chairperson of the Disciplinary Board. It is integral to a fair process that the decision-maker apply the legislative criteria free from the pressures of institutional bias, with an impartial weighing of the competing interests of prisoners and prison administrators. Mr. Oag's continued segregation in the 1990s resulted from the deadlock between the wardens of Kent Institution, William Head Institution, and Mountain Institution on the appropriateness of transferring him to medium security, even though he was deemed a medium security prisoner. At many other points during Mr. Oag's long segregation it was precisely such institutional pressures that perpetuated his segregation.

Under the procedures in the Model Segregation Code, there would have been a legal requirement to formulate a plan for presentation to the independent adjudicator early on in the segregation. Once that plan was approved by the independent adjudicator, subsequent reviews would be required to document the steps taken to implement it. Such a procedure would avoid situations in which plans are not implemented for reasons that, although understandable in the context of institutional life—a change in assignment of case management officer or staff members taking annual leave—are simply not legitimate reasons for maintaining a prisoner in long-term segregation.

Locating the decision-making power in an independent adjudicator would also provide a trigger absent under the existing procedures. Segregation Review Board discussions were often unfocussed and shapeless, particularly in cases of long-term segregation, where the very existence of a lengthy segregation almost fatalistically provided the evidence of its future inevitability. In many cases the decision to maintain segregation emerged not as a decision but as a *fait accompli*. In other cases, prisoners were left with vague promises that the institution would "try to do something"—to overcome the resistance of other institutions to accepting a prisoner; to ensure that a progress summary required for a transfer application was completed before the next review; to see that the institutional preventive security officer visited the prisoner to try to resolve problems of incompatibility. In these and myriad other situations, the prisoner was, in fact, "sloughed off." Under the Model Segregation Code, the independent adjudicator at Segregation Review Board hearings would have both the legal authority and the obligation to "do something."

The second feature of the Model Segregation Code that would have made a difference to Mr. Oag's case is the ninety-day limitation I proposed on the overall duration of segregation. Operationally, this would have meant that Kent Institution had no more than ninety days from the time Mr. Oag was first segregated to find an alternative placement for him. This would have created some urgency in presenting his case for transfer to another institution, and it would have put the decision about transferring Mr. Oag into a framework in which the "least restrictive alternative" was recognized as a legal imperative, not seen as an administrative option. In the absence of both time constraints on the duration of administrative segregation and the other protections contained in the Model Segregation Code, Donnie Oag finally left Kent Institution on statutory release on February 8, 1997, straight from his cell in segregation, having spent the last 1,000 days of his sentence in a "prison within a prison."

## CHAPTER 3

# The Arbour Report:
# The Indictment of a System

In April 1994, a series of events began to unfold at the Prison for Women in Kingston (P4W) that exposed to public view and scrutiny, in a manner unprecedented in Canadian history, the relationship between the Rule of Law and operational realty. The videotaped strip-searching of women prisoners by a male emergency response team shocked and horrified many Canadians, including correctional staff, when it was shown a year later on national television. The strip search and the subsequent long-term segregation of the prisoners became the subject of both a special report by the Correctional Investigator and a report by the Commission of Inquiry conducted by Madam Justice Louise Arbour. Both reports condemned the correctional practices that occurred in the Prison for Women, but Madam Justice Arbour's report contained the clearest indictment of the Correctional Service of Canada.

Following the submission of her report, Madam Justice Arbour was appointed Chief Prosecutor for the International War Crimes Tribunal, established to bring to trial those accused of crimes against humanity committed during the hostilities in Rwanda and the former Yugoslavia. It would be unfair to compare the murder and torture of men, women, and children under the guise of ethnic cleansing with what happened to a small group of prisoners at the Prison for Women; it is not unfair, however, to conclude from Madam Justice Arbour's findings that, at the beginning of the twenty-first century, Canadian correctional practices associated with the use of segregation continue to dehumanize and degrade prisoners and are inconsistent with fundamental principles enshrined in international human rights covenants, the *Canadian Charter of Rights and Freedoms,* and correctional law.

The Arbour Report (*Commission of Inquiry into Certain Events at the Prison for Women in Kingston* [Ottawa: Public Works and Government Services Canada, 1996] [Commissioner: Louise Arbour]) is a critical document in the history of Canadian corrections, opening a window onto correctional practices and attitudes beyond the narrow and little publicized view provided by individual judicial challenges by prisoners. In many respects, it provides for the 1990s what the report of the House of Commons Sub-Committee on the Penitentiary System in Canada did for the 1970s; indeed, the findings of the Arbour Report serve as an important measure of how far the correctional system has progressed in bringing its operations into compliance with two of the fundamental principles pronounced by that Parliamentary subcommittee: that "The Rule of Law must prevail inside Canadian penitentiaries" and that "Justice for inmates is a personal right and also an essential condition of their socialization and personal reformation" (*Report to Parliament* at 86–87).

The Arbour Report also provides a window onto the world of Canadian women in prison and their experiences of justice. There is an important and growing literature on women's experience of imprisonment and the struggle to develop a women-centred model reflecting empowerment, choice, and healing. Readers are referred to Kelly Hannah-Moffat, *Punishment in Disguise: Penal Governance and Federal Imprisonment of Women in Canada* (Toronto: University of Toronto Press, 2001) and the resource links in the Internet version of this book.

My observations and inquiries in this book are focussed on correctional practices at Matsqui and Kent Institutions, prisons for men. The Arbour Inquiry focussed on practices at the Prison for Women, more than two thousand miles from the Fraser Valley. To the extent that Madam Justice Arbour's findings regarding disrespect for the law and continuing abuse of discretionary power parallel my own, they provide compelling evidence that these are systemic issues. To the extent that the Arbour recommendations for reform parallel those I have made, they suggest that these pathways to reform are not the idealistic musings of a civil rights lawyer but rather a principled and practical agenda for entrenching the Rule of Law in the Canadian prison system.

## What Happened at the Prison for Women

The chronology of the events leading to the Arbour Inquiry is outlined in the following passage from the Commissioner's report:

> On the evening of Friday, April 22, 1994, a brief but violent physical confrontation took place between six inmates at the Prison for

Women and a number of the correctional staff. The six inmates were immediately placed in the Segregation Unit at the Prison for Women. Criminal charges were laid against them; and five of the six inmates ultimately pleaded guilty to offences connected to the incident.

Tension was very high at the prison—particularly in the Segregation Unit. In the subsequent days, behaviour in that unit was very agitated. On Sunday, April 24th, three inmates who had not been involved in the April 22nd incident, but who were already in segregation when the six were brought in, variously slashed, took a hostage, and attempted suicide.

On Tuesday, April 26, 1994, correctional staff demonstrated outside the Prison for Women demanding the transfer of the inmates that had been involved in the April 22nd incident.

On the evening of April 26, 1994, the Warden of the Prison for Women called in a male Institutional Emergency Response Team ("IERT") from Kingston Penitentiary to conduct a cell extraction and strip search of eight women in segregation; the six who had been involved in the April 22nd incident, and two others. As is customary when the IERT is deployed, the cell extractions and strip searches were videotaped. At the end of the lengthy procedure, which finished early in the morning of April 27th, the eight inmates were left in empty cells in the Segregation Unit wearing paper gowns, and in restraints and leg irons.

On the evening of Wednesday, April 27th, seven of the eight inmates were subjected to body cavity searches.

On Friday, May 6, 1994, five inmates, four of whom had been involved in the April 22nd incident, were transferred to a wing of the Regional Treatment Centre, a male psychiatric treatment facility within Kingston Penitentiary. Two of these women subsequently launched *habeas corpus* applications, and on July 12, 1994, they were ordered returned to the Prison for Women. Four inmates were returned to the Prison for Women between July 14th and 18th, 1994, while another was transferred to the Regional Prairies Centre.

The six women who had been involved in the April 22nd incident remained in segregation for many months. On December 1, 1994, the women's agreement to plead guilty to related criminal charges was publicly announced. They appeared in court and pleaded guilty to the agreed charges on December 22, 1994.

The women were released from segregation between December 7, 1994 and January 19, 1995 . . .

On all the evidence before me, I am satisfied that the guilty pleas, and the facts tendered in support of these pleas, present a reliable summary of the significant elements of the events on April 22nd. These facts are as follows.

The incident took place shortly before 6:00 p.m. on April 22nd. The B range inmates were attending the hospital area, as is routine, to receive prescribed medication. Inmates Young and Shea approached the hospital barrier and inmate Young began to demand her medication in a loud and aggressive voice. The two inmates were quickly joined by inmates Twins, Morrison, Emsley and Bettencourt. Most of the inmates wore street clothes.

There were six inmates in an area controlled by four correctional officers—Vance, Boston, Metivier and Fabio. Officer Vance questioned the group at which point the inmates jumped the officers on what appeared to be a signal from Ms. Twins. Ms. Morrison attacked Office Vance, striking her a number of times in the upper abdomen, left arm and left thigh area with an instrument, which was never recovered, capable of making puncture marks. Ms. Young also jumped Officer Vance and during the course of the assault, the officer recalls hearing the words "kill you" spoken by one of the inmates.

Inmate Young turned to inmate Twins and said: "Where is the scissors? Give me the scissors so I can stick her." Inmate Twins reached for a pair of hobbycraft-sized scissors and tried to pass them to inmate Young, but they were knocked clear and taken by Officer Boston . . .

Ms. Twins grabbed Officer Fabio, who had gone to assist Officer Vance, around the neck and said to her: "You're my fucking hostage. We're going out through the front door." Officer Fabio was able to break free and was attacked by Ms. Young, Ms. Bettencourt and Ms. Morrison, who grabbed her and struck her. Inmate Young said: "Grab the telephone cord. We'll string the bitch up, right here." Inmates Young and Bettencourt tried to pull Officer Fabio onto B range and were heard yelling: "We've got her. She's coming with us. Let's get her." Inmate Young pulled Officer Fabio by the hair and clumps of hair similar in colour to that of Officer Fabio were later found on the floor.

Correctional Supervisor Gillis arrived, armed with mace, and ordered the inmates to release Officer Fabio. They wouldn't, and Correctional Supervisor Gillis maced both inmates, thereby freeing Officer Fabio who remembers thinking that she was going to be killed.

Officer Boston had attempted to go to Officer Fabio's aid and was grabbed around the throat by Ms. Twins who said: "Give me your keys. We're going out the front door. Don't push me, Boston. I've got a shiv, and I'll stick you." Ms. Twins then attempted to get Officer Boston's key from her pocket. Correctional Supervisor Gillis attempted to control the situation and Ms. Twins kicked him in the groin area, whereupon he maced her.

After the immediate situation was controlled, the inmates were removed from the area to the Segregation Unit . . . During the course of the removal to the segregation area, Ms. Bettencourt became violent, biting, kicking and spitting at the escort officers. She kicked Officer Smith in the left knee. Officer Smith had previously had medical problems with the knee. The doctor later diagnosed a torn cartilage, and placed Officer Smith in a hip to ankle cast. She was subsequently rushed to hospital as a result of blood clotting.

The incident was very brief, lasting a minute and a half to two or three minutes at most. (at 27–29)

The charges to which the women pleaded guilty included attempted prison breach, assault with a weapon, assault, possession of a weapon for a purpose dangerous to the public peace, and threatening serious bodily harm. The report observes that Union of Solicitor General Employees argued that the events under investigation began with a planned, deliberate attempt at escape by six prisoners and that it involved an attempted murder. However, Madam Justice Arbour found that although the evidence suggested the events of April 22 were not entirely spontaneous, it did not support the conclusion that there was much planning beyond a short caucusing between inmates a few minutes before they came to blows with correctional officers. Furthermore, she rejected union submissions that the assaults perpetrated by the inmates revealed an intent to kill, adding that no inmate was ever charged with attempted murder.

In her report, Madam Justice Arbour addressed each stage of "The Events," including the strip search by the male Institutional Emergency Response Team (IERT), the body cavity searches carried out after the women were segregated, the transfer to the male Regional Treatment Centre, and the subsequent long-term segregation of the women. She also addressed the manner in which CSC carried out its internal investigation and edited its report, noting in particular the inaccurate and misleading description of the IERT intervention. Her findings in each of these areas were integral elements of her conclusion that CSC's culture did not respect the Rule of Law. In this chapter I will concentrate on her findings in relation to segregation and strip searching: segregation because of its direct relevance to my research and the strip search because it presages events at Kent Institution two years after the publication of the Arbour Report.

## The Segregation Unit at the P4W, April 22–26, 1994

The Arbour Report recounts developments at the P4W in the aftermath of the attack on staff.

> The April 22nd incident was seen as an unprecedented assault on staff. It produced tremendous hostility, resentment and fear among members of the staff at the Prison for Women. The staff response was itself unprecedented, and included an unwillingness to act upon the Warden's order to unlock the ranges, and the holding of a demonstration demanding the transfer of the women involved in the incident out of the Prison for Women and into a special handling unit . . . While some steps were taken to try to reduce the level of trauma—debriefings, further meetings with staff, sick leave for those most affected—it is clear that those reactions persisted among staff in the days and weeks that followed . . .
>
> It is also evident that for the inmates involved, there were not the comparable opportunities to reduce the emotional stress of the events which were available to the staff who had debriefings, informal social gatherings, and the opportunity to leave the institution to go home. On the contrary, the inmates were placed in constant contact with the other inmates involved in the incidents (together with a small number of other inmates already in the unit by reason of individual personal crises), thereby making it impossible to distance themselves from the events, and producing an inevitable solidarity among them.
>
> From the evening of April 22nd to the evening of April 26th, there were extraordinary levels of unrest in the Segregation Unit. There were also periods, sometimes whole shifts, that were quiet or normal . . .
>
> From the beginning of these events, there were periods in which the inmates were acting out, and engaging in verbal abuse ranging from demands (for amenities or rights to which they thought they were entitled and which were being denied), through insults, and threats. Sometimes the noise level was so high that the entire unit seemed to vibrate . . .
>
> Commencing on April 25th, the periods of acting out in the Segregation Unit included, on occasion, the setting of small fires.
>
> On the afternoon of April 26th, Dr. Robert Bater, the Chair of the Citizens' Advisory Committee, visited in the Segregation Unit and talked to a number of the inmates. He testified that he did not feel threatened and was made to feel welcome by the inmates.

Later, on the afternoon of April 26th, Officer Ostrom, while patrolling the unit alone, was confined at the end of the upper range by threats, apparently accompanied by the swinging of items thought to be weapons. She was escorted from the range by Correctional Supervisor Warnell, who was armed with a mace can . . .

One question raised by the evidence is whether or not the collective behaviour of the inmates was of a scale so unprecedented as to be unmanageable, and in my opinion the answer to that is no. Each inmate was lodged individually in a segregation cell, and although at times their collective behaviour was highly disruptive and, in some cases, assaultive to persons who approached their cells, it is inconceivable to suggest that between the evening of April 22nd up until the evening of April 26th, when the IERT was called in to intervene, nothing could have been done to bring the situation in that unit under control. (Arbour at 36–38)

In addressing the segregation of the prisoners from April 22 to 26, Madam Justice Arbour found that there were serial violations of basic legal rights. The first violation was in relation to a prisoner's right to counsel when placed in administrative segregation.

Throughout the period April 22nd to April 26th, inmates were neither advised of their right to counsel, nor given access to counsel. Inmates' specific and repeated requests for lawyers were denied. Indeed, this denial continued until April 29th. (Arbour at 41)

Madam Justice Arbour found that the legal obligation set out by the CCR *Regulations* to "ensure that every inmate is given a reasonable opportunity to retain and instruct legal counsel without delay and that every inmate is informed of the inmate's right to legal counsel where the inmate (a) is placed in administrative segregation" (CCR *Regulations* 97(2)) was largely unknown to the staff at the P4W. When this legal right was brought to staff's attention during the inquiry, they failed to appreciate the purpose of such legal entitlement or the need to comply with it. The other violation of the law found by Madam Justice Arbour was the denial of daily exercise for over a month, from April 22 until May 24, 1994. The CCR *Regulations* provide that "the Service shall take all reasonable steps . . . to ensure . . . that every inmate is (d) given the opportunity exercise for at least one hour every day outdoors, weather permitting, or indoors where the weather does not permit exercising outdoors."

The prolonged deprivation of daily exercise to inmates in segregation was in serious contravention of the Regulations and, I would have thought, was a serious departure from Correctional Service policy. I hesitate in the latter conclusion because of the suggestion, in the evidence of many Correctional Service witnesses, that the operational policy of the Service is that daily exercise is always subject to security concerns, and that the security concerns perceived to exist in this case justified the denial of exercise. Indeed, in written submissions, the Correctional Service puts forward the following proposition:

> An interpretation of "recreational activities" that requires exercise to be given irrespective of security requirements is absurd and would exceed the "all reasonable steps" requirement of the Regulations.

In response to that position, I can only say that I do not think it is absurd to suggest that a person should not be kept locked up in a small cell 24 hours a day, and that if there were security concerns, they should be dealt with otherwise than by simply denying an inmate an opportunity to step out of her cell. Moreover, if security considerations were to prevent the removal of a segregated inmate from his or her cell for one hour on a given day, I see no basis for that ever to be more than occasional. In any event, I find nothing in this case to suggest that there were ever security concerns of such magnitude that exercise should have been denied on any single day, to all segregated inmates . . .

. . . Once again it seems that even if the law is known, there is a general perception that it can always be departed from for a valid reason, and that, in any event compliance with prisoners' rights is not a priority. At best, denial of exercise can be attributed here to inadequate staffing. More realistically, it was part of a general punitive attitude which required inmates to earn entitlements to everything perceived as a privilege, rather than a right. (Arbour at 46–47)

A further, more pervasive violation of the law related to *CCRA* requirements that prisoners in administrative segregation be given the same rights, privileges and conditions of confinement as the general inmate population, except for those that cannot reasonably be given owing to limitations specific to the administrative segregation area or security requirements (*CCRA* s. 37).

In this case, the governing direction from the Warden in place from early April 23rd was that nothing was to be given to the inmates. The interpretation of this instruction varied somewhat depending upon who was on duty. In general, though, the regime was one of denial.

Virtually none of the rights, privileges and conditions of confinement available in the general prison population or ordinarily available in segregation were provided . . .

In addition to being denied their legal entitlements with respect to access to lawyers and exercise, they were denied telephone calls to others, including to the Correctional Investigator, books and activities, showers, cleaning, and the removal of garbage accumulation. As well, the segregation logs record frequent refusals of their requests for socks, clothing, ice, lights, pop and toilet paper.

They were denied visits from the Inmate Committee members, from members of the Peer Support Team (a group of specially trained inmates who support each other in times of crisis), and spiritual support.

On the evening of Sunday, April 24th, officers were directed not to speak to the inmates, and two days later they were directed not to do rounds.

That same evening, the water was shut off and remained off until Monday afternoon, when it was turned on and the inmates were advised that if there were any problems, it would be turned off again. The evidence indicated that the only reason for turning off water would be flooding, although there was no indication that flooding had occurred. Indeed, turning off the water appears to have aggravated the behaviour of the inmates and increased the throwing of urine.

In general terms, the reasons advanced for the denial of these rights and privileges were linked to the behaviour of the inmates. Not all these restrictions can be rationally attributed to security or safety concerns. They were more an attempt to reward good behaviour and punish bad . . .

The denial of rights and privileges in the Segregation Unit between April 22nd and April 26th was in contravention of the applicable law and policy. This was clearly based on a managerial strategy for handling the situation in the unit. It was an ill advised strategy which, in my opinion, contributed to an escalation of the situation . . . The fact that the policy of "they get nothing" was never changed, even after the intervention of the IERT, raises serious questions as to whether it was indeed merely a managerial strategy to control the unit, or whether it was, in part, the manifestation of a punitive attitude which would be a more serious contravention, not only of the policies, but of the law. (Arbour at 51–55)

As readers will recall, Bill Frederick's account of his harrowing experiences in H unit at Kent in 1983 also reflected an institutional strategy of "they get nothing," which precipitated prisoner protests, "justifying" more punitive responses from the staff.

Madam Justice Arbour commented on the CSC's general attitude regarding non-compliance with the law, as reflected in the witnesses who testified before her:

> The most troubling from my point of view, is the attitude of CSC, throughout this inquiry, *vis à vis* these issues. It is only when virtually all the evidence had been thoroughly scrutinized at the hearings that CSC conceded that access to counsel during the period of April 25th to 29th was improperly denied. Even then, counsel for CSC urged the Commission not to conclude that the denial of right to counsel was reflective of the usual standards met by the Correctional Service staff with regard to observance of legal and policy requirements. It was not within the ambit of this inquiry to scrutinize the level of legal compliance throughout the Service and I therefore have little basis upon which to conclude that the shortcomings at the Prison for Women were an aberration . . . Certainly with respect to right to counsel, access to daily exercise, daily visits to segregation by institutional heads, and so on, the evidence indicates that these legal requirements were largely unknown, virtually at all levels, at the Prison for Women . . .
>
> . . . Significantly in my view, when the departures from legal requirements in this case became known through this inquiry's process, their importance was downplayed and the overriding public security concern was always relied upon when lack of compliance had to be admitted. This was true to the higher ranks of the Correctional Service management, *which leads me to believe that the lack of observance of individual rights is not an isolated factor applicable only to the Prison for Women, but is probably very much part of CSC's corporate culture.* (Arbour at 56–57, emphasis added)

## The Strip Search of April 26–27, 1994

As Madam Justice Arbour found, the law is quite clear that men may not strip-search women. The only exception is where a delay in locating women staff to conduct the search would be dangerous to human life or safety or might result in the loss of evidence. The decision to deploy a male emergency response team to strip-search the women in segregation at the P4W was made following a recommendation of Correctional Supervisor Warnell:

Given the fragile psyche of the officers at the institution at this time, I strongly recommend that an IERT cell extraction team be brought in and all inmates in the dissociation side be taken from their cells, strip searched and placed in strip cells. I do not feel that our Officers should have to continue to suffer this type of abuse when we have the means to put a stop to it. Otherwise, I fear that we will have more staff requesting stress leaves and a diminished credibility toward management. (cited in Arbour at 65)

The Warden concurred with that recommendation and did not consider negotiating with the prisoners prior to the deployment of the team. Neither were the prisoners advised that the team would be put into action if they did not stop their disruptive activities. The manner in which the IERT subsequently carried out its mandate is captured on the videotape of the exercise.

Prior to the video being turned on, the IERT marched into the Segregation Unit in standard formation, approached Joey Twins' cell and banged on the bars of her cell with the shield. She immediately did as she was ordered, and when the video begins she is lying face down in her cell surrounded by IERT members who are holding her down. An officer now identified as a female member of the Prison for Women staff, cuts off Ms. Twins' clothing with the 911 tool [a curved knife], while IERT members hold her down. The extent to which they are assisting the female officer in the actual cutting and removal of the clothes is difficult to tell from the tape. Ms. Twins' hands are cuffed behind her back and her legs shackled. She is marched backwards out of her cell naked, and led to the corner of the range. There she is held against the wall with the clear plastic shield, with her back against the wall. Some IERT members stand around her while the IPSO, Mr. Waller, and maintenance men from the prison enter the Segregation Unit to begin stripping Ms. Twins' cell. The corner where Ms. Twins is standing is visible to anyone in the unit or standing in the doorway separating the dissociation side from the protective custody side of the Segregation Unit . . . The Warden and Deputy Warden were not in the dissociation side during the strip searches.

While she is still being held in the corner, a paper gown is brought to Ms. Twins and tied around her neck. The effect is something like that of a bib. The paper gown neither covers her, nor provides warmth.

Upon her return to the cell, an IERT member begins the extremely lengthy process of attempting to apply a body belt in substitution of her handcuffs, during which procedure her gown comes off . . .

Finally, this lengthy procedure is completed and she is left lying on the floor of her cell in restraints—body belt and leg irons—and with a small paper gown . . .

The video and the evidence reveal that the cell extraction and strip search of the remaining inmates was substantially similar to those of Ms. Twins', with certain exceptions.

. . . The video shows the last inmate who was strip searched, Brenda Morrison, with her clothes on when the IERT enter the cell. In response to their order for her to kneel and remove her clothing, she asks questions about what will happen if she does not remove them. The questions are not answered. Rather, restraint equipment is applied over her clothing, at which point she offers to take her clothes off. They direct her to lie face down. She does not immediately do so and they force her to the ground. Three IERT members hold her down and rip and then cut her shirt open at the back while the female correctional officer cuts her pants off. (Arbour at 71–73)

The graphic depiction of these events is supplemented in the report by Ms. Morrison's testimony.

I felt very degraded and pissed off. I don't know—I don't know how anybody can do that to somebody and live with themselves. How they can walk in there, rip my clothes and say "It's okay, I was doing my job; it was professional." Maybe if the tables were turned they wouldn't think so, but the tables aren't. I don't know how any man can do that to any woman and say it was their job. As far as I know, it's a crime. A crime was committed there. And if something like that happened down the street, that's a crime. If you go in an apartment and rip girls' clothes off, that's a crime. That's sexual assault . . .

If somebody can stand here and tell me, look me in the eyes and tell me that's right, I ask myself: where is justice? What about justice inside the institution? Is there any for us inside? We must not, because we are criminals.

The report continues with its summary of events as depicted on the videotape.

Throughout the strip searches, there is a fairly constant level of talking and calling in the Segregation Unit. Inmates are heard to call out their requests that the windows be closed. These had been opened prior to the IERT attendance to clear out the remaining smoke from the earlier fires. Although the smoke had already cleared when the operation began at 11:40 p.m., the windows were left open until after 2 in the morning, notwithstanding the fact that the temperature was between 11 and 12 degrees. Other requests, for tampax, medication, eye glasses, are called out, as are comments which were interpreted by some who were present in the unit to be flirtatious, joking or defiant in nature. Some called out that they were being raped. In addition, questions about what was happening and about whether the IERT were all male were directed to IERT members. Some expressed their fear at the memory of previous sexual assaults. Consistent with IERT training, questions and requests were not answered . . .

There was no security reason not to give the women more appropriate gowns for covering themselves immediately after the strip search. Nor was there a security or any other reason offered for leaving the windows open for almost three hours after the smoke in the unit had cleared.

At the end of the procedure, pursuant to the Warden's instructions, the women were left on the cement floor of their cells in body belts, leg irons, paper gowns, and with nothing else. The bolted beds had been removed from the cells and there was nothing left but a sink and a toilet. They remained in that condition until the early afternoon of the following day when each was given one security blanket. While there was some attempt to suggest that this state of affairs was due to security concerns, no plausible explanation was offered for keeping the women in leg irons and depriving them of any means of keeping warm. (Arbour at 74–77)

The then Commissioner of Corrections testified before the inquiry that while he was shocked when he first viewed the video of the strip search, he believed the video was unfair since it did not depict the circumstances immediately preceding the search. Had these been portrayed with the same detail as the search itself, he said, it would have coloured the public's view of these events. Madam Justice Arbour disputed that interpretation:

I understand his comment to suggest that the shock upon viewing this amount of brutality would be greatly diminished if one were equally apprised of the ongoing level of disruption, vulgarity and verbal violence which had taken place in the larger timeframe preceding the IERT intervention. I disagree . . . I believe that even if all that had been captured on film, it would not have detracted from the

shocking effect and the indignation generated by seeing men handling naked women in that fashion.

*. . . The process was intended to terrorize, and therefore subdue.
There is no doubt that it had this intended effect in this case.* It also,
unfortunately, had the effect of re-victimizing women who had had
traumatic experiences in their past at the hands of men. Although
this consequence was not intended, it should have been foreseen.

I find that the conditions in which the inmates were left in their
cell at the completion of the IERT intervention were, frankly, appalling and I see nothing in the evidence to indicate that these conditions were genuinely dictated by a serious security concern. (Arbour
at 87–89, emphasis added)

## Segregation Post-April 26: The P4W and the Penthouse at the B.C. Penitentiary

The women involved in the April 22 incident remained in segregation from that
date until December 1994 or January 1995. The Arbour Report traces the conditions of their confinement, the reasons given by the CSC for its necessity, the segregation review process through which it was maintained, and the impact of the
segregation on the women.

On April 27, 1994, the Warden's order that the inmates in segregation were to get nothing without specific direction from her, was
forcefully repeated in the segregation log, and even more stringently
interpreted than in the days before the IERT attendance. The resulting regime of denial continued for an extended period of time . . .

. . . Mattresses were not reintroduced in segregation at the Prison
for Women until May 10th. Restrictions on the availability of clothing continued for some period of time, and even included the failure
to comply with Unit Manager Hilder's direction that women be provided with street clothes prior to attending in court. In the period
immediately following April 27th, toilet paper was restricted to "one
or two squares" per inmate. Underwear was denied, even in the circumstance of an inmate who required the use of a sanitary pad with
vaginal cream. Regular cleaning of the segregation area, garbage
removal and laundry was very slow to resume. At the Prison for
Women, showers were not regularly provided in the initial weeks.
Phone calls (including calls to the Correctional Investigator) were
denied, as were specific requests for cigarettes, ice and face cloths . . .

While there was some attempt to suggest that the basis of the

overall regime was grounded in security concerns, most witnesses
who testified appeared to concede that there was little in the way of
specific security justifications for the deprivations noted above . . .
(Arbour at 132)

This deprivation of basic amenities replicated the conditions I observed at
Kent Institution in H unit in 1983 and in the Penthouse at the B.C. Penitentiary
a decade earlier. The regime of reducing prisoners to a Hobbesian state of brutish
nature to demonstrate that they are under the total control of their jailers has
long been a cornerstone of the customary law of segregation units. What Madam
Justice Arbour found was that at the P4W, customary law had little difficulty
maintaining its ascendancy over the provisions of the CCRA.

There were other elements of déjà vu at the Prison for Women.

When the inmates who had been transferred to the Regional Treatment Centre were returned, heavy treadplate was welded to the bars
of all cells in the dissociation unit. This was done to discourage the
throwing of objects or fluids from the cells. There had been no incidents of throwing anything through the bars after April 27th, either
at the Regional Treatment Centre or at the Prison for Women. The
effect of the addition of the treadplate was to increase markedly the
oppressiveness of the dissociation unit cells, and the isolation of their
inhabitants. Although almost $38,000.00 was spent installing the
treadplate, it was not considered appropriate to spend the $2,000.00
which had been estimated as necessary to provide electricity to the
cells so that televisions or radios could be provided, until late
November or early December of 1994. (Arbour at 133)

This "improvement" to the segregation unit mirrored a similar "improvement" made to the Penthouse in the wake of the 1975 Federal Court judgement
in *McCann.* The tiny windows in the cell doors were enlarged to permit more
light into the interior, but within months these were covered with a heavy steel-
wire grill, isolating prisoners even further from the outside world.

Madam Justice Arbour was especially critical of the Segregation Review
process at P4W.

It is difficult to discern any indication in the segregation review
process or otherwise, that any assessment was made of whether the
statutory requirements for continued segregation were met.

. . . There is little, if any, consistency in the reasons for continued
segregation recorded in the segregation review documents. Nor do

the reasons advanced in the segregation reviews specifically address the question of whether or how those reasons relate to the statutory standards.

Throughout the segregation reviews, there is repeated reference to the significance of the outstanding criminal charges to the ongoing segregation of these women. In a number of instances, the outstanding charges are identified as the significant, and in some cases the only reasons for the continued segregation. This is so notwithstanding that it was conceded, as it must be, that the existence of such outstanding charges cannot by itself justify continued segregation.

The Regulations contemplate that an independent assessment of whether the statutory requirements for continued segregation have been met will occur every 60 days at the Regional Headquarters. The evidence raises a serious question as to whether such independent reviews occur . . .

It is apparent that the person conducting the review at the Regional Headquarters is heavily influenced by the judgement of the institution as reflected in the paper or electronic record of the segregation review. Indeed, there was evidence that insufficient attention was paid even to that record. (Arbour at 136–37)

Madam Justice Arbour's findings regarding the deferential nature of regional reviews parallel my observations at Kent. Similarly, justifying segregation on the basis of outstanding charges reflects the persistence of customary law at Kent, notwithstanding the provisions of the CCRA.

Madam Justice Arbour concluded her review with an assessment of the impact of prolonged segregation on the prisoners at the P4W.

In October of 1994, the prison's psychologists advised the prison staff of the psychological ill effects being suffered by the women. Their report read:

Many of the symptoms currently observed are typical effects of long-term isolation and sensory deprivation. One thing which seems to have increased the deprivation in this current situation is the new grillwork which has been put up on the cells. The following symptoms have been observed: perceptual distortions, auditory and visual hallucinations, flashbacks, increased sensitivity and startle response, concentration difficulties and subsequent effect on school work, emotional distress due to the extreme boredom and monotony, anxiety, particularly associated with leaving the cell or seg area, generalized emotional lability at times, fear that they are "going crazy" or "losing their minds" because of limited interaction with others which results in lack of external frames of reference, low mood and generalized sense of hopelessness.

Part of this last symptom stems from a lack of clear goals for them. They do not know what they have to do to earn privileges or gain release from segregation . . . Their behaviour had been satisfactory since their return from RTC but has not earned them additional privileges, nor have they been informed that their satisfactory behaviour will result in any change of status.

If the current situation continues it will ultimately lead to some kind of crisis, including violence, suicide and self-injury. They will become desperate enough to use any means to assert some form of control of their lives. The constant demands to segregation staff [are] related to needs for external stimulation and some sense of control of their lives.

The segregation of these inmates continued for between two and a half to three months after these observations were made. (Arbour at 139–40)

The psychologists' report reiterates the conclusions of psychologists at the *McCann* trial that "sustained punishment without escape, without any instrumental response to terminate it . . . where there is nothing to learn" will generate violence and mental illness (cited in Jackson, *Prisoners of Isolation* at 74). As with Jack McCann, whose ongoing assessment as "quiet and cooperative" did not result in his release from segregation, the good behaviour of the prisoners at the P4W did not provide them relief from their continued detention.

In summation, the Arbour Report made these findings:

The prolonged segregation of the inmates and the conditions and management of their segregation was again, not in accordance with law and policy, and was, in my opinion, a profound failure of the custodial mandate of the Correctional Service. The segregation was administrative in name only. In fact it was punitive, and it was a form of punishment that courts would be loathe to impose, so destructive are its consequences . . .

The most objectionable feature of this lengthy detention in segregation was its indefiniteness. The absence of any release plan in the early stages made it impossible for the segregated inmates to determine when, and through what effort on their part, they could bring an end to that ordeal. This indefinite hardship would have the most demoralizing effect and, if for that reason alone, there may well have to be a cap placed on all forms of administrative segregation . . .

If the segregation review process was designed to prevent endless, indeterminate segregation, by imposing a periodic burden on the prison authorities to justify further detention, it proved to be a total failure in this case. Essentially, the segregation review process reversed the burden and assumed, in virtually every instance, that release had to be justified. In many instances, the reasons advanced for maintaining the segregation status would have been entirely unacceptable to trigger segregation in the first place. The frequent reference to the disposition of criminal charges as a landmark for de-segregation indicated that a wrong test was being applied. Worse, and even if not intended to do so, it could be objectively viewed as an inducement for the inmates to expedite the disposition of charges against them.

Eight or nine months of segregation, even in conditions vastly superior to those which existed in this case, is a significant departure from the standard terms and conditions of imprisonment, and is only justifiable if explicitly permitted by law. If it is not legally authorized, it disturbs the integrity of the sentence . . .

In this instance, this prolonged period of segregation was aggravated by the conditions that prevailed in the Segregation Unit at the Prison for Women at the time. The physical layout of the cells created the worst possible environment. The addition of the treadplate in front of the open bars created a massive visual obstruction which rendered the cement interior of the small cell darker and more claustrophobic. On the other hand, it did not shelter each individual inmate from the noise generated in the adjacent cells. For most of their time in segregation, these women had virtually no access to any form of external stimuli. Apart from the painful deprivation of human contact which segregation necessarily entails, they had no access to television and were limited for a time to a communal radio (only introduced in September) and some sparse reading materials.

There was no effort on the part of the prison to deal creatively with their reintegration. There were no programs available to them, and they were left idle and alone in circumstances that could only contribute to their further physical, mental and emotional deterioration. The period of segregation was not meant, in law, to serve as punishment for offences to which they had not yet pleaded guilty. They eventually did plead guilty and most of them were sentenced to additional time to be served consecutively to their current sentences. The bitterness, resentment and anger that this kind of treatment would generate in anyone who still allows herself to feel anything, would greatly overweigh the short-term benefits that their removal from the general population could possibly produce . . .

If prolonged segregation in these deplorable conditions is so common throughout the Correctional Service that it failed to attract anyone's attention, then I would think that the Service is delinquent in the way it discharges its legal mandate. (Arbour at 141–43)

For those who would argue that the conditions endured by prisoners in the Penthouse at the B.C. Penitentiary can safely be consigned to the lessons of history, Madam Justice Arbour's findings stand as an indictment of a failure of the Correctional Service of Canada to take those lessons seriously. Without a fundamental change in the culture of corrections, these practices, which harken back to the nineteenth century, will persist well into the twenty-first.

## Measuring csc's Performance against Its Mission Statement

At the conclusion of the first part of her report, Madam Justice Arbour reviewed her findings in the context of the Mission Statement of the Correctional Service of Canada and the core values to which the Service commits itself, values now incorporated into the *CCRA*. Her conclusions were unambiguous.

In its Mission Statement, the Correctional Service of Canada commits itself to "openness," "integrity," and "accountability." An organization which was truly committed to these values would, it seems to me, be concerned about compliance with the law, and vigilant to correct any departures from the law; it would be responsive to outside criticism, and prepared to engage in honest self-criticism; it would be prepared to give a fair and honest account of its actions; and it would acknowledge error. In this case, the Correctional Service did little of this. Too often, the approach was to deny error, defend against criticism, and to react without a proper investigation of the truth . . .

The deplorable defensive culture that manifested itself during this inquiry has old, established roots within the Correctional Service, and there is nothing to suggest that it emerged at the initiative of the present Commissioner or his senior staff. They are, it would seem, simply entrenched in it.

I believe that it is also part of that corporate culture to close ranks, and that the defensive stance of senior managers was often motivated by a sense of loyalty to their subordinates. This otherwise admirable instinct should, however, always defer to the imperatives of scrupulous commitment to the truth which must be displayed by those entrusted with people's liberty. (Arbour at 173–74)

## The Arbour Recommendations: Developing a Culture of Rights

In the second part of her report, Madam Justice Arbour made recommendations on some of the broad policy issues which underlay her examination of events at the Prison for Women. The primary issue—and the one also central to this book—deals with the role of the Rule of Law in the corporate philosophy of the Correctional Service of Canada. Madam Justice Arbour began with an analysis of the fundamental values underlying the Rule of Law:

> Reliance on the Rule of Law for the governance of citizens' interactions with each other and with the State has a particular connotation in the general criminal law context. Not only does it reflect ideals of liberty, equality and fairness, but it expresses the fear of arbitrariness in the imposition of punishment. This concept is reflected in the old legal maxim: *nullum crimen sine lege, nulla poena sine lege*—there can be no crime, nor punishment, without law.
>
> In the correctional context, "no punishment without law" means that there must also be legal authority for all State actions enforcing punishment.
>
> It is apparent that the legal order must serve as both the justification and the code of conduct for correctional authorities since the confinement of persons against their will has no other foundation; it is not justifiable solely on self-evident moral grounds; it is not required on medical, humanitarian, charitable or any other basis. The coercive actions of the State must find their justification in a legal grant of authority and persons who enforce criminal sanctions on behalf of the State must act with scrupulous concern not to exceed their authority. (Arbour at 179)

Madam Justice Arbour drew the important distinction between the Rule of Law and the existence of rules. In her view, the evidence at the inquiry demonstrated that "The Rule of Law is absent, although rules are everywhere." The multiplicity of rules and the proliferation of Commissioner's Directives and standing orders obscured "the fundamental premise that all correctional authority must find its roots in enabling legislation, and that it must yield to the legislated rights of prisoners." Ironically, the very multiplicity of rules "largely contributed to the applicable law or policy being often unknown, or easily forgotten and ignored." In finding "little evidence of the will to yield pragmatic concerns to the dictates of a legal order," Madam Justice Arbour concluded that the absence of the Rule of Law was not something confined to line staff at the

Prison for Women but was "most noticeable at the management level, both within the prison and at the Regional and National levels" (Arbour at 180–81).

Madam Justice Arbour concluded that the enactment of the CCRA, the existence of internal grievance mechanisms, and the existing forms of judicial review had not been successful in developing a culture of rights within the Correctional Service of Canada. She also expressed deep scepticism that the Service was able to put its own house in order. She cited a 1984 report prepared by the Service for the Solicitor General which contained the following exhortation:

> It must be made clear to staff and inmates alike, while the Service will protect them, it will not condone any unwarranted and unlawful use of force. Both staff and inmates must realize that violations will be resolved in swift and certain disciplinary action. (*Report of the Advisory Committee to the Solicitor General of Canada on the Management of Correctional Institutions* [Ottawa: Solicitor General of Canada, Communications Division, 1984] [Chairman: John J. Carson], cited in Arbour at 180)

Madam Justice Arbour's response to this left little room for ambiguity.

> In my view, if anything emerges from this inquiry, it is the realization that the Rule of Law will not find its place in corrections by "swift and certain disciplinary action" against staff and inmates . . . *The Rule of Law has to be imported and integrated . . . from the other partners in the criminal justice enterprise, as there is no evidence that it will emerge spontaneously.* (Arbour at 180, emphasis added)

## Managing Segregation within a Framework of Legality

Madam Justice Arbour made a separate body of recommendations concerning segregation and the legal and administrative regime she deemed necessary to bring its management into compliance with the law and the *Canadian Charter of Rights and Freedoms.* She recommended that the management of administrative segregation be subject preferably to judicial oversight but alternatively to independent adjudication. Her preferred model would permit the institutional head to segregate a prisoner for up to three days to diffuse an immediate incident. After three days, a documented review would take place. If further segregation was contemplated, the administrative review could provide for a maximum of thirty days in segregation, no more than twice in a calendar year, with the effect that a prisoner could not be made to spend more than sixty nonconsecutive days annually in segregation. After thirty days, or if the total days served in segregation during that year already approached sixty, the institution would have to apply other options, such as transfer, placement in a mental health unit, or forms of intensive supervision, with all to involve interaction with the general population. If these options proved unavailable, or if the Correctional Service thought a longer period of segregation was required, it would have to apply to a court for this determination (Arbour at 191).

Failing a willingness to put segregation under judicial supervision, Madam Arbour recommended that segregation decisions be made initially at the institutional level, but that they be subject to confirmation within five days by an independent adjudicator who should be a lawyer and who would be required to give reasons for a decision to maintain segregation. Thereafter, segregation reviews would be conducted every thirty days before a different adjudicator (Arbour at 192 and 255–56).

These recommendations for the administrative segregation process were unambiguously related to her general findings that "the facts of this inquiry have revealed a disturbing lack of commitment to the ideals of justice on the part of the Correctional Service" and her judgement that "there is nothing to suggest that the Service is either willing or able to reform without judicial guidance and control" (Arbour at 198). Nonetheless, Madam Justice Arbour held no illusions about how the Correctional Service would respond to her recommendations. In predicting that "the Correctional Service may not share my view of the need for judicial supervision," she cited the trenchant comment of Professor Hélène Dumont, former Dean at the Faculty of Law, University of Montreal:

> It is self-evident to students of Penal Law that correctional authorities do not take at all kindly to judicial admonitions regarding their abuse of discretion and legendary contempt for inmate rights. (Hélène Dumont, *Pénologie: Le droit canadien relatif aux peines et aux sentences* [Montréal: Les Éditions Thémis, 1993], cited in Arbour at 185)

In the next chapter we will see how "kindly" the Correctional Service of Canada took to Madam Justice Arbour's recommendation for judicial supervison and independent adjudication of administrative segregation.

## CHAPTER 4

# The Task Force on Administrative Segregation, 1996–97

The Arbour Report had an immediate effect when it was released in April 1996. The Commissioner of Corrections, John Edwards, tendered his resignation to the Solicitor General, and two months later Ole Ingstrup was appointed in his place. Mr. Ingstrup, who had held the position from 1988 to 1992, was the driving force behind the Service's Mission Statement and had been at the helm during development and passage of the *Corrections and Conditional Release Act.* One of Mr. Ingstrup's first initiatives on his reappointment was to set up a task force to conduct a comprehensive review of the use of segregation. The mandate of the Task Force on Administrative Segregation (commonly referred to simply as the Task Force on Segregation) was to address the recommendations and issues raised by the Arbour Report; to examine the extent to which the Arbour findings at the Prison for Women were applicable to other institutions; and to ensure both that all staff members and managers were knowledgeable about legal and policy requirements and that measures were in place to ensure continuing compliance with these.

Members of the Task Force on Segregation were drawn from both within and outside the Correctional Service. The outside membership consisted of the Office of the Correctional Investigator's legal counsel, Todd Sloan, and two consultants, including myself. The chairperson was Dan Kane, who brought to the role extensive experience at the institutional, regional, and national levels. The Task Force adopted a three-phased approach to its work. In the first phase, a preliminary assessment was undertaken to measure how fully the operation of

segregation units across the country complied with the basic procedural requirements set out in the CCRA, the CCR *Regulations*, and the Commissioner's Directives. Small audit teams visited each institution with a segregation unit to review
the documentation relating to its operation, together with a small sample of cases
taken from the files of segregated prisoners. Task Force members then visited
each institution and were debriefed by the audit team regarding any deficiencies
that had been noted, as well as with any "best practices" that could provide
models for other institutions. At each institution, the Task Force met with managers and staff involved in segregation, and a representative from the CSC's Legal
Services gave an orientation lecture on the legal principles and provisions governing segregation. Task Force members toured each segregation unit and met
with representatives from staff unions, inmate committees, and Native Brotherhoods. At the end of each visit, the warden, who had earlier received a copy of
the audit team's report, was asked to provide the Task Force with an action plan
identifying measures to correct procedural deficiencies.

The second phase of the Task Force involved the completion of a "formal
compliance audit," in which an audit team re-visited each institution to review
the extent of its compliance with the procedural requirements relating to segregation (for example, those requiring written notice of the reasons for segregation
and a hearing within five days). The Task Force's third phase addressed policy,
operational, and research issues relating to the fairness and effectiveness of the
segregation process and reviewed the recommendations of the Arbour Report
relating to independent adjudication.

## A Chairperson's Perspective

As a member of the Task Force, I participated in the visits to Matsqui, Kent,
Mission, and Mountain Institutions in the Pacific Region; Renous, Springhill,
and Dorchester Institutions in the Atlantic Region; and the newly opened
Edmonton Institution for Women in the Prairies Region. By the time the Task
Force visited the Pacific Region institutions in September 1996, preliminary
audits and visits to the Ontario, Prairies, and Quebec Regions had been completed, and it was clear that the lack of legal compliance found by Madam Justice
Arbour at the P4W was a systemic national problem for the CSC. Dan Kane
painted the contours of that picture at a briefing at Matsqui on September 3,
1996. His first response to the Arbour Report, he said, like that of many CSC staff,
had been that the events at the Prison for Women were an aberration. While this
was true in one sense—the strip-searching of women prisoners by male staff could
not happen anywhere except at a women's prison and at the time it occurred
there were no other institutions for women—the other elements of correctional
operations that had drawn Madam Justice Arbour's condemnation, particularly
the lack of adequate legal grounds for segregation and the denial of prisoners'

legal rights in segregation, were things that, based on the Task Force's preliminary review, did happen at other institutions.

Mr. Kane, reflecting his own experiences as a warden, suggested that the CSC was a pragmatic, operationally driven culture, and that this operational pragmatism undermined CSC's ability to comply with what the law requires. For example, when a correctional supervisor came on shift in segregation, he or she checked to see how many prisoners were there, how many hours were available for exercise and showers, which prisoners could exercise together, how long it would take to provide meals, and what security escorts were required: all this determined how much exercise each prisoner would get, whatever the law might say. As he expressed it, based on Task Force observations, "If the Service were charged with lack of respect for the law, it would be found guilty." Mr. Kane stressed that the CCRA was not something imposed upon the Service; at all stages, the Service was involved in the development and drafting of the legislation, and therefore it was hardly unreasonable to expect its operations to be consistent with the law's requirements. Yet staff often reacted to the CCRA as if it were an alien force.

## The Preliminary Findings of the Task Force and the Legal Compliance Audit

The initial audits and visits to the institutions yielded significant findings for the Task Force on Segregation.

> The findings of the preliminary assessment (Phase 1) confirmed Madam Justice Arbour's findings that CSC did not fully appreciate the obligation to rigorously comply with legislative and policy provisions in its management of administrative segregation. Overall, CSC staff members and managers demonstrated a casual attitude towards the rigorous requirements of the law, both in terms of their understanding of the law and their sense of being bound by it.
>
> The compliance shortcomings that were observed were both systemic and significant. The Task Force recorded the following:
> - Formal documentation indicated that CSC had segregated inmates for reasons that did not meet legislative criteria . . .
> - Time frames governing the one hour of daily exercise, the three-day written disclosure notice, and the five- and thirty-day hearings, were more likely to be seen as "guidelines" than mandatory regulatory provisions requiring compliance.
> - Inmates were not well informed of their legal rights and privileges with respect to administrative segregation procedures and conditions of confinement.

(*Task Force Report on Administrative Segregation: Commitment to Legal Compliance, Fair Decisions and Effective Results* [Ottawa: Correctional Service of Canada, March 1997] at 12–13. Online: <http://www.csc-scc.gc.ca/text/publct/taskforce/toc_e.shtml> [last modified: October 22, 1999])

Based on the findings of Phase 1, the Task Force launched several initiatives to address the areas of non-compliance. All wardens were required to submit detailed action plans outlining the steps they intended to take to deal with the deficiencies identified at their institution. Changes were made to the electronic filing system (OMS) to enable staff to document decisions taken at key stages in the administrative segregation review process. The Task Force also issued an administrative segregation process checklist to staff and management and a handbook to be given to all segregated prisoners. Finally, in order to answer all questions raised by the institutions, the Task Force and the CSC's Legal Services department issued a consolidated document entitled "Administrative Segregation: Answers to Most Frequently Asked Questions."

A comprehensive national legal compliance audit was conducted by the Task Force in early 1997, to ensure that the operation of all segregation units was now in compliance with the basic legal procedural requirements and that deficiencies identified in Phase 1 had been addressed. The audit instrument was circulated to all institutions well in advance of the visits of the audit teams. Pre-audits were performed to assess readiness for the formal compliance audit, and an extension of two months was granted to provide more time for corrective action. As stated later in the Task Force's report:

> It should have been possible, and this was the Task Force's expectation, that all institutions would have been able to achieve 100-percent compliance with the basic procedural requirements of the law . . .
> . . . [T]he goal of 100-percent compliance, 100-percent of the time, as articulated by the current Commissioner, is the only acceptable goal for an organization which exercises such strong controls over the liberty of individuals. (at 15, 18)

Yet audit results showed that the Service failed to measure up to this expectation. The Task Force provided this assessment:

> The results of the audit can be viewed from a number of perspectives. From the perspective of where CSC was when the Task Force was established in June 1996, there has been significant positive change in the extent of CSC's compliance with the law, an achievement in which the Service can take justifiable pride. At the time of the initial

assessment, procedural compliance shortcomings were significant and systemic across all regions and in almost every aspect of the administrative segregation process. The compliance audit revealed an overall pattern of compliance. From another perspective, the fact that the compliance audit revealed less than 100-percent compliance in all institutions is a concern . . .

. . . The fact that non-compliance spanned a number of areas in the administrative segregation review process in several of the institutions is a cause for concern, especially in maximum-security institutions where intrusiveness can be the most severe . . .

On the one hand, CSC has demonstrated that, given the necessary corporate will, leadership, and resources, it can significantly improve its ability to comply with the basic procedural requirements of the law. On the other hand, considering the scope of the compliance audit, which was directed only to compliance with the basic procedural requirements of the law, and the fact that it was conducted at a time when full attention was being given to the issue of segregation, CSC's performance falls short of full compliance.

Since CSC's focus could easily shift to other areas in the future, the Task Force believes it critical that mechanisms be put in place to ensure that recent progress is sustained. Consequently, the Task Force recommends that a Segregation Advisory Committee be created with membership from inside/outside CSC to continue to shape an effective and compliant administrative segregation process within a fixed time frame.

This action, coupled with other recommendations related to an enhanced segregation review process and experimentation with independent adjudication, will contribute to public confidence that CSC is maintaining its corporate commitment to respect the "Rule of Law." (*Task Force Report* at 17–18)

## The Task Force Recommendations: Enhanced Internal Review or Independent Adjudication?

One of the Task Force's mandates was to review the recommendations of Madam Justice Arbour for judicial supervision or independent adjudication of segregation decisions and to make recommendations for improving the effectiveness of the segregation review process. In our initial meetings, a clear division of opinion on the issue of independent adjudication emerged between members from within the ranks of the Service and those drawn from outside. The CSC members argued vigorously that the necessary reforms could be achieved through "enhancing" the existing internal model of administrative decision-making, in which the

Segregation Review Board, chaired by institutional managers, made recommendations and the warden had the ultimate authority.

The CSC members' argument had several strands. Under existing law, the warden was the person held accountable for the security of the institution and the safety of staff and prisoners. The decision to segregate a prisoner involved critical issues of safety and security. The staff's understanding of the dynamics of an institution and the personalities of the prisoners was integral to making the right decision in a situation where the wrong decision could be fatal; no outsider, however well-educated in the law, could provide an adequate substitute for correctional experience and understanding. Furthermore, transferring decision-making for segregation from institutional managers to outside adjudicators would have a corrosive effect on institutional morale and add to existing staff dissatisfaction with the independent adjudication of disciplinary hearings. The final strand to the argument was that the Service, having been made aware of the extent of its non-compliance with the law and the deficiency of its existing procedures, should be given the opportunity to put its own shop in order.

Task Force members from outside the Service set out the competing arguments. There was first the compelling historical record, which demonstrated that over the twenty-year period since the *McCann* decision, the Service's efforts to reform itself had consistently failed. The Arbour Report documented the latest chapter in that history. Second, principles of fairness require that the legislative criteria for a decision that affects the institutional liberty of a prisoner and consigns him to "a prison within a prison" be applied free from the pressure of institutional bias, with an objective weighing of the competing interests of prisoners and prison administrators. Principles of fairness had underpinned the introduction of independent adjudication for serious disciplinary offences and were no less compelling in the case of administrative segregation. In a working paper I prepared for the Task Force, I referred to some of the case studies documented in this book to illustrate how, under prevailing operational reality, justice was mediated by institutional politics and convenience rather than by the law.

The Task Force spent many hours debating the relative merits of an enhanced internal segregation review process and a system of independent adjudication. Members from within the Service developed a model for enhancing the internal review process; I developed the ideas for independent adjudication first put forth in my Model Segregation Code, revising the model to recognize the important distinctions between involuntary and voluntary cases. From our debate emerged a consensus that the Task Force recommend that the Service reform the segregation process along parallel paths, one path being the enhancement of the internal review process and the other an experiment with independent adjudication. As Dan Kane noted in his introduction to our report, "The fact that consensus was achieved out of views that were so disparate, yet passionately held, testifies to the value of open and honest discussion" (*Task Force Report* at 2).

The enhanced internal model for segregation review recommended by the Task Force had eight elements, including a legal education initiative, improved procedures for segregation review hearings, the development of better alternatives to segregation, and the establishment of regional Segregation Review Boards. The legal education initiative came both from recommendations in the Arbour Report and from feedback received by the Task Force that correctional staff and managers received insufficient training in administrative law and the principles enshrined in the *Charter of Rights and Freedoms*. In the Task Force's view, and based upon its interviews with Native Brotherhoods across the country, this legal education needed to include training on the distinct constitutional and legal rights of Aboriginal people and, more specifically, on their access to spiritual and cultural possessions and ceremonies and to the spiritual and cultural support provided by Elders and Native Liaison officers. The most critical part of the enhanced segregation model was directed to improving the conduct of segregation review hearings, and the CSC's Legal Services developed a twelve-step procedural guide for these hearings which was appended to the report of the Task Force. The Task Force also recommended that the chairperson of the Segregation Review Board undergo specialized training through a formal certification program such as those adopted in some jurisdictions in the United States.

The external members of the Task Force supported the development of these initiatives, which would improve the Service's ability to make fair and effective segregation decisions. The enhancement of this internal ability through legal education and certification in the conduct of hearings could serve as a model in other decision-making areas that affected the rights and liberties of prisoners. But the limitations of these initiatives were clear: they assumed that training in the substantive and procedural requirements of the law would be enough to ensure fairness. However, if fairness requires an *objective* balancing of competing interests—those of prison administrators to manage a safe and secure institution and those of prisoners not to suffer the loss of their institutional liberty except in strict accordance with the criteria and procedures set out in the law—how could fairness be achieved, and be seen to be achieved, where decisions were made by the correctional administrators themselves? Even assuming that the CSC could demonstrate through training and education that it had developed a corporate culture which respected the Rule of Law, the issue of bias would continue to cast a long shadow over the substantive justice of the process.

The model of independent adjudication I developed for the Task Force was designed to build upon and be integrated into CSC initiatives. In voluntary cases, the initial decision to segregate would remain with the warden. The five-day review would be chaired by the warden or deputy warden, which would elevate the importance of the segregation decision. The thirty-day review would be chaired by an independent adjudicator, and the institution would be responsible for developing and presenting at the hearing a plan to reintegrate the prisoner.

The adjudicator's role would be to ensure that a plan had been developed and that all reasonable alternatives to segregation had been explored. Where the plan for reintegration involved a negotiated return to the population of the parent institution, requiring the assistance of the Inmate Committee, the Native Brotherhood, or an Elder, the hearing should include these parties. If the plan involved a transfer to another institution, the adjudicator would ensure that the necessary progress summaries were prepared and that transfer time frames were complied with. If the transfer was rejected, the adjudicator could order the convening of a regional segregation/transfer board chaired by the deputy commissioner of the region or a delegate with the legal authority to order a transfer.

In involuntary cases, the warden would also retain the initial authority to segregate the prisoner. However, here the independent adjudicator would conduct the five-day review as well as any subsequent thirty-day reviews. In an involuntary case, the burden is on the institution to demonstrate that there are grounds justifying segregation and that there are no reasonable alternatives. Because this position is likely to be contested, independent adjudication is required early in the process. Furthermore, where the institution's case for segregation is based on an ongoing investigation, the independent adjudicator could establish a reasonable time frame for the completion of the investigation. At the thirty-day review, the onus would be on the institution to demonstrate a continuing need for segregation and to present a plan for reintegration. Subsequent reviews would monitor the implementation of the plan.

An integral part of the experiment the Task Force proposed would be to determine how the best blend between an enhanced segregation review process and independent adjudication could be achieved. In identifying the contours of the experiment, the Task Force considered a number of issues, including the authority of the adjudicator.

In both my original Model Segregation Code and the model I developed for the Task Force, as well as in Madam Justice Arbour's model, the independent adjudicator has the final legal authority. However, to enable the experiment with independent adjudication to be implemented immediately, indeed fast-tracked, the Task Force agreed it would have to be done within the framework of the existing law, under which the warden retains ultimate legal authority to make segregation decisions. The results of the experiment would thus be relevant in determining whether it was necessary to change the law so that the adjudicator was given the power to make decisions rather than just recommendations. The Task Force recommended that the experiment with independent adjudication take place in four institutions, two of which would have independent adjudicators and two of which, for comparative purposes, would not. It was recommended that the enhanced internal review process be initiated in all institutions.

It was the Task Force's considered view that our proposed model of reform, encompassing an enhanced internal review process and an experiment with independent adjudication within the existing framework of the law, would contribute to the development of a fair and effective segregation process. In keeping with the clarion call of the House of Commons Sub-Committee on the Penitentiary System in 1977 and the report of Madam Justice Arbour in 1996, it would also encourage the development of a correctional culture and operational practice that respected the Rule of Law.

## Conditions of Confinement: Giving Effect to Legal Rights

As discussed, the CCRA provides that prisoners in administrative segregation shall be given the same rights, privileges, and conditions of confinement as the general population, except for those rights, privileges, and conditions that can only be enjoined in association with other prisoners or cannot reasonably be given owing to limitations specific to the administrative segregation area or security requirements. The Task Force found that "the operational reality, however, has been that inmates, their advocates or program staff have had to demonstrate why they *should* be provided the same rights, privileges and programs. The legal reality is that CSC has to demonstrate why they should *not* be provided" (*Task Force Report* at 50). To get a more informed picture of the national situation, the Task Force distributed a questionnaire to all segregated prisoners in late 1996 and received responses from almost four hundred. The purpose of the questionnaire was to determine whether prisoners had the same, less, or more access to rights, privileges, and services while in segregation. The responses confirmed that, under current practice, administrative convenience and security considerations had all but eclipsed legal programming requirements. This confirmation has important implications for the issue of independent adjudication. Just as independent adjudicators are not likely to allow administrative convenience to overshadow the requirements of justice, so also would they be less likely to permit the abridgement of the Service's lawful requirements regarding programming for administrative convenience or ill-defined security considerations.

At the time prisoner Glen Rosenthal responded to the questionnaire, he had served a year in segregation at Edmonton Max. In addition to checking off the list of questions, he offered these reflections:

> In the course of completing this survey I have found it extremely difficult to convey the reality of living in this segregation unit for nearly a year. I have spent fifteen years in many different prisons and have found myself in the segregation units of most of them at one time or another. Never have I experienced anything remotely comparable to what I am experiencing now. It is one thing to be locked in a cell for a year, and that of itself is bad enough. Add to that the fact that you have no idea how long it will continue . . . And add to that the fact

that your health has deteriorated to the point where you doubt you will ever be healthy again . . . You can't sleep more than three or at best four hours at a time. You are constantly getting awoken by music blasting, barriers clanging open and shut. You are always tired. You have gone from a hundred and fifty pounds to a hundred and ninety pounds and every muscle in your body is either knotted or atrophied. The Warden told you he would transfer you to B.C., so your wife moved there six months ago and you have watched your marriage fall apart one piece at a time since then. You have been wearing stinking rags for so long you don't notice it anymore. You look older, fatter, disgusting to yourself when you look in the mirror. Your self-esteem is sub-zero . . .

You want to complain about the rags you get for clothes but you know the cleaners will spit in your food or urinate in your coffee if you do. You want to complain about the guard who miscounted your phone calls for the month, only giving you one or two, but you know next month you won't get any if you do. You want to complain about not being transferred but you know that this will piss somebody off and you will never get out. You can't bear the thought of people you love seeing you in this condition so you don't take any visits. Your life is so static there is nothing, absolutely nothing left to write to anyone about. Your once passionate and hopeful phone conversations with your wife turn into a string of uncomfortable silences and misdirected frustrations. But she is the only one who will listen, and then one day there is no one. You spend twenty hours a day on your back, somewhere between waking and sleeping, trying to keep your mind out of the dark places but you can't. Your mind seems full of thoughts that don't belong there. You can't carry a conversation anymore because you are afraid one of them will slip out. You don't tell anyone because you are even more afraid of the medication they might think you need.

I don't use words like "afraid" easily. I have always identified myself with being up to whatever challenge came my way, and so far I have. I have never faced a challenge that threatens who and what I am more than this last year in this segregation unit. It is no exaggeration to call this cruel and unusual punishment. Though the circumstances here are likely more the product of indifference than malice, it is no less insidious and destructive. My health is gone, my life has fallen apart, parts of me that words can't describe will not recover from this. And I did nothing wrong. All this is happening to me because the machine isn't working and no one seems obliged to fix it.

## A Profile of the Segregated

The Task Force on Segregation found that segregated prisoners were higher risk and higher need than non-segregated prisoners. According to the Offender Intake Assessment Process (a collection of historical and current information on each offender admitted to a federal correctional institution), segregated prisoners have been found to be high need in six of the seven need categories assessed at admission. They are more likely to experience difficulties than non-segregated offenders in relation to: (1) employment (less than grade 10 education; lacking skills, trade, or profession; unemployed at the time of arrest; unstable job history); (2) associates and social interaction (socially isolated; associated with substance abusers and criminal acquaintances; easily influenced by others; difficulty in communicating with others); (3) substance abuse (abuse of alcohol and drugs at an early age); (4) community functioning (unstable accommodations; financial difficulties); (5) personal and emotional orientation (cognition problems; hostility; poor conflict-resolution skills; low frustration tolerance; thrill-seeking), and (6) attitude (negative attitudes towards the criminal justice system; pro-criminal attitudes; disrespectful and lacking direction; non-conforming).

The paradox emerges that the regime and conditions in segregation units are peculiarly well suited to aggravate and even intensify these characteristics. Where else in the prison system can a prisoner who is socially isolated feel even more isolated? Where else can a prisoner with cognition problems, poor conflict-resolution skills, and a low frustration tolerance experience conditions in which these are put to the most severe test on a daily basis? Where can a prisoner with a negative attitude towards the criminal justice system find more reinforcement for that attitude than in a segregation cell, in which, locked up for twenty-three hours a day, he is able to focus unwaveringly on his treatment?

The measure of justice accorded prisoners in segregation must not only reflect the fact that segregation is the most intrusive form of imprisonment but also demonstrate the legitimacy of state authority to prisoners for whom that legitimacy is severely compromised.

## The csc's Response to the Task Force on Administrative Segregation: A Study in Resistance

The report of the Task Force was filed with the Commissioner of Corrections at the end of March 1997. Task Force members expected that the report would then be made public; it was not, and the reason given was that it was necessary to brief the Solicitor General on the report prior to its public release. In late April, before this could be done, the federal government called an election, and Ottawa went into full election gear. The release of the *Task Force Report* was put off until after the election would be completed and a new cabinet sworn in. That new cabinet involved a shuffle, with the position of Solicitor General being assigned to Andy Scott. Task Force members were advised that the release of the report would have to await briefings of the new minister. Those briefings, which included a separate briefing on the government's response to the Arbour Report, came and went, but the *Task Force Report* was still not released. Although there was no formal communication between Commissioner Ingstrup and the Task Force regarding the report's recommendations, external members received the clear message that there was serious resistance, tantamount to rejection, at the senior management level to the recommended experiment with independent adjudication. Once it became clear that the csc did not intend to implement the experiment with independent adjudication or establish a Segregation Advisory Committee, the external members insisted that Commissioner Ingstrup make good on a commitment to meet with Task Force members to discuss the Service's response to the report.

That meeting took place on December 17, 1997, in Ottawa. Commissioner Ingstrup raised a number of concerns with the Task Force recommendation for expanding the scope of independent adjudication to segregation cases; these were clustered around interrelated issues of consistency, competence, and credibility. Many csc staff perceived that the independent adjudication of disciplinary boards suffered from a lack of these attributes. If the existing system had these problems, the commissioner suggested, expanding independent adjudication to other areas might only compound them. The commissioner expressed his preference for a national or a regional oversight mechanism which would not take away line responsibility from wardens but would still provide an avenue for review to prevent abuses.

The commissioner stated that he had not yet taken a final position on the recommended experiment with independent adjudication, and that before doing so he would like to have his concerns addressed. It was agreed that Todd Sloan and I would prepare a written response, following which a decision would be made on whether the experiment would take place and within what parameters.

Our written response was submitted in mid-February of 1998. With regard to Commissioner Instrup's concern that the expansion of independent adjudication might compound existing problems, we highlighted both my research on the disciplinary process at Kent and Matsqui Institutions and the csc's internal evaluations, both of which indicated that the system of independent adjudication, as a whole, operated fairly and in conformity with the law. Acknowledging that there were staff and prisoner concerns, we then suggested how some of these could be addressed through improvements to the existing process. These improvements included the requirement that the Independent Chairperson's reasons for decision be reduced to writing in all cases and that these reasons be made available to staff and prisoners; the dedication of a staff position to the co-ordination of disciplinary hearings and the provision of suitable legal training to that person to improve the efficiency of the process and consistency in staff recommendations; and the development of a clear set of criteria for the appointment of Independent Chairpersons of disciplinary boards with a level of remuneration commensurate with their responsibilities. (These recommendations for improvements to the disciplinary process are discussed more fully in Sector 3, Chapter 4, of this book.)

In response to the commissioner's arguments for national or regional oversight mechanisms that would maintain the wardens' authority, we pointed to a major difference between the two models. The independent adjudication model requires a case-by-case review of segregation decisions in the institution at the time these decisions are being made. Independent adjudication is built into the process at the front end to achieve fairness and effectiveness. The external oversight model, whether in the form of audits or reviews, involves a retrospective assessment of a body of cases to ensure that they have been decided fairly and effectively. In other words, in the first model the features of independent review are brought to bear on the case at the decision point; in the second, these features are applied after the fact, with a view to correcting errors that have been made in the past and/or to making recommendations to prevent these errors in the future. We also emphasized that these models should not be viewed as alternatives, with the CSC choosing one or the other. Rather, they should be viewed as cumulative avenues through which the CSC would uphold its Mission and ensure full compliance with the CCRA, the *Charter of Rights and Freedoms,* and Canada's international human rights obligations. Seen in this way, independent adjudication of segregation cases and oversight through regional or national reviews become part of a continuum of review mechanisms.

At about the same time he met with the Task Force in December 1997, Commissioner Ingstrup received a copy of the report of the Working Group on Human Rights. The Working Group had been established by the commissioner in May 1997 under the chairmanship of Max Yalden, former Chief Commissioner of the Canadian Human Rights Commission. It had been given a mandate "to review CSC systems for ensuring compliance with the rule of law in human rights matters; to provide a general strategic model for evaluating compliance within any correctional context; and to present recommendations concerning the Service's own ability to comply and to effectively communicate such compliance" (Working Group on Human Rights, *Human Rights and Corrections: A Strategic Model* [Ottawa: Correctional Service of Canada, 1997] [Chairman: Max Yalden] at 2. Online: <http://www.csc-scc.gc.ca/text/pblct/rights/human/toce.shtml> [last modified October 22, 1999]). The Working Group's recommendations are addressed more fully in Sector 6 of this book. However, it is important to mention here that in reviewing the necessary balance between internal and external mechanisms to ensure compliance with human rights obligations, the Working Group specifically addressed the recommendation of the Task Force on Segregation that there be an experiment in independent adjudication.

> Since, in Canada, administrative segregation may affect inmates' liberties even more than disciplinary segregation, which has an upper limit of 30 days, and given the fact that institutional authorities may have a vested interest in the outcome of their decisions, we believe the [Task Force] recommendation should be pursued. (*Human Rights and Corrections* at 33)

One other outstanding issue raised at the December 1997 meeting with Commissioner Ingstrup was the fact that the report of the Task Force on Segregation still had not been made available to CSC staff, prisoners, or the public. The commissioner agreed that the report should be made public. Early in the new year, instructions were given for copies to be distributed, and the document, in both official languages, was posted electronically on CSC's internal infonet and the Service's public website in February 1998, almost a full year after it was first delivered to the commissioner.

In April 1998, I was advised by senior officials that while the commissioner had not yet made a decision on the experiment with independent adjudication, the expectation was that it would go ahead, having the accumulated weight of support in the reports of Madam Justice Arbour, the Task Force on Segregation, and the Yalden Working Group on Human Rights. However, in early May my sources informed me that Commissioner Ingstrup had decided there would *not* be an experiment with independent adjudication. Instead, the Service would proceed with an oversight mechanism based at each regional headquarters.

This regional oversight mechanism would involve the appointment of a senior official who would work directly with wardens to ensure that institutions were in full compliance with the law with respect to managing the administrative segregation review process. This would be accomplished not only by discharging the existing sixty-day review but also by reviewing a sample of cases that had reached the thirty-day hearing point. In addition, the person holding this new position would work directly with wardens and colleagues in other regions to find timely reintegration solutions; conduct reviews of segregation units to ensure that prisoners were housed safely and humanely; provide training to chairpersons of Segregation Review Boards to ensure that they remained fully knowledgeable of the law; act on behalf of regional deputy commissioners to resolve issues raised by the Office of the Correctional Investigator in relation to segregation; and contribute to an annual national report to the Solicitor General on the Service's performance with respect to the use of administrative segregation.

When it was suggested to me by senior officials that this regional oversight model was a form of "independent" review—in the sense that the new position was located outside of any institution—my disappointment crystallized into a deepening scepticism about the Service's commitment to the values of openness and integrity so prominently proclaimed in its Mission Statement. The regional oversight model is a worthwhile initiative. As part of an enhanced segregation review process, it could make a valuable contribution. But the essential thrust of both the Arbour recommendations and the Task Force on Segregation's analysis was that a decision which drastically curtails the rights and liberties of a prisoner should be made by a person who is independent from the pressures and biases which drive institutional and regional decision-making. The appointment of a new regional official who would inevitably be part of the culture and hierarchy of the Service entrenches, rather than redresses, exactly the kind of bias against which independent adjudication is directed. There was also the important distinction, clearly identified in our paper responding to the commissioner's concerns, between independent adjudication at the hearing stage and a review function after the fact. The Service's regional oversight mechanism conveniently ignores this distinction.

My feelings of disappointment and scepticism were only intensified following further discussions with Mr. Ingstrup at his Commissioner's Forum held in Kingston in May 1998. (The Forum was established by Mr. Ingstrup to provide him with advice on public policy issues relating to the mandate of the Service.) When the Task Force met with the commissioner in December 1997, he had articulated his concerns about independent adjudication. The paper Todd Sloan and I had prepared, at Commissioner Ingstrup's express invitation, addressed these concerns one by one. We had received no response to that paper, suggesting that we had not satisfactorily addressed the issues or that our paper raised other issues that required further analysis. In my discussions with senior officials I had been given no explanation for the decision not to proceed with the experiment on independent adjudication beyond the statement that the commissioner had decided against it. At the very least, I expected that my meeting with the commissioner at the Forum would yield his explanation for the decision, particularly with regard to why he had found our response to his concerns less than compelling. His answer to my question took my breath away, and I was left speechless for one of the few times in my life. He advised me that he had not read our paper and then went on to express the same concerns he had voiced at the meeting in December—the very concerns our paper addressed. When I reminded him that the paper had been prepared at his request, and that he had stated the final decision on whether to proceed with the independent adjudication experiment would be contingent on its preparation and consideration, he assured me that upon his return to Ottawa he would read it. I knew it would not change his opinion regarding independent adjudication, of course, because the decision not to proceed with the experiment had already been made.

In a perverse way, more than anything I have so far described, the commissioner's response makes the case for independent adjudication. The principal criticism of prisoners is that the segregation review process is a sham; the Segregation Review Board comes to the hearing with an agenda, places primary reliance upon its own sources of information, heavily discounts the prisoner's own statement of events and, under the veil of a review, recommends a course of action which is predetermined. In this scenario, nothing the prisoner says makes much difference to the result. Consider the scenario I have described of the commissioner's decision not to conduct an experiment with independent adjudication. The Task Force had been advised through a number of channels that the commissioner had come to this conclusion; a meeting was called to review the issue; at the meeting Commissioner Ingstrup advised Todd Sloan and me that he was prepared to reconsider provided we addressed his concerns with the proposal; we addressed all of his concerns in a paper that was sent to him; without even reading it, the commissioner affirmed his earlier decision not to conduct the experiment. Lawyers have a phrase for this: *res ipsa loquitor*, which translates as "the scenario speaks for itself."

## An Appeal to "Slumbering Humanity"

My position on the need for independent adjudication also received powerful reinforcement from a visit to Kingston Penitentiary that had been arranged on the evening before the Commissioner's Forum in May 1998. Most of the Forum members had never set foot inside a prison. We were met at the front gate by the warden, Monty Bourke, who set out the penitentiary's history from its opening in 1835; part of that history included the terrible events that took place within the walls in the late 1840s, when children as young as eleven were barbarously flogged for whispering to each other in violation of the rule of silence. The penitentiary's massive front gate is relieved by a portico of limestone columns which, as one member of the Forum observed, would not be out of place at the entrance to a major bank. However, these recently restored columns led not to the vaults of power but to the places of confinement of the powerless. They heralded not privilege but pain.

The visit began at seven in the evening. After dinner in the officers' mess, we broke into small groups and were taken to different areas of the penitentiary. I was a part of a group guided by the warden, which included Commissioner Ingstrup, Chief Justice Edward Bayda of the Saskatchewan Court of Appeal, Pamela Wallin (one of Canada's most respected TV journalists), and Graham Stewart, the Executive Director of the John Howard Society of Canada. At around 9:00 p.m. we arrived in one of the two segregation areas. Built in 1958, it is the most recent addition to the penitentiary. It consists of a single range of cells facing each other, into which little natural light enters. The cells have double doors: an inner door of bars and an outer door of 4-inch solid oak with a food slot. As recently as the 1980s, the oak doors would be closed after suppertime, completely isolating the prisoners from human contact. Those doors are now left open, but even so the cells are like dark caverns. High on the back wall of each cell are a light and an observation window through which the staff, patrolling on an elevated catwalk behind the cells, can observe the prisoners. The flicker of a television set in one of the cells, depicting cartoon characters, only intensified the hideous nature of this most modern of Kingston's chambers of punishment. The members of the Forum were visibly shocked at what we saw. The staff member in charge advised us that most prisoners did not spend long in this unit, although he acknowledged that some prisoners were quite psychologically disturbed. One prisoner motioned to Graham Stewart and me as we walked down the range. His cell—the observation cell—was completely devoid of personal effects. He told us he had been there for four months and was due to be released to the street within the next four months. He was serving a three-year term for robbery and was extremely worried about facing life in the community after his extended period in the segregation unit. The staff later told us this man was a behavioural problem and had been setting fires in his cell in the general population.

At the end of our tour of Kingston, Warden Bourke gave each member of the Forum a binder containing a profile of the prisoners in the institution, together with a newsletter that is distributed to all staff. Under the heading "Historical Fact," the newsletter noted that in May of 1842, 156 years before our visit, Charles Dickens had visited Kingston Penitentiary as part of his tour of North America. Although impressed by Kingston, which he described as "an admirable jail, well and wisely governed"—a characterization he likely would not have made a few years later, when the savage regime of Warden Smith held sway—Dickens recorded in his *American Notes* his indictment of solitary confinement. His words appear at the beginning of my book *Prisoners of Isolation*, and they were read in court in the 1975 challenge to the conditions in the solitary confinement unit in the B.C. Penitentiary.

> I hold this slow and daily hampering with the mysteries of the brain to be immeasurably worse than any torture of the body; and because its ghastly signs and tokens are not so palpable to the eye and sense of touch as scars upon the flesh, because its wounds are not on the surface and it extorts few cries that human ears can hear; therefore, I denounce it as a secret punishment which slumbering humanity is not roused to stay. (Charles Dickens, *American Notes for General Circulation* [London: Chapman and Hall, 1842] at 119–20)

At next day's meeting, I expressed to the Forum my deep disappointment that Commissioner Ingstrup had not seen fit to initiate the experiment with independent adjudication of segregation decisions. I suggested that the conditions we had seen in the segregation unit the evening before were fully deserving of Dickens' indictment, and I urged the commissioner, on behalf of "slumbering humanity," to take immediate measures to close the dungeon at Kingston. Mr. Instrup advised us that he had been sufficiently shocked by what he saw to ask Warden Bourke for an action plan for closing the unit. A year later, the unit was closed permanently.

## The Equation for Reform

On June 15, 1998, Todd Sloan and I wrote to Commissioner Ingstrup. We reviewed the history of the Task Force recommendation on independent adjudication and expressed our profound disappointment that he had rejected it. We gave appropriate credit to the initiatives the Service had introduced as a result of the Task Force's work but argued that they were not enough on their own.

> The development of a segregation review handbook in conjunction with legal training sessions for managers and supervisors working in segregation units; the improvements to the OMS system designed to improve the written sharing of information with prisoners; the initiatives to develop better alternatives to segregation: these are all important steps in reducing the use of segregation and ensuring that when used it is done fairly. However, they are only one half of the equation. The other half is clearly set out in Madam Justice Arbour's report, the Task Force on Segregation's recommendations and their most recent endorsement by the Working Group on Human Rights. Your resistance to the implementation of this recommendation for independent adjudication, in the face of this trilogy of a Royal Commission and your own Task Force and Working Group, will be seen by many of your critics as a symbol of operational reality failing to conform to the principles of openness, integrity and accountability. As Madam Justice Arbour observed, placing a prisoner in segregation is the most intrusive decision the Service can make affecting a prisoner's liberty. The legitimacy of that decision in terms of fairness and conformity with the law is in many ways a litmus test for the legitimacy of the correctional system. Your decision not to implement the experiment with independent adjudication in segregation cases should also be judged as a litmus test of the Service's commitment to changing its corporate culture to one which not only professes but demonstrates its respect for the Rule of Law. (Letter from Michael Jackson and Todd Sloan to Ole Ingstrup, Commissioner of Corrections, June 15, 1998)

The commissioner replied to our letter on July 15, 1998. He stated:

> After carefully assessing the deliberations of the Task Force and con-
> sidering the changes already implemented, the EXCOM [Executive
> Committee of CSC] has decided that instead of proceeding with the
> limited experiment with independent adjudication as recommended
> by the Task Force, the most effective way of ensuring legal compli-
> ance is to appoint a dedicated senior employee in each region to
> ensure compliance with legal, policy and procedural requirements
> and provide effective and timely solutions to release and reintegra-
> tion of segregated offenders . . .
>
> It is important to acknowledge that the recommendations of the
> Task Force have resulted in numerous other significant changes in
> how the Service manages administrative segregation. These initia-
> tives, complemented by the strengthening of regional oversight, go a
> long way to ensuring that the Service is compliant with its legal obli-
> gations . . .
>
> The Service is confident that these changes will ensure that segre-
> gated offenders are treated in a fair and forthright manner. As you
> are aware, in parallel to an enhanced segregation review process, seg-
> regated offenders have access to lawyers, judicial review, members of
> Parliament as well as the Correctional Investigator. The initiatives
> noted above, paired with existing external remedies, will assure the
> Canadian public that the Service is managing administrative segre-
> gation in compliance with the law. (Letter from Ole Instrup, Com-
> missioner of Corrections, to Michael Jackson, July 15, 1998)

The confidence the commissioner places in the Correctional Service of
Canada to put its own house in order can be assessed from two perspectives. The
first is historical. Twenty years earlier, the House of Commons Sub-Committee
on the Penitentiary System, in its 1977 report, had accepted those same assurances by not recommending that independent adjudication be used for administrative segregation until the Service had had an opportunity to implement
Segregation Review Boards, which would conduct regular reviews of segregated
prisoners. In the mid-1980s, several of the Correctional Investigator's annual
reports chastized the Service for its lack of compliance with the Commissioner's
Directives in the operation of segregation units and particularly condemned the
practice of double-bunking in segregation. The Correctional Investigator called
for a comprehensive review of the operation of segregation. The reply from the
Service, as recorded by the Correctional Investigator in his 1984–85 report, was
this:

[W]e were advised that the last six months had been spent drafting explicit policies and guidelines regarding administrative segregation which included minimum standards for showering, exercise, visits, etc. As well, to ensure compliance, that a "Manager, Administrative Segregation" had been appointed at the National Headquarters and a Regional Co-ordinator had been appointed in each Region to assist in the implementation of the new policies and procedures. Also, that workshops had been held to familiarize staff, and that future monitoring would address the type of problem outlined in the [Correctional Investigator's report]. (*Annual Report of the Correctional Investigator, 1984–85* [Ottawa: Supply and Services Canada, 1986] at 19–20)

A decade after the 1985 action plan of new policies, national and regional managers to monitor segregation operations, and better staff training, the events at the Prison for Women shattered any pretence that real reform had taken place.

The other perspective from which to assess the commissioner's assurances are the changes made by the csc following the Task Force on Segregation's report. According to the commissioner, the objectives of fairness, effectiveness, and compliance with the law can all be achieved without independent adjudication at any stage of the segregation process. In the next chapter, I trace the developments in the administration of segregation at Kent Institution in the two years after the Task Force's first visit to test the commissioner's confident assertion.

# A Deadly July: Prison Politics, Staff Realities, and the Law

In the summer of 1997, a crisis erupted at Kent Institution which led to the segregation of a large number of prisoners. A crisis provides an acid test of any organization's mettle. For the CSC, it also tests the organization's commitment to the Rule of Law. The Arbour Report had demonstrated that when a situation is characterized by the the CSC as an emergency, that commitment can falter. In its place arises a default mode based on institutional customary practices designed to assert control and maintain order. Viewed as an epilogue to my analysis of the law and practice of segregation, the events at Kent invite reflection on the relationships between prison politics, staff realities, and the law. Taking place three months after the completion of the Task Force on Segregation's report, the events also provide a measure of the CSC's efforts to "enhance" the segregation process.

On Thursday, July 10, 1997, twenty-seven months after Gary Allen was carried from the inner courtyard at Kent Institution, another prisoner, Christian Grenier, lay dying in the outer exercise yard. The institution was locked down while the RCMP and correctional staff began their investigation. Kent did not, however, experience the unnatural quiet which often follows the death of a prisoner. On July 11, two prisoners from A unit, Kenny Makichuk and Neil Simpson, were taken to segregation after a review of the videotape of the incident and witness statements implicated them in the killing. In the following days, six more prisoners were segregated. The lock-down continued throughout the weekend and, as prisoner unrest mounted, objects were thrown out of cell windows, including a shirt that was set on fire and landed on the cellblock roof, causing several thousand dollars' worth of damage. On Monday evening, July 14, a group of prisoners in A unit began smashing their cells, setting fires, damaging sprinklers, and flooding the range. The glass and in some cases the frames were kicked out of the cell windows, leaving just concrete cylinders in the window openings. The decision was made to remove the disruptive prisoners from A unit to segregation, and the Emergency Response Team, led by Officer Mark Noon-Ward, was called in to effect the removal. Once the team appeared in the unit suited up with their shields and batons, the prisoners quieted down, and it was clear they were not going to fight all the way to segregation. Each prisoner was told to strip in his cell. They were taken naked except for their shoes to the common room at the end of the range, where they were searched, given coveralls, and then taken to J unit. There were no incidents during this operation. After the prisoners involved in the smash-up were taken out, a clean-up began that had not been completed by the time I arrived the next morning, July 15. There was still water and debris on the upper range. I inspected the cell belonging to the prisoner believed to have triggered the smash-up. The walls and the ceiling were fire-damaged, the sprinkler was smashed, and the window frame lay on the grass below the cell. The sink and toilet had not been damaged, but little else had withstood the trashing.

During the course of the day, I was given several accounts of what had led to the killing and the subsequent smash-up. According to Acting Unit Manager Mike Csoka, the previous summer a power struggle had begun between two rival factions on the general population side. He referred to the factions as the "French guys" and the "junkies." A struggle for power and drugs was at the centre. A series of incidents and consequent lock-downs late the previous summer and into the fall were all part of this conflict; they centred on A unit, where the junkies lived, and C unit, which housed most of the French-Canadian prisoners. Jean-Louis (Cacane) Tremblay was the acknowledged leader of C unit, and Jimmy Whitmore, of A unit. Both were former chairpersons of the Inmate Committee. A series of verbal confrontations occurring in early July in the courtyard finally erupted on July 10. A large amount of Valium had been smuggled into the institution by a visitor to a prisoner in A unit, and these pills were intended for a prisoner in C unit. However, instead of reaching their destination, most of the pills were consumed or otherwise distributed. During a meeting in the C unit pool room between some A unit and C unit prisoners, an apparent resolution was reached. However, a few hours later there was a flurry of activity in the outside exercise yard involving a small group of prisoners from C unit and a larger group from A unit. At first confined to heated exchanges, this activity exploded into an armed battle. One prisoner from C unit, Christian Grenier, was stabbed to death, and another, Claude Forget, was dealt a severe blow to the head with a baseball bat.

## July 17: The Five-Day Reviews—Clearing the Legal Hurdles

On July 17, Mike Csoka conducted fourteen five-day reviews, all involving prisoners allegedly involved in either the incident in the exercise yard or the smash-up in A unit—by far the largest number of such reviews done at one sitting during my five years of research at Kent. This correctional tour de force was a fitting match for the thirty-eight minor disciplinary charges Mr. Csoka had adjudicated in one afternoon four years earlier at Matsqui Institution. He completed the review of these fourteen cases in about an hour and a half. A number of prisoners were extremely angry and still pumped up from the previous Monday's smash-up. Although there were security officers posted outside the room, Mr. Csoka conducted the review without reinforcements; he kept his cool even when subjected to considerable verbal abuse. His handling of the cases portrayed a correctional practitioner with confidence in his position and authority, ready to do a tough job under difficult circumstances. In a correctional context, he was the proverbial man for all seasons.

But how well did this second marathon measure up to the standards of the law and due process? Each review followed the same format under Mr. Csoka's chairmanship. He began by asking the prisoner whether he had received seventy-two hours' written notice of the review and had agreed to come to the review. Each one had. In several cases, he prefaced these questions with the comment: "But first there is some legal stuff to go over." This was revealing, since it implied that the legal requirements were procedural hurdles which, having been cleared, allowed the real business—the exercise of administrative discretion unconstrained by law—to get underway.

Having cleared these legal hurdles, Mr. Csoka informed each prisoner that he would remain in segregation pending an investigation, in some cases of his involvement with the incident in the yard and in the others with the destruction of property in A unit. This signalled to prisoners that the determination for continued segregation had already been made; whatever they said would make no difference to this outcome. Mr. Csoka was up front about this, a quality much respected by prisoners. However, the legal function of the five-day review is to consider whether there are continuing grounds for segregation, not simply to announce this determination to the prisoner.

The following exchange from the review of prisoner Glen Rosenthal (taken from my notes) captures the nature of Mr. Csoka's review process:

> MC: Mr. Rosenthal, we are going to maintain you in segregation pending the investigation of your involvement in the yard.
>
> GR: I would like to request specific information about what has been alleged against me regarding my involvement in the yard.

MC: I can't tell you that. It's up to the IPSOs. They're the ones doing the investigation with the RCMP.

GR: So I'm in seg for allegations but you can't tell me what they are?

MC: That's right.

Mr. Rosenthal and several other prisoners complained bitterly about the conditions in segregation: specifically, they had been given no change of clothes. Prisoners brought down after the smash-up on Monday were still in the coveralls they had been given when they were taken out of their cells. They had no underwear, and their cells were bare except for bedding. Mr. Rosenthal asked Mr. Csoka why Kent was not complying with the CCRA provisions requiring that a prisoner admitted into segregation be given the same rights, privileges, and conditions of confinement as the general inmate population. Mr. Csoka's response was that prisoners receive their effects only after the five-day review. Mr. Rosenthal asked, "Where in the CCRA does it say that prisoners in segregation are not entitled to all their rights in the first five days?" Mr. Csoka said the recent audit done as part of the Task Force on Administrative Segregation had approved the practice of not giving prisoners their effects until after the five-day review; however, Mr. Rosenthal still wanted to know where in the law this was authorized. The segregation staff had told him and other prisoners that they would get their clothes and tobacco only when they started to behave themselves. Mr. Rosenthal questioned, "Where does it say in the CCRA that you can use our rights as behaviour modification?" (In her report the previous year, Madam Justice Arbour had given her unequivocal answer that this was not legally permissible.)

Mr. Rosenthal inquired whether the five-day review was being tape-recorded. When told it was not, he asked how the review was documented. Mr. Csoka said the clerk was keeping a record. Mr. Rosenthal questioned this: "She hasn't written down anything that I have said, so how is she keeping a record?" Mr. Csoka explained that the clerk wrote down only the reasons for segregation. Mr. Rosenthal's characterization of this was: "So none of what went on here is on record. It's like it never happened."

Two of the reviews conducted by Mr. Csoka on July 17 had a compelling quality. Mr. Forget had seen his friend Christian Grenier dying in the yard and had himself been hit in the head with a baseball bat. Mr. Csoka showed compassion and empathy, asking Mr. Forget how he was coping with his friend's death and commenting that it must be very hard on him. Mr. Forget explained that the Valium which had come into the institution was supposed to reach Mr. Grenier. When it did not, Mr. Grenier and his friends were prepared to write it off. But on Thursday, while Mr. Forget and Mr. Grenier were walking around the yard, they had been approached by other prisoners and confronted with threats. Mr. Forget had taken a defensive position, which he now regretted because his friend was dead. Mr. Csoka told him he would be kept in segregation pending the outcome of the investigation; the institution was concerned that if Mr. Forget went back to the population there was a risk of further assaults.

Jimmy Whitmore's five-day review was compelling for different reasons. In Sector 2, Chapter 2, "The Life and Death of the Electric Man," I described Mr. Whitmore's physical intensity when he gave evidence in Hughie MacDonald's murder trial. On this occasion, he was infused with an anger that filled the small interview room. Mr. Whitmore was told by Mr. Csoka that he would be maintained in segregation pending the investigation of the incident in the yard. When Mr. Whitmore questioned why that required him to be segregated beyond five days, he was given the additional information that the IPSOs and the RCMP had asked that he be kept there until the investigation was complete. When Mr. Whitmore asked what the particular allegations were against him, he was advised, as were the other prisoners who asked this question, that this information was not available to him. He protested angrily, saying the institution must know from the videotape that he had taken a baseball bat out of a prisoner's hands and thrown it over the fence, and that he had tried to calm things down rather than incite matters. He and some of the other prisoners had got everyone to lock up without further problems. "We did your job for you," he thundered, "and now we look like goofs." Two months before, an understanding had been struck between the warden and prisoner representatives that there would be a protocol if lock-downs were imposed; this protocol involved communicating with the prisoners. Yet this had not been respected the previous week, he said, and that had the predictable effect of getting prisoners riled up. When the lock-down continued after the weekend, visits were cancelled, showers were limited, and tobacco was scarce. He had written to the warden early Monday morning and the prisoners expected a response, but it never came. He maintained that the smash-up on Monday evening was as much the administration's responsibility as it was the prisoners'. He went on to protest the conditions in segregation: the lack of clothes, the limited showers, the restrictions on visits. He told Mr. Csoka that he had a private family visit in three weeks and proclaimed, with his body wound tight, "I won't see my child crying because he can't touch his dad because you Nazis have me locked up in segregation."

Mr. Csoka let Mr. Whitmore finish what he had to say, although he must have been very discomforted. He then promised to talk to the Visit Review Board and get back to Mr. Whitmore before the end of the day with their response to whether more visiting blocks could be opened up, given the large numbers of prisoners in segregation.

It was still only 1:30 p.m., and Mike Csoka's day was not yet over. Neither was mine. Later that afternoon, I returned to segregation and taped an interview with Jimmy Whitmore. His speech was quieter, in part a conspiratorial function of having a microphone on the table, but his anger was still pulsating. He began by calling the review a sham. Two days before, one of the IPSOs had told Mr. Whitmore he was in segregation because several hours before the smash-up in A unit, some guards had heard him shouting out his cell window, and he was therefore believed to have incited the destruction. He had been through major smash-ups in Millhaven and elsewhere and he knew how little they accomplished and how much prisoners were made to pay later. None of the cells on his range, which included Hughie MacDonald's and Darryl Bates', had been trashed, he said, because prisoners with as much time in as they had knew how little was achieved by such "punk action." He had been shouting out his window that afternoon to tell the other prisoners about his letter to the warden and was actually trying to keep a lid on the situation. A lot of people were shouting that afternoon, and he questioned how any officer could distinguish who was saying what. He suspected he had been fingered because he was the acknowledged spokesman for A unit.

Jimmy Whitmore then explained to me the nature of his involvement with the incident in the yard:

> I went out to the yard that afternoon. I left my visit early. I went out because I knew there was a trip. But I was sure it could be mediated and solved and that's the way I like to work things. I'm sick and tired of seeing people dying in here. No one wants to die in prison. I believed that the problem was squared off, it was mediated, it was over. Then all of a sudden somebody grabbed some bats, threw them to the guys, and the next thing you know I'm standing between a guy with a knife and another guy with two bats trying to keep them from fighting, right? It's all on camera. They can't dispute that. I had no weapons. I mean, I put my life on the line . . .
>
> My involvement there was taking the bat out of a guy's hand and throwing it over the fence and getting the guys to go in quietly. That's wrong? I also took [Claude Forget] to the gym. He had a big cut on his head . . . If we didn't do that, take the bats away from the guys and tell them to calm down, what do you think would have happened? I know what would have happened because I've seen it happen before. Hey, there's a bunch of guards out there. They've got no weapons. There's one guy in the tower with a gun. A couple of us would have got shot. Probably quite a few of them would have got hurt. A few more of our guys would have been killed or stabbed. And we stopped that. And we're locked up now? Where's the logic? And what they tell me in seg review is "I don't have an answer for this" and "I don't have an answer for that." (Interview with Jimmy Whitmore, Kent Institution, July 17, 1997)

Mr. Whitmore's five-day review, like the other hearings that day, did not conform to the basic requirements of the law. When he was first placed in segregation and at the five-day review, Mr. Whitmore was told he would be maintained in segregation pending the completion of investigations into the incident in the yard. This is not a sufficient ground under the CCRA. An ongoing investigation justifies segregation under s. 31(3)(b) only if that investigation could lead to a criminal charge or a serious disciplinary offence *and*—this is critical—if the continued presence of the prisoner in the general population would interfere with that investigation. This interference could be caused by intimidation of other prisoners the police or the IPSOs want to interview or by the destruction of evidence.

The five-day review of Mr. Whitmore's case should have addressed these issues, and Mr. Whitmore should have received notice in writing of whatever information the institution had to support his segregation. Yet all he and the other prisoners were provided with was a segregation notice containing the following:

> You have been placed in segregation pending investigation into your involvement in the recent sports field incident. All alternatives to segregation were explored, as none were found, your placement in segregation was actioned. You will be seen by the Segregation Review Board on July 17, 1997. (Five-Day Review of Offender's Segregated Status, Kent Institution, July 17, 1997)

The five-day reviews of Jimmy Whitmore and the other thirteen inmates illustrate more than the continuing issue of non-compliance with the CCRA requirements for administrative segregation; they also underline why independent adjudication is crucial to the justice of both the process and the result. The current provisions of the CCRA assume that correctional administrators are capable of conducting the review of segregation cases fairly and impartially. Yet a close examination of the situation in the aftermath of Christian Grenier's murder reveals the fallacy of this assumption.

Based on a review of the videotape evidence and the observations of correctional officers, a small group of prisoners were identified as the primary participants in the melee. Given that the authorities already knew of the ongoing power struggle between the prisoners in A unit and C unit, it does not take a Ph.D. in Correctional Administration to recognize that the institution needed to get matters under control, and quickly. This was accomplished effectively by the lockdown, which contained the situation and enabled the investigation to begin. However, the problems which gave rise to the hostilities remained, so opening up the units and returning the prison to normal routine presented a real risk of renewed conflict and further violence by way of retaliation or pre-emptive strike.

The segregation of prisoners identified by video and other evidence as primary players in the assault and murder is justified during the initial period of investigation, during which the institution explores the conditions under which the lock-down can be ended. In these initial stages, it may be reasonable to segregate individuals whose activity on the videotape is ambiguous but who could well be implicated in the assaults by virtue of their close relationship with other participants. For some of these prisoners, immediate segregation may be justified because of a reasonably based fear that, even in a lock-down situation, their presence in the general population may be a source of further disturbance. For others, while their presence is no threat to the security of the institution during a lock-down, their presence in the general population thereafter may undermine the prison's return to normal operations because of the prisoners' willingness to carry on the war or their vulnerability to retaliation by the other side.

There is no doubt that these are very difficult judgement calls, with a heavy premium on "getting it right." "Getting it wrong" could result in another body in the yard. Kent Warden Brenda Marshall, together with senior staff including Mike Csoka, the IPSO, and experienced correctional supervisors, determined which prisoners should be immediately and subsequently segregated to both contain the war zone and prevent further conflict. After the smash-up in A unit, they segregated the prisoners directly involved, to prevent further damage to the institution and a further delay in ending the lock-down of the general population. None of these decisions were taken lightly, and they were made in good faith based on the best information available to the warden and her staff.

The segregated prisoners were then entitled to a five-day review. The Segregation Review Board was chaired by the person who was simultaneously Co-ordinator of Case Management and Acting Unit Manager of Segregation and who the previous week had also been acting as Deputy Warden. Mike Csoka, in all of these capacities, played a central role in developing correctional strategies following the killing and subsequent smash-up. It defies reason, correctional or otherwise, to expect him to conduct these five-day reviews with an open mind, unbiased by the previous decisions and the flow of information to which he had been privy. When he announced to the prisoners that they would remain in segregation pending completion of the investigation, he was, from his senior administrator's perspective, stating the obvious. That is the way things work in a maximum security institution after a major incident, especially one involving a killing. From Mr. Csoka's perspective, you would have to be from Mars to expect anything different. In that sense, the five-day reviews were conducted only because they were required by the CCRA, not because any decision other than maintaining the prisoners' segregation might be reached.

Under these circumstances, there is clearly no possibility that the review contemplated by the CCRA can be carried out. A "review" requires a consideration of the facts measured against the lawful grounds for segregation, and a determination whether, in light of any reasonable alternatives, continued segregation is justifiable. A "review" requires an evaluation by someone whose mind is not already made up on the issue. This fatal flaw in the current form of review cannot be side-stepped by the assertion that the Segregation Review Board simply makes a recommendation which is then referred to the warden for the ultimate decision. In the cases we are considering here, and indeed in most cases of a similar nature, the warden is part of a collective decision-making process in which the five-day reviews are an element.

It was not surprising that the majority of the prisoners in this instance viewed their five-day reviews with scepticism, even contempt. The requirements of the law were invoked solely to ensure that prisoners had their three days' notice of the review and their right to appear. But that right meant nothing in the context of a decision already made. These are men already deeply suspicious of and resistant to authority. For them to be told, in the name of fairness and the law, that they have a right to a hearing, and then to be told a decision has been made in advance, is worse than giving them no hearing at all—and it does greater damage to the legitimacy of correctional authority.

A year later, I shared with Mike Csoka my perception that he saw the legal requirements of the CCRA regarding segregation as a set of procedural hurdles to be cleared before he got down to the real business at hand. He replied, with his usual candour.

> My reputation and my word mean more to me than that I fill out all these boxes. Sometimes I'll give that air that I've got to get all this out of the way. Do I disagree with the law? Do I think it's a waste of time? No, because some guys won't do it, some guys will screw an inmate around. I won't. I live by my reputation. So, you call them hurdles, I wouldn't call them hurdles; I call them necessary steps I have to go through, that I will go through because it's the law. But sometimes I feel that there's just too many of them. (Interview with Mike Csoka, Kent Institution, July 1998)

The role of an independent adjudicator is not to replicate the hard-won knowledge and experience of correctional administrators like Mike Csoka. It is to examine the legal criteria for segregation within a procedural framework which allows the institution to present its case and the prisoner to answer it. Given the broad criteria in the CCRA (sometimes overly broad, as I have commented elsewhere), the institution in this case would have had little difficulty in persuading an independent adjudicator of the lawful justification for segregating the primary participants in the Grenier homicide and the A unit smash-up. The institutional case would involve a review of the videotape and other evidence implicating particular prisoners and a justification of why anything short of segregation would prejudice the security of the institution, compromise the safety of other prisoners, or jeopardize the ongoing investigation. If the disclosure of any evidence (for example, information from prison informants) posed a danger to the safety of prisoners, the institution could make out a case for non-disclosure to the independent adjudicator. As long as the institution did its job in presenting reasonable grounds for maintaining segregation, it is difficult to imagine that an independent adjudicator would not weigh these points heavily in maintaining segregation, *unless* a prisoner presented a credible argument that he was mistakenly implicated or that his presence in the population would not prejudice security or safety, or compromise the investigation. An independent adjudicator would *not* turn a blind eye to the realities of a maximum security prison in the aftermath of a homicide precipitated by a power struggle between rival groups. But his or her determination, measured against the criteria of the law, would be made free from correctional judgements formed in the adrenaline rush of crisis and emergency and with due regard to the submissions of prisoners.

Other important aspects of the independent adjudicator's role are illustrated in these cases. Several prisoners complained during their hearings that their rights and privileges were being denied in administrative segregation. For example, they were kept in the same clothes or coveralls for five days, were denied access to daily showers, and were having difficulty in making legal calls. Under my Model Segregation Code, the independent adjudicator would ensure full compliance with the law regarding the conditions of segregation and report serious violations to both the warden and the commissioner.

The presence of an independent adjudicator would not undermine or straitjacket the authority of wardens and staff to manage their institutions decisively at times of crisis, maintaining a precarious balance of control and security. Independent adjudication is designed to safeguard another kind of precarious balance, one likely to be upset at times of crisis and emergency: the balance between correctional discretion involving the most intrusive form of imprisonment—administrative segregation—and the rights of prisoners to the full protection of the law.

## July 22: Who's on First?

The process set in motion by the murder of Christian Grenier and the A unit smash-up had only begun with the segregation of prisoners and the five-day reviews. When I returned to Kent on Tuesday, July 22, I spoke with Cacane Tremblay about the events leading up to Mr. Grenier's death. Some prisoners in A unit had drug debts with prisoners in C unit, and although a meeting between them seemed initially to resolve the matter, it escalated into a situation in the yard in which threats were uttered and knives were flashed. Claude Forget, who was serving a 20-year sentence for the attempted murder of two police officers, made it clear that anyone threatening Mr. Tremblay would have to go through him first. Knives were drawn, and Mr. Forget defended himself with a baseball bat. When Mr. Grenier came to his assistance, he was knifed. Mr. Forget was struck on the back of the head with a baseball bat. Mr. Tremblay told me that the A unit prisoners involved were in deep trouble. They could not return to the population without risking death or serious assault, and, given how well connected Claude Forget was, Mr. Tremblay could not think of any maximum security institution to which they could be sent without encountering major problems.

On July 23, I interviewed Glen Rosenthal and Pat McKenna in segregation. Mr. Rosenthal provided me with a running commentary on the events in the exercise yard, concluding with these words:

> When you're on one team in a situation like this, you tag someone on the other team before they tag you. That's what happened. That's why Christian got killed.
>
> The honest-to-god truth was that this Christian was a nice guy. There was nobody involved on our side [in A unit] that had any ill intentions towards him whatsoever. But the guy's got a baseball bat and he's swinging it at Kenny Makichuk and the person who stabbed him cared a lot about Kenny. They were in a relationship, and what are you going to do? It's a husband-and-wife kind of thing, and if someone is swinging a baseball bat at your wife or your husband and you're standing behind them with a knife, what are you going to do? It's like the sparks in a gas tank, and that's what erupted here. (Interview with Glen Rosenthal, Kent Institution, July 23, 1997)

At the beginning of my interview with Pat McKenna, I told him I had received information from the institution that he was the trigger for the smash-up in A unit. I asked if he could explain how he saw his role in it, and also what had caused the rage that led to such extensive damage and destruction. His explanation painted a very different picture from the institutional images of a rogue prisoner out of control.

> I had got married just before the murder and I was in a private family visit with my wife in the trailer when it happened. I came out of the trailer on Friday and walked straight into a lock-down. My wife was scheduled to come out on Saturday, Sunday, and then again on Monday. Because of the lock-down, we didn't get Saturday's visit, which was to be expected because there was just a murder. That's fine. Then comes Sunday's visit. That's cancelled. That's pushing it a bit, but still the administration is doing its investigation, and so that's fine too . . .

All that weekend and into the Monday we'd been trying to get the administration's attention and it hasn't worked. The biggest thing was the visits. The whole smash-up could have been avoided if they had given us the visits. They could have ten less guys in the hole if they had given visits, because as soon as I walk into a visit, the first thing my wife is telling me is to calm down, chill out, don't let this bother you. And everybody's visitor does that. So for them to take that away is mind-boggling.

So now you're locked in your cell and your efforts to get their attention is exhausted, so what else are you going to do? So yes, I did set a fire. Now the fire is an easy way to get their attention. Smoke comes out onto the range so they're going to come down. Well, they came down, looked at the fire and said, "Let them burn" and left. I couldn't believe it. So I set the sprinkler off to try and put out the fire and that didn't work too good, so now I've got a cell filled with smoke. That's how come the window got taken out. Because I couldn't breathe in there. I kicked the window open to get some air. I was pretty desperate. And it's self-preservation now.

When the guards were taking me out of my cell to segregation, they had this video camera on me. So I figured that I hadn't had a chance to talk to the warden before, so this was going to be my only opportunity to speak to her and I did—on camera. I spoke into the camera like a fool, and I said to the warden that this concern is not with the guards and I told the guards that "this isn't with you guys. This isn't personal. We're not doing this because of something you did on shift today. We don't expect you to clean it up. This is for the warden, and this is to let the warden know that there is a serious problem here in population." I probably shouldn't have done it, because now they've got me under investigation for inciting a riot. When she saw that tape it probably looked pretty bad. I'm covered in water and black smoke and I'm naked, walking backwards down the hall, giving my fifteen-second message into a videotape. And I've got six guards around me with cameras and shields and sticks. I probably look like a maniac. The fact is I'm probably one of the more reasonable guys down here. I'm not an animal. This whole smash-up could have been avoided if we'd had some communication. (Interview with Pat McKenna, Kent Institution, July 23, 1997)

## July 29–30: Who's on Second and Third?

During the week of July 29, I sat in on a meeting held in segregation between Deputy Warden Doug Richmond, Unit Manager Lin Wallin, and Jimmy

Whitmore. Mr. Richmond advised Mr. Whitmore that the RCMP and CSC investigation was dealing with two different theories regarding his involvement in the murder—one being that he had played a peaceful mediation role, the other that he was the instigator of the crime. Until the institution was debriefed on the results of the investigation, they would be maintaining Mr. Whitmore's segregation. Mr. Richmond also indicated staff had received information that Mr. Whitmore's safety in the general population would be in jeopardy.

Mr. Whitmore responded that surely the evidence on the videotape validated one theory and negated the other. Both Mr. Richmond and Mr. Wallin had seen only portions of the video, but those pieces suggested that Mr. Whitmore was going from group to group in what seemed to be a mediation role. Mr. Wallin acknowledged that in the years he had known him at Kent, Mr. Whitmore's role had been one of mediation, and that on many occasions his involvement had prevented violence. (Mr. Whitmore was not told at this meeting that the RCMP had obtained a statement from another prisoner alleging that, on the evening prior to the death of Christian Grenier, Mr. Whitmore had said, "The Frenchmen are dead tomorrow. I'm not going to do it, but I will get someone to kill them." Mr. Whitmore became aware of this allegation only several months later.)

Addressing the issue of his own safety, Mr. Whitmore said there were elements in the population who were quite happy to see him in segregation and would like him shipped out of the institution. Although it was in their interests to "talk up" the danger he would encounter, to ensure his continued segregation and thereby consolidate their power in the institution, the serious threats in prison came not from the loudest mouths but from those who kept their intentions close to their chests. Mr. Richmond said he would continue to evaluate the reliability of his information.

Later that afternoon, I met with Darryl Bates and Alan Nicol. Mr. Nicol summed up what he had been told by C unit: "You don't kill a Frenchman in Kent." The way he read the situation, regardless of Jimmy Whitmore's actual involvement in the incident, some in C unit were holding him responsible and saying they would move against him if he came back. There had been a real hardening of attitudes in C unit against all prisoners believed to be involved in the attack on Mr. Grenier and Mr. Forget, and he could not say with any confidence that the threats were paper ones. Neither he nor Mr. Bates felt comfortable telling Jimmy Whitmore he could safely come out into the population, if what he risked was having a knife in his back or facing another trip to the SHU for defending himself. I asked whether Claude Forget's return to the population might contribute to a peaceful resolution. Both Mr. Bates and Mr. Nicol thought it would; they had relatively good relations with Mr. Forget and felt his attitude might be less inflexible than those of his brothers in C unit.

On Wednesday, July 30, I met with Dan Kane, head of the CSC national investigation team, who gave me his assessment of the situation. A large quantity of

Valium had come into the institution at a social on July 6. The pills were destined for prisoners in the francophone group, but most of them never reached C unit. Some information suggested that the person the drugs were destined for was Christian Grenier, although this might be a case of using the dead man to insulate others. Because this posed a potential source of conflict, there was a meeting between prisoners from A unit and C unit to settle this issue and it was resolved. The francophone prisoners decided they would not take retaliative action for the non-delivery of the drugs but would treat it as a debt to be made good in the future. The investigation team was satisfied that what followed in the yard was not related to the undelivered Valium. Instead, the team related it to a confrontation between Kenny Makichuk and Cacane Tremblay which had occurred earlier on the day of the murder. Mr. Makichuk had threatened Mr. Tremblay with a knife and said he was prepared to kill him. Mr. Makichuk's subsequent apology had been rebuffed. He went back to A unit to muster support, and after lunch a number of prisoners from A unit armed themselves and went out to the yard in anticipation of a fight with the prisoners in C unit. However, because the C unit prisoners believed there had been a resolution of the issue involving the Valium, only Mr. Forget, Mr. Grenier, and Mr. Shropshire went out to the yard. Some information suggested that other C unit heavies were high on drugs that day and that was why they did not go outside. In the yard, Mr. Makichuk was told by another prisoner from A unit that the French Canadians had armed themselves with baseball bats, and at that point he attacked Mr. Forget. When Mr. Grenier came to Mr. Forget's assistance, Mr. Makichuk stabbed him in the chest. Mr. Simpson, Mr. Makichuk's partner, stabbed Mr. Grenier in the back.

## August 3–5: A Correctional Officer's Laying on of Hands

Over the long weekend marking the celebration of B.C. Day, Kent Institution experienced two further incidents in which prisoners came perilously close to death. This time the events involved protective custody prisoners and resulted in the lock-down of that side of the house.

On Sunday, August 3, in the exercise yard where Christian Grenier had been killed three weeks earlier, Mr. Acheson, armed with a knife and a weight bar, attacked another prisoner. A staff member managed to confiscate the bar, but Mr. Acheson continued slashing the other prisoner with the knife, inflicting several cuts on his arms. Despite being asked repeatedly to give up his weapon, Mr. Acheson refused to do so. As Officer Noon-Ward, the head of the Emergency Response Team, explained to me, the prisoner at that point ran the serious risk of being shot by the officer in the gun tower. To avoid this, Officer Noon-Ward struck Mr. Acheson with the weight bar. He fell to the ground, where he was restrained. Normally gas would have been available to disable the prisoner, but the gas canister had been moved from its accustomed location and the officers had to improvise an alternative method. Officer Noon-Ward told me he had placed himself between the tower officer's line of sight and the prisoner, and as a consequence, the prisoner had suffered some bruised ribs but had not been shot. Prisoners observing the confrontation expressed surprise that an officer would use a weight bar to strike a prisoner. As described by Officer Noon-Ward:

> "Did you see that pig? He piped him." Several inmates approached me and said, "You've got a guy with a gun up there. Why didn't he use the gun?" My response was "Would you rather that one of your confreres gets shot, possibly killed, as opposed to a non-lethal strike with a weight bar used like a baton? Give your head a shake." The officer in the gun-walk would have been fully within his rights to fire a warning shot and, after the warning shot, if Acheson didn't drop the knife, because of the proximity of staff, he would have been fully justified in using lethal force on that inmate. Luckily it didn't come to that. (Interview with Mark Noon-Ward, Kent Institution, August 28, 1997)

The next day, Monday, August 4, Officer Noon-Ward was again on duty, this time with several other officers observing prisoner movement in the inner courtyard. Prisoner Sean Blair was sitting on the steps of the courtyard when he felt a burning sensation in his back. As he looked around, he saw another prisoner walking away, carrying a knife by his side that was dripping blood. Mr. Blair realized he had been stabbed. Rather than alerting the guards, he made his way across the courtyard towards the Health Care Unit. He collapsed as he reached the door leading from the courtyard and was rushed to Health Care, where an ambulance was called. Officer Noon-Ward accompanied him to the Chilliwack Hospital, where he was operated on in the emergency room for a punctured lung. His condition did not permit a general anaesthetic, so only a local anaesthetic was administered. At the request of the surgeon, Officer Mark Noon-Ward held Mr. Blair down to prevent him from moving during the operation.

In a period of less than three weeks, Correctional Officer Mark Noon-Ward had found himself leading the Emergency Response Team into A unit to extract prisoners involved in the smash-up; packing and documenting the water-damaged personal effects of segregated prisoners; stepping into the line of a fire of an officer in the gun tower to disable a defiant, knife-wielding prisoner with a weight bar; and assisting in a life-saving operation. Rarely can the phrase "the laying on of hands" have contained such diverse meaning.

The prisoner who stabbed Mr. Blair did this so quickly—literally without breaking his stride—that not only the four officers in the yard but also Sean Blair himself missed the play. The video cameras recorded only dark shadows, so that the assailant remained anonymous to the authorities.

Back on the other side of the prison, the national team investigating the A unit smash-up and the murder of Christian Grenier had delivered its debriefing on the previous Thursday, July 31. On Friday, August 1, two of the prisoners involved in the smash-up were released from segregation. However, Mr. Forget, whom the investigation team had confirmed was to be viewed as a victim, not an aggressor, was not released. Cacane Tremblay spoke to Unit Manager Wallin and was advised that Mr. Forget would remain in segregation until after the long weekend, because senior management wanted to be on the scene when he was released to ensure there were no problems.

Mr. Forget's expected release from segregation on Tuesday, August 5 did not happen. At the end of that day I spoke with Doug Richmond, the acting warden, about the developments. Because of the two assaults on the protective custody side over the weekend, he had been fully occupied with initiating the necessary internal investigations and had not yet given consideration to the release of Mr. Forget or the other prisoners who remained in segregation. He advised me that these decisions would probably await the determination of the Segregation Review Board, although he acknowledged that the original justification for keeping Mr. Forget in segregation no longer sufficed, in light of the national investigation's confirmation that Mr. Forget was a victim.

## August 11–12: The CSC and the CYA Principle

The Segregation Review Board met on August 11 to conduct a number of reviews, including the cases of Mr. McKenna and Mr. Forget. The Board recommended that both prisoners be released from segregation. The warden, back after a week's vacation, accepted the recommendation in relation to Mr. McKenna, and he was released from segregation that day. In the case of Mr. Forget, the warden asked the IPSO to prepare a risk/threat assessment prior to making her final decision.

The next day, I asked Warden Marshall for her assessment of the situation at Kent in the aftermath of the Grenier murder. She was acutely aware of the critical nature of her decision on Claude Forget's release from segregation. Many prisoners had told the administration that Mr. Forget's release would not pose a risk to him and that it could help to resolve some outstanding problems in the population, but there was other information to the effect that "blood will flow if Forget is released." That was the reason she had asked the IPSO to prepare a statement of risk. Gary Allen's death two years earlier, within hours of his release from segregation, was very much on her mind.

It is not difficult to understand the warden's response. She is accountable to the Commissioner of Corrections for her judgements. There was enormous pressure on her to ensure that decisions made following the incidents of "Deadly July" did not precipitate further incidents compromising safety or security. If

Brenda Marshall approved the release of Claude Forget and there was further bloodshed, she would wear it. This was the inescapable reality that Warden Marshall faced: like any other warden, in making decisions she had to take her job into account. In addition to the legal criteria for segregation, there is, therefore, an important criterion that remains unwritten: "The prisoner's release to the population shall not jeopardize the security of my position as warden." In most hierarchical structures of management, including the Correctional Service of Canada, this is known as the CYA (Cover Your Ass) principle.

It is precisely *because* of the immense responsibility and accountability that rests on a warden's shoulders that decisions which have a major impact on a prisoner's rights and liberties should be made by an independent adjudicator, someone who can exercise the best possible judgement in light of the available evidence, weighing the competing risks involved, without the fear that his or her job is on the line.

## August 14: The Thirty-Day Reviews—A Legal Milestone?

The Segregation Review Board which met on August 14 did not have to consider the cases of any prisoners involved in the A unit smash-up. All of them had already been released except for one who remained in segregation, serving out a sentence of 30 days' punitive segregation imposed at a disciplinary hearing on charges preceding the smash-up.

Seven prisoners alleged to be involved in the incident in the exercise yard remained in segregation. As I have described, Mr. Forget had been seen by the Board two days prior to the regular thirty-day reviews, and the Board recommended to the warden that he be released back to the population. The warden determined that this should take place and late in the afternoon of August 14, Mr. Forget returned to his cell in C unit.

The thirty-day reviews were chaired by Unit Manager Wallin, who had been asked to take on this responsibility at the last moment. All of the prisoners attended their reviews except for Mr. Makichuk. Under new procedures, each prisoner's CMO was supposed to be at the review, together with the IPSO; however, at the August 14 reviews, none of the prisoners' CMOs were present and neither was the IPSO, despite the fact that information he had collected was critical to the reviews. Because Mr. Wallin had had no time to prepare in advance, at the beginning of each review he consulted the bare-bones summary on the prisoner's index card. Although the prisoners had been given three days' notice that the hearing would be conducted, they were provided with no written information regarding their cases. It could hardly be maintained that there was no information to share. During the month since the Grenier killing, there had been a constant flow of information between prisoners and the administration regarding the climate in the population and the risks associated with the release of the segregated prisoners. The national investigation had been completed two weeks earlier, and senior management had been debriefed by the investigation team. This new information was the basis on which the Segregation Review Board should have assessed the justification for continued segregation of the prisoners. The information should also have been reduced to writing and shared with the prisoners. The thirty-day review should be a significant milestone for the gathering of evidence and its assessment against the legal criteria. However, the August thirty-day reviews bore none of these markings.

In several cases, when prisoners inquired when they would be released now that the national investigation was over, they were told that the RCMP investigation was ongoing and they would be maintained in segregation pending its completion and the IPSO's assessment of their risk. After informing Shawn Preddy of this, Mr. Wallin asked him whether he had been questioned by the RCMP. Mr. Preddy said no; in fact, nobody from *either* outside or inside the institution had questioned him about the incident in the yard. (Mr. Preddy, like Mr. Whitmore, was a player in the events of both Deadly July and the Life and Death of the Electric Man.) Mr. Wallin said he would ask the IPSO to speak with Mr. Preddy.

There was one obvious question which occurred to me during the hearings and which was voiced by several prisoners. Why was the Board maintaining their segregation at this stage pending an assessment by the IPSO of their risk if released to the population? There had been more than enough time to do this assessment, and one primary purpose of the thirty-day review should have been to consider it.

The thirty-day reviews of these prisoners, like the five-day reviews, utterly failed to fulfil the purposes of a review as envisaged by the CCRA. Prisoners had not been given the legally required written information about their cases; there was no review or assessment of the available evidence, and no inquiry was directed to the legal grounds for segregation. While it could not be said, as in the five-day reviews, that the thirty-day reviews were conducted by a chairperson who had prejudged the issue, they *were* conducted by a chairperson who (through no fault of his own) was totally unprepared for the hearing.

The legislative purpose of the thirty-day reviews had also been undermined by the musical chairs played over the previous month in key management positions. For two weeks after the death of Christian Grenier, Mike Csoka (in his various capacities), IPSO Jim Farrell, and Warden Brenda Marshall were the principal institutional figures to and through whom information flowed. All three were there during the national investigation and had participated in the debriefing. Following that, the warden went on a week's annual leave. Mike Csoka and Jim Farrell went on three weeks' leave, and Unit Manager Lin Wallin and IPSO Wayne Culbert, who had been on annual leaves of absence themselves during the critical period and missed the national debriefing, returned to their positions. Claude Demers, Acting Unit Manager of Segregation, had been absent for six weeks previous to that. Deputy Warden Doug Richmond was in the institution for only part of the two weeks following the murder, and he too missed the national debriefing. These comings and goings resulted in people making decisions without being in possession of the entire picture.

Correctional staff, like all workers, are certainly entitled to their holidays. July and August, for obvious reasons—good weather, kids out of school—are the prime months for annual leave. But the law is not supposed to go on holiday. In July and August of 1997, Kent maintained the skeletal framework of segregation review, but the reviews did not meet the legal standards of a fair and effective process.

It is worth examining how these thirty-day reviews could have been conducted with the benefit of independent adjudication. The administration would have been compelled to prepare a written review of all information it believed would support the case for continued segregation. That information would have been shared with prisoners, subject to any justifiable statutory claims for exemption. Given the completion of the national investigation, the institution would have been able to justify continued segregation for investigatory purposes only if it could show that the release of prisoners to the population would interfere with the ongoing RCMP investigation—something I very much doubt it could have shown. Thus the institution's case for continued detention would have focussed primarily on the belief that the release of prisoners would endanger their safety. In support of its position, the administration would have presented information collected from other prisoners that the release of the men believed to be involved in Christian Grenier's death would result in retaliation against those men. The prisoners in segregation would undoubtedly have argued that much of this information came from prisoners in C unit with a vested interest in ensuring that the segregated prisoners did not come back into the population—their continued segregation would help consolidate C unit's power in the institution. They would further have argued that the rhetoric of retaliation should be assessed in this light and therefore be heavily discounted. The administration might have argued that the C unit prisoners making the threats had proven themselves capable of violent retaliation in the past, spending long periods in the Special Handling Unit in Quebec as a result. The prisoners in segregation would likely have countered that precisely *because* these prisoners had come out to western Canada from the SHU to escape their reputations, they were not likely to instigate a battle. (The segregated prisoners might also have been tempted to respond—although this would have been ill advised—that in terms of firepower, A unit and their friends were more than a match for C unit and their allies. The potential resulting war was in fact the worst-case scenario feared by the warden.)

An independent adjudicator fully briefed on the volatility of the situation would likely have concluded that the institution had reasonable grounds to believe the release of the segregated prisoners, at this juncture, would pose a serious risk to both their safety and the security of the institution. However—and this is extremely significant—the independent adjudicator would then turn the legal inquiry towards alternatives to segregation and the development of a plan for reintegration. Within that framework, consideration would be given to the proposals of the prisoners for mediation. Over the past month, prisoners had suggested, to me and others, a number of scenarios for a mediated settlement of the dispute between the two units. The early release of Claude Forget was one of those. In this case, in fact, the process of mediation could have been started shortly after the five-day review, with some reasonable expectation that a plan be developed and presented at the thirty-day review.

Let us be clear about the complexity of the situation at Kent as "Deadly July" continued into August. The risk of further violence was very real. Various postures were taken by prisoners, some talking up the risk of retaliation and others the possibilities for a truce. No one could say with any confidence what the real risks were. The person with primary responsibility for risk assessment was the IPSO, who was not only completely overwhelmed with other work but, by his own admission, still getting up to speed on what had happened in the prison during his annual leave. Even more important, as the institution's point man, he was not someone in whom most prisoners would confide. I had little doubt that the information I was receiving was much closer to the mark. In such a situation, an independent adjudicator could play a crucial role by ordering the appointment of a mediator from outside the institution at an early stage of the process. The most positive outcome would be a mediated settlement to which all parties could commit. If that settlement proved impossible to achieve, the only remaining alternative to long-term segregation would be transfers to other institutions.

## August 19–23: Negotiating a Peace Treaty

On August 19, my next visit to Kent, I checked with IPSO Wayne Culbert on the developments since Claude Forget's release from segregation. Officers' observation reports indicated that there had been some tense moments and some stare-downs between the prisoners in C and A units, but nothing more. Mr. Forget was keeping a low profile, spending most of his time in his cell.

I spoke next with Darryl Bates and Pat McKenna. Each of them had spoken to Claude Forget, and both were satisfied that he had no "beef" with either Jimmy Whitmore or Glen Rosenthal. Those two prisoners could be brought back into the population without reigniting the conflict. I explained to them that no prisoners would be returned to the population unless the warden was satisfied there would be no retaliation on either side. Their task was to assure her she could leave the institution at the end of the day without worrying about finding an armed camp or more dead bodies the next morning. Mr. Bates suggested a meeting of selected GP prisoners, which I would attend, to see if some agreement could be reached for the gradual release of the prisoners in segregation. With someone who had the confidence of all parties and was seen as independent of the administration, the prisoners involved might be prepared to put their cards on the table. I agreed, contingent on a consensus among the principals that this would be a useful and desired process.

I returned to Kent on August 22. I began the day by talking with Pat McKenna, who filled me in on his recent discussions with the players in C unit. There were some common messages from these conversations. All agreed that Kenny Makichuk and Neil Simpson could not return to the population at Kent, but since they were facing transfer packages to the SHU, this was not an issue. The two prisoners who had struck Mr. Forget with baseball bats would be in danger if they returned to the population. However, one of these prisoners had just received his statutory release from Kent and the other was due for release in less than a month. It made sense therefore for him not to come back to the population to face the risk of possible retaliation with so little time left on his sentence. The other prisoners, including Jimmy Whitmore, Glen Rosenthal, and Shawn Preddy, would face no problems in the population, but C unit wanted no role in securing their release.

I then went to C unit to talk with Cacane Tremblay and Claude Forget. Before our meeting began, Mr. Tremblay showed me his most recent paintings. The canvasses featured a complex landscape of characters and creatures within an urban architecture which moved from the real to the surreal. As remarkable as the compositions themselves was the layering and moulding of the paint, so that the canvas took on the characteristics of a sculpture or carving. In one of the paintings, there was so much activity that exploring the canvas almost required a map. Mr. Tremblay took me through the characters and gave me a partial key to understanding what I was seeing. In many ways, his painting was a metaphor for what had been happening at Kent Institution. A surface understanding was not difficult to achieve, but a deeper understanding required divining artistic intention and the hidden meanings of subtle interactions between characters. Depending upon one's perspective, the same picture bore many different interpretations.

During the meeting with Cacane Tremblay and Claude Forget, I explained why I thought that mediation involving people independent of the administration might help to resolve problems which otherwise could be resolved only through segregation or transfer. While they might see mediation in this case as potentially benefiting prisoners they had no interest in helping, in the long term mediation was a process that could benefit many other prisoners, including their friends. Cacane Tremblay had no difficulty understanding the larger, long-term implications and impressed upon me that his own approach in dealing with the administration when he was on the Inmate Committee was to look at the larger picture and what would ultimately benefit "the guys." I then asked Mr. Tremblay whether he would participate in a meeting with his people on one side and Pat

McKenna and his people on the other, with my role that of exploring the possibilities of a peaceful settlement or treaty. He told me frankly that such a meeting would not be helpful to a real, lasting settlement. His statements at such a meeting would be political, and all he could promise was that he would do nothing to prevent the release of the prisoners. He could make no promises as to what would happen after that. However, the reality as he saw it was that for all the prisoners implicated in the killing of Christian Grenier, their days were numbered. While there might be other situations in which independent mediation was effective, in this case the lines had already been drawn. After my meeting in C unit, I returned to A unit and advised Pat McKenna that I did not believe that a joint meeting would be productive in producing a peace treaty.

## September 16: The Sixty-Day Reviews

With the exception of Mr. Forget and Mr. Thornber, the prisoners who had been segregated following the murder of Christian Grenier were still in segregation when the Segregation Review Board conducted its sixty-day reviews on September 16 under the chairmanship of Mike Csoka. Mr. Thornber, who had been in the exercise yard when Christian Grenier was killed, had been released in the first week of September, having served the 30 days' segregation he received for damaging the roof during the A unit smash-up. His release was without incident. In the second week of September, a decision had been made to release Mr. Arneil, whom the national investigation team had concluded was only peripherally involved in the yard incident, but before that release could be effected the institution received information that he would be harmed if returned to general population. Voluntary transfers had been approved for two prisoners: Mr. Shropshire, who was in protective custody after providing the RCMP with a statement implicating Mr. Makichuk and Mr. Simpson in the killing, and Mr. Hepburn, who had also provided a statement. The segregation review hearings for these men were extremely brief, advising them only that their transfers had been processed and that they would be leaving Kent in the near future. The review of Jeremy Adams was also abbreviated; since he was due to be released from Kent in ten days' time, it was decided he would remain in segregation until that date for his own safety.

Shawn Preddy's review did not last much longer than Mr. Adams'. Mr. Csoka informed him that according to the IPSOs, Mr. Preddy's life would be in danger if he were returned to the population. Mr. Preddy said that since being placed in segregation in July, the only written information he had received was the original segregation notice, which indicated he was being segregated pending an investigation into an incident in the exercise yard. Since that date, he had been given no further information, and neither of the IPSOs had interviewed him or explained the basis for their belief that his life would be in jeopardy in the population. Mr. Csoka said he would ensure that the IPSOs came down to talk to Mr. Preddy—which was exactly what Mr. Preddy had been told by Mr. Wallin at his thirty-day review.

Only Mr. Whitmore and Mr. Rosenthal had been provided with a written gist of the information that led IPSO Jim Farrell to conclude their safety would be compromised if they were returned to the population. The gist in Mr. Whitmore's case concluded:

> Numerous sources have told staff that WHITMORE would be harmed if released to the open GP units. Source information has recently been received that WHITMORE could be released to the open units but would not guarantee his safety.
>
> The fact of having conflicting reports on the safety of inmate WHITMORE being released causes great concern with the Preventive Security department. In the past, members of the GP population have guaranteed the safety of certain inmates that can be released to the open GP units. In this case while we have had information that WHITMORE can be released no guarantees have been given even when asked for. Due to the above information, the writer recommends that WHITMORE remain in segregation. (Gist of Information, Kent Institution, September 8, 1997)

At the beginning of his sixty-day review, Mr. Whitmore was told by Mr. Csoka that the institution would be pursuing his involuntary transfer to Edmonton Institution. Mr. Whitmore insisted that the information about the threats to his safety were inflated and self-serving and asked why, if a transfer was being considered, he could not be transferred to a medium security institution within the Pacific region, so he could remain close to his wife and son. Mr. Csoka responded that reduction in Mr. Whitmore's security classification was not in the cards because of his involvement in the Grenier murder. Mr. Whitmore challenged that statement, saying, "You know I wasn't involved." Mr. Csoka, returning Mr. Whitmore's eye-to-eye challenge, responded, "I don't know that. I'm just going on what the IPSOs tell me. If you disagree with what we are saying, you or your lawyer will have a chance to rebut it when you get the transfer package." The following exchange ensued:

JW: It doesn't matter what I say, you people will do whatever you want.

MC: That's your interpretation.

JW: It's not my interpretation, it's my experience. How do I prove to you people that I'm not in danger? The only way I can convince you is if you let me out. There is no other way so long as there are people out there who have an interest in keeping me in here and keep telling you that my life is danger.

MC: I can't go against what the IPSOs tell me.

JW: But the IPSOs are talking to the people who want to keep me in here. It's not just me you're affecting, you're affecting my family and my son.

MC: I'm well aware of your family, and I want to make sure that your son has a father. If I let you back in the population and someone stabs you, I have to think of how I'm going to explain to your son that he no longer has a father.

JW: That is not going to happen. Don't you think I've thought about that? I'm not going to press to get myself back into the population if I thought that there was a serious risk that I'd die.

The review ended with Mr. Csoka informing Mr. Whitmore that the IPSOs' assessment would prevail and that he would remain in segregation pending the completion of the involuntary transfer package.

Mr. Rosenthal came to his sixty-day review with a copy of the gist of information he had received. The gist concluded:

> Numerous source information has been received stating that ROSEN-THAL would be harmed if released to the open GP units with the most recent being this past weekend. We have not received any information to date to state that ROSENTHAL could be released to the open GP population. Due to the above information the writer recommends that ROSENTHAL remain in segregation. (Gist of Information, Kent Institution, September 8, 1997)

At the beginning of his review, Mr. Rosenthal stated, "I get the impression from everybody else who's been here today that you have already decided before we get here what you intend to do with us." Mr. Csoka responded, "That's not true." Mr. Rosenthal then presented Mr. Csoka with a copy of a letter he had written to Warden Marshall and asked that Mr. Csoka read it as the basis for discussion about his case. Mr. Csoka said he would pass the letter on to the warden but he did not have time to read it at the review. I later obtained a copy of Mr. Rosenthal's letter. It read in part:

> I was not involved in the death of inmate Grenier in any capacity. There was no conspiracy or premeditation in Grenier's death. The incident itself was recorded on videotape and at no time am I anywhere near it. I am told that even the RCMP and the CSC National Investigative Team make this same determination. Any other con-

struction of events is nothing but a house of smoke and mirrors.

By this point in this writing I would hope that you have gathered that I am not foolhardy enough to want to run headlong to my death. I am not. I have my own sources of information amongst the population in whom I have every reason to have every confidence. I have communicated directly with all the parties in this incident, all of whom have made it very clear that they have no problem with me. I don't hold everyone here in high regard nor they me. Everyone here is not my friend. I don't expect that everyone here would take an active role in getting me released from segregation and neither should your administration. If that were the standard no one would ever get released from segregation.

It has recently been suggested to me that my security level is going to be raised to maximum and that an involuntary transfer to another max. is being considered. In making this determination, I'm asking that you also consider that my whole life is now in the B.C. region. My family and my wife live here. My release plans are all for this region. In all my 17 years of imprisonment I have never had nearly the good things in and good prospects for my life that I have now. In my short time here, I completed the GED with the highest marks possible. I've been a medium for over a year and at the time of this incident was waiting for a transfer to Matsqui which was already approved. I am also awaiting acceptance at RHC. I worked in the library, studied in my cell and jogged for exercise every day. I wasn't involved in anything in any capacity. An out of region transfer would be devastating to me, my wife and my family. It would also be unfair, unjust and completely unnecessary. (Letter from Glen Rosenthal to Warden Brenda Marshall, undated)

Faced with Mr. Csoka's refusal to read the letter at the segregation review, Mr. Rosenthal attempted to highlight his central point: the gist of information stated that he was "one of the key players in the murder of Grenier and a contract was out on him." Mr. Rosenthal said this information was false, and the idea of any preplanned conspiracy had been rejected by the national investigation. This gave rise to the following exchange between Mr. Csoka and Mr. Rosenthal:

MC:  We're not saying that there was a conspiracy. However, the perception of prisoners in the population is that there was a conspiracy and that you were involved in it.

GR:  Well, that was not the way it was, and that perception is wrong.

MC: So what do you expect? That I should go out there and tell the prisoners that their perception is wrong so that they shouldn't kill you? I don't think so.

Mr. Csoka advised Mr. Rosenthal that he would be staying segregated.

## September 25: Checking out of Segregation and into PC

At the completion of a private family visit following his sixty-day review, Jimmy Whitmore made what is probably the most agonizing decision a GP prisoner ever has to make: he agreed to sign "Annex A," a document in which he acknowledged that his safety in the general population was at risk and he agreed to become a protective custody prisoner. As a result, instead of remaining in segregation with the prospect of an involuntary transfer to Edmonton Institution, he moved into B unit on the PC side of the house at Kent. Our interview on September 25 was difficult for him to give. He was now a member of that part of prison society he had long despised and differentiated from himself and his "solid" brothers. He confirmed what I had suspected: his reason for taking this drastic step was fear not for his life or safety but for the future of his relationship with his wife and son. Prisoners' Legal Services had advised him that the chances of a successful legal challenge to either his segregation or his involuntary transfer were very slight. During the private family visit, he had discussed his options with his wife and decided to put his family before his reputation. He was concerned that some prisoners would misinterpret his move, believing that he would now be providing information to the institution about what had happened in the yard in July. He asked me to convey to the prisoners still in segregation that he would never become an informer.

## The Way out of Segregation: Go East, Young Man

By early October, the Kent administration had resolved that the only alternative to long-term segregation for those involved in the Grenier incident was involuntary transfers out of the region. The cases of Kenny Makichuk and Neil Simpson were easiest to resolve; both had been charged with the first-degree murder of Christian Grenier, and involuntary transfer packages were prepared recommending their transfer to the Special Handling Unit in Quebec. Other maximum security institutions were being sought for Messrs. Rosenthal, Preddy, and Arneil. The administration's position was that the lives and safety of these prisoners would be in jeopardy if they were returned to Kent's general population.

In challenging this basis for maintaining them in segregation and seeking their transfers, the three men believed that a recent development would strengthen their hand. Back in July, Jeremy Adams, one of the prisoners originally segregated, had been released from segregation but had been returned just a few hours later when an officer stated that he had personally seen Mr. Adams hit Mr. Forget with a baseball bat and his release to the population would likely result in immediate retaliation. Mr. Adams remained in segregation until his statutory release in September. A few weeks later he was returned to Kent for violation of his statutory release conditions. He was placed in the temporary detention unit and, as part of that unit's usual routine, permitted to mix with GP prisoners in the yard. His return was met with no threats of violence. The three prisoners remaining in segregation argued that this was the best evidence that the administration's fears of retaliation against all prisoners implicated in the Grenier killing were unfounded. If Mr. Adams could be reintegrated into the population without incident, clearly the risk of retaliation was overblown and the basis for continued segregation or involuntary transfers undermined.

Those arguments found no favour with the Segregation Review Board. However, Mr. Preddy and Mr. Arneil prepared written rebuttals to the involuntary transfer packages served on them in November. Mr. Preddy's rebuttal, supported by submissions from Prisoners' Legal Services, pointed out that his gist of information was virtually identical to the gist given to Mr. Adams; if Mr. Adams could interact in the population without incident, it logically followed that Mr. Preddy could as well. Prisoners' Legal Services also referred to a discussion with IPSO Wayne Culbert, who "advised that he had not spoken to the informant sources for approximately one and a half months. Since that time Mr. Adams' contact with population prisoners has been without incident. It would suggest that the information received was either not reliable and/or is now outdated" (Letter from Beth Parkinson to Warden Brenda Marshall, Kent Institution, December 5, 1997). Notwithstanding these objections, Warden Marshall affirmed her recommendations that both Mr. Preddy and Mr. Arneil be transferred. The transfers were upheld by Regional Headquarters, and in February 1998, Mr. Preddy and Mr. Arneil were flown to Edmonton Institution.

On the day before the transfer I spoke with Mr. Preddy during his last visit with his wife in the Kent visiting area. At both his thirty-day day review in August and his sixty-day day review in September, Mr. Preddy had been told by the Segregation Review Board that one of the IPSOs would be down to explain to him the reasons why they believed his safety was in jeopardy. Mr. Preddy confirmed for me that since the day he was placed in segregation in July 1997, the IPSOs had never spoken with him personally about their concerns for his safety. He had received a bare bones gist of information in late September and the notice of involuntary transfer in late November, but even these had not led to any face-to-face discussion.

Mr. Rosenthal had fully expected to receive the same involuntary transfer package served on Mr. Preddy and Mr. Arneil. However, the correctional dice rolled in his favour. Barry Owen, his case management officer, instructed to prepare an involuntary transfer package to another maximum security institution, recommended instead that Mr. Rosenthal be transferred to Matsqui. Mr. Owen reasoned that Mr. Rosenthal had previously been positively considered for a medium security institution; the limited evidence of his involvement in the Grenier incident should not impede his descent down the security ladder. Matsqui initially turned down the application, citing the fact that Mr. Rosenthal was found to be in possession of a knife during the Grenier incident; when asked to hand it over by an officer, he had refused to do so. This, Matsqui said, was incompatible with medium security status. Mr. Rosenthal's response, supported by the Kent officer involved, was that he had not refused to surrender the knife but rather thrown it to the ground to avoid handing over a weapon to staff in front of other prisoners. In the context of maximum security, this was a way of demonstrating that he was "solid," and it had not been seen by the officer as an aggressive act. Following some politicking between the wardens of Kent and Matsqui, Mr. Rosenthal's transfer was approved. Still, it was not until early February of 1998, almost seven months after he had first been segregated, that Mr. Rosenthal left his segregation cell at Kent for Matsqui.

If the new year brought some positive change in Mr. Rosenthal's life, it brought an ill wind for another prisoner segregated after the Grenier killing. Crown counsel, as part of its legal obligation under s. 7 of the *Charter of Rights and Freedoms,* had disclosed to the lawyers representing Kenny Makichuk and Neil Simpson, both charged with the first-degree murder of Christian Grenier, the statements taken from various prisoners as part of their investigation. One of those statements was from Claude Forget. Nowhere in Mr. Forget's statement did he identify either Mr. Makichuk or Mr. Simpson as the perpetrators of the attack on Mr. Grenier. He also made it very clear to the RCMP that he would not testify at any criminal trial. The RCMP report of Mr. Forget's statement included the comment that "this, of course, was due to the fact that he is an inmate and it is not acceptable to help police. If he did co-operate and testify, he could not return to general population."

The irony for Mr. Forget was that, when Mr. Makichuk and Mr. Simpson received copies of the Crown disclosure documents and saw that Mr. Forget had spoken to police, the word was quickly sent out that Mr. Forget *had* co-operated with police and was therefore a "rat." As the word circulated through the GP units, Mr. Forget, acutely aware from what had happened over the past several months that perception was everything, accepted the inevitable and on January 14, 1998, asked to move to segregation for his own safety. The initial reintegration plan for Mr. Forget involved an involuntary transfer to Port-Cartier Institution in Quebec; instead, he requested a transfer to the Regional Health Centre to participate in the Violent Offender Program. The RHC accepted Mr. Forget, and early in May 1998 he was transferred there from Kent segregation.

Kenny Makichuk and Neil Simpson remained in segregation at Kent until

February 1998, when they were transferred to the Special Handling Unit in Quebec. They were returned to the Pacific Region in early May so that their lawyers could prepare for the court hearing on their murder charges. The twists and turns in the course of justice that had characterized the events of "Deadly July" from the very beginning took another unexpected path on the morning of the May 26: while the two prisoners were waiting in the holding cells beneath the courtroom, the Crown entered a stay of proceedings of the murder charges. Although the legal effect of this is merely to suspend proceedings, leaving the Crown with the option of renewing them within a year, in the great majority of cases the entering of a stay marks the end of the prosecution's trail, as it did in this instance. Crown counsel's reasons as conveyed both to Defence counsel and to the administration at Kent, were these: The videotape of the incident and the observations of correctional officers on duty at the time were not sufficiently clear to support the criminal charges against Mr. Makichuk and Mr. Simpson. The evidentiary vacuum could only be filled by the evidence of other prisoners prepared to testify for the Crown. As an essential part of its case, Crown counsel had intended to call Mr. Shropshire and Mr. Hepburn. Both had been present at the meeting in the C unit pool room when the issue of the missing Valium was discussed and supposedly resolved; both had been in the yard and witnessed what took place. Prior to the preliminary inquiry, however, Mr. Shropshire had advised Crown counsel that he was not prepared to testify, and counsel felt that his evidence would not be helpful to their case if he was compelled to attend court. Mr. Hepburn had advised Crown counsel before the preliminary inquiry that he would testify the prisoners in C unit planned to attack and kill Mr. Makichuk and his friends in A unit. This evidence would support the anticipated self-defence argument of Mr. Makichuk and Mr. Simpson. Under the circumstances, Crown counsel decided there was no reasonable prospect of succeeding in the prosecution.

After the stay of proceedings had been entered, Mr. Makichuk and Mr. Simpson, through their lawyers, argued that they should not be returned to the Special Handling Unit on the following analysis: their transfers had been based on the allegation that they were involved in an unprovoked attack on Mr. Grenier, resulting in his death; the murder charges had been based on the same allegation; the murder charges had now been stayed on the grounds that these allegations could not be supported through sworn evidence and there was a reasonable prospect a defence of self-defence would be successful; Mr. Makichuk and Mr. Simpson should therefore be treated as if they had acted in self-defence and so their actions were not culpable. This line of argument was no more successful with Kent authorities in 1998 than had been the argument raised two years earlier on behalf of Hughie MacDonald, who, it will be remembered, had been acquitted by a jury of the murder of Gary Allen on the basis of self-defence. It had taken a *habeus corpus* application to B.C. Supreme Court to secure the release of Mr. MacDonald from segregation, and certainly the institution's position was that it would take no less than a court order to stop the transfer of Mr. Makichuk and Mr. Simpson back to the Special Handling Unit. The transfers were arranged before any court proceedings could be launched.

## Enhancing Segregation Review

By the time the Grenier murder charges were stayed in the spring of 1998, the CSC could present a report card showing that, a year after the completion of the report of the Task Force on Segregation, it had taken specific, focussed measures to enhance the segregation review process. It had conducted training workshops in all regions, developed the Draft Administrative Segregation Handbook, re-engineered an electronic recording system built around the pivotal legal points of reference, and provided a set of tools to take staff through the process review by review, literally day by day. The whole package was further reinforced by a series of regular audits.

All of this was impressive. But to use the question that Dan Kane, Chair of the Task Force on Segregation, regularly asked in staff briefings, "What does it look like where the rubber meets the road?" In other words, were segregation decisions and segregation reviews conducted differently at Kent a year after the Task Force report? The audit in January 1998 had found that Kent was not providing sufficient information to prisoners and that segregation review records were not adequately justifying the rationale for segregation, or demonstrating no reasonable alternatives, or documenting a reintegration plan (deficiencies I had also observed in the segregation reviews conducted in the aftermath of "Deadly July"). Following the audit, there was an exchange of correspondence among National Headquarters, the deputy commissioner for the Pacific Region, and the warden of Kent, setting out an action plan to address the deficiencies. That plan included intensive training on the revised OMS segregation module, the assignment of a full-time CO-II dedicated to ensuring that information was documented and shared with prisoners, and the assignment of a full-time case management officer whose only responsibility would be for segregated prisoners. In addition, it was agreed that the warden or the deputy warden of Kent would monitor case development for administratively segregated prisoners on a daily basis and that Regional Headquarters would review cases weekly to ensure that compliance measures were in effect. The final element of the plan was that a national audit team would revisit Kent in March 1998 to conduct a follow-up audit. Using the vernacular of parole, it would be fair to say that the Kent administration was placed under intensive supervision in relation to segregation practices.

In May and June 1998, I attended a number of segregation reviews. In the wake of the January audit, the scheduling of thirty-day reviews was now done on an individual basis. Instead of holding a once-monthly review board at which as many as thirty cases might be reviewed, the Board now met throughout the month, reviewing smaller clusters of cases each time. The other major change was in the sixty-day reviews. Formerly, these had involved a larger cast of characters than the thirty-day reviews, including a representative from Regional Headquarters. The regional aspect of the sixty-day review was now performed electronically at Regional Headquarters.

The Segregation Review Board was now chaired by Kevin Morgan, who had taken over as the unit manager for segregation at Kent in December 1997. Kent was Mr. Morgan's first assignment as a unit manager, and he was therefore on a very steep learning curve. He had participated in the segregation training workshop in January 1998 and had assumed primary responsibilities for implementing the action plan established following the January audit. From 1994 to 1996, the thirty- and sixty-day reviews had usually been held in the boardroom adjacent to the segregation unit, which doubled as the hearing room for disciplinary court and National Parole Board hearings. As their frequency increased, the thirty- and sixty-day reviews were shifted to the small interview room in J unit. The move lessened the demands on staff providing escorts. But while it was administratively more convenient to hold the hearings in J unit, there were considerable costs. The interview room was approximately 13 feet by 10 feet; it contained only a small desk and two chairs, one of which (the one used by prisoners) was bolted to the floor. In 1997, the room's already meagre dimensions contracted by a third, when it was divided by a metal partition which better controlled prisoner movement from the exercise yard. As a result, the weight of institutional authority in a typical segregation review hearing was pervasive, and the limited space allowed little opportunity for a formal hearing process. The Board typically consisted of Mr. Morgan, Mr. Yarwood—the case management officer responsible for the management of segregated prisoners ("Institutional Parole Officer" after January 1998)—and the segregation clerk. Mr. Morgan's hearing style was unstructured, with some hearings directed by him, others by Mr. Yarwood.

The Draft Administrative Segregation Handbook, a copy of which was given to all staff attending the training workshops, sets out guidelines for Segregation Review Board hearings. These include the following:

> The hearing should be recorded on audio tape, to ensure an accurate record is available . . . A statement explaining the purpose of the Segregation Review Board should be read out loud to all participants at the beginning of the hearing. The procedural safeguards checklist should be reviewed (out loud) to ensure that appropriate requirements have been fulfilled. The chairperson should describe circumstances giving rise to the inmate's placement in Administrative

Segregation, and indicate that the SRB would decide whether there are adequate grounds to justify keeping him or her there, based on those grounds. (Draft Administrative Segregation Handbook, Annex A, December 1997)

In the segregation review hearings I observed in May 1998, none of these guidelines was followed.

According to the Draft Administrative Segregation Handbook, the purpose for regional participation at the sixty-day review is to act "as a court of sober second sight, ensuring that Administrative Segregation is being used as a last resort and is based only on one of the valid grounds set out in the CCRA." In May 1998 in the Pacific Region, this "court of sober second sight" took the form of a project officer reviewing the OMS record on his computer at Regional Headquarters.

## Assessing the Reforms

Much of my criticism of the reforms introduced in response to the Task Force on Administrative Segregation's recommendations has been directed to the failure to implement the most critical part of a reformed system—independent adjudication. However, it would be unfair to suggest that the improvements made to the segregation review process at Kent Institution by 1998 were not significant. The most important qualitative improvement was in the preparation and sharing of detailed, written information within the time frames set out in the CCRA. This was the full-time responsibility of CO-II Stan Beacon, working in close conjunction with Segregation Unit Manager Kevin Morgan. They gave the document preparation the kind of attention the CCRA required, which, hitherto, it had never received.

The other important improvement was quantitative: a reduction in the overall number of placements in segregation. The Task Force on Segregation first visited Kent in September 1996. That month, 42 prisoners were placed in segregation. A year later, the number for the same month was 36, and in September 1998 it was 20. In aggregate terms, for the whole of 1997 there were 308 placements into segregation at Kent Institution, with an average stay of thirty-nine days; for the whole of 1998, the number was 218, with an average stay of twenty-two days. There was also a reduction in the number of prisoners in long-term segregation. In 1997, 15 prisoners served between sixty-one and ninety days in segregation; in 1998, only 7 prisoners did so. Five prisoners spent between 91 and 120 days in segregation in 1997, 6 prisoners in 1998. For prisoners who served more than 120 days in segregation, the numbers had shrunk from 38 prisoners in 1997 to 7 in 1998.

Stan Beacon and Kevin Morgan were justifiably proud in December 1998 when they presented me with the statistical verification of Kent's reduced use of segregation. That pride was soured, however, by the failure of National Head-quarters to provide the further training promised at the workshop on Segregation and the Law held in January 1998. The Task Force on Segregation had recommended a certification program for chairpersons of Segregation Review Boards, and at the January workshop CSC representatives had confirmed this was in preparation. Yet a year later, no word had filtered down from National Head-quarters on the status of this initiative. A new position had been established at Regional Headquarters to better fulfil the legal requirement of a regional review of cases of prisoners segregated for more than sixty days; part of that officer's responsibilities would be to provide ongoing training for the institutional Segregation Review Board. The person appointed to that position in the Pacific Region was Bob Lusk, who had been warden of Kent Institution from 1993 to 1997, when he transferred to Regional Headquarters. His assignment in 1999 to the new position of Regional Co-ordinator of Segregation was seen not so much as the designation of a high-profile and experienced correctional practitioner (which Mr. Lusk certainly was) but rather as a pre-retirement secondment. The creation of the position of Regional Co-ordinator provided staff with as little assurance that their needs for ongoing training in the law and procedures governing segregation would be met as it gave me in representing a real alternative to independent adjudication.

My scepticism about the capacity of the CSC to reform itself without independent adjudication should not be read as a slight to the integrity of individual correctional staff and managers. Rather, it flows from my concern about how personal and professional relationships within the CSC affect fairness and justice behind the walls. Over the six years of research for this book, I observed and talked to the key players at Kent and Matsqui Institutions on many occasions. I came to respect their professionalism and in some cases to know and like them as good people. That is not a remarkable outcome. Indeed, it is perhaps an inevitable feature of this kind of fieldwork; as you get to know the people with whom you are working, there develops a level of mutual respect, and indeed friendship, that makes the research encounter more rewarding and revealing. What I did find remarkable, however, was how these developing relationships affected my feelings about what I was writing. I have related how uneasy I became about my account of Mike Csoka's handling of minor disciplinary court at Matsqui in 1993 as I came to know him better when he assumed the responsibilities of unit manager at Kent during 1996–98. I worried he would feel betrayed by the strong criticisms I had expressed about those hearings and the five-day hearings I later observed him chairing at Kent. My concern led me to re-interview him, both to explain what I had written and to give him an opportunity to respond. In one sense, this can be viewed as a research version of the duty to act fairly. Yet when I explained my actions to students in my Penal Policy seminar at the University of B.C., several of them diplomatically suggested that my concern for Mike

Csoka's feelings might have blunted my criticism and caused some self-censorship in my written observations. Although I had not changed the text of my original critique, only added Mr. Csoka's commentary on my observations, the students' criticism reinforced my views that professional and personal relationships do affect judgement.

If I, as an independent researcher and thirty-year advocate for prisoners' rights, was concerned that publication of my research would affect my relationship with a correctional administrator I had come to like but with whom I would have only intermittent professional contact in the future, how much more so would this be the case if our relationship was career-long and situated within the same inner circle? Yet this is the environment within which correctional staff must make their decisions. The inescapable fact is that the relationships staff members form with their peers and superiors is of far more importance to their careers than the relationships they have with prisoners. This professional reality is reinforced by the personal relationships many correctional staff and administrators have with one another outside of prison. There are many examples of spousal and family relationships within the system, and friendships take the form of membership in the same legion, bowling alley, or gym and of involvement in the many other areas of shared interest that develop in a workplace. The pressure against second-guessing your colleague in a work situation may be very strong when that colleague is someone you have known for twenty-five years and with whom you and your family have ties of affection and respect.

It might be suggested that the same is true for judges. They also move within a circle involving recurring contact and ongoing professional, social, and personal relationships. The difference is that within the judiciary—recognizing that individual judges have personal and ideological biases—there is a long and well-entrenched tradition of independence; furthermore, the transparency of published reasons for decisions is buttressed by an independent bar asserting and defending the competing interests at stake. It is the absence of this tradition and these same hallmarks of justice within the prison that anchors the case for independent adjudication of those decisions that critically affect the rights and liberties of prisoners.

## Postscript

In March 2001, I returned to Kent to observe a series of five-day reviews held following an assault on a staff member by a prisoner. The prisoner was overpowered and immediately taken to segregation. Subsequently, five other prisoners were segregated based on allegations that they had been present at a Lifers' group meeting in B unit immediately prior to the assault and had conspired to have the assault carried out. Each of the prisoners received a segregation notice that stated:

The date and timing of this meeting is significant as shortly afterwards an officer was attacked with a wooden paddle similar, if not the same one, given to the attacker during the meeting. The inmates who attended this meeting are believed to have conspired and pre-planned the violent physical assault upon a staff member in the evening and directly participated by arranging for the aggressor to have possession of the wooden paddle which was used as a weapon. (Segregation Notice, Kent Institution, March 22, 2001)

The five-day reviews for the segregated prisoners were scheduled for Thursday, March 28. When I arrived at Kent that day, I was told that three of the prisoners had been transferred that morning on an emergency basis to other maximum security institutions across the country. As I observed the reviews of the two remaining prisoners and five others, a clear pattern emerged as a basis upon which to measure the changes in the segregation review process at Kent since 1998.

The reviews were chaired by Irv Hammond, the unit manager for segregation. Also present was Darryl Broadbank, the programming co-ordinator for segregation who, beginning in 1999, initiated cognitive living skills and anger management modules for segregated prisoners. This had been one of the recommendations of the Task Force on Segregation. Other staff members at the reviews were the institutional parole officers (IPOs) specifically assigned to the segregation unit and the IPOs assigned to individual prisoners. The only IPO who had been at Kent during the Task Force on Segregation's work was Barry Owen, one of the two veteran case management officers.

None of the guidelines set out in the Draft Administrative Segregation Handbook was observed at the five-day reviews. Procedural safeguards were not reviewed to ensure that prisoners had received both three days' notice of the hearing and written information; there was no tape recording of the hearing; and the chairperson did not describe the circumstances leading to each prisoner's segregation. Thus, even what Mike Csoka had described as "clearing legal stuff out of the way" was omitted, on the assumption that these procedural requirements had been observed.

Unit Manager Hammond began each hearing by introducing himself and asking whether the prisoner knew the other staff members in the room. He introduced me as an observer, then asked the prisoner's IPO to summarize why the prisoner had been placed in segregation. In Mr. Ellis' case, when there was some hesitation as to who would present this summary, the prisoner himself jumped in, taking the initiative with the comment, "Do you want me to run this show? The reason I'm down here is that they say I threatened to slit a staff member's throat." Mr. Ellis then read from the report he had been given as part of the written sharing of information. This alleged that Officer Jones had heard a prisoner from a cell in the lower range of B unit call out, "Who is that on the camera? Is that Jones? I'm going to slit your fucking throat." Officer Jones asked Officer Head which prisoner had called out, and he identified Mr. Ellis. Mr. Ellis acknowledged that he had mouthed off at Officer Jones in the past but said they had resolved their differences and he had not made the threats attributed to him on this occasion. Mr. Ellis challenged the reliability of this identification by pointing out that at the time of the incident he had moved to the upper range of B unit, and Officer Jones had identified the threatening voice as coming from the lower range. Furthermore, from Mr. Ellis' cell on the upper range, it was physically impossible to see who was shown on the camera located on the lower range. Mr. Ellis asked that he be released from segregation since he had already spent six days in the hole without justification. Mr. Hammond said he would follow up Mr. Ellis' version of events with the IPSO and convene another hearing once that investigation was complete, so Mr. Ellis would not have to wait for his thirty-day review. Mr. Ellis challenged the need for further investigation; there could be no argument about where he lived, and clearly Officer Head had made a mistake. Mr. Hammond said it was his job to review the reports and further investigate the matter. Mr. Ellis pointedly retorted, "Why wasn't this done during the last six days? Why didn't the IPSO come down and hear my side of the story? I've shared it with other staff."

Mr. Ellis' comments recalled those of Glen Rosenthal at his five-day review following the Grenier killing in July 1997. They exposed the continuing failure of the five-day review process to measure up to the legal requirements of a "review," at which specific allegations are tested in the crucible of evidence and judgements are rendered on the basis of that evidence. While in some cases judgements may not be possible at the five-day review, since the facts are still being investigated, in Mr. Ellis' case segregation was based on a specific allegation to which he had a very specific answer. His defence could easily have been investigated before the five-day review.

The same flaw was exposed in the review of Mr. Gibson. His segregation notice said Mr. Gibson was believed to be part of the conspiracy to assault a staff member. The observation reports included in the sharing of information alleged he had been present at the meeting in the Lifers' office in B unit. Mr. Gibson acknowledged that he was president of the Lifers' group and that he had been in B unit prior to the assault on official business, gathering signatures for some proposals that were going to the warden. However, he had not attended any meeting in the Lifers' office. He acknowledged that he had been in the pool room immediately beside the Lifers' office, and suggested that his mistaken identification may have stemmed from that. (The staff office, the Lifers' office, and the pool room are separated by walls with large glass windows which enable staff to see into both the other rooms.) Mr. Gibson also pointed out that the observation report he received was dated *before* the meeting in the Lifers' office was supposed to have taken place, suggesting that the officer may have been confused on a number of matters. Mr. Gibson's third point was that after leaving B unit he had returned to his own unit and made a phone call to a friend. The institution could confirm from his PIN number that at the time the meeting in B unit supposedly took place, he was on the phone in another part of the prison. Mr. Gibson said that Mr. Laverty, the prisoner who had committed the assault, was his partner and best friend. However, Mr. Laverty had never spoken to him about planning to assault an officer, presumably because Mr. Gibson would have tried to dissuade him from this course of action.

Mr. Hammond told Mr. Gibson he would investigate the matter further with the IPSO. As with Mr. Ellis, the IPSO had not yet spoken to Mr. Gibson, even though there were significant elements of his defence, in particular the phone call, which could have been verified prior to the five-day review.

The other prisoner who remained in segregation as part of the assault investigation was Mr. Miller. Mr. Miller acknowledged he had been in the Lifers' office in B unit but stated this was solely for the purpose of giving a tattoo and had nothing to do with the planning of an assault. He was told by Mr. Hammond that he would remain in segregation pending the completion of the investigation. Mr. Miller had not yet seen anyone from the IPSO's office, nor had he been asked by any other staff member to account for his activities in the unit.

In addition to the five-day reviews, I also observed several thirty-day reviews. Mr. Colluney's case illustrated how institutional politics can undermine compliance with the law, again reinforcing the need for independent adjudication. Mr. Colluney had been placed in segregation at Mission Institution following the interception of drugs his visitor had tried to smuggle in. After spending two months in segregation, he was involuntarily transferred to Kent, where it was discovered that he had a listed incompatible in the open PC population. He therefore remained in segregation while the IPSO's office explored the possibilities of mediation. Such mediation did not prove feasible, and Mr. Colluney, notwithstanding his cooperative behaviour, remained in segregation. At his ninety-day review, he was advised that Kent would seek his re-transfer to Mission Institution. This plan was pursued with the full support of his case management team. The Mission administration, however, was not prepared to accept Mr. Colluney back for at least six months. Given his incompatibility in the open population, he would have to serve those six months in segregation at Kent.

Several staff members at Kent had already raised Mr. Colluney's case with me; they believed he was being unfairly kept in segregation while the wardens of Kent and Mission played hardball with each other. At Mr. Colluney's segregation review hearings from December 2000 to February 2001, the same entries appeared on his file:

His behaviour continues to be fully satisfactory and his case will be pursued for a return to medium security to alleviate long-term segregation. A check with the preventive security officer does not identify any additional information at this time. (Review of Offender's Segregated Status—Institutional Review, Kent Institution, December 2000–February 2001)

At the time of his segregation review on March 28, 2001, Mr. Colluney had been in segregation for 146 days. Mr. Hammond advised him that the Kent administration was still endeavouring to have him transferred back to Mission. Almost despairingly, Mr. Colluney reminded the Segregation Review Board that he had been in segregation at Kent for five months, on top of the two months he had spent in segregation at Mission. In the middle of February he had been reclassified to medium security, and he was now only six months from his release date from prison.

Mr. Hammond acknowledged all of these facts. Tellingly, he concluded the review by saying, "We are doing everything we can, and I realize that we're getting close to the end of our legal rope."

After Mr. Colluney left the room, I engaged Mr. Hammond and other staff members in a discussion of his case. I suggested that since Mr. Colluney was a medium security prisoner and a transfer to Mission was a reasonable alternative to segregation, the warden of Kent had no legal rope at all left under the CCRA. Under amendments to the transfer process introduced in 1999 (the subject of Sector 5 of this book), the warden now had the decision-making authority to transfer Mr. Colluney to Mission. Mr. Hammond said he had impressed upon the warden the inappropriateness of keeping Mr. Colluney in segregation and this case had become an embarrassment to his staff.

In a later conversation with one of those staff members it became clear it was more than just embarrassment. I was told staff understood Mr. Colluney was being held illegally, given the existence of a reasonable alternative. Yet because of institutional politics, the warden of Kent seemed unable to pull the decision-making trigger to get Mr. Colluney to Mission. How could staff be expected to give high priority to compliance with the law when the wardens of Kent and Mission were prepared to allow institutional politics to compromise it? It was a good question, and one I posed to the warden of Kent when I spoke to him later that day.

The end-of-the-legal-rope metaphor seemed to have an energizing impact. Telephone calls and e-mails flew between Kent and Mission, and arrangements were made for Mr. Colluney's transfer, which took place two days later. Under a system of independent adjudication along the lines I have recommended, that transfer would have taken place at least two months earlier.

# SECTOR 5

## CHAPTER 1

# Involuntary Transfers: Greyhound Therapy Then and Now

Transfers from one institution to another are an integral part of a modern prison regime. One hundred years ago, five bastilles—Kingston, Dorchester, Laval, Stony Mountain, and the B.C. Penitentiary—constituted the carceral landscape of maximum security in Canada. Today there are forty-seven federal institutions for men that cover a spectrum of security, from the most intensive in the Special Handling Units to the least intrusive in minimum security camps without fences. A Correctional Service of Canada report explains the hierarchical nature of the federal prison system and the role of transfers within it:

> The Correctional Service of Canada has jurisdiction over a vast net-
> work of inter-related institutions. This network is organized in a
> hierarchical fashion based on a highly elaborated punishment/reward
> structure that holds out the incentive of minimum security living
> conditions in exchange for co-operation with the administration.
> Social control exists not with the individual institution but with the
> system as a whole. Each institution is defined by its security level and
> transfers between institutions are commonplace in a centralized hier-
> archical system.
>
> Very directly related to transferring is csc's "cascading" policy.
> Cascading, begun in 1979, is the practice of transferring inmates to
> the lowest security level possible insofar as is practical, respecting the
> Service's mandate to protect the public. The cascading practice is also
> consistent with the opportunities model. An inmate's reward for

good behaviour is a transfer to a lower level of security . . . Reverse cascading can also occur and is consistent with the punishment/ reward system. (*Report of the Study Group on Murders and Assaults in the Ontario Region* [Ottawa: Correctional Service of Canada, 1984] at 37–38)

What the report did not identify is the pervasive sense among prisoners that the process of reverse cascading—of returning prisoners to higher security, in particular to maximum security—is a major source of injustice. It has been left to other reports, most significantly the annual reports of the Correctional Investigator, to highlight this sense of injustice, reflected in the fact that involuntary transfers are consistently the single greatest cause for complaints.

As the Study Group's report indicates, the practice of reverse cascading is explicitly tied to the punishment/reward system in the penitentiary. Prisoners convicted of disciplinary offences involving assault, attempted escape, threats, drug dealing, or other behaviour viewed as disruptive to the regime of a medium security institution are regularly transferred to maximum security. These are labelled "involuntary administrative transfers," but they are seen by everyone as being an additional disciplinary measure. In cases where the prisoner's conduct is viewed as immediately prejudicial to the personal safety of staff or prisoners, an emergency transfer to maximum security is made before any disciplinary hearing has been held.

In a significant number of cases, prisoners are transferred from medium to maximum security in the absence of formal disciplinary charges on the basis of allegations and the suspicion of misconduct. The justification for involuntary transfers without formal proof of a disciplinary offence was expressed by the warden of Joyceville Institution in 1981 in this way:

One personal observation I have made is that, as a consequence of the expansion of individual rights, a lot of inmates are actually losing certain rights, for example: the right to do their time as they see fit; the right not to have someone muscle them for their canteen— I know of many cases in which an inmate has gone for months without cigarettes, chocolate bars or shampoo, because someone on the range who was bigger, stronger and smarter than he was, simply told him to turn it over. The Warden cannot prove anything in such cases any more than he can prove, for example, that one inmate is raping another inmate every second night. Now how do you deal with that kind of problem? You cannot do it capriciously, nor do I think that we should be able to but, at the same time, when we know that an inmate is harming others in a prison population, I think it is incumbent on us to move that person into another institution. And we do know when and how much harm is being done, not from court-room-like evidence but from the experience of working in the institutions and from a knowledge of the prison population. The type of action that is required has been referred to over the years as "Grey-hound therapy." You back the bus up, you throw five or six inmates in the bus, you drive them 40 miles down the road to increased security, and the whole tone of Joyceville, the medium security institution I work in, mellows. Those inmates who were stealing cookies and chocolate bars are now gone. It might be six months before someone else starts stealing cookies and chocolate bars. (Ken Payne, "Inmates' Rights: The Implications for Institutional Managers," in *National Parole Board Report on the Conference on Discretion in the Correctional System* [Ottawa: Minister of Supply and Services, 1983] at 2)

From Warden Payne's perspective, discretionary decision-making is used to secure the protection and safety of prisoners. He expressly disavows the capricious exercise of discretion, yet it would be difficult to persuade a prisoner rounded up as one of the five or six prisoners suspected of muscling (but who in fact is *not* involved) that his transfer to maximum security without a charge, without a hearing at which he can hear the case against him and present evidence in response, is not the very definition of capriciousness.

For Warden Payne, any harm caused through an error in judgement in the exercise of discretionary power is a necessary cost of doing the business of corrections.

> Given the reality of penitentiary life, we have to be given the opportunity to err on the side of caution. It is better to move five or six people, four of whom you are certain are doing nasty things in your institution, and a couple of whom you suspect might be, to another institution, than to gamble and leave a couple of inmates behind, and perhaps later pay the price of more riots or another assault . . . Without the power to act on experience and "gut" intuition, you might end up knowing who is responsible for a stabbing or a beating, but be unable to do anything about it. Because you lack solid proof, the responsible inmate will be cleared in the hearing, and the next thing you know he is in the institution, smiling and grinning at the staff. (at 4)

Since 1981, there have been important developments in both the law and the administrative practice relating to involuntary transfers, the purpose of which has been to provide prisoners with greater protection against arbitrary transfers. In this chapter, I will trace these developments, explore the role "Greyhound therapy" continues to play in correctional management, and evaluate whether the route traversed is marked with greater justice.

## The Schiere Case

The involuntary transfer of Dick Schiere and two other prisoners from Matsqui to Kent Institution in 1984 vividly illustrates the interests at stake in transfers from medium to maximum security, the balance drawn by prison administrators between crime control and due process values, and the impact this has on prisoners' perception of prison justice. The facts and documents referred to in this case study are taken from the affidavit material in a 1986 Federal Court action, filed after the prisoners involved had exhausted the internal grievance procedure (*Schiere et al.* v. *The Commissioner of Penitentiaries* (F.C.T.D. No. 735-86).

In February 1984, John Paul Belliveau, a prisoner in Matsqui Institution, was murdered. Six weeks later, on April 5, three prisoners—Dick Schiere, Robert Pelletier, and Mike Angus—were informed by the administration that, as a result of new information, they were being reclassified from the S5 medium security level to an S6 maximum security level, and hence being transferred to Kent Institution. They were placed in restraint equipment (handcuffs and leg irons), and each of them was handed a memorandum stating that he was being transferred to Kent "for the good order of Matsqui Institution." They were given neither the 48 hours' notice of the intention to transfer nor the opportunity to present reasons for reconsideration of that decision, as required by the Commissioner's Directive in force at the time.

On April 7 at Kent Institution, the three men were told verbally that their transfers had to do with an ongoing investigation by Matsqui police into Belliveau's murder. Prior to the transfer, none of the three had been questioned by Matsqui police or any institutional staff regarding Belliveau's death. On April 14, each of them filed an inmate complaint form, the first step in the Correctional Service's grievance procedure, in which they denied involvement in Belliveau's death and requested, first, that they be transferred back to Matsqui while the investigation continued and, second, that they be given substantial and specific reasons for the transfer. On April 26, they received this answer from the assistant warden at Kent:

> The Regional Classification Board advises that you have been
> reclassified to S6 level security—Kent Institution. I am not at
> liberty to release the reasons for your reclassification to you
> until the Regional Classification Board forward their written

comments to us. You can review the written comments with your Living Unit Development Officer when they arrive at the institution. If you wish to directly contact the Regional Classification Board for an explanation, please feel free to do so.

On May 10, the three prisoners sent a letter to the Regional Classification Board requesting specific reasons for their reclassification to maximum security. The answer they received from the Regional Transfer Officer, dated May 23, stated:

> You are involved in an investigation by Matsqui police into the murder of inmate Belliveau, John Paul, at Matsqui Institution. Because of this suspected involvement, your security classification was reviewed and resulted in a reclassification to S6.

In a letter dated August 9, Mr. Schiere presented his view on the adequacy of this response:

> I can easily understand the need for an investigation, and how this would take time, but I fail to see any ethical, moral or legal justice in how my "involvement" has been automatically taken for granted. The administration, while the investigation remains open and incomplete, has judged me guilty and is treating me as such. In effect, the administration has arrested and jailed me on the basis of suspicion, hoping that eventually (more than four months have already passed) something might turn up to support the case it wishes to make. My rights, legal or otherwise, are being trampled in the meantime. If my present situation can be seen as an indication of what to expect, the degree of justice I can look forward to, then the future looks pretty grim to me. What will happen if this matter is never resolved? If the administration fails to find anyone else to blame, do I then remain an administrative next-best-bet for them?

This resulted in a further response from the Regional Transfer Officer:

> I regret to inform you that you will not be considered eligible for transfer to lower security until the investigation into the circumstances surrounding the death at Matsqui Institution of inmate John Paul Belliveau is complete. As soon as this office receives information from Matsqui Police Department that they have concluded their investigation, your case management team will be informed.

On August 20, the prisoners filed an inmate grievance with the warden of Kent. They reiterated that they were being deemed guilty of involvement in the Belliveau murder without a hearing, prior to the completion of an investigation, and requested that they be returned to medium security. In denying the grievance, the warden stated:

(a) The Administration at Matsqui Institution deemed it appropriate to transfer you to increased security while the investigation was under way. I am not in a position to explain the rationale.

(b) Information concerning the entire case is being reviewed—some of which may or may not be substantiative [sic]. Until such time as the case has been concluded, I would expect that you would remain at Kent Institution.

(c) I cannot foresee your former security status being reinstated at this point. I am sure you will have the opportunity to defend yourself against specific allegations if they are made.

The prisoners then moved to the second level of the grievance process, appealing to the Regional Director General. His response, dated September 6, was:

Your grievance has been thoroughly reviewed at the second level. The responses you received at the complaint stage and grievance level one adequately answered your questions. Matsqui Municipal Police are still investigating the circumstances surrounding the death of an inmate in Matsqui Institution. When their investigations are completed your case will be thoroughly reviewed by your case management team.

The prisoners then appealed to the third and final level of the grievance procedure, the Commissioner of Corrections in Ottawa. On November 10, Mr. Schiere and Mr. Angus received the following response:

As you were advised at previous levels, you were transferred to higher security for the good order of Matsqui Institution pending the completion of a police investigation into the murder of an inmate. As this police investigation is not yet complete, no decision can yet be taken on your request to be returned to lesser security. I regret that my response cannot be more definitive at this time. As you are probably aware, the Correctional Service of Canada has no control or authority over police investigations. The authorities therefore had two choices while awaiting the results of the police investigation. They could transfer you to an institution of a higher security level or segregate you. They chose the first alternative, which I believe was in your best interest.

On December 7, Mr. Schiere, on behalf of himself and the other two prisoners, wrote to the Correctional Investigator informing him of the denial of their grievance by the Commissioner of Corrections. In that letter, he ably summarized how the prisoners viewed their treatment.

> The authorities claim to have had only two choices while awaiting the results of the police investigation: transfer me to an institution of higher security level or segregate me. Either proposal, raising my security or segregating me, amounts to the same thing—an automatic presumption of guilt. It is true that, prior to the conclusion of any investigation, the authorities had two options open to them, to presume my innocence or guilt, and it is quite obvious that they decided on the latter of these two. Furthermore, to add insult to injury, the Commissioner of Penitentiaries now wishes to convince me that the Correctional Service of Canada acted in my best interests when deciding to presume guilt, raising my security status rather than segregating me. This is strictly nonsense. In my particular case it makes no difference whether I am locked up in segregation or sitting where I am now. The inference is the same, I am losing hard-earned time while never having had as much as a disciplinary charge over the last two and a half years. It is not my physical environment which is at stake in this case, the real issue is being accused of something I am not guilty of.
>
> Thus far, the authorities, by the way of predetermining guilt, have only acted unfairly and have managed to cause irreparable damage and grief—my name will forever be associated with this incident at Matsqui. Ask anyone, staff or inmate, and you will be told how Dick Schiere was transferred back to Kent for murdering Belliveau, a presumption which is now generally accepted as fact. Under these circumstances, being dealt with as unfairly as I have, I don't know if I can guarantee my own behaviour to remain rational. I might be better off locked up in segregation—the worst harm I could do there is to hang myself. I am not exaggerating my feelings here, I am literally sick and tired of all the nonsensical excuses which have been offered to me over the past eight months. What does the Correctional Service of Canada expect of me, just to sit here while they run roughshod over me? Is it right that my guilt be presumed while being

denied the right to defend myself? Is it right that I have been detained and punished while this so-called investigation remains incomplete, let alone without formal charges being laid?

The Correctional Investigator replied to the prisoners in the following terms:

Our inquiry into your transfer from Matsqui to Kent Institution has been completed. I should indicate to you that the *Penitentiary Act* authorizes the Commissioner or his delegated official to place an inmate in the institution which is considered most suitable to his needs and security level. As well, you should be aware that the authorities can act on suspicion, and the proving of guilt or innocence is not necessarily the determining factor in reaching a decision to transfer. Based on our review of the circumstances surrounding your transfer I have found nothing on which to base a recommendation for a further review by the Correctional Service and consequently I am unable to be of any further assistance on this matter.

Certain procedural discrepancies were noted in our review of the documentation and these have been referred to the attention of the Commissioner. As a consequence, further instructions have been issued to all regions to ensure the Correctional Service acts fairly in all transfer decisions. I realize this action will be of no benefit to you, but hopefully it will provide safeguards in the future. [The "procedural discrepancies" were the failure to give two days' prior notice of the transfer in April 1984, as required by the Commissioner's Directive on Transfer.]

The prisoners continued to press for a re-transfer to medium security. Mr. Schiere, after having been told by correctional staff at Kent that he had been cleared for transfer to Mission Medium Security Institution, was informed in August 1985 (eighteen months after the murder was committed) that as long as the investigation into Belliveau's death was ongoing, he could not be considered for transfer to lower security. Yet without further explanation, on September 10, Mr. Schiere was told by the assistant warden at Kent that his transfer to Mission would be activated, "even though the police investigation was not concluded." However, "should you be charged and found guilty of any offence in relation to the incident at Matsqui, you could be returned to maximum security."

On September 12, Mr. Schiere was transferred to Mission and placed in the Induction Unit, where he remained double-bunked for three weeks. The day after he left the Induction Unit and was given his own cell, he was transferred back to Kent. He was not given 48 hours' notice of the transfer as required by the Commissioner's Directives, and written notification of the transfer was served on him at the same time as the transfer was effected, replicating the initial "procedural discrepancy" that had happened at Matsqui. The notification contained the following reasons:

> Your current involvement in an ongoing police investigation raises questions as to the appropriate level of security in which you should be held. Until your status as to this investigation is clarified to the satisfaction of the Warden of Mission Institution, you are being moved to Kent Institution on a temporary administrative basis for the good order of the institution.

Mr. Shiere was not informed of any new developments in the police investigation that could explain his transfer back to Kent. On his return, he was required to double-bunk in the Induction Unit. His visitors were required to reapply for visitors' status and, until they had completed this and gone through security clearance, they were not permitted to visit Mr. Schiere, even though they had been security-cleared by Kent only three weeks previously. On November 6, again without explanation, Mr. Schiere was re-transferred to Mission Institution. Mr. Angus and Mr. Pelletier remained imprisoned in Kent throughout.

The three prisoners initiated legal action challenging the legality of their initial transfers, on the basis that the institutional authorities had violated both the common law duty to act fairly and s. 7 of the *Canadian Charter of Rights and Freedoms*. In their affidavits, the prisoners set out the impact of the transfers on their institutional liberty and on their opportunities for rehabilitation and eventual reintegration into society. They described the differences in the institutional regimes of a medium and a maximum security institution, particularly regarding freedom of movement, visiting programs, work, and recreational opportunities. Mr. Schiere also identified more pervasive differences.

> A prisoner is under considerably greater stress when dealing with every day situations in a maximum security setting. The potential for violence is much higher at Kent than at Matsqui. Whether or not an individual prisoner is directly involved in violence, it is very difficult for him not to be touched by this more violent atmosphere in which he exists. Prisoners at maximum security institutions are eventually shaped by such an experience and are more likely to become aggressive in reacting to particular situations. The stress of life in maximum security was, in my particular case, aggravated by the fact that I am required to live under a cloud of presumptive guilt for the killing of another prisoner. It has become a common assumption among prisoners and staff alike that if I were not guilty of this crime, I would not have been transferred from Matsqui. My protestations of

innocence fall on ears which have already predetermined my criminal involvement in this incident. This affects in a very negative way my relationship with both staff and other prisoners and renders it much less likely that I will be given favourable consideration in any decisions affecting my institutional program.

The *Schiere* case never went to trial. A few days prior to the hearing date, the Department of Justice agreed to a consent order setting aside the transfers and returning the three prisoners to their medium security status.

In seeking to construct a fair transfer process, it is important to understand how far the standards of justice that prevail inside prison depart from those outside. Had Mr. Schiere, Mr. Pelletier, and Mr. Angus been free men, their liberty could not have been curtailed on the basis of an ongoing criminal investigation. The limits on police powers of investigatory arrest were set out by Mr. Justice Martin in *R.* v. *Dedman:*

> A peace officer has no right to detain a person for questioning or for further investigation. No one is entitled to impose any physical restraint upon the citizen except as authorized by law, and this principle applies as much to peace officers as to anyone else. Although a peace officer may approach a person on the street and ask him questions, if the person refuses to answer the police officer must allow him to proceed on his way, unless of course, the officer arrests him on a specific charge or arrests him pursuant to section 450 of the Code where the officer has reasonable and probable grounds to believe that he is about to commit an indictable offence. (*R.* v. *Dedman* (1981), 23 C.R. (3d) 228 at 242–43)

In *R.* v. *Duguay,* Chief Justice Mackinnon identified the fundamental principle involved here:

> It is repugnant to our concept of the administration of criminal justice and to the rights of citizens in the free and democratic society to make them subject to arbitrary arrest for investigative purposes. (*R.* v. *Duguay* (1985), 45 C.R. (3d) 140 at 150)

Had Mr. Schiere, Mr. Pelletier, and Mr. Angus been arrested, they would have been told the reasons for their arrest and have had the right to be brought before a judge within twenty-four hours; at that point, these charges would have to be brought forward and the men would have the right to seek bail. They would have the right to test the cases against them at a preliminary inquiry, and ultimately the Crown would bear the burden of proving its case beyond a reasonable doubt at a trial with the full protection of criminal due process.

But Mr. Schiere, Mr. Pelletier, and Mr. Angus were not free men. As prisoners, their institutional liberty could be severely curtailed by a transfer from medium to maximum security without a charge and without any procedure for testing the case against them. The existence of a police investigation was deemed sufficient to maintain their maximum security status, even though police acknowledged that the investigation was open ended and would be concluded only when a charge was laid. Mr. Schiere and Mr. Pelletier were both serving life sentences. If the power to transfer them to maximum security pending the completion of an investigation of a criminal offence was subject to no substantive limits, they could be kept in maximum security for many years, In fact, Mr. Schiere spent nineteen months in maximum security, Mr. Angus and Mr. Pelletier twenty-two months. Had legal action not been initiated, their maximum security confinement would likely have been much longer.

The prisoners in the *Schiere* case, in their grievances and affidavits, clearly set out their sense of injustice in being transferred without the laying of specific charges or the benefit of a hearing at which they could defend themselves. What interests of correctional authorities could be presented as a counterpoint?

It is no doubt important that wardens have the authority to remove prisoners they see as serious threats to the stability of the institution, whether those threats take the form of violence, intimidation of other prisoners, introduction of or trafficking in contraband (particularly drugs), undermining of staff authority, or breaches of physical security. Some of these threats take the form of overt action that is witnessed by staff members and can be dealt with through a formal charge, either under the prison disciplinary code or in outside court. Following conviction on such a charge, a transfer to higher security can be justified as flowing from the clearly adjudicated finding of guilt.

In some cases, the threat is not witnessed by staff but comes to their attention in the form of a prisoner victim. The victim may not be able, as in the case of the murdered Belliveau, to give information on the attack, or he may be unwilling to provide it because of the prisoner code's prohibition on "ratting." Other prisoners who have witnessed the events or have information about them may be prepared to breach the prohibition on ratting under a promise of informant confidentiality, coupled with the expectation (whether express or implicit) of consideration for institutional benefits such as transfer to lesser security or recommendation for parole. There is a constant flow of information in a prison, and prison authorities develop a sense of the reliability of different sources.

Let us return to the Belliveau situation. Let us hypothesize (and I emphasize, these are not the facts) that, sometime after Belliveau's murder, information is given to the warden of Matsqui by an eyewitness informant that Mr. Schiere, Mr.

Angus, and Mr. Pelletier were involved in the killing; that this informant has supplied reliable information in the past; that there is a reasonable explanation for why this information was not forthcoming earlier (for example, the informant has since been transferred to another prison or been released from prison and is therefore less concerned about suspicion falling upon him); and that further inquiry of other prisoners corroborates that there was bad feeling between the deceased man and these three prisoners. Let us further hypothesize that information is received from other prisoners that the continued presence of the three men in Matsqui is intimidating; prisoners fear the same fate may befall them if they cross these men. But since the primary informant makes it clear he will not testify against the three men in a criminal or disciplinary hearing, in the absence of other evidence no charge can be laid against them.

Under these circumstances, is it reasonable for the warden, charged with maintaining the safety of staff and prisoners, to act as if Belliveau was killed by phantoms? Is it not reasonable for him to assert that he has reasonable grounds to believe these three men were involved in the killing, and that their presence in a medium security institution will jeopardize other prisoners and staff, and that these prisoners need the additional control of a maximum security regime?

The warden's need for authority in these circumstances is reinforced if we consider the implications of doing nothing. Other prisoners will see the warden's impotence as a demonstration that major crimes can be committed in the penitentiary with impunity. Staff will see his impotence as indicative of the absence of law and order inside the walls, contributing to their feelings of insecurity. Viewed from these perspectives, a lack of action could be seen as contributing to increased tension and as undermining both security and institutional authority at Matsqui.

The warden's case is not one that can be summarily dismissed. But neither can that of the prisoners. Leaving aside the particulars of this case, prisoners could offer the rejoinder that, outside of prison, police may be satisfied that an individual has committed a crime yet be unable to lay a charge for lack of evidence amenable to formal proof. For example, their information may come from an informant not prepared to testify at a trial. Their inability to take coercive measures against the suspect may undermine police confidence in the efficacy of penal sanctions and reinforce the perception among the suspect's peers that crime is not always punished. Members of the community aware of the real circumstances may fear for their safety because of the continued presence among them of the suspect. However, none of these concerns are viewed by the law as sufficiently compelling to override the fundamental principles that a person's liberty cannot be taken away unless he or she is charged with an offence and that such charges cannot be based on suspicion but must be founded on evidence amenable to proof in a court of law. Underlying these principles is the deep conviction that in a free and democratic society our liberty must not be curtailed on the basis of secret allegations made to the authorities. The apparatus of the criminal justice system seeks to enhance our sense of security in this, by requiring that allegations of wrongdoing be measured against the specific criteria of crimes and be proven before an independent tribunal in accordance with legally defined rules of evidence.

As Madam Justice Arbour made clear in her 1996 report, it is not sufficient to assert that prisoners fall outside the protective veil of due process by virtue of having committed crimes for which they are sentenced to imprisonment. The need to feel that one's life will not be subject to arbitrary assertions of power, that it cannot be reordered on the basis of secret allegations, is no less important to prisoners than it is to free men and women. Indeed, a strong case can be made that because of the already circumscribed nature of prisoners' lives, their institutional or residual liberty is of special import.

The statements made by Dick Schiere, Mike Angus, and Robert Pelletier bear eloquent testimony to the depth of their feelings of injustice. They also indicate the effect such treatment had upon them as prisoners: it reinforced their scepticism about the nature of carceral authority, their sense of the hypocrisy of the "justice" system, and their deep alienation from the rest of society. Their feelings are no different from those we would have as free citizens were the police to come in the dead of night and, on the basis of allegations that we had been involved in a deadly assault, take us away from friends and family to a place of detention and let us know that we could be detained there indefinitely while the police pursue their investigations, that there might never be a trial before a judge or an opportunity to hear the case against us and present a defence. This nightmarish scenario is a hallmark of totalitarian regimes, reflected among other places in the anguished accounts of the mothers of the "disappeared" in Argentina and Chile in the 1970s.

But although it would be unfair to tell Messrs. Schiere, Angus, and Pelletier that they are without a claim to justice because they are prisoners, the special nature of prison cannot be ignored in meeting the legitimate needs of the warden for the authority to deal with disruptive behaviour. The closed nature of prison society is such that prisoners, and to a lesser extent guards, cannot take steps, as the rest of us in the larger society can, to change their life circumstances so as to remove themselves from the danger zone. Prison society is a pressure cooker in which hostilities and paranoia are intensified and in which personal insecurity and physical risk loom large. As with administrative segregation, the real issue is how the competing claims of prisoners and prison administrators can be balanced to produce a decision-making process which is just and fair for both the keepers and the kept and enhances both sides' sense of security and respect for authority.

## Transfers under the *CCRA*

The principal change introduced by the *Corrections and Conditional Release Act* in 1992 was that transfer provisions were elevated from their prior status as non-legally binding Commissioner's Directives to legislation and regulations backed by the force of law.

Section 28 of the *CCRA* sets out the criteria for placement and transfer:

> Where a person is, or is to be, confined in a penitentiary, the Service shall take all reasonable steps to ensure that the penitentiary in which the person is confined is one that provides the least restrictive environment for that person, taking into account
> (a) the degree and kind of custody and control necessary for
>     (i) the safety of the public
>     (ii) the safety of that person and other persons in the penitentiary, and
>     (iii) the security of the penitentiary;
> (b) accessibility to
>     (i) the person's home community and family,
>     (ii) a compatible cultural environment, and
>     (iii) a compatible linguistic environment; and
> (c) the availability of appropriate programs and services and the person's willingness to participate in those programs.

Section 18 of the *CCR Regulations* sets out the criteria for classification into maximum, medium, and minimum security based on three factors: the probability of escape, the risk to the safety of the public in the event of escape, and the degree of supervision and control required within the penitentiary. Other provisions in the *CCR Regulations,* supplemented by the Commissioner's Directives, set out a procedural code for transfers that distinguishes between voluntary transfers (those made at the request of the prisoner) and involuntary ones (those initiated by the warden), and between non-emergency and emergency transfers. Commissioner's Directive 540 sets out the step-by-step procedures for both non-emergency and emergency involuntary transfers that were in force during the period of my research from 1992 to 1999:

> NON-EMERGENCY INVOLUNTARY TRANSFERS
> The institutional head shall:
> a.   advise the inmate, in writing, of the reasons and destination of the proposed transfer;
> b.   give the inmate 48 hours to prepare a response to the proposed transfer;

c.   meet with the inmate to explain the reasons for and give him or her an opportunity to respond to the proposed transfer, in person or, if the inmate prefers, in writing;

d.   forward the inmate's response to the regional transfer authority [the Regional Deputy Commissioner] for a decision;

e.   give the inmate written notice of the final decision and the reasons therefor upon receipt, and

  1)   at least two (2) days before effecting the transfer, unless the inmate consents to a shorter period; and

  2)   within five (5) working days of the decision being made, where the decision is not to transfer.

EMERGENCY INVOLUNTARY TRANSFERS

Where, in an emergency situation, an involuntary transfer takes place without prior notification to the innate, the institutional head of the receiving institution shall:

a.   meet with the inmate within two (2) working days of his or her placement in the receiving institution to explain the reasons for the transfer;

b.   give the inmate 48 hours to respond to the transfer, in person or, if the inmate prefers, in writing;

c.   forward the inmate's response to the institutional head of the sending institution;

d.   give the inmate written notice of the final decision and the reasons therefor upon receipt and within five (5) working days of the decision being made. (c.d. 540, November 1, 1992, paras. 14–16. The current procedures are set out in *Standing Operating Practices*—700-15, February 20, 2001, paras. 9–19.)

The procedures I observed during my research at Matsqui and Kent included a further step in the process. In non-emergency cases, the initial notification of an intended transfer was reviewed at the institutional level to allow for any rebuttal the prisoner prepared. In almost all cases, that review resulted in a confirmation of the original recommendation, and this, together with the prisoner's response, was forwarded to the Regional Deputy Commissioner for decision. It is within this procedural matrix that the transfers described in the following pages occurred.

## The Matsqui Transfers

On June 15, 1994, a number of prisoners were involuntarily transferred on an emergency basis from Matsqui to Kent. In the weeks that followed I spoke to staff at both institutions about what lay behind these transfers. I also interviewed some of the prisoners involved, reviewed the documentation supporting the transfers, and, in one case where disciplinary charges were laid, observed the hearing of those charges before the Independent Chairperson.

The IPSOs at Matsqui provided this background to the transfers. There had been a number of assaults by prisoners on both staff and other prisoners, and some staff were concerned that, with the summer coming up, there was potential for a disturbance or even a riot. Weapons were known to be in circulation in the living unit. The warden imposed a week-long lock-down, during which time a general search took place and a number of weapons were discovered. Staff were canvassed about which prisoners they felt were prime candidates for transfer because of their disruptive impact at Matsqui, and this generated a target list of twelve prisoners. The IPSOs were asked for the information they had on these prisoners. For some of them, the IPSOs had no information. There were several other prisoners whom the IPSOs did not see as high priorities for transfer but who had established a negative reputation among staff, particularly in relation to drug activity. In addition, there was a third group of prisoners who were found with weapons or were disruptive during the lock-down. The lock-down and targeting followed a remarkably similar pattern to that which preceded Operation Big Scoop at Matsqui in August 1993.

## The Heide Case

Mr. Heide was one of the prisoners in whose cells weapons were found. Three days after the search, on June 15, Mr. Heide was taken to segregation, where two hours later he was served with a Notification of Recommendation for Involuntary Transfer to Kent. On his arrival at Kent, he was placed in segregation, where he remained for the next three weeks. The reasons for his transfer, set out in the notification, were these:

> (1) During a search of your cell on 94.06.12 a piece of contraband metal was found. This item has been examined by several staff members knowledgeable in firearms and it is believed to be a firing pin; (2) Several other items of contraband were seized including screwdrivers, pliers, a nut driver, scissors and a handmade hammer; (3) You have been charged with possession of these items; (4) Your behaviour is considered to be unacceptable at a medium security facility. Your security classification has been revised to maximum security. (Notification of Recommendation for Involuntary Transfer, Matsqui Institution, June 15, 1994)

On June 17, Mr. Heide received a progress summary supporting the recommendation of involuntary transfer. It stated:

Mr. Heide is currently serving a sentence for numerous impaired driving offences (times 12), theft under, driving while disqualified (times four), breach of conditions, driver with over 80 mg, fail to stop at the scene of an accident, and escape lawful custody. To date Mr. Heide has completed the offender substance abuse program and participates in institutional Alcoholics Anonymous meetings but he continues to pose a high risk of re-offending as he only recently began addressing his problems. During his previous incarcerations Mr. Heide did not address his alcohol abuse which he had denied until now. Mr. Heide is volatile to re-offend and is considered a high risk to the public safety. Furthermore, it appears that Mr. Heide is involved in the manufacturing of "zip guns" within the institution which could present serious concerns to the public safety. (Progress Summary, Matsqui Institution, June 17, 1994)

Mr. Heide prepared a written rebuttal disputing the allegation that he was a high risk to public safety.

The issue I'm deeply concerned of is where it states; it appears that Mr. Heide is involved in the manufacturing of zip guns. How, where or why they'd ever place that in a report about me is beyond me because I've never, ever owned a gun in my entire life let alone tried to build one, so that affected me harshly as I definitely do not have any use for such an object and definitely wouldn't jeopardize my release by doing it for someone else. If such an object were in my cell, knowing fully that there was a major search in effect, I'm sure I wouldn't of had something like that out in the open because I could have thrown it out the cell window before my cell was searched. The object they claim to be a firing pin is a countersinker for my hobbies as I have a wood permit and build little boxes for nails and screws as well as the odd jewellery box, so that also is why I had a home-made hammer, screwdriver, socket driver and scissors. I just inherited these from someone who got released and had no real use for them so they simply just laid around. I'd like to also mention all these contraband items are contraband seemingly while in my possession, but it's not contraband if you purchase them from Canadian Tire or Pro Hardware and had them in your cell for hobbies. So I'll admit I'm guilty of having these items in my possession but I won't admit to what they claim is a firing pin. I'd like to mention on numerous amount of times my cell was searched and none of these items were then confiscated or even brought to my attention, but yet now I've lost my security rating, pay, job and a chance of going to camps. (Rebuttal of Roy Heide, July 4, 1994)

On June 22, Mr. Heide, along with a number of the other prisoners who had been transferred from Matsqui to Kent, appeared before a special sitting of the Disciplinary Board at Kent Institution presided over by Mr. Routley. Mr. Heide's case was set down for hearing at Matsqui on July 6. Prior to that, there were some remarkable developments. Maria Parton, the Transfer Co-ordinator at Matsqui, came to Kent to serve Mr. Heide and the other prisoners who had been transferred with their progress summaries. In the middle of her interview with Mr. Heide, one of the Kent unit managers came into the room and advised her that Matsqui had agreed to take Mr. Heide back. Ms. Parton had no prior knowledge of the decision, and she told me later that she was embarrassed by this announcement in the middle of the interview.

Ms. Parton told me this sudden reversal likely stemmed from an incident at Matsqui the previous week, in which a prisoner had assaulted a staff member and then been placed in segregation. When he flooded his cell, a decision was made to transfer him to Kent. But because both Matsqui and Kent were full, transfers could be made only on a one-for-one basis. In other words, if Matsqui wanted to transfer another prisoner to Kent, someone from Kent had to be transferred back to Matsqui. Ms. Parton's theory was confirmed by a unit manager at Kent. Mr. Heide's transfer package was the weakest of those recently transferred, he said, and his return to Matsqui was a practical expedient for having Kent accept a more urgent involuntary transfer. Mr. Heide was supposed to be transferred on June 30, but due to a clerical error this did not take place until July 5. He therefore spent Canada Day 1994 in a segregation cell at Kent instead of in his cell in the general population at Matsqui.

On July 6, Mr. Heide appeared in disciplinary court at Matsqui before Mr. Routley on the charge that had precipitated his transfer to Kent. Mr. Heide said he was prepared to plead guilty to possession of all of the items except the alleged firing pin. He said he worked in the prison garage and collected pieces there for his hobby work. Mr. Routley—who in his pre-lawyer life had been a mechanic—examined the piece of metal as Mr. Heide explained it was a piece taken from an old lawn-mower motor that he used as a countersink. Mr. Routley said he doubted the piece of metal had sufficient weight to be used as a firing pin, and in light of Mr. Heide's explanation he reduced the charge to a minor one. As to sentence, Mr. Routley said, he felt a warning would be appropriate.

The IPSO office at Matsqui had not been directly involved in Mr. Heide's transfer, and prior to the discovery of the alleged firing pin they had no information on him. When I asked the charging officer why he thought the piece of metal might have been a firing pin, he replied that he had searched dozens of cells that week. When he found the items in Mr. Heide's cell he didn't think too much about the piece of metal. While he was writing up the charge, however, he looked at it again and thought it could be in the process of being made into a firing pin. He had not come to any definite conclusions, and that was why he had used the words "possible firing pin." The officer had had no previous dealings with Mr. Heide and had nothing to do with the transfer recommendation. Nobody had consulted him after he filed the offence report.

I completed my investigation by talking to Warden Brock about the case. He told me that the lock-down and general search had resulted in the seizure of about twenty shanks, which indicated to him a lamentable lack of contraband control. When he was advised that the piece of metal in Mr. Heide's cell was likely a firing pin for a zip gun, he felt no hesitation in determining that a transfer to Kent was necessary and justified.

In a climate of institutional crackdown, a piece of metal for which there was a perfectly legitimate explanation—a countersink for hobby work—had been re-imaged as a "metal scribe which had been fashioned into what appeared to be a firing pin for a zip gun." As a result, Mr. Heide—whose record revealed a recurring problem with impaired driving, and who was ninety days away from the end of his sentence—was elevated to a maximum security risk as an arms manufacturer and confined in a segregation cell for twenty-one days. When he was finally returned to Matsqui, he was placed in a double-bunked cell; he had lost his job, and his pay level was reduced from four (the maximum) to zero. Yet the same evidence, when placed under the scrutiny of an Independent Chairperson, resulted in a rejection of the firing pin theory and an appraisal of the other items found in the cell as warranting only a minor charge deserving of nothing more than a warning.

## The Tucker Case

A second prisoner transferred to Kent after the lock-down at Matsqui was Mr. Tucker. At the time of his transfer, Mr. Tucker was a twenty-seven-year-old first-time federal offender serving 6½ years for break and enter, attempted robbery, and robbery. The general search conducted in June 1994 had revealed what was alleged to be drug and gambling paraphernalia in Mr. Tucker's cell, as a result of which he was segregated. A progress summary gave the following grounds for his transfer to Kent:

> While at Matsqui, according to security information, in January 1994 Mr. Tucker's communications were monitored and conversations were overheard in reference to moneys owing to other inmates. Furthermore, in April 1994 Mr. Tucker was identified by a reliable source as selling cocaine within Matsqui Institution. Once again, in May 1994 Mr. Tucker's communications were monitored and conversations were overhead in reference to moneys owing by other inmates. Additionally, a cell search was completed on 94-06-13 of Mr. Tucker's cell and correctional staff found pills which tested

positive for codeine, one complete syringe, a notebook detailing drug debts, gambling markers and a pair of scissors . . . Mr. Tucker has failed to conduct himself within the rules and regulations of Matsqui Institution and, at the present time, his case management team does not feel that a medium security environment is suitable for Mr. Tucker. (Progress Summary, Matsqui Institution, June 17, 1994)

The offence report, supporting a charge of possession of contraband, indicated that officers found "a complete hype kit wrapped in a Kleenex and tucked inside a lip on the metal cell cabinet and two beige coloured pills inside the lip on the cell ceiling light." The pills were tested by the IPSO at Matsqui and registered positive for codeine. This charge was initially set down for hearing on July 13, then made peremptory on Matsqui on July 27. On that date, the charge was administratively withdrawn. The reason listed on the offence report was "no physical evidence."

In his written rebuttal, Mr. Tucker denied any knowledge of the drug outfit. With regard to the pills that had tested positive for codeine, he explained that these could have been from a pack of sinus Tylenol which another prisoner had left in his cell and he had thrown in the garbage. In response to the allegation that he was using and dealing in drugs, he stated that he had taken the Relapse Prevention Program and had signed an agreement to participate in urine analysis but had never been asked for a sample. He asked, "If some inmate had said to you that I was selling cocaine, why wasn't I approached by staff for a search or asked for a urine sample?" He also denied any involvement in gambling within the institution:

My involvement in gambling is nil. I was not once found with playing cards. What was involved in the notebook was that I lent out bales and asked for extra back, something like a bank. So that I am guilty of, but I would never pressure anybody if they owed me and couldn't pay right away. In all institutions tobacco is very hard to come by because of the pay inmates make and the lack of work available . . . people have to pick up cigarette butts off the ground and out of ash trays, it's actually a very sad situation. It also said I had gambling markers in my house. Well, they are for my courses in horticulture and business management for lining out things, nothing more. If I was involved in gambling, why wouldn't you have staff and inmate reports on me? (Rebuttal of Tracy Tucker, June 1994)

Warden Brock, in reviewing and confirming his recommendation for transfer, responded to Mr. Tucker's rebuttal in this way:

- You were involuntarily transferred to Kent Institution on 94-06-15.
- I have reviewed the documentation mentioned above and have given consideration to your rebuttal. I note that you deny all knowledge of the syringe which was found in your cell. However, it is your responsibility to ensure that your cell does not contain contraband items. Furthermore, as stated in the documentation provided to you, reliable information dated April 1994 indicated that you were selling cocaine within Matsqui Institution.
- You state that the pills were sinus Tylenol and that you had thrown them in the garbage. Again, as I state above, you must accept responsibility for the contraband found in your cell whether it is drug related, scissors or items which appear to be gambling markers.
- It is of concern that in your rebuttal you admit to lending bales of tobacco and then "ask for extra back, something like a bank." This is a flagrant breach of expected conduct and is known in other circles as "loan sharking." This type of conduct will not be tolerated in an institution.
- I have given serious consideration to your rebuttal and the related documentation. I have considered your previous involvement in drug usage in the community and other security information which indicates you are involved in drug activity in the institution. While I appreciate your honesty, I have serious concerns about your lending bales of tobacco and then expecting something extra in return. This is not acceptable behaviour. (Notification of Recommendation for Involuntary Transfer, Matsqui Institution, July 13, 1994)

The Deputy Commissioner, in upholding Mr. Tucker's involuntary transfer to Kent, stated:

I have carefully reviewed the transfer documentation and Mr. Tucker's responses. There is sufficient information to justify a high rating under institutional adjustment concern which results in an overall classification of maximum security. Therefore I approve transfer to Kent Institution. (Final Decision, August 5, 1994)

The allegation of Mr. Tucker's involvement in drugs seems referable to a single reliable source, but he was provided with no gist of this information beyond its assertion in the progress summary. There is no information about the time frame in which this involvement is alleged to have taken place, the sources through which Mr. Tucker is alleged to have introduced the drugs, or the quantities of drugs alleged to be involved. There is no answer to Mr. Tucker's question about why he was never given a urine analysis or subjected to a search if the institution suspected his involvement with drugs. The allegations of gambling are linked to a notebook containing debts owed and to gambling markers. Mr. Tucker's explanation of his use of the markers for highlighting course materials is never addressed, yet this would have been easy for the authorities to corroborate.

Mr. Tucker's transactions in lending other prisoners tobacco with the expectation that he would be paid "extra back" is characterized by Warden Brock as "loan sharking" and "a flagrant breach of expected conduct." These allegations seem exaggerated. There is no evidence that Mr. Tucker was charging an unconscionably high rate of interest. He asserts that he never put undo pressure on prisoners who owed him, and the institution did not come forward with evidence suggesting otherwise. If lending tobacco in prison was sufficient grounds for transfer to maximum security, Greyhound therapy would require investment in a whole new fleet of buses.

This leaves the allegations of possession of drugs and drug paraphernalia. Warden Brock asserts that Mr. Tucker is responsible for whatever is found in his cell. This is true as a matter of institutional policy but not as a matter of legal possession. In Sector 2, Chapter 2 of this book, I recounted the clash between the institutional perspective on a prisoner's responsibility for objects found in his cell and the legal prerequisites to prove possession of them. In the absence of proof, a prisoner cannot be found guilty of the disciplinary offence of possession of contraband or an unauthorized item. The disciplinary charge against Mr. Tucker was withdrawn because the institution, by its own admission, could not meet the legal test of possession. Had Mr. Tucker faced a charge of possession of drugs on the street and the charge been withdrawn for lack of evidence, he would have left the courtroom a free man. However, in the prison world, that lack of evidence—while preventing Mr. Tucker's conviction on a disciplinary charge—did not limit the institution's power to punish him by raising his security level and transferring him to Kent. Mr. Tucker was denied the chance to establish his innocence and, for the purpose of his transfer, treated as if he had been found guilty.

## The Fitzgerald Case

In July 1994, Mr. Justice Thackray of the B.C. Supreme Court issued a judgement that illustrates how the courts approach the review of correctional administrators' decisions and the difference in how judges evaluate what constitutes reliable and compelling evidence of security risk justifying transfer to maximum security. Gary Fitzgerald, a prisoner who had served eleven years of a life sentence for first-degree murder imposed in 1981, was transferred from William Head Institution to Kent in October 1992 based on information from a prison informant that Mr. Fitzgerald was planning to escape from William Head.

Because the 1992 transfer was an emergency one, Mr. Fitzgerald was given his notification of reasons for transfer after his arrival at Kent. He filed a petition in B.C. Supreme Court challenging the transfer, primarily on the basis that he had not received sufficient information about the alleged escape plan to enable him to make a full answer and defence. Mr. Justice Gow agreed that the information provided to Mr. Fitzgerald was insufficient and ordered the warden of William Head to file a supplementary affidavit providing the full information. If the warden felt the disclosure of information critical to his decision would imperil the safety of the informant, Mr. Justice Gow suggested he follow the Federal Court practice of filing a sealed envelope for the court's perusal, together with an explanation about why it could not be revealed to the prisoner. The warden filed a supplementary affidavit to be shared with Mr. Fitzgerald, together with a sealed internal investigation report into the alleged escape plan. Mr. Justice Gow held that this constituted a sharing of information to the greatest extent possible and that Mr. Fitzgerald should be given an opportunity to respond to it. Mr. Fitzgerald, through his counsel, filed such a response, and the warden at William Head upheld his initial recommendation to transfer the prisoner to Kent. His recommendation was approved by the Assistant Deputy Commissioner. That decision was challenged again in B.C. Supreme Court and was the subject of Mr. Justice Thackray's ruling on July 7, 1994.

His Lordship first addressed the appropriate standard for judicial review of a transfer decision. Mr. Fitzgerald's argument was that the transfer was made in violation of the common law duty to act fairly and of the principles of fundamental justice required by s. 7 of the *Charter of Rights and Freedoms* for any decision which affects the liberty of the subject. He argued that in the case of *Demaria* v. *the Regional Transfer Board and Warden of Joyceville Institution* ([1988] 2 F.C. 480), Madam Justice Reed had expressed the view that both the Federal Court of Appeal and the Supreme Court of Canada had interpreted s. 7 of the *Charter* as requiring not only that there be procedural fairness, in the narrow sense, but also that decisions not be made in an unreasonable or arbitrary manner.

Mr. Justice Thackray held that the appropriate standard for judicial review was the "patently unreasonable test," which Mr. Justice Seaton of the B.C. Court of Appeal had expressed in this way: "Is this a decision that we can let stand?" Mr. Justice Thackray ruled that it was up to correctional authorities to establish, on a balance of probabilities, that the ultimate decision to transfer was not patently unreasonable. In applying this test, he reviewed a number of the judicial authorities which have addressed "the delicate balance to be maintained" in the review of correctional decisions:

> I must keep in mind that the decision to transfer was made by authorities who know infinitely more about the incarceration and

correction systems than does the court. The authorities should be secure to think that if they act in accordance with fundamental principles of justice within the legislative requirements, that their decisions will prevail . . . The court should stand poised to intervene only in those cases where either breaches of fundamental justice have occurred or there is such unreasonableness to a decision that it amounts to unfairness. The error should be egregious or equivalent to bad faith. (*Fitzgerald* v. *Trono,* [1994] B.C.J. No. 1534 at 19)

It was within these confines that Mr. Justice Thackray reviewed the facts in the *Fitzgerald* case. The reasons given by the Assistant Deputy Commissioner for approving Mr. Fitzgerald's transfer to Kent were these:

Mr. Fitzgerald was transferred on an emergency involuntary basis, to Kent Institution, based upon believed, reliable, detailed inmate informant information indicating that Mr. Fitzgerald was planning to escape from William Head Institution with other inmates. A brief summary of this information is as follows: the escape plan was reported to have involved Mr. Fitzgerald acquiring false identification, being picked up by boat from William Head Institution, travel to Vancouver and air travel to, eventually, Costa Rica. This informant information was reportedly supported by the discovery of correspondence from Mr. Fitzgerald to the consulates of various countries, including Costa Rica, inquiring about residency criteria. The inmate informant was not identified out of consideration for the individual's safety. The other inmates involved were not identified as it was believed that this information would cause the informant to be identified . . .

A summary of the information submitted on Mr. Fitzgerald's behalf is as follows: Mr. Fitzgerald denies any intent or plan to escape from William Head Institution; he references his positive behaviour over the last eight years; treatment at the Regional Psychiatric Centre; institutional support for transfer to minimum security; and family support. Mr. Fitzgerald's submissions, in addition to those of others, provide his explanation of letters to foreign consulates. Those individuals identified in the community who were reported to be of assistance to Mr. Fitzgerald in the escape plan have submitted statements denying knowledge of such a plan and willingness to participate. Mr. Fitzgerald, in his own submissions and in those prepared on his behalf, has addressed, in detail, the information presented in the Warden's supplementary affidavit.

While submissions presented by both Mr. Fitzgerald and his legal counsel do provide alternate explanations for much of the information and present the theory that the escape plan was a hoax, the informant information is considered credible, primarily due to the level of detail provided. Mr. Fitzgerald's escape attempt in 1984, and the discovered correspondence to foreign consulates does support the belief that Mr. Fitzgerald was planning to escape. I am not convinced that the escape plot was a fabrication by the informant. Information that would indicate the informant's motivation to provide false information has not been presented. I am also concerned about the level of risk Mr. Fitzgerald would present to the community should he escape. (*Fitzgerald*, at 16–17)

In one of the affidavits submitted on Mr. Fitzgerald's behalf, Mr. Fitzgerald said that he intended to renounce Canadian citizenship and to this end had written to the consulates of several countries, including Costa Rica. He also noted that he had been scheduled to see the transfer board from Ferndale minimum security institution four days after his transfer to Kent, and that he had the full support of his case management team at William Head for the transfer to minimum security. Given the realistic prospect of his being transferred to a prison with no fence, situated a hundred yards from a public road, why would he be planning a highly risky escape by sea from William Head? Mr. Fitzgerald's affidavit was supplemented by one from the William Head chaplain, who acknowledged that Mr. Fitzgerald had discussed with him his plans to seek citizenship in another country.

In determining "whether the reasons given for Mr. Fitzgerald's transfer were patently unreasonable," Mr. Justice Thackray cited first the transfer summary prepared by the case management team supporting Mr. Fitzgerald's transfer to Ferndale minimum security. This, he said, "makes it difficult to understand the basis for the conclusion of the Assistant Deputy Commissioner which suggests some significant level of risk to the public from Mr. Fitzgerald." Because the criteria for minimum security require an assessment that the prisoner presents a "low risk to the safety of the public in the event of escape," the recommendation that Mr. Fitzgerald be transferred to minimum security negated a finding that he represented a "significant level of risk to the public."

Next, Mr. Justice Thackray had this to say about the Assistant Deputy Commissioner's finding that an "escape plot was very real":

The plan is so inept as to put its existence into doubt. The petitioner was to be picked up in a small boat off the shore of William Head Institution. The likelihood of this event being observed seemed significant. Mr. Fitzgerald was then to make his way to Nanaimo and then, by way of B.C. ferries, to Vancouver. He would then, accompanied by his wife, depart on an international flight with the ultimate destination being Costa Rica.

Mr. Denis [the acting warden] found that the "explanation in relation to correspondence with various countries as to residency is simply unbelievable, at best naive." There is, in my opinion, a vast difference in the context of this case between "unbelievable" and "naive." If it is unbelievable, then Mr. Denis would be justified in concluding that it was part of an escape plot. However, if it was simply naive, then it can have no bearing on the authenticity of the alleged plot.

The Assistant Deputy Commissioner then concluded that he is "not convinced that the escape plot was a fabrication by the informant. Information that would indicate the informant's motivation to provide false information has not been presented." It would be more convincing if he had concluded that the plot *was* a fabrication. Furthermore, in that the authorities could not provide the name of the informer, it was hardly open to the petitioner to provide information that would indicate the informant's motivation to provide false information.

There is also the problem created by the fact that much "material" is contained in a sealed envelope. I am not suggesting that the contents should be revealed to the petitioner. In any event, Mr. Justice Gow held that information has been shared with the petitioner to the greatest extent possible. However, that does not change the situation created by the concealment of information. There can be no doubt but that the petitioner is in a disabled position to respond fully to the concerns of the authorities. This, in my opinion, puts more of an onus on the authorities to ensure that the procedures followed are in keeping with the regulations and the procedures set forward. Further, that the reasons given for decisions are sound, and as revealing as possible as to the foundations therefor. In this case, I am unable to conclude that the reasons properly reflect the evidence, including what is contained in the sealed envelope.

While the authorities chose to find the informant reliable, and this is a subjective judgement, I cannot uncover any basis for this. Nothing in the informant's background suggests to me that he is a person to be relied upon. (*Fitzgerald,* at 22–23)

Significantly, Mr. Justice Thackray's Reasons for Judgement concluded with an acknowledgement of the climate within which contemporary courts must adjudicate issues of prisoners' rights:

The climate today is against a "soft" attitude towards prisoners' rights. This is understandable in view of the crimes apparently committed by persons on parole or who have escaped from corrections institutions. However, I cannot allow this atmosphere to govern the outcome of this petition.

It appears to me, in keeping with the submissions of counsel for the petitioner, that the decisions to transfer have been extremely arbitrary and, as such, unfair to the petitioner. The reasons and decisions do not conform to the principle of natural justice which, after all, is only "fair play in action."

The decision to transfer is not, to again return to the words of Mr. Justice Seaton, "a decision that we can let stand." I am of the opinion that it has not been demonstrated that the decision was arrived at fairly. It is therefore "patently unreasonable." (*Fitzgerald*, at 24)

The court ordered that Mr. Fitzgerald be returned to William Head Institution.

## A Model Transfer Code

Gary Fitzgerald was fortunate in finding John Conroy, one of the few lawyers who specialize in correctional law, to challenge his transfer. Most transfers go unchallenged in the courts, not because there are no meritorious grounds for the challenge but because of the woeful inadequacy of legal aid for prisoners and the low priority given to such litigation by the legal profession. There is the additional problem, reflected in the Reasons for Judgement in the *Fitzgerald* case, that the courts have extended a significant degree of judicial deference to correctional administrators and will usually interfere only where the decision is patently unreasonable. To look to the courts as the ultimate vindicator of fairness in transfer decisions is to cast prisoners' rights to the winds of litigation. As with administrative segregation, the achievement of a fair transfer process requires a transfer code designed specifically to legislate the appropriate balance between the interests of prison administrators in exercising correctional authority to ensure safety and security and the interests of prisoners in being free from the arbitrary exercise of that authority.

The first component of such a code would be the substantive criteria for transfer. As outlined earlier in this Sector, some essential contours of these criteria are already set out in s. 28 of the *CCRA* and s. 18 of the *CCR Regulations*. Section 28 articulates the least restrictive environment concept and sets out the factors for determining the least restrictive environment for any particular prisoner. Section 18, which sets out the criteria for the tripartite classification of maximum, medium, and minimum security, focusses on the escape-risk potential, the associated potential degree of danger to public safety, and the degree of supervision required for the prisoner. Thus, placement in or transfer to maximum security requires that the prisoner presents "a high probability of escape and a high risk to the safety of the public in the event of escape" or "[requires] a high degree of supervision and control within the penitentiary." Under these criteria, the involvement of a medium security prisoner in offences such as hostage-taking, violence against other prisoners or staff, escape or attempted escape, or trafficking of drugs or other contraband would *prima facie* be grounds for transfer to higher security. A transfer code would also authorize transfer where a prisoner's disciplinary offences form a pattern of behaviour that demonstrate his unwillingness or inability to abide by the rules of the institution.

Where transfer to maximum security is authorized upon conviction of a designated offence, the issue becomes whether or not the convicted prisoner should be permitted to remain in medium security. This judgement is best left to correctional authorities because of the many considerations to be taken into account. Under a transfer code, the warden's application for transfer would be reviewed by a Regional Transfer Board, who would make their decision after a hearing at which the prisoner had a right to appear with a representative of his choosing. This representative would help the prisoner marshal facts and arguments supportive of his case to remain in medium security. The role could be filled by a lawyer or by someone else—a prisoner's wife, for example, upon whom a transfer might fall most harshly. The Board would also assess the impact of a transfer on the prisoner's institutional programs and release plans and consider whether a less restrictive alternative would be appropriate—for example, a suspension of the transfer under specific conditions. The Board's decision, and the reasons for it, would be supplied in writing.

In cases where a warden seeks to transfer a prisoner to higher security pending investigation of a disciplinary or criminal charge, the decision-making function shifts to the adjudicatory end of the spectrum, where competing interests become more acute. In the instance of transfer pending an investigation, such as in the *Schiere* case, the decision-maker must determine whether there are reasonable and probable grounds for implicating the prisoner in an offence qualifying for transfer and must ensure compliance with the time line on the conclusion of that investigation. Since this is a situation in which factual allegations are likely to be in conflict, and also one in which there are competing interests— the warden's in acting upon information he feels reliably implicates the prisoner, and the prisoner's in relying upon the presumption of innocence—the decision-maker should be independent of the correctional administration and the procedure should parallel that set out in my Model Segregation Code for pre-trial and investigatory segregation.

The case for an independent adjudicator is even more compelling where the institution seeks to justify an involuntary transfer on the basis of serious allegations which, because of the need to protect prisoner informants, are not the subject of disciplinary or criminal charges. The *Fitzgerald* case fits into this category. In this situation, the institution judges the prisoner to be guilty even though that cannot be proved in either a court of law or disciplinary court. In these cases, the process of notice, rebuttal, and review represents little more than a formality where the end result is never in doubt. That result is not just that the transfer is affirmed but that the allegations are presumed to be true so that the prisoner thereafter is judged as if he were found guilty. Dick Schiere, in his grievance documents, spoke of the depth of prejudice this caused in his interactions with correctional staff and other prisoners. Judicial review of transfer decisions is problematic not only because of the limitations of legal aid and the judicial deference extended to correctional administrators but because even a successful challenge takes an inordinate amount of time, particularly when measured from a segregation cell or a maximum security institution. In *Fitzgerald,* Mr. Justice Thackray's judgement came down almost two years after Mr. Fitzgerald had been transferred from William Head to Kent. What is required, as in the case of segregation reviews, is a front-end review process in which the institution's case and the prisoner's answer can be assessed, in which claims to maintain confidentiality of information can be weighed and measures taken to ensure that deprivations of liberty are not founded on the quicksand of secret information.

## Disclosure of Information: Faceless Informers and Barbarian Princes

The adage that information is power is as compellingly relevant in the cells, ranges, and courtyards of penitentiaries as it is in the corridors and suites of legislative buildings and corporations. In prison, as elsewhere, information is not only part of the calculus of power but also an essential component of fairness. The achievement of a fair balance between the claims of prisoners to disclosure of information and the competing claims of the prison administration to the confidentiality of that information is another measure of a just decision-making process.

The case for disclosure has deep historical and contemporary roots. A lead editorial in the *New York Times,* in supporting the publication of the report of Special Prosecutor Kenneth Starr and the details of the relationship between then President Bill Clinton and Monica Lewinsky, commented:

> The nation should rely on the principles that have served the country well throughout its history. One of the most important is that full disclosure and the free flow of information are the oxygen of a democracy. (*New York Times,* September 20, 1998)

Prisons are not democratic institutions, but they are one of the agencies of a democratic society. Within their walls the disclosure of information upon which decisions about a prisoner's liberty are made is no less vital to breathing the air of justice.

The issue of disclosure has also been addressed by the courts. Lord Edmund-Davis, in a House of Lords judgement, cited the following passage as expressing the competing interests involved:

> Few situations in life are more calculated to arouse resentment in a person than to be told that he has been traduced, but cannot be confronted with his traducer. It is submitted that, ideally, nothing but the very pressing demands of public security, where vital interests of the community are unquestionably involved, can require that private individuals should be expected to acquiesce in their vulnerability by an invisible foe. (H. G. Hanbury, "Equality and Privilege in English Law" [1952] 68 L.Q.R. 173 at 181, cited in *D.* v. *National Society for the Prevention of Cruelty to Children* [1977] 1 All E.R. 589 at 615)

The issue has also been confronted by the U.S. courts. In *Peters* v. *Hobby* (349 U.S. 331 (1955)), the Supreme Court heard the case of a professor of medicine who was barred from federal employment by the Federal Civil Service Commission's Loyalty Review Board. Dr. Peters had been given a hearing on charges relating to his alleged membership in the Communist Party and alleged association with communists and communist sympathizers. At the hearing, the sources of the information supporting the charges were not identified or made available to Dr. Peters' counsel for cross-examination. Justice Douglas had this to say of the process:

> Dr. Peters was condemned by faceless informers, some of whom were not known even to the Board that condemned him. Some of these informers were not even under oath. None of them had to submit to cross-examination. None had to face Dr. Peters. So far as we or the Board know, they may be psychopaths or venal people like Titus Oates. They may bear old grudges. Under cross-examination their stories might disappear like bubbles. Their whispered confidences might turn out to be yarns conceived by twisted minds or by people who, though sincere, have poor faculties of observation and memory . . .
>
> We have here a system where government with all its power and authority condemns a man to a suspect class and the outer darkness, without the rudiments of a fair trial . . . When we relax our standards to accommodate the faceless informer we violate our basic constitu-

tional guarantees and ape the tactics of those whom we despise. (*Peters*, at 351–52)

Justice Douglas' comments have a particular significance in the context of life inside a prison. Prisons are rife with rumours; within such a world, it is not difficult to find prisoners who are anxious to cascade down through the system, who wish to even old scores or remove potential or actual rivals, for whom a carefully revealed piece of information is a strategy for advancing their own interests. The prison has its own brand of Titus Oates. Within such a world, the policy of preserving the anonymity of informants, far from contributing to the authorities' ability to gather the whole truth, provides incentives for the propagation of false allegations.

The claim on justice made by prisoners seeking to know the full extent of the case against them where a negative decision could lead to the deprivation of their liberty has been recognized by Canadian judges. Madam Justice Reed of the Federal Court expressed it this way:

> The requirement that an individual is entitled to know, and be given an opportunity to respond to the case against him is essential not only to prevent abuses by people making false accusations but also to give the person who has been accused the assurance that he or she is not being dealt with arbitrarily or capriciously. A particularly eloquent history of the principle is found in de Smith's *Judicial Review of Administrative Action* (4th ed., 1980) at pages 157–158:
>> 'That no man is to be judged unheard was a precept known to the Greeks, inscribed in ancient times upon images in places where justice was administered, proclaimed in Seneca's Medea, enshrined in the scriptures, mentioned by St. Augustine, embodied in Germanic as well as African proverbs, ascribed in the Year Books to the law of nature, asserted by Coke to be a principle of divine justice, and traced by an eighteenth-century judge to the events in the Garden of Eden.' (footnotes omitted) [*Gough* v. *Canada (National Parole Board)*, [1991] 2 F.C. 117 at 125–26]

In highlighting the importance of disclosure of information to prisoners, I am not suggesting that the well-established common law rule regarding the secrecy of police informers has less application in prison. This very issue was considered by Mr. Justice Muldoon in the following terms:

> The reason for the secrecy rule is abundantly clear and it operates in any civilized society, be it a free and democratic society like Canada,

or a totalitarian one like many other countries in the world. It resides in the very real, and realistic, fear of retaliation in an aggressive society, which, in this instance, is the population of a maximum security penitentiary . . . That fear of retaliation is so well known and its realistic, factual basis is such that the court would be wilfully blind not to take judicial notice of that savage, unwritten "code" of conduct which is kept alive by the dominant inmates in those "aggressive (inmate) communities" in Canadian prisons. The so-called "convict code" was in no way ameliorated by the state's adoption of either the Canadian *Bill of Rights* or of the Canadian *Charter of Rights and Freedoms*. That abominable "code" makes an offence of seeking protection from, or co-operating with, the prison administration; and even though Parliament has eschewed capital punishment, the supporters and enforcers of the "convict code" do not flinch at murder, maiming, wounding, beating, or sometimes sexual indignities according to "culpability" in the administration of their brand of rotten injustice . . .

In the "aggressive society" of prisons, the "convict code" is an attempt to establish, to honour and to exact fearing tribute, and obedience, to the savagery of the barbarian princes among the inmate population . . . So for this reason, ultimately the probability of retribution, have courts defined, developed and upheld the rule of nondisclosure of the identity of informants . . .

The Court observes that given the common law rule of secrecy of the identity of informers, given the reality of that well-known abomination—the "convict code"—and given the historic and subsisting duty of a custodial authority to keep those prisoners committed into his, her or its charge in safe custody, only the most cogent and compelling evidence should ever persuade the Court that a Deputy Commissioner or Warden would be taking an alarmist, frivolous or careless view of the risks. (*Gill and Gallant* v. *Trono,* [1988] 3 F.C. 361 at 368–70)

This notion of a prison run by "barbarian princes" ruthlessly applying a monolithic "convict code" stems from American maximum security penitentiaries with populations running in the thousands; it has little relevance in the much smaller, contemporary Canadian prison. Even as an American phenomenon, this depiction is more the stuff of which movies are made than a realistic description of prison. Jerome Washington, in his book *Iron House,* relates a story from the annals of Attica that captures the extensive trade in information between prisoners and the administration, belying Mr. Justice Muldoon's description:

The last time we tried a hunger strike the warden stormed into the mess hall and ordered us to eat. When no one made a move to break our solidarity by eating, the warden dragged a large chalk board into the middle of the mess hall. "This is your last chance," the warden shouted as he held up a piece of chalk for all to see, and then prepared to write. "If you men don't start eating right now," the warden screamed, "I'm going to write the names of every informer, snitch and rat in the prison." Before the chalk touched the board nearly every plate was clean. (at 70)

The issue of disclosure in the context of a transfer from medium to maximum security was addressed by the Federal Court of Appeal in the *Demaria* case. Mr. Demaria and his lawyer had sought to obtain from prison officials the particulars of allegations that he had had cyanide brought into the prison. These requests were refused. One reason given was that all preventive security information acquired by the CSC was confidential and could not be released to an inmate's legal representative. The Court ruled that this was not sufficient compliance with the legal duty to act fairly, stating:

The purpose of requiring that notice be given to a person against whose interests it is proposed to act is to allow him to respond to it intelligently. If the matter is contested, such response would normally consist of either or both a denial of what is alleged and an allegation of other facts to complete the picture. Where, as here, it is not intended to hold a hearing or otherwise give the person concerned the right to confront the evidence against him directly, it is particularly important that the notice contain as much detail as possible, else the right to answer becomes totally illusory. Indeed, the present case is an excellent example of the right to answer being frustrated and denied by the inadequacy of the notice. The appellant is told that there are reasonable grounds for believing him to have brought in cyanide. He is given no hint of what those grounds are. The allegations against him are devoid of every significant detail. When? Where? How? Whence came the poison? How was it obtained? For what purpose? How much? The allegation is said to be based on information obtained by the Millhaven staff and the Ontario Provincial Police. What information comes from which source? Is there an informer involved? If so, how much of the substance of his statement can be revealed while protecting his identity? Have the police pursued their inquiries? Have they made any arrests? The list of questions is almost endless. In the absence of anything more than the bald allegation that there were grounds to believe that he had brought in cyanide, the appellant was reduced to a simple denial, by itself almost always less convincing than a positive affirmation, and futile speculation as to what the case against him really was.

There is, of course, no doubt that the authorities were entitled to protect confidential sources of information. A penitentiary is not a choir school and, if informers were involved (the record here does not reveal whether they were or not), it is important that they not be put at risk. But even if that were the case, it should always be possible to give the substance of the information while protecting the identity of the informant. The burden is always on the authorities to demonstrate that they have withheld only such information as is strictly necessary for that purpose. (*Demaria* v. *Regional Classification Board and Payne,* [1987] 1 F.C. 74 at 77–78)

Based on the jurisprudence of cases such as *Demaria,* s. 27 of the CCRA now contains specific provisions dealing with the disclosure of information to prisoners:

(1) Where an offender is entitled by this Part or the regulations to make representations in relation to a decision to be taken by the Service about the offender, the person or body that is to take the decision shall, subject to subsection (3), give the offender, a reasonable period before the decision is to be taken, all the information to be considered in the taking of the decision or a summary of that information.

(2) Where an offender is entitled by this Part or the regulations to be given reasons for a decision taken by the Service about the offender, the person or body that takes the decision shall, subject to subsection (3), give the offender, forthwith after the decision is taken, all the information that was considered in the taking of the decision or a summary of that information.

(3) Except in relation to decisions on disciplinary offences, where the Commissioner has reasonable grounds to believe that disclosure of information under subsection (1) or (2) would jeopardize:

(a) the safety of any person

(b) the security of a penitentiary, or

(c) the conduct of any lawful investigation,

the Commissioner may authorize the withholding from the offender of as much information as is strictly necessary in order to protect the interest identified in paragraph (a), (b) or (c).

The faultline in these provisions is that decisions relating to non-disclosure continue to be made by correctional administrators. In commenting on the new provisions when they were before Parliament, I argued that disclosure of information is critical to the operation of a fair system. Where a prisoner's rights are at stake and correctional administrators have made a preliminary decision not to disclose relevant information to him—specifically in the context of administrative segregation or involuntary transfer—the issue should be referred to an independent adjudicator who, under my proposed Segregation and Transfer Codes, would assess the justification for these decisions.

Both the nature of the disclosure inquiry and the rationale for it being conducted by an independent person can be understood from a comparative review of the inquiry conducted by the courts in relation to searches or arrests without warrant. In *R* v. *Debot,* Mr. Justice Martin of the Ontario Court of Appeal described it this way:

> Unquestionably, information supplied by a reliable informer, even though it is hearsay, may in some circumstances provide the necessary "reasonable grounds to believe" to justify the granting of a search warrant . . . It would seem to be entirely logical and reasonable that such information can also provide the necessary "reasonable ground to believe" to justify a warrantless search, where a warrantless search is authorized by law. On an application for a search warrant, the informant must set out in the information the grounds for his or her belief in order that the justice may satisfy himself or herself that there are reasonable grounds for believing what is alleged. Consequently, a mere statement by the informant that he or she was told by a reliable informer that a certain person is carrying on a criminal activity or that drugs would be found at a certain place would be an insufficient basis for the granting of the warrant. The underlying circumstances disclosed by the informer for his or her conclusion must be set out, thus enabling the justice to satisfy himself or herself that there are reasonable grounds for believing what is alleged. I am of the view that such a mere conclusionary statement made by an informer to a police officer would not constitute reasonable grounds for conducting a warrantless search or for making an arrest without warrant. Highly relevant to whether information supplied by an informer constitutes reasonable grounds to justify a warrantless search or an arrest without warrant are whether the informer's "tip" contains sufficient detail to ensure it is based on more than mere rumour or gossip, whether the informer discloses his or her source or means of knowledge and whether there are any *indicia* of his or her reliability,

such as the supplying of reliable information in the past or confirmation of part of his or her story by police surveillance. I do not intend to imply that each of these relevant criteria must be present in every case, provided that the totality of the circumstances meets the standard of the necessary reasonable grounds for belief. (*R.* v. *Debot* (1986), 30 C.C.C. (3d) 207 at 218–19)

Madam Justice Wilson, in her judgement in the Supreme Court of Canada in the same case, developed what has become known as the "Triple C" test:

First, was the information predicting the commission of a criminal offence *compelling?* Second, where that information was based on a "tip" originating from a source outside the police, was that source *credible?* Finally, was the information *corroborated* by police investigation prior to making the decision to conduct the search? I do not suggest that each of these factors forms a separate test. Rather, I concur with Martin J.A.'s view that the "totality of the circumstances" must be the standard of reasonableness. Weakness in one area may, to some extent, be compensated by strengths in the other two. (*R.* v. *Debot,* [1989] 2 S.C.R. 1140 at 1168, emphasis added)

The Court here was articulating a line of inquiry directed to the power to search or arrest without warrant. In neither situation can the informant's information, unless corroborated by legally admissible evidence, form the basis for further deprivations of liberty. An arrest without warrant based on information from an undisclosed informant may be lawful, but it cannot justify further detention unless a charge is laid, based on evidence presented to a court in the presence of the accused. The threshold inquiry for prisoners facing deprivation of their institutional liberty on the basis of undisclosed information should be at least as rigorous, requiring undergoing impartial, independent review.

During my research at Kent and Matsqui, it was a frequent refrain at Segregation Review Boards that the basis of the information could not be disclosed because it had been collected by the IPSOs; in due course, those officers would determine how much of the information would be shared. Where a written gist of information was provided, it often lacked the detail necessary for an effective response from the prisoner. During my many discussions with them, the IPSOs at both institutions asserted that their training and experience had taught them to assess the reliability of their sources of information; their work involved corroboration where that was possible and also piecing together information from anonymous "kites," officer observations, interviews with prisoners, intercepted telephone conversations or letters, and police intelligence from the street. They maintained that their operating procedures ensured a prisoner's rights and liberties were not interfered with on the basis of mere rumour or unsubstantiated allegations.

In April 1995 I interviewed Peter Thorpe, the IPSO at William Head and at that time acting IPSO at Kent. We discussed the frequent claim by prisoners that prison informants had personal agendas and that some prisoners were easy targets since their reputations kept them under suspicion. Mr. Thorpe acknowledged that these concerns about the unreliability of informer information were sometimes well founded. For example, a prisoner at Kent had told him that drugs were brought into the institution on particular days by a named prisoner through particular visitors. Mr. Thorpe's check of the records showed that, on the days in question, the named prisoner had had no visitors. A recent case had involved a prisoner transferred from Elbow Lake to Kent after a weapon was found in his room. Based on Mr. Thorpe's discussions with this prisoner (whom he had known at William Head) and on other information he received, he believed the prisoner had been set up. While at Elbow Lake, the prisoner had been lending bales of tobacco to be repaid with interest, and Mr. Thorpe believed those indebted to the prisoner had planted a weapon in his room as a way of avoiding repayment. He also confirmed that some "high profile" prisoners were the subjects of a disproportionate amount of informant information, much of which was not substantiated. He identified Robert Martineau as one such prisoner at Kent.

The clandestine nature of preventive security work and the "deep throat" character of some information-gathering is not only a source of concern to many prisoners, but is viewed with scepticism by some correctional staff. In January 1994, Matsqui Case Management Officer Dave Sinclair described to me the situation surrounding Mr. Baker's proposed transfer to minimum security. A progress summary had been prepared supporting the transfer, but the IPSOs told Mr. Sinclair they had received information that Mr. Baker had brought drugs into the institution after an escorted temporary absence pass in November 1993. Mr. Baker vehemently denied this accusation, and Mr. Sinclair believed it to be inconsistent with his knowledge of the man. Accordingly, he prepared a memorandum to that effect.

> After hearing the IPSOs' information and where they obtained it, this writer's opinion is that there does not appear to be enough credible information to support this accusation.
>
> Mr. Baker currently has an outside grounds clearance and goes to work in the outside warehouse on an almost daily basis. As well, he has been diligent in completing his Correctional Plan. There is no indication from any source that Mr. Baker is involved in the "drug scene" here at Matsqui either as a user or as a dealer. The CMT [Case Management Team] continue to support Mr. Baker's request for

transfer to Ferndale as we do not find there is enough hard evidence of wrongdoing to override the great gains Mr. Baker has made. In our opinion he has earned enough credibility to warrant our continued support. (Memorandum, Dave Sinclair, Matsqui Institution, January 24, 1994)

Without such intervention, the preventive security information would have been highly prejudicial to Mr. Baker's transfer prospects. Given the open nature of minimum security institutions, the wardens there are unlikely to accept prisoners about whom there is IPSO information regarding active drug involvement or muscling.

Mr. Sinclair, as an experienced case management officer, brought to this work several attributes which are increasingly rare within the CSC. He was not afraid to advocate on behalf of a prisoner who had earned the case management team's support; he was therefore not afraid to "butt heads" with correctional staff when he perceived improper interference with a fair and principled decision. He also possessed a degree of scepticism regarding the information gathered by preventive security officers (the "secret squirrels," as he called them); he was therefore not afraid to challenge that information where it contradicted his own opinions, which were based on interaction with and knowledge of prisoners. I saw no other instances at either Matsqui or Kent in which a case management officer provided a written evaluation of why preventive security information was not sufficiently credible to hold up a transfer to lower security.

Dave Sinclair was also critical of the practices of some IPSOs in fostering a network of informants. Many of the prisoners he dealt with had very low self-esteem and a lack of respect not just for others but for themselves. For the CSC to turn them into informants, valuing and rewarding them only for "ratting" on other prisoners, was, in Mr. Sinclair's opinion, subversive of a positive correctional mission.

Earlier in this book, I compared looking at life inside a penitentiary to looking through a kaleidoscope. One prisoner I interviewed used the image of a blurred video picture. Ray Enright had been a professional football player back in the 1970s. A sharp focus and broad peripheral vision were part of his stock in trade, and they proved essential assets for survival in prison. At the time of our interview in September 1993, he had served thirteen years for murder, mostly in the maximum security Edmonton Institution. On his recent transfer to Matsqui, he had been surprised at the pervasiveness of the drug scene, and found it difficult to sort out what was going on. Life at Matsqui, he said, was "like watching a video screen in which the images are blurred so that you're not quite sure of what is happening." This image evokes well the nature of preventive security. When the administration takes decisive action because of a play that has gone down, they in effect freeze the picture, and the people they identify as players are those who happen to be in the frame at the time. In the shadowland of drug dealing, the images are often out of focus, however, even for other prisoners, and there is an inherent danger that the wrong people will be identified.

It is within this highly complex context of covert intelligence gathering that a model of fairness must be fashioned within the prison. In many of the cases I reviewed, the allegations against prisoners were based on "information received from a reliable source." Very rarely were reasons given for finding this information compelling or credible. The present procedures surrounding both segregation and involuntary transfer involve no legally anchored, independent determination of whether information is sufficiently reliable to justify interference with a prisoner's liberty. Independent adjudication would provide a framework for achieving a balance between the claims of confidentiality and fairness; under the present practice, in a contest between the two, it is fairness that almost always suffers defeat.

In several recent high-profile criminal cases, innocent people were found to have been wrongfully convicted on the evidence of "jailhouse informants." The wrongful conviction of Guy Paul Morin was the subject of a Royal Commission conducted by Mr. Justice Kaufman. The resulting report highlighted the extreme dangers of relying on prison informants:

> In-custody informers are almost invariably motivated by self interest. They often have little or no respect for the truth or their testimony or oath or affirmation. Accordingly, they may lie or tell the truth, depending only upon where their perceived self-interest lies. In-custody confessions are often easy to allege and difficult, if not impossible, to disprove. The evidence at this enquiry demonstrates the inherent unreliability of the in-custody informant's testimony, its contribution to miscarriages of justice and the substantial risks that the dangers may not be fully appreciated by the jury. In my view, the present law has developed to the point that a cautionary instruction is virtually mandated in cases where the in-custody informant's testimony is contested. (*Report of the Commission on Proceedings involving Guy Paul Morin* [Toronto: Ontario Ministry of the Attorney General, 1998] [Chairman: Fred Kaufman] at 602, 638)

The Kaufman report recommended a long list of factors to be considered in assessing an informer's reliability. These include the extent to which the statement attributed to the accused is confirmed by independent evidence; whether the alleged statement contains detail that could be known only to the perpetrator; any request the informer has made for special benefits and any promises that have been made; whether the informer has given reliable information to authorities in the past; whether the informer made a written or other record of words attributed to the accused and, if so, whether that record was made contemporaneously with the alleged statement; and the nature of the relationship between the accused and the informer (Kaufman Report at 607–9). The Ontario Ministry of Attorney General has since revised its internal policies to incorporate many of the report's recommendations. New policies include the establishment of an In-Custody Informer Committee, which will review all criminal trials using in-custody informers as witnesses to determine whether this is in the public interest.

Two years after the Kaufman Report, the Supreme Court of Canada addressed the issue of jailhouse informants. In *R. v. Brooks*, Mr. Justice Binnie had this to say:

> "Jailhouse informant" is a term that conveniently catches a number of factors that are highly relevant to the need for caution. These include the facts that the jailhouse informant is already in the power of the state, is looking to better his or her situation in a jailhouse environment where bargaining power is otherwise hard to come by, and will often have a history of criminality. This is not to deny the possibility that a jailhouse can on occasion produce a trustworthy witness. The trigger for caution is not so much the label "jailhouse informant" as it is the extent to which these underlying sources of potential unreliability are present in a particular case. (*R. v. Brooks*, [2000] 1 S.C.R. 237 at para. 129)

In the most recent public inquiry into a wrongful conviction, that of Thomas Sophonow, the retired Supreme Court Justice Peter Cory was far more scathing in his condemnation of the use of jailhouse informants, describing them as "a uniquely evil group" who "should as far as it is possible, be excised and removed from our trial process" (*Report of the Inquiry Regarding Thomas Sophonow* [Winnipeg: Manitoba Department of Justice, 2001] [Chairman: Peter Cory] at 40. Online: <http://www.gov.mb.ca/justice/sophonow/>).

The need for extreme caution in relying on informers is even greater in the correctional context. In a criminal trial, the informer must take the witness stand and is subject to vigorous cross-examination by defence counsel. As the Guy Paul Morin case demonstrates, even this protection may not be enough to challenge the credibility of a well tutored and experienced informant; hence there is a need for special procedures to review the use of an informant and special instructions to the jury in considering the evidence. A prisoner facing segregation or involuntary transfer based on information from an informant is not given an opportunity to cross-examine his accuser; indeed, in most cases the informant's identity remains concealed from the prisoner. Yet there are no special committees evaluating the use of the informant's information nor any process in which the equivalent of a warning to the jury can be given.

While it is the high-profile criminal trials such as Guy Paul Morin's that have become the lightning rod for critical concern, the use of jailhouse informants in criminal proceedings is an exceptional event. The use of such informants in correctional decision-making is commonplace, however, and thus the occasions for possible miscarriage of justice are multiplied. For this reason, independent adjudication of decisions that rely upon such information must be entrenched in correctional law. It is only within such a framework that the scrutiny and caution which accompanies the use of jailhouse informants in a criminal context will be given meaning behind the walls.

## 1999—Streamlining the Transfer Process

In October 1999, significant revisions were made to transfer procedures. The principles articulated in the 1999 version of Commissioner's Directive 540, as implemented in detailed *Standing Operating Practices,* were "to ensure that offenders serve their sentences at the lowest level security necessary to meet their individual program needs and security requirements, to ensure that transfers are carried out in a fair, efficient and secure manner that meets the requirements of both the offender and the institutions involved, and that offender rights are protected" (c.d. 540, para. 1). From an operational standpoint, the most significant change was that the decision-making for intra-regional transfers, whether voluntary, involuntary, or emergency, was given to the warden of the institution initiating the transfer. Prior to 1999, in the case of voluntary intra-regional transfers down the security ladder, the wardens of the receiving institution made the decision; in the case of involuntary transfers up the security ladder, the warden of the sending institution made the recommendation but the Regional Deputy Commissioner had final authority. Under the new procedures, the warden of Kent has the authority to effect a transfer from Kent to lower security, although he or she must consult with the receiving institution before the transfer is implemented. More significantly, the warden of William Head or Matsqui now has the authority to transfer a prisoner to Kent (that is, up the security ladder) without the involvement of the Regional Deputy Commissioner.

This change with regard to voluntary transfers down the security ladder is consistent with the csc's reintegration strategy, to ensure that prisoners are not warehoused in higher security facilities because the wardens of lower security institutions are reluctant to accept them. (Readers will remember that in Donny Oag's case, that reluctance was the principal contributor to his four years in segregation.) In a voluntary transfer to lower security, the prisoner and the correctional authorities at the sending institution have similar interests, and there are no conflicting factual issues to be resolved. The prisoner wants to go to lower security, and the case management team, supported by the warden, believes that lower security is suitable and will further the prisoner's reintegration.

However, the cases I am concerned with in this chapter, involuntary transfers up the security ladder, are altogether different. They typically involve serious conflicts between institutional and prisoner interests and highly disputed factual issues relating to the prisoner's involvement in alleged wrongdoing. Under pre-1999 procedures, a warden seeking an involuntary transfer made a recommendation to the Regional Deputy Commissioner's Office. The process ostensibly provided "a court of sober second thought" by someone removed from the cut and thrust of daily operations. But while there were cases in which involuntary transfers were not approved by regional headquarters, in the great majority of cases the warden's recommendation was confirmed. This is hardly surprising. The task of preparing the regional decision was often assigned to a staff person with a lower rank in the correctional hierarchy than that of the warden, and career advancement argued strongly for deference. Even where the Regional Deputy Commissioner or his delegate became actively involved in the decision-making, there were career-related reasons for extending deference to the warden. There is regular movement at the csc senior management level both between institutions and between institutions and regional headquarters, so that a former warden reviewing a warden's recommendation for involuntary transfer knows full well that the following year their roles may be reversed. As at all levels of the process, professional judgements are inevitably affected by a sense of trust and confidence in a colleague's capacity to make sound correctional decisions. This fact of correctional life is the reason I have argued so strongly for a system of independent adjudication. Yet the 1999 "reforms," far from moving in that direction, remove even the limited protection of the oversight of regional headquarters, allowing the warden to, in effect, legislate his or her own recommendation.

The 1999 changes purport to better protect "offender rights" by requiring that the written notice of an involuntary transfer recommendation contain "enough information to allow the offender to know the case against him."

> To meet this standard, the details of the incident(s) which prompted the transfer recommendation must be provided to the greatest extent possible. This may include providing the offender with the following information regarding the incident(s): where it occurred, when it occurred, against whom it occurred, the extent of injury or damage which resulted, the evidence or proof of its occurrence, and any further relevant information which may elaborate on the incident(s). In cases where sensitive information exists which cannot fully be shared, the offender shall be provided with a gist. (Transfer of Offenders, *Standard Operating Practices*—700-15, October 5, 1999, para. 12; revised February 2, 2001)

This passage must be viewed with a degree of scepticism, however. First, it restates what the Federal Court of Appeal in *Demaria* already requires under the duty to act fairly and s. 7 of the *Canadian Charter of Rights and Freedoms*. Furthermore, the new procedures do nothing to ensure that informant information meets the necessary threshold of reliability. Most significantly, they make no provision for independent review of claims to maintain confidentiality of "sensitive information." A measure of how well the new transfer procedures protect prisoners' rights is a security gist prepared by the preventive security office of William Head Institution in support of an involuntary transfer in July 2000, nine months after the required procedures came into effect.

> The Preventive Security Office at William Head has long believed that Weaver was involved with a lot of the problems within population. He always seems to be involved in situations even though he may be actually removed from the situation physically. Weaver appears to be a puppeteer pulling the strings that cause things to happen. There has been a number of people that have implicated Weaver in their problems, but refuse to name him officially as they are terrified of him. The statement has been made that it is easier to just avoid Weaver than it is to name him and deal with the consequences. Although Weaver has been named unofficially no one will name him so that the information can be used. He is a problematic inmate that has worn thin his time at William Head. His reputation is that if he cannot get you one of his associates will. It is the belief of the Preventive Security Officer that things at William Head would cool down considerably once Weaver is transferred elsewhere. (Memorandum, William Head Institution, July 28, 2000)

Far from providing "enough information to allow the offender to know the case against him," this memorandum is evidence that faceless informers continue to adversely affect the lives of other prisoners. The only difference is that, post-1999, a warden is the final judge of this information's reliability as it affects a decision regarding involuntary transfer. The 1999 reforms, touted as an advance in the protection of prisoners' rights, in fact mark a regression.

## 2001—A Return to Expediency-Based Corrections

Early in 2001, the csc introduced a new policy affecting security classification that resulted in the transfer of prisoners. This initiative illustrates how the politics of law and order can override principles entrenched in the law.

This policy, announced in February 2001, stated that prisoners sentenced to life in prison for murder must serve the first two years of their sentence in a maximum security prison. Furthermore, offenders in this category would have their security classification reviewed only every two years, rather than every year, the policy applied to all other offenders. The policy change was accomplished by a simple mathematical mechanism. The "Custody Rating Scale," a tool which assigns values to the three elements of offender security classification—public safety risk, escape risk, and institutional adjustment—was revised so that a life sentence automatically results in a high public safety rating for a two-year period. The trigger for this new policy appears to have been media accounts of the negative reaction of families of murder victims to the knowledge that some murderers, shortly after their conviction, were sent to medium security institutions. The Solicitor General announced the new policy without consultation with agencies such as the John Howard or Elizabeth Fry Societies, and indeed without the involvement of the Ministry's Secretariat, which normally advises on the implications of major new policy. The rationale given for the policy was as follows:

> Since first and second degree murder are the most serious crimes that can be committed in Canada, and are subject to the most severe penalty in the *Criminal Code*, CSC's policies and procedures must more clearly reinforce this aspect of our criminal justice system. (Policy Bulletin 107, February 23, 2001, amending *Standard Operating Practices—700-14*)

As we have seen, s. 28 of the CCRA requires that "the penitentiary in which [a prisoner] is confined is one that provides the least restrictive environment" having regard to a number of specified factors, including public and personal safety, security of the penitentiary, geographical accessibility, a compatible cultural and linguistic environment, and availability of appropriate programs. The *CCR Regulations*, in setting out the tripartite classification of maximum, medium, and minimum security, require an assessment of the prisoner's probability of escape, the risk to the safety of the public in the event of escape, and the degree of supervision and control required within the penitentiary. Two features of this classification should be noted. First, it is intended to be an assessment of each individual prisoner. Second, the seriousness of the offence and the length of the sentence are not factors specified in the CCRA or the *CCR Regulations;* although they are clearly relevant to making an individual assessment of escape and public safety risks, they are not determinative. Prior to the new policy, many convicted murderers admitted to the penitentiary under a life sentence were assessed as medium security. For instance, a person convicted of the murder of a family member, with no prior criminal convictions, would not be deemed a high risk for escape, a danger to public safety in the event of escape, or a prisoner requiring a high degree of supervision and control. One example would be Robert Latimer, convicted of the murder of his daughter in 1994. Under the new policy, however, such a prisoner is automatically deemed to be maximum security and will serve at least two years in a maximum security facility.

A study done by the CSC after the fact, under pressure from agencies such as the John Howard Society, found that 50 per cent of prisoners considered under the new policy to be maximum security would have been assessed as no more than medium security under previous security assessment criteria.

The John Howard and Elizabeth Fry Societies, along with the Canadian Bar Association, quickly marshalled principled criticisms of the new policy. First, the *CCRA* specifically required the CSC to place an offender in the least restrictive environment, and the *CCRA* and *CCR Regulations* set out the legislative criteria for an individualized assessment. The new policy overrode that legislative principle by seeking to determine, for a whole class of prisoners, a security classification based on the nature of their offence. Second, the CSC's rationale for doing this was to reinforce the denunciatory aspect of the sentence. Yet while denunciation of a crime was a legitimate, legislated objective of the sentencing process, it was not part of the statutory mandate of the CSC under the *CCRA*. Section 3 of that *Act* requires the Service to carry out the sentence imposed by courts in a safe and humane way and to assist in the rehabilitation and reintegration of offenders.

The criticisms also pointed to the particular consequences of the new policy for female, Aboriginal, and young offenders. Because the new facilities built to replace the Prison for Women at Kingston were not deemed suitable as maximum security prisons, women prisoners designated as maximum security were housed in separate ranges in men's prisons, where there was very little freedom of movement and limited access to programs and meaningful employment. For northern Inuit prisoners, the result would be massive cultural dislocation, over and above the experience of their removal from Nunavut. Prior to the new policy, Inuit prisoners convicted of murder served their sentences at Fenbrook, a medium security institution in Ontario, where they had some access to culturally appropriate food and services. To require such prisoners to serve the first two years of a life sentence in maximum security—in cultural and linguistic isolation—was excessively harsh and punitive. For young offenders raised to adult court, and thus required to serve the first two years of their sentence in an adult maximum security prison, the correctional consequences of the new policy were even more damaging. The young offender would be in considerable danger of sexual predation and/or of developing a hard-core attitude towards incarceration. Either prospect was inconsistent with the statutory goals of humane confinement and reintegration.

Several months after the new policy was announced, I participated in an annual consultation meeting between the National Associations Active in

Criminal Justice (NAACJ) and the CSC. The members of the NAACJ expressed their unanimous denunciation of the policy as a violation of the *CCRA*, the Mission Statement, and the CSC's public statements as an organization that practised progressive and principled corrections. A representative from the Psychological Association of Canada challenged the policy as inconsistent with the scientific and research basis for the security assessment process. What was the point of conducting research on risk and needs assessment, he asked, if individual assessments could be overriden by the simplistic classification of prisoners based on their offences? He also questioned how the CSC could maintain the position, reflected in its training materials, that offenders come to prison *as* punishment and not *for* punishment, when it was now saying that one group of prisoners should suffer the particular harsh punishment of maximum security for at least two years.

Graham Stewart, Executive Director of the John Howard Society and one of Canada's most respected voices in criminal justice reform, suggested that the implications of the new policy went far beyond the unjust treatment of prisoners captured by it. The complete disregard it showed for the express provisions of the *CCRA* and the *CCR Regulations* represented a fundamental breach of trust in the CSC's commitment to respect for the Rule of Law. In his view, the policy marked a regression to "expediency-based corrections," in which politics rather than the law determined the CSC's interpretation of its mandate.

Several staff and administrators at Kent had told me that the new policy would not only add to the problems of overcrowding but was blatantly inconsistent with a correctional philosophy which respected the least restrictive alternative principle and emphasized reintegration. The wardens of maximum security facilities had not been consulted on the new policy, and the warden of Kent was hard pressed to explain to his staff how it could be implemented in a manner consistent with the *CCRA*. At the consultation meeting in Ottawa, I suggested the clear message conveyed by the new policy was that, when the Solicitor General was subject to enough political pressure, correctional policy could be changed regardless of the law.

The Arbour Report referred to a pervasive attitude among CSC staff that "even if the law is known, there is a general perception that it can always be departed from for a valid reason, and that, in any event compliance with prisoners' rights is not a priority" (Arbour, at 47). The new policy requiring murderers to serve the first two years of their sentences in maximum security reflected this same attitude; s. 28 of the *CCRA* could be dispensed with in the interests of political expediency. If that attitude was good enough for the Solicitor General, why should CSC line staff believe that adherence to the law was an essential element of the correctional enterprise?

The issues of both the legality and the implications of the two-year policy for "lifers" was the subject of critical comment by the Correctional Investigator in his 2000–2001 annual report. He wrote:

> If this kind of measure can be adopted in such a hasty and unconsidered fashion over such a discreet aspect of the correctional system, what message does this send:
>
> • to the line staff person who has been told, since Arbour, to observe the spirit and the letter of the law in his/her every action, even where this is extremely inconvenient?
>
> • to the inmate who wants to believe that his/her expectations about basic aspects of custody and release will not be suddenly modified for no apparent reason?
>
> • to the community representative whose ability to effect solutions in cooperation with the Service must be based on some reasonable assurance the Rule of Law will not be ignored?
>
> (*Annual Report of the Correctional Investigator, 2000–2001* [Ottawa: Minister of Public Works and Government Services Canada, 2001] at 36–38)

The Correctional Investigator concluded that the new policy was "contrary to the law, unreasonable, and improperly discriminatory to specified offender groups" (at 38).

In answer to the Commissioner's rationale for maintaining the policy as an appropriate reflection of the seriousness of the offence and the sanction imposed, the Correctional Investigator wrote:

> As to the argument that a retributive measure such as this policy is only just and appropriate, I can only say that this argument does not appear to reflect the intentions of Parliament in enacting the CCRA. As well, it just doesn't make sense in the context of a reasonable and coherent approach to corrections. (at 39)

The Correctional Investigator concluded his call for the rescinding of the new policy with this caveat from history:

> We must not forget that when every material improvement has been affected in prisons, when the temperature has been adjusted, when the proper food to maintain health and strength have been given, when the doctors, chaplains and prison visitors have come and gone, the convict stands deprived of everything that a free man calls life. We must not forget that all these improvements, which are sometimes

salves to our consciences, do not change that position. (Winston
Churchill, Speech to the House of Commons, 20 July 1910, cited in
*Annual Report of the Correctional Investigator, 2000–2001* at 39)

Not for the first time, Winston Churchill's oratory has important messages for
upholding freedom and decency at times when these values are most deeply challenged.

## CHAPTER 2

# The Power to Search and the Protection of Privacy

Many prisoners are able to complete their sentences without running afoul of the disciplinary process and to manage their affairs so as to avoid placement in administrative segregation or transfer to higher security. But no prisoner, however well-behaved and compliant with the rules of the institution, can avoid the intrusions into personal privacy that are part of the daily ritual of prison life. On any day, a prisoner can expect to have his cell searched and may have his personal possessions, such as family photographs, posters, and other ornaments, "rearranged" or discarded; he may be physically searched by a scanner or frisked by means of a hand search from head to foot; he may be ordered to submit to a strip search in which he is required to undress completely before staff members, open his mouth for examination, and allow a visual inspection of his genital and anal area. All of his clothing may be searched. He may be asked to provide a sample of urine for urinalysis. Superimposed on this, the prisoner, while in his own cell, is subject to surveillance at any time by staff and may be observed engaging in the most intimate bodily functions.

These intrusions have been appropriately described by sociologists as "status degradation ceremonies," in that their daily repetition reinforces a prisoner's feeling of being less than human. In the context of growing societal concern about the right to privacy in the modern technological world, it is not surprising that prisoners have demanded their privacy no longer be treated as a disposable commodity. From the perspective of a prison administrator, however, the power to search is not an attempt to degrade prisoners but a necessary, indeed indispensable, strategy for maintaining a safe community and ensuring adherence to institutional rules about possession of contraband, particularly weapons and drugs. For a prison administrator, given the realities of the prison environment, the prisoner's right to privacy must be compromised and large and liberal powers of search must be authorized.

## From Untrammelled Discretion to a *Charter*-Driven Regime

Most of the prisoners I spoke to at Kent after the televising of the videotape from the Prison for Women (P4W ) were angered by the treatment visited on their sisters. They were well aware, however, that the humiliation and degradation they too experienced during strip searches did not register on the seismograph of public opinion. The issue of respect for human rights of all prisoners—men and women—engaged by the practice of strip searching, emerged in my study at Kent Institution and became the subject of a further round of intense scrutiny, albeit far less public than that which followed the events at the Prison for Women.

The scant recognition of prisoners' rights under the pre-1992 *Penitentiary Act* is nowhere better reflected than in the total absence of provisions addressing the power to search. It was left to the *Penitentiary Service Regulations* to fill the void; they did so by casting the power in the broadest possible terms, authorizing a staff member to search "any inmate or inmates, where a member considers such action reasonable to detect the presence of contraband or to maintain the good order of the institution" (s. 41(2)(c)).

The Correctional Law Review Working Group, established in 1983, recognized that the open-ended power to search allowed by the *Penitentiary Service Regulations* did not meet the standards and protections the Supreme Court of Canada had established in some of its first decisions on the *Charter of Rights and Freedoms*.

> The Supreme Court of Canada has stated that the purpose of constitutionalizing the right to be secure against unreasonable search or seizure is to protect individuals from unjustified state intrusion upon a reasonable expectation of privacy. In effect, the court has established a minimum privacy threshold to be protected by the *Charter*. According to the Supreme Court of Canada, section 8 protects "persons not places" and the *Charter* then applies where there is a reasonable expectation of privacy, rather than being limited to the more narrow protection of property or privacy interests traditionally associated with a dwelling.
>
> It is clear that while incarcerated a person does not have as great an expectation of privacy as he or she would have in a dwelling house or private office. Nevertheless an inmate retains an expectation of

privacy based on what is reasonable in the circumstances. The test of what is reasonable in the circumstances is not necessarily limited by present penitentiary conditions, under which inmates retain little privacy. Such deprivations of privacy are arguably a "functional pre-requisite to the institutionalizing operation, deriving from the social organization of prisons and not from the legal status of persons found in them" . . .

It should be remembered that today the right to privacy is recognized as fundamental in Canadian society, and protection of privacy is being accorded increased legal safeguards and protections. In line with this approach, every effort should be made to provide an inmate with as much privacy as possible.

A further reason for protecting an inmate's reasonable expectation of privacy relates to the statement of purpose and principles of corrections, which recognize the importance of a safe and healthful environment in encouraging offenders to prepare for successful reintegration into the community. A reasonable expectation of privacy is an element of the kind of institutional environment which is conducive to this goal. Moreover, social scientists studying the escalation of violence in prisons have suggested that dealing with this problem through increases in search and seizure may be counterproductive. Increases in search may lead to increased violence by interfering with whatever amount of privacy an inmate may reasonably expect. Without legal protection, an inmate's rights in this regard may be thoroughly eroded and at the expense, rather than the benefit, of prison security. (CLR Working Paper No. 5 at 65–66)

The Working Group went on to articulate the nature of the *Charter*-driven inquiry required in the context of prison searches:

The issue then is the degree to which the safeguards and protections afforded individuals outside prison must be applied within prisons . . . It is obvious that the state would have a great deal of difficulty in operating a secure prison system if all search and seizure protections of open society, such as a requirement for a search warrant, were to be imposed before every search of an inmate. There is a strong need for the state's conduct in the prison context to be regulated under a different, more flexible standard. (at 68)

That a more flexible standard was constitutionally permissible had already been recognized by the Supreme Court of Canada in relation to the powers of Customs officers to conduct border searches. The Court established that there was a sliding scale of reasonableness which corresponded with the degree of intrusion that particular searches involved. Thus, a routine search of luggage or walking through a scanning device was at one end of the spectrum; a strip search was considerably more intrusive on personal dignity, and at the far end lay a body cavity search. All along the spectrum, the requirements for prior authorization and threshold standards to justify the search must be proportionate to the degree of intrusion. The Working Group's paper recommended adopting this approach for prison searches.

> The sliding scale of reasonableness adopted in the border search cases shows that there exists a "middle ground" between, on the one hand, saddling the government with an unrealistically high standard of proof, such as individualized reasonable grounds to believe, and on the other, allowing officials unfettered discretion to conduct searches. The sliding scale of reasonableness that balances the interests of the state and the individual and that recognizes how these interests change in varying circumstances has been adopted in the proposed procedures for search of inmates. (at 69)

In line with the Working Group's recommendations, the CCRA replaces the extraordinarily broad power to search contained in the pre-1992 regime with carefully structured provisions that distinguish between routine, administrative, and investigative searches and sets out specific criteria for different kinds of searches, depending on the degree of intrusiveness involved. The legislation also lays out procedures for prior authorization for other than routine and administrative searches, requiring that receipts be given when objects are seized and that reports be filled out when more intrusive types of searches are conducted. Section 46 of the CCRA distinguishes between "non-intrusive searches," "frisk searches," "strip searches," "body cavity searches," and "urinalysis"; sections 49 and 53 provide for emergency and exceptional searches. The "prescribed manner" for carrying out the various kinds of searches is covered by the CCR Regulations.

The particular provisions of the legislative regime implicated by events at Kent in 1998 were section 53 of the CCRA and sections 45 and 46 of the CCR Regulations. Section 53 of the CCRA, which deals with exceptional powers of search, provides:

(1) Where the institutional head is satisfied that there are reasonable grounds to believe that
    (a) there exists, because of contraband, a clear and substantial danger to human life or safety or to the security of the penitentiary, and

    (b) a frisk search or strip search of all the inmates in the peni-
        tentiary or any part thereof is necessary in order to seize the
        contraband and avert the danger,

the institutional head may authorize in writing such a search,
subject to subsection (2).

(2) A strip search authorized under subsection (1) shall be conducted
    in each case by a staff member of the same sex as the inmate.

Sections 45 and 46 of the *CCR Regulations* set out the prescribed manner for carrying out strip searches:

    45. A strip search shall consist of a visual inspection of the person by
        a staff member, in the course of which inspection the person
        being searched shall undress completely in front of the staff
        member and may be required to open the person's mouth, dis-
        play the soles of their feet, run their fingers through their hair,
        present open hands and arms, bend over or otherwise enable a
        staff member to perform a visual inspection.

    46. A strip search and a body cavity search shall be carried out in a
        private area that is out of sight of every other person except for
        one staff member of the same sex as the person being searched,
        which staff member is required to be present as a witness unless,
        in the case of a strip search, the search is an emergency as
        described in subsection 49(4) of the *Act.*

## The Strip Searches at Kent

On Thursday, March 19, 1998, the warden of Kent authorized an exceptional search of the institution. The IPSO had received information from a prisoner believed to be reliable that he had recently seen a .22 calibre revolver and ten to twenty rounds of .22 ammunition. The source believed that the weapon and ammunition were in the possession of a protective custody prisoner, but there were plans to sell them to the GP Native Brotherhood, and a down payment of seven points of heroin had already been paid to the PC Brotherhood. The search authorization form recited the provisions of s. 53 of the *CCRA;* and since there were reasonable grounds to believe the weapon and ammunition constituted "a clear and substantial danger to human life or safety or to the security of the penitentiary . . . a strip search of all the inmates in the penitentiary or any part there-of is necessary in order to seize the contraband and avert the danger" (Exceptional Search Authorization Form, Kent Institution, March 19, 1998).

Because it was believed that the weapon and ammunition were still on the PC side, most likely with particular prisoners in F and G units, it was determined that the search would begin there. A decision was made to deploy the Emergency Response Team (ERT) to remove these prisoners from their cells and conduct the strip searches. The previous week, there had been a disturbance in G unit which resulted in lock-down of the PC population. The prisoners in E and F units were locked down without any problems, but one of the G unit prisoners overturned a table and openly incited other prisoners to join him in resisting the staff. The "insurrection" was resolved through negotiations, but the prisoners in G unit had advised the administration that the next time they wanted to lock down the unit, they had better come "with all of their friends." In light of that, the use of the ERT was deemed appropriate. Because the team would already be suited up, it was decided they should extract and search the targeted prisoners from F unit as well.

ERT leader Officer Mark Noon-Ward was called into the institution along with other members of the team. He was briefed by the warden and the co-ordinator of correctional operations. All prisoners housed in G unit and two targeted prisoners from F unit were to be extracted, strip-searched, and escorted to K unit. In accordance with ERT procedures, Officer Noon-Ward drew up an operational plan. He requested that, in addition to team members wearing bulletproof vests, the teams for both F and G units be armed with a rifle in case they confronted a prisoner with a loaded gun. The warden rejected this on the grounds that there was an armed officer in the control bubble on the units. Other elements of the plan were that each prisoner was to be strip-searched, given coveralls, and scanned with a metal detector, and that each cell was to be searched by hand-picked staff after the ERT was clear. There was no specific discussion during the briefing session about the method of strip searching, and it was Officer Noon-Ward's understanding that this would be done in accordance with normal ERT procedures.

Officer Noon-Ward then briefed members of the ERT. The briefing was video-taped, as would be the rest of the operation. Officer Noon-Ward reiterated the grounds for the operation—it was believed there was a weapon and ammunition in the institution. Two separate teams would be deployed, each consisting of six members. Each prisoner would be instructed to strip in his cell prior to the cell door being opened. He would then be instructed to place his hands behind his back to be handcuffed. He would be escorted to the common area at the end of the tier, where a thorough search would be conducted using a hand-held metal scanner. Once the team was satisfied the prisoner was not in possession of any unauthorized items, he would be placed in coveralls, handcuffed again, and escorted to the entrance of the unit by the team, then turned over to other staff for escort to K unit. One team member would be equipped with a gas launcher and other designated officers would carry a distraction device to use in the event that the team encountered a serious threat. (These devices, when detonated, make a very loud noise and are intended to distract anyone in close proximity, allowing team members to move in and "take down" a prisoner.) The team members were advised that if they heard the word "gun," they were to move quickly away from the cell doors so that the distraction devices could be deployed. Officer Noon-Ward, in reviewing strip-search procedures, stated that prisoners would be asked to lift their "nut sacks." This colloquialism was not used in a salacious or flippant way and elicited no inappropriate response from team members. Officer Noon-Ward also emphasized that team members marching in formation across the courtyard to the units were to bang their shields loudly.

In a later interview, Mr. Noon-Ward explained the reason for the latter procedure. It sends a clear signal to prisoners that the team is on its way and is intended to intimidate them into compliance with the team's instructions, thereby minimizing the need for resorting to force; it also reinforces the concept of members working as a team and allows a measured release of adrenaline so that there is no build-up of tension that may result in precipitate action.

The cell extractions and strip searches began in F unit with Mr. Garnell. The videotape shows Mr. Garnell taking off his clothes in his cell, as ordered, then being placed in handcuffs behind his back and led, facing backwards, by the team to the common area. Though the prisoner is naked, the video shows him only from the waist up. This is standard operating procedure for videotaping strip searches and is done to protect the prisoner's dignity in the event that the tape is viewed by others. In the common area, Mr. Garnell was surrounded by ten officers: team members, an officer designated as the "scribe" to document the team's activities, and a correctional supervisor, Mr. Cole. He was also under observation by the officer in the control bubble. Mr. Garnell was searched with a metal wand detector and was then asked to open his mouth, run his fingers through his hair and lift his scrotum. According to Officer Noon-Ward's plan, after the strip search a prisoner was to receive a set of clean coveralls. However, during the first searches the coveralls had not yet been delivered, so Mr. Garnell stood naked while his clothes were retrieved from his cell and carefully inspected by a staff member. He was then given his shorts and shirt, taken to the door of the unit and escorted by other staff to K unit. The time that Mr. Garnell stood naked in front of staff was about seven minutes. (Once the coveralls arrived, this time was reduced to between three and four minutes.) At no time were disparaging comments made to Mr. Garnell; Officer Noon-Ward's firm instructions on several occasions were coupled with the word "please" and Mr. Garnell was fully co-operative in the procedure. The cell extractions and strip searches of the rest of the prisoners also took place without incident. The extractions began at 10:20 p.m., and by 11:00 p.m. all twenty-six prisoners from F and G units had been removed by the two teams to K unit. The gun and ammunition were not found.

The next day, Friday, March 20, the strip-search operation for the rest of the

PC population continued. This time, the searches were carried out by regular line staff under the direction of correctional supervisors. Because the ERT operation had proceeded so smoothly, the correctional supervisor in charge of the search, Officer Cole, determined that the same procedures should be followed, with one important modification: as a range was searched, two officers would be assigned to stand in front of each cell to ensure that prisoners did not dispose of items while other prisoners were being searched. This modification meant that prisoners being escorted naked down the range to the common area walked past other correctional officers. By the end of the weekend, all PC prisoners had been strip-searched without discovery of the gun or ammunition. However, some other weapons, drugs, and drug paraphernalia were recovered.

On Monday, March 23, the search moved to the GP ranges. In B unit, for the first time the staff encountered a challenge to their procedures from prisoner Greg Hanson, a challenge that would lead to both an internal grievance and a lawsuit. In a later interview, Mr. Hanson (one of the prisoners also segregated at Matsqui in Operation Big Scoop) gave me this account of his experience with the strip search:

> On Thursday night [March 19] we were locked down. The adminis-tration worked really well to start with, using a new process we had negotiated in which they issue a written communiqué why we are locked down. That written communiqué was slipped under our doors and said that they were looking for dangerous contraband. So right away we know that they are looking for a gun or a bomb and we knew that this was going to be a long lock-down. So we hunkered in. On Friday they came back with another communiqué that we were going to be allowed out for showers, six prisoners at a time. So we were getting the feeling that this may be an emergency but it's not one of gargantuan proportions. On Saturday we were allowed out of our cells, and Sunday we were allowed out twelve at a time to go to the common room, so again it does not seem to be that big of an emergency.
>
> On Monday morning my door cracks at eight o'clock. I've got four guards standing in my doorway. Mr. Nelson told me that there was a search of the institution to locate contraband and told me to strip down, balls-naked, and to walk down the hallway to the com-mon area with my clothes in my hand. I said, "Ain't happening, boys." I don't even know that once I step out of the cell, there's a gauntlet of twenty guards lined up down the hall that I'm about to walk through. But while I don't know this, I do know enough about the law to know that a strip search has to be conducted by two staff members in a private area, no female staff allowed, etc. And what

they are asking me to do is completely against the law. But I've got four staff standing in my doorway who were physically able to cause me some pretty good grief, so I asked them to call down the keeper. Correctional Supervisor Kevin Cole came down and repeated the order and said, "Listen, Greg, it has to happen this way." I said, "This is bullshit, Kevin, this is against the CCRA. Who ordered this? Are there any women out there?" I'm asking these questions because I'm scrambling to try and find a reason to not to have to go through this embarrassing indignity. Now I'm really raging and all the blood's now in my muscles, my brain, and I'm pumping and I'm naked. I'm embarrassed, and it was a really humiliating thing to have to go through even having these four guys in my doorway. Now I pick up my clothes and I step into the hallway and there is literally a gauntlet lined up along the right side of the wall of about twenty staff, all looking at me in my total state of nakedness and embarrassment. And I know this is illegal, smacks of P4W all over again. I was so mad all I wanted to do was kill and, having killed before, I know that feeling. It was an over-the-top feeling of rage, where you've made the decision that this person is about to die, damn the consequences. Now that's right-brain thinking. My left brain was going, "Greg, shut up. You've worked so hard for four years to get where you are, don't give it up, don't give it to them. You punch them out, you're giving in. They know how to deal with that and now you're going them a reason to deal with you in that way." But I couldn't shut up. As I was walking along I was swearing and I don't usually swear. But I was so mad, I was breathing threats.

After I passed the line of officers and I was in the common area, there were eight staff members all standing there looking at me. I see another prisoner come down the gauntlet on the other side of the tier and he's covering his private parts and trying to be discreet. It looks like they're herding us like cattle. One of the staff members says, "Over here, drop your clothes." He waves the scanner over my body and down around my private area. Then he starts searching my clothes. He picks up one shoe and I shout, "Listen, do my underwear," and I threw them right in his face and now he's really angry and I'm really raging. The keeper says, "Calm down, calm down, everybody." He's trying to keep the situation under control. The officer then did my underwear and I put them on. I was given back my clothes and told to proceed to the gymnasium and outside yard. When I got outside it was cold and it was raining, but I was so hot that I didn't even feel the rain. I was so mad I hadn't even grabbed warm clothing, and I was just in my shorts and a pair of shoes. As I walked to the gymnasium, I was so angry I drove the window of the door opposite the gym with all I had and I didn't even feel it. I was so angry I couldn't talk any more. I went outside in the yard and there was a big blue garbage can that's like half a barrel, weighs about thirty pounds, and I kicked it all the way around a half-a-mile field. I felt total, uncontrollable hatred for them, and this is something that I have really worked hard over the past four years to try and control. I didn't do a very good job of it that day. But I didn't fight that day, because of the dignity that I raised in myself in the past four years. I have learned how to deal with things not in a violent manner. Is that my left brain thinking? I don't know. But it took over and I didn't embarrass myself that day. (Interview with Greg Hanson, Kent Institution, April 14, 1998)

Mr. Hanson filed a grievance and then a lawsuit (today still in the pre-trial process) in which he sued for damages for the "humiliating, degrading, illegal and immoral" treatment involved in the strip search. A month earlier, there had been an announcement by the Solicitor General that each of the women who had been illegally searched and segregated at the Prison for Women would be receiving $50,000. Many of the staff at Kent believed that Mr. Hanson's lawsuit was an attempt to get a similar settlement for himself and doubted his professed feelings of degradation and humiliation. Based on our interview, I had no doubt about the depth of his feelings. However, he had also explained to me a larger reason for the lawsuit.

This is why I have to do this. We live in a country governed by the Rule of Law. I have been encouraged to participate in a society governed by the Rule of Law. I have to win this by law. If I don't, there will be a tremendous feeling inside of me that this is all bullshit. I already have that feeling. I grew up with that feeling. I never did believe in the law, in the government, or in state-sponsored sanctions. I always thought it was bullshit. I'm trying to convince myself now that the law is a means to an end. The end being a happier life. I have to convince myself by the Rule of Law. Someone, somewhere has to say that this was wrong. Someone in authority has to say that this was wrong. I'll accept that. Internally I'll accept that. I'm paying the price for my breaches of the law, somebody has to, to build up my confidence in the system.

Because this is how it works in my world: you screw me like that, I put you in a trunk and sink the car. I don't want to live like that any more. But believe me, that solved the problem before. Nobody ever screwed me around again. I have to assure myself that the law is at least as powerful, that no one will ever screw with me in that manner again. That's why it's so important.

In an interview with Unit Manager Mike Csoka, I learned that Officer Cole had consulted him following Mr. Hanson's objections that the manner of the strip search was in violation of the CCRA. Mr. Csoka was not able to cite chapter and verse of the *Act*, but he knew intuitively that parading naked prisoners down the range was not permitted. He therefore instructed Officer Cole to change the procedures so that prisoners were brought out of their cells with their shorts on, taken to the common area and then subjected to the strip search. He instructed one of his staff to review the provisions of the CCRA regarding the conduct of strip searches and, having satisfied himself that there had been unintended violations of the law, he issued Officer Cole a verbal reprimand.

The warden of Kent, Brenda Marshall, had been unaware of the manner in which the strip searches in the GP units were being conducted, and she had not realized that prisoners would be required to walk naked from their cells to the common area. She ordered an internal investigation, which confirmed that there had been violations of the CCRA. In upholding Mr. Hanson's grievance, she wrote:

> You are correct in stating that the strip search procedures used on March 23, 1998, were in contravention of both the law and policies. It is unfortunate that the Acting Correctional Supervisor determined the potential for a weapon and ammunition in the institution to be serious enough to take the drastic measure of having you strip in the cell and then searched in the presence of other staff before permitting you to dress.
>
> We have taken measures to ensure this type of strip search is not conducted in similar circumstances in the future. The Acting Supervisor and other staff involved have been dealt with, however any actions taken cannot be shared with you, as that would be a violation of the Privacy Act. I can assure you this situation will not happen in this manner again. As Warden of Kent Institution, and on behalf of the staff involved, apologies are offered for the affront to your personal dignity.
>
> We have conducted an investigation and taken appropriate measures with staff as requested in your grievance. This grievance is upheld. (Grievance Response from the Warden, Kent Institution, June 23, 1998)

The warden's response afforded a measure of vindication for Mr. Hanson, but the blame she placed on the shoulders of Acting Correctional Supervisor Cole was not well received by Kent staff. In their view, Officer Cole had been following the procedures adopted by the ERT, and it was therefore unfair to suggest that he had made the determination as to how the strip search would be carried out. Staff felt that if a mistake had been made and a breach of the law had occurred, the responsibility should be assumed by the warden herself.

The repercussions of the March emergency strip search were more far-reaching than the rumblings of staff at the warden's response to Mr. Hanson's grievance. The filing of the internal investigation and the subsequent filing of Mr. Hanson's lawsuit triggered anxious reviews at both the Regional Headquarters and the Commissioner's Office in Ottawa. The accounts and videos of prisoners being paraded naked down the corridors of a maximum security institution sent off fears of another "Arbour," with the CSC again being pilloried for its inability to comply with the law. The warden of Kent and the Regional Deputy Commissioner were summoned to Edmonton on August 21, 1998, to meet with the Commissioner and the Senior Deputy Commissioner. From all accounts, the Commissioner expressed his extreme displeasure at what had transpired at Kent and, in particular, that it had taken so long for the matter to be reported to him. Upon Warden Marshall's return, rumours flew that there would be an inquiry conducted either by the Correctional Investigator or by the CSC's National Investigation Team; there was also talk of staff being subject to disciplinary hearings.

On August 31, Warden Marshall advised Officer Noon-Ward that he was being suspended as ERT leader. According to Officer Noon-Ward and others at the meeting, the warden said she had lost confidence in his abilities as an ERT leader, that on the night of March 19 he had showed fear, and that he did not display the values and attitudes of the modern CSC.

Mr. Noon-Ward contacted me following this meeting. He knew that I held him in high regard as an officer, and he was upset about his demotion from "hero to heel." He asked whether I could represent him in a grievance he had filed regarding his suspension, as well as advise him should he be called to answer questions by a national inquiry. I gave him the same answer I had given a number of prisoners, including Mr. Hanson in relation to his lawsuit: it was not appropriate for me to represent either staff or prisoners in a dispute with the administration while I was conducting my research. However, I said I was prepared to talk to the warden and other senior managers to get a better understanding of the dynamics behind his suspension; furthermore, in the event of an investigation, I would make available copies of my favourable observations on Mr. Noon-Ward's performance in the line of duty. Within days of Mr. Noon-Ward's suspension, it was confirmed that a national investigation team would come to Kent, headed by the Assistant Commissioner for Performance Assurance.

On my next visit to Kent, I spoke with Unit Managers Mike Csoka and Kevin Morgan, both of whom had been at the warden's briefing on March 19 in which

Mark Noon-Ward received the mandate to deploy the ERT. I spoke to Deputy Warden Doug Richmond and to Correctional Supervisor Mackie, who had been at the meeting in which Mr. Noon-Ward was handed his suspension. I also met with several members of the ERT. Finally, I spoke with the warden herself.

The unit managers who had been at the March 19 briefing were astonished that the warden would later have faulted Mr. Noon-Ward for having displayed fear. Not only was Mr. Noon-Ward universally recognized as one of the most fearless officers at Kent, but his suggestion on the night of March 19 that the ERT be permitted to have firearms was prompted by legitimate caution, given that there were reasonable grounds to believe that a prisoner might be in possession of a loaded gun. What Mr. Noon-Ward had displayed that evening was a concern for the safety of team members. If he could be faulted, it was not because he had displayed fear but because he had challenged the warden's judgement; his final comments when informed that the team would not be armed were, "If anything happens to one of my men, it will be on your head." After the completion of the operation, Mr. Noon-Ward had apologized to the warden for these comments and she had accepted that apology, saying that she appreciated staff speaking their minds. The unit managers' assumption was that the warden's meeting with the Commissioner and Senior Deputy Commissioner had precipitated Mr. Noon-Ward's suspension. They now found themselves in the invidious position in which, as unit managers, they could not be seen as undermining the warden's decision by showing support and confidence in Mr. Noon-Ward's abilities but, privately, they did not believe that the warden's actions were justifiable.

Mr. Noon-Ward pushed for an early hearing of his grievance. The date was finally set for late November, but on the morning of the hearing he was advised by the warden that, effective immediately, he would be reinstated as ERT leader.

## Balancing Prisoners' Dignity and Staff Safety

The events stemming from the March exceptional search—the Hanson grievance and lawsuit, the suspension of the ERT leader, and the national investigation—generated a great deal of discussion both at Kent and in Ottawa on the legality of the search procedures. There was no issue as to the lawful justification for conducting the search; there can hardly be more compelling grounds than a reasonably grounded belief that a gun and ammunition are in the possession of prisoners in a maximum security institution. Neither were there procedural irregularities in the advance written authorization or the post-search report sent to Regional Headquarters. The issue was whether the strip search had been carried out in conformity with the law and with the policy expressed in the Commissioner's Directive that "searches shall always be conducted with due regard for privacy and for the dignity of the individual being searched" (C.D. 571, January 24, 1997, para. 4, replaced by C.D. 566–67, October 17, 2001, para. 2).

The case made by the unit managers was that s. 46 of the *CCR Regulations*, while providing that a strip search "shall be carried out in a private area that is out of sight of every other person except for one staff member of the same sex as the person being searched," specifically provides for an exception where "in the case of a strip search, the search is an emergency." The situation in March was such an emergency, and the exceptional measures taken could therefore be justified. Mark Noon-Ward forcibly made the point that if the RCMP or another police ERT were required to conduct strip searches of suspects where it was believed one might have a loaded firearm, they would ridicule the suggestion that the search team consist of no more than two persons. Indeed, a police ERT would ridicule the idea that they go into such a situation without weapons. For only two officers to conduct a strip search of a prisoner who might have a gun on his person or within close reach would seriously compromise the safety of staff. Surely, said Officer Noon-Ward, in a case where there was a conflict between protecting the safety of staff and preserving the privacy and dignity of prisoners, the *CCRA* would support preference being given to staff safety. This is not an argument lightly dismissed. Each member of the six-person ERT was assigned specific responsibilities. Conducting the strip search in each prisoner's cell was problematic both because there was not enough room for all team members and because the metal in the door frames would not permit the effective operation of the metal scanner. Having the prisoner proceed naked to the common area not only enabled the ERT to assume full control of the situation but, by virtue of the proximity of the armed officer in the control bubble, ensured maximum protection for staff if the prisoner offered resistance.

What this argument does not consider, however, is whether less restrictive measures could have been taken to allow the physical presence of more than two officers while restricting the sight of the naked prisoner being searched to no more than two officers. In fact, provision for such a procedure had been made almost a decade earlier. In 1987, following a large influx of female correctional officers, a privacy screen had been installed in all units at Kent. This consisted of a floor-to-ceiling curtain that could be moved into place along a track; the bottom four feet of the curtain were opaque and the top was transparent. Prior to a prisoner being required to strip, the screen could be moved into place. However, before March 1998 the screens had never been used. Prisoners brought into the segregation unit, for example, were required to strip in the open area adjacent to the control bubble in the presence of at least three and often many more officers.

Following the events of March 1998, strip searches in the segregation unit were conducted using the privacy screen. Two staff members conducted the strip search and others stood behind the screen, ready to intervene if there were any problems. This procedure could easily have been adapted for the emergency searches by the ERT in F and G units. In other words, the legitimate concerns Mr. Noon-Ward expressed for the protection of staff could have been respected, while also protecting the dignity of the prisoners, through less intrusive and restrictive measures.

## The Case for Legal Training

During the Task Force on Administrative Segregation's visits to Mission Institution in 1996, Warden Ken Peterson had commented: "CSC has done a good job of giving its staff ongoing training in the use of firearms but has neglected training them in the use of the law, even though it is the law and not guns that they draw upon the most." "CSC and the Law" training sessions have since been introduced, but the analogy drawn by Warden Peterson is still useful. Correctional staff need more than a knowledge of what the search provisions of the *CCRA* and *CCR Regulations* specify. Staff must gain an appreciation of how correctional law evolved as part of an endeavour to reflect *Charter* values and, in the case of search provisions, to achieve a principled balance between privacy, dignity, safety, and security. Many staff still believe the *CCRA* operates as a set of legal handcuffs on correctional operations. Consequently, as with any other kind of handcuffs, there is great incentive to try to wriggle out of them when they cut too tight. Well-conceived and well-executed legal training would have little difficulty demonstrating that the legislation is not there to handcuff staff or to place correctional decision-making in a straitjacket; it is to ensure that the experience of justice which sustains democracy outside of prison is not abandoned when the keeper and the kept encounter each other inside.

## Enforcing the "Bend Over" Rule

Although the *CCR Regulations* specifically provide that in the course of a strip search a prisoner "may be required to . . . bend over or otherwise enable a staff member to perform a visual inspection," it had not been the practice to make this demand of prisoners at Kent. Even the strip searches conducted in March 1998 by the ERT did not involve this procedure. However, following the filing of Greg Hanson's grievance and subsequent lawsuit, prisoners were increasingly asked to bend over as part of a strip search. Mr. Hanson had this demand made of him when he came out of the visiting area following an open visit. Although he did strip and comply with all other aspects of the search, he refused to bend over and so was charged with the minor disciplinary offence of refusing a direct order. Prisoners who complained about the procedure were told that they had Mr. Hanson to thank for the staff now applying strip-search requirements "to the letter of the law." From the prisoners' perspective, this was a clear message that challenging the administration involved some pay-back. The full measure of that pay-back became clear in October 1998.

On Monday, October 17, the warden of Kent authorized an exceptional search involving a strip search of all GP prisoners together with a search of their cells. The order came following a series of drug overdoses, the seizure of several containers of home brew, and staff observations of a number of prisoners being under the influence of drugs or alcohol. The search procedures adopted in October were modified to bring them into conformity with s. 46 of the CCR *Regulations*. Prisoners were required to strip and be searched in their cells, under the observation of two officers; they were then allowed to dress and were taken to the common room while their cells were searched. The strip-search procedure included a requirement that the prisoner bend over to permit a visual inspection of his rectum.

The search commenced in A unit. Officers completed the strip and cell searches of three ranges and began procedures on the fourth. Five of the six prisoners there complied with the strip-search procedures and were placed in the common room. The sixth prisoner, Jason Gallant, complied fully with the procedure until asked to bend over and touch his toes. He refused to do so. Officer Laurie, the officer supervising the search, showed Mr. Gallant a copy of the section of the CCR *Regulations* authorizing officers to make this demand. Mr. Gallant read the document, handed it back and stated, "Yeah, well, it doesn't make it right." He was advised that if he refused to comply, the officer would have to suspend the search of A unit. Mr. Gallant held firm. Officer Laurie then told the prisoners in the common room that the search was being suspended and they were placed back in their cells without those cells having been searched. Mr. Gallant requested that Officer Laurie move him to segregation so that his protest would not operate to the prejudice of other prisoners. Officer Laurie declined, on the basis that he did not feel Mr. Gallant presented a risk to staff, the institution, or himself. The general search continued over the weekend without incident until officers reached the cell of Darryl Bates in D unit. Mr. Bates also declined to bend over. He too was shown a copy of the CCR *Regulations;* he responded that this procedure had never been part of the strip-search routine at Kent.

On October 19, three staff members arrived at Mr. Gallant's cell in A unit and advised him that he was going to segregation. He was not given any reason. Mr. Gallant was then handcuffed and escorted to J unit. Upon arrival, he was taken to the common area next to the control bubble, where he was asked to submit to the routine strip search required of all prisoners on admission to segregation. As he entered the common area, Mr. Gallant observed that a six-member squad of the ERT was standing fully suited behind the privacy curtain. The prisoner was placed behind the curtain in the presence of two officers. He was asked to strip; he complied. He was asked to open his mouth and extend his arms; he complied. He was told to run his fingers through his hair; he complied. He was asked to turn around and show the balls of his feet; he complied. He was asked to bend over; he refused. He was then asked whether this was going "to be the easy way or the hard way." He responded, "Let's try the hard way." At that point the correctional supervisor overseeing the search motioned to the ERT squad; the privacy curtain was lowered and the squad immediately moved towards Mr. Gallant and took him to the ground. He was handcuffed behind his back and his legs were forcibly pried apart. The videotape of the procedure did not show Mr. Gallant offering any resistance to the officers either physically or verbally. A member of the ERT holding Mr. Gallant to the ground is heard asking an ERT member kneeling between Mr. Gallant's legs, "Do you have a good visual?" "I am satisfied with the visual," the officer responded. Mr. Gallant was then allowed to get up. He was placed in a segregation cell and the handcuffs were removed.

Following the segregation and search of Mr. Gallant, the same three staff members went to Mr. Bates' cell and advised him that he was going to segregation. Mr. Bates was told this was because of his non-compliance with the search the day before. Once in the segregation unit, Mr. Bates was placed behind the privacy curtain and asked to strip. He complied with every demand until he was asked to bend over. At that point he refused and pulled his underwear back on. Again the correctional supervisor motioned to the ERT squad, who immediately overpowered Mr. Bates and took him to the ground. The videotape, in the brief seconds before the ERT's swarming of Mr. Bates, showed Mr. Bates facing towards them with a look of disbelief on his face. As Mr. Bates lay on the ground, he was handcuffed behind his back. One of the ERT officers then cut off his underwear and his legs were pried apart to permit a visual inspection. The videotape also showed that a metal detector was passed over Mr. Bates' buttocks. During this procedure, Mr. Bates was heard shouting at the officers, "You fucking skin hounds." He was obviously enraged, although he did not strike out against any officer. After Mr. Bates was assisted to his feet, the videotape clearly showed his features contorted with anger. There was blood on his face from a cut caused by contact with an ERT officer's shield. Mr. Bates was placed in a segregation cell and his handcuffs were removed.

Both Mr. Gallant and Mr. Bates were kept in segregation until their five-day review and then released. Shortly thereafter, Mr. Gallant filed a complaint, the first step in the grievance procedure. The text set out why he and other prisoners considered the "bend over" rule to be so deeply offensive.

> Until some lawsuits were brought against Kent, arising from the strip searches that took place here last March, the general practice at Kent Institution when conducting strip searches was not to require prisoners to bend over, whatever might be written down in the CCRA. Clearly correctional supervisors and other staff members conducting searches did not believe that requiring prisoners to bend over so that staff could look up their asses was a necessary aspect (legal or otherwise) of skinning down the incarcerated. It would therefore appear

that this added humiliation . . . is intended to send a signal that CSC will not tolerate challenges to their power and authority over the prison population. This practice is calculated—if not by intent, then certainly by consequence—to humiliate, degrade, demean and dehumanize prisoners. Skin searches carried out in this manner are calculated to deny and to desensitize a captive population to its basic humanity and thus to "bend" both literally and symbolically to correctional authority's need to dominate and control . . .

When I was taken to segregation, I was again asked to submit to a strip search. I complied by removing my clothes but refused to bend over. The notice states "force was used to complete the search. You physically resisted staff while they conducted the search." This last allegation is unfounded. The Emergency Response Team descended upon me, forced me to the ground and forcibly spread my legs. I did not so much as raise a hand . . . I merely did not comply with the command that I bend over. The video will show that I offered no assaultive or resistant behaviour . . .

Since the "take down" I have been suffering from considerable neck and back pain and cannot maintain my spine in an upright position. What I need is access to a physiotherapist or a specialist of comparable skills to determine the extent of my neck injury and to ensure proper treatment.

Corrective Action Requested
1. That there be a National Review or Investigation of the need for prisoners to "bend over" and spread their ass cheeks, in light of the Mission Statement Core Value 1 that "we respect the dignity of individuals, the rights of all members of society and the potential for human growth and development" and in light of the Universal Declaration of Human Rights and other international covenants to which Canada is a signatory. I believe this review is particularly appropriate in light of the fact that 1998 is the 50th anniversary of the Universal Declaration and that CSC has now accepted the Yalden Report of the Working Group on Human Rights.
2. That I be permitted to see a physiotherapist or a specialist of comparable skills for the neck injury.
3. That I be permitted to pack my cell effects and be returned to segregation but without the need to comply with the bend over command.

The explanation for this third request is that in segregation, the prisoner understands that he has no privileges and there is nothing to lose because quite simply he has nothing. In segregation it is understood that a prisoner is less than a human being and can therefore be locked up twenty-three hours a day in a cage. In general population, even in maximum security, there is a semblance of humanity, some rights and privileges and some respect for human dignity. However, if while in general population I must live with the ever present threat that, upon demand, I will bend over and, if I refuse, will be taken to segregation each time and violence will be done to me so that my legs can be pried apart and a guard can look up my rectum, I would prefer that I be placed in segregation where there is no pretence for respect for human rights. At least then I will have no sense of loss. (Complaint filed by Jason Gallant, Kent Institution, October 26, 1998)

## The Values of a "Barbarian Prince"

During the course of my work at Kent, I spent many hours with Jason Gallant, tracing his long and tumultuous career as a prisoner. He began his first life sentence in 1977, following his conviction for a killing that took place in a bar in British Columbia. In 1982, following a riot at Archambault in which three officers died, he pleaded guilty to three counts of first-degree murder. He spent three years in the Special Handling Unit. Following that he was at Kent until 1988, when he was readmitted to the SHU following an allegation of involvement in extorting funds from prisoners and their families. After five years there he was transferred back to Kent in 1993 and had been there ever since, apart from a four-month stay at Matsqui in 1996–97. He was one of the "barbarian princes" referred to in the 1988 judgement of Mr. Justice Muldoon. In one of my early interviews with Mr. Gallant, I asked whether the judge's comments were a fair characterization of his values and orientation to life in prison. That question became a trigger for a wide-ranging discussion of his experiences.

The unofficial punishment inflicted upon Mr. Gallant in the aftermath of his conviction for the murder of three prison guards was etched deep in his body and psyche. He had pleaded guilty to those murders; however, it was generally accepted in the prison population that he was not the perpetrator but had agreed to accept responsibility for the killings to save another prisoner from the fate to which he was already assigned—twenty-five years before parole eligibility. That interpretation was not shared by prison guards, however, and Mr. Gallant described to me the painful retribution he had suffered over and above his lawfully imposed sentence: how correctional officers had come into his cell and beaten him; how he had been scalded with hot water and hit so hard with a billy club that his intestine was driven up to his diaphragm, perforating it and causing a reversal in his digestive process, with the result that he was bringing up his bodily wastes. He also described how he was made to feel the guards' hatred and contempt.

> I don't know what the hell they did to me but I see these red bikini briefs and urine in my face and I can hear it. My mouth's open, I can't close it. When I was in the shower and they were fire-hosing me, they'd throw some type of bleach, Javex bleach, on me. So when they were doing what they were doing to me, I could hear the powder fizzing in my hair.
>
> It was during this time that my eyes were open to a depth of hatred, and I know hatred. I'm well acquainted with the bitch because I've lived on it. You can live on it like food. Because of the torture trips I went through I had difficulty allowing anyone to come near to me. I could not bear anyone's touch. Because of what went down, I cannot sit down with a guard and discuss my private life, my history, and open up and reveal confidences, which is required in this new way of doing things in programs. (Interviews with Jason Gallant, Kent Institution, February–May 1994)

Because Mr. Gallant had been brought up by foster parents who were deeply religious, he was able to relate this period in his life to some scriptural teachings.

> The scriptures tell us to stand diligently at the door of your heart; that out of it comes the issues of life. From the time that these incidents happened until the time that I was able to forgive, I didn't guard diligently at the door to my heart because a lot of bad stuff got in and it was watered with my hatred. I have struggled to allow that to flow out of me.

That struggle was intensified in the context of the Special Handling Unit.

> It was the mindless compliance to something I believe violates a person's right to control their own lives. Every time you leave your cell there is the handcuffs, the pat-down searches. Even in your own cell there is no place to hide because every two or three days they come down and they strip search you, take your clothes off, put you in handcuffs again or put you in that little interview booth and then go through your cell. There's a constant sense of bombardment. A lot of guys can't handle the pain any more so they comply, and after a while they don't need to be told anything. It just becomes routine and they

put their hands up, down, out, in, whatever is required. They
become conditioned to it. I could not let myself do that. I said,
"Somebody's got to stand up and say this is wrong." I did it head on
by resisting.

The intrusion of unwanted hands and what it symbolized were things Jason
Gallant still struggled with at Kent.

I go to a social and they're skinning me down afterwards and asking
me, "Did you have a nice social?" The social was pleasant enough,
but I'm standing in front of them, naked, and I'm expected to relate
to them like they care about how I feel. They're trying to be civil and
I have a hard time relating to that. I could if I believed they cared,
but I don't believe that. So I say to them, "You're trying to bust me,
I'm standing here before you naked and you want social interaction?
Give your fucking head a shake."

Jason Gallant had never read Dostoyevsky's *House of the Dead*, based on the
Russian novelist's experiences in a Siberian labour camp in the 1840s. Dostoyevsky
wrote:

Everyone, whoever he is and however lowly the circumstances into
which he has been pushed, demands, albeit instinctively and unconsciously, that respect be shown for his human dignity. The convict
knows he is a convict, an outcast, and he knows his place *vis-à-vis* his
superior officer; but no brands, no fetters will ever be able to make
him forget that he is a human being. And since he really is a human
being, it is necessary to treat him as one. (Fyodor Dostoyevsky, *The
House of the Dead*, trans. David McDuff [London: Penguin, 1985]
at 145)

Although separated by language, geography, and a century and a half, the
words of both Dostoyevsky and Gallant go to the heart of contemporary prison
conditions. As Jason Gallant told me:

If you want to change a man, you must change his thoughts. And
you don't change thoughts by appealing to a man's fear of reprisal.
You have to appeal to his humanity no matter how far we fall. In
order to appeal to a prisoner's humanity, you must first believe and
accept that he has some. If you have an attitude, a perspective and a
perception of prisoners as having humanity—not necessarily being

humane because by and large most of us aren't—I believe there's very few of us that will not respond in time to humane, fair, and kind approaches. If you're going to have any chance at all of turning men like me around, you must treat us fairly, you must treat us kindly. And yes, you must treat us with discipline and continuity in all that you do, and all but those who suffer from dementia cannot help but respond to kindness and fairness. That is the most dangerous weapon you have against the criminal element. But you can't get me to buy into a system where you tell me no violence should ever be used when the first time I do not do what you say, you come down with gas masks and clubs and beat the living shit out of me.

To survive in prison the prisoner must come up with his own values that give him self-esteem, a sense of purpose, a sense of direction. You don't dole these out like they're privileges. The need to love and the need to be loved, a sense of direction, of self-worth, of purpose, those are indigenous to the human being. This is what raises us above the beasts. You don't tell us to act human and then you will give us back those things as privileges. Those things that you are willingly prepared to give us if we act human are the things we need to be human, free of the fear of reprisal.

I asked Jason Gallant, as one of the "barbarian princes" identified by Mr. Justice Muldoon, to talk about "that savage, unwritten 'code' of conduct which is kept alive by the dominant inmates in those 'aggressive (inmate) communities' in Canadian prisons."

The con code in the strictest sense is to make sure that you don't mess with anybody else's time. The violence as enacted by some of us guys on the inside isn't because we hold to a code of ethics that extols violence; the nastiness in the con code doesn't find its origin in the heart of a callous prisoner. That's not it at all. The cons know they're not far removed from society in wanting vengeance. When somebody rapes your child or another loved one, even law-abiding citizens just lose it. It seems to me that Judge Muldoon was making this connection that all violence on the inside is a result of the con code. It may have nothing to do with the con code whatsoever . . .

Society says we're riffraff. They relegate us to the realms of second-class citizenship. We can't very well, individually or collectively, accept that view. I think the con code in its infancy stage was to give us a sense of value and identity that was more consistent with our view of ourselves as people with some dignity and worthy of respect. As it has developed in terms of justifying retaliation against informants, is that so unreasonable? It's not that the stool pigeon is necessarily at fault, because the person informed on may have done something wrong. But for whatever reasons this man pulled us down. Is it a realistic expectation that we can live with that man? Is it so unreasonable that we would be angry and vengeful at somebody who is responsible, directly or indirectly, for our freedom, even within the prison, being further taken away? How is that different from society on the outside exacting retribution and punishment on us, for infringing on their freedom? Inside, we're outside of the law, and we do not have available to us the means to enforce our values and mores in any lawful structure. The violent aspect of the con code is our way of adapting to the system being willing to sacrifice some prisoners in order to have a flood of information whereby they think they will have better control.

After one of our first interviews, Mr. Gallant found himself unsatisfied with how he had answered some of my questions. He offered me a set of poems he had composed which he felt better captured the essence of his experiences as a prisoner and a human being. Here is one of them.

### Escape from the Demon's Lair

They've ravished my soul and raped my mind.
My spirit they try to take.
For once behind these prison walls,
they think we're theirs to break.

It was accepted, in times past,
we had rights; with freedom of choice
But once these doors to gloom slam shut,
we're robbed of even voice.

We can file complaints—policy claims,
on forms, with procedures fair.
But to the very ones found hounding us—
what's the odds you think they'll care?

I stand in awe of noble law—
more pointedly of its Spirit.
But caught up in its written word,
most people just won't hear it.

The Spirit corrects the heart of man,
while the Letter disciplines the mind.
The Letter comes easily from the hand of man,
but the Spirit is hard to find.

I first read this poem in 1994. When I reread it in 1998, following Mr. Gallant's account of his strip search by the ERT, its phrasing seemed even more relevant. How *should* we balance the letter and the spirit of the law to ensure that the guidance it provides does not become a source of oppression? It is to that question I will now turn in discussing the merits raised by Jason Gallant's complaint.

## The "Bend Over" Rule: The Constitutional Framework

At the beginning of this chapter, I set out the critical line of inquiry for determining whether a prison search is constitutionally permissible. That inquiry hinges on s. 8 of the *Charter* and requires an analysis of whether a particular search power or the manner in which that power is exercised constitutes an "unreasonable search." The Supreme Court in its 1987 decision in *R.* v. *Collins* stated that "a search will be reasonable if it is authorized by law, if the law itself is reasonable and if the manner in which the search was carried out is reasonable" ([1987] 1 S.C.R. 265 at 278). The first of these requirements is met with regard to the "bend over" rule, since the *CCR Regulations* authorize both investigative and routine strip searches under certain circumstances and specifically state that as part of the "prescribed manner" for carrying out a strip search, a prisoner may be required to "bend over or otherwise enable a staff member to perform a visual inspection."

The second requirement is that the law authorizing the search itself be reasonable. The Supreme Court jurisprudence on this aspect of reasonableness has hinged the analysis on a purposive approach to the value protected by s. 8 of the *Charter:* "a reasonable expectation of privacy." In determining what that is, an assessment must be made as to whether the individual's interest in being left alone is outweighed by the government's interest in intruding on privacy. Just what that means in the prison context has been the subject of court decisions in both Canada and the United States.

The U.S. Supreme Court in *Bell* v. *Wolfish,* while assuming that prisoners retain some measure of Fourth Amendment rights—guaranteeing protection from unreasonable search and seizure—stated that in determining whether a particular prison search was reasonable the courts "must consider the scope of the particular intrusion, the manner in which it was conducted, the justification for initiating it, and the place in which it was conducted" (441 U.S. 520 (1979) at

559). A court engaged in this balancing must evaluate "prison practice . . . in light of the central objective of prison administration, safeguarding institutional security," and "prison administrators . . . should be accorded wide-ranging deference in the adoption and execution of policies and practices that in their judgement are needed to preserve internal order and discipline and to maintain institutional security" (at 547). The U.S. Supreme Court, in *Wolfish,* upheld strip searches involving visual inspection of body cavities that were conducted after every contact visit in a pre-trial detention centre. Following *Wolfish,* U.S. courts have found prison strip searches to be "reasonable" under the Fourth Amendment for prisoners entering or leaving living units, the prison law library, the infirmary, or a segregation unit and also for prisoners leaving the units' visiting rooms after receiving visitors (*Arruda* v. *Fair,* 710 F.2d 886 (1st Cir. 1983); *Peckham* v. *Wisconsin Department of Corrections,* 141 F.3d 694 (7th Cir. 1998)). While the U.S. courts in *Arruda* recognized "the severe if not gross interference with a person's privacy that occurs when guards conduct a visual inspection of body cavities" (710 F.2d 886 at 887), and the Supreme Court in *Wolfish* acknowledged that this practice "instinctively" caused it "the most pause" (441 U.S. 520 at 558), strip searching under the circumstances and in the manner authorized by the CCRA has passed constitutional muster in the United States.

Canadian courts, like their U.S. counterparts, have acknowledged that while prisoners do not forfeit the right to privacy when they enter through prison gates, the expectation of privacy is much diminished by the fact of incarceration and the realities of correctional administration. The issue has come before the courts in a variety of contexts, including a challenge to the strip search procedures protested by Jason Gallant.

In *Warriner* v. *Kingston Penitentiary,* Mr. Warriner, after a contact visit with his wife, was asked to submit to a strip search. He removed his clothing and did everything expected of him until he was directed to bend over and touch his toes, so that his anal cavity was exposed for inspection. This he refused to do. He was then taken to segregation, where he was asked to submit to a second strip search. He co-operated but again refused to bend over. The pattern of Mr. Warriner's co-operation and refusal at this point replicates the facts in Mr. Gallant's case. However, those facts then quickly diverge. Mr. Warriner, following his refusal to bend over, was placed in a segregation cell and charged with the disciplinary offence of failing to obey a lawful order. After conviction by an Independent Chairperson, Mr. Warriner appealed to the Federal Court, arguing that the order to bend over constituted an unreasonable search contrary to s. 8 of the *Charter.* Mr. Warriner argued that the bend-over procedure was by design and effect degrading and humiliating. Correctional authorities, in justifying the reasonableness of strip search procedures, relied principally on the need for this technique in controlling the flow of contraband, including drugs and weapons, into penitentiaries. In his affidavit, Warden Payne of Kingston Penitentiary set out the reasons he believed a skin frisk, including a visual rectal search, was necessary for all prisoners returning from an open visit.

> Inmates have a strong desire to obtain mood-altering drugs, and these drugs often make them more physically violent and dangerous. I am familiar with Dr. Donald George Workman's study on the relationship between aggression and the taking of certain drugs, and I can confirm from my experience that what he has documented is fact. Drug-induced violent events are a major problem in the penitentiary. An example may be useful. When I was Warden at Collins Bay Institution, a medium security institution, I was aware of at least two deaths there that were drug initiated and drug related. In one case, a young inmate paid with his life for failing to give up ten Valium.
>
> Open contact visits, while undoubtedly important in rehabilitating, also present a major opportunity for smuggling contraband into a penitentiary . . . It is regrettably not uncommon for an inmate and his family to have pressure put on them to smuggle in contraband for other inmates. Naturally, the selected "mule" tends to be someone who one would not normally suspect of concealing contraband.
>
> Inmates are most ingenious when it comes to introducing contraband into an institution and known incidents include everything from condoms and balloons full of drugs to an actual working small calibre (.22) handgun, rectally packed. It is imperative, I believe, that the management of an institution retain the right to at least put up a barrier against inmates easily introducing contraband into the institution in order to protect the lives and safety of both staff and inmates. (*Warriner* v. *Kingston Penitentiary*, [1991] 2 F.C. 88 at 106–7)

Dr. Workman, in his affidavit, referred to research he had conducted at Millhaven in 1975 which found a significant increase in violent tendencies in prisoners receiving minor tranquillizers and other medications.

> We have found the majority of inmates are more interested in mood-altering drugs than the average patient in the private sector. I believe it is paramount to control the use of such drugs, either prescribed or otherwise, within the institution, and it is especially paramount to attempt to prevent any illicit trafficking in such drugs. When we couple the results of our study with the fact that inmates on the whole are more aggressive and violent than the average citizen in the general population, the above measures are absolutely essential. It is

> my considered opinion that, for the safety of inmates and staff, it is essential that prison authorities conduct complete skin searches after contact visits including the requirement that inmates bend at the waist, touching their toes so as to expose their anal cavity. (at 107)

Neither Mr. Payne nor Dr. Workman were cross-examined on their affidavits, and Mr. Warriner did not present any evidence that rebutted their conclusions. Mr. Justice MacKay concluded that the skin search, including the visual rectal search, "was based on reasons related to the safety of inmates and staff and to the good order of the institution, and that it was not an unreasonable search contrary to Section 8 of the *Canadian Charter of Rights and Freedoms*" (at 113).

Where does this finding leave the merits of Jason Gallant's grievance? In light of the *Warriner* decision, the demand made of Mr. Gallant that he submit to a strip search, including the requirement that he bend over, would appear to be constitutional. However, this conclusion requires more careful examination. The evidence of Warden Payne and Dr. Workman in *Warriner* was that the requirement to bend over was necessary to deter and detect the introduction of contraband, particularly drugs, into institutions. In the absence of any competing evidence, Mr. Justice McKay accepted this necessity, and it was a major premise in his conclusion that the strip-search procedure, including the "bend over" rule, constituted a reasonable search under s. 8.

There are three distinct steps in the institution's argument. The first is that the introduction and distribution of drugs within a prison has a negative effect on the safety of prisoners and staff, the peaceful management of the institution, and the promotion of rehabilitative programs. This step is clearly supported by the evidence in *Warriner*. In the course of my own research, the events of "Deadly July" at Kent Institution illustrate the dangers that drugs can introduce into the life of a penitentiary.

The next step in the institutional argument is that a strip search, including the requirement to bend over, is a reasonable strategy to deter and detect the possession of contraband. This requires an assessment first of whether the occasions on which a prisoner is required to submit to a strip search are reasonably related to opportunities to obtain contraband, and second, whether it is reasonable to believe that the strip-search procedure will reveal evidence of contraband. On the first question, the CCRA specifically limits the circumstances in which routine strip searches are authorized to those situations "in which the inmate has been in a place where there was a likelihood of access to contraband that is capable of being hidden on or in the body, or when the inmate is entering or leaving a segregation area" (s. 48). The factual context of *Warriner*—an open visit in which the prisoner and visitor sit in close proximity and may have physical contact—is a clear example of a situation where the opportunity to obtain contraband exists.

The second question requires an assessment of the means—strip-search procedures—as directed to the ends—the detection of contraband. In the Jason Gallant case, this assessment must be focussed on the bending over requirement of the strip search. The question can be posed in this way: is it reasonable that requiring a prisoner to bend over to allow a visual inspection of a body cavity will reveal contraband concealed in that cavity? The search for an answer is not for the squeamish, requiring as it does an examination of the way prisoners and their visitors "suitcase" drugs within their bodies. The principal method is to place drugs in condoms or balloons and insert these into the rectum or vagina. Requiring a prisoner to bend over, even if this is accompanied with an order to "spread them," will not reveal a suitcased package except where it has been hastily inserted or where circumstances have not provided the opportunity to insert the package fully. That the bend-over requirement as implemented in Canadian penitentiaries is *not* reasonably related to the detection of contraband is confirmed by several pieces of evidence. First, in the *Jackson* case, Mr. Justice MacKay summarized the evidence of Mr. R. Harvey, the CSC's Director of Custody and Control:

> Despite internal intelligence, searches by detectives, frisking and even skin or nude searches, especially related to pre-release programs and major visitor occasions, it seems little contraband is actually found and forfeited. Harvey indicated that those responsible for safety and security in the Institutions believe that most drugs are transported by inmates themselves and by family members and other outsiders, in body cavities, principally the anus and vagina, hidden so as not to be detected by visual search. (*Jackson* v. *Joyceville Penitentiary*, [1990] 3 F.C. 55 at 78)

The second piece of evidence is reflected in the long-standing correctional practice at Kent of not requiring prisoners to bend over as part of strip-search procedures. This represented a judgement by line staff that the bend-over rule was futile, since contraband was not going to be discovered except in the most exceptional circumstances. Most correctional officers at Kent, like most prisoners, saw the requirement as degrading, and therefore to be avoided if it did not serve any useful purpose. The practice at Kent was consistent with both the letter and the spirit of the law, since s. 45 of the CCR *Regulations* is cast in permissive terms: "the person being searched shall undress completely in front of the staff member and may be required to . . . bend over." According to my conversations with staff, the change in practice at Kent after March 1998 did not bring with it any confidence that more contraband would be discovered, nor was it. From the time the "bend over" rule was reinstated until the completion of my research, there was no instance in which drugs or other contraband was discovered as the result of a prisoner's bending over.

The combined weight of this evidence compels the conclusion that the requirement to bend over adds nothing to the deterrence and detection of contraband by strip searches. Additionally, the Supreme Court of Canada in the *Sue Rodriguez* case, albeit in the context of s. 7 of the *Charter,* has held that:

> Where deprivation of the right in question does little or nothing to enhance the state's interest (whatever it may be) it seems to me that a breach of fundamental justice will be made out, as the individual's rights will have been deprived for no valid purpose. (*Rodriguez* v. *A.G.B.C.,* [1994] 3 S.C.R. 519 at para. 147)

Extrapolating from this judgement, requiring Jason Gallant to bend over advances no correctional purpose. Indeed, the bend-over requirement achieves quite the opposite. Mr. Gallant's grievance says it all. The requirement undermines a prisoner's dignity, self-respect, pride, and sense of being in control of the most intimate parts of his body. It also undermines the possibility of respectful relations between prisoners and correctional officers by symbolically demonstrating to prisoners that they are pariahs worthy of such degrading treatment.

The outrage expressed by Mr. Gallant finds some resonance in a judgement of the Supreme Court of Canada dealing with the power of police to demand and seize samples of hair and body fluids for DNA analysis. Mr. Justice Cory, in ruling that such samples obtained without specific statutory authorization amounted to conscriptive evidence, the admission of which would render a trial unfair, had these comments about the values at stake:

> Canadians think of their bodies as the outward manifestation of themselves. It is considered to be uniquely important and uniquely theirs. Any invasion of the body is an invasion of the particular person. Indeed, it is the ultimate invasion of personal dignity and privacy. No doubt this approach was the basis for the assault and sexual assault provisions. The body was very rightly seen to be worthy of protection by means of criminal sanctions against those who assault others. The concept of fairness requires that searches carried out in the course of police investigations recognize the importance of the body.
>
> Traditionally, the common law and Canadian society have recognized the fundamental importance of the innate dignity of the individual. There is little likelihood of maintaining any semblance of dignity where, without consent and in the absence of any statutory authorization, intrusive procedures are employed to take bodily substances. For example, can there be any respect demonstrated for an individual if against their will women and men accused of a crime

can be compelled to provide samples of their pubic hair to the police? (*R. v. Stillman*, [1997] 1 S.C.R. 607 at paras. 87–88)

As a prisoner, is Jason Gallant disentitled to think of his body as the outward manifestation of himself? Must he, for no legitimate correctional purpose, be prepared to suffer without complaint the "ultimate invasion of personal dignity and privacy"?

In considering how to answer these questions and many others this book raises, the framework of inquiry suggested by Nils Christie, an eminent Norwegian criminologist and philosopher, is very useful. In his book *Crime Control as Industry*, he has written:

> Punishment can then be seen to reflect our understanding and our values, and is therefore regulated by standards people apply every day for what it is possible and what it is not possible to do to others . . . More than a tool for social engineering, the level and kind of punishment is a mirror of the standards that reign in a society. So the question for each and every one of us is: would it be in accordance with my general set of values to live in a state which represented me in this particular way? (Nils Christie, *Crime Control as Industry: Towards Gulags, Western Style*, 2d enlarged ed. [London: Routledge, 1994] at 185–86)

At a conference in Barcelona in 1995, Professor Christie described how such a question can be approached. He and I had taken a walk the day before along La Rambla and Passeig de Gràcia, two of Barcelona's most elegant boulevards. La Rambla, lit at night by finely wrought iron lamps, is framed by tall trees whose branches arch to shelter those walking arm in arm beneath; Passeig de Gràcia is the site of Antoni Gaudí's *Casa Milá* and *Casa Batlló*, both celebrations of the harmony of art and architecture. During the conference's keynote address, Professor Christie said Barcelonans are justifiably proud of the contributions they have made to expressing the human spirit. By contrast, Professor Christie pointed to the prison in Barcelona, which he had just visited. While no worse than many other overcrowded prisons in Europe, as an artifact of punishment it was at war with everything La Rambla and Passeig de Gràcia represented. Barcelonans should be ashamed, he said, to tolerate within their city a place that so tortures the human spirit.

How well do the videotapes of the strip searches of Jason Gallant and Darryl Bates at Kent Institution mirror the standards that reign in Canadian society? The *Charter of Rights and Freedoms* provides the basis for what we hope is a just and peaceful society that respects human dignity and protects against the abuse of power. How well are these visions reflected when, on no reasonable grounds, two prisoners are asked to expose their rectums to correctional officers and when, on their refusal to do so, six officers tackle each of them, wrestling them to the ground and forcibly prying their legs apart for a visual inspection? Is this an image that mirrors the standards of decency we want in the Canada of the twenty-first century?

## CHAPTER 3

# Super Max to Club Fed:
# The Journey from
# Outlawry

Shortly after I began my work at Kent Institution in 1994, Gary Weaver was placed in the segregation unit there and informed that he was being considered for a transfer to the Special Handling Unit. Mr. Weaver was twenty-five years old and had served five years of a life sentence for second-degree murder. He had spent the entire period in either maximum security or the Special Handling Units, including a significant amount of time in segregation. Between April 1994 and September 2001, I interviewed Gary Weaver on twelve occasions, and the transcripts of those interviews run close to 600 pages. Our interviews were supplemented by many informal conversations. I also reviewed his extensive correctional files. During the seven-year span of our interviews Mr. Weaver traversed the length and breadth of the carceral archipelago: he was transferred from Kent to the Special Handling Unit in Quebec, then returned to Kent, completed the Violent Offender Program at the Regional Health Centre, crossed the Strait of Georgia to the medium security William Head Institution and received approval from the National Parole Board for a series of escorted temporary absence passes. Three days after his first pass—marking the first occasion he had been outside of prison in ten years—he was placed in segregation for an alleged assault on another prisoner. He spent the next eighty days protesting his innocence, before being released on the eve of a *habeas corpus* court hearing challenging his detention.

While traversing this difficult terrain, Gary Weaver developed his talents as an artist, became a practising Buddhist, found a soulmate, and struggled to change his values from those of an outlaw to those of a man with a realistic, realizable future outside of prison. Along the way he encountered the full spectrum of the discretionary forces *Justice behind the Walls* has addressed; therefore, the recounting of his journey provides a final opportunity to unravel the DNA of contemporary imprisonment and determine whether justice is part of its genetic imprint.

## Rage and Resistance

Gary Weaver was born on December 1, 1968, in Peterborough, Ontario, and adopted at nine weeks of age. Early on in his schooling he displayed symptoms of Attention Deficit Disorder, and in Grade 4 he was put on the medication Ritalin. By the time he was fourteen, Gary had become a social misfit, rebellious and resistant to authority. From 1983, when he first experienced detention in training school, his life consisted of increasingly long periods of secure custody in juvenile institutions. Eventually he graduated to the penitentiary on a variety of charges, including breaking and entering and possession of narcotics for the purpose of trafficking. In 1989 he pleaded guilty to the charge of second-degree murder in the fatal stabbing of an elderly man he believed to be a sex offender. He was high on cocaine at the time. He received a life sentence without eligibility for parole for ten years.

Mr. Justice Mason, in imposing the sentence, had this to say about Gary Weaver:

> One could class [Mr. Weaver] as a complete addict to cocaine and other drugs of that nature. My appreciation of Mr. Weaver from his appearance as a witness in this case is that of an angry and confused young man, ruthless, without direction, addicted to drugs, and bordering on self-destruction.
>
> The character of this offence was a brutal killing, sudden and violent, but mercifully according to the evidence, Mr. Marsh died quickly. The offender was at the time a drug addict acting under a personality disorder and a misguided sense of values fuelled by the drug abuse. (Reasons for Judgement of Mr. Justice Mason, Queen's Bench of Alberta, November 3, 1989)

Almost a decade later, in a treatment program, Gary Weaver for the first time acknowledged that as a young boy he had been sexually abused by an older cousin. While not excusing his offence, this admission went some way in explaining the rage that had been unleashed in the stabbing of his victim.

When I met Gary Weaver, he had been in segregation at Kent for two months. During our first interview, I mentioned that I had written a book about solitary confinement. He was keen to read it, so I brought a copy out to Kent on my next visit. He devoured it in twenty-four hours. When *Prisoners of Isolation* was published in 1983, Gary was fourteen years old. He had not experienced solitary confinement in a federal prison, but was already familiar with the degradation of "the hole":

> I was in the digger in training school when I was fourteen . . . Every place I've been, I've been in seg. We had a riot in the Young Offender Unit in Peterborough Jail and they shipped a bunch of us out. Some guys went to the Toronto East Detention Centre, some of us got sent to the Detention Centre in Napanee. They ran out of shackles so they used our pants. They yanked our pants and underwear down to our ankles, and tied our hands behind our backs with those garbage bag ties. They told us to get face down on the floor, and I'd never seen these sticks and shields to that degree. I'd seen the sticks and the shields in Peterborough during that riot, because I got a few whacks, and I thought that wasn't so bad, but these guys looked dead serious. I was thinking, how serious can they be? We're just kids. We were face down on the floor, bang, bang, bang. Now I know how serious it gets. My face is kicked in. We get to the hole. You've got to walk through these big, long hallways. I've got my pants at my ankles, garbage bags on my hands, those hard ties, so we go down and all the nurses are standing there, female nurses, female guards. They are laughing that they are bringing kids down like that. We had no clothes so they gave me a dress. (Interview with Gary Weaver, Kent Institution, August 23, 1994)

Gary also described for me his experience of "the hole" in Peterborough when he was sixteen:

> They only had one cell for the hole, and I'm just a kid with an attitude in the Young Offenders' Section. They kept putting me in this box until it would work to break down this attitude. I was wearing just a pair of boxer shorts. They take the mattress from you first thing in the morning until night and I'm basically conditioning myself to hole-time. Maybe deep down inside I know I'm going to see plenty more of this twenty-three-hour lock-up. I remember it got to the point where I strengthened myself in seg. At first I'd cry at night and think, "Why are they doing this to me?" I'm really emotional and fucked up thinking I'm being tortured here. Why? What did I do that was so bad? . . . There was a toilet in the cell so I'd use that to sit on. The only other thing was the steel bed frame, and that gets really uncomfortable. It's all rivets, the whole thing. I used to count these things. It goes right up in the thousands. I was thinking, "What the fuck did I do?"

Now when they come with the mattress at night I said, "Shove the mattress. Look, you paid to see this, now you've got it." They are having physical beefs with me to get the mattress in the cell and I'm having physical beefs with them throwing it back out first thing in the morning. I wouldn't use it all night. Now I've conditioned myself to sleep on rivets and you get these little bruises and welts on your skin from the lack of circulation. The more I rebelled the better I felt. (August 23, 1994)

Gary Weaver's experiences years later in the Special Handling Unit in the Saskatchewan Penitentiary would parallel these early ones: the more oppressive his treatment was, the more rebellious he became.

Gary confided that what had most affected him in *Prisoners of Isolation* were the quotations from prisoners in the first generation of Special Handling Units—"I read that and it was like I wrote it myself." What he particularly picked up on were statements made by Edgar Roussel:

The system aims to reduce the criminal to nothing, restrain the slightest initiative, and in one word, assassinate his personality to make him conform to a microcosm in which he is forced to develop. When the prisoner has become sufficiently conniving, hypercritical and lying that he can pretend to acknowledge the assassination to his executioners, then he is eligible for a transfer. (cited in Jackson, *Prisoners of Isolation,* at 176)

Gary gave me his theory of what the second-generation SHUs were all about:

Their whole objective is to put you in a situation where you feel like it's all over, you have nothing to live for, they have totally destroyed your identify and now you're hanging off the edge of a cliff. You might just drop into a total abyss, and then some guard or Case Management Officer is there pulling you back over, and it's the same person that pushed you off the edge. (August 23, 1994)

In the course of another interview, Gary and I discussed the film *Murder in the First,* which depicts the solitary confinement cells in Alcatraz and the cruel and barbaric treatment of Henry Young when he was confined there in the 1940s. Henry Young had been not only isolated but kept in a dungeon cell from which light and hope were excluded.

That darkness in that empty cell, well, we had that darkness and empty cell in our head in the Prince Albert SHU. You were so constrained and calloused in a sterile environment. Sure we had a light, but we also had that same sense of hopelessness. I remember the goon squad coming down and putting a licking on me, and I thought for sure they were just going to kill me and that was that. I pictured myself in a body bag, getting zipped up and carted out. I was thinking it was almost like a cryogenics warehouse, where they freeze you and forget about you and then one day when there's a fix they'll let you out, but nothing's a fix. It's a dysfunctional environment. They've created the illusion that they have kept you stamped for such a long time that it's going to make all the difference in your life. Sure it makes a difference, but not the way they wanted. (Interview with Gary Weaver, Kent Institution, April 19, 1996)

Gary Weaver had much to say about the distance between the rhetoric and the reality of change in the Canadian correctional system from his time in the Special Handling Units.

There's a good possibility I could have been reached if they would've helped me wrap my mind around the fact that "Look, man, you've got some problems and you need to change here. Society can't manage a person like you amongst them." But it was this, "We're going to fucking break you. We're going to knock that chip off your shoulder and hammer you down until you get up and crawl." It was just so in your face. They would always say things about security. Well, I remember reading the Mission Statement when it first came out. It said there would be a plausible balance of control and assistance, which led me to believe that there would be security—there would be walls and there would be guns to prevent escapes and threats to the community—but there would also be assistance at that same level. The way it's written it presents this real nice ideology, things are going to change and be better, but I never saw the assistance. Every time I was in trouble they just rained fire and brimstone on me. I couldn't believe it. Like, for being disrespectful in language to an officer. I'm in my cell after what I deemed to be an argument with my keeper and they show up at my door with Mace and five or six guards telling me to get down on my hands and knees and face the wall and do I surrender? Put my hands behind my back. Every time they come to take you to segregation it's like Vietnam. They come whipping down your range with all their artillery and "do you surrender." It's a break-you-down attitude. I'm still affected by a lot of that even today. (April 19, 1996)

Life in the Special Handling Unit as described by Gary Weaver was an acid mix of anger and hopelessness.

> There's no rhyme or reason to it, there's no explanation for what they're doing or why they're doing it, and they deny they're doing it. And I tried the appropriate channels. I was putting in complaints and I was writing letters to the Deputy Commissioner and I was staying away from all the shock-talk and bitterness, trying to address things maturely and responsibly. And he would write back not addressing the complaint or what I had to say but with stuff like "it's good that you're taking an interest in your rehabilitation. I strongly recommend that you involve yourself in the necessary programs." It was just like talking to a bunch of robots. I eventually stopped putting in grievances because I would sit down and put my heart and soul into explaining what the problem was and they would send me this goofy response and I would literally see red. This envelope would come under the door and my physical cues would just start going. One day I was reading an answer to a grievance and my whole body started shaking and everything in the cell was red, I mean crimson, blood-fucking red. Everything, and it was like I was looking through glass, and I started kicking this toilet with my bare feet. I remember that like yesterday, because you sleep with your head close to the door and the mail would come under the door and I jumped out of bed and I went nuts. I was kicking the shit out of a stainless steel toilet and I started kicking the door. I never even hurt my foot. Then I started smashing things up. (Interview with Gary Weaver, Kent Institution, June 3, 1996)

On other occasions, Gary would destroy his personal possessions as part of a strategy for self-preservation. In his cell at the SHU he was permitted to have personal photographs. The ones he most treasured were of his family and his girlfriend. When he knew the guards were coming to take him to segregation, he would take down the pictures, tear them up and flush them down the toilet. This served two purposes. First, it prevented the guards from desecrating what was most dear to him; second, having removed everything that gave him an identity as a member of a human family, he could play the role assigned to him, a violent prisoner, to the hilt.

> I just destroyed everything so that when they came, they would have nothing to hold against me and I would have nothing to hold myself back. I've got nothing to safeguard. (June 3, 1996)

Gary Weaver was never imprisoned in the Penthouse in the B.C. Penitentiary or in H unit at Kent. At Matsqui and Kent, prisoners in segregation now had televisions and sometimes stereos. Interviewing him at Kent on two occasions in 1994, I asked Gary to explain why members of the Canadian public or the legal profession should be concerned about the conditions in segregation units.

> Slowly but surely, you lose your sense of self and your sense of community. You feel incommunicado while you still have some communicado efforts to make. You still write your family, you can still make your phone calls, you can still wave to the guard when he goes by, you can still see the guys in the yard, but it's like you've taken a move to another planet. It's not simply what do you lose, but what do you gain? What you're losing is not just your sense of self but any sense of direction that you could be doing something else with your life, because you're stuck down here. If I'm out in population and I'm going to school, I'm focussed on something and I'm learning. When I'm in segregation, I feel I'm being treated unfairly, and I'm focussed on thinking on how to pay people back. All I'm thinking about is bitterness, because that's the only way to keep going . . . Something's been exacted on me that's unjust so why should I sit down here and think justly? Why should I sit down here and think about returning to this wonderful society and being a well-behaved guy when society is saying, "Go with it, do this to him and that's fine by us." (May 10, 1994)
>
> The public says we've got TVs and stereos, so why are these guys whining? Things like TV and stereos make it look like it's getting better, but in fact they are the things that make it worse, especially to a guy like me. I know a lot of guys respond to all this physical comfort. I say fuck the TV and the stereo, because it gets away from the real issues. It's another thing that's being held above your head and it can drop at any time, so psychologically it's the same, if not worse. Take my TV, take the stereo. It just means I'm going to have a lot more energy to think about what's happening around me than to be brainwashed by some form of entertainment. (August 23, 1994)

## Back to the SHU: An Opening Salvo in the War on Drugs

A common theme in my interviews with prisoners who have undergone extended imprisonment in segregation or Special Handling Units is that their experiences from these periods have a long afterlife. Often it is difficult to outdistance the attitudes and survival strategies they develop in these alien environments. One of Gary Weaver's coping strategies precipitated his return to the Special Handling Unit. Gary was placed in segregation following his visit with Ms. S.R. on February 17, 1994. His case was being considered by the Warden for transfer to the SHU based on allegations that he was actively involved in the drug trade and was prepared to use violence against other prisoners. The conversations during his February 17 visit had been monitored due to information obtained at an earlier monitored visit that Mr. Weaver had asked Ms. S.R. to bring drugs into the institution. On February 17, Ms. S.R. had gone to the washroom to remove an internally concealed package. She was confronted as she left the washroom and 15.3 grams of marijuana was found in her bra. The RCMP were called and Ms. S.R. was charged with possession for the purpose of trafficking.

At his five- and thirty-day segregation reviews, Mr. Weaver was informed that:

> You are segregated because of alleged involvement in the institutional drug trade. You have not yet been charged with anything. You are currently being reviewed for transfer to H.M.S.U. [High Maximum Security Unit] and the investigation is ongoing. Your segregation will be maintained pending this review and investigation. (Review of Inmate Segregated Status, Kent Institution, March 14, 1993)

On May 5, 1994, seventy-eight days after he was first placed in segregation, Gary Weaver was served with a notice of Warden Lusk's recommendation for a transfer to the Quebec Special Handling Unit. The recommendation was explicitly tied to the "War on Drugs," which became a significant part of correctional policy in 1994–95.

1) On 94-02-17 your visitor was arrested at Kent Institution for attempting to introduce contraband narcotics into the institution. She has been charged with possession of narcotics for the purpose of trafficking.

2) The seizure of the narcotics was a direct result of monitored conversations that took place on 94-01-20 and 94-02-17 in the V&C area of Kent Institution. These conversations, particularly the one that occurred on 94-01-20, demonstrated quite clearly, that you intended to introduce a variety of illegal drugs into Kent Institution, that you intended to introduce as large a quantity of drugs as you could obtain, that you viewed yourself becoming an important drug dealer within the institution and that you would not hesitate to engage in violent acts, including murder, in order to further your objectives.

3) You have a lengthy well-documented history of institutional violence including a stabbing, assaults, threatening, muscling

and robbing other inmates. This past history clearly shows your propensity to commit serious violent acts. It is your past history that leads one to conclude your threats to kill, as recorded in your 94-01-20 conversation, must be taken very seriously.

4) The traffic of narcotics within correctional facilities is a leading cause of violence. If this violence is to be controlled, the dealers and those responsible for the introduction of the narcotics must be placed in a very controlled, restricted environment to severely limit their activities. I believe these requirements can best be met in a Special Handling Unit. (Annex A to Notice of Involuntary Transfer Recommendation, Kent Institution, May 5, 1994)

Supporting the recommendation was a progress summary prepared by Barry Owen, Mr. Weaver's case management officer, which cited extracts from the monitored conversation of January 20. One group of extracts is cited to demonstrate Mr. Weaver's willingness to use violence in pursuit of his planned drug trade activities. In one passage, he states, "Nobody burns me. I'd fuckin' cut their throat in a second." A second group of extracts is cited to demonstrate "the depths of [Mr. Weaver's] obsession with violence and abject coldness":

> I could sit here and torture a cop for a week in a garage . . . see what I could do with a cop. I could give him some fucking tranquillizers so he can't go into shock and some local anaesthetic, like I can freeze his legs up, and I can tie his head and I could clip his eyes open and I could hack his fucking legs off and he's gotta watch and he can't go unconscious and he can't go into shock because the tranquillizers stop him from going into shock and with the anaesthetic you can't feel a fucking thing.

Gary Weaver provided me with the copy of the transcript of his conversation with Ms. S.R. After reading the document, I put it to him that the language seemed to paint a picture of a violent, hateful man, justifying Mr. Owen's characterization. I asked him why the Warden should not conclude that these conversations did reveal "the depths of his obsession with violence and abject coldness." He responded:

> It is not an obsession with violence; I would say that it is more an admission of my being desensitized to talking about violence and hearing about violence. You hear so much about it you could put together any scenario in your head, and it's no different than creative writing. If you read a poem like—who would be a good example— Jim Carroll, *The Basketball Diaries*. He is a heroin addict who wrote

a really good book of poems. It's vivid. Who else? William Blake, he's written some pretty serious stuff. Jim Morrison, now there's some heavy shit. Now if society were to buy into all that, they would have grabbed all the poets and the musicians and thrown them in prison.

I picked up all kinds of wild stuff in the SHU. I pick up all kinds of wild stuff in books and in movies. When you're sitting in the SHU you're listening to talk about heads going off or people eating the wildest poisons, guards getting sliced and people licking knives. I've got a million horror stories in my head and I can articulate them and tell them to anybody. Why do people go see the *Terminator II: Judgement Day* movie? It's a turn-on to some degree, or it wouldn't sell millions of tickets and people wouldn't go and see it two, three or four times and then buy the video and add it to their collection. It's not reality. That day I ran down the scenarios in a couple of movies I had seen, including *True Romance* with Christian Slater and Dennis Hopper, which is a pretty violent film. The other stuff with the cop was another movie that nobody has made yet. (Interview with Gary Weaver, Kent Institution, May 3, 1994)

## Portrait of the Artist as a Young Prisoner

One of Gary Weaver's criticisms of the correctional authorities was that they saw him only in shades of black. Nothing he had read in his files suggested any features in his character that were redeeming or of positive value to humanity. He deeply resented the portrait the progress summary had painted and rejected it as being unfair. I asked him to identify how he saw the real Gary Weaver, and he proceeded to tell me about his painting.

I was in the Quebec SHU and there was this guy, he'd been in a lot of years. He was painting and his paintings looked good and I told him that. I started hanging out with him a little bit. He couldn't draw, and so he stencilled pictures onto a canvas and then painted. One day he saw me drawing, it was wolves. He asked me if I could draw some wolves for him. You don't ask guys for things in the SHU without offering something back, so he told me he'd give me a small canvas. It was about 8" x 10", and I could have use of some of his paints. So I drew his wolves and then he showed me how to mix acrylic paint. Honest to God, this guy cried tears when he saw what I had drawn. He was really moved. He said, "You keep that up, you'll be better than me." This guy had been painting for ten years plus. He had done hundreds of paintings, and yet he's telling me that in a couple of weeks I am going to be better than he's ever been, because I'm an artist and I didn't realize what I've got. He wrote out for me a whole list of all the paints I'd need and the kind of canvases, and I promised that when I got to Millhaven I would take up painting. At Millhaven I never got into it, but when I came out to Kent my mom sent me some money. Now, I can't take money from my mom and spend it on drugs, so I ordered all the paints I needed. We had a culture night with the Native Brotherhood, and I was getting bored and I didn't like to leave because people might think that I had no respect. So I grabbed a paper plate, and all the kids were hanging around me while I was drawing on this paper plate. I was drawing an eagle head because I have tattooed it so many times. This one little boy, Ira, he said, "Can I have that?" I said, "Sure" and gave it to him. His mom came to a healing group meeting the next Tuesday and she told me that Ira put it up on his wall. He made a cover for it out of Saran Wrap to preserve it like a glass on a painting. She asked me if I could paint him another eagle. I got all my painting stuff and I sat up all night because I couldn't say no. (Interview with Gary Weaver, Kent Institution, May 25, 1994)

One of Gary's canvases showed a pack of wolves peering out from a forest of silver birches. He explained that one of the wolves had not turned out very well, and initially he was going to paint over it. However, he decided not to do this, because the animal deserved to be allowed to live. He nicknamed this wolf "The Retard" because it was not quite right, yet it still belonged with its more per-fected brothers and sisters. Another painting was of a Bengal tiger. I told Gary that its detail and coloration reminded me of the paintings by Fleur Cowles in *Tiger Flower* and *Lion and Blue,* books I had often read to my children when they were young.

Gary explained his paintings showed a side of him not recognized in any progress summary.

It's hard to explain, because when I paint I'm thinking about those animals, who I love more than anything. When you bring them to life it's not just a cartoon, it's not an animated face on a canvas or a drawing or a tattoo. When I'm painting I'm sitting there, my mind is off with rivers and forests and the cottage when I was a kid, all the things that make you look back and say, "How the fuck did I get here?" I could have been in Rwanda with Dian Fossey. When I paint it's just a whole different world, and then when I stop painting I stare at it for hours. I was thinking of asking my dad to sign his name to my paintings, so that they could be exhibited at art shows. My dad would get the credit, but people could see some of the goodness in me. I don't paint evil things . . . Okay, maybe they got my body here for now, but all my thoughts aren't killing cops and selling drugs. (May 25, 1994)

To contradict the negative progress summary, Gary described some of the changes he believed he had made during his years in prison.

I believe I've changed within myself . . . Before, I'd get involved with this and that, and all of a sudden it's just a pumped-up fantasy, because you meet guys that are really in that life. They're sitting right beside you and they're eating at the same table as you and who are they? Where's all the special things? Where's all those great things that were going to come? Where's the flash? It doesn't even shine.

Years ago I went with the flow because you don't want to be the odd man in your crew when you know that your crew is your salvation. Without them, you could just walk out in the yard and get dumped by a rival clique. . . I always wanted to be a man, and back when I started doing time, being a man was being able to pick up a knife and being able to take care of things on behalf of your crew. Whereas now, the manly thing is having the strength to go against the odds, even if it's a real heavy personal cross or if your friends all laugh and joke about something and you know they're wrong, you're risking your position right there. When people say "Fuck pigs," I used to be that guy. Although I can still get into that, like I did in that conversation they've got on tape, it no longer represents where I'm really at. (May 25, 1994)

Gary told me that a few years previously, he had sought to explain himself to his father.

My dad had a heart attack a couple years ago, and I was freaking because my mom said, "Your dad might be dying." I'm adopted, but I really love these people as my parents. All of a sudden I thought, I've got to get something through to him so he knows, and I picked a card that looked like a city skyline in the dark and I said, Well, Dad, I picked this card because this is my life, "Downtown Gary," but I want you to know that this isn't my life. I don't want you to feel that you raised me in a bad way. I don't expect you to respect the things I did but I'm asking you, if you've got to go, go with the sense of respect that your son didn't follow everybody else's footsteps. As much as some of the things that I did were wrong, I did a lot of good things. I always helped bums on the street. I would give them the last penny out of my pocket. I would give my clothes to strangers. I remember while the police were investigating me on this murder I ran into this little black girl runaway. She was about ten years old, and I gave her all the money out of my pockets. I told her I'd take her to my place but I got heat on a suspected murder, so I gave her the address to a hostel. I went out of my way for a lot of things out there which were totally inconsistent with what these people paint up of a guy like me. Like I'm just a monster. I just wanted to break free. I admit, I broke free in the wrong direction. I was stupid. I saw something, it turned me on and now I pay the price, and I'm expected to do that. (May 25, 1994)

A passage from Dylan Thomas' *Under Milk Wood* captures Gary Weaver's perception—and my own—that the case management process seems to focus primarily on a prisoner's weaknesses, rarely identifying his strengths. In the poem, the Reverend Eli Jenkins makes this appeal to God:

> We are not wholly bad or good
> Who live our lives under Milk Wood
> And Thou, I know, wilt be the first
> To see our best side, not our worst.

Gary Weaver may have persuaded his father that despite his criminal lifestyle he had displayed some redeeming human qualities—to see his best side not his worst—but he faced a more daunting task in persuading the correctional authorities at Kent that the true measure of Gary Weaver was not to be found in the transcript of his conversation on January 20.

## Rebuttal and Decision

On June 9, 1994, Gary Weaver's lawyer, Kate Ker, submitted a rebuttal to the Notice of Involuntary Transfer Recommendation. She pointed out that Mr. Weaver had not been involved in any incidents of violence or assaultive behaviour since his transfer from the Saskatchewan SHU in 1991. Between January 20 and February 17, 1994, the date on which Ms. S.R. was arrested and Mr. Weaver segregated, eight to ten more visits had taken place between them. No transcripts of communications intercepted during those visits had been produced by the institution, underscoring the unusual nature of the conversation on January 20 and exposing Mr. Weaver's talk of violence as "con puffery" and bravado designed to impress his visitor. In particular, the expression of wanting to do physical harm to a police officer was

> nothing more than a means of releasing tension through fantasy which is a by-product of the overall process of desensitization to violence the longer one spends in SHU and segregation units. It is a coping mechanism for [Mr. Weaver] given the extreme brutality and violence he has had to witness and endure in SHU and segregation units. (Submission of Gary Weaver in response to Notice of Involuntary Transfer Recommendation, Kent Institution, June 9, 1994)

Warden Lusk, in a decision dated June 13, 1994, advised Mr. Weaver that he intended to uphold his recommendation for transfer to the SHU. He concluded, "After reviewing all of the materials submitted, I remain convinced that Mr. Weaver's direct involvement in the drug traffic at Kent Institution and the threat that such action presents, indicate that the level of risk he presents to the good order of the Institution can only be managed in the Special Handling Unit" (Notice of Involuntary Transfer Recommendation, Kent Institution, June 13, 1994). On August 31, 1994, the Deputy Commissioner for the Pacific Region approved the transfer of Mr. Weaver.

## Assessing Assessment at the SHU

On September 5, 1994, Gary Weaver was transferred from Kent to the Special Handling Unit at Ste.-Anne-des-Plaines, Quebec. Prior to 1990, prisoners transferred to the Special Handling Units typically spent a minimum of two years there before being transferred back to a maximum security institution. During this time, according to the official rhetoric, they were expected to progress through a three-phase reintegration process. In fact, many prisoners spent far longer periods in the SHUs. The hollowness of the phase program was heavily criticized by the Correctional Investigator, and in *Prisoners of Isolation*, where I devoted a whole chapter to the reality of life in the first generation of Special Handling Units. By 1990, the CSC itself was forced to acknowledge that the rhetoric surrounding Special Handling Units bore little relationship to the reality.

> The phases of gradual reintegration existed only on paper. Meaningful activities were limited. These were essentially non-contact prisons. The regime was a repressive one. Control had become the sole watchword. When the current operation of the Special Handling Unit was examined in light of the Mission, the justifications for the

types of controls now practised became questionable. The Mission's first two core values speak to the dignity of individuals, the rights of all members of society, and the recognition that the offender has the potential to live as a law-abiding citizen. The Mission promotes an active intervention ideology in a safe, secure and humane environment. Control, according to our Mission, is best assured through positive interaction between staff and inmates and not by mere reliance on static security. Human relationships are to be the cornerstone of our endeavours. csc has committed itself to this course of action. Every policy, every decision, must be looked at in the light of its consistency with the philosophy set out in the Mission.

Clearly, the control philosophy that had evolved in the Special Handling Units was not consistent with the Mission. It was, therefore, unacceptable and had to be changed. (*Our Story: Organizational Renewal in Federal Corrections*, Jim Vantour, ed. [Ottawa: Correctional Service of Canada, 1991] at 84–85)

The resulting new Commissioner's Directive 551 stated that the Mission-driven objective of the sHUs was "to create an environment in which dangerous inmates are motivated and assisted to behave in a responsible manner so as to facilitate their integration in a maximum security institution."

Once new policy directives were introduced in 1990, the first three months after admission to the sHU were designated an "assessment period." The Directive in force at the time of Gary Weaver's transfer required that "Each inmate transferred to a Special Handling Unit shall undergo a comprehensive assessment to determine an appropriate intervention strategy and the required level of control" (c.d. 551). Based on this assessment, a detailed correctional treatment plan was to be developed to address the prisoner's violent behaviour and other criminogenic factors. Both the assessment and the treatment plan were to be completed within the initial three-month period. Within one month of the assessment's completion, the sHU National Review Committee was required to review the recommended treatment plan to determine if the prisoner should remain in the sHU or be transferred to another institution (c.d. 551, October 29, 1993. The latest version of c.d. 551, dated February 20, 2001, retains these timeframes, but shifts authority from the National Review Committee—renamed the sHU Advisory Committee—to the Senior Deputy Commissioner).

By the time Gary Weaver was transferred to the sHU in September 1994, he had already spent six and a half months in segregation at Kent. Once transferred, he was placed on the assessment range, which also operated as a twenty-three-hour lock-up. His comprehensive assessment and correctional treatment plan were not completed within the three months specified by the Commissioner's

Directive. On January 19, 1995, a progress summary and a correctional plan were produced; they concluded that it was not necessary for Mr. Weaver be detained in the SHU and recommended his return to Kent. In a decision dated February 27, 1995, the National Review Committee approved that recommendation and "strongly encouraged [him] to participate in institutional programming to address criminogenic needs." On March 8, 1995, Gary Weaver was returned to Kent. He had spent his entire six months away on twenty-three-hour lock-up, bringing the total duration of his segregation at Kent and the SHU to almost thirteen months.

After his return to Kent, Gary Weaver showed me a letter he had written to his case management officer in the SHU after receiving her progress summary. It read in part:

> In approximately 138 days I had been interviewed for "assessment evaluation purposes" for less than eight full hours. Add 138 hours for one hour a day fresh air and you can conclude that out of 3,312 hours, I spent 3,166 hours in my cell during the assessment evaluation period all by myself, and doing what, being assessed??? I certainly don't think so, and I can't imagine anyone else thinking so either. I never once refused an interview and you can see in my files that I asked to see you a lot more than you asked to see me. The same thing goes for the psychologist. I saw the psychologist for about 20 minutes shortly after my arrival here in the first week of September, 1994. Even with having sent two or three requests in writing or verbally through you asking when I could see her for the assessment evaluation and psychological testing, I never saw her again until the second week of January 1995. For those four months of no psychological interviews was I being psychologically assessed? (Letter from Gary Weaver, February 20, 1995)

In an interview with me in April 1995, Gary described a dramatic escalation in the level of violence at the SHU since he had been there in 1992. He described stabbings in the exercise yard and the showers, even though both areas were supposedly under surveillance; one incident even took place during a lock-down. Serious threats had been made against his own life, and once again he found himself having to prepare to meet violence with violence.

> You've got to think murder because there's no way out in a place like that. Every time you get your meal you've got to wonder if somebody's in the shower waiting to stab you. (Interview with Gary Weaver, Kent Institution, April 25, 1995)

Gary told me that in addition to the stabbings, some compression bombs made with pop cans had exploded in the unit. And it was not only the level of violence among prisoners that undermined the ideal of the SHU to help prisoners become "pro-social." Gary described an incident in which he and other prisoners were moved from the assessment unit to segregation to enable some renovations to be made after bullets were discovered behind a toilet bowl:

> This PC [Protective Custody] was in the hole. He was there the last time I was in the Quebec SHU. This man's gone. He comes out and throws shit at people through the bars. I mean, he breaks everything he gets his hands on, he screams almost twenty-four hours a day. The guards go down and fire-hose him and gas him and kick his face off on a very steady basis, and as much as I don't like PCs, what the fuck are they doing? That's a human being in that cell. (April 25, 1995)

The distance between what actually faced him and what should have been happening to Gary Weaver during his assessment phase at the SHU could not have been greater. Gary Weaver had been sent to the Quebec SHU to undergo a comprehensive assessment and to develop a correctional treatment plan to assist him "to modify his behaviour . . . and become pro-social" (C.D. 551, October 29, 1993, para. 5). What he encountered instead was the most violent, anti-social environment in the entire prison system, where the principal lessons to be learned were how to survive a raised blade or an exploding pop can.

The Quebec SHU had not only become a more dangerous place than it had been in 1992, but in that time it had also become physically more confining.

> They used to have real nice cells where the windows went from the floor to the ceiling and you could stick your arm out. Cats could come in and so it was pretty cool. Everyone buys special food for the cats. Then they found some bars cut and knives in the windows so they changed the windows. You can still crank the window open but now you've got three or four layers of wire screens that have little tiny holes. Not only can't the cats come in, but you can't even get air in there, and what you see out of the window is just so distorted it's not worth the look. (Interview with Gary Weaver, April 25, 1995)

Even the one positive thing Gary Weaver had learned in the Quebec SHU in 1992 was now denied him. Because some prisoners had used paints to cover up the windows in their cell, all painting material was removed. Denied an opportunity to create a natural world inhabited by wolves and eagles, Gary Weaver was left to cope with an unnatural world from which even the cats of Ste.-Anne-des-

Plaines were excluded. His experiences in the "Mission-driven" Special Handling Unit, and the experiences of many other prisoners, justify the judgement of the Correctional Investigator that the SHU remains little more than disguised segregation, whose real purpose is to intensify the pains of imprisonment.

## Wrapping Your Mind around Fairness

Following his return to Kent, Gary Weaver began a determined and focussed effort to place himself on a path leading to the street rather than to segregation and the Special Handling Unit. He dug deep within, questioning the directions his life had taken.

> I've been basically challenging all my lifestyles from the past. Like it used to be real appealing to wind up downtown. You know, the flashy lights and the women and the bars and the action. There was a real draw for that. I think of that stuff and it's with disgust. I question how did I ever get attracted to that in the first place. I saw my whole world as just a mission to score drugs and rock 'n' roll. The image is you're going to have a great time, but then you see people doing dirty moves all the time over dope. It takes away all their class and respect. They sell it for dope. I've come to question all that.
>
> My values are changing these days towards positive things, because I've got a perspective toward the future now, whereas when I was sitting in the SHU you can't possibly hope for the future. You might be dead the next day. It's as simple as that. (Interview with Gary Weaver, Kent Institution, March 27, 1996)

Gary completed Kent's Substance Abuse Treatment Program in December 1995. The following April he graduated from the Anger and Emotions Management Program, and in July he finished Cognitive Skills Training. He received excellent evaluations, and his instructors were impressed with both his commitment to change and his ability to take concrete steps to demonstrate it. According to one report:

> [He] challenged thoughts and beliefs which he had lived by for years only to realize that in some cases, they actually create or escalate emotions. Mr. Weaver explored this area with amazing sincerity in exercises. His input during the sessions was also beneficial to other group members. (Program Performance Report, Kent Institution, April 30, 1996)

I asked Gary how realistic it was to expect that two or three programs could change such long-entrenched attitudes. This was his answer:

It's not realistic in itself. But it's not just the programs that elicited change. I was sick of living my life the way I was living it, and I recognized a need to change that. If I kept going the way I have been going, I was just going to bury myself. I'd be better off dead. But there's a level of fairness that I've experienced here since I came back [from the SHU] that's opened a lot of doors for change.

. . . My mind has been helped a lot over the past year to be wrapped around the idea of fairness. I feel that I've been treated fairly on a pretty consistent basis in my interactions with staff. The drug counsellor is a good example. I got to know him as a person and I told him that his group was just incredible, although I didn't expect much out of eighty-three hours of training on substance abuse and pre-release programming. When I first went in there I thought, he's a former guard teaching a course and he probably doesn't know his head from his asshole. When I went for my first day I was expecting him to be standing up there reading stuff out of a textbook and trying to help us identify and deal with problems that he couldn't possibly grasp. When was he ever in the street shooting coke out of mud puddles, and when was he in the sleazy, seedy neighbourhoods and motels with the whores, the bikers, the weirdos, and everything? I went in and this guy, he knew this program like the back of his hand. He was well organized. When you asked a question he could give you an answer, and if he couldn't give you an answer he didn't bullshit you. He shared a little bit about himself on pretty much a daily basis. I like this guy. I regard him as good people, and I didn't see him as a guard teaching a program because, for the first time in my life, here's a guy that's talking about what's going on at his home, how he's dealing with situations with his wife and his kids and how a lot of this program helps him in his day-to-day living.

I find that when you help guys wrap their minds around fairness, changes occur. For the years when I felt that I was being dealt a bad hand, I thought, "Fuck 'em. I'll get out of this someday. I'll get out and do whatever I want, like I did before I came in." They're supposed to be the law. They're supposed to be role models. They're supposed to be upstanding. They're supposed to be people that didn't do to their lives what we did to ours. Yet here they are in their roles committing assault causing bodily harm, extortion, threatening, on a daily basis. It's just the regime itself, just the way it operates. To grab you and forcibly confine you and give you very little, if any, reason at all as to why you're in seg, and then even more far-fetched reasoning for why you're not getting out of seg. You just think "fuck 'em." With me, all of that seems to be over, this going to segregation and fucking up and getting charged and being in their faces and their being in mine. (March 17 and 27, 1996)

Gary Weaver's concept of fairness went beyond the conventional legal definition. He emphasized that the staff members in his programs showed respect for him as a person, not as a prisoner. In turn, he was able to extend a reciprocal respect to them as "good people" rather than as guards. Part of this respect came from honesty: "There was a strong level of honesty there, and I never saw honesty before in any situation with a guard and a prisoner, since I came to the pen" (March 27, 1996).

Respect is a concept many prisoners have talked about in my interviews with them. Respect can mean many different things. It can refer to what those who live outside of prison might think to be a corrupted courage to maintain the self-respect of a career criminal. Many older prisoners use the term to differentiate themselves from a younger generation of prisoners who do not understand the "traditional" values of convicts. This concept of respect requires maintaining a division between prisoners and guards. Although it can tolerate a level of day-to-day informality in communication, beneath the surface the lines are clearly drawn. It was to this version of respect Gary Weaver had subscribed for most of his life as a prisoner. It was an important part of both how he saw himself and how he believed maximum and super maximum security must be survived. He had now come to a concept of respect large enough to include staff as part of the prison community, provided—and it is a big proviso—that they saw him as a person with strengths, with a capacity to learn and grow, and not as a prisoner to be written off as incorrigible.

Gary Weaver's wider concept of respect is, in essence, humanistic, and as such, places great value on respect for human rights. He was in the Quebec Special Handling Unit when he saw the shocking images of the strip searches at the Prison for Women on television. Gary Weaver's girlfriend was in the P4W at the time, although she was not among the prisoners strip-searched. "I saw that as nothing but a mass sexual assault," he told me in a later interview. "It was sick and twisted. Just seeing that I wanted to smash my cell up."

For Gary Weaver, as for many other prisoners, the events at the P4W were seen not as an aberration but as the expected result of a system which had no respect for legal rights.

> The guards will do as they're told. Rights don't have anything to do with it. If his boss tells him to do that, he's going to do it because he doesn't know what rights are. He doesn't know how to enforce peoples' rights. It's not a concern. (Interview with Gary Weaver, Kent Institution, April 19, 1995)

Over the years Gary had given a great deal of thought as to why certain guards acted as they did; to his mind, a lack of respect for legal rights was only part of the explanation.

In the Prince Albert SHU I had numerous conversations with the other prisoners because of the little things that guards would do which would send me and other prisoners into a rage. They'd come and slam my tray slot shut and I would take it personal. And I used to say to the guys, "Do these people take courses and learn how to fuck with people's minds like this?" And I determined that they couldn't possibly, that human beings couldn't possibly treat people like that on a regular and consistent basis. I just don't think that human beings could learn to and agree to go and treat people like that all day long. I don't think they realized the damage they were doing.

A good example is when I was in the Prince Albert SHU and I was in the hole and I had done about seventy days of hole time and I had promised my mom, I gave her my word, that I would try and bite my tongue because my mouth was getting me in a lot of trouble. One morning, and I was very consciously aware and thinking what I had told my mom, they passed me my breakfast tray and one of the guards had rubbed butter all through my cereal bowl. I tried to take the butter out—it was a Styrofoam bowl—but the bowl got cracked so I couldn't put my milk in and I can't eat my cereal. I pushed the button in my cell thinking, "Stay cool, remember what you promised Mom and just deal with this appropriately," and the guard comes over the speaker and says right away, "What the fuck do you want?" And that set me off. I wanted to respond immediately but I'm saying, "No, just be cool." I felt my voice shaking, but I said, "I need a new cereal bowl." He said, "What's your fucking problem?" I told him that somebody had rubbed butter through my cereal bowl and that I had tried to get the butter out but the bowl had got cracked and so I needed another bowl. He came back on the speaker: "Listen, you fucking punk, you were probably eating out of garbage cans on the street and now you come here and complain." I just went ape-shit. I kicked that door until the goon squad came. And when they came, there were two hot coffees on the tray and I threw both cups at them.

Looking back, do you think that the guard that was standing there with all his buddies preparing the meal trays knew that by rubbing butter in that bowl he was going to set the situation off where

I wouldn't give a fuck if they came in and killed me in the cell? That guard was being a smart-ass, and he's trying to impress his buddies with how much he hates prisoners and to get them snickering. I suppose it's the camaraderie they try to impress upon each other and they bring it into our arena. But I don't think they've got a clue what they're playing with there. If they did, they wouldn't do it. I just can't see that human beings would do that to other people. (Interview with Gary Weaver, Kent Institution, June 3, 1996)

In August 1996, Gary Weaver's case management officer, Stephanie Hronek, prepared a progress summary recommending his transfer to William Head medium security institution. The normal process of "cascading" for general population prisoners at Kent is to Matsqui or Mission Institutions. Although not unprecedented, because William Head is the most open of the mediums, a transfer to it is unusual, particularly for a prisoner with Gary Weaver's institutional record. But Ms. Hronek was very impressed with the changes she had seen in Mr. Weaver. Her summary read in part:

WORK PERFORMANCE:
Mr. Weaver has been employed as the Grievance Clerk since 96-01-15. His work supervisor was contacted and asked for her assessment of Mr. Weaver's performance as Grievance Clerk. She stated that Mr. Weaver conducts himself in a very professional manner and that she credits him with the significant reduction in grievances that are being submitted because of his good communication skills and calming influence with the general population inmates. She further stated that Mr. Weaver has a real grasp of the skills taught to him in the programs he has taken and that he uses these skills in resolving problems. She believes that Gary Weaver is making a sincere effort to make changes in his attitude and his behaviour.

PROGRAM PARTICIPATION:
The Facilitator for [the Anger and Emotions Management Program] has had several discussions with the writer about Gary Weaver and his level of understanding and commitment to learning the skills taught in the Program. Seldom has she seen one so driven to challenging his attitudes and beliefs; she was highly encouraged by Gary Weaver's effort and productivity. (Progress Summary, Kent Institution, August 14, 1996)

The warden of William Head rejected the transfer, recommending that Mr. Weaver first spend time in a more closely controlled medium security institution such as Mission or Matsqui. Mission had a six-month waiting list due to overcrowding. As for Matsqui, both Mr. Weaver and his case management officer felt the staff there would likely view him with suspicion because of his reputation, and this could be easily fuelled by informant information. However, Mr. Weaver was accepted for the Violent Offender Program at the Regional Health Centre scheduled to begin in February 1997, and so he accepted a transfer to Matsqui in the interim. After spending six weeks there, he was transferred to the RHC.

Generally regarded by CSC staff and by prisoners as "the mother of all programs," the eight-month Violent Offender Program at the RHC consists of treatment modules designed to get to the roots of violence and to help prisoners develop cognitive and behavioural controls to prevent future violent acts. In April 1997, I met with Gary Weaver and asked him to describe his first three months in the program.

> When I first came here I couldn't even sit still. I was just psyched, ready for action all the time, and in people's faces. I thought a lot of the guys in the group [PC prisoners] were people that I could never relate to, and now I genuinely care about these guys. When we started this group there was a lot of fronts, and mine was one of the best. "You f-ing rats and f-ing creeps, I'm unapproachable. Don't even try it." Now I'm walking laps with these guys and thinking, How would I ever explain this in a place like Millhaven as to where I used to be then and where I am now? Then I said, What do I have to explain? I'm growing as a human being and letting go of some of this stigmatized prison bullshit. My life doesn't revolve around the prison scene. (Interview with Gary Weaver, Regional Health Centre, April 21, 1997)

Gary was also deeply engaged in disciplining his mind and body during his time at the RHC.

> I've been getting heavy into the martial arts. Every day the stretching, the discipline, the meditation. I'm reading tons of Buddhist literature and some stuff by Jung and Wilhelm Reich. Some of the breathing exercises I'm doing are helping me to get in more control of myself. I don't get so emotional and erratic and things that would normally set me off are now under better control. I keep walking forward and looking behind me at the same time, and every day is a new experience. (April 21, 1997)

## Life at Club Fed

On November 30, 1997, Gary Weaver, after successfully completing the RHC's Violent Offender Program, was transferred to William Head Institution. A few months later, I travelled there to see him. It had been ten years since I had visited William Head, and during that time the institution had undergone a complete makeover. It had originally been a quarantine camp for new immigrants to Canada, and until 1992, the housing for prisoners consisted of dormitory-style huts with prisoners eating their meals in a common dining room. Since then, prisoners have lived in small duplexes where they make their own meals, do their own laundry and take on the everyday living responsibilities which traditional prisons strip away. It is not the duplexes, however, that have given William Head its "Club Fed" designation. That is largely attributable to the site on which the institution is located: a rocky promontory with magnificent vistas of water, wooded coves, and coastal mountains. Once through the main gate and a security fence topped with razor wire, visitors could easily be led to believe they had arrived at an oceanfront retreat with modest but comfortable housing. Within the eighty acres, there are lofty Douglas fir, western red cedar, and Garry oak trees. A meandering road follows the contours of the coast. The duplexes, which each house six to eight prisoners, are organized in cluster formation, with each cluster sharing a common community building with laundry room and offices for staff and programs.

Gary Weaver took me on a walking tour of the site, which included a carving shed built by Aboriginal prisoners with a house front and two house posts carved in traditional West Coast style and a wood salvage area where prisoners cut up driftwood for use in sweat lodges and carving. The tour ended at Gary's favourite place, a Buddhist shrine of which he was the caretaker.

Despite the improved surroundings, Gary Weaver's first five months at William Head had been anything but ideal. From the day of his arrival he was a primary target for informant reports. In January, the IPSOs had confronted him with "reliable information" that he was muscling in on the drug action at William Head; by March, these allegations had escalated to claims that he was not only selling but using heroin. He denied these allegations and offered to provide urine samples, as he had done at Kent and the RHC, to prove that he remained drug free. He was told that only prisoners in programs involving community contact could be placed on voluntary urinalysis. He then offered to provide urine samples on demand at any time and challenged the IPSOs to make such a demand each and every time they received what they regarded as "reliable information" that he was using drugs. No such demand was ever made of him, yet he continued to be under a cloud of suspicion. His case management officer said she could not support his reclassification to minimum security until this cloud was removed.

During our interview, Gary expressed his mounting frustration at these correctional roadblocks.

> At one meeting I was told by the IPSO that I was number 4 on his top 10 list. Then, two weeks later, my case management officer told

me that I was down to number 10. Later the chief IPSO told me that I could be at that number 10 for up to a year. He went on to tell me that people have gotten away with things at William Head and sometimes it takes them a year to catch them. He said, "Time will tell if you're sincere, but if you're not, we'll burrow you out." I said, "Well, I don't have a year to spend playing your stupid games. It's not fair that with zero substance to your so-called reliable information I should have to sit here in this joint and do more time in prison."

It seems that everything I do comes under suspicion. I was teaching a guy Tai Chi at the Buddhist grounds, and they gave me a bunch of heat for that because it makes the staff uneasy. I used to practice Tai Chi with other prisoners at Kent, at Matsqui and RHC, and there never was a problem. They get paranoid here. They think martial art and they've got this negative perception, but if they'd only sit down and talk to me about it they would realize that it's based upon a whole philosophy: if the hand moves forth, hold back the temper, if the temper moves forth, hold back the hand. It's not about kicking the shit out of people and it's not really about fighting. It's about stopping harm from being done. It's about balancing yourself, balancing the yin and yang influences. I've got the Tai Chi bible in my cell. It's called *T'ai Chi Classics* by Master Wai Sun Lao that's revered throughout the world. It talks about the roots of Tai Chi and what Taoists figured out thousands of years ago. And they don't even want to sit down and discuss it with me. They choose to be ignorant. However, it allows me an opportunity, like the Dalai Lama would say, to practise patience, because I sure need patience to deal with these people. (Interview with Gary Weaver, William Head Institution, April 16, 1998)

After lunch at his duplex, Gary Weaver, Unit Manager Marge Fletcher, and I had an extended discussion. Ms. Fletcher believed, as did Gary, that the information the IPSOs were receiving was probably coming from some PC prisoners seeking revenge on Gary for things he had done in the past. In the course of our discussion, a solution emerged. Stephanie Hronek, Gary's case management officer from Kent, was now a CMO at William Head. She would be in the best position to assess the recent changes in Gary. Particularly, she was well placed to assess how his participation in the Violent Offender Program had brought about further developments in his attitude, values, and commitment to change his life. As an experienced case management officer, she would be able to challenge the IPSOs on the reliability of their information.

Before I left, Gary showed me a drawing of a golden eagle he was working on. He explained the picture reminded him of himself. "I was trying to capture the true characteristics of the golden eagle, the intensity which you see in the eyes but at the same time the patience. The intensity and the patience are held in balance. That is what I am trying to do. I've always had the intensity and it's always caused me problems, but it's part of who I am. If I can balance it with patience in working towards what I want in life, I will be like the golden eagle. My vision will be focussed but it will also be broad, and I will see the big picture." Later he took me up to his room to show me the books he had been reading to discipline his art, his mind, and his spirit. He had spent some of his limited money on a book on Rembrandt, and he had just finished reading George Orwell's *1984*.

Over the summer of 1998 things started to look up for Gary Weaver. He completed the Healthy Relationships Program and the Violent Offender Follow-Up Program. He was taken off the IPSOs' "Top 10" list as mysteriously as he had appeared on it. Ms. Hronek recommended that his security classification be lowered to minimum security and that he be transferred to Elbow Lake. Her logic was that Mr. Weaver had completed every aspect of his correctional plan and had served ten months at William Head demonstrating his ability to use the skills he had learned. She noted that "although there have been numerous reports received by the IPSO department suggesting Mr. Weaver is involved in the use of and distribution of drugs and alcohol and the 'muscling' of other inmates, there has been no proof to support any of the allegations" (Progress Summary, William Head Institution, August 21, 1998). Ms. Hronek's recommendation did not carry the day, however, and the deputy warden of William Head, Mr. Denis, determined that Mr. Weaver would remain a medium security prisoner.

## An Elder-Assisted Parole Hearing

After receiving the deputy warden's decision, Gary Weaver's spirits slumped. Stephanie Hronek decided to refocus his "reintegration strategy" on an application to the National Parole Board for escorted temporary absence passes for personal development purposes. Gary had served ten years on his life sentence and was therefore eligible for parole. His pass program would include such activities as psychological counselling, meditation at the Buddhist Dharma Centre, participating in Aboriginal spiritual and cultural activities with the Native Liaison Officer, and attending the Bridge Program in Victoria, which was designed to help prisoners prepare for a return to the community. Ms. Hronek noted that Mr. Weaver's application for two eight-hour escorted passes a month was in keeping with his correctional plan and that the suggested activities would address his criminogenic factors.

Gary Weaver's application also received written support from the Buddhist Chaplain at William Head Institution, Lama Margaret Ludwig, and the Native Liaison Officer, William Bellegarde. In his letter, Mr. Bellegarde wrote:

Over a period of ten months Gary and I have established a trusting relationship that now includes one-on-one sessions covering many topics and interests that pertain directly or indirectly to his eventual and gradual release . . . Gary views the management of his personal life through a holistic process. He is constantly creating a balance with his mental, spiritual, emotional and physical domains. Buddhism is a spiritual philosophy that Gary has taken a strong interest in and one that gives him an alternative belief system that he slowly explores and incorporates. He sees "Natural Law" as a correlation between Buddhism and Native spirituality . . . Whenever there are ceremonies or guests that come to the Native Health Trailer Gary is responsive and responsible in his approach and involvement. He supports in ways that are asked of him and gives of his time freely. For this I am thankful and again I realize that Gary demonstrates honour for other cultures and their beliefs. I will continue to be of support to Gary in his journey of self-evaluation, self-improvement and his reintegration to community, and I can foresee this support extending to working with him in the community. (Letter from William Bellegarde, Native Liaison Officer, to National Parole Board, November 4, 1998)

Shortly after I met Gary, I had offered to act as his legal assistant in his first appearance before the National Parole Board. When the time came in November 1998 to think about that first appearance, I suggested he might want to request an Elder-Assisted Hearing.

Elder-Assisted Hearings began in 1991 in the Prairie Region. There are a number of significant differences between Elder-Assisted Hearings and regular parole hearings. In a regular hearing, the offender appears before two or three members of the Board. Typically, the offender sits on one side of the table and Board members on the other. Some offenders have the support of an assistant, who may be a friend or family member or, in relatively few cases, a lawyer. The regular hearing is inquisitorial in nature; Board members maintain tight control, asking questions relating to the prisoner's offence, institutional history, understanding of his criminogenic factors, and progress towards rehabilitation and reintegration. Elder-Assisted Hearings are conducted in a circular arrangement. Participants include Board members, an Aboriginal Elder retained by the Board as a resource person, the Native Liaison Officer, and the institutional Elder who has been involved in the spiritual and cultural growth of the offender, together with institutional case management staff and the offender's assistant. The hearing begins with a smudging ceremony and a prayer to cleanse the hearts and minds of those participating and to open the road to clear, honest communication. All participants in the circle are encouraged to speak, and while Board members ask the questions they would in a regular hearing, the manner of inquiry tends to be less confrontational (Kathy Louis, "Elder and Community Assisted Hearings" [Paper presented to the International Indigenous Symposium on Corrections— Effective Corrections through Indigenous Wisdom, Vancouver, March 23–25, 1999] at 5–6).

Although Elder-Assisted Hearings were originally intended for Aboriginal offenders, they have also been used by non-Aboriginal offenders who have participated in Aboriginal ceremonies to benefit from the spiritual strength and guidance they offer. Gary had done this for many years and had worked closely with institutional Elders and Aboriginal liaison officers. It was for this reason I suggested he might want to consider an Elder-Assisted Hearing.

Gary Weaver appeared before the National Parole Board at an Elder-Assisted Hearing on January 6, 1999. I was there as his assistant. The hearing lasted several hours, during which Gary took the Board through the twists and turns of his life, tracing his transformation from a rudderless, drug-addicted, and callous punk capable of murder to a reflective, introspective man with both a purpose and a direction. William Bellegarde, Lama Margaret, Stephanie Hronek, and I related our experiences with Gary and expressed our conviction that his remarkable energy, intelligence, and insight held out enormous promise for his future outside prison. Gary answered the Board's questions in detail, answers using the arcane language he had been taught regarding "criminogenic factors," "crime cycles," "thought-stopping" techniques, and a dozen other concepts. I have attended many parole hearings, and I felt Gary gave as good an account of himself as any offender I had ever heard.

The Board members decided to recommend the escorted temporary absence program as proposed by the case management team and approved by the warden. The Board congratulated Gary on his remarkable progress over the last several years, but they also questioned whether his understanding of his violent behaviour was overly intellectualized. These concerns are captured in their written reasons for the decision:

> At today's hearing you, your assistant and the case management team, confirmed much of the filed documentation outlining the miraculous change that you have effected over the past three to four years. Unfortunately, your attempts at responding to the Board's questions in the areas of self-understanding of the root causes of your violent behaviour and victim empathy were intellectualized, lacking true feeling, and bordering on seeming to be well-rehearsed. However, the Board has taken into consideration the lengthy period of solid time you have done segregated in Special Handling Units in

maximum security prisons. Although you are responsible for spending much of your sentence in those facilities, the isolation from normal community values and adherence to the "con code" can have an emotionally flattening effect. The Board therefore accepts your positive change as genuine and concurred the time is right for you to commence an extremely gradual release into the community . . . The Board is satisfied you need to commence implementing your new-found behavioural skills in the community as well as developing a community support network for future assistance as you slowly work towards reintegration into society. (National Parole Board Decision, January 6, 1999)

Most prisoners at Parole Board hearings are interested in the bottom line. For Gary Weaver the bottom line was in the black: the Board recommended the conditional release program he had put forward. Gary Weaver is not like most prisoners, however; he was distressed that his efforts to explain himself had appeared to the Board to lack "true feeling." Lama Margaret, William Bellegarde, and I also found the Board's statements puzzling, knowing how deeply Gary Weaver had gone into himself compared to many offenders. I hypothesized that perhaps Gary's facility at incorporating intellectual, emotional, and spiritual dimensions into his self-analysis was so exceptional and unusual that it had seemed to Board members too good to be true.

## February 2: The First Foray into the Community

The paperwork was processed for Gary's first escorted pass, an expedition involving a half-hour car ride into Victoria for a counselling session with a psychologist. February 2, 1999, marked the first occasion in ten years that Gary Weaver was outside of prison without being in handcuffs and leg irons. As Gary described it:

I'm looking out the car window, I'm seeing grass and trees, and farms, I'm seeing everything—it's so fine—unbelievable. When we get to Victoria I'm looking in stores and at people. The cars look like spaceships, like you see in commercials. (Interview with Gary Weaver, William Head Institution, March 19, 1999)

Three days later, another journey began, one that would plunge Gary back into the abyss of segregation. This journey would also chart how, four years after the Arbour Report and two years after the report of the Task Force on Segregation, segregation review at William Head Institution flagrantly failed to comply with the *Corrections and Conditional Release Act.* Far from illustrating the

CSC's reintegration strategy, the events that followed provide a compelling case for independent adjudication to bring the Rule of Law into "Club Fed."

## February 5: The Assault of Curtis Caziere

On Friday, February 5, at around 9:30 p.m., Curtis Caziere, a prisoner at William Head, was viciously attacked in Upper G Tier by a group of prisoners armed with knives and a steel bar. He suffered extensive injuries, including a deep gash to his head and multiple stab wounds to his arms and hands; a sharpened piece of metal was left embedded in his back. Gary Weaver was one of the prisoners segregated after the attack, based upon the institution's belief that he was involved. On April 7, I filed on Mr. Weaver's behalf a petition for *habeas corpus* in B.C. Supreme Court that was set down for trial on May 3 and 4. On April 28, Warden Gallagher released Mr. Weaver from segregation on the advice of the Department of Justice, thus avoiding a full hearing of the merits and legality of his segregation. The following account of events is drawn from the documents filed in the *habeas corpus* petition of *Gary Weaver* v. *The Warden of William Head Institution* (B.C. Supreme Court, Vancouver Registry cc990462).

After the attack on February 5, Mr. Caziere—bleeding profusely and with the knife still embedded in his back—made his way to the end of Upper G Tier corridor, down two flights of stairs, and into the C-Unit Community Building, a distance of some 200 yards. There he sought assistance from Officer Draibye. Ms. Draibye phoned for the back-up of other officers. Her observation report stated that Mr. Caziere had arrived in her office at approximately 21:40 (9:40 p.m.). Officers Whitten and Higgins, the first officers to arrive on the scene, stated respectively in their reports that they had heard the call for assistance at approximately 21:40 and approximately 21:45 and responded immediately. An observation report by Officer Shular, who was on duty at the front gate, stated that Officer Draibye's call for help came over the radio at 21:37 and that at 21:38 the front gate was contacted to phone 911. Her report went on to record the imposition of a lock-down at 21:49 and the arrival of an ambulance at 21:54. Because Officer Shular was not preoccupied with the immediate task of assisting the badly injured prisoner, her report provides the most accurate time frame for the events.

For reasons that will become apparent, the time frames in this case are of great significance. According to Officer Shular, Mr. Caziere had arrived in the C-Unit Community Building at 21:37 (9:37 p.m.). Given the serious nature of his injuries and the distance between the site of the assault and C unit, it would have taken him no less than five minutes to get to C unit. It could well have taken him much longer, particularly if he had rested, fallen down or passed out on the way. This suggested that the attack on Mr. Caziere was completed no later, and possibly earlier, than 9:32 p.m.

## February 5: Gary Weaver's Initial Segregation

In accordance with standard procedure after an incident of this kind, a lockdown was announced and all prisoners were ordered to return to their houses. Also as part of standard procedure, a search was conducted involving the visual scanning of prisoners for marks such as cuts or abrasions that might indicate involvement in an assault. Shortly after 10:15 p.m., Officers Heck and Miller came into the house in which Gary Weaver resided, F-7. In his *habeas corpus* affidavit, Mr. Weaver described what happened.

> At approximately 10:15–10:25 p.m. I was sitting at the kitchen table in F-7. CO-II Heck and CO-II Miller entered the house. They told me to remove my clothing so that my body could be inspected for wounds, as is the normal procedure when an inmate is assaulted. I did this, and Mr. Heck inspected me from the waist up, using his flashlight. He saw a small scab on my right wrist which had pink, dry scar tissue on it. He stated that it looked "fresh" and that I would be taken to SCU [the Special Correctional Unit] for further examination. He also noticed faded black ink stains on my shirt and said that it looked like blood. He then left to check upstairs. I asked CO-II Miller if CO-II Heck was "for real," and showed him how old the wound was. When I asked him why he didn't stand up to CO-II Heck, he asked me to be patient and to co-operate since they had a major incident to deal with. He said that I would be examined at SCU and probably would be back in a couple of hours. He allowed me to get a cigarette to bring with me. (Affidavit of Gary Weaver, April 1, 1999, para. 18)

Upon arrival at the segregation unit, Gary Weaver and prisoner Scott Carter—also taken to segregation on the basis that he appeared to have recently inflicted cuts; he claimed they were old punching-bag wounds—were placed in the indoor exercise room. Within minutes of their arrival, the two prisoners asked to see a nurse so that a medical professional could confirm there were no fresh cuts on their bodies. They were told someone would be down to see them shortly. The two prisoners also sought to exercise their legal right to make a phone call to their lawyers. Despite repeated requests, they were not allowed to make those calls until 3:50 a.m., five hours after they were taken to the segregation unit. During this period a phone was readily available, and there was no other prisoner movement within the segregation unit that would have made facilitating legal calls impractical.

At around 3:30 a.m. on February 6, Gary Weaver, who had gone to sleep on the floor of the exercise room in the segregation unit, was woken up and told that the RCMP wanted to interview him. He agreed to the interview but requested that he be allowed to contact his lawyer to seek advice. He was permitted to make a phone call and spoke to a Vancouver Island criminal lawyer. Having done so, he went into the interview room. When Mr. Weaver was first seen by the RCMP, Ken Williams, the IPSO, was also present; after Mr. Weaver agreed to talk to the police Mr. Williams offered to leave, but Mr. Weaver asked him to remain during the questioning so he could "hear the truth first hand."

Gary Weaver gave the RCMP the following account of his activities on the previous evening. At around 8:50 p.m. he had phoned Lama Margaret Ludwig, and he had been on the phone with her until around 9:30. The length of the phone call was not unusual; in addition to meeting with Lama Margaret on her twice-weekly visits to the institution, Mr. Weaver spoke to her on a regular, sometimes daily, basis by phone. Their conversation on the evening of February 5 covered Mr. Weaver's reaction to his first pass into the community and his plans for his second pass, which would involve participating in a meditation service with Lama Margaret at the Buddhist Centre in Victoria. His phone call ended when another prisoner, George Storry, came into the F-Unit Community Building to phone his wife. Mr. Weaver and Mr. Storry were regular users of this phone, and they had a courtesy arrangement in which each of them would cut short his phone call when the other person came in to use it. After finishing his phone call to Lama Margaret, Mr. Weaver went into the laundry room in the F-Unit Community Building. He took his clothes out of the washer, where he had placed them before getting on the phone, and put them into one of the dryers. He then left the F-Unit Community Building to return to his residence in F-7. Mr. Weaver was dressed only in a shirt and light pants. Although it was a cold night, he had no coat because it was only a short distance between his house and the Community Building.

Upon returning to F-7, he met three other prisoners outside, Kenny Sutherland, Scott Carter, and Kevin Sims, who had come from their residence in B-2 to borrow some tobacco. Mr. Weaver invited them in. Shortly thereafter they were joined by another prisoner, Ron Perras. At the time Mr. Weaver and his friends entered F-7, two other residents, Ray Bouchard and Robert Scott Terry, were inside watching a film on television that had begun at 8:00 p.m. Mr. Weaver, Mr. Sutherland, Mr. Sims, Mr. Carter, and Mr. Perras were at the kitchen table drinking coffee until around 9:40 p.m., when another prisoner, Chris McCullough, came into F-7 and told everybody that a prisoner had been attacked and there would likely be a lock-down of the institution. Mr. Weaver and several of the other prisoners then left F-7 so that Mr. Weaver could pick up some cigarette tubes at B-2, where the other prisoners lived, before the lock-down came into effect. On the way they stopped at the C-Unit Community Building and peered into the office window, where they could see Curtis Caziere slumped in a chair. At that point, Officer Heck told the prisoners they should return to their units, and Gary Weaver and the others complied.

At the end of his interview with the RCMP, Mr. Weaver was asked to hand over his clothes so they could be checked for blood stains. He took off his clothes, with the exception of his underwear, and was given institutional coveralls in return. These clothes, including his boots, were the same ones he had been wearing from the time he got dressed on Friday morning.

After the completion of his interview with the RCMP, Mr. Weaver was given a Segregation Placement Notice which stated that he was being placed in segregation pursuant to s. 31(3)(b) of the *CCRA*, on the basis that there were reasonable grounds to believe "that the continued presence of the inmate in the general inmate population would interfere with an investigation that could lead to a criminal charge or a serious disciplinary offence." Mr. Weaver was not given any information to explain these "reasonable grounds."

At 4:50 that afternoon Mr. Weaver was released from segregation and told to return to his unit in the general population. He was given no reasons verbally or in writing for his release. He assumed correctional authorities had checked out his story and accepted the truth of what he had told them about his whereabouts at the time Mr. Caziere was assaulted.

## February 8: Return to Segregation

Shortly after lunch on Monday, February 8, Mr. Weaver was in the shower in his house in F-7 when three guards came to tell him he was being returned to segregation. He was escorted to the segregation unit and served with a second Segregation Placement Notice virtually identical to the one he had received two days previously. Even though he had been in the general population for over thirty-six hours since his release from segregation on Saturday and had in no way interfered with the investigation into the assault on Mr. Caziere, he was given no further reasons to explain why the institution now believed his presence in the population would interfere with that investigation. Mr. Weaver was advised that the five-day segregation review required by the *Corrections and Conditional Release Act* would be held on February 15.

Mr. Weaver contacted me to ask if I would represent him in challenging the basis for his segregation. Up to that point, my policy while conducting research was that I would offer advice to prisoners and refer them to other lawyers but would not undertake representation. I had been given complete access to files and been permitted to attend meetings and conduct interviews with staff on the basis that the information was for research purposes and would not be used in the legal representation of prisoners in disputes with the institution. The only exceptions to that rule had been a number of cases involving representation for the purposes of parole, an application to reopen a murder conviction on the basis that the prisoner was wrongly convicted, and an appeal against a Canadian Metis prisoner's extradition to Alabama to serve a 120-year sentence for attempted extortion. Gary Weaver was now asking me to represent him in a full advocacy role challenging the basis for his segregation. I agreed to do this for two reasons. First, the stakes could not have been higher. Just three days after going out on his first pass following ten years of imprisonment, Mr. Weaver was facing segregation on the basis of an accusation that could send him back to maximum security or the Special Handling Unit, with no prospect for release from prison for probably another decade. On the phone he swore he had not been involved in the assault. Second, because I had not conducted research at William Head Institution or interviewed any staff or administrators, I would not, in my advocacy, be making use of material gathered in the course of research.

As Gary Weaver's lawyer, the first thing I did was to contact the warden and the IPSOs at William Head to find out why Mr. Weaver was believed to be a suspect in the assault on Mr. Caziere. I was told there was a "concern" with the credibility of his alibi. Even though Lama Margaret had sent a letter to the Warden confirming that she and Mr. Weaver had been on the phone during the time period he specified, the administration felt she was mistaken about the time frame, and there was the inference that she might be providing Mr. Weaver with an alibi. There was similar scepticism about the corroboration offered by other prisoners who said they were in Mr. Weaver's presence after 9:30 p.m.

The most obvious way to corroborate Mr. Weaver's account of his telephone call to Lama Margaret was to obtain the official Millennium telephone records. The Millennium System had been introduced, over prisoners' objections and after an unsuccessful legal challenge, to enable the CSC to track phone calls made by prisoners; the CSC claimed this would prevent prisoners from using the phone system to make threatening or indecent calls, engage in telephone fraud, or facilitate drug deals. The system allowed correctional authorities to pinpoint any call made on the system to a specific phone and, through the use of PIN numbers, to particular prisoners. When I asked Warden Gallagher to provide me with copies of the Millennium phone records on the evening in question using Mr. Weaver's PIN, I was informed that for technical reasons it was not possible to determine the length of time Mr. Weaver had been on the phone with Lama Margaret. Richard Montminy at CSC National Headquarters, the "guru" of the Millennium System, subsequently advised me that the system was specifically set up to enable a call made on any institutional phone to be traced, identifying the number called, the time the call began, and the length of time it lasted. All of this could be accessed through the prisoner's PIN. Since Warden Gallagher still did not believe it was possible to do this sort of tracing, Mr. Montminy, with Mr. Weaver's consent, accessed the Millennium System and provided the Warden and me with a detailed telephone log.

Before obtaining Mr. Montminy's assistance, I had asked Gary Weaver to review for me his phone call with Lama Margaret on the evening of February 5. He said the call had begun around 8:50 p.m. and continued with a one-minute break until around 9:30. The break occurred when another prisoner's name came up in their conversation. Mr. Weaver had heard that the prisoner, who was on parole at a halfway house in Victoria, may have been suspended. He asked Lama Margaret if she would call the halfway house to see if the prisoner was still a resident there, and he simultaneously made a call to the Victoria Parole Duty Office to find out whether the prisoner had been suspended. After being told he could not get this information over the phone, Mr. Weaver redialled Lama Margaret's number and their call continued until George Storry came into the F-Unit Community Building to use the phone. Mr. Weaver told me he thought he had made all of the calls on his authorized PIN, but it was possible he might also have used an unauthorized one.

I had given Mr. Montminy both PINs, and the official log he provided corroborated Mr. Weaver's account. The log shows that Mr. Weaver phoned Lama Margaret at 20.53.23 (8:53 p.m.) and that this call lasted for eighteen minutes. At 21.12.30 (9:12 p.m.) he phoned the Victoria Parole Office, and this call lasted for forty-two seconds. At 21.13.37 (9:13 p.m.), he phoned Lama Margaret again, and this call lasted for thirteen minutes and fifty-four seconds. Mr. Weaver was therefore on the phone with Lama Margaret (except for the break at 9:12 for less than a minute), from 8:53 p.m. until almost 9:27 p.m. The Warden's response to this verification was that it still left Mr. Weaver with enough time to have taken part in the assault on Mr. Caziere. The new information would be considered by the Segregation Review Board at Mr. Weaver's five-day review, he said.

## February 11–18: The Five-Day Review Process

On February 11, Mr. Weaver was provided with a document entitled "Sharing of Information—Fifth Working Day Review." This failed to set out any substantive reasons why Mr. Weaver was still being held in segregation. It stated only that he was placed in segregation on February 8 and that since his admission he had had access to legal and personal telephone calls, showers, meals, and exercise, and that he continued to abide by the rules and regulations that govern administrative segregation. There was no mention of his interview with the RCMP in the presence of the IPSO, in which he had described his telephone conversation with Lama Margaret and his activities in F-7 afterwards as witnessed by other prisoners. This was all information known to the institution and relevant to Mr. Weaver's segregation review.

On February 15, Mr. Weaver was summoned to what he was told was his five-day segregation review. The Review Board was chaired by Unit Manager Callahan. Mr. Weaver stated that the written Sharing of Information did not contain information relating to the reasons for his continued segregation and that therefore he could not present a proper case to the Board. He was told that the five-day review would be postponed for a further three days in order to provide him with information from the IPSOs. He agreed to this postponement under protest, arguing that the information should have been provided to him on February 11 to enable his five-day review to proceed on the legally required date.

The information Mr. Weaver was promised on February 15 was not given to him until February 17. It came in the form of a memorandum from IPSO Hamer. Under the heading "Gist of Reasons for Continued Segregation," it stated the institution had received information from a number of sources, believed to be reliable, that indicated Mr. Weaver had been involved in the assault on Mr. Caziere. According to the memo, "The only variation in the provided information is your exact involvement whether directly as an assailant or indirectly as a party to the incident." The memo then set out information from several sources. Three of these were anonymous inmates. The first indicated that "while three inmates were in the process of assaulting inmate Caziere in Upper G Tier, you and another inmate were positioned at each end of the corridor keeping watch for the assailants." The second source "provided staff with the information that three inmates were involved in the assault and that you were one of the participants in this assault." The third source "provided staff with information about three inmates directly involved in the assault on inmate Caziere, specifically naming yourself as one of those involved." These three inmate sources are set out in the memo as if they corroborated each other to make a case against Mr. Weaver. What the memorandum failed to acknowledge was that one of these sources was inconsistent with the other two. If Mr. Weaver was directly involved in the assault, he could not have been positioned at the end of the corridor keeping watch. Both accounts cannot be "deemed reliable."

The final source cited in the IPSO's memo offers double hearsay to substantiate the allegations against Mr. Weaver. The memo stated, "A staff member reported that his source who is considered reliable indicated that another inmate told him that there were going to be three assaults on different inmates and that you were involved in this action and that you had another inmate prepared to report to the IPSO that you were elsewhere at the time of the incident." In one fell swoop, this source claims to implicate Mr. Weaver not only in the assault on Mr. Caziere but in two other planned assaults, and it is also designed to invalidate his alibi. Yet in addition to referring to assaults that never happened, it fails to explain how not one but five other prisoners, one of whom had no relationship with Mr. Weaver apart from a telephone courtesy arrangement, corroborated Mr. Weaver's explanation of his whereabouts at the time of the incident.

The five-day review reconvened the next day, February 18. The Board was again chaired by Unit Manager Callahan. The following account by Mr. Weaver describes the manner in which the Board carried out its statutory mandate.

The Review Board informed me that I would be kept in segregation pending the outcome of the investigation into the assault. I protested that I was in no way involved in the assault on Mr. Caziere. I pointed out that the information in the IPSO report was both internally inconsistent and false. I stated that I had been fully honest and truthful in my dealings with the RCMP and with C.S.C. I requested a polygraph be administered in order to establish the truthfulness of my statements. My statements did not elicit any response from the Board. They simply repeated that I would be kept in segregation pending the outcome of the investigation. The Board did not address the issue of why it was believed that my presence in the population would interfere with the ongoing investigation. It was clear to me that the Segregation Review Board had made up its mind that I was to remain in segregation before the hearing even started. (Affidavit of Gary Weaver, April 1, 1999)

## The RCMP Investigation

Following Mr. Weaver's five-day review, I spoke with the RCMP officers conducting the investigation into the assault on Mr. Caziere. Sergeant Bruce Brown and Corporal Gordon Gavin are veteran officers with over fifty years between them in the Force, and they have conducted a number of investigations at William Head. Their preliminary investigation had led them to the view that Mr. Weaver was not involved in the assault on Mr. Caziere. This was based on a number of factors. Sergeant Brown advised me that no blood stains had been found on Mr. Weaver's clothing, nor did his boots match any of the bloody footprints at the scene of the crime. A search of Mr. Weaver's room at F-7, pursuant to a search warrant executed on February 16, had found no incriminating evidence.

The RCMP had also interviewed several of the prisoners Gary Weaver said could corroborate his whereabouts on the evening in question. They had found that these prisoners' accounts were credible and therefore confirmed Mr. Weaver's alibi. Of importance in their assessment that Mr. Weaver was not implicated was the high degree of improbability that he could have committed the assault given (a) his corroborated telephone calls to Lama Margaret until 9:27 p.m. and (b) his corroborated presence in F-7 from 9:30 to 9:40 p.m. Even discounting (b), the RCMP pointed to the virtual impossibility that Mr. Weaver could have completed his telephone call to Lama Margaret, gotten to Upper G Tier, participated in the assault, gotten rid of any incriminating evidence, gotten back to F-7, showered, dressed and then made his way over to C unit to inspect the damage he was supposed to have done—all by 9:37 p.m.

There was another highly significant element in the RCMP's belief that Mr. Weaver was not involved in the assault. The RCMP had first interviewed

Mr. Caziere shortly after the assault, when he was taken to an outside hospital. He had told them then that he could not identify his assailants. Seven days later, following his return to the institution's Health Care Unit, he was re-interviewed by the RCMP and at that time identified Gary Weaver as one of his assailants. Sergeant Brown and Corporal Gavin told me they had the gravest concerns about the reliability of this identification. Prior to their second interview with Mr. Caziere, he had been visited by a William Head staff member who told him which prisoners had been placed in segregation following his assault. In the RCMP's view, this communication not only made the identification unusable in a court of law but rendered it unreliable in assessing the allegations against Mr. Weaver. It also came to light in the second interview that the assailants had been masked. This further undermined the reliability of Mr. Caziere's identification. The RCMP also advised me that to further their investigation and to provide Mr. Weaver with an opportunity to clear his name, they would arrange for him to be assessed by a polygraph examiner. Everything the RCMP told me they had already conveyed to the IPSOs' office at William Head.

## The IPSOs' Investigation

The IPSOs had been conducting their own investigation. Pursuant to a Notice of Intercept of Communications, Mr. Hamer had monitored all of Gary Weaver's telephone calls (including those to his spiritual adviser, Lama Margaret) from February 9, the day after he was returned to segregation, until February 23. In an interview with Mr. Weaver on March 5, Mr. Hamer said he had listened to seven of the fifty tapes and had not heard anything that suggested Mr. Weaver was implicated in the assault of Mr. Caziere. He told Mr. Weaver he had advised the warden of the results of his monitoring and recommended that he not listen to the rest. Mr. Hamer's opinion was reflected in his handwritten notation on the Notice of Intercept: "Seven of fifty calls monitored. No need to transcribe or keep recordings." In a separate conversation I had with Mr. Hamer, he advised me that, in his experience, prisoners involved in wrongdoing will say something that corroborates this over the course of extensive monitoring. In his monitoring of Mr. Weaver's conversations, this did not occur.

The other information Mr. Hamer shared on March 5 related to a hand-written letter Mr. Weaver had sent Warden Gallagher on February 14 in which he unequivocally stated his innocence. Although Mr. Weaver was not told this at the time, the IPSOs' office had sent the letter to the Laboratory for Scientific Interrogation for analysis. In a memorandum dated March 3, 1999, the following assessment was provided: "The subject used very strong denials in regard to being involved in the assault on Curtis Caziere. Such denials are usually associated with being truthful. Please note that the subject's denials do not rule out that the subject might have some knowledge of the identity of the ones who assaulted Caziere." The results of this analysis clearly supported Mr. Weaver's assertions of innocence. The comment made in the last sentence in no way implicated Mr. Weaver, because many other prisoners at William Head had some knowledge (or thought they had) of the identity of Caziere's attackers.

## A Lawyer's Investigation

As part of my investigation, I went to William Head and interviewed the prisoners whose names Mr. Weaver had given to the RCMP to corroborate his alibi. I spoke separately to Mr. Bouchard and Mr. Terry, who had been watching a movie that evening since 8:00 p.m.; each of them remembered Mr. Weaver coming back to the house at around 9:30 with his friends and remaining until around 9:40, when Mr. McCullough came in and announced that a prisoner had been piped. Mr. Sutherland, Mr. Sims, and Mr. Perras all confirmed Mr. Weaver's account, with some differences in the details they remembered. These differences, far from undermining, enhanced the credibility of their accounts. Mr. Sims' statement had some important additional relevance. About half an hour before he went to see Gary Weaver that night, he had met up with Curtis Caziere, who said he was expecting some trouble later that evening and asked Mr. Sims to "back his play," a prison reference to standing by him in the event of a confrontation. Mr. Sims asked Mr. Caziere what the play was and who the players would be. Mr. Caziere refused to give any details, and Mr. Sims replied that he was not prepared to walk in blind. Mr. Caziere knew that Mr. Sims was a good friend of Gary Weaver; it was inconceivable that he would have asked Mr. Sims to back his play if he believed Gary Weaver would be involved.

I also interviewed George Storry, who confirmed the courtesy arrangement he had with Mr. Weaver regarding the use of the phone in the F-Unit Community Building. He remembered that after Mr. Weaver hung up the phone he went over to the laundry room, briefly scanned the bulletin board and then exited the building in the direction of F-7. He also remembered that Mr. Weaver was wearing a shirt and pants but no coat, and that he did not appear to be in a hurry. Of particular significance, Mr. Storry remembered that Mr. Weaver had not left the F-Unit Community Building until after he began his call to his wife. With Mr. Storry's consent, I obtained a copy of his Millennium telephone log from Mr. Montminy at National Headquarters; it showed that his call to his wife began shortly after 9:29 p.m., a fact that reduced the already narrow window of opportunity within which, theoretically, Mr. Weaver could have participated in the attack on Mr. Caziere. Mr. Storry's statements confirmed that Mr. Weaver's behaviour and activities in the F-Unit Community Building were inconsistent with those of a man getting ready to participate in a murderous attack on a prisoner in another part of the prison; furthermore, the fact that Mr. Weaver's telephone call came to an end only with Mr. Storry's arrival was inconsistent with the theory that Mr. Weaver had an appointment to keep with alleged co-conspirators.

Mr. Storry had at first been reluctant to meet with me, but on further reflection agreed because, as he explained, he had himself been the subject of false allegations that resulted in his transfer from William Head several years previously. Warden Gallagher had received "reliable information" that Mr. Storry was plotting to escape from William Head. As a result, Mr. Storry was transferred to Mission Institution. He initiated a court case. A Federal Court judge found the warden's belief that Mr. Storry was involved in the escape "patently unreasonable" and ordered that he be returned to William Head. Apart from the courtesy arrangement over access to the phones, he had no dealings with Mr. Weaver. Mr. Storry, like the other prisoners I interviewed, agreed to swear an affidavit confirming what he had told me.

## March 4–9: The Thirty-Day Review: A Minimalist Approach

On March 4, Mr. Weaver received another Sharing of Information document. This advised him that his thirty-day segregation review would be on March 9, 1999. The document stated that the original Segregation Placement Form, the five-day review, and a psychological assessment would be considered at the hearing. No reference was made to the preliminary results of the RCMP's investigation, the results of the analysis performed on Mr. Weaver's letter to Warden Gallagher, or the negative results of the interception of his telephone calls.

Mr. Weaver's thirty-day segregation review was chaired by Unit Manager Callahan. Mr. Callahan denied Mr. Weaver's request to have me present as legal counsel at the hearing, on the grounds that a lawyer's presence was not necessary considering the Board's duties and functions. Mr. Callahan informed Mr. Weaver that the Board was recommending he remain segregated while his case was reviewed for a transfer to a maximum security institution. Mr. Weaver protested that the Board had come to a decision without giving him an opportunity to present his case. Mr. Callahan said the Board's primary function was to review any concerns Mr. Weaver had with regard to his segregated status, including such things as meals, showers, exercise, and legal calls. Mr. Weaver asked the Board whether it was taking the new information into account: the RCMP's conclusions that his boots did not match any footprints at the scene of the crime, the RCMP's concerns about the reliability of Mr. Caziere's identification of his assailants, and the RCMP's overall conclusion that Mr. Weaver was not involved in the assault. He also asked whether the Board was taking into account the results of the hand-writing analysis and the interception of his telephone calls. Mr. Weaver was told that all of this would be dealt with in the documents being prepared for his

Involuntary Transfer and he would have a chance to present a rebuttal in due course. Although Mr. Weaver pointed out that all the evidence was consistent with his innocence rather than his guilt, the Board reiterated that he would be maintained in segregation pending a decision on his transfer to Kent maximum security.

Mr. Callahan's minimalist statement of the Segregation Board's functions—to review prisoners' concerns about such things as meals, showers, exercise, and legal calls—failed to include the Board's primary function, which is to review whether there are reasonable grounds for continued segregation of a prisoner and reasonable alternatives to such segregation. Mr. Callahan began the hearing by advising Mr. Weaver that he would be maintained in segregation while his case was reviewed for a transfer to higher security. The original legal justification for Mr. Weaver's segregation was to prevent interference with an ongoing investigation. Segregation for the purposes of reviewing a prisoner's security classification is not an authorized basis for segregation under s. 31(3) of the *CCRA*. As he had done at his five-day review, Gary Weaver protested his innocence of any wrongdoing in the assault of Mr. Caziere, and he sought to bring to the Board's attention the preliminary results of the RCMP investigation and the IPSOS' investigation, which corroborated his innocence. The Segregation Review Board made no efforts to respond to Mr. Weaver's arguments.

## March 15: Notice of Involuntary Transfer

On March 15, Gary Weaver received a Notice of Involuntary Transfer Recommendation for Kent maximum security, signed by Unit Manager Callahan. The Notice stated:

> As a result of this incident there has been an extensive investigation and information gathered from various sources. While the information does vary somewhat, there is no doubt that from every source of information Weaver is identified as having had some part in the assault. We may never know the extent of Mr. Weaver's involvement in this assault but I sincerely believe he played some part. (Notice of Involuntary Transfer Recommendation, William Head Institution, March 15, 1999)

Quite apart from the inaccuracy of Mr. Callahan's statement that every source of information identified Gary Weaver as being involved with the assault—this completely disregarded both the information from the RCMP and the results of the handwriting investigation and the monitoring of tapes—this notice clearly revealed that Mr. Callahan had already considered Mr. Weaver to be guilty at the time he chaired the thirty-day review.

The initiation of Gary Weaver's involuntary transfer to Kent required my immediate attention. Under *CCR Regulations,* prisoners have two days to prepare a written rebuttal to a recommendation for transfer. Because of the complexity of the case, and because Mr. Weaver was scheduled for a polygraph examination on March 25, I requested and received an extension until the end of March for the preparation of the rebuttal. I also requested further written information regarding the various "reliable" sources identified in the IPSO's memo of February 15, which were also referred to in the transfer recommendation. In response, I received a Security Intelligence Report, dated February 26, 1999, in which the names of prisoner informants were blanked out to protect their identity.

On March 25, Gary Weaver was taken under escort to the Victoria RCMP detachment, where he was interviewed and tested by Sergeant Hunter of the Vancouver RCMP Polygraph Section. Sergeant Hunter later reported to Sergeant Brown and Corporal Gavin that, although the results of the test itself were "inconclusive," his intensive questioning of Mr. Weaver and Weaver's demeanour during and after the test led him to agree that Mr. Weaver was not involved in the assault on Curtis Caziere. The results of the test and Sergeant Hunter's opinion were relayed to the IPSOS' office at William Head.

## The Same Rights, Privileges, and Conditions of Confinement

The provisions of the *CCRA* make it clear that prisoners in administrative segregation shall be given the same rights, privileges, and conditions of confinement as the general inmate population, except for those that can only be enjoyed in association with other inmates or cannot reasonably be given owing to limitations for security requirements. The William Head Segregation Unit Inmate Handbook specifically provides that inmates will receive their cell effects as soon as this can be arranged, but not later than two days after admission to segregation. The Handbook also states that individuals held in segregation are entitled to wear personal clothing. The only items which a prisoner is not entitled to possess in segregation are those "construed as dangerous, or as having the potential to be used as a weapon."

Notwithstanding the provisions of the *CCRA* and the Inmate Handbook, Gary Weaver was not provided with his personal effects until March 25, forty-five days into his segregation, even though he had made several requests for them. The IPSO, Mr. Hamer, had told Mr. Weaver on March 5 that he was denied his personal clothing and effects at the beginning of his segregation because of the existence of a search warrant for certain specified items, including clothing and footwear. That search, however, had been executed on February 16, so there was no reason they could not be released to him. Yet it took another twenty days for that to happen. In his affidavit Mr. Weaver described how his belongings had been treated.

Everything I owned, including clothes, books and my Buddhist and Aboriginal spiritual items, had been carelessly and haphazardly packed in boxes and garbage bags. When I looked through my personal effects I was outraged at the total disrespect that had been displayed toward my religious and spiritual items. A tapestry valued at $400.00, that I use for Tantric practice, was stuffed in one of the bags as if it were a dishcloth. An eagle feather, which is of great significance in Aboriginal ceremonies, was crushed under other items. The disrespect shown to my spiritual items matched the disrespect the Correctional Service of Canada has shown to my legal rights in continuing my placement in Segregation and failing to comply with the provisions of the c.c.r.a. (Affidavit of Gary Weaver, April 1, 1999, para. 67)

## March 31: The Rebuttal to the Involuntary Transfer Notice

On March 31, I travelled to William Head, my fourth trip within a month, and delivered to Warden Gallagher the rebuttal to the recommendation for Gary Weaver's involuntary transfer to Kent. Accompanying the rebuttal were the affidavits of Mr. Storry and the other prisoners who swore Mr. Weaver was with them from 9:30 p.m. to around 9:40 p.m. In the rebuttal, I first set out the facts that I believed were not in dispute and asked the question, "How credible and reasonable is the allegation that Mr. Weaver was involved in the assault on Mr. Caziere?"

> According to the information that I have obtained from the RCMP the attack on Mr. Caziere was well planned. They believe he was lured to the Upper G unit at an appointed time and his attackers had their faces masked and were armed with knives and a steel pipe. A number of prisoners were involved, some of them as the actual perpetrators of the assault and others may have been stationed at either end of the corridor to prevent Mr. Caziere's escape or to act as lookouts in case officers or other prisoners came by . . . It is established that Mr. Weaver was on the phone until shortly before 9:27 p.m. According to both Mr. Weaver and Mr. Storry he terminated his phone call only because Mr. Storry at that point came in to use the phone. He then attended to the mundane activity of taking his clothes out of the washer and putting them in the dryer without any hint of being in a hurry. He then left the F-Unit Community Building. Even though February 5 was a cold and windy day Mr. Weaver was dressed lightly, consistent with his making the short trip from F-7 to the Community Building and back again . . . According

to Mr. Storry's Affidavit Mr. Weaver did not leave the F-Unit Community Building until after 9:29 p.m.

It is clearly established that Mr. Caziere did not arrive at the C-Unit Community Building until 9:37 p.m. Both the RCMP and IPSOs believe that in light of the extensive injuries suffered by Mr. Caziere it is likely to have taken him at least 5 minutes after he was attacked to get from the Upper G Tier to the C-Unit Building. I have myself retraced the route that Mr. Caziere would likely have taken; walking slowly, but without a knife in my back and without feeling the effects of a steel pipe over my head and a deep gash in my face and multiple cuts on my hands and arms, it took me 5 minutes to make the trip. This means that the attack on Mr. Caziere must have been completed no later than 9:32 p.m. In all likelihood it was completed before that.

For Mr. Weaver to be one of the participants in the assault on Mr. Caziere after leaving the F-7 Community Building at 9:29 p.m. he would have had to go somewhere else to pick up a mask and a weapon and make his way over to the Upper G Tier with the supreme confidence that all of the other pre-planning for the attack, including luring Mr. Caziere to the Upper G Tier and the positioning of lookouts, was in place, ready for him to perform his assigned role. Having fulfilled that role he would then have had to dispose of his mask and weapon. Since the physical evidence shows that there was a lot of blood at the scene of the crime, some of which would have likely been splashed on the assailants' clothing and hands, he would also have had to dispose of any blood-stained clothes, return to his Unit, shower and change into fresh clothes. Having done so, he would then have gone over to the C-Unit Community Building, conspicuously presenting himself to the Officers attending to Mr. Caziere, to see what state Mr. Caziere was in after the attack, having only minutes before himself participated in the attack which left a knife in Mr. Caziere's back. It is hard to imagine a scenario or theory more preposterous or more removed from any air of reality. Far from supporting a belief based on reasonable and probable grounds that Mr. Weaver was involved in the assault, it defies any such belief.

At the risk of repetition I would underline the fact that three days prior to the assault on Mr. Caziere Mr. Weaver had participated in his first temporary absence pass, representing the first time he had been outside of prison in ten years, and was eagerly awaiting his next pass at which he would be participating in a Buddhist spiritual ceremony, with the prospect of further release from imprisonment. First and foremost on his mind were the possibilities of the rest of his life outside of prison; furthest from his mind were the violence and mayhem within which he had lived much of the previous ten years. I emphasize also the fact that Mr. Weaver's conversation only ended when Mr. Storry came into the F-Unit Community Building to make his call; had he not done so, Mr. Weaver would have continued to talk to Lama Margaret and in all likelihood would have been on the phone, as was Mr. Storry, when Mr. Caziere staggered into the C-Unit Building. (Letter from Michael Jackson to Warden Gallagher, March 31, 1999)

The next part of my rebuttal addressed the institution's case against Mr. Weaver. I first reviewed the so-called "reliable information" contained in the security gist given to Mr. Weaver on February 15, to which reference was made in the transfer recommendation. I suggested that the sources were inconsistent with one another and were unsworn hearsay accounts flatly contradicted by the sworn affidavits I had gathered.

My rebuttal specifically addressed the information contained in the Security Intelligence Report dated February 26. Far from supporting the allegations against Mr. Weaver, this document further demonstrated that there were no reasonable grounds to believe he had been involved in the assault. The sources cited contradicted one another on essential issues. For example, on page 3 the report stated that Officer Heck received information "believed to be reliable" that five offenders were involved in the assault. Later on that page the report said another officer received information from a "reliable source" that three offenders were involved. On page 5, another source "known to Officer Heck" stated that four offenders were involved in the attack. Several sources said that Mr. Weaver stabbed Mr. Caziere, others that he kept watch. Yet all of these sources were uncritically cited as "reliable." There were multiple theories about the motive for the attack as well. On page 3, one source suggested that it had happened because Mr. Caziere owed three bales of tobacco; on page 5, a second source stated that Mr. Caziere was supposed to move drugs inside but failed to do so; on the same page another source "hypothesized" that the attack related to rivalry in the drug trade within William Head. Another theory, given on page 4, was that Mr. Caziere had befriended a prisoner "fingered as a rat."

My rebuttal then reviewed the results of the RCMP and IPSO investigations. I argued that both the monitoring of Mr. Weaver's telephone calls and the analysis of his letter to the warden supported the case for his innocence. In addition, every line of the RCMP investigation corroborated Mr. Weaver's innocence and provided no evidence of his involvement in the assault.

The final part of my rebuttal involved an analysis of the report prepared by Stephanie Hronek, Mr. Weaver's Institutional Parole Officer. In my discussions with her, she had made it clear she believed Mr. Weaver was not involved in the assault and there was no justification for either segregation or transfer. However, as his IPO, she had been instructed by the warden to prepare the documents to support a recommendation for transfer. In her report, using the CSC's security rating scheme, Ms. Hronek rated Mr. Weaver as a medium security prisoner, but she concluded that because of an "override factor, based upon Mr. Weaver's involvement in an assault causing serious physical harm to another inmate, he is to be rated a maximum security prisoner." Ms. Hronek set out the basis for the institution's case and compared it with the information provided by the RCMP.

> Several inmate sources deemed to be reliable, implicate Mr. Weaver as one of the perpetrators in the physical attack on another inmate on 99-02-05. The police are continuing their investigation of this assault, however it will be several more weeks before their investigation will be concluded. However, the RCMP Officer leading the investigation into the assault on inmate Caziere does not believe that Gary Weaver was involved. Sergeant Brown bases his professional opinion on several facts that have arisen, i.e. that Gary Weaver was on the telephone to his Buddhist teacher when the assault is believed to have occurred, that Gary Weaver's footwear does not match any of the footprints at the scene of the attack, that none of Gary Weaver's clothes appear to have blood stains on them. Additionally Sergeant Brown has serious concerns about the truthfulness of Curtis Caziere's statement to police. In the interim, Mr. Weaver cannot be returned to the general population due to security concerns he is viewed as presenting at William Head Institution. There is a great deal of animosity that has arisen within the inmate population and by staff, as a result of the attack on inmate Caziere and the segregation of Gary Weaver. Given that the police have all but ruled out Gary Weaver as one of the perpetrators in the attack on Curtis Caziere, it would appear that the least restrictive alternative to continued placement in the Segregation Unit is Mr. Weaver's voluntary placement in another medium security environment. An involuntary transfer to Kent Institution in the face of strong police information indicating that Mr. Weaver was not involved in the assault on inmate Caziere would be regarded by this writer to be unjust. The security classification supports a medium rating but with the override factor due to the assault on another offender, a maximum rating is achieved. (Notice of Involuntary Transfer Recommendation, William Head Institution, March 15, 1999)

I argued in my rebuttal that Ms. Hronek's conclusions demonstrated the fatal flaw in the recommendation for Mr. Weaver's transfer to Kent.

How can it be argued that a prisoner who on every scale is rated as a medium security prisoner, can be considered maximum security on the basis of an "over-ride" factor that assumes his involvement in an assault on another prisoner where, in the very same paragraph, it is stated that the RCMP have all but ruled out his participation in this assault and that in light of this it would be "unjust" to transfer him to a maximum security institution. Not only would it be, as Ms. Hronek rightfully states, "unjust," it would be a violation of fundamental principles of justice contrary to Section 7 of the *Canadian Charter of Rights and Freedoms,* and inconsistent with the explicit provisions of the *CCRA* regarding security classification.

## March 31 to April 8: The Sixty-Day Review— "Some Little Things"

On March 31, the same day I delivered my rebuttal to Warden Gallagher, Gary Weaver received a Sharing of Information document advising him that his case would be reviewed by the Segregation Review Board on April 8. He was also given the results of his sixty-day regional review. This review had been conducted by Bob Lusk, Regional Oversight Co-ordinator for Administrative Segregation. This was the regional oversight mechanism the Commissioner of Corrections had suggested was a sufficient alternative mechanism to independent adjudication to ensure compliance with the law. Mr. Lusk's review had been completed on March 30. Yet Mr. Weaver had not been notified that this review would take place; he was not asked to present any submissions, nor was he given the opportunity to appear in person. According to the new procedures, the review was done electronically, using the file maintained by the Offender Management System. Mr. Lusk's decision was as follows:

> Mr. Weaver is a suspect in the stabbing of another offender at William Head Institution. The assault was serious and the victim required extensive hospitalization before he could be spoken to. The police investigation and interviews of other witnesses continue while he is isolated from the general population. Additional information and determination of criminal charges will be examined prior to any security classification review or transfer actions. Administrative Segregation is justified. (Regional Review of Offender's Segregated Status, March 30, 1999)

Mr. Lusk's decision makes no reference to the results of the police investigation referred to in Ms. Hronek's assessment in the involuntary transfer package. Mr. Lusk states that "interviews of other witnesses continue while he [Mr.

Weaver] is isolated from the general population," yet police had already completed their interviews and had informed the institution that, for the purposes of their ongoing investigation, it was not necessary that Mr. Weaver be maintained in administrative segregation. Had Mr. Weaver been given an opportunity to present his case before Mr. Lusk, he could have brought these facts to his attention, along with the other evidence that supported his innocence. This evidence could have been taken into account by Mr. Lusk in conducting his regional review of the justification for Mr. Weaver's continued segregation. As it was, the new "enhanced" regional review process provided no more protection for Gary Weaver than the institutional reviews.

On April 8, 1999, Mr. Weaver appeared before the Segregation Review Board for his second thirty-day review. The Board was chaired by Unit Manager Cawsey. At the outset, Mr. Weaver requested that the hearing be tape-recorded so that there was an accurate record of the proceedings. His request was in accordance with the policy set out in the *Administrative Segregation Handbook* provided to participants, including Mr. Cawsey, at a regional legal education workshop held in January 1998. The policy states, "Hearings should be recorded on audio tape, to ensure an accurate record is available. The audio tape should be retained for at least two years" (*Administrative Segregation Handbook,* December 1997, Annex A: Detailed Timelines and Procedures). According to Mr. Weaver's sworn statement, Unit Manager Cawsey rejected Mr. Weaver's request, "because basically what we are doing is some little things." Mr. Cawsey then informed Mr. Weaver that the Board had to "get some administrative stuff out of the way" and proceeded to ask him if he had received visits from Health Care and had access to showers, phone calls, and visits. When Mr. Weaver sought to raise the issue of his innocence in the assault on Mr. Caziere, arguing that therefore there was no basis for his segregation, he was advised by Mr. Cawsey, "That's for you to deal with with your lawyer." Mr. Weaver was advised that no recommendation would be made for his release from segregation until a decision was reached about his involuntary transfer to maximum security. Mr. Weaver submitted that this was unfair and that once again he was being denied the opportunity to have his case considered on its merits by the Segregation Review Board. Mr. Weaver asked if Mr. Cawsey was aware of the information that had come to light since his initial segregation, including the confirmation of his alibi and the results of the RCMP investigation. Mr. Cawsey said he was not. Mr. Weaver referred Mr. Cawsey to the rebuttal to the involuntary transfer package, submitted March 31. Mr. Cawsey said he had not seen this document. Mr. Weaver requested that Mr. Cawsey review the document, then reconvene the Segregation Review Board prior to making a recommendation regarding his segregated status. Mr. Cawsey agreed to obtain a copy of the rebuttal. If after having read it he felt there was a need to reconvene the hearing, he would do so.

Later that same day, Mr. Weaver received the written recommendation of the Segregation Review Board that he be maintained in segregation and the warden's decision accepting that recommendation. The Segregation Review Board gave no reason for its recommendation, and the warden's final decision stated that Mr. Weaver would remain in segregation until the transfer process was completed. Needless to say, the Segregation Review hearing was never reconvened.

As with the previous Segregation Review hearings of Mr. Weaver's case, the hearing on April 8 was not the hearing contemplated by the legislative framework of the CCRA and CCR *Regulations,* nor did it conform with any model of a fair hearing. As with the other hearings, the decision to maintain Mr. Weaver in segregation was a foregone conclusion, and the Board did not consider any of the relevant information in assessing the lawful justification for segregation under s. 31(3) of the CCRA. As both the recommendation of the Segregation Review Board and the warden's decision make clear, the segregation review process was entirely subordinated to the outcome of the involuntary transfer process. There was no independent inquiry into the lawful grounds for segregation.

## A Petition for *Habeas Corpus*

On April 7, the day before Mr. Weaver's second thirty-day review, I had filed in B.C. Supreme Court a petition for *habeas corpus* seeking an order for the release of Gary Weaver from unlawful segregation. The petition claimed there was no evidence to support a belief on reasonable grounds that there was a legal basis for segregation under s. 31(3) of the CCRA; that Mr. Weaver's continued segregation had been in contravention of the mandatory provisions of the CCRA in respect to the written sharing of information and the conduct of segregation reviews; and that he had been denied the rights, privileges, and conditions to which he was entitled in administrative segregation. There was a further ground for the petition: that the CCRA, by not providing for a segregation review process that was independent and impartial, violated the principles of fundamental justice, contrary to s. 7 of the *Charter of Rights and Freedoms.* The petition was set down for hearing for May 3 and 4.

## April 20: The Warden's Response to the Rebuttal

On April 19, Warden Gallagher responded in writing to my rebuttal, informing Mr. Weaver that he would be recommending his involuntary transfer to Kent. In two and a half pages, the warden addressed only a few of the arguments I had set out in my twenty-five-page rebuttal. Surprisingly, he challenged my contention that the time frame for the attack on Mr. Caziere was best gauged by the times the officer on the front gate had recorded.

This conclusion is only warranted if all other time references are specifically related to timekeeping as maintained by Officer Shular, and if one has confidence that hers was a completely accurate reference in the first place. Indeed, Ms. Shular indicates in subsequent inquiries that she is uncertain about what timepiece she used to note the time reference, although she believes it was her personal analog wristwatch. She states she habitually keeps it five minutes fast. As the timepiece she believes she used for the reference is an analog variety, her observations are, almost by necessity, estimates, due to the nature of the faces of analog timepieces. (Notification of Review of Recommendation Relative to Transfer, William Head Institution, April 19, 1999)

Ironically, just the day before the warden expressed his view that Officer Shular's observations were estimates "due to the nature of the faces of analog timepieces," David Gelernter, a professor of computer science at Yale, had written in a special edition of the *New York Times Magazine* devoted to "the best ideas, stories and inventions of the last thousand years" that his vote for runner-up for best invention of the millennium went to the analog clock face.

Two hands trace out different scales; you would think such a gadget would be too tricky to use. In fact, it's the best "interface" ever designed. No other device can transmit such complex information so precisely, so fast. (David Gelernter, "Bound to Succeed," *New York Times Magazine*, April 18, 1999, at 132)

Certainly Officer Shular, when she was on duty on February 5, did not believe that she was only estimating time when she wrote down that the call for help over the radio came at 21:37, that the front gate was contacted to phone 911 at 21:38, that a lock-down was imposed at 21:49, and that the ambulance arrived at 21:54.

Warden Gallagher also challenged my assumption (one shared by the RCMP) that it must have taken Mr. Caziere at least five minutes to get from the site of his attack to the C-Unit Community Building. He suggests, "It is equally conceivable that, being fully conscious during this fight, and driven by fear and adrenaline, the victim could have traversed the distance between Upper G Tier and the C-Unit Community Building in considerably less time, perhaps stumbling due to the speed of his movement as well as his injuries." Conceivable, yes, but highly improbable. Indeed, subsequent to my receipt of the warden's recommendation, I interviewed another prisoner at William Head who had observed, from a window in his house, Mr. Caziere coming up the path very slowly and stumbling. Moreover, according to this prisoner's observations, instead of proceeding straight to C-Unit Community Building, Mr. Caziere went to his own house and sat on the porch for several minutes before moving slowly over to the C-Unit Community Building. If that was the case, my original estimate that it took him five minutes to get from Upper G Tier to the C-Unit building was on the low side.

Even more surprising than Warden Gallagher's reliance on the necessary imprecision of an analog timepiece was his suggestion that the phone calls made to Lama Margaret, as verified by the Millennium phone records, may have been made by another prisoner. He stated that the use of the second PIN number "does not irrefutably mean Offender Weaver in fact made the calls." The implication here is either that Lama Margaret Ludwig lied when she said she spoke to Gary Weaver or that she *mistakenly* believed the prisoner she spoke to for forty minutes was Gary Weaver. In response to this incredible assertion, I obtained an affidavit from Lama Margaret in which she swore the conversation she had between 8:53 p.m. and 9:27 p.m. on February 5 "was with Mr. Weaver and no other prisoner" (Affidavit of Lama Margaret Ludwig, April 30, 1999). Her affidavit also stated that the conversation was particularly memorable since it concerned Mr. Weaver's reflections on his first pass into the community and his forthcoming pass to the Buddhist Dharma Centre.

Warden Gallagher also took issue with my argument that George Storry had no motive for providing Gary Weaver with a cover story because they were not friends or associates. He stated that Mr. Storry may have harboured ill will towards the administration due to his own involuntary transfer from William Head and pointed to the fact that Mr. Storry initially told the IPSOs his telephone conversation with his wife began at 9:15 p.m. The Warden failed to realize, however, that this last factor supported my contention that Mr. Storry was not trying to provide Mr. Weaver with an alibi; otherwise, he would have chosen a time much closer to when Mr. Caziere was attacked. In any event, the Millennium record shows definitively that Mr. Storry began his phone call at 9:29 p.m. Mr. Storry had already told me that his willingness to swear an affidavit supporting Mr. Weaver's account was born of his concern that Warden Gallagher not be permitted to unfairly accuse another prisoner and thereby destroy all that the prisoner had worked for.

For Warden Gallagher, the bottom line was "the essential fact . . . that the victim has repeatedly identified Offender Weaver as one of his assailants." He suggested Mr. Caziere's initial reluctance to identify his assailants likely stemmed from a hope he could "fix" the difficulty and re-enter the general population. Mr. Caziere had told staff that the meeting in Upper G Tier was pre-arranged to conclude a drug transaction, and therefore the Warden found it "quite conceivable that all of the necessities to commit the assault, including weapons and protective clothing, were in place before the assault."

Putting aside the important fact that this was only one of three different accounts Mr. Caziere gave to staff to explain his presence in Upper G Tier, Mr. Weaver's activities from 8:50 until 9:27 are inconsistent with his participation in this conspiracy. He was engaged in an extended telephone conversation with a Buddhist nun about his future outside of prison; the call was terminated by the unpredictable timing of Mr. Storry's arrival to use the phone.

The RCMP's opinion regarding Mr. Weaver's innocence was given short shrift by the Warden.

> The rebuttal comments on the fact that the RCMP investigating officer, Sergeant Brown, and the polygraph operator have made comments about their opinions regarding the involvement of Offender Weaver in the assault. In the case of Sergeant Brown, his opinion may reflect the extent to which he believes a prosecution would be successful. To simply offer the opinion that Offender Weaver was not involved in the assault ignores the fact that Caziere has maintained he was an assailant and that he was implicated by others. The polygraph results have been characterized as inconclusive. It is again, only the administrator's unsubstantiated opinion based on extraneous information that Offender Weaver was not involved. (Notification of Review, William Head Institution, April 19, 1999)

This dismissive commentary mischaracterizes what the RCMP conveyed both to me and to the IPSOs. They had not concluded that Mr. Weaver was involved in the assault but that there was not enough admissible evidence to secure a conviction. Their opinion, based on a full investigation, was that Mr. Weaver was *not* involved in the assault. The Warden incorrectly states that the RCMP ignored Mr. Caziere's identification of Mr. Weaver as one of his assailants. The RCMP interviewed Mr. Caziere on two occasions, and they made it clear that they discounted his identification because his assailants were masked and the institution had supplied him with information about the suspects. It was Warden Gallagher who ignored the opinions of highly experienced RCMP investigators, based on interviews with the principals, an analysis of Mr. Weaver's clothing, the corroboration of his alibis, and the sheer implausibility that Mr. Weaver could have participated within the likely time frame. Ironically, in the court proceedings in which George Storry successfully challenged his involuntary transfer from William Head, Warden Gallagher had based his assessment of the reliability of informant information on the fact that the RCMP believed it to be reliable; in the case of Gary Weaver, where the RCMP consistently expressed their opinion that the information implicating him was not credible or reliable, the Warden chose to dismiss this without providing a scintilla of evidence to the contrary.

Prior to receiving Warden Gallagher's recommendation that Mr. Weaver be involuntarily transferred, I had asked Sergeant Brown and Corporal Gavin if they would prepare an official report on the state of their investigations. I put it to them that, as key players in the administration of justice, it was their duty not only to ensure that the guilty parties were prosecuted but also to ensure that punishment was not inflicted upon those wrongly accused. The Warden's belief that Mr. Weaver had participated in the assault, if left unchallenged, would result in Mr. Weaver being treated as if he were guilty and consequently in his spending many more years in prison. Sergeant Brown and Corporal Gavin agreed this would be unjust. In a letter dated April 20, 1999, they wrote to the IPSOS at William Head confirming that they had completed their investigation into the assault on Mr. Caziere and that there was insufficient evidence to support criminal charges. The letter went on to state:

> When Mr. Caziere did agree to provide details of his recollection it was seven days after the assault. By this time the names of several persons had been provided to him as possible suspects. Even at this point in the investigation Mr. Caziere continued to withhold crucial information, particularly, that the suspects were wearing balaclavas at the time of the attack. These actions diminished the value of Mr. Caziere's identification of the suspects and detracted from his credibility.
>
> Several search warrants were effected during the course of this investigation, and items of clothing and footwear were seized as exhibits. These exhibits have been scanned by our Forensic Services Personnel, with negative results in either locating suspect DNA evidence or in physically matching footwear impressions to the scene.
>
> Gary Weaver [was] given polygraph tests on March 25, 1999 by Sergeant Hunter of Vancouver polygraph section. [The test] was deemed inconclusive by Sergeant Hunter. Sergeant Hunter did provide his professional opinion, that it was his belief that Weaver [was] not involved in the assault on Caziere.
>
> Numerous inmates were interviewed to check alibis provided by . . . Weaver. The alibis as provided were confirmed through these interviews. It is our belief that Inmate X [for legal reasons, X has been substituted for the name given in the letter] was involved in the assault on Caziere. He has been interviewed on two separate occasions and on each occasion he denied any knowledge or involvement. Unfortunately there is insufficient evidence to proceed against X. (Letter from RCMP to William Head Institution, April 19, 1999)

## April 28: Release from Segregation

Given Warden Gallagher's determination to proceed with his recommendation for transfer (which had gone to Regional Headquarters for a final decision) and Gary Weaver's continued segregation, the matter now headed for court. For the last two weeks of April I worked on the preparation of my legal argument, culminating in a sixty-six-page brief. I also awaited receipt of the material to be filed by the Department of Justice in support of Warden Gallagher's decision to maintain Mr. Weaver in segregation. On the evening of April 27, I was advised by counsel for the Department of Justice that she would not be filing any material; on her advice, the warden would be releasing Mr. Weaver from segregation the next day and withdrawing his recommendation for involuntary transfer to Kent. On Wednesday, April 28, Gary Weaver was released to the general population after having served eighty days in segregation.

His time in segregation took a heavy toll on Mr. Weaver. In his first affidavit in support of the petition for *habeas corpus,* he described the conditions in segregation and his reaction to his false imprisonment.

> During the ten years I have served on my life sentence I have spent many days in Segregation units in other prisons. However, the 50 days I have so far spent in Segregation at William Head is in many respects the most difficult and damaging. On February 2, 1999 I was in the community on a pass with other citizens, beginning a new life. Since February 8, I have been confined in a cage with no furnishings except a steel double bunk, a desk welded to the floor and a steel sink and toilet. I am not even allowed to sleep in darkness because there is a light which remains on throughout the night. This light is bright enough to read from and it makes sleep fitful and at times impossible. Most distressing is the fact that I have been placed in Segregation for something I did not do and that the RCMP do not believe that I did. The Warden of William Head and Unit Manager Callahan, the Chair of the Segregation Review Board, have failed to take into account any of the evidence that the RCMP find compelling and continue to treat me as if I am guilty of the assault. From day to day I tell myself, "Be patient, hang on, justice will prevail, the truth will be revealed," but I still remain in Segregation. When I first came down to Segregation, for the first 10 days I imagined every time I heard a noise in the hallway, that my cell door was going to open and there was going to be either the Warden, Mr. Callahan or someone else saying, "Look, Gary, there's been a mistake here, you're going back to population, we're going to restore everything." That has not happened and I do not believe it will happen without the intervention of this Court. (Affidavit of Gary Weaver, April 1, 1999, para. 69)

## A Report Card on Legal Compliance

There is little doubt that Gary Weaver was right. Without the filing of the *habeas corpus* petition, he would have remained in segregation and, depending on

Regional Headquarters' response to my rebuttal, would likely have been transferred back to Kent Institution. The Department of Justice's advice to Warden Gallagher was likely based on their assessment that if the matter proceeded to court, a judge would order Mr. Weaver's release from segregation. From their perspective, releasing Mr. Weaver before the *habeas corpus* petition could be heard would avert an embarrassing precedent documenting the illegality of his segregation.

The segregation and attempted involuntary transfer of Gary Weaver show clearly the faultlines identified by the Arbour Report, the Task Force on Segregation's report, and my own analysis of correctional practices. Moreover, since his segregation occurred two years after the Commissioner of Corrections had received the recommendations of the Task Force on Segregation and a year after correctional officials, including those at William Head, participated in a workshop specifically addressing the legal requirements of segregation review, it serves as a report card on how well, in the absence of independent adjudication, the CSC can ensure that its officials comply with the law.

The segregation of Gary Weaver involved serial violations of the *Charter* and the *CCRA*. The preliminary assessment of the Task Force on Segregation had been that "staff members and managers demonstrated a casual attitude towards the rigorous requirements of the law, both in terms of their understanding of the law and their sense of being bound by it" (*Task Force Report* at 12). These words describe exactly the behaviour of staff members and managers at William Head. Staff violated Mr. Weaver's rights under the *Charter* and *CCR Regulations* when they denied him his legal right to contact a lawyer without delay during his first four hours in segregation. Only through the intervention of the RCMP was he able to exercise his right. Correctional staff violated s. 37 of the *CCRA* in denying Mr. Weaver access to his spiritual advisor during his first week in segregation; correctional staff also violated s. 37 by not providing Mr. Weaver with any of his personal cell effects until forty-five days after he was placed in segregation.

Correctional managers at William Head failed to conduct segregation reviews in accordance with the *CCRA*. The written Sharing of Information given to Gary Weaver before his five-day, thirty-day, and sixty-day reviews contained none of the information relevant to a consideration of whether it was reasonable to believe that lawful grounds existed for his segregation. The inadequacy of the sharing process at William Head reflected practices at both Kent and Matsqui prior to the Task Force on Segregation. As I have described in Sector 4, there have been significant improvements in the sharing of information process at Kent; by comparison, at William Head managers were not even aware that their processes failed to comply with the law. The conduct of the five-day, thirty-day, and sixty-day reviews also demonstrated an abject failure to fulfil the legislative mandate of the *CCRA*. There was no attempt at any of these reviews to relate the information and evidence to the legal criteria for segregation; the Chairperson of the Segregation Review Board in each case announced at the beginning of the hearing that Mr. Weaver would be maintained in segregation. No consideration was given to the information Mr. Weaver attempted to provide to the Board, drawn from the RCMP's and the IPSOs' investigations, which pointed to his innocence of any wrongdoing. Similarly, the decisions of the warden of William Head that Mr. Weaver be maintained in segregation were made without reference to the legal standards of s. 31(3). There was no attempt to justify how Mr. Weaver's presence in the general population would interfere with an ongoing investigation; at the five-day review the mere existence of the investigation was seen as sufficient to justify segregation, and at the thirty- and sixty-day reviews the fact that Mr. Weaver was being considered for involuntary transfer—not a legally sufficient basis for segregation under the CCRA—was cited.

## The Gary Weaver Case and Independent Adjudication

Had Gary Weaver's *habeas corpus* petition gone before the courts, I intended to raise the argument that independent adjudication of segregation decisions was an essential element of fairness and a principle of fundamental justice within s. 7 of the *Charter*. The facts suggested that Warden Gallagher had at an early point determined Gary Weaver was involved in the assault on Mr. Caziere, and Mr. Weaver was no longer welcome at William Head. Nothing revealed by the unfolding investigation was able to challenge that belief. Although Warden Gallagher never interviewed Mr. Weaver or any of the other material witnesses, he stood firm, basing his belief on "reliable sources" without ever stating why he believed them to be reliable. He maintained that belief in the face of the opinions of two highly experienced RCMP investigators who had interviewed Mr. Weaver and found him credible, and who had interviewed Mr. Caziere and found his account lacking in credibility. What better demonstration of a decision-maker who would be unable to review the matter in an impartial and objective manner?

In March 1999, I appeared on behalf of the Canadian Bar Association before the Sub-committee of the Parliamentary Standing Committee on Justice and Human Rights conducting the Five-Year Review of the CCRA. The centrepiece of my presentation was the importance of independent adjudication. I advised the Sub-committee of the Bar's position, in light of the recommendations of Madam Justice Arbour and the Commissioner's failure to implement the experiment on independent adjudication as recommended by the Task Force on Administrative Segregation, that the CCRA be amended to provide for independent adjudication of administrative segregation. I reviewed the facts of Gary Weaver's case and suggested that if I had an opportunity to present my full argument, I was confident I could persuade the MPs on the Sub-committee—even those who had publicly expressed antipathy to the cause of prisoners' rights—that under the CCRA there were no lawful grounds to segregate Mr. Weaver. Yet under the existing provisions, I had no impartial decision-maker to whom I could make my argument.

# SECTOR 6

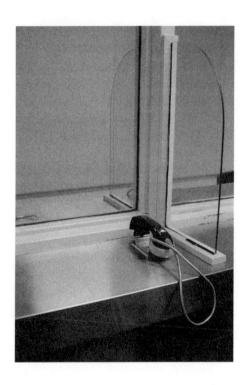

## CHAPTER 1

# Correcting Corrections:
# The Remedial Tool Box

The traditional legal maxim that where there is a right there is a remedy has had, until quite recently, little relevance to prisons and prisoners. Today, the recognition of the duty to act fairly, the constitutional entrenchment of rights in the *Canadian Charter of Rights and Freedoms,* the establishment of the Office of the Correctional Investigator, the creation of an internal prisoner grievance mechanism, and the enactment of the *CCRA* have changed the legal landscape and together have established a constitutional, legal, and administrative infrastructure of rights and remedies.

Yet that infrastructure, impressive when read in judicial pronouncement, legislative text, or administrative policy, is less so when viewed from a prisoner's cell. Although the pace of judicial review has quickened as an avenue for the vindication of rights and the prevention of abuses, litigation still remains an exceptional strategy. That is not to deny that litigation has a part to play nor that some court judgements have provided significant landmarks, but the intermittent, exceptional, and delayed nature of judicial intervention necessarily limits its capacity to achieve compliance with the law and the constitution on a day-by-day, prison-by-prison basis. For this reason, administrative remedies, particularly those provided by the internal grievance mechanism and access to the Office of the Correctional Investigator, assume particular significance in the lives of prisoners. Utilizing these avenues does not require the assistance of a lawyer; sophisticated legal training is not necessary for the initiation of a complaint or grievance or a letter or phone call to the Correctional Investigator. For the

overwhelming majority of prisoners, therefore, the responsiveness of the grievance mechanism and the timely intervention of the Correctional Investigator are
the measure of their ability to achieve a fair and effective remedy.

## The Grievance System: Through the Eyes of a Prison Ombudsman

In Sector 1, I traced the legal and administrative provisions establishing the
Office of the Correctional Investigator (CI) and the inmate grievance process.
Since 1973, the CI has produced an annual report which is filed with the Solicitor
General. The dominant theme of these reports has been the CSC's lack of respon-
siveness, both internally and externally, to the CI's recommendations. Inger
Hansen (now Judge Hansen) served as Canada's first Correctional Investigator,
from 1973 to 1976. She was succeeded by Ron Stewart, who has held the position
ever since. In his first report, Mr. Stewart addressed this lack of responsiveness.

> There is an overwhelming tendency within the Service to "cover" for
> one another, a practice which makes the job of the Correctional
> Investigator more difficult than it should be. There is less difficulty
> when a recommendation is applied to the grassroots level; the
> response received from the institutions is usually fairly good. A prob-
> lem occurs when an ombudsman is not successful at this level and
> must move up the administrative ladder.
>
> The director [warden] and other supervisory levels are often
> caught in the trap of having to back staff to retain support. This atti-
> tude is detectable even in Ottawa. There is no doubt that in any
> organization it is desirable for supervisors to support employees, but
> not when it perpetrates mismanagement and poor administration.
> This office dealt with cases where even the most simple recommen-
> dations met opposition. It often appeared that administrators were
> reluctant to make a change because it was a change. I am under no
> illusion that a recommendation by this office is the ultimate answer
> but I am troubled when a recommendation is rejected because clear-
> ly either my letter was not read or not understood. Frequently, the
> replies bear no relationship to the problems described in my letters.
> (*Annual Report of the Correctional Investigator, 1977–78* [Ottawa:
> Information Canada, 1978] at 3)

The first annual report of the CI, in 1973–74, had contained extensive discussion of the conditions in segregation and recommended a special study on its
use. The 1984–85 report focussed on double-bunking.

One of the most serious problems that we have encountered is that of double-bunking and especially in segregated cells where in some cases inmates are confined for more than 23 hours a day. Life in a segregation or dissociation cell is hell at the best of times; however, we are aware that in some institutions because of staff shortages they are unable to provide such basics as daily showers and the minimum one hour exercise per day for inmates in these special cells. The problem is of course compounded when these cells hardly big enough for one man are double-bunked.

I recommended:

(a) that the Correctional Service of Canada review its present segregation/dissociation operations to ensure that they are in compliance with the requirements enunciated in the Commissioner's Directives;

(b) that the Correctional Service of Canada cease immediately the practice of double-bunking in segregation and dissociation areas.

After a lengthy delay of almost three months we received from the Inspector General comments of the Deputy Commissioner Offender Programs but there was no mention of the review we had recommended. Instead we were advised that the last six months had been spent drafting explicit policies and guidelines regarding administrative segregation which included minimum standards for showering, exercise, visits, etc. *As well, to ensure compliance, [that] a "Manager, Administrative Segregation" had been appointed at the National Headquarters and that a Regional Co-ordinator had been appointed in each Region to assist in the implementation of the new policies and procedures. Also, that workshops had been held to familiarize staff and that future monitoring would address the type of problem outlined in the recommendation.*

As for the second part of the recommendation, it was agreed that double-bunking in dissociation was undesirable, that the issue was to be presented to the Dissociation Policy Board for consideration and that we would be advised of the status of part (b) by October 31, 1984 . . .

[In March 1985] I was advised that the Senior Management Committee had approved in principle my recommendation but that it would probably take a long time to resolve. Would I consider the matter complete? However after reading a copy of the Senior Management Committee minutes which indicated that double-bunking was not about to cease I certainly was not about to consider the matter closed.

It is interesting to note that according to the Correctional Service of Canada statistics there were 124 inmates double-bunked in segregation when the recommendation was made in June, 1984. As of January 30, 1985 that number had increased to 198.

It still remains my position that it is inhumane to lock two people up in one cell twenty-three hours a day, especially when you have cells in the general population which are not double-bunked and so I re-submitted the matter, this time to the Commissioner of Corrections.

Unfortunately, the recommendation has not been implemented because of the acute shortage of cells in most institutions. (*Annual Report of the Correctional Investigator, 1984–85* [Ottawa: Supply and Services Canada, 1985] at 19–20, emphasis added)

A careful reading of the passage I have italicized is instructive. The reform offered to the Correctional Investigator in 1984 to address systemic problems in administrative segregation was the appointment of regional and national co-ordinators and staff training workshops. Fast-forwarding a dozen years, we find that the Commissioner of Corrections, faced with his own Task Force's report documenting continuing systemic problems in segregation, rejects the recommendation for an experiment in independent adjudication in favour of the appointment of regional co-ordinators of segregation and more staff training workshops.

By 1989–90, the Correctional Investigator was able to refer to "a tradition in each annual report" that the 1984 recommendation to end double-bunking in segregation was restated. With more than a little sarcasm, he remarked, "It has as well become a tradition to record each year CSC's latest response to this issue: 'Efforts are currently underway to reduce the number of double-bunked protective custody inmates at Kent Institution'" (*Annual Report of the Correctional Investigator, 1989–90* [Ottawa: Supply and Services Canada, 1990] at 26).

A year later, the CI was pleased to break with this tradition by reporting "the resolution of a long-standing problem which began in 1986, that being the double-bunking situation within the segregation/protective custody area at Kent Institution. I have been advised by the Commissioner that the vacant unit at Kent Institution will be finally opened and the double-bunking of administrative segregation cases at that institution will cease as of June, 1991" (*Annual Report of the Correctional Investigator, 1990–91* [Ottawa: Supply and Services Canada, 1991] at 30). How well placed the Correctional Investigator's confidence in this assurance was can be assessed by looking at the reality: when I began my study at Kent in January 1994, K unit, the protective custody segregation unit, was almost completely double-bunked.

In 1989–90, the CI had these highly critical comments to make about the grievance process, sixteen years after its inception:

> The effectiveness and credibility of any levelled redress mechanism is dependant upon a combined front-end process which is capable, in a participative fashion, of thoroughly and objectively reviewing the issue at question. It also requires a final level within the process which has the courage to take definitive and timely decisions on those issues which are referred to its attention for resolution. At the present time, the Service has a grievance process which at the front-end does very little to encourage offender participation. This in turn seriously compromises the objectivity and the thoroughness of its review. In addition, the final level of the process sometimes has shown itself to be unable to make timely and definitive decisions.
>
> I feel the difficulties with the current grievance process are not directly related to its structure or its existing procedures but rather to the lack of commitment and acceptance of responsibility on the part of csc's senior management for its operation. An improvement in the effectiveness and credibility of the process will only happen when those responsible for its operation decide to make it work. (*Annual Report 1989–90* at 29)

In 1990–91, the Correctional Investigator assessed the impact of the csc's Mission Statement:

> The Service's Mission Statement has projected a positive public image and established a sound framework of core values, guiding principles and strategic objectives for the management of its operation. But a Mission document, regardless of its detail and eloquence, cannot be seen or accepted as a replacement for sound policy and clear direction. Nor can it be seen as reflective of an organization's operational reality. The operational reality from my perspective is that the number of complaints have increased significantly, and that some areas of complaint, again from my perspective, are slow to be resolved. We continue to stress at the national level the significance these issues hold for the offender population and the impact that non-action has on decisions taken at the operational level . . . It is important that the Correctional Service continue to strive to improve its responsiveness to inmate concerns. Delays, defensiveness and non-commitment are inconsistent with the Service's stated Mission and the basic concept of administrative fairness and I sincerely hope

that our comments are taken in the constructive way they are offered. (*Annual Report 1990–91* at 43)

The CI's annual report for 1992–93 marked the first full reporting year under the provisions of the CCRA. The report characterized the changes introduced by the *Act* in this way:

> The *Act* has not significantly added to the powers which the Correctional Investigator previously possessed. Rather, the legislation has clearly established the "function" of the Correctional Investigator as that of an Ombudsman and clarified the authority and responsibilities of the Office within a procedural framework which both focuses and paces our activities. In essence, Parliament has provided the Correctional Investigator, not with new powers, but with specific direction and momentum. (*Annual Report of the Correctional Investigator, 1992–93* [Ottawa: Supply and Services, 1993] at 1)

The report, while noting that responses from the Service "continue to be excessively delayed, defensive and non-committal," expressed hope that "as the appreciation and understanding of the new legislation increases all parties involved in the correction process would accept their responsibility in ensuring that offender concerns are addressed in a thorough, timely and objective fashion" (*Annual Report 1992–93* at 45). Sadly but predictably, the 1993–94 report opens with these sobering comments:

> The majority of the issues detailed in last year's report have not been resolved, and given the time elapsed since initially recommending action on these issues and the reality of staff and funding reductions, I see little evidence that these areas of legitimate inmate concern will be given the priority which they require. (*Annual Report of the Correctional Investigator, 1993–94* [Ottawa: Supply and Services, 1994] at 1)

The report for that year also found the enactment of the CCRA had done little to improve the effectiveness of the grievance process:

> The grievance process, despite years of internal review and past commitments, displays, at the national level, little if any evidence of effective management of the system or management commitment to the system. Grievance responses continue to be delayed well beyond the timeframes of the policy, and the thoroughness and objectivity of the reviews undertaken in many instances is wanting. The automated reporting system has yet to come on line and as such, the process

continues without the capacity to provide relevant information on its own operations or management with ongoing information capable of identifying inconsistencies concerning the interpretation and application of the Service's policies.

The *Corrections and Conditional Release Act* requires of the Service the establishment of a "procedure for fairly and expeditiously resolving offender grievances." The current procedure does not meet this requirement. The process is anything but expeditious, with offender grievances taking up to six months to work their way through the process. The current process as well cannot be seen as directed towards fair resolution, it is rather an adversarial, win-lose exercise played out on a very uneven playing field with the offender having limited input at the higher levels of the procedure . . .

In conclusion on this matter, I return to my comments of 1989, that improvement in the effectiveness and credibility of this process will only happen when the senior management of the Service accepts responsibility for the operation of procedure. (*Annual Report 1993–94* at 23)

The 1994–95 annual report detailed the continuing "excessive delay, defensiveness and non-commitment" of the Service, especially at the National Headquarters level, and concluded with this observation:

The Service's responses over the course of this reporting year are consistent with their past performances. The responses have avoided the substance of the issues at question including a failure to address the specific observations and recommendations contained in last year's Annual Report. The responses are defensive, display little if any appreciation for the history or significance of the issues at question and provide at best a further string of endless promises of future action, with no indication as to expected results or how the results of these proposed actions will be measured or analyzed. (*Annual Report of the Correctional Investigator, 1994–95* [Ottawa: Supply and Services Canada, 1995] at 57)

## The Grievance System: Through the Eyes of the Arbour Commission

The effectiveness of the grievance system came under particular scrutiny in the course of the Arbour Commission's inquiry into events at the Prison for Women in 1994. Madam Justice Arbour noted that "virtually all of the issues that have arisen in the course of this inquiry were raised in the first instance by the inmates in complaints, grievances, and in some cases, in letters addressed to senior Correctional Service officials" (Arbour Report at 150). Some of her harshest criticisms concerned the ineffectiveness of grievance procedures:

> Some of these grievances were never answered at all. Those that were answered were almost always answered late, in some cases several months after the answers were due. In a number of instances, the grievances were responded to by an inappropriate person: either someone not at the appropriate level to respond, or someone who could not be expected to have access to the relevant facts. There is no system to effectively prioritize those grievances where the only effective response would be one received on an urgent basis.
>
> However, by far the most troubling aspect of the responses to these grievances, which raised important issues of fundamental inmate rights, was the number of times in which the responses failed to deal properly with the substance of the issues raised. In some cases, the responses failed to appreciate the legal significance of the issues raised by the inmates. In some cases, the responses indicated a failure to properly ascertain the underlying facts. In many instances, one was left with the impression that an inmate's version of events was treated as inherently unreliable . . . (Arbour Report at 150–51)

Madam Justice Arbour noted that the Correctional Investigator "has pointed out for years the chronic untimeliness of the response to the complaints and grievance process in the Correctional Service" and concluded:

> As revealed in this case, the process is highly bureaucratic. Particularly at the appellate level, both Regional and National, responsibility for the disposition of grievances is often given to people with neither the knowledge nor the means of acquiring it and, worse, with no real authority to remedy the problem should they be prepared to acknowledge its existence. This could be redressed by the current initiative to promote lower level resolution. However, this strategy will be equally ineffective unless there is a profound change in the mindset of the entire organization. At present, it would seem that the admission of error is perceived as an admission of defeat by the Correctional Service. In that climate, no internal method of dispute resolution will succeed. (Arbour Report at 162)

As an essential part of a reformed grievance process, Madam Justice Arbour recommended that the Commissioner of Corrections "personally review some, if not all, grievances brought to him, as third level grievances, as the most effective, if not the only method for him to keep abreast of the conditions of life in institutions under his care and supervision"; she further recommended that "should the Commissioner be unwilling or unable to participate significantly in the disposition of third level grievances, such grievances be channelled to a source outside the Correctional Service for disposition, and that the disposition be binding on the Correctional Service" (Arbour Report at 257). This recommendation for binding independent arbitration can be traced to the earlier recommendation of the Correctional Law Review that binding arbitration, as a necessary part of a fair and effective grievance process, be incorporated into the *CCRA*. That recommendation was not adopted as a result of the CSC's resistance to it. The CSC was no less resistant to Madam Justice Arbour's recommendations with respect to the grievance process; they too were rejected.

## The Arbour Proposal for a New Judicial Remedy

The great difficulty the Correctional Investigator had experienced in getting the Service to respond to his recommendations over the years led Madam Justice Arbour to recommend a larger role for the courts.

> It is only because of the Correctional Investigator's inability to compel compliance by the Service with his conclusions, and because of the demonstrated unwillingness of the Service to do so willingly in many instances, that I recommend greater access by prisoners to the courts for the effective enforcement of their rights and the vindication of the Rule of Law. (Arbour Report at 195)

One of Madam Justice Arbour's major recommendation had not previously appeared as part of a reform agenda: she suggested that prisoners who had experienced illegalities, gross mismanagement, or unfairness in the administration of their sentences (for example, by being detained for a lengthy period in administrative segregation in violation of the law) be able to apply for a judicial remedy to reduce the period of their imprisonment.

> Ultimately, I believe that there is little hope that the Rule of Law will implant itself within the correctional culture without assistance and control from Parliament and the courts. As a corrective measure to redress the lack of consciousness of individual rights and the ineffectiveness of internal mechanisms designed to ensure legal compliance in the Correctional Service, I believe that it is imperative that a just and effective sanction be developed to offer an adequate redress for the infringement of prisoners' rights, as well as to encourage compliance . . . *One must resist the temptation to trivialize the infringement*

*of prisoners' rights as either an insignificant infringement of rights, or as an infringement of the rights of people who do not deserve any better. When a right has been granted by law, it is no less important that such right be respected because the person entitled to it is a prisoner. Indeed, it is always more important that the vigorous enforcement of rights be effected in the cases where the right is the most meaningful . . .*

Respect for the individual rights of prisoners will remain illusory unless a mechanism is developed to bring home to the Correctional Service the serious consequences of interfering with the integrity of a sentence by mismanaging it. The administration of a sentence is part of the administration of justice. If the Rule of Law is to be brought within the correctional system with full force, the administration of justice must reclaim control of the legality of a sentence, beyond a limited traditional scope of *habeas corpus* remedies . . .

It would be unthinkable that the Correctional Service could illegally modify the duration of a sentence with impunity. This is the essence of *habeas corpus*. It is difficult to comprehend why there should be more tolerance for the disregard of other terms and conditions of a sentence which are as essential to its integrity as is its duration. As a means of preserving the integrity of a sentence which can be threatened by illegality, a provision should be enacted to give effect to the following principle:

> If illegalities, gross mismanagement or unfairness in the administration of a sentence render the sentence harsher than that imposed by the court, a reduction of the period of imprisonment may be granted, such as to reflect the fact that the punishment administered was more punitive than the one intended.

(Arbour Report at 182–83, emphasis added)

Let us consider how the remedy envisaged by Madam Justice Arbour might apply to some of the case studies I have documented in earlier parts of this book, in which prisoners were kept in segregation or transferred to higher security in violation of the law. A judicial remedy ordering a release from segregation or a return to lower security would not sufficiently respond to the deprivation of liberty inflicted, and in the few cases where prisoners have filed civil lawsuits claiming damages for wrongful confinement, the awards have usually been derisory, giving little incentive to prisoners and even less to their lawyers. Hence, in cases like Donnie Oag's and Hughie MacDonald's, where unlawful segregation continued not only for days or months but for years, the just and appropriate remedy would be one also measured in the currency of time. For Mr. Oag, the appropriate remedy would have been to accelerate his statutory release. Since he was released straight to the street from segregation without the benefit of any programs, it could hardly be argued that his release at an earlier point would have aggravated any risk he posed.

Because Mr. MacDonald was serving a life sentence with no fixed expiry date, his remedy would have to be more flexibly conceived. There are a number of possibilities. At the time he was charged with the murder of Gary Allen, Mr. MacDonald was working towards a return to the Regional Health Centre to participate in the Violent Offender Program. Completion of this program would have been an important factor in the judicial review to which he was entitled after serving fifteen years of his sentence for first-degree murder. By virtue of his detainment in segregation, that program opportunity was denied him, and his fifteen-year review was delayed. Mr. Justice Wilson, in ordering Mr. MacDonald's release from segregation in August 1996, sought to address this by adding at the end of his judgement, "I would certainly encourage the Service to endeavour with all deliberate speed to get Mr. MacDonald to the Regional Health Centre" (*MacDonald* v. *Warden of Kent Institution*, August 21, 1996, Vancouver cc951235 (B.C.S.C.)). That judicial encouragement was of no avail; Mr. MacDonald remained at Kent until July 1998, and even then he was transferred not to the Regional Health Centre but to Matsqui. It was not until October 2001 that he was transferred to the RHC. Since he had served twenty-one years of his sentence by then, his fifteen-year review was rendered meaningless. Under an Arbour-type remedy, the court could order that the CSC give Mr. MacDonald a high priority for placement in the Violent Offender Program. Another possibility, in Mr. MacDonald's case and that of other "lifers," would be to provide for a statutory adjustment to potential parole eligibility dates. Although Madam Justice Arbour did not address this issue in detail, she did suggest that the law could require Parole Boards to consider legally harsh conditions as a factor weighing in favour of an earlier release.

Consider also how an Arbour-type remedy could have availed Gary Weaver. The month before Mr. Weaver was segregated, he had been approved by the National Parole Board for twice-monthly temporary absence passes. As a result of his illegal segregation for eighty days, he was denied the opportunity to participate in five of these passes. Even though he was released from segregation in late April of 1999, it was mid-June before he enjoyed another pass. An appropriate remedy in this case could include the provision of additional passes. Mr. Weaver might also have been given priority for placement in other programs. Prior to his segregation, Mr. Weaver's case management officer had recommended him for a work-release program. Yet despite continued support from his CMO following his release from segregation, Mr. Weaver was told he would not be eligible for the program for another six months, during which time he should demonstrate good behaviour. That decision completely disregarded the fact that he had spent almost three months in segregation without just cause. A judicial remedy could be framed to prevent such further discriminatory treatment.

It is important to recognize that Madam Justice Arbour did not see the judicial remedy as sufficient in itself to ensure compliance with the Rule of Law. Her proposals for a grievance process subject to binding arbitration and an administrative segregation process subject to independent adjudication were other vital components of creating a correctional culture driven by the Rule of Law rather than by expedience. As she made clear, it was her scepticism that these other measures would be accepted by the CSC that prompted her proposal for a judicial remedy. However, even if these other reforms were implemented, the existence of a judicial remedy along the lines of the Arbour model would provide the necessary underpinning to ensure compliance with the law. The judicial remedy is designed to buttress, not displace, other administrative processes that seek to institutionalize fairness and respect for the law and would permit a full measure of restitution for significant harm not addressed or redressed by these other processes.

## The Correctional Investigator's Proposed Remedy

Madam Justice Arbour's report applauded the work of the Correctional Investigator, particularly his initiative in issuing the Special Report which forced the issues of P4W into the public domain. She recognized that "of all the internal and external mechanisms or agencies designed to make the Correctional Service open and accountable, the Office of the Correctional Investigator is by far the most efficient and the best equipped to discharge that function" (Arbour Report at 195). In his 1995–96 report, published just a few months after the release of the Arbour Report, the Correctional Investigator reviewed the record of the CSC in dealing with the recommendations of the CI's office and emphasized yet again the failings of the Service.

> The authority of the Office within [the legislative framework of the CCRA] lies in its ability to thoroughly and objectively investigate a wide spectrum of administrative actions and present its findings and recommendations initially to the Correctional Service of Canada. In those instances where the Correctional Service of Canada has failed to reasonably address the Office's findings and recommendations, the issue is referred to the Minister and eventually to Parliament and the public, generally through the vehicle of our Annual Report. The Office, as such, in attempting to assure administrative fairness and accountability within correctional operations is dependent in large part on the willingness of the Correctional Service to approach the findings and recommendations of this Office in an objective, thorough and timely fashion.
>
> I have been singularly unsuccessful over the past few years, as evi-

denced by my previous Annual Reports, in causing a change in the
Correctional Service's approach in dealing with matters raised by this
Office. (*Annual Report of the Correctional Investigator, 1995–96*
[Ottawa: Supply and Services Canada, 1996] at 1)

On the basis of this record, the Correctional Investigator went on to recommend the establishment of an administrative tribunal to overcome the road
blocks thrown up by the csc.

On the basis of my own experience over the past few years and without limiting the judicial guidance and control called for by Justice
Arbour, I believe there is a need for a mechanism between this office
and the courts with the authority to order timely corrective action in
instances of illegalities, gross mismanagement or unfairness. The correctional environment, the impact of administrative decisions on
individuals within that environment and the consistent failure of the
Correctional Service to approach individual and systemic areas of
concern in an objective, thorough and timely fashion demands that
a timely and responsive binding avenue of redress be available.
  As such I recommend:
  a) that an administrative tribunal be established with the
     authority both to compel Correctional Service compliance
     with legislation and policy governing the administration
     of the sentence and to redress the adverse effects of non-
     compliance, and
  b) that access to the tribunal be provided for in those instances
     where if within a reasonable time after receiving a recom-
     mendation from the Correctional Investigator pursuant to
     section 179 of the *Corrections and Conditional Release Act*,
     the Commissioner of Corrections takes no action that is
     seen as adequate or appropriate.
  The above recommendation is intended to support and complement, not attenuate or replace, the function of the Office in ensuring that areas of offender concern are decided on in an objective and
timely fashion consistent with the Service's legislative responsibilities. (*Annual Report 1995–96* at 2)

The rationale for, and advantages of, access to an administrative tribunal are
directly related to the limitations of existing remedies, both administrative and
judicial. The tribunal would have jurisdiction to deal with the whole range of
non-compliance issues. Through the development of specialized expertise, it
could also fashion a wide range of remedies, tailored not only to redressing harm

but also to compelling administrative solutions to intractable problems. Thus, in addition to having general jurisdiction to make any order or recommendation to the Service concerning the matter before it, the tribunal would have specific authority to order the Service to pay compensation to any offender adversely affected by illegal or unfair treatment. This would include reimbursement for allowances, wages, or other payments lost as a result of the treatment as well as "special compensation" up to a maximum of $5,000 (similar to the provisions of the *Canadian Human Rights Act*). The tribunal would have the authority to recommend to a court that the offender's imprisonment be modified in line with the Arbour recommendations. It would also have specific authority to recommend to the CSC, the police, or the Attorney General that disciplinary or criminal proceedings be instituted against any person.

One of the most important advantages of the tribunal remedy is that it would bring closure to those issues, often of a system-wide nature, that have filled up the annual reports of the Correctional Investigator. The very existence of such an avenue for resolution would provide a major incentive for the Service to resolve these issues at an early stage.

To forestall critics concerned about the expense of creating such a tribunal, the CI suggested that it could be constituted as part of an existing tribunal, such as the Canadian Human Rights Tribunal, which has an existing national administrative infrastructure. Hearings could therefore be held at the site of the dispute, much the same as Parole Board hearings. Another potential objection to the proposal is that the tribunal would be swamped with complaints from prisoners, overwhelming its resources. However, the tribunal is conceived primarily as a vehicle for resolving issues within the legislative mandate of the Correctional Investigator which that office has been unable to resolve using its normal procedures; prisoners would have access to it only indirectly, through referral of their cases by the CI. Some prisoners' advocates have objected that this access would be too restrictive, and in my judgement, the tribunal should have a discretionary jurisdiction to accept direct references from prisoners where the case raises a serious issue of general importance to prisoners. Jason Gallant's case, which involves both domestic and international human rights standards, would be one example.

## The Correctional Investigator's Millennium Report

The Correctional Investigator's 1998–99 annual report provided an overview of systemic issues detailed in previous reports; it identified specific areas of concern associated with each of these issues and presented a series of recommendations designed to address them.

In October 1999, the Office of the Correctional Investigator signed a Memorandum of Understanding with the Correctional Service of Canada. The memorandum was intended to provide "a structure for interaction between the two agencies during the course of the OCI's investigations into offender concerns." To this end, it set out procedures to ensure that "the CSC provide accurate information in a timely manner to the OCI in response to requests which stem from matters under the OCI's jurisdiction" and that "timely corrective action in relation to valid offender concerns is taken by the CSC."

In order to bring "closure" to the issues raised and recommendations made by the Correctional Investigator, the parties agreed "to attempt resolution on points on which agreement has not been achieved"; disputes could be referred to "mediation, facilitation, non-binding arbitration or other alternative dispute resolution mechanism" (Memorandum of Understanding between the Office of the Correctional Investigator and the Correctional Service of Canada, October 1999; Appendix A, *Report of the Correctional Investigator, 1999–2000* [Ottawa: Minister of Public Works and Government Services Canada, 2000]. Online: <http://www.oci-bec.gc.ca>).

If the Memorandum of Understanding was expected to bring a new responsiveness on the part of the CSC to the CI's recommendations, that expectation was quickly dashed. The CI's first report of the new millennium proved to be one of the most damning in the twenty-seven years of the Office's existence.

> Although progress has been made on a number of issues, I am quite frankly disappointed in the results of the Service's efforts to address these systemic areas of concern. While I believed last year that our agencies had come to an agreement on what needed to be done to begin addressing these issues, the Service's undertakings appear to have been overwhelmed by a bureaucratic process of excessive review, consultations and endless study . . .
>
> I stated in my Annual Report a decade ago that "the Correctional Service of Canada is a direct service agency whose policies and decisions impact directly and immediately on the offender population. There is a need, and an urgent need for the Service to take steps to ensure that its review and decision-making processes, especially at the national level, are capable of responding and resolving issues in a timely fashion . . ."
>
> The concerns of the offenders tend to be forgotten at times during the review of these issues . . .
>
> The positive impact on the offender population of the Service's efforts to address these systemic issues over the past year, I suspect, has been negligible. (*Annual Report 1999–2000* at 5–6)

In relation to the inmate grievance process, the report acknowledged significant improvements in the system's operations over the years but identified three remaining areas of concern.

- continuing instances of excessive delay in responding at the institutional and regional levels of the process; . . .
- the non-acceptance by senior management of the responsibility and accountability for specifically addressing offender concerns as recommended by Madam Justice Arbour; and
- the effectiveness of the current procedure in addressing the concerns of Female and Aboriginal offenders. (*Annual Report 1999–2000* at 11)

The report also commented on the Service's own characterization of "improvement."

In terms of delays in responding last year, the Service indicated that 48% of the grievances at the regional level were late. We are advised that this year 33% of the regional level grievances were late. Although this is an improvement, having one in three grievances responded to outside of the established timeframe, a timeframe which has been extended by fifteen working days, is unreasonable and does little to promote offender confidence in the process. (*Annual Report 1999–2000* at 11)

Another systemic problem identified was that of double-bunking. During 1999–2000, the percentage of federal prisoners double-bunked increased from 21.2 per cent to 23.1 per cent. This increase was even more significant in segregation.

Although the Service advised that "*systemic double-bunking in segregation has been eliminated in three regions,*" I note that the percentage of segregated inmates double-bunked over the course of this year increased from 12.9% to 15.7%. I note as well that the number of inmates admitted to segregation has measurably increased and that a significant number of inmates in segregation have been double-bunked for well in excess of thirty days. (*Annual Report 1999–2000* at 16)

The 1999–2000 annual report also addressed two issues that figure in this book's earlier chapters. One of these is the accuracy of preventive security information. In previous reports, the CI had identified "the absence of any clear national direction concerning the co-ordination, verification, communication and correction of this information or who is responsible and accountable for the accuracy of this information" (*Annual Report 1999–2000* at 19). In 1996, the CI recommended that preventive security standards and guidelines be developed to bring some clarity to this matter. The CSC undertook to produce these by the fall of 1997. Yet in his millennium report the CI writes:

> On March 8, 2000, representatives from this Office met with the Service's Security Division to review draft policy. I am now advised that "*it is anticipated that these SOP's will be presented for approval to the Services Executive Committee by the Fall of 2000.*" It has now been four years since the Service's initial commitment to produce guidelines and standards in this area. (*Annual Report 1999–2000* at 19)

The use of force also features in the millennium report, both as a systemic issue and in the form of a specific investigation carried out by the CI, arising from the use of force against Jason Gallant and Darryl Bates. Addressing the issue first as a matter of policy, the CI writes:

> The Service's 1997 Interim Policy on Videotapes, in response to Madam Justice Arbour's recommendation, requires that all videotapes of use of force incidents and supporting documentation be forwarded to this Office and the Service's National Headquarters within fifteen days of the incident. During the course of a year, we review in excess of three hundred incidents involving the use of force.
>
> This Office's review of these incidents has noted a disturbingly high rate of non-compliance with the Service's policy related to the use of force. Our findings have been shared with the Service and, in large part, are not inconsistent with the results of its own review. A recent CSC internal memorandum, in commenting on a specific incident, noted:
>
>> The staff in the Security Division who review incidents involving use of force have indicated repeatedly the areas of non-compliance. While there have been some improvements in dealing with incidents of use of force, it seems this incident underscores the fact that there are serious problems with respecting basic rights of inmates.
>
> While it is encouraging that the Service acknowledges that there are serious problems, it is obvious that its current review process is neither ensuring compliance with policy nor reducing the number of incidents resulting in the uses of force. The process is not working, in part, because senior line managers do not see themselves as either responsible or accountable for ensuring compliance with law and policy. When the review policy leaves the institution, the identified areas of non-compliance become discussion points between regional and national functional staff, rather than action points resulting in

specific direction from senior line authority at the regional and national level. (*Annual Report 1999–2000* at 20–21)

After reviewing the videotape of the enforced rectal inspections of Jason Gallant and Darryl Bates, the CI concluded in May 1999 that "the authorized use of force to facilitate a visual inspection of the rectum in these cases was excessive, contrary to policy and unreasonable." The CI recommended that:

- an apology be offered to the inmates; and
- the Service immediately review its policies and procedures related to the use of force and strip-searching and issue clear direction to the field with respect to:
  - the considerations to be given prior to authorising the use of force to facilitate a strip search, inclusive of options;
  - the utility of a visual inspection of the rectum in finding contraband;
  - the requirement for specific written authorisation, with reasons, from the Warden; and
  - the provision of these reasons to the inmate prior to using force, and the role of medical staff in both the authorisation process and the use of force itself. (*Annual Report 1999–2000* at 36)

As documented in the CI's 1999–2000 report, the CSC rejected the need for specific risk assessment or authorization at the time of the use of force, since the searches were "routine" and required no "individualized suspicion of contraband." However, "without admitting that the force used was unreasonable or excessive," the Service did "recognize that the matter should have been handled differently." This meant there should have been "better communication" at the time of the incident, with the prisoners receiving a warning that force would be used if they did not comply with the order to submit to a complete strip search. To bring closure to the issue and clarify the relevant law and policy, the CI suggested in his millennium report that the matter be referred to non-binding dispute resolution, as permitted by the Memorandum of Understanding. Thus far, CSC has not responded to this suggestion.

At the conclusion of his 1999–2000 annual report, Correctional Investigator Stewart appealed to the public interest that underlies his Office's functions.

It is important for all parties to appreciate that the Correctional Investigator is neither an agent of the Correctional Service of Canada, nor the advocate of every complainant or interest group that lodges a complaint. The Office's mandate is to investigate complaints from an independent and neutral position, to consider thoroughly the Service's action and the reasons behind it, and to either endorse or explain that action to the complainant, or, if there is evidence of unfairness, to make appropriate recommendations concerning corrective action. The interest of the Correctional Investigator lies in ensuring that offender concerns are objectively and fairly addressed in a timely fashion. This interest cannot be met without a consistent level of responsiveness on the part of the Correctional Service to these concerns that is and is seen to be fair, open and accountable. The Service's responses to offender concerns, raised by this Office, continue to be excessively delayed, overly-defensive and absent of commitment to specific corrective action. (*Annual Report 1999–2000* at 59)

## The *CCRA* Five-Year Review

On May 29, 2000, the House of Commons Standing Committee on Justice and Human Rights tabled the report of its subcommittee formed to conduct a comprehensive review of the provisions and operations of the *CCRA*. The report specifically identified the work of the Correctional Investigator as important in maintaining Canada's commitment to respecting the rights of prisoners.

The Sub-committee believes, it is essential that correctional authorities respect offenders' rights, particularly since the principles and provisions incorporated in the *CCRA* "derive from universal human rights standards supported by all the advanced democracies with which Canada compares itself." The Sub-committee is therefore convinced that it is important to support independent organizations that are authorized to monitor respect for human rights, in particular the Office of the Correctional Investigator, which has the specific mandate to defend the rights of federally sentenced offenders. (*A Work in Progress* at 61)

The Sub-committee had heard evidence from the Correctional Investigator and other witnesses regarding the CSC's lack of responsiveness to recommendations. To enhance the independence of the Correctional Investigator, more readily bring to light issues his Office raised, and improve the resolution of disputes between the CI and the CSC, the Sub-committee's report recommended that the *CCRA* be amended so that the annual and special reports of the CI be submitted simultaneously to the Solicitor General and to Parliament. Furthermore, they recommended that these annual and special reports be automatically referred to the Standing Committee on Justice and Human Rights. This procedure would "give more authority to the Correctional Investigator's recommendations and improve the Correctional Service's accountability" (*A Work in Progress* at 66).

The Solicitor General's response to these two recommendations, issued in October 2000, was a simple "Considered, but not pursued at this time." Despite the unequivocal evidence documented in the annual reports of the Correctional Investigator over almost thirty years, the authors of the government response unconvincingly asserted, "The Government believes that the current structure enables the Correctional Investigator to effectively act as an ombudsman on behalf of offenders" (Government Response to the Report of the Sub-Committee on *Corrections and Conditional Release Act,* October 2000 at 22).

*A Work in Progress,* like the report of the 1977 House of Commons Sub-Committee on the Penitentiary System in Canada, devoted a chapter to the issue of "Fair and Equitable Decision Making." The chapter discussed several components of the remedial tool box I have identified. Most significantly, in *A Work in Progress* the Sub-committee addressed the case for independent adjudication of administrative segregation. At an appearance before the Sub-committee on behalf of the Canadian Bar Association, I had reviewed the history of this issue, citing evidence in *Prisoners of Isolation* and the more recent recommendations of the Arbour Report, the Task Force on Administrative Segregation, and the Task Force on Human Rights. The Sub-committee, after reciting this history and commending the csc for taking steps to enhance and monitor the segregation review process, agreed in their report that these initiatives are "a complement to, and not a replacement for, the independent adjudication of actions affecting the residual rights and freedoms of inmates" (*A Work in Progress* at 48). In the words of the Sub-committee,

> . . . The physical and program constraints on administratively segregated inmates are severe. This was obvious to the Sub-committee in each of the segregation units it visited during its penitentiary tours . . . Administrative segregation removes inmates from normal daily contact with other offenders. It has the effect of making their access to programs, employment, services and recreation more difficult than it is for inmates in the general prison population. It has a dramatic impact on their residual rights. It makes the conditions of incarceration more stringent than they are for other inmates . . .
>
> For these reasons, the Sub-committee believes there is a need for the insertion of an independent decision-maker who will take into account all factors related to administrative segregation cases. (*A Work in Progress* at 48–49)

The Sub-committee recommended that the independent adjudication process kick in at the thirty-day review for involuntary cases and the sixty-day review for voluntary cases. The thirty-day period was selected both because this is the maximum period of segregation allowed as a punishment imposed by the Independent Chairperson for a serious offence and because "there is little or no difference in the stringency of living conditions to which inmates administratively or punitively segregated are subject" (*A Work in Progress* at 49). The Sub-committee went on to recommend that the present Independent Chairpersons of disciplinary boards also be empowered to exercise the adjudicative authority for administrative segregation, "since they would already be knowledgeable of and familiar with the law and day-to-day reality of federal penitentiaries" (*A Work in Progress* at 49). The report suggested the CCRA be amended to specify not just the authority but also the criteria for the appointment of Independent Chairpersons.

> The additions to the functions to be performed by independent chairpersons proposed by the Sub-committee demonstrate the importance it attributes to this position. The duty to act fairly is not just a series of procedural rules applicable to decision-makers. It also imposes an obligation on policy-makers to ensure that decision-makers exercising adjudicative authority do so in a fair and unbiased manner, indeed, in the absence of even an appearance or apprehension of bias.
>
> One way for policy-makers to do this is to provide a clear statutory basis for the independent exercise of adjudicative functions. Including the process and criteria in the *Act* for the appointment of independent chairpersons will enhance their authority, provide permanence to the functions they perform, and make their adjudicative functions more open and transparent to those who want to scrutinize them. (*A Work in Progress* at 55)

The response from both the Correctional Service of Canada and the federal government was less than enthusiastic. With regard to the recommendation that the CCRA be amended to provide for the adjudication of administrative segregation cases by Independent Chairpersons, the response was this:

> The Government proposes an Enhanced Segregation Review process that includes external membership. This model will attempt to balance independent adjudication with the promotion of appropriate operational accountability by the Correctional Service of Canada. This model will be implemented on a pilot basis in all regions and detailed independent evaluation will be undertaken. The development of the pilot may be guided by a Steering Committee comprised of internal and external members. (Government Response at 18)

In response to the recommendation that the *CCRA* be amended to allow for the appointment of Independent Chairpersons for five-year renewable terms and that the *Act* set up criteria for selection and appointment of such chairpersons, the Government suggested that its proposals to conduct the pilot project was a full answer to this recommendation. Far from being such an answer, this response completely evaded the recommendation.

The government's proposal for this pilot project in 2000 is one more egregious example of bureaucratic foot-dragging. In 1975, the federally appointed Study Group on Dissociation, building on my 1974 study, had recommended that Independent Chairpersons be appointed for disciplinary hearings on a pilot project basis. No action was taken by the government, and in 1977 the House of Commons Sub-Committee on the Penitentiary System found the case for Independent Chairpersons sufficiently compelling to recommend that they be appointed in all institutions immediately. The government responded by implementing independent adjudication for serious disciplinary cases only in maximum security institutions. Twenty years later, the Task Force on Segregation recommended a pilot project of independent adjudication for administrative segregation, a recommendation endorsed by the Task Force on Human Rights. In 2000, the Parliamentary Sub-committee on the *CCRA* was sufficiently satisfied of the need for independent adjudication that, like its predecessor in 1977, it recommended immediate implementation of a full model. The government's response—a pilot project for an enhanced segregation review process that included external membership—was inconsistent with both these recommendations. The CSC's plans for this pilot, to be implemented over a six-month period in 2001–2, are for a segregation review board, composed of a deputy warden and an external member, to sit once a month in one institution in each of the five regions, to review a small sample of cases. Contrary to the Government's response to the Sub-committee's recommendation, the design of the project was not guided by a Steering Committee that included external members. (The results of the pilot project and any further developments in implementing independent adjudication will be available through the Internet version of this book.)

## Judicial Review: The Residual Role of the Courts

At the beginning of this sector, in advancing the need for more effective administrative remedies, I remarked on the limitations of judicial review as the primary vehicle for redressing injustices behind the walls. These limitations flow in part from the small number of lawyers interested in the work and the non-existent or low level of legal aid coverage—the latter contributing to the former. However, in setting the legal thresholds for judicial review, the courts play an important part in ensuring that the writ of justice follows prisoners into the prison. In Sector 5, in describing the case of *Fitzgerald* v. *Trono* ([1994] B.C.J. No. 1534), I explained how judges, when faced with the argument that a correctional administrator has made the wrong decision regarding transfer or segregation, will not substitute their own view of what, on the facts, the "correct" decision might be; rather, they will interfere only if the decision is "patently unreasonable," in the sense that no reasonable administrator could have come to that decision on the evidence before him or her. By this standard of patent unreasonableness, a correctional administrator has "the right to be wrong." In recent years, however, the Supreme Court of Canada has articulated the concept of a "spectrum of standards of review." Prior to the Supreme Court decision in *Southam,* there had been two standards of judicial review, the "correctness" standard and the "patent unreasonableness" standard, the latter representing the most deferential standard and the former the least deferential. Within this dichotomy, most of the case law involving decisions of correctional authorities—like *Fitzgerald*—had applied the patent unreasonableness standard. In the *Southam* case, the Supreme Court articulated a middle ground of "reasonableness *simpliciter,*" which it described this way:

> This test is to be distinguished from the most deferential standard of review, which requires courts to consider whether a tribunal's decision is patently unreasonable. An unreasonable decision is one that, in the main, is not supported by any reasons that can stand up to a somewhat probing examination. Accordingly, a court reviewing a conclusion on the reasonableness standard must look to see whether any reasons support it. The defect, if there is one, could presumably be in the evidentiary foundation itself or in the logical process by which conclusions are sought to be drawn from it. An example of the former kind of defect would be an assumption that has no basis in evidence, or that was contrary to the overwhelming weight of the evidence. An example of the latter kind of defect would be a contradiction in the premises or an invalid inference. (*Canada (Director of Investigation and Research)* v. *Southam Inc.,* [1997] 1 S.C.R. 748 at para. 56)

In *Southam* and subsequent cases, the Supreme Court has identified the critical path of inquiry in determining the appropriate standard of review. The most important factor, and the one most often referred to in cases dealing with judicial review of the decisions of correctional officials, is the expertise of the tribunal or official whose decision is being reviewed.

> If a tribunal has been constituted with a particular expertise with respect to achieving the aims of an Act, whether because of the specialized knowledge of its decision-makers, special procedure, or

non-judicial means of implementing the Act, then a greater degree of deference will be accorded . . .

. . . Making an evaluation of relative expertise has three dimensions: the court must characterize the expertise of the tribunal in question; it must consider its own expertise relative to that of the tribunal; and it must identify the nature of the specific issue before the administrative decision-maker relative to this expertise. (*Pushpanathan* v. *Canada (Minister of Citizenship and Immigration)*, [1998] 1 S.C.R. 982 at paras. 32–33)

The deference the courts have traditionally extended to administrative tribunals is premised on the sophisticated role that these tribunals play in the modern Canadian state. For example, in relation to decisions of labour boards, the Supreme Court has stated:

The rationale for protection of a Labour Board's decisions within its jurisdiction is straightforward and compelling. The Labour Board is a specialized tribunal which administers a comprehensive statute regulating labour relations. In the administration of that regime, the Board is called upon not only to find facts and decide questions of law, but also to exercise its understanding of the body of jurisprudence around the collective bargaining system, as understood in Canada, and its labour relations sense acquired from accumulated experience in the area. (*Canadian Union of Public Employees Local 963* v. *New Brunswick Liquor Corporation,* [1979] 2 S.C.R. 227 at 235)

In applying these statements to the correctional context, there are a number of distinguishing factors. While, as in labour legislation, the CCRA represents a comprehensive statute, in this case governing the administration of penitentiaries, neither the Segregation Review Board nor the warden is allocated the responsibilities of a labour relations board; neither is "called upon not only to find facts and decide questions of law, but also to exercise its understanding of the body of jurisprudence" relevant to the field of expertise. Indeed, the major finding of the Arbour Report was that correctional administrators lacked even a basic understanding of the law governing their actions. Only recently has the CSC developed a rudimentary form of legal training for correctional administrators, and as evidenced in the facts in Gary Weaver's case, the Segregation Board at William Head had a woeful lack of understanding of the legal functions of the Board under the CCRA. The Task Force on Segregation's recommendation that specialized training be given to the chairpersons of Segregation Review Boards and that a process of certification be introduced to test their legal and administrative competence has not been implemented, and Segregation Review Boards can make no claim to the kind of expertise that characterizes specialized boards such as labour boards.

One of the other factors identified in the Supreme Court jurisprudence is the purpose of the legislation constituting the administrative tribunal.

> The purpose of the statute is often indicated by the specialized nature of the legislative structure and dispute-settlement mechanism, and the need for expertise is often manifested as much by the requirements of the statute as by the specific qualifications of its members. Where the purposes of the statute and of the decision-maker are conceived not primarily in terms of establishing rights as between parties, or as entitlements, but rather as a delicate balancing between different constituencies, then the appropriateness of court supervision diminishes . . . In *Southam,* the Court found (at para. 48) that the "aims of the *Act* are more 'economic' than they are strictly 'legal'" because the broad goals of the *Act* "are matters that business women and men and economists are better able to understand than is a typical judge" . . . While judicial procedure is premised on a bipolar opposition of parties, interests, and factual discovery, some problems require the consideration of numerous interests simultaneously, and the promulgation of solutions which concurrently balance benefits and costs for many different parties. (*Pushpanathan* at para. 36)

While the general management of a penitentiary may be viewed as "a delicate balancing between different constituencies"—in terms of protecting public safety, maintaining good staff relations, and providing for the rehabilitation of prisoners—the particular provisions of the CCRA governing administrative segregation and involuntary transfers have everything to do with "establishing rights as between parties" and setting out "entitlements," in terms of providing for a right to notice, a sharing of information and written reasons for the decision. There are many instances in which a person trained and experienced in "corrections" has a better understanding of the issues than a "typical judge"—for example, in deciding whether a particular offender could benefit from a specialized program. However, the decision to segregate a prisoner or transfer him to higher security is "correctional" only in the sense that the activity takes place inside a correctional facility. In all other respects, the decision, involving as it does the deprivation of residual liberty, and attracting as it does s. 7 of the *Charter,* is quintessentially "legal." While many decisions made by correctional administrators require the consideration of numerous interests simultaneously, the decision to segregate a prisoner or to transfer him to higher security based on alleged wrongdoing, as in Gary Weaver's case, is very much premised on a "bipolar opposition of parties," with the institutional authorities seeking to deprive the prisoner of his residual liberty and the prisoner resisting that deprivation. Factual discovery, far from being peripheral to the issue, lies at the heart of the inquiry.

A further relevant factor identified in the Supreme Court jurisprudence is the nature of the problem, particularly whether it is a question of law or of fact.

> In general, deference is given on questions of fact because of the "signal advantage" enjoyed by the primary finder of fact. Less deference is warranted on questions of law, in part because the finder of fact may not have developed any particular familiarity with issues of law. (*Canada (Attorney General)* v. *Mossop*, [1993] 1 S.C.R. 554 at 599–600)

The "signal advantage" referred to here is the privileged position of the tribunal with respect to the assessment of evidence, in that it sees and hears witnesses. In the correctional context, while this is true for the decisions of Independent Chairpersons of disciplinary boards, it is not the case for decisions regarding administrative segregation and involuntary transfers. Consider again the facts in Gary Weaver's case. In none of the hearings of the Segregation Review Board were any witnesses called, and at Mr. Weaver's second thirty-day review the chairman of the Segregation Review Board acknowledged he was not aware of the underlying facts, nor had he read any of the written documentation relevant to lawful justification for continued segregation. In the case of the warden of William Head Institution, the situation was even further removed from the "signal advantage" of a fact-finding tribunal. The warden did not meet with Gary Weaver at any time during the eighty days he was confined in segregation.

There is a final factor which must be considered in determining where to locate correctional decision-making on the spectrum of standards of judicial review. The continuing pattern within the CSC of disregard for the law and the absence of a culture of respect for individual rights demonstrates a need—highlighted in the Arbour Report—for the intervention of the judiciary. Locating the standard of review at the most deferential point of the spectrum, that of patent unreasonableness, militates against the ability of the judiciary to maintain a high degree of vigilance in ensuring that the Rule of Law prevails in prisons. Shifting the standard to either reasonableness or correctness, depending upon the nature of the particular decision, would enable the judiciary to take a vital place in the remedial tool box. (A recent example of applying the spectrum of standards approach to correctional decision-making is *Tehrankari* v. *Canada*, [2000] F.C.J. No. 495 (F.C.T.D.).)

## Lawyer's Dream or Correctional Administrator's Nightmare?

This elaboration of remedies to vindicate prisoners' rights and ensure compliance with the law may seem to some readers a lawyer's dream come true: Independent

Chairpersons for serious disciplinary cases; independent adjudicators for segregation, involuntary transfers, and visit reviews; grievance processes with binding arbitration; an administrative tribunal; judicial review; the Arbour remedy of revision of sentence. For correctional administrators, this scenario might seem to evoke a nightmare world in which their principal preoccupation is preparing for and appearing at a succession of proceedings in which their decisions are challenged and redress for alleged or perceived injustices is sought. In this world, prisoners would become full-time grievors/appellants, with no time left for participating in programs aimed at their rehabilitation.

The way this array of remedies would operate in the real world bears little relationship to either the lawyer's dream or the correctional administrator's nightmare. In the recommendations I have made throughout this book, primary reliance for entrenching the Rule of Law and ensuring compliance with the law is on what lawyers call "first instance" processes. If disciplinary hearings, segregation reviews, and involuntary transfers are conducted with the appropriate balance between correctional expertise and independent adjudication, most cases will not proceed beyond this point. If the grievance process is underpinned by the possibility of independent binding arbitration, the incentive to resolve grievances at an early stage will ensure that only the exceptional case proceeds beyond there. In the same way, recourse to the administrative tribunal proposed by the Correctional Investigator would be reserved for those cases in which the CI has exhausted all other avenues in seeking to have the Service respond to his recommendations. Judicial review is not about second-guessing the decisions of correctional administrators; it interferes only when the decision is unreasonable or where there is a violation of the rules of procedural fairness and will not suddenly take over the agenda in wardens' offices. The judicial remedy proposed by the Arbour Report will be an even more exceptional event, because in most cases non-compliance with the law will not rise to a sufficient level of gravity to meet the threshold test of interfering with the integrity of the original sentence. In those exceptional cases, however, it will provide both an essential form of redress and a judicial indictment of the correctional practice which has made such redress necessary.

A final issue that must be addressed in contemplating enlargement of the remedies for the vindication of prisoners' rights is the cost. The Correctional Investigator has suggested that an administrative tribunal would be cost-effective because, in providing parties with ongoing clarification of the law, it would avoid the needless expense of revisiting unresolved issues with the Correctional Service. In proposing her judicial remedy, Madam Justice Arbour acknowledged the additional burden this could place on the courts but made the trenchant observation, which can be applied to every remedy considered in this chapter, that any additional burden "would only be so in proportion to the Correctional Service's non-compliance with the law" (Arbour Report at 184). The reforms the Correctional Investigator, Madam Justice Arbour, and I have proposed all seek to draw the operations of the Correctional Service of Canada into the gravitational pull of a culture that respects legal and constitutional rights. The more fully the Service brings itself within this legal orbit, the less need there will be for prisoners and the Correctional Investigator to seek redress.

In Sector 1, I quoted from the 1977 report of the House of Commons Sub-Committee on the Penitentiary System on the consequences, in the pre-*Martineau* era, of judicial non-intervention in the administration of justice in prisons. To recap:

> . . . The present judicial policy invites the perpetuation by the authorities of a system that is so far removed from normal standards of justice that it remains safely within the class of matters in which the imposition of judicial or quasi-judicial procedures would clearly be, in most instances, inconceivable . . . The worse things are in the penitentiary system, therefore, the more self-evident it is to the courts that Parliament could not possibly have intended for them to intervene. Injustice, as well as virtue, can be its own reward. (*Report to Parliament* at 86)

In a post-*Martineau*, post-*Charter*, post-*CCRA* era, it is now self-evident that outside intervention is a necessary prerequisite to the attainment of justice behind the walls. To turn the Sub-Committee's comment on its head, if the Correctional Service of Canada does "good corrections" within the letter and spirit of the law, *justice* can be its own reward, in the form of avoiding prisoners' grievances, adverse reports from the Correctional Investigator, unnecessary appearances before administrative tribunals, and criticism from judicial reviews.

For those who remain sceptical about the need for the expansion of remedies to vindicate the rights of prisoners, it may be helpful to reflect on the words of Mary Campbell. Ms. Campbell, as a senior official with the Secretariat to the Solicitor General, had an inside track in both the creation of the *CCRA* and the monitoring of its implementation. In commenting on the Arbour Report, she had this to say:

> The Arbour Report amply demonstrates the frailty of the recognition of inmates' rights in this country. Notwithstanding the years of litigation, policy development and legislative reform, the lack of a genuine commitment to a culture of human rights behind bars can swiftly return prison culture to the "dark ages" where expediency rules rather than the law. The answer is not to abandon the norms, but rather, as Arbour has recommended, to shore up the practices so

as to bring them into line with the law and an acceptable standard of prisoners' rights . . .

It is important to pay attention to how the Prison for Women abuses came to public attention: through *habeas corpus* application in the courts and through a special report by the Correctional Investigator which contradicted the findings of the Correctional Service's internal investigation. Consequently, when the argument is made that a strong, multi-facted legal framework is essential for the protection of inmates' rights, this means not just the substantive law but also the support mechanisms that allow that law to be monitored and tested in the open light of day. Had the women not had adequate access to the courts, had the Correctional Investigator not existed, the events at the Prison for Women might well have been simply one more anecdote in prison history behind the walls. (Mary E. Campbell, "Revolution and Counter-Revolution in Canadian Prisoners' Rights" [1996] 2 *Canadian Criminal Law Review* 285 at 324)

The remedial measures advanced in this chapter are intended to ensure that the experiences of Hughie MacDonald, Donnie Oag, Jason Gallant, Gary Weaver, and all the other prisoners whose cases I have chronicled do not become just further anecdotes in this history. Rather, they are offered as legal antidotes to the practice of injustice.

# CONCLUSION

# Human Rights and the
# Prison at the Beginning of
# the Twenty-First Century

In December 1998, Canada joined other countries in celebrating the fiftieth anniversary of the *Universal Declaration of Human Rights* (G.A. res. 217A (III), U.N. Doc A/810 at 71 (1948), reprinted in [1948] U.N.Y.B. 465). We did so with the knowledge that, as much as any country, we have endeavoured to live up to the ideals and standards set by this statement of fundamental human rights, and with added pride that a Canadian, John Humphrey, played a leading role in drafting and guiding the *Declaration* through the United Nations in 1948. Article 1 of the *Universal Declaration* affirms that "All human beings are born free and equal in dignity and rights." As Max Yalden, former Chief Commissioner of the Canadian Human Rights Commission and a current commissioner with the United Nations Human Rights Commission, stated at the time, this "fundamental statement of humanity's goals and aspirations for a fairer and more humane future, is nowhere more applicable than in the world of corrections" (Maxwell Yalden, "Canada, the CSC and Human Rights" [November 1998] 23 (no. 4) *Let's Talk* [Correctional Service of Canada] 12 at 13). Mr. Yalden went on to assert that "no moment in history could be more appropriate" for the Correctional Service of Canada to re-commit itself to respecting the provisions of the *Declaration*. In Mr. Yalden's judgement, that would "require ongoing and vigilant attention at every level of the Service" (Yalden at 13).

As I have outlined in Sector 4 of this book, in 1997 the CSC had invited Mr. Yalden to chair the Working Group on Human Rights. The group's mandate was to review the Service's systems for ensuring compliance with the Rule of Law in human rights matters; to provide a strategic model for evaluating compliance within a correctional context; and to present recommendations concerning the Service's ability to comply and to effectively communicate such compliance. The report of the Working Group was completed in December 1997, along with two guides setting out international and domestic human rights obligations with respect to prisoners and CSC employees.

The Yalden Report tracks the principles of the *Universal Declaration* through the subsequent UN covenants and conventions to which Canada is a party that have shaped international human rights law, in particular the *International Covenant on Civil and Political Rights* (19 December 1966, CAN.J.S. 1976 No. 47, 999 U.N.T.S. 171). Articles 7 and 10 of the *International Covenant* provide:

7.  No one shall be subjected to torture or to cruel, inhuman or degrading treatment or punishment . . .
10. All persons deprived of their liberty shall be treated with humanity and with respect for the inherent dignity of the human person.

The *Universal Declaration* and the *International Covenant* have been influential in shaping Canadian domestic law, and many of their provisions are the source of the constitutional protections entrenched in the *Canadian Charter of Rights and Freedoms*. As we have seen, the *Corrections and Conditional Release Act* was drafted to ensure that the correctional legal regime was consistent with the *Charter*, and thus it is possible to trace a lineage through the four documents. As the Working Group concluded:

. . . One must acknowledge what the *CCRA* does do to lay out a correctional regime that will be respectful of Canada's obligations in human rights matters . . . Over and above the general right to safe and humane custody, sections 3 and 4 of the *Act* specifically identify: the right to be dealt with in the least restrictive way; the residual rights which are those of any member of society, except those necessarily restricted or removed by virtue of incarceration; the right to forthright and fair decision-making, and to an effective grievance procedure; the right to have sexual, cultural, linguistic and other differences and needs respected; and the right to participate in programs designed to promote rehabilitation and reintegration. These broad principles can be readily traced back to their international and constitutional roots. (Yalden Report at 24)

There is no binding international treaty that deals exclusively with the treatment of prisoners and the conditions of imprisonment. However, in 1955, the first United Nations *Congress* on the Prevention of Crime and the Treatment of

Offenders adopted the *Standard Minimum Rules for the Treatment of Prisoners*. These rules were approved by the United Nations Economic and Social Council in 1957 (Resolution 663 CI (XXIV) of 31 July 1957), with the recommendation that all states adopt the rules and conduct compliance surveys every five years. It was not until 1975, at the Fifth UN Congress, that Canada endorsed the *Standard Minimum Rules* and committed itself to ensuring full compliance and implementation.

A 1998 CSC report has suggested that three fundamental human rights principles emerge from the ninety-five individual articles of the *Standard Minimum Rules*. First, a prisoner's dignity and worth as a human being must be respected through the entire course of his or her imprisonment. Second, the loss of liberty through the fact of incarceration is punishment enough. Third, prisons should not be punishing places; rather, they should help prisoners rehabilitate themselves. The report observed:

> The fact that many states, including Canada, have incorporated [this] set of principles and rules in the legislative design of their correctional systems may be taken as evidence that the SMRs are now considered an essential element of international and, indeed, domestic human rights standards. Still, 40 years after their initial adoption, certain rules have not been fully implemented and remain a challenge to correctional authorities. For instance, Canada still practices *"double-bunking"* of inmates in cells designed for one; permits some young offenders to serve their prison sentences in adult institutions; does not use the SMRs in the training of correctional personnel; and does not distribute the rules to every prisoner upon their initial reception. (*50 Years of Human Rights Developments in Federal Corrections* [Ottawa: Correctional Service of Canada, Human Rights Division, August 1998] at 15)

Although the Yalden Report concluded that "Canada is generally compliant with all the relevant international and domestic human rights norms, as are most other advanced democracies in terms of their legal and policy frameworks" (Yalden Report at 8), it noted that the CCRA did not invoke or even allude to those international obligations and norms. The Report therefore recommended that the *Act* be amended to say explicitly that its principles and provisions are aimed at meeting Canada's international commitments. That way, correctional staff could see their mandate in its full human rights dimensions.

Part of the Yalden Working Group's mandate was to compare the CSC's legislative and policy framework with those of other countries demonstrating a strong commitment to human rights. Surveying the regimes in France, Germany, the Netherlands, the United Kingdom, Denmark, Norway, Sweden, Australia, and the United States, it found that virtually all of these jurisdictions made use of parallel mechanisms for the protection of human rights: an internal monitoring mechanism that includes a grievance redress system and an external monitoring mechanism that makes or reviews decisions seriously impinging on prisoners' rights to fair and humane treatment. In concluding that a system of independent oversight is necessary to ensure "an unbiased reading on the extent of a system's compliance with its lawful obligations," the Yalden Report observed that, generally speaking, such oversight was "*not* intended to provide an additional level of operational management" (Yalden Report at 16). However:

> In instances where significant loss of prisoners' rights is at stake, the simple monitoring of a correctional authority's decisions by an external entity may not be sufficient to ensure compliance; it is arguable that the decision itself should be made by some external entity. Currently, most jurisdictions we have reviewed recognize that serious disciplinary matters and parole decisions should at least involve some authority independent of the correctional service. We believe this requirement should be a component of any effective correctional model. (Yalden Report at 17)

In keeping with this statement of principle, the Working Group recommended, as discussed in Sector 4, that the experiment on independent adjudication put forward by the Task Force on Segregation be implemented. However, even Mr. Yalden's endorsement of this recommendation failed to convince the Commissioner of Corrections that the experiment on independent adjudication should proceed.

In identifying a strategy for improving CSC's communication of its mandate regarding human rights to the general public and the international community, the Yalden Report acknowledged that the Service was "caught in a cross-fire between those who perceive the correctional system as soft on criminals and those who worry that incarceration further degrades them, or fails to assist them in becoming more positive members of society" (Yalden Report at 36). Based on the results of a 1996 CSC staff survey, the Report also observed that a substantial proportion of staff either do not accept the rationale for their professional conduct or question its effectiveness. The Report concluded:

> If staff are to see themselves as part of a lawful and socially constructive enterprise, they not only need a firm grasp of clear and practical professional guidelines, they must also have some personal understanding of why such rules are lawful and the social purpose that they serve. (Yalden Report at 37)

The Report offered what it saw as the best argument for observing human rights in a correctional context:

> [It] is not merely that [these rules] are required by international convention or domestic law, or even that they are intrinsically more civilizing, but that they actually work better than any known alternatives—for inmates, for staff and for society at large. By preserving such fundamental social rules within the institutional setting, so the argument goes, one improves the odds of eventually releasing a more responsible person. (Yalden Report at 40)

The Yalden Report proposed a broad platform of reforms, all premised on a "rights-related strategy." In addition to those already mentioned, these included improvements in the quantity, quality, and accessibility of rights-related training, particularly for front-line staff, and the establishment of a Human Rights Unit, headed by an individual with appropriate seniority, to monitor compliance with human rights standards.

The Yalden Report was generally well received by the Commissioner of Corrections, and one of the first recommendations to be implemented was the establishment of a Human Rights Unit at National Headquarters. However, far from being given the profile and resources suggested by the Yalden Report, the csc's Human Rights Unit has a smaller staff than any other at National Headquarters and remains outside the loop of decision-making. Ivan Zinger, the first Human Rights Officer and himself one of the three members of the Working Group on Human Rights, resigned from his position within a year, in large measure because of the csc's resistance to his recommendation that new policy initiatives be reviewed and "signed off" by the Human Rights Unit.

The Human Rights Unit has initiated workshops with senior managers and staff in every region of the country to promote greater understanding of the human-rights-related strategy. However, as with the one-shot legal workshops conducted in the wake of the Task Force on Segregation, these workshops reach very few line staff. The extent to which the strategy endorsed by the Yalden Report has seeped into csc operational reality can be assessed by my own experience at a training session held for Matsqui staff in September 1999. The session was for all staff and managers at the Regional Reception and Assessment Centre, located within the institution. Because the Reception Centre contains in its upper ranges the segregation unit for Matsqui, I was asked to speak on the changes that have occurred in the segregation regime. In the course of my presentation, made to about fifty staff members, I asked whether any of them had read either the report of the Task Force on Administrative Segregation or the report of the Working Group on Human Rights. No hands were raised. Both documents are posted on the Service's Intranet, and the deputy warden advised me that a few copies of each were "floating around" the institution. Yet few staff were even aware that they existed. For them, the human-rights-related knowledge, perspective, and strategy of the Yalden Report was still out there in the ether.

These were the staff members who have the first contact with prisoners when they come into the penitentiary system. Their case management manuals provide systematic guidance for preparation of intake assessment interviews, detailed protocols for the completion of criminal profile reports, coverage of the factors to be included in risk/needs assessments, and the litany of other critical documents that must be entered in the computerized Offender Management System. The professed aim of the assessment process is to provide the fullest possible information base on which correctional staff and managers may make informed decisions during the course of a prisoner's sentence. Underpinning the assessment process is staff training in the risk management model. There is, however, no parallel training in the human-rights-related model. I suggested to staff at the session that as the front line of the Service's interface with prisoners, their professional mandate embraced more than the protection of the public through informed risk management; it also embraced the protection of human rights to which Canada is committed by international covenant and by its own legislation.

After my presentation, a staff member spoke to me informally about the difficulty he faced in accepting the human rights agenda. It was not that he did not understand it, he said; indeed, he understood it all too well. But enhanced segregation reviews did not change the physical conditions of the segregation unit, and it was difficult, if not impossible, to reconcile the reality of men confined for twenty-three hours a day in a small cage with an elevated sense of human dignity and respect for human rights.

The often enormous distance between professed intentions, even those enshrined in binding legal texts, and the real world of imprisonment is a fact of life no less today than at the end of the eighteenth century when John Howard, in *The State of the Prisons,* penned his blueprint for radical transformation to ensure that the sentence of imprisonment observed the strictest standards of justice and morality. This inherent duality is found in the pages of the official news magazine of the Correctional Service of Canada, *Let's Talk,* in the issue commemorating the fiftieth anniversary of the *Universal Declaration of Human Rights.* Ivan Zinger ended his contribution on this cautionary note:

> . . . We must not allow celebrating our progress and accomplishments in the human rights field to overshadow the important work and challenges that lie ahead. Our criminal justice system is far from perfect. Canada's incarceration rate continues to rank among the highest in the industrialized world. Many of our penitentiaries are

full beyond capacity. The majority of our prison population is drawn from the ranks of the economically and socially disadvantaged; a disproportionate number of minorities, including Aboriginal persons, are locked up in our prisons. HIV infection rates and incidence of AIDS among Canadian offenders continues to far exceed prevalence rates in the general population. As for its employees, the Correctional Service of Canada still has a long way to go in becoming a more inclusive and representative workplace free of practices that undermine a person's sense of dignity. Clearly, there is room for improvement. (Ivan Zinger, "Human Rights for All" [November 1998] 23 (no. 4) *Let's Talk* 4 at 6)

Kim Pate, the Executive Director of the Canadian Association of Elizabeth Fry Societies, also contributed an article to this issue of *Let's Talk*. Ms. Pate, whose unflagging work on behalf of women prisoners was acknowledged by Madam Justice Arbour in her report, provided a much starker reminder of why celebration must be tempered with a constant questioning of the system's willingness and ability to practice internally what it professes internationally.

Since the Arbour Commission Report chronicled extensive human rights abuses and other reprehensible transgressions of law and policy have again surfaced. Why have women prisoners been stripped, shackled and left chained naked to a metal bed frame, without a mattress, in segregation? Why have minimum security women been sent into the community in shackles on various forms of temporary absences? Why do we continue to use classification tools that disproportionately discriminate on the basis of race, class, gender and sexual orientation? Why have perimeter and razor wire fences, additional alarms and total surveillance cameras been installed in the new regional facilities that were supposed to be modeled on international examples of women-centred minimum security facilities? Why are women with mental health problems and maximum security women imprisoned in all-male prisons? Why are so few federally sentenced Aboriginal women placed in the Okimaw Ohci Healing Lodge, a facility designed specifically for them? How can these situations persist in a country that is touted around the globe as having one of the most humane and progressive correctional systems in the world? (Kim Pate, "Correcting Corrections for Federally Sentenced Women" [November 1998] 23 (no. 4) *Let's Talk* 16 at 16)

In October 1999, Michael Ignatieff began a magazine article about Louise Arbour with these words: "Louise Arbour arrived in The Hague with high-minded beliefs about international justice. She's leaving with an education in politics, hypocrisy, and the limits of the West's moral indignation" (Michael Ignatieff, "The Trials of Louise Arbour," *Saturday Night,* October 1999). He was, of course, referring to the massive human rights abuses in the former Yugoslavia and Madam Justice Arbour's role as Chief Prosecutor for the International War Crimes Tribunal. In commenting on the work of Louise Arbour and her predecessor, Judge Goldstone, in turning "an institution which had no real precedent in international law and precious little actual backing from Western governments" into a real-time law-enforcement agency, Ignatieff suggested that "in the process they both discovered the huge gap that separates what Western states preach about human rights and international law from what they actually practice." As Ignatieff pointed out, the disputes that would come before Madam Justice Arbour "as a robed judge in the Supreme Court of a peaceable kingdom [are] a long way away from ravines where children are murdered." However, the common thread is that it takes vigilance and courage, both individual and collective, to ensure that human rights are protected at those points where they become most vulnerable. Within Canada, that vulnerability is nowhere more evident than inside penitentiaries.

In a May 1997 article about Vaclav Havel, Czech President and former political prisoner, Paul Berman wrote these provocative words:

> It is fine and good to speak about human rights, laws, constitutions, non-governmental organizations . . . The world is full of countries that adopt the best of constitutions and proclaim the rights of man from here to the horizon, yet fail to achieve very much democracy. And why is that?
>
> It is because democracy requires a certain kind of citizen. It requires citizens who feel responsible for something more than their own well-feathered little corner; citizens who want to participate in society's affairs, who insist on it; citizens with backbones; citizens who hold their ideas about democracy at the deep level, at the level that religion is held, where beliefs and identity are the same. (Paul Berman, "The Philosopher-King Is Mortal," *New York Times Magazine,* May 11, 1997, at 32)

In Canada at the beginning of the twenty-first century, the fertile ground of a democratic, peaceful kingdom, so well entrenched in the Constitution and the law, is in danger of serious erosion as the politics of fear escalates demand for increased punitiveness against prisoners with a remarkable indifference to the fact that crime rates are declining. Indeed, for some proponents of stepping up the war against crime, a repudiation of the fundamental premises of international human rights law is an acceptable price to pay.

In September 1999, the Canadian Institute for the Administration of Justice sponsored a conference in Saskatoon at which participants were asked to reflect on the changing nature of punishment. Jim Gouk, a Reform (now Canadian Alliance) Member of Parliament and a member of the House of Commons Committee on Justice and Human Rights, offered these comments:

> Canada has long been known as the land of rights and equality. If we are to make meaningful changes to the effectiveness of the punishment of crime, we must put those principles aside . . . To develop a new and effective approach to the punishment of criminals, it is necessary to accept to some degree that the rights of those who obey the laws of this country are different from the rights of those who do not. The system currently approaches the punishment of criminals from the point of view that criminals still have almost all of the rights of a law-abiding citizen. I fundamentally reject that approach. I believe that any person who has been convicted in a Canadian court gives up their rights as a Canadian with the sole exceptions of the right to humane and healthful treatment. I define this as the right to be incarcerated in accommodations with reasonable environmental control, to be provided with basic personal care supplies, to be fed according to the Canadian Nutrition Guide, and to be provided with access to basic medical treatment. Beyond this, prisoners should have the ability to earn other rights such as more freedom within the prison, transfers to more desirable facilities, training programs, sports programs, visitor privileges, payment for work performance, canteen privileges, temporary absences and parole. Each of these rights must be earned by appropriate behaviour which in turn means they can also be taken away for inappropriate behaviour. (Jim Gouk, "A New Approach to the Punishment of Crime in Canada" [Paper presented at Changing Punishment at the Turn of the Century: Finding a Common Ground, Saskatoon, September 27, 1999])

Following his presentation, I asked Mr. Gouk from the floor whether he was aware that his "new approach" was inconsistent not only with the decisions of the Supreme Court of Canada and the *Corrections and Conditional Release Act*, but also with principles enshrined in international human rights covenants to which Canada was a party. What meaningful changes in justice behind the walls would come from putting these principles aside? What evidence did Mr. Gouk have that rescinding fundamental human rights would result in a safer and more secure democracy? I neither expected nor received a response.

At the same conference, Commissioner of Corrections Ole Ingstrup and I were part of a panel with the theme "The Ongoing Struggle for Justice." The

Commissioner, in reflecting on changes within the Correctional Service of Canada, began with a quotation from the 1977 report of the House of Commons Sub-Committee on the Penitentiary System in Canada.

> [The] fundamental absence of purpose or direction creates a corrosive ambivalence that subverts from the outset the efforts, policies, plans and operations of the administrators of the Canadian Penitentiary Service, saps the confidence and seriously impairs the morale and sense of professional purpose of the correctional, classificational and program officers, and ensures, from the inmate's perspective, that imprisonment in Canada, where it is not simply inhumane, is the most individually destructive, psychologically crippling and socially alienating experience that could conceivably exist within the borders of the country. (*Report to Parliament* at 156)

The Commissioner went on to make the case that corrections in Canada had come a long way since 1977, and that nobody today could use those words to describe imprisonment in a federal institution. In place of a corrosive "absence of purpose," there was now the Mission Statement—which he had animated—and the statement of purpose and principles set out in the *Corrections and Conditional Release Act*. He pointed to minimum security healing lodges for Aboriginal women and men; a correctional strategy based on the earliest reintegration of the prisoner back into the community; a research-based spectrum of correctional programs designed to address prisoners' needs and risks; and an array of oversight mechanisms that included the Auditor General of Canada and the Office of the Correctional Investigator in addition to the Service's internal grievance mechanisms and audit procedures. Altogether, it was an impressive list. Indeed, the Commissioner ventured to suggest to an audience including representatives from both the judiciary and law enforcement that federal corrections had changed more than any other part of the criminal justice system.

As I listened to Commissioner Ingstrup, I thought about the history of the penitentiary and the different ways that history can be read. The Commissioner had told what English criminologist Stanley Cohen would have called "a good story," the latest chapter in the progression from barbarism to civilization, from arbitrary and inhumane imprisonment to principled corrections. When it was my turn to speak, I acknowledged that much in the Commissioner's story deserved recognition, and that on the basis of those changes Canada is seen as an international leader in corrections. I suggested, however, that his story, while an important tributary of change, had to work hard against the main flow of penitentiary history. That history had demonstrated that "conscience"—whether manifest in the professed desire to rehabilitate prisoners or the professed commitment to protect their human rights—seemed time and again to be trumped by "convenience," in which the exigencies of prison administration prevailed over the practice of justice. As a counterbalance to the Commissioner's story, I offered some of the stories I have presented in this book.

One of those stories was Gary Weaver's. After outlining the events at William Head, I told the audience how, early in March 1999, I had picked a blue wild-flower on the grounds of William Head and taken it to Gary in segregation, as a symbol of the impending spring. Unknown to me, Gary kept the flower alive for the next sixty days, carefully changing the water in the cup in which it sat. When he was finally released from segregation, just days before his *habeas corpus* petition was due to be heard in B.C. Supreme Court, he gave the flower to the man in the cell next to him as a small floral torch of hope. I asked the Commissioner and the audience, as I would ask anyone, why a man like Gary Weaver, hardened beyond belief by the rigours of maximum and super-maximum security, could find so much solace in a single wildflower. Might it not be that for all the physical splendour of William Head, for all the progressive developments in the last twenty years, Gary Weaver's imprisonment was as much an "individually destructive, psychologically crippling and socially alienating experience" as imprisonment had been for Jack McCann and his brothers in solitary in the B.C. Penitentiary almost twenty years before? In Gary Weaver's case, the gift of a flower, the support of those who believed in his innocence, and the prospect of justice through a *habeas corpus* petition were strong enough to sustain him in his struggle. But flowers do not often make their way inside segregation units, *habeas corpus* petitions are few and far between, and not many prisoners have the forti-tude of Gary Weaver. The cords that link a sentence of imprisonment to the practice of justice must not only be girded with the steel of the law but must also be subject to the most careful scrutiny, because it is at precisely this juncture that the greatest strains will occur. What happened to Gary Weaver and the other prisoners whose stories I have presented should not be seen as the correctional equivalent of metal fatigue in the otherwise robust metallurgy of modern cor-rections but instead as a flaw encoded in a system that in every generation has trampled on human rights.

Two weeks after the Saskatoon conference, I travelled to Paris on my way to a meeting with the international representatives of *Avocats Sans Frontières*. Inscribed in stone high on the splendid façade of that city's Hotel de Ville is the *cri du coeur* of the French Revolution: "*Liberté, Egalité, Fraternite.*" Imprison-ment may take away a prisoner's freedom, but it does not nullify a prisoner's right to equal treatment under the law, and it must never be allowed to sever the ties that link a prisoner to the brotherhood and sisterhood the *Universal Declaration of Human Rights* accords us all.

# Acknowledgements

Many years ago, shortly after I began teaching, I received a letter from a prisoner asking the pointed question, "As a law professor, what do you profess?" It was a question I have grappled with ever since, and *Justice behind the Walls* represents my attempt to answer it.

In searching for that answer, I must acknowledge the hundreds of prisoners, prison administrators, and staff whose experiences and perspectives have given shape to my mapping of the borders of prison justice. I would also acknowledge the contributions of students at the U.B.C. Faculty of Law who have participated in my Penal Policy seminar and of colleagues and friends who have provided valuable commentary on earlier drafts. During the years of research and the demanding process of turning thousands of pages of notes and journals into this book, I was fortunate to have the assistance of Karen Toop, Sandra Redekop, Rachel Maté, Craig Walker, Deanna Clark, Cythe Gogan, and Michele Vernet. I was also fortunate in drawing upon the enthusiasm and commitment of Michael Bromm and Paddy Long in facilitating the transition of *Justice behind the Walls* to the Internet. To my editor, Barbara Pulling, I am deeply appreciative for her flexing of considerable intellectual and technical muscle in what was a most challenging but rewarding editorial experience from which the book has benefited. Further refinement is to be credited to the eagle eyes of Robin Van Heck. To Scott McIntyre, it is a privilege to be on the list of a Canadian publisher who, despite the demands of the bottom line, has retained a vision of social justice and artistic integrity.

To Shane, whose photographs grace the cover and sector headings, it is a true pleasure to acknowledge a son's contribution to a father's work. To my daughter, Melissa, who, on hearing of the awful abuse some prisoners had experienced as young children, urged me to redouble my efforts to protect them from further abuse, I have tried my best to reflect your heartfelt concern. To Marcy, who was with me on the first part of my journey behind the walls, I thank you for providing the safe haven of home and family. To Surjeet, who has been with me during this part of the journey, and who heard many of these stories in their raw form before their retelling for publication, I hope this work honours our relationship and your own abiding concern for a world free of discrimination and violence.

Financial support for the initial stages of my research was provided by the Social Sciences and Humanities Research Council, which in 1993 awarded me the Bora Laskin National Fellowship in Human Rights Research (named after the former Chief Justice of the Supreme Court of Canada). The creation of the website was made possible by grants from U.B.C.'s Faculty of Law and the Law Foundation of B.C. I am indebted to Dean Joost Blom for his support. The final stages of the project were assisted by the financial contributions of Joseph and Vera Zilber; I am very grateful to you both for easing the burdens of publication and for your unconditional respect for my work.

To my mother, Hilda Jackson, whose passion for righting wrongs has inspired me, and to my father, Ralph Jackson, whose capacity for patience I have aspired to, thank you for the treasured moments of last summer and for the memory of you walking, hand in hand, by the sea wall.

# Index